ENGLISH EPISCOPAL ACTA

II

CANTERBURY 1162–1190

ENGLISH EPISCOPAL ACTA

II

CANTERBURY 1162–1190

EDITED BY

C. R. CHENEY

AND

BRIDGETT E. A. JONES

LONDON · *Published for* THE BRITISH ACADEMY
by THE OXFORD UNIVERSITY PRESS
1986

Oxford University Press, Walton Street, Oxford OX2 6DP

London New York Toronto
Delhi Bombay Calcutta Madras Karachi
Kuala Lumpur Singapore Hong Kong Tokyo
Nairobi Dar es Salaam Cape Town
Melbourne Auckland

and associate companies in
Beirut Berlin Ibadan Mexico City Nicosia

Oxford is a trade mark of Oxford University Press

Published in the United States by Oxford University Press, New York

© *The British Academy, 1986*

British Library Cataloguing in Publication Data
English episcopal acta
2: Canterbury, 1162–1190
3: Canterbury, 1193–1205
1. Catholic Church — England — Bishops — History — Sources
2. Catholic Church — England — Dioceses — History — Sources
I. Cheney, C.R.   II. Jones, Bridgett E.A.
262'.3   BR750
ISBN 0–19–726022–5

Printed in Great Britain
at the University Printing House, Oxford
by David Stanford
Printer to the University

CONTENTS

LIST OF PLATES   *page* vi

PREFACE   vii

MANUSCRIPT SOURCES CITED   x

PRINTED BOOKS AND ARTICLES CITED,
  WITH ABBREVIATED REFERENCES   xiv

OTHER ABBREVIATIONS   xxi

INTRODUCTION
  The archbishops and their staff   xxiii
  Contents of the acta   xxxiv
  The diplomatic of the acta   xli
  Editorial method   lxxv

PLATES   lxxix

THE ACTA
  Thomas Becket   nos. 1–45   1
  Richard of Dover   nos. 46–232   28
  Baldwin of Forde   nos. 233–326   203

APPENDICES
  I. Reginald elect of Canterbury, 1191   276
  II. Itineraries of the archbishops, 1162–1190   277

Combined indices to this volume and the next are contained in volume III.

LIST OF PLATES

(between page lxxviii *and page* 1)

I.   ACTUM OF ARCHBISHOP THOMAS
        (no. 3)

II.   ACTA OF ARCHBISHOP RICHARD
        (nos. 77, 80, 211: scribes **III, II, IV**)

III.   ACTA OF ARCHBISHOP BALDWIN
        (nos. 264, 311, 312)

IV.   (*a*) COUNTERSEAL OF ARCHBISHOP THOMAS
        (no. 23)
      (*b*) SEAL AND COUNTERSEAL OF ARCHBISHOP
        RICHARD
        (no. 215: scribe **I**)

V.   ACTUM OF ARCHBISHOP HUBERT
        (no. 489: scribe **III**)

VI.   ACTUM OF ARCHBISHOP HUBERT
        (no. 550: scribe **V**)

VII.   ACTA OF ARCHBISHOP HUBERT
        (nos. 355, 387: scribe **IV**)

VIII.   ACTA OF ARCHBISHOP HUBERT
        (nos. 549, 555, 558: scribes **I, II, VI**)

Facsimiles of other original acta have been published elsewhere, as noted in the descriptions below of nos. 34, 206, 276, 495, 597. See no. 597 for facsimiles of Hubert's seal, obverse and reverse.

PREFACE

by C. R. CHENEY

The two volumes of Canterbury acta, 1162–1190 and 1193–1205, are here published and indexed as one work, to bridge the gap between Professor Saltman's *Theobald* and Dr Major's *Acta Stephani Langton*. The final editorial responsibility rests with me, and a few words about the background of publication are called for. The collection began in a tentative way at Oxford in 1938, when I included in a course on medieval diplomatic a section about English episcopal documents of the twelfth and thirteenth centuries. My collecting of acta — not for Canterbury alone — was resumed after the Second World War and has never really stopped since then. But the finished work is not all my own: it results in large measure from the labours of two scholars, Bridgett Jones and Eric John. Their contributions must be clearly stated before I acknowledge my obligations to others.

Dr Jones prepared a full edition of the texts of archbishops Richard and Baldwin as part of her doctoral thesis for the University of London, 1964 (deposited in the Institute of Historical Research, London). This has provided a solid basis of annotated texts, comprising a large majority of those which survive. At the same time her dissertation contains a substantial study of the two archbishops, their activities as judges, their households, and the diplomatic of their acta. When the present volume was planned in 1976, Miss Jones graciously gave me *carte blanche* to use her thesis, and I have drawn on all parts of it freely. Coming to archbishop Hubert — whose acta equal in number those of his three predecessors — my *English bishops' chanceries*, published in 1950, utilized the material I had accumulated by then, and I made it available to my pupil, Eric John. In the following few years Mr John carried out a much more thorough and systematic scouring of manuscripts for Hubert's acta, including all the cartularies of the southern province in the British Museum and Public Record Office and the collections at Canterbury and Lambeth Palace. Later in the fifties other interests supervened, and in 1961 Mr John most generously made over to me all his transcripts and notes, very copious but admittedly incomplete, for me to use at my discretion. I was able to draw on all this material when preparing a book on Hubert Walter (1967) and it lies behind the present revised and enlarged collection. When Professor Charles R. Young published his well-documented *Hubert Walter, lord of Canterbury and lord of England* in 1968, his book provided very few but welcome additions to my existing catalogue of acta.

As always, my wife, Mary Cheney, has been the best of collaborators. She has been at my side at every stage of the protracted editorial process, transcribing manuscripts and correcting my transcripts, criticizing and improving the notes and introduction, giving the support and encouragement I needed. I am grateful to many other scholars, too, for help in collecting and assessing the material: to Mr T. A. M. Bishop for discrimination of scripts of the archbishops' clerks; to Dr Pierre Chaplais and Dr Neil Ker for advice on particular points of diplomatic and palaeography; to Dr Anne Duggan and Professor Raymonde Foreville for comments on the acta of Thomas Becket. Others I remember gratefully for help with particular documents: Miss Melanie Barber, Dr Martin Brett, Dr J. H. Denton, Mr T. A. Heslop, Miss Vera London, Mr John Moule, Mrs Dorothy Owen, Sir Richard Southern, Mrs S. Stallworthy, Mr Colin Taylor. Mr Martin Snape brought no. 419 to my notice. Professors Foreville and Van Caenegem and Drs D. Lambrecht, D. E. Bates, and Margaret A. Harris have been instrumental in procuring photocopies of documents in French and Belgian archives.

In addition, I offer thanks to private owners for allowing access to manuscripts and permission to publish: to His Grace the Duke of Rutland (and his former archivist, Dr L. A. Parker), Commander M. Saunders Watson, and Messrs R. J. R. Arundell, David Rogers, and Geoffrey D. Roper, and to the authorities of those public libraries and archive offices and private institutions whose manuscripts we have used, for permitting publication. Transcripts of Crown copyright records in the Public Record Office appear by permission of the controller of HM Stationery Office. The index of manuscripts on pp. x–xiii below shows how much the editors have drawn from institutional collections throughout the country. What that list fails to disclose is the unstinted help received, over forty years and more, from certain individuals in charge of various ecclesiastical and collegiate archives and from officials in public libraries and record offices. At Canterbury especially, I have made many demands on the time and unfailing patience of Dr William

Urry and Miss A. M. Oakley successively; for the rest I must record thanks in general terms to the custodians past and present to whom this edition owes so much. To borrow the words of Thomas Fuller, thanking Master Sherman, the archbishop's registrar of his day: 'may my candle go out in a stench, when I will not confess whence I have lights'.

Finally, I am deeply obliged to those who have read the whole work in typescript with critical eyes: Professor C. N. L. Brooke, Dr Kathleen Major (members of the Academy's Episcopal Acta Committee), Dr David M. Smith (General Editor of the series), and my wife. They have effected many significant improvements and corrected countless mistakes.

Postscript by the General Editor: This volume and the next were completed and delivered for publication early in 1981. Subsequent delays in production have given opportunities to incorporate a few editorial revisions.

MANUSCRIPT SOURCES CITED

Aberystwyth, Nat. Libr. of Wales: 7851: *616*.

Alençon, Archives dép. de l'Orne: H 905: *598*.

Bedford, Beds. Record Office: DD GY 9/2: *363*.

Belvoir Castle: 3/43/106: *56*; Add. 105: *56, 57, 234*.

Birmingham Reference Libr.: 473629: *228*.

Bruges, Grand Séminaire: 169: *449–50*.

Burton-upon-Trent Libr.: D 27/15 and 16: *63n.*; D 27/42: *63, 360*; D 27/164: *63, 240*.

Caen, Archives dép. du Calvados: H 1884: *64*.

Cambridge,
– Christ's Coll. mun.: Manorbier box no. A: *231–2, 650*.
– Corpus Christi Coll.: 134: *30n.*; 189: *394–5*; 266: *214n.*
– Jesus Coll. mun.: Cambr. ch. A 2: *3*.
– King's Coll. mun.: 2 W 3: *271*; 2 W 10: *270*; 2 W 13: *272*.
– Trinity Coll.: R 5 33 (James 724): *481*.
– Univ. Libr.: documents 42: *160n.*; Ee 4 20: *200*; Ee 5 31: *138, 144–5, 285, 289, 352, 368, 450, 518–20*; Ll 2 15: *92–4, 258, 397, 399–401*; EDC 1B/1/81: *453*; EDR G 1/2: *453*; EDR G 3/28: *453–4*.

Canterbury, D. & C. Archives and Libr.: Lit. C 16: *398*; Lit. D 4: *125, 442*; Lit. E 28: *85*; Lit. E 30: *96*.
– – Chartae Antiquae (C.A.): A 5: *383n.*; A 27: *79*; C 106: *532*; C 115: *532n.*; C 179: *77*; C 1112: *78n.*; C 1261: *341*; D 7 and 8: *81*; D 19: *80*; D 95: *442*; D 113: *65*; E 176 and 178: *82*; E 186: *383*; E 189b: *84*; F 4: *85*; F 85: *390*; G 187: *474*; H 89: *248n.*; H 90: *248*; H 91: *388*; H 94: *388*; L 4: *249n.*; L 39: *249*; L 129–133: *383n.*; L 136: *382*; L 376: *512*; P 50: *384*; R 70a and b: *595n.*; S 8: *387*; S 269: *396*; S 354: *72*; T 34: *90n.*; T 35: *90*; Z 134: *588*; Z 144: *535*.

– – Ch. C₁. Letters vol. II: 02: *intro. p. xlix n. 62*, 03: *468*; 214: *550*; 225: *603*; 226: *420–1*; 228: *404*; 231: *418*; 233: *649*; 234: *460–1*; 235–6: *548–9*; 238: *456*; 239: *543*; 240: *570*; 241: *p. xlix n. 62*; 244: *487*; 245: *645*; 248: *485*; 250: *475–7*; 252: *562*; 254: *637*.
– – Eastbridge mun.: A 1 & 2: *403*.
– – Eastry corr.: group III 25: *546*; group VI 1: *355*.
– – Ecclesiastical suits: 341: *577n.*
– – Sede Vacante Scrapbook I: 50 (ii): *536*; 50 (iv): *549n.*; 132 (i): *478*; 132 (ii): *422–3*; 133 (i): *653*; 133 (iii): *634*; 134 (ii): *547*; 154 (ii): *489*.
– – Sede Vacante Scrapbook III: 7 no. 20: *546*; 156 no. 447: *536*; 157 (i): *595n.*
– – Reg. A: *86, 256, 387–8*;
   Reg. B: *80, 84–5, 257, 387*;
   Reg. C: *82*;
   Reg. D: *89*;
   Reg. E: *80, 86, 89, 256, 388*;
   Reg. H: *76*;
   Reg. I: *80, 82, 84–5, 388–9*;
   Reg. O: *388*.
– – Black Book of the Archdeaconry: *66, 75*.

Chelmsford, Essex Record Office: D/DP TI/274: *215*.

Chichester, W. Sussex Record Office, Dioc. archives: Ep. i/1/5: *452*; Ep. vi/1/6: *103, 408*.

Colchester, Colchester & Essex Museum: Cart. of St John's: *107–8, 412*.

Combermere Abbey: Cotton mun. (lost): *263, 416*.

Coventry, John Hales Hospital: register (lost): *116*.

Douai, Bibl. municipale: 887: *383*.

Durham Cathedral Libr.: C IV 24: *419*.

Ellenhall: Harcourt mun. (lost): *301*.

Ely: *see* Cambridge, Univ. Libr.

Eton College mun.: ECR 4/1: *601n.*; 18/1–3: *621*; 47/94: *208, 601*.

Évreux, Archives dép. de l'Eure: H 10: *335*; 1 M 2: *259*.

Exeter, D. & C. mun.: 303: *455n.*; 810: *413*; 811, 813: *414*; 3672: *413, 414*.
– Devon Record Office, City archives: misc. deed 226: *298*.
Forde Abbey, Geoffrey Roper, Esq.: cartulary: *470–1*.
Gent, Rijksarchief: Lewisham cartulary: *275*.
Gloucester, County Record Office: D 678: *324, 648*.
– – D. & C. Reg. A: *506*.
Hereford, D. & C. mun.: 722: *136n.*; 1364: *490n.*; 1386: *490n.*; 2770: *136*.
Kew (Surrey): B.S. Cron, Esq., 351 Sandycombe Road: *159*.
Lichfield, D. & C. Libr.: Magnum reg. album: *154–6, 265, 527–9*.
Lincoln, Lincs. Archives Office, D. & C. mun.: A/1/5: *533*; A/1/6: *13, 131*; D ii/73/1/31: *191*.
London, BL: Add. mss. 5706: *295*; 5948: *503*; 6037: *388*; 6159: *82, 84–5*; 14847: *362*; 32098: *320, 632*; 32100: *576*; 33182: *295, 538*; 35170: *173*; 46353: *432–6*; 46701: *619*; 47677: *115, 140–2, 366*; 50121: *21, 157, 291, 530–1*; 53710: *394–5*.
– – Add. charters 15238: *334*; 15688: *p. xlix n. 53*; 33596: *494*; 47397: *177A*; 47398: *177A, 297A*.
– – Arundel 68: *164*.
– – Campbell ch. xxii 6: *411*.
– – Cotton,
– – Appendix xxi: *41, 130, 620*; Aug. ii 26: *411n.*; Calig. A xiii: *576*; Claud. A vi: *5, 59, 71, 236–7, 342*; Claud. C vi: *164*; Claud. D x: *78, 91, 390, 392–3*; Claud. D xii: *120*; Cleop. B i: *607–15*; Cleop. C vii: *544–5*; Domit. A v: *356*; Domit. A x: *188–92, 194–7, 244, 303–5, 371–3, 590, 594*; Faust. A iv: *205–6, 599*; Faust. B v: *591–2*; Galba E ii: *137, 495*; Julius D ii: *91, 390*; Nero C iii: *411*; Nero D iii: *45*; Nero E vi: *42, 139, 213, 317–8, 630*; Otho B xiii: *Hubert app. 3–4*; Otho B xiv: *259, 499*; Otho D iii: *37, 198–9*; Tib. A ix: *394–5*; Tib. B xiii: *353–4*; Tib. C ix: *427, 640–2*; Tib. E v: *176*; Titus C ix: *427*; Vesp. A xxii: *371*; Vesp. E v: *585*; Vesp. E xiv: *290, 522–3*; Vesp. E xv: *178*; Vesp. E xvii: *174*; Vesp. E xix: *27*; Vesp. E xx: *1, 49–50*; Vesp. E xxiii: *129, 269*; Vesp. E xxv: *185, 302,* *452, 584–7*; Vesp. F xv: *133, 153*; Vit. A i: *415*; Vit. A x: *528*; Vit. A xi: *238, 346–7*; Vit. D ix: *14, 457–9*; Vit. D xviii: *415*; Vit. E xv: *178*.
– – Egerton 3031: *35, 185, 302, 584–7, Hubert app. 8–9*; 3033: *367*; 3126: *58, 313–4*; 3316: *332*; 3712: *325, 651*; 3772: *2, 60–1, 358*.
– – Harley 391: *224, 640, 641n., 642–4*; 468: *607–15*; 662: *139*; 1708: *302, 585–7*; 1885: *11–12, 127–8, 451*; 1965: *99–100, 260*; 2071: *102*; 2110: *98, 405–6, 557*; 2188: *552–4*; 3602: *426*; 3650: *17, 115, 140–2, 262*; 3656: *171, 171A*; 3688: *167*; 3697: *220–3*; 3868: *291, 530*; 4714: *338*; 6976: *239*; 7048: *92, 94*.
– – Harley charters 43 G 23: *170*; 43 G 24: *169*; 43 G 25: *365*; 43 G 26: *315*; 43 I 18: *364*; 75 A 13: *109*; 83 C 27–8: *597*; 84 C 42: *338*.
– – Lansdowne 448: *23*.
– – Loan 30: *63, 240, 360*.
– – Royal: 5 A iv: *194, 304, 594*; 11 B ix: *174*.
– – Stowe: 925: *238, 346–7*; 935: *138*.
London, Coll. of Arms: Arundel 59: *217–9*; Arundel 60: *173*; Combwell ch. V/96: *113*; XXIX/20: *114*; XXX/103: *110*; XL/2: *264*.
– Greater London Record Office: Acc. 312/214: *16n.*
– Guildhall Libr.: 9531/6: *33, 109n., 580, 622*.
– Inner Temple: Petit 511.18: *209*.
– Lambeth Palace: 8: *533B, 658*; 20: *164*; 241: *9, 122–6, 267A, 268, 437–47*; 415: *241–3, 246, 248–55, 327, 374, 391*; 419: *394–5*; 582: *388*; 719: *510*; 1131: *96*; 1212: *66–8, 75, 91n., 184, 295, 300, 344, 370–2, 387, 389, 412*.
– – TT. 1: *348–9, 351*.
– – Reg. W. Warham: *18, 23, 54, 91, 95, 111–2, 114, 121, 138, 144–7, 151, 162–3, 267, 281–3, 285, 287, 289, 294, 310, 333, 351–2, 370n., 371, 373–83, 402, 408, 430, 511, 518–21, 534, 600*.
– – Carte antique et misc. (CM): V/97: *537*; V/111: *18–9, 143–5, 147–50, 284, 286, 288, 511, 513–21*; XI/17: *371*; XI/18: *372n.*; XI/19: *370*; XI/20, 21: *370n.*; XI/32: *495*; XI/45: *519*; XIII/6 (ii): *6*; XIII/15: *82–3, 85, 87–8*.

London (*cont.*):
- Lincoln's Inn: Hale 87: *54, 233, 333.*
- Public Record Office: C 53/76: *484;*
  53/124: *43;* 53/150: *519;* 54/46: *525;*
  66/178: *623;* 109/86/39: *186;* 115/K
  1/6681: *508–9;* 115/K 2/6683: *487n.,*
  505–6; 115/L 1/6689: *505, p. xlvi n.*
  52; 115/L 1/6687: *506;* 115/L 2/6690:
  506; 146/5124: *340;* 150/1: *506;*
  270/30/27: *467n.*
  - - DL 25/8: *639;* 25/3394: *556;* 27/4:
    467; 27/5: *639n.;* 36/1/203: *467;*
    36/3/210: *62.*
  - - E 36/137: *66, 183, 300, 389, 400;*
    36/138: *389;* 40/4913: *23;* 40/5269:
    232; 40/6693: *p. xlvi n. 52;* 40/14000:
    617; 40/14001: *617n.;* 40/14414: *34;*
    40/14542: *650;* 40/14631: *165;*
    40/15418: *497;* 40/15466: *153;*
    164/20: *134;* 164/22: *323, 646–7;*
    164/27: *390, 394–5;* 164/28: *34,*
    581–2; 164/29: *172, 281, 500–2;*
    210/119: *168;* 315/31/45: *581;*
    315/45/139: *54, 333;* 315/46/68: *54,*
    333; 315/49/219: *635–6;* 315/61: *31,*
    181, 563–8; 326/4895: *636n.;*
    326/10443: *235;* 326/11667: *585n.;*
    326/11845 and 11852: *341n.;* 327/39:
    216n., 321; 327/94: *168, 296.*
  - - KB 136/1/1(2): *Hubert app. 7.*
  - - P.R.O. 31/8/140B: *64, 343, Hu-*
    bert app. 6; 31/8/144: *39–40,*
    202–4, 307; 31/140/1: *598.*
  - - S.C. 1/1/3: *605n.;* 1/1/17: *Hubert*
    app. 2; 1/1/18: *407;* 1/1/19: *507;*
    1/47/2: *Hubert app. 5;* 7/1/3: *617n.*
- St Bartholomew's Hosp.: Coke's cartulary: *24.*
- St Paul's Cathedral: Liber A (WD 1):
  158, 160; A/78/3016: *160.*
- Westminster Abbey mun.: book 11:
  69–70.
Maidstone, Kent Archives Office: DRc
  L 10/2: *589;* L 16/1: *193;* L 17: *194;* R
  3: *193, 245, 368–9, 371, 593, 629;* R
  4: *520n., 540, 623, 625–8;* R 9: *193,*
  593; T 54/1: *372;* T 54/2: *371;* T
  54/3: *370n., 371n.;* T 54/4: *373;* T 55
  and 55A: *594;* T 56: *194, 594n.;* T 57:
  595; T 264/12: *187;* T 293: *303;* T
  572/1: *628n.;* T 572/5: *627n.;* T
  572/7: *625n.;* T 572/8: *624;* T 572/9
  and 10: *629;* T 572/13: *626n.*
  - - Reg. John Fisher: *22, 520n.*

- - U 120/Q 13: *18, 144, 146–7, 151,*
  282–3, 285, 287, 289, 512, 518–21.
Northampton, Northants Record
  Office: Montagu (Buccleuch) 25/6:
  206.
Norwich, Norfolk Record Office, Nor-
  wich D. & C.: ch. 953: *558;* Reg. V:
  558; Reg. VII: *558–9.*
Orléans, Bibl. de la ville: 490–1: *38.*
Oxford, Bodleian Libr.: Ashmole 790:
  15; 1527: *154.*
- - Bodley 509: *30.*
- - Bucks. ch. a. 4: *16.*
- - Carte papers 108: *239.*
- - dep. deeds, Ch. Ch. O 627: *178.*
- - Digby 36: *607–15.*
- - Dugdale 12: *323, 575;* 15: *551.*
- - Essex ch. a. 2: *496.*
- - Fairfax 7: *499A.*
- - Glouc. ch. 21, 22: *276–7.*
- - Gough Kent 18: *348, 351.*
- - Hatton 23: *25.*
- - James 23: *182.*
- - Laud misc. 582: *426;* 625: *20, 152;*
  642: 329.
- - Loan (Stowell Park) Reg. A: *8,*
  104–5, 409–10, Hubert app. 1; Reg.
  B: *8, 105, 410.*
- - Lyell 15: *46.*
- - Northants ch. 2: *428.*
- - Rawl. B 329: *490;* B 333: *34;* B 336:
  351–2; B 461: *348–51;* Essex 11: *139.*
- - Tanner 18: *82, 84, 87;* 223: *66, 75,*
  183, 295, 300, 387, 389; 425: *492–3.*
- - Top. Northants c. 5: *176;* Yorks c.
  72: *10, 448.*
- - University Coll. 170: *473.*
- - Wood empt. 10: *319, 631.*
- - David Rogers Esq., c/o Bodleian
  Libr.: *2, 60–1, 358.*
Oxford, Balliol Coll.: 271: *491.*
- Christ Church: Chapter Libr. 31:
  132, 273, 462–6; 224: *29, 180, 561.*
- - Archives: Notley roll: *560.*
Oxford, Magdalen Coll.: 273: *345;* 274:
  211.
- - Deeds: Brackley 1a: *345;* Brackley
  76a: *117;* Durrington 3, 4: *211;* Rom-
  ney 59: *306;* Southwick 3, 15: *606A;*
  Estate Paper 137/1: *117.*
Oxford, New Coll. mun.: 12014: *55;*
  Liber Niger: *297.*
Oxford, University Coll.: *see* Bodleian
  Libr.

Paris, Archives nationales: L 968 no. 225: *311*.
– Bibl. nationale: fonds lat. 12775: *38*; Collection de Bourgogne vol. 81 nos. 284–9: *524–6*.
Peterborough, D. & C. Libr. 1: *569, 571–3*; 5: *570–2*.
Rochester, D. & C.: *see* Maidstone, DRc.
Rockingham Castle, Comdr M. Saunders Watson: muniments C 10: *429, 467A*.
Rouen, Archives dép. de la Seine-Maritime: G 9425: *486*; 7 H 57: *578–9*.
– Bibl. municipale: Y 200: *299*.
St-Lô, Archives dép. de la Manche: H 838A (lost): *Hubert app. 6*.
St-Omer, Bibl. municipale: 746: *40, 202–4*; 803: *39–40, 202–4, 307*.
Salisbury, Cathedral Libr.: 188: *Hubert app. 6*.
– D. & C. mun.: Liber evid. C: *209, 604*.
San Marino, Calif., H. Huntington Libr.: Battle 29: *54, 233, 333*; Battle 30: *54, 333*; Stowe 1: *28*.
Shrewsbury, Public Libr.: 1: *278, 488, 583*.

Spalding, Gentlemen's Soc.: Crowland cartulary: *118–9, 424*.
Stafford, County Record Office: 938/5: *312*.
Stowell Park: *see* Oxford, Bodl. Loan.
Stratford, Shakespeare Birthplace Trust: DR 10/195: *262*.
Taunton, Somerset Records Office: DD/SAS SX 133: *279*.
Trowbridge, Wilts Record Office: Acc. 128: *469*.
– Salisbury Dioc. Records: Liber evid. B: *209, 602, 604*; Reg. rubrum: *209, 602, 604*.
Vatican, Biblioteca Apostolica: Reginensis 470: *354*.
Wells, D. & C. mun.: charter 17: *337*; Reg. I: *51, 225–7*; Reg. III: *225–7*; Reg. IV: *226*.
Westminster: *see* London.
Winchester, Hants Record Office: Southwick Reg. I and Reg. III: *618*.
Windsor, St George's Chapel, mun.: XI G 11: *335–6*; XI G 13: *55*.
Woburn Abbey: Tavistock cartulary: *212, 316*.
Worcester, Cathedral Libr.: F 92: *574*.
– D. & C. mun.: A 4 (Reg. I): *326*.

PRINTED BOOKS AND ARTICLES CITED,
WITH ABBREVIATED REFERENCES

(references are to pages or columns, unless otherwise stated)

Acta Stephani Langton Cantuariensis archiepiscopi a.d. 1207–1228 ed. K. Major (CYS 50, 1950).

Adams *see Canterbury cases.*

Anglia sacra   [ed. H. Wharton]. 2 vols. (1691).

Ann. mon.   *Annales monastici* ed. H. R. Luard. 5 vols. (RS 1864–9).

Bec documents   *Select documents of the English lands of the abbey of Bec* ed. M. Chibnall (Camden 3s. 73, 1951).

Bernard, A. and Bruel, A. (ed.) *Recueil des chartes de l'abbaye de Cluny* (Coll. de docts inédits sur l'hist. de France. 6 vols. 1876–1903).

BIHR   *Bulletin of the Institute of Historical Research.*

Bishop, T. A. M. *Scriptores regis.* (Oxford 1961).

BJRL   *Bulletin of the John Rylands (University) Library.*

Black Book of St Augustine's   *The register of St Augustine's abbey, Canterbury, commonly called the Black Book* ed. G. J. Turner and H. E. Salter (Brit. Acad. Records of the social and econ. hist. of England and Wales. 1915–24) 2 vols.

Book of Seals   *Sir Christopher Hatton's Book of Seals* ed. L. C. Loyd and D. M. Stenton (Northants Record Soc. 15 and Oxford 1950).

Boxgrove chartulary   *Chartulary of Boxgrove priory* ed. and transl. Lindsay Fleming (Sussex Record Soc. 59, 1960).

Bradenstoke cartulary   *The cartulary of Bradenstoke priory* ed. V. C. M. London (Wilts. Record Soc. 35, Devizes 1979).

Bresslau, H. *Handbuch der Urkundenlehre für Deutschland und Italien* 2nd ed. (Berlin 1912–31, repr. 1958, and Register 1960).

Brooke, C. N. L. 'Episcopal charters for Wix priory', *Medieval miscellany for Doris Mary Stenton* (PRS n.s. 36, 1962) 45–63.

Bruton cartulary   *Two cartularies of the Augustinian priory of Bruton and the Cluniac priory of Montacute* ed. H. C. Maxwell-Lyte et al. (Somerset Record Soc. 8, 1894).

Buckland cartulary   *Cartulary of Buckland priory* ed. F. W. Weaver (Somerset Record Soc. 25, 1909).

Burton charters   *Descriptive catalogue of the charters and muniments belonging to the marquis of Anglesey* ed. I. H. Jeayes (Staffs. Record Soc. Collections, 61, 1937).

Burton chartulary   *Abstract of the contents of the Burton chartulary* (Wm Salt Archaeol. Soc. Collections 5. i, 1884).

Bushmead cartulary   *Cartulary of Bushmead priory* ed. G. H. Fowler and J. Godber (Bedfordshire Hist. Record Soc. 22, 1945).

Cal. Ch. Rolls   *Calendar of the Charter Rolls* (1226–1516). 6 vols. (HMSO 1903–27).

'Canterbury archbishopric charters, Table of' ed. I. J. Churchill *Camden miscellany XV* (Royal Hist. Soc. Camden 3s. 41, 1929).

Canterbury cases   *Selected cases from the ecclesiastical courts of the province of Canterbury c.1200–1301*, ed. Norma Adams and Charles Donahue Jr. (Selden Soc. 95, 1981).

Canterbury professions   ed. Michael Richter (CYS 67, 1973).

Canterbury see also *Black Book*, Churchill, Du Boulay, *Ep. Cant.*, *St Gregory's cartulary*, Somner, Urry.

CDF   *Calendar of documents preserved in France . . . a.d. 918–1206* ed. J. H. Round (HMSO 1899).

Chartes de St-Bertin (Les), d'après le grand cartulaire ed. D. Haigneré. 4 vols. (Soc. des antiquaires de la Morinie. St-Omer 1886–99).

Cheney, C. R. *English bishops' chanceries 1100–1250* (Manchester 1950).

Cheney, C. R. *Hubert Walter* (1967).

Cheney, C. R. *Pope Innocent III and England* (Päpste und Papsttum. 9. Stuttgart 1976).

Cheney, C. R. 'On the acta of Theobald and Thomas archbishops of Canterbury', *Journal of the Society of Archivists*, vol. 6 no. 8 (Oct. 1981) 467–81.

Cheney, M. G. *Roger, bishop of Worcester, 1164–79* (Oxford 1981).

Chester chartulary   *The chartulary or register of the abbey of St Werburgh, Chester* ed. J. Tait. 2 vols. (Chetham Soc. n.s. 79, 82, 1920–1).

Chichester acta   *The acta of the bishops of Chichester 1075–1207* ed. H. Mayr-Harting (CYS 56, 1964).

Chichester chartulary   *The chartulary of the high church of Chichester* ed. W. D. Peckham (Sussex Record Soc. 46, 1946).

Christ Church cartulary   *Cartulary of the mediaeval archives of Christ Church [Oxford]* ed. N. Denholm-Young (Oxford Hist. Soc. 92, 1931).

Chron. mon. de Bello   *Chronicon monasterii de Bello* ed. J. S. Brewer (Anglia Christiana Soc. 1846). Also, *Chronicle of Battle Abbey*, ed. and transl. E. Searle (Oxford 1980).

Churchill, I. J. *Canterbury administration.* 2 vols. (1933).

Cirencester cartulary   *The cartulary of Cirencester abbey* ed. C. D. Ross and Mary Devine. 3 vols. (Oxford 1964–77).

Clerkenwell cartulary   *Cartulary of St Mary Clerkenwell* ed. W. O. Hassall (Royal Hist. Soc. Camden 3s. 71, 1949).

Colchester cartulary   *Cartularium monasterii sancti Iohannis baptiste de Colecestria* ed. S. A. Moore. 2 vols. (Roxburghe Club 1897).

Colvin, H. M. *The white canons in England* (Oxford 1951).

CPL   *Calendar of entries in the papal registers relating to Great Britain and Ireland: Papal letters* ed. W. H. Bliss et al. 14 vols. in 15 (HMSO 1893–1960).

CRR   *Curia Regis rolls . . . preserved in the PRO.* 15 vols. (HMSO 1922–72).

CYS   Canterbury and York Society publications.

Danelaw docts   *Documents illustrative of the social and economic history of the Danelaw* ed. F. M. Stenton (Brit. Acad. Records of the social and econ. hist. of England and Wales 5, 1920).

Diceto, Ralph de *Opera historica* ed. W. Stubbs. 2 vols. (RS 1876).

Domerham, Adam de *Historia de rebus gestis Glastoniensibus* ed. Thomas Hearne. 2 vols. (Oxford 1727).

Du Boulay, F. R. H. *The lordship of Canterbury* (1966).

Duckett, G. F. (ed.) *Charters and records of Cluni* (1888).

Dunstable cartulary   *A digest of the charters preserved in the cartulary of the priory of Dunstable* ed. G. H. Fowler (Bedfordshire Hist. Record Soc. 10, 1926).

EBC see Cheney *English bishops' chanceries 1100–1250.*

EEA   *English episcopal acta*: i. *Lincoln 1067–1185* and iv. *Lincoln 1186–1206*, ed. David M. Smith (Brit. Acad. 1980–).

EHR   *English Historical Review.*

Elmham, Thomas of *Historia monasterii S. Augustini Cantuariensis* ed. C. Hardwick (RS 1858).

Ep. Cant.   *Epistolae Cantuarienses: Chronicles and memorials of the reign of Richard I*, vol. 2, ed. W. Stubbs. (RS 1865).

Evesham chronicle   *Chronicon abbatiae de Evesham ad an. 1418* ed. W. D. Macray (RS 1863).

Extra   *Decretalium Gregorii pp. IX compilatio* ed. E. Friedberg (Corpus iuris canonici vol. ii. Leipzig 1881).

EYC   *Early Yorkshire charters* vols. i–iii ed. W. Farrer (1914–16) vols. iv–xii ed. C. T. Clay, and index to vols. i–iii by C. T. Clay and Edith Clay (Yorks. Archaeological Soc. Record series, extra series. 1935–65).

Eynsham cartulary   *The cartulary of the abbey of Eynsham* ed. H. E. Salter. 2 vols. (Oxford Hist. Soc. 49, 51. 1907–8).

Eyton, R. W. *The court, household, and itinerary of king Henry II* (1888).

Fasti ecclesiae anglicanae 1066–1300 by John Le Neve, ed. Diana E. Greenway. vols. 1–3 (1968–77).

Foliot   *Letters and charters of Gilbert Foliot* ed. A. Morey and C. N. L. Brooke (Cambridge 1967).

Foreville, Raymonde *Un procès de canonisation à l'aube du xiii* *siècle (1201–1202): le livre de S. Gilbert de Sempringham* (Paris 1943).

Foreville, Raymonde 'Lettres "extravagantes" de Thomas Becket, archevêque de Canterbury' *Mélanges d'histoire dédiés à la mémoire de Louis Halphen* (Paris 1951) 225–38; reprinted in Foreville, *Thomas Becket dans la tradition historique et hagiographique* (Variorum Reprints, 1981).

Formulare anglicanum [ed. Thomas Madox] (1702).

GEC   G. E. C[okayne] *Complete peerage.* New ed. 13 vols. (1910–59).

Gervas. Cant.   *Hist. works of Gervase of Canterbury* ed. W. Stubbs. 2 vols. (RS 1879–80).

Gesta regis Henrici II ed. W. Stubbs. 2 vols. (RS 1867).

Giraldus Cambrensis *Opera* ed. J. S. Brewer et al. 8 vols. (RS 1861–91).

Glastonbury chartulary   *The great chartulary of Glastonbury* ed. A. Watkin (Somerset Record Soc. 59, 63, 64. 1947–56).

Gloucester cartulary   *Historia et cartularium monasterii sancti Petri Gloucestriae* ed. W. H. Hart. 3 vols. (RS 1863–7).

Hereford charters   *Charters and records of Hereford cathedral* ed. W. W. Capes (Cantilupe Soc. Hereford 1908).

HMCR   *Reports* of the Historical Manuscripts Commission.

Holme St Benets *see St Benet's.*

Holtzmann, Walther *see PUE.*

Hoveden, Roger de, *Chronica* ed. W. Stubbs. 4 vols. (RS 1868–71).

HRH   D. Knowles, C. N. L. Brooke, V. C. M. London (eds.) *The heads of religious houses: England and Wales 940–1216* (Cambridge 1972).

Itinerary of king Richard I by Lionel Landon (PRS n.s. 13. 1935).

JL   *Regesta pontificum Romanorum . . . ad annum 1198*, ed. Ph. Jaffé 2nd ed. S. Loewenfeld et al. 2 vols. (Leipzig 1885–8).

John of Salisbury   *The letters of John of Salisbury* ed. W. J. Millor, H. E. Butler, and C. N. L. Brooke. 2 vols. (Nelson's Medieval Texts (vol. i) London 1955, Oxford Medieval Texts (vol. ii) Oxford 1979).

Kennett, White *Parochial antiquities attempted in the history of Ambrosden, Burcister (etc.)* 2nd ed. 2 vols. (Oxford 1818).

Kent fines   *Calendar of Kent feet of fines* ed. F. W. Jessupp et al. (Kent Archaeol. Soc. Records Branch 15, 1956).

Langton *see Acta Stephani Langton.*

Leiston cart.   *Leiston abbey cartulary and Butley priory charters* ed. R. Mortimer. (Suffolk Records Soc.: Suffolk charters i. 1979).

Letters of pope Innocent III concerning England and Wales ed. C. R. and M. G. Cheney (Oxford 1967).

Lewes chartulary   *The chartulary of the priory of St Pancras of Lewes (Sussex portion)* ed. L. F. Salzman. 2 vols. (Sussex Record Soc. 38, 40. 1933–5).

Lewes chartulary: Norfolk portion   *The Norfolk portion of the chartulary of the priory of St Pancras of Lewes* ed. J. H. Bullock (Norfolk Record Soc. 12, 1939).

Lichfield M. R. A.   *The great register of Lichfield cathedral known as Magnum Registrum Album* ed. H. E. Savage (Wm Salt Archaeol. Soc. Collections for 1924, 1926).

Lincoln reg. ant.   *The Registrum Antiquissimum of the cathedral charch of Lincoln* ed. C. W. Foster and Kathleen Major. 10 vols. and plates (Lincoln Record Soc. 1931–73).

Madox *see Formulare.*

Mon. Ang.   W. Dugdale *Monasticon Anglicanum* ed. J. Caley, H. Ellis and B. Bandinel. 6 vols. in 8 (London 1817–30, and 1846).

Mon. Exon.   G. Oliver *Monasticon diocesis Exoniensis* (Exeter 1846) and *Additional supplement* (Exeter 1854).

Morey, Adrian *Bartholomew of Exeter* (Cambridge 1937).

MTB   *Materials for the history of Thomas Becket* ed. J. C. Robertson and J. B. Sheppard. 7 vols. (RS 1875–85).

Newcourt, Richard *Repertorium ecclesiasticum parochiale Londinense.* 2 vols. (1708–10).

Newington Longeville charters ed. H. E. Salter (Oxfordshire Record Soc. 3, 1921).

Newnham cartulary   *Cartulary of Newnham priory* ed. Joyce Godber (Bedfordshire Hist. Record Soc. 43, 1963–4).

Nichols, John *Bibliotheca topographica Britannica.* 10 vols. (1780–1800).

Northants charters   *Facsimiles of early charters from Northants collections* ed. F. M. Stenton (Northants Record Soc. 4, 1930).

Oseney cartulary   *Cartulary of Oseney abbey* ed. H. E. Salter. 6 vols. (Oxford Hist. Soc. 1929–36).

Owen, D. M. *Catalogue of Lambeth mss. 889–901: Carte antique et miscellanee* (1968).

Paris *Chron. Maj.*   Matthew Paris *Chronica maiora* ed. H. R. Luard. 7 vols. (RS 1872–83).

Petri Blesensis opera omnia ed. J. A. Giles. 4 vols. (Patres ecclesiae anglicanae. Oxford 1846–7). Also in *PL* 207.

PL   *Patrologiae latinae cursus completus* ed. J. P. Migne. (Paris 1844–64).

Pleas before the king or his justices 1198–1202 ed. D. M. Stenton. vols. 1–2: 1198–1202 (Selden Soc. vols. 67–8. 1952–3); vols. 3–4: 1198-1212 (ibid. vols. 83–4. 1966–7).

Pott.   *Regesta pontificum romanorum a.d. 1198–1304* ed. A. Potthast. 2 vols. (Berlin 1874–5).

PRS   Pipe Roll Society publications.

PUE   *Papsturkunden in England* ed. W. Holtzmann. 3 vols. (Abhandlungen der Gesellschaft der Wissenschaften zu Göttingen phil.-hist. Kl. N.F. 25, 1930–1; 3 Folge 14–15, 1935–6; 3 Folge 33, 1952).

Ramsey cartulary   *Cartularium monasterii de Rameseia* ed. W. H. Hart and P. A. Lyons. 3 vols. (RS 1884–93).

Recueil des actes de Henri II roi d'Angleterre et duc de Normandie concernant les provinces françaises et les affaires de France ed. L. Delisle and É. Berger. 4 vols. and album (Chartes et diplômes. Paris 1909–27).

Regesta regum anglo-normannorum ed. H. W. C. Davis et al. 4 vols. (Oxford 1913, 1956, 1968–9).

Register of St Osmund ed. W. H. Rich Jones. 2 vols. (RS 1883–4).

Registrum Hamonis Hethe dioc. Roffensis ed. Charles Johnson. 2 vols. (CYS 48, 49, 1948).

Registrum Roffense ed. John Thorpe (1769).

Rot. ch.   *Rotuli chartarum . . . 1199–1216* ed. T. D. Hardy (Record Commission 1837).

Rot. lit. pat.   *Rotuli litterarum patentium . . . 1201–16* ed. T. D. Hardy (Record Commission 1835).

RS   Rolls series: The chronicles and memorials of Great Britain and Ireland during the Middle Ages published under the direction of the Master of the Rolls (HMSO 1858–96).

St Benet's register   *St Benet of Holme 1020–1210. The eleventh and twelfth-century sections of Cotton ms. Galba E ii, the register of the abbey of St Benet of Holme* ed. J. R. West. 2 vols. (Norfolk Record Soc. 2, 3, 1932).

St-Bertin *see Chartes de St-Bertin.*

St Frideswide's cartulary   *The cartulary of the monastery of St Frideswide at Oxford* ed. S. R. Wigram. 2 vols. (Oxford Hist. Soc. 28, 31, 1895–6).

St Gregory's cartulary   *Cartulary of the priory of St Gregory, Canterbury* ed. A. M. Woodcock (Royal Hist. Soc. Camden 3s. 88, 1956).

Salisbury charters   *Charters and documents . . . of the cathedral, city, and diocese of Salisbury . . .* ed. W. Rich Jones and W. D. Macray (RS 1891).

Saltman, Avrom *Theobald, archbishop of Canterbury* (Univ. of London Hist. Studies 2, 1956).

Sandford cartulary (The) ed. A. M. Leys. 2 vols. (Oxfordshire Record Soc. 19, 22, 1938–41).

SLI   *Selected letters of Pope Innocent III concerning England 1198–1216* ed. C. R. Cheney and W. H. Semple (Nelson's Medieval Texts 1953).

Somner, William *Antiquities of Canterbury* 2nd ed. by N. Battely (1703), repr. with introduction by W. Urry (1977).

Thame cartulary (The) ed. H. E. Salter. 2 vols. (Oxfordshire Record Soc. 25, 26, 1947–8).

Tutbury cartulary   *Cartulary of Tutbury priory* ed. A. Saltman (Staffordshire Record Soc. 4s. 4 and HMC JP2, 1962).

Twysden, Roger (ed.) *Historiae anglicanae scriptores decem* (1652).

Urry, William   *Canterbury under the Angevin kings.* 2 vols. (1967).

VCH   The Victoria History of the counties of England.

Wardon cartulary   Cartulary of the abbey of Old Wardon ed. G. H. Fowler (Bedfordshire Hist. Record Soc. 13, 1930).

Welsh ep. acts   Episcopal acts relating to Welsh dioceses ed. J. Conway Davies. Vols. i–ii. (Hist. Soc. of the Church in Wales. 1946–8).

Wilkins, David (ed.) *Concilia Magnae Britanniae et Hiberniae a.d. 446–1717.* 4 vols. (1737).

Winchcombe cartulary   Landboc sive Registrum monasterii beatae Mariae virginis et sancti Cénhelmi de Winchelcumba ed. David Royce. 2 vols. (Exeter 1892).

Winchester chartulary   Chartulary of Winchester cathedral ed. in English by A. W. Goodman (Winchester 1927).

Worcester cartulary   The cartulary of Worcester cathedral priory (Register I) ed. R. R. Darlington (PRS n.s. 38, 1968).

York minster fasti ed. C. T. Clay. 2 vols. (Yorks Archaeol. Soc. Record Series 123–4, 1958–9).

Young, C. R. *Hubert Walter, lord of Canterbury and lord of England* (Durham, N. Carolina 1968).

OTHER ABBREVIATIONS

add	addition
archbp	archbishop
archdn	archdeacon
Arr.	Arrouaisian
Aug.	Augustinian
Ben.	Benedictine
BL	British Library, formerly British Museum
BN	Bibliothèque Nationale, Paris
Bodl.	Bodleian Library, Oxford
bp	bishop
card.	cardinal
ch.	church
Cist.	Cistercian
clk	clerk
Clun.	Cluniac
D. & C.	Dean and chapter
dioc.	diocese
d. q.	sur double queue (cf. Introduction p. xlvi)
Gilb.	Gilbertine
HMSO	Her (His) Majesty's Stationery Office
kg	king
Mun.	Muniments
m.	membrane
om.	omit, omission
P. & C.	Prior and convent
Pd	Printed
pr.	priest
Prem.	Premonstratensian
PR	Pipe Roll
PRO	Public Record Office, London
reg.	Regesta, regestum, register, etc.
s. q.	sur simple queue
UL	University Library

INTRODUCTION

THE ARCHBISHOPS AND THEIR STAFF

This period begins with normal church government disrupted by the clash of archbishop Thomas Becket and king Henry II, and ends when archbishop Hubert Walter's death leads to the election of Stephen Langton, obstructed by king John, and a papal interdict on England. These dramatic events were not matched by sudden changes in the method of internal government of the Church. The provincial organization of Canterbury in Stephen's day was very different from that of Theobald's; but this resulted from a gradual evolution of offices, institutions, and customs in Latin christendom. Contact between England and the Roman Curia increased, ecclesiastical litigation increased, more regularity was introduced into diocesan practice; and all this is reflected in the surviving documentary records. We are not dealing with a long span of time, in terms of human life. There were four archbishops of Canterbury in this period and the longest pontificate — that of Hubert Walter — lasted less than twelve years. A clerk ordained when Thomas became archbishop might well be active, if past his prime, when archbishop Hubert died forty-three years later. The career of Mr Peter of Blois is a case in point, and other clerks might be named who had a comparable length of activity.[1]

The occupants of the see present strong contrasts. Thomas, with a secular career behind him, was an exile for more than two-thirds of his short pontificate and seems to have had little contact with his monastic chapter. His administrative acta are far less bulky than the diplomatic correspondence which records his estrangement from Henry II and his uneasy relations with the pope. The next two archbishops were monks, one Benedictine and one Cistercian. Richard of Dover, formerly a monk of Christ Church, left records of an active routine throughout a fairly peaceful pontificate of nearly ten years. Baldwin of Forde, active but indiscreet, departed on

---

[1] Mr Silvester was a clerk of bishop Roger of Worcester by 1165, followed bishop Baldwin to Canterbury (1185–90), and was probably the archdeacon of Chichester of that name *c.*1196 — after 1213 (see H. M. R. E. Mayr-Harting in *Studies in Church History* ii (1965) 186–96). Mr Ralph de Sancto Martino is recorded from 1177 to 1207 and Robert of Bristol from 1193 to 1225 (see Index below, vol. III).

crusade in his fifth year as archbishop after angry exchanges with his chapter, and never came back. Hubert, who had the background of a civil servant, was made justiciar of England as soon as he was translated from Salisbury to Canterbury, and within a few months of resigning that secular office became king John's chancellor.

Thanks to the fact that more copious records and fuller narratives by contemporary historians survive than are available for the early twelfth century, we are fairly well informed about the activities of these archbishops in politics and diplomacy. It is less easy to discover signs of their impact on the routine ecclesiastical business. It is impossible to prove, and dangerous to speculate upon, what influence—if any—an individual archbishop had on office practice.

A few able clerks with long experience, sometimes enjoying the trust of two or three prelates in turn, might make more of a mark on the administration than did their employers. They ensured some continuity and, probably, conservatism; at the same time, they might take responsibility for innovations. The witness-lists of the archbishops' acta throw light, though only faint light, on the persons in question. The following table will give a rough idea of the continued service, not only of several distinguished *litterati*, but of humbler clerks, often known to us only by their presence in the lists. Allowance must be made, of course, for the risk of confusing, in this state of obscurity, different men of the same name.

Thomas	Richard	Baldwin	Hubert
Gerard Pucella	—		
William, chaplain	—		
Alexander Walensis	—		
	Peter of Blois	—	—
	Geoffrey Fortis	—	—
	Henry of Northampton	—	
	William of Northolt	—	
	Roger of Rolleston	—	
	Ralph de S. Martino	—	
	William of Shottenden	—	
	Solomon (of Dover?)	—	
		Robert of Bristol	—

Two of these archbishops came to Canterbury after ruling dioceses in the province — Baldwin at Worcester 1180–84 and Hubert at Salisbury 1189–93 — and they brought with them to Canterbury some of their former clerical staff. For Baldwin we can point to John of Exeter, Mr Godfrey, Mr Samson, and Mr Silvester. Hubert employed in both his sees Roger of Bassingham,

Mr Edmund, Mr Elias 'medicus', Mr Gervase, Mr William of Necton, Ranulf the treasurer of Salisbury, Mr Simon de Scalis, Mr Reiner of Stamford. There was also a coming and going between the service of the metropolitan and that of his suffragans; and clerks divided their careers between English and Norman churches.

When all this is said, the unfortunate fact remains that not much light can be shed on the office staff which drafted and wrote the acta assembled here. Much has been written about the persons composing the *familiae* or households or retainers of medieval prelates, and on this basis conclusions have been drawn about episcopal secretariats. It is not, however, always realised how little solid evidence on this matter can be gained from twelfth-century records.[2] A profusion of names, even names of persons frequently found in a bishop's company as witnesses of his acta, does not always prove that they comprise his permanent staff. Still less is it axiomatic that they include the very clerks who draft and write. Speaking of the see of Lincoln, Dr David Smith says: 'The actual organization of the clerical side of the household defies investigation for lack of evidence.'[3]

For the see of Canterbury, we have the exceptional chance to make a list — albeit a discontinuous list — of officially designated chancellors;[4] presumably these men were in some way heads of the secretariat, but we seldom see them at work and their functions are nowhere spelt out.[5] Most other English sees managed without an officer with this title.

A chancellor of archbishop Thomas is mentioned by Peter Cantor and by Gerald of Wales.[6] Peter names him 'Mr Arnulf' and perhaps it was he who witnessed Thomas's charters for St-Bertin in November 1164 without using the title (nos. 39–40, cf. Diceto i 307). One Roger *cancellarius* occupies the same place, after Mr Gunther, in the witness-list of a charter for Minster (no. 26).

When the pope instructed archbishop Richard, probably at his consecration, to entrust his seal to one of his monks,[7] Richard took

---

[2] Cheney, *EBC* ch. 1–2 and *Hubert Walter* ch. 8, and especially D. M. Smith, *EEA* i *Lincoln 1067–1185* pp. xxxix–xlvii. For earlier times see M. Brett, *Engl. church under Henry I* (Oxford 1975) 173–85 and Saltman, *Theobald* 165–77. For the Canterbury household in later times see K. Major in *EHR* xlviii (1933) 529–53 and *Acta S. Langton* xlviii–li, and C. H. Lawrence, *St Edmund of Abingdon* (Oxford 1960) 138–55.

[3] *EEA* i p. xlv.   [4] For the sequence from 1121 see *EBC* 28–37.

[5] Churchill, *Canterbury administration* i 16.

[6] Thomas is said to have required his chancellor to swear to take nothing ('usque ad cnipulum') for his official services. *MTB* iv 265, Gir. Cambr. *Opp.* ii 292.

[7] *PUE* ii 329–30 no. 137 (11 May 1174): a letter close, probably impetrated by the monks of Christ Church.

Benedict, monk of Christ Church, for chancellor. As chancellor Benedict proclaimed the statutes in the Council of Westminster in 1175 and attested at least eight acta of the archbishop. He probably ceased to hold the office after becoming prior of Canterbury c.July 1175.[8] Not long afterwards Mr Peter of Blois, presenting his *Compendium in Iob* to king Henry, describes himself as chancellor of the archbishop of Canterbury, and refers to his office in a personal letter to his friend John of Salisbury between August 1176 and October 1180 (ep. 130).[9] But the appointment did not limit his tasks to those of an active head of the secretariat. He was sent to the Roman Curia in autumn 1177 and was there the following April. He also represented the absent archbishop in the Third Lateran Council in March 1179, and we have no trace of him in England for the next two years. Between 1181 and 1184 he was in England and in Normandy, often in the archbishop's company. During these years pope Lucius III refers to him as archbishop Richard's chancellor (*Extra* 3 22 3) and Peter attests three acta of the archbishop as 'Mr P. Blesensis cancellarius noster archidiaconus Bathoniensis.'[10] None of these acta survives in original. On the other hand, five originals which can be certainly dated in these years (nos. 64, 85, 113–4, 206) and very many others in reliable copies name the archdeacon as witness without the title of chancellor. One can but conclude that the title of chancellor was not taken very seriously (unless by the bearer of the title) and that at this time its use in witness-lists depended on the draftsman or the scribe.

Baldwin's pontificate shows equal laxness. There are exiguous traces of John, his chancellor, in two witness-lists (nos. 323, and †304, spurious) and in one other list (no. 262) he appears as John de Exonia 'cancellarius domini archiepiscopi'. But John of Exeter also appears without the title of chancellor at intervals throughout the pontificate.

Under archbishop Hubert references to 'Mr Richard our chancellor' are abundant in witness-lists, but nowhere else. All, or almost all, of these references could be no later than 1198 (no. 484, dated 1204, is a most dubious document). The copy of a lost original (no. 504) may conceal his name under the entry: 'Ricardus cancellarius de Brandeston''. Did the office lapse in or before 1198? We shall not

---

[8] Cf. nos. 111n., 215. Benedict witnesses two of Richard's acta as abbot, both before Sept. 1181 (nos. 95, 204).

[9] *EBC* 33–34, where some correction is needed in the light of the acta printed here.

[10] Nos. 54 (1183×4), 66 (1182×4), 167 (1183), the last two transposing the titles. In Apr. × May 1183 the archbishop describes Peter as 'our clerk Mr Peter of Blois, archdeacon of Bath' (no. 156). He became archdeacon in 1182.

hear of an archbishop's chancellor again until late in Stephen Langton's pontificate.

Nor do Canterbury records refer often to officials who might be the chancellor's deputies or subordinates. Mr Walter *scriptor* is mentioned with Amicus and William *domini Cantuariensis notarii* in the context of an award by archbishop Richard about two Gloucestershire churches.[11] Mr Henry Pigon is described in 1187 by a Roman cardinal as *secretarius domini Cantuariensis*.[12] Geoffrey *noturius* witnesses a charter of archbishop Baldwin (no. 303). A papal letter of 1202, which speaks of Mr Simon, vice-chancellor of archbishop Hubert, may refer to Mr Simon of Sywell, who was entrusted with the archbishop's counterseal while he was overseas in that year.[13] In general, this meagre summary of named officials throws little light on the way in which the archbishop's chancery operated and the way in which secretarial work was allocated. One recalls that John of Salisbury, who wrote so many official letters for archbishop Theobald, had no official title in the primate's *familia*. What can be learnt about the *familia* as a whole?

The household of an archbishop of Canterbury — a churchman and statesman of the first importance — was likely to be a gathering place for scholars and others who had ambitions in the Church, offering the chance of a *carrière ouverte au talent*. There was work to do for which the archbishop would reward his clerical assistants with benefices and prebends. The entourage therefore attracted the attention of contemporaries, so that we get some light upon it from biographies and letters and chronicles of the time. These refer at least to the most distinguished of the archbishop's counsellors and give scraps of information about the elusive secretariat. Notable literary figures, John of Salisbury, Herbert of Bosham, Peter de Blois, are recorded in the service of archbishop Theobald and his four successors; and because their letters were collected, we have the evidence of letters they wrote in the names of their employers and patrons. Besides this, in Bosham's life of St Thomas, is a precious list of twenty 'eruditi' (including Herbert himself and John of Salisbury) who belonged to Becket's household for some parts of his pontificate.[14] Eight of them appear as witnesses to the few witnessed

---

[11] No. 136, cf. *Hereford Charters* 27–8. [12] *Ep. Cant.* 80.

[13] *Letters of Innocent III* no. 452, cf. *EBC* 13. William Thorne's chronicle calls Simon de Camera the archbishop's vice-chancellor, but he probably refers to the royal chancery under Hubert, when Simon de Camera was a frequent datary. *EBC* 35–6.

[14] *MTB* iii 523–9. Diceto (i 307) names those who fetched the archbishop's pallium from the pope at Montpellier in June 1162: John Bellesmains, John of Salisbury, Jordan of Chichester, abbot Adam of Evesham, Mr Arnulf (Thomas's chancellor), and Simon monk of Canterbury.

acta of the archbishop. One of these, Mr John of Tilbury, is described by Herbert of Bosham as 'scriba doctus et velox' and point is given to the description by his reputed authorship of a work on shorthand.[15]

Under Thomas's successor a few famous scholars appear among the witnesses of archbishop Richard's acta. One of Becket's 'eruditi', Mr Gerard Pucella, a considerable canonist, attests dozens of acta of archbishop Richard, where he is accorded precedence over all but the most notable personages. Even Mr Peter of Blois, the chancellor, gives place to Gerard. He travelled with Peter to Rome in 1177 to fight the archbishop's battle against St Augustine's abbey, and the abbey chronicler, while likening them to fierce wolves, concedes that 'these two were considered — not without reason — the most eloquent men in all the world.'[16] Mr Peter, speaking immodestly as one of the circle, observes that archbishop Richard's household was 'an assembly of cultivated and acute minds' (ep. 6).

Archbishop Baldwin, himself a distinguished scholar, was a patron of scholars, in the persons of his nephew, Joseph of Exeter, Peter of Blois, and Gerald of Wales. Neither Gerald nor Joseph figures often as witness of his official business (nos. 276, 268, 287), but Gerald accompanied the archbishop on his visitation of Wales and Joseph set out with him for the Holy Land.[17] Mr Peter of Blois witnesses many of the archbishop's charters, and his own epistolary collections preserve three letters in Baldwin's name (nos. 247 261, 322). Peter remains at the service of archbishop Hubert in the early years of his pontificate and assures us that Hubert valued his company and found his services useful (epp. 109, 124). So far as the evidence goes, he continues to act as he had done for Baldwin. He writes several letters for Hubert (nos. 605, 655) and occasionally attests other acta. Other scholars in Hubert's service who are named by contemporaries are mostly men employed in lawsuits, Mr John of Tynemouth and Mr Honorius, archdeacon of Richmond, being the most prominent. There is also Mr Simon of Sywell, a canon of Lincoln who becomes a canon of the ill-fated chapel at Lambeth and treasurer of Lichfield in 1198 (nos. 491, 568). According to Gerald of Wales he acted as the archbishop's *generalis officialis* in England during Hubert's absence abroad in 1202, when he wrote on his master's business 'nomine archiepiscopi' and sealed mandates

---

[15] M. Manitius, *Gesch. der latein. Literatur des MA* (Munich 1911–31) iii 311–2; A. B. Emden, *Biog. register . . . Oxford* (Oxford 1957–9) iii 1876.
[16] Twysden 1821.   [17] *PL* ccxi 1305–8; cf. Gir. Cambr. *Opp.* i 79.

with the archbishop's counterseal. These were notable canonists and were both teachers and practitioners.[18]

LISTS OF WITNESSES

For light on the archbishop's clerical staff the chief source must be the witness-lists of his acta.[19] But are witness-lists safe guides? The question is as hard to answer as that which arises over the practice of the Angevin royal chancery. Witness-lists are resistant to statistical analysis, presenting many traps, of which some must be briefly mentioned here. Do the lists indicate those present at the trans-action or those present when it was recorded? We seldom know.[20] We can seldom assign exact dates, so that the frequent appearance of a witness does not necessarily prove long periods of service at the archbishop's side; many acta may have been issued together on one day. Scribal inconsistency or ignorance probably explains why witnesses are not always assigned their identificatory dignity or office and why their names (particularly in copies) are garbled. Moreover, personal names were unstable. Mr Gerard was seldom, but occasionally, described as 'Pucella'. Among the inferior staff the use of surnames, especially those drawn from places, was erratic, as the following examples show. Thirteen of archbishop Richard's acta are attested by both Richard and Geoffrey 'clerks' (and once 'chaplains', no. 92). Another eight are attested by Richard of London and Geoffrey; and two late acta (nos. 96, 114) are attested by Richard of London and Geoffrey Fortis. Some of these same acta have Roger 'dean' among the witnesses, in near proximity to Richard and Geoffrey; and in nos. 54, 114 and 213 appears Roger the dean of 'Cranbroc' or 'Cranewer'. When other coincidences are noted (cf. nos. 154, 155) it is hard to believe that Richard of London and Geoffrey Fortis are not the same as the other Richards and Geoffreys. Roger dean who attests more than twenty of archbishop Richard's acta thus, may well be the man whose deanery is named in nos. 54, 114, 213. The household of archbishop Baldwin provides another case of varying practice over nomenclature: in two original acta which may have been drawn up on the same occasion, and certainly at no great distance of time, the Mr Henry and the Eustace of no. 248 are evidently the Mr Henry of Northampton and the

---

[18] See S. Kuttner and E. Rathbone, 'Anglo-Norman canonists of the twelfth century', *Traditio* vii (1949–51) and sources there cited.

[19] For lay officers one must generally look elsewhere. Cf. *EEA* i p. xli, and cf. below, no. 68.

[20] A. de Boüard, *Manuel de diplomatique* i (1929) 76–8.

Eustace of Wilton of no. 249. Inconsistency also appears when a clerk is called *magister* in early lists and denied the title in later ones. Roger of Norwich is a case in point, where we almost certainly have to do with one man only.

Any figures which aim to show frequency of attendance upon the archbishop, depending as they must in large part on cartulary-copies, are further vitiated by the scribal habit of curtailing, if not omitting, witness-lists. This is striking in cases where original and copy, or several copies, can be compared (e.g. nos. 233, 506, 519, 642).

It is another measure of our ignorance of the rules and customs of the writing-office that we cannot say why some acta have lists of witnesses whereas others exactly comparable do not. Nor can we do more than guess on what principle names were selected for inclusion. They may include both the archbishop's clerks and visitors, picked arbitrarily and without rigid observance of rank.[21] This apparently arbitrary selection of certain names, taken from among those eligible to appear in a witness-list, prevents us from determining how many of the acta were written at one time. It is excessively rare to find precisely the same list twice; but it is inconceivable that the archbishop's clerks never produced more than one document a day. Differences between lists — which are sometimes very slight — do not prove separate occasions. A glance at the royal charters of king Richard I and king John, which bear full dates, show a variety of witnesses named by the scribes of different charters dated on one day at one place. The clerks who made up the lists in the archbishop's charters may have exercised equal freedom of choice or have operated according to rules unknown to us.

Some documents, issued when the archbishop was at the king's court or a legatine council (e.g. nos. 227, 623), only record very important persons and exclude the mere clerical staff. In charters concerning the temporalities of the see, on the other hand, the scribe may list none but local bailiffs and suitors of a hundred court. For normal ecclesiastical business, however, most witnesses of a charter of confirmation or a judicial settlement are drawn from the household, apart from a few visitors of distinction, judicial assessors, or chief clerks of the great men present. Used cautiously, these lists

---

[21] Cf. Foliot, *Letters and charters* pp. 26–7 and no. 391 for an act containing both sorts. C. L. Lewis rashly treats Mr Richard de Mores, canonist and later prior of Dunstable, as one of Hubert's *familia* on the strength of his attestation of no. 467 (*Traditio* xxii (1966) 469–71); but he never appears again in the archbishop's company. On these critical questions cf. Smith, *EEA* i p. xl.

may yield useful evidence. Save for indications to the contrary, we may expect the archbishop's own trusted advisers to head the list. Mr Gerard Pucella heads forty-eight lists of archbishop Richard's acta. Benedict the chancellor, monk and later prior of Christ Church is the only regular witness to take precedence before him (nos. 111, 209, 215, 228). The placing of extraneous witnesses is less certain. When archbishop Hubert was justiciar his clerks seem to have had difficulty in deciding where to inscribe royal judges who were in his entourage. And below the more eminent, the order of attesting was not uniform. Two original charters of archbishop Baldwin (nos. 248–9) present the witnesses, common to both, in the sequence 1–7 and 1, 2, 4, 3, 5, 7, 6 respectively. In Hubert's acta William of Somercotes usually takes precedence before William of Calne, but not always (cf. nos. 403, 551). Witnesses can be fairly safely assigned to the archbishop's household when their names recur over a long time in acta for different beneficiaries. Perhaps a score come in this category. A few of them, though rewarded by ecclesiastical promotion for unspecified merit or service to the archbishop continue to attest when they become archdeacons or dignitaries outside the. diocese of Canterbury.[22]

The same names are naturally encountered among the witnesses of other deeds which interested the archbishop (and to which he sometimes allowed his own name to be appended, cf. below, p. xlv). When Hubert acquired a London house from Boxley abbey in exchange for land in Romney marsh, the abbot and convent recorded the exchange in letters patent of which the witness-list, headed by the archbishop's personal friends, the abbots of Reading and Waltham, and the Cluniac prior of Thetford, continues with ten names, all belonging to the archbishop's usual staff, headed by his chancellor.[23]

Many of the archbishop's clerks were *magistri*; this argues a qualification in letters and sometimes in the law. A few are designated *capellani*, and other information may identify among them the two or three chaplains whom the archbishop, like other prelates, was supposed to keep as constant companions. At Canterbury they were sometimes recruited from Christ Church: Richard of Dover, as a monk of Christ Church, had been chaplain to archbishop Thomas. In earlier days, the monk-chaplains might be

---

[22] E.g. Robert Foliot, William of Northolt, Waleran, Peter of Blois, archdns of Oxford, Gloucester, Bayeux and Bath respectively, and Ranulf and Simon of Sywell, treasurers of Salisbury and Lichfield. Diceto describes archdn Waleran as 'allateralem archiepiscopi clericumque domesticum' (*Op.* ii 13). See Hubert's letter to the chapter of Salisbury (written suitably enough by Peter of Blois) on absentees in the archbishop's service (no. 605).

[23] Lambeth Palace ms. 1212 fo. 107v (p. 207); cf. ibid. fo. 66v (p. 128).

concerned with the secretariat, as were royal chaplains with the royal chancery;[24] but we cannot tell whether and to what extent chaplains of these four archbishops helped with secretarial work. They cease to figure much in the witness-lists after archbishop Richard, and never appear in Baldwin's acta. Unlike bishops with secular chapters, the archbishop had no reservoir of clerks who were prebendaries. He may have drawn helpers from the cloister, but there is little sign of this, except for a monastic almoner. Perhaps he put more faith in secular clergy, and it was need to reward them with benefices that led Baldwin and Hubert into trouble with their chapter over the establishment of a collegiate church at Lambeth and over the patronage of certain parish churches.

It is tempting but dangerous to assume that the names of draftsmen and scribes regularly appear in these lists. The words 'qui hoc scripsit' and the like, sometimes found after the last witness of a private charter, never appear in the archiepiscopal acta.[25] The scribes are anonymous. Even if their names do in fact lurk in the lists, we normally have no means of distinguishing them. As we shall see in looking at arengas (p. lxi below), stylistic similarities between two acta for different beneficiaries may point to a single draftsman for both, but not to his name. Supposing draftsman and scribe to be separate persons, who shall say that a single draftsman only employed one scribe? And when the archbishop confirms his predecessor's grant without change of wording, the composition could be left to an inferior clerk.[26] The growing popularity of the inspeximus towards the end of the twelfth century simplified the drafting of confirmations and discouraged originality.

Finally, there remains the baffling problem of 'external' writing.[27] Were all the acta composed and/or written by clerks in the archbishop's regular employment? Which, if any, display the work of an outside draftsman or scribe? One can envisage the situation where a

---

[24] EBC 9–10; cf. Brett, *Engl. church under Henry I* 108, 180.

[25] Cf. Smith, *EEA* i p. lii. Only two witness-lists in the following collection describe a man as *scriptor*, both between 1174 and 1177: no. 228 closes the list with 'Rogerio, Amicio scriptoribus'; no. 136 has 'magistro Waltero scriptore' third from the end, the last being 'Amico clerico'. Mr Walter does not appear again; Amicus or Amicius witnesses ten more acta as 'clericus'. For the time of archbishop Theobald Mr Bishop tentatively ascribes twenty-nine to the hand of Peter scriptor, a former scribe of the royal chancery, attesting two of the archbishop's acta where he appears as the last, or the last clerical, witness. *Scriptores regis* p. 8 and pl. XVII(b) and note; cf. Saltman, *Theobald* 273 no. 46 and 474 no. 250.

[26] E.g. nos. 125, 126 for Dover, explicitly based on no. 9, retaining the Becket *intitulatio*, and no. 142 which quotes Theobald's confirmation. Exemplars exist but are not mentioned in nos. 1, 5, 258. In other cases the presence of archaisms point to an exemplar now lost (e.g. no. 601, and see below, p. lxi (arenga)).

[27] Cf. *EBC* 44–5, 55–6, 97 and Smith, *EEA* i pp. li–lii. Similar problems about the royal chancery are subtly discussed by Bishop, *Scriptores regis* esp. 9–10, 14–15.

monastery or individual petitions the archbishop for a favour and presents an acceptable draft for engrossment or sealing. The archbishop may be importuned for a charter when his usual staff is not at hand and he relies on a colleague's clerk or the beneficiary's. The charter of archbishop Richard for Daventry (no. 120) has unusual and anomalous features; it only survives in cartulary copies. Hubert's confirmation for Beauport, in Britanny (no. 334), is an original in a hand recognizable in other of Hubert's acta, therefore presumably written by one of his scribes. But it is diplomatically odd in having a full date and no witnesses and no valediction. Was it perhaps drafted by a canon of the abbey? A particular original deed which shows uncharacteristic formulae or style of writing may justify speculation on these questions. Even so, in view of the apparent lack of regularity of practice and of central control in the 'chancery', it is dangerous to impute novelties only to strangers. After all, by the latter part of the twelfth century the archbishop's household was probably the most literate and highly cultivated in the country; he travelled with a large retinue and would seldom need the help of others. But we are hampered in this enquiry by almost total ignorance of the detailed working of the secretariat. It will be necessary to come back (pp. xlii–iii) to the problem of 'external' writing.

Returning now to the question of drafting, it must be admitted that we can rarely discover who composed the contents of this volume. Positive pointers are limited to the epistolary collections of the celebrated literary men named above, who were used for the purpose by the archbishops, and who preserved compositions written in their masters' names: John of Salisbury, Herbert of Bosham, Peter of Blois. The letters of the first two of this trio written for, and in the name of, Becket, are personal in tone or have a strong political cast; relatively few deal with normal diocesan or metropolitan business. Although the distinction between this group of correspondence and the acta printed below is at times somewhat artificial, it seems reasonable and convenient to lighten this volume by omitting the very numerous Becketian letters put together by contemporary and sub-contemporary collectors, which are distinct in their tradition, are already in print, and demand separate treatment.[28]

[28] See Anne Duggan, *Thomas Becket: a textual history of his letters* (Oxford 1980). Only one of John's collected letters shows him writing for Becket: John of Salisbury ii 64–7 ep. 157, to Nicholas de Monte (ed. Giles no. 232, *MTB* v 360 no. 184). During most of the exile he was writing *to* the archbishop, and letter no. 228 to Becket (John of Salisbury ii 400, Giles no. 232, *MTB* vi 220 no. 318) shows that Becket sent him, perhaps for approval before despatch, letters addressed to Cardinal William of Pavia: John replies: 'Nec priorum nec posteriorum michi placet conceptio litterarum.'

CONTENTS OF THE ACTA

The archbishop's correspondence included more topics than can be enumerated here; but they may be touched on briefly before we turn to the diplomatic aspect of the survivals from his secretariat.

This correspondence divides broadly into several categories. First come the letters which any bishop of this period might issue in the discharge of his ecclesiastical duties. These include grants and confirmations of churches and letters of protection for religious houses in the diocese of Canterbury, appropriations of parish churches, letters of institution and admission to benefices in the diocese, mandates to subordinates on discipline, on tithe, and so on. Here, as in other English dioceses, one can trace in the formulas the evolution of episcopal control over parish churches, canonical institution, and the regulating of vicarages. Secondly come those acta which — as in other sees — arise from the diocesan's position as a lord and landholder: enfeoffments, leases, exchanges. Under the heading 'Lands of the see' are assembled transactions with various tenants, mostly undistinguished people (nos. 5, 67–72, 244, 368–73, 385–6).

These two categories of diocesan business account for between a quarter and a third of the surviving material. A third group includes acta which show the archbishop as metropolitan, or as legate of the apostolic see. Charters which confirm with the archbishop's authority the grants of his suffragans are very numerous, and Baldwin and Hubert confirm grants they had themselves made as bishops, of Worcester and Salisbury respectively. Exceptional duties engage the archbishop in the dioceses of his suffragans, proceedings for a canonization (nos. 607–15, 652), the ordering of a diocese in the vacancy of a see. When he is legate he may hold visitations, even beyond the limits of his own province if his commission allows. As the highest ordinary authority in the southern province, the archbishop of Canterbury entertains appeals from inferiors and receives the pope's orders to transmit to them.[29] Increase of appeals to the pope brings with them appeals for tuition to the archbishop[30] and requires correspondence with Rome both in particular lawsuits and on legal problems about which the local church looks for clarification from the fount of law. Every pope from Alexander III to Innocent III addresses many decretals to the archbishop.

[29] The mandate no. 30 below is an early instance of the employment of the bishop of London as dean of the province to receive and transmit sentences of excommunication.
[30] Cheney, *Innocent III and England* 118–9.

At the same time, the official business of the archbishop in his province was far from being all-embracing; and the reader of these acta cannot hope to see in them all aspects of ecclesiastical government in twelfth-century England. They leave large areas unreported, for which an historian has to look elsewhere. To begin with, he will find little or nothing about the ancient exempt Benedictine abbeys or the exempt houses of the Cluniacs, Cistercians, and Premonstratensians, except in so far as they were objects of the personal patronage of an archbishop. This simply reflects the fact that these powerful bodies keep the archbishop and his jurisdiction at arm's length, if they can. Seldom if ever do the older exempt houses ask for confirmation of their rights and property; they are more likely in defence of their privileges to confront the archbishops in the court of Rome. It is noticeable that a house like St Augustine's, Canterbury, appears far less often in these pages than some less highly privileged establishments. St Albans is represented by archiepiscopal confirmations of an agreement with its diocesan and by two letters of protection (nos. 37, 198–200); Bury St Edmunds and Westminster appear not at all. Moreover, among the non-exempt institutions in the province, not every one troubled to go to the metropolitan for protection; and when trouble arose among them, it was not always to Canterbury that they turned. Appeals from the courts of the suffragans were often made directly to Rome. The evidence, indeed, suggests that the archbishop was not very active in his suffragans' dioceses *sede plena* as a matter of course. The suffragans' inferiors were more inclined to have recourse to him *sede vacante* or in the absence of their own bishop. This may explain (and help to date conjecturally) the numerous archiepiscopal acta which concern the diocese of Lincoln, where protracted vacancies and absences left much diocesan administration to the dean of Lincoln and the archdeacons.

A fourth category of acta concerns politics and diplomacy. The archbishop's office compels him to be a statesman, and critical issues which arise between Church and State require his intervention. In this colourless statement is concealed all the conflict of principle, the friction and the uneasy adjustment between the Angevin kings and the primates; but these matters are more evident in the narratives of the time than in the relatively few exchanges of letters, except for the Becket correspondence, while the collection in Lambeth ms. 415 and the St Augustine's cartularies yield a very few revealing letters from archbishop Hubert to the kings (nos. 379–81, 395). Finally, there are letters with a more personal colour: an excuse for absence on account of illness (no. 532), a report on a journey (no. 257), letters of recommendation (nos. 230, 550) or of advice (nos. 377, 394). These letters of political or private character come under the head described by a thirteenth-century writer on dictamen as *missiles littere*. They form, he says, not a *species* of letters, but a whole *genus*, for which no strict rules other than purely literary ones can be formulated.[31]

THE SURVIVING ACTA

Survivals, including the mere mentions of acta, give a distorted picture of the output of the archbishop's office. The bulk of them record grants and confirmations of property and privileges or else settlements of disputes by judges or arbitrators which called for permanent memorial.[32] These all had the quality of title-deeds or muniments, affording legal proofs for centuries to come; they have mostly survived because the beneficiaries had an interest in preserving them and copying them, and most of the beneficiaries were undying corporations which were already beginning to marshal their muniments more systematically than were the archbishops themselves.[33] At the visitations of archbishop William Warham in Kent, in the sixteenth century, his clerks copied with commendable accuracy the original charters then extant in the religious houses, which his predecessors had granted more than three hundred years earlier. Many more are preserved in inspeximus charters of the intervening centuries. A few cartularies record with their title-deeds occasional copies of related documents: mandates to archdeacons or rural deans to take action on a monastery's behalf (nos. 115, 123, 141, 178, 438–40) or to judges delegate to hear a case recorded by the victorious party (nos. 213, 465–6). The start of the Curia Regis rolls during the justiciarship of archbishop Hubert provides traces of this archbishop's administrative correspondence with the civil courts on ecclesiastical matters: significations of excommunication and certificates of marriage and legitimacy, of kinds hitherto

[31] Quoted from L. Rockinger (ed.), *Briefsteller u. Formelbücher xi–xiv Jh.* (Quellen u. Erörterungen zur bayer. u. deutschen Gesch. IX. Munich 1863–4) i 260 by Giles Constable, *Letters and letter-collections* (Typologie des sources du moyen âge occidental, fasc. 17. Turnhout. 1976) 12. See ibid. 56–62 on the formation of collections.

[32] The remainder include about a sixth of the acta of Thomas, Richard, and Baldwin, and about a third of Hubert's acta.

[33] Some institutions took the precaution of getting duplicates of important documents (e.g. no. 597 and cf. Cheney, *Med. texts and studies* 102 n. 2). This may explain why texts sometimes turn up twice in a cartulary. The parts of a chirograph sometimes came together later on (e.g. no. 81).

unrecorded, These same records sometimes include copies of archiepiscopal charters produced as evidence in court.

Apart from this material we must fall back on the archiepiscopal archives. They are disappointing. We know little or nothing of how and where the twelfth-century archbishops kept their records, though title-deeds of the see and some documents of a public character were certainly laid up in the mother church.[34] Nothing shows what system, if any, was adopted to keep record of acta despatched. There is no description, no inventory, few recognizable survivals from this source. We can infer a little — but not much, and not safely — from what is known from thirteenth-century usage.[35] The inference is that from Thomas to Hubert no official registers of letters-out were prepared, such as the papal chancery had long maintained, and no enrolments comparable to those which begin in the English royal chancery towards the end of the century. Single-sheet duplicates of important letters despatched might be kept, but it seems unlikely that a comprehensive classified record was aimed at. Occasional use of the ancient form of bipartite chirograph (which will call for later notice) safeguarded some few documents against both loss and fraud. The bulk of the archives probably consisted of drafts and botched originals. Indications of this state of affairs survive exclusively from the latter years of Hubert Walter. Because the appointment of his successor was delayed and because of the still longer delay before Langton got possession of his see, some current business records of 1202–5 were left in the muniments of Christ Church, Canterbury. They include a unique series of forty-four mandates, judgments, and draft letters which range over the archbishop's usual business as diocesan and metropolitan. They give an inkling of what we lack for the preceding century.[36]

The epistolary collections of scholars in the archbishops' service, already mentioned, supplement official archives. Nearly 200 letters of archbishop Thomas of a political or personal nature were

[34] *EBC* 139 and *Med. texts and studies* 100–1. For the second type of record see Dr Duggan's important analysis of the origins of the Becket collections (op. cit. above, p. xxxiii n. 28) especially pp. 25–33, 167–8. Cf. nos. 164, 389.

[35] Jane Sayers, 'The medieval care and custody of the archbishop of Canterbury's archives' *BIHR* xxxix (1966) 95–107, D. M. Owen, *Catalogue of Lambeth mss. 889–91 (Carte antique et miscellanee)* (Lambeth Palace Libr. 1968) p. 1 and works there cited. Cf. *EBC* 130–41.

[36] No. 398 is possibly a draft. A sealed duplicate was retained of an important letter to the pope (no. 383). For more of Hubert's archives see *Canterbury cases* pp. *104–14*, nos. *1–48*. A grant of a tenement by archbishop Conrad of Mainz, 1189, was made and sealed in duplicate, and one text kept in the cathedral treasury 'ne quis dolus hinc inde queat intercedere et huic nostre donationi refragari'. *Mainzer Urkundenbuch* II ii (ed. P. Acht 1971) 844 no. 513.

assembled by his staff and biographers; the acta of his successors among the collected letters of Peter of Blois amount to no more than a dozen. By contrast with the Becket letters, there are good practical reasons for calendaring these letters here, even those which lie outside the ordinary run of the archbishop's acta. They are important letters addressed to important people, the pope, the young king, the archbishop of Reims. Though the matter of the letters is overlaid with a prodigious amount of rhetoric, they deserve inclusion as genuine business-correspondence of the metropolitan. We know from witness-lists of other acta of archbishops Richard and Baldwin that Peter was often at their side, and (as we have seen, above, p. xxvi) enjoyed the title of chancellor in Richard's pontificate. It may be well to insist on this, since there has been a tendency to dismiss some of these letters as the literary exercises of a loquacious individual, expressing private opinions and personal prejudices. In fact, there is no ground for supposing — to take one instance — that the letter to pope Alexander III against the abbot of Malmesbury (no. 165) does not reflect the views held by archbishop Richard on monastic exemption, in which views Peter concurred. This is an early and discursive example of a recognized type of formal report from an inferior judge to his superior — *apostoli refutatorii*.[37] For one reason only, apart from their literary distinction, do these letters contrast with the other acta printed below: their tradition is different. They have not survived in the sparse archives of Peter's employers; nor is there evidence that any of them reached their destinations. They are preserved solely in the collection of Peter's letters which he himself made and revised and enlarged in several editions.[38] The letters are certainly genuine, that is, Peter was their author, and the later recensions show no signs of significant re-touching. There is no reason, then, to deny them the evidential status of official correspondence, prompted and sanctioned by the archbishops' authority, comparable to those letters which John of Salisbury and Herbert of Bosham wrote in the names of their employers, archbishops Theobald and Thomas. An element of doubt must always remain, however, whether they were actually despatched.[39]

---

[37] D. Knowles, *Monastic Order in England* (Cambridge 1940) 590, describes this as 'the *ex parte* presentation of a case from the pen of one known from his other writings to have lacked both a sense of responsibility and a judicial temper of mind.'

[38] R. W. Southern, *Medieval humanism* (1970) 104–32 and literature there cited.

[39] The calendaring below of the letters from Peter's collection does not try to convey their literary quality or go beyond their main administrative or political topics. The full texts are fairly accurately presented by Giles, *P. Blesensis opera* and in *PL* ccvii.

The preservation of these special letters by Peter himself does not preclude the possibility that he drafted many other letters in the archbishops' office which he did not choose to put out under his name. He kept those he was proud of. We lack means to detect others for which he may have been responsible. There were other capable draftsmen besides, who cannot be identified. Some few other letters of the archbishops in this edition display equal grandiloquence and hover on the boundary of business letter and literary effusion.[40] One of Hubert's letters (no. 419) only survives because its eloquence gained it a place in a formulary a century later. Pantin remarked a propos the fourteenth-century letters of John Mason that 'the prosecution of a great lawsuit needed rhetoricians as well as lawyers'.[41]

Special topics, stirring episodes, could prompt the making of special dossiers. In Lambeth Palace ms. 415 a monk of Canterbury compiled an epistolary record of the battles waged by the convent against archbishops Baldwin and Hubert over the chapels of Hackington and Lambeth. It comprises 557 documents, including nineteen of the archbishops' letters. Again, we owe to the assiduity of a canon of Sempringham who assembled the dossier of St Gilbert's canonization no less than nine of archbishop Hubert's letters on this matter.[42]

This lucky abundance gives the historian a hint of the magnitude of the losses elsewhere. It contrasts with the total lack of letters at Worcester and Canterbury about the canonization of St Wulfstan, although both bishop Mauger and archbishop Hubert played leading parts in the process. On many other topics little or nothing has survived. The notorious preaching missions of the abbot of St-Germer-de-Fly in England leave no trace in our acta. An even more striking lacuna concerns the Third and Fourth Crusades. Although Baldwin and Hubert were deeply involved in preaching and regulating the expeditions, the records in the acta are meagre in the extreme. Mandates which must have been sent to prelates throughout the province are found only in solitary copies in unexpected places (e.g. 419, 574). Chronicles and papal letters imply constant correspondence on the crusades between the popes and the archbishops. Hubert sought clarification from Rome on various points

---

[40] Edited here, since they are unlikely to call for separate treatment elsewhere: nos. 103, 254, 383, 550, 656.

[41] *Essays in medieval history pres. to Bertie Wilkinson* (Toronto 1969) 197–8. For some more prosaic letter-books see *EBC* 119–30.

[42] *Ep. Cant.*; Foreville, *Procès de canonisation.*

of law which affected the status and obligations of those who took
the cross. But we have none of his enquiries and do not know how
he raised these questions; so that we cannot treat the papal
consultationes as grounds for assuming lost archiepiscopal letters
which would call for 'mentions' here.

The decretals of Celestine III and Innocent III on crusades and
crusaders illustrate a deficiency in the archiepiscopal acta which
extends to all the correspondence with Rome. Out of 75 extant
letters addressed by Innocent III to archbishop Hubert on all
manner of topics, sixteen are plainly in response to enquiries or
petitions by the archbishop, yet in no case is a letter from the
archbishop known.[43] What is not usually made plain is the way by
which the archbishop conveyed his enquiries and petitions. Were
they sent under his seal, or did he instruct proctors? Only two of the
papal responses use wholly unambiguous words: 'Ex litteris tuis,
frater archiepiscope' and 'de qua tua fraternitas nobis scripsit' (cf.
nos. 339, 498), while some others point to a different procedure: 'Ex
parte tua fuit in audientia nostra propositum'.[44] This state of things
obtained in earlier times. No fewer than forty decretals of Alexander
III addressed to archbishop Richard occur in *Compilatio prima* or
other decretal collections. Many of them presuppose an enquiry
from Canterbury, and some begin with such words as 'Cum te
consulente postulas edoceri', 'Quoniam nos consulere voluisti',
'Super eo quod quesivisti'. But these leave the procedure uncertain.
I have found only four explicit mentions: 'Ex litteris quas . . .
transmisisti', 'Accepimus litteras ven. fr. n. R. Cant.', 'sicut ex tuis
litteris intelleximus', 'Ex litteris fr. tue' (nos. 47–48A, cf. 322A). In
short, papal letters imply a steady traffic of Canterbury proctors to
the Curia who pose the archbishops' questions; it remains impossible to guess what proportion of the questions took the form of letters
written in an archbishop's name, under his seal. The history of the
papal chancery suggests that it may have been more usual to leave
the final drafting of supplications to the proctor in the Curia, on the
basis of memoranda and notes, than for the petitioner to provide
him with formal sealed letters before he left home.

The foregoing brief view of the provenance of surviving acta is an
essential preliminary to any critical assessment of particular items.
If they — or their originals — can be traced to the archives of the

---

[43] *Letters of Innocent III* nos. 51–2, 143*–4, 150, 160–1, 167, 261*, 333, 347, 350*, 413,
548, 550*, 638*. (asterisked items are decretals).
[44] JL 17307, *Letters of Innocent III* nos. 333, 413. Cf. 'nos duxisti per nuntium tuum
consulendos' (JL 17614, 17679) and 'Cant. archiepiscopus nobis intimare curavit' (*SLI* 38).

beneficiary or addressee, they are at least known to have reached their destination. Supposing, however, that they are in any sense beneficial documents, we must reckon with the possibility of deliberate falsification by the beneficiaries. Texts which give point to this warning are a group of acta of Richard, Baldwin, and Hubert laid up in the archives of Rochester (some in *soi-disant* originals) which must be classified as spurious (nos. 194–7, 304–5, 591–5). A slightly different sort of forgery is seen in the 'Magna carta sancti Thome', manufactured by the monks of Christ Church in the 1230s (no. 6). This was not only repeatedly copied into Christ Church cartularies, long after its condemnation, but was successfully foisted on the compilers of the thirteenth-century muniment-book of the archbishops, Lambeth Palace ms. 1212, and was copied into the fourteenth-century register of archbishop William Courtenay.

Acta in original or contemporary copy which come from the archbishops' archives may be trusted implicitly as products of their administration, but they raise another problem. Various reasons may explain their presence in the issuing office. They may be untidy drafts of which improved versions were later despatched; they may have been defective in substance and have been suppressed (see no. 398 and cf. 397). On the other hand, fair copies were deliberately multiplied with the object of retaining duplicates for future reference, in days before official enrolment or registration. This uncertainty means that the provenance offers no guarantee that they were despatched unaltered or, indeed, despatched at all.

THE DIPLOMATIC OF THE ACTA: I. EXTERNAL FEATURES

The known surviving original acta of the four archbishops amount to about 120, apart from four or five spuria. These are the documents on which we rely for guidance to the physical appearance of the acta and, since all copyists are fallible, for the surest evidence of internal features.

FORMAT AND SCRIPT

By the time of archbishop Thomas the format of English episcopal acta was tending towards standard shape and size, within the limits imposed by the length of the text. The Canterbury acta are neither extremely narrow nor extremely broad; indeed, most routine documents are roughly square in size and no more than 200 mm. broad. Most of them are broader than they are long. The biggest example by far is the detailed and elaborate record of archbishop Hubert's purchase of Lambeth from the monks of Rochester (no. 371), a bi-partite chirograph of which the parts measure 495 × 242 mm. and 495 × 235 mm. Even the grandest documents have narrow margins.

It has been remarked above (p. xxxiii) that the archbishop's household was probably the most literate and highly cultivated in the country. The archbishop could probably command the services of clerks for performing all the operations required in producing his official acta; in other words, drafting and writing and sealing of acta could all be carried out by his staff. Even when he was on his travels he might, according to canon 4 of the Third Lateran Council, have a retinue of 40 to 50 horse. On the other hand, the recipients of the beneficial acta were often ecclesiastical institutions or prelates who themselves had competent clerks in their employment. So who, in fact, did the work?.Contemporaries did not discourse on the subject for our benefit. On general grounds, it seems probable that many of the beneficial acta and most administrative mandates were written by the archbishop's scribes (cf. pp. xxxii–iii above). If we wish to proceed beyond mere supposition, we must turn for enlightenment to the original acta themselves.

As in other English sees, by the second half of the twelfth century the script has become usually small and neat and sophisticated, devoid of the papal features which had appeared in the preceding generation and which continue to prevail in many episcopal chanceries abroad. (The tittle is the one papal feature which is in increasingly frequent use for beneficial acta, as elsewhere in English ecclesiastical and secular charters). To distinguish on purely palaeographical grounds how much writing was done by the archbishop's scribes, how much by outsiders, is beyond our powers; and since we know practically nothing about the terms of service of the clerical staff or the arrangements for casual hiring, we may be posing the question in the wrong terms. We cannot write off as 'external' work all which shows abnormalities of script and format, for the organisation of the secretariat was not so rigid, nor were its products so invariably well penned, that we can confidently dismiss all idiosyncrasies as outsiders' work. On the other hand, we cannot assign a script to an archbishop's clerk rather than to the hand of an outsider on grounds of general style and family likeness. All we can do is to search for individual characteristics, the clear mark of a single scribe, in several acta addressed to different beneficiaries or concerned with totally different transactions. The discovery of several such acta shows an archiepiscopal scribe, even though it does not permit us to attach a name to the writer. The accumulation of groups of such acta provides sufficient evidence that our preliminary supposition is justified: a majority, if not all, of the acta were written by scribes in the archbishop's office.

The following particulars I owe to the kindness of Mr T. A. M. Bishop, who has very generously applied his time and his expertise to the examination of photocopies and to the discussion of them.

THOMAS Unfortunately the four originals surviving are too few to make an analysis by peculiarities of script very rewarding for the purpose of determining whether 'internal' writing was the rule. Even so, the scrutiny shows that not only is no. 3, for St Radegund's, Cambridge, in the script of no. 34 for Ramsey; the hand reappears in 1177 in a charter of archbishop Richard for Hereford (no. 136). No. 16, for the nuns of Ivinghoe, is of interest for another reason. Mr Bishop identifies the hand as that of a royal scribe who wrote ten early charters of Henry II, during the chancellorship of Thomas, whom he presumably followed to Canterbury.[45]

RICHARD Of 37 originals Mr Bishop identifies twenty-four in five groups of the type mentioned: i.e., acta for diverse beneficiaries written by the same scribe. They are

I	153, 215, 228
II	80, 90, 159, 168, 169, 178, 187
III	77, 79, 85, 109, 117
IV	84, 114, 160, 211, 232
V	55, 113, 186

BALDWIN The evidence is meagre: sixteen acta (for thirteen beneficiaries). No. 264 for Combwell is in the hand of one of archbishop Richard's charters for the same house (no. 113) which appears in Richard's acta for Bec and Repton. A single scribe wrote charters of Baldwin for Monks' Kirby and Savigny (nos. 296, 311). This is the more interesting because the sealing of the Savigny document has been tampered with, inviting comparison with the Savigny-manufactured charters of king Henry II which Delisle discussed.[46] Were it not that the hand is found in no. 296, one would suspect external writing. Nos. 270–2 are in a style of script unlike any found in others of Baldwin's acta; they may be external work.

---

[45] *Scriptores regis* pl. XXVI(a), scribe **xxvii**; cf. *Lincoln reg. ant.* ii pl. XIII(a). On the other hand, no. 23 below (Thomas for Holy Trinity, Aldgate), is in Bishop's view a scribe of Holy Trinity.   [46] *Recueil des actes . . . Introduction* 278–9, 326–9.

HUBERT   The harvest is more copious. There are 64 originals, of which Mr Bishop places no fewer than 38 in six groups:

   I   360, 373, 414, 467, 469, 494, 496, 512, 549, 589, 597, 617, 621, 639

   II 453, 507, 558, 581

  III 489, 524

  IV 334, 337, 355, 387, 407, 418, 525, 536, 537, 578

   V 456, 535, 550, 649

  VI 474, 495, 555, 579

Of the many acta which cannot be grouped in this fashion, no positive statement can be made. Many of them may be the work of the archbishops' clerks, including occasionally scribes represented in the groups set out above; but some may be by beneficiaries' scribes. In some cases certainty might perhaps be achieved by comparison with contemporary texts in the beneficiaries' archives; but this has proved to be too big an undertaking. Fruits of this method in the field of royal charters may be seen in *Scriptores regis* pp. 9–10, 14–5.

In the second half of the twelfth century the bi-partite or tri-partite chirograph was occasionally used by English bishops' clerks.[47] We possess ten acta of archbishops Richard, Baldwin and Hubert cast in this form. Most surviving originals divide the identical texts by a straight cut, which bisects the word 'Cyrographum'.[48] In each case a seal was appended, double queue. Only one of the originals (no. 387) announces in its corroboration-clause that it is made 'in modum cyrographi'; one other speaks (no. 370) of 'mutua scripta'. It may be, therefore, that many similar settlements — perhaps, indeed, all others — which only survive in cartularies, were in the same form.[49] The known chirographs mostly record settlements by the archbishop as judge or arbitrator between disputants over parish churches. They were a convenient means of providing authentic duplicates for both parties, and they take the usual form of a notification addressed to all the faithful (nos. 81, 90, 170, 211, 387, 536). The only surviving chirograph of Baldwin,

---

[47] *EBC* 57–8. Cf. *Acta S. Langton* p. xxxvii; *Chichester acta* nos. 42, 47, 119–20, 132.

[48] No. 536 (a draft) is indented, 370 and 387 are cut by a wavy line. No. 170 has a longer inscription.

[49] See a rubric in the Red Book of St Augustine's, Canterbury: 'carta cyrographata Theobaldi' (Saltman, *Theobald* 284 no. 58). The actum has a corroboration clause, followed by 'Tradidimus etiam Rogero aliam cartam nostro sigillo sigillatam hec eadem verba continentem'.

similar in matter, retains the ancient impersonal form, and begins with a date and a *narratio* (no. 262, cf. *EBC* 40–1). Exceptionally imposing specimens were drawn up in 1197 and 1201, to record transactions which involved the archbishop, once as a party, once as arbitrator. They are both cast in impersonal form and begin with an invocation.[50] The first (no. 370) records the archbishop's purchase of the manor of Lambeth from the monks of Rochester, and twin texts were first sealed by the parties alternately. Then another bipartite chirograph was prepared for the reception of a great many seals of bishops and magnates to add weighty corroboration (no. 371). In 1201 a magnificent tripartite chirograph recorded a settlement in which the archbishop appears as arbitrator with the bishop of Ely and the justiciar of England, in a dispute between the abbot of Cluny and the earl of Warenne over the appointment of the priors of Lewes. Each of the two surviving parts carried six seals (no. 525).

Besides the Lewes chirograph, it is convenient to note here a few other acta in which the archbishop has other prelates associated with him. The Lewes case produces two such (nos. 524, 526), in which the bishops of Ely and Chichester appear. Earlier documents issued jointly by the archbishop and other prelates are uncommon; but the occasion might arise when he and colleagues acted as papal judges delegate (nos. 182, 227), and joint action by metropolitan and suffragans might produce a call for documents drawn up in the names of the participants. Thus Hubert holds visitations and issues written injunctions twice with diocesans (nos. 410, 582), records with other prelates settlements made in their presence about disputed churches and tithes (nos. 424, 576), and takes action in the process of canonization of Gilbert of Sempringham (nos. 610–1). He associates his brother with him in a charter to his foundation at Dereham (no. 435).

Finally, as a pendant to acta which associate the archbishop with other prelates, one remarks that the archbishop may attach his seal, or be named as witness, to someone else's charter. His name is common on royal charters when he is at court. Others are generally charters of persons of consequence and the other attestations to them often indicate an important occasion. Thus both king Henry and archbishop Richard put their seals to a chirograph between Christ Church, Canterbury and Gervase of Cornhill.[51] Laymen's

---

[50] An earlier example of the impersonal form is archbishop Theobald's chirograph ratifying a settlement, in Saltman 535, suppl. doct. A. The invocation and impersonal form appear in two acta of the Lambeth case which are not chirographs (nos. 382–3).

[51] Urry, *Canterbury* 409–10 nos. XXIX–XXX. Cf. M. G. Cheney, *Roger of Worcester* 144.

grants to the church of Lewes and the bishop of Worcester not only show archbishop Richard as first witness but follow with the names of men who are frequently at his side, the bishop of Rochester, Mr Gerard, and others.[52] Archbishop Baldwin attests two grants to religious houses by Richard de Redvers and by Margaret de Bohun.[53] Attestations by archbishop Hubert are too numerous to be listed.[54] In 1201 he adds his seal, with that of Geoffrey FitzPeter, the justiciar, to the treaty of king John and prince Llewelyn ap Iorwerth. He also puts his seal to an appeal by Mr Peter of Blois, as parson of Shoreham, to the Curia.[55]

SEALING

For seals and sealing the actual evidence in hard wax is rather scanty; but remains of seals — often mere fragments — exist: one of archbishop Thomas (*secretum* only), twelve of Richard, eight of Baldwin, ten of Hubert. Moreover, although a few surviving documents have been so mutilated as to obscure all mark of sealing, most extant originals show how they were once sealed. Sealing 'sur simple queue' (on a tongue cut at the foot of the sheet, attached at the left hand) and 'sur double queue' (on a tag drawn through a fold at the foot of the sheet) were both used for beneficial acta apparently indifferently until the end of Richard's pontificate. Thereafter, simple queue sealing may have been reserved for mandates and letters missive.[56] A few solemn acta were sealed with silk cords (nos. 64, 311-2, 337, 371-2). Only one highly exceptional document received the archbishop's signature: the settlement in 1200 by arbitrators of the protracted dispute between Hubert and the convent of Christ Church bears the autograph subscriptions of the archbishop and the prior, and bore the seals of the parties with those of the arbitrators, appended double queue.[57]

---

[52] Round, *Ancient charters* (PRS 10) 71-2 no. 44 (PRO E 40/6693), and PRO C 115/L 1/6689 fo. 52v. The former records that the archbp put his seal to a composition.

[53] BL Add. ch. 15688, for Quarr abbey, with the archbp of Rouen; PRO C 115/L 1/6689 fos. 27r, 32v for Lanthony, with bp William of Worcester and Ranulf de Glanvill. He witnesses an agreement between Cirencester and Bradenstoke in *Bradenstoke cartulary* 34 no. 21.

[54] E.g. *Bec documents* 20-1 no. XXXVIII, Round, *Ancient charters* 103 no. 63, *Cal. ancient deeds* (HMSO) ii 503, iii 338, *EYC* vii 79-80 no. 35, and below, nos. 641n., 648n.

[55] Rymer I i 84; *HMCR Var. coll.* i 240. Another actum concerns a clerk of the archbp, Roger of Bassingham (*Reg. S. Osmundi* (RS) i 299-300).

[56] Examples of simple queue for Richard: nos. 79-80, 169, 178, 186-7, 206; for Hubert: 355, 414, 456, 532, 550, 555, 579. No cases are discernible for Baldwin.

[57] *EBC* pl. VI, cf. ibid. 47, 159-60. This was not, of course, an act of the archbishop, but of the arbitrators. Cf. no. 383 below. For impressive examples of multiple sealing see no. 371 and the engrossment of the arbitrators' award (1200) in Canterbury, D. & C. C.A. L 130.

Those acta sealed 'sur double queue' were normally sealed in one of two ways; in all cases the attachment was strengthened in the traditional fashion by a fold at the foot of the parchment sheet. (1) One method involved simply a single horizontal incision through the two thicknesses of parchment in the fold. Then a parchment tag was drawn through the slit to carry the seal. (2) Another method, found on nearly half of Richard's acta, and on all of Baldwin's which are sealed double queue, made for greater stability. Two parallel incisions were made through the two thicknesses of the fold and a third was made on the crease itself. The tag then passed through the two thicknesses at the upper slit, its tails then turned inwards at the lower slit and emerged together at the slit on the crease to receive the seal.[58] Plate XIX below illustrates the second method. In our descriptions of the acta, these methods are indicated as 'd.q. 1' and 'd.q. 2'. It will be seen that Hubert's chancery most often used the simpler method 1 which had been used in the times of Theobald and Thomas.

LETTERS CLOSE

There remains the vexed question of the method of closure by sealing. How or on what occasions were missives with personal address closed by a seal rather than sent open with seal appended?[59] Since the formulae of acta provide no guidance — those sent patent and close are in this respect indistinguishable — we look for originals which bear the impression of a seal and for extraneous references to the use of seals for closure. First to take possible references to archiepiscopal letters close. From the early twelfth century comes a letter of king Henry I to archbishop Anselm in 1106, which acknowledges 'littere reposite in tuo sigillo' received from the archbishop.[60] Late in the century, archbishop Baldwin wrote in August 1187 from Alençon to bishop Gilbert of Rochester, instructing him to put into effect the archbishop's unpopular appointments at Christ Church (no. 253). Gervase of Canterbury (i

---

[58] No. 303 is exceptional in having no slit in crease. The method described above is common in other classes of charter (*Guide to seals in the PRO* (1954) 15) and is usual in the chanceries of Henry II and Richard and John as count of Mortain (not as king). It is found in other English episcopal acta late in the twelfth century, e.g. of Coventry and of Lincoln, and a good example of archbp Rotrou of Rouen, 1182, is given by J. J. Vernier, *Recueil de facs. de chartes normandes* (Soc. de l'hist. de Normandie 1919) pl. VI.

[59] 'Litere extra sigillum pendentes', 'littere patentes': cf. no. 338. See the valuable discussion of letters patent and close by P. Chaplais, *English royal documents King John – Henry VI* (Oxford 1971) 7–11, and cf. *Pleas before the king* i 28–9.

[60] Eadmer, *Hist.* (RS) 176; *S. Anselmi opp.* (ed. F. S. Schmitt) v 337 no. 392.

381) speaks of the receipt of the order: 'When the archbishop's letter was opened ('confractis autem litteris'), the men he sent to the bishop of Rochester on this business found . . . '. This indicates more definitely than Henry I's words to Anselm a letter closed by a seal in the shape of letters close. Likewise, Gerald archdeacon of Brecon tells us that he got a mandate in the shape of letters close to the clergy of St David's from Mr Simon of Sywell, when Simon was acting as the archbishop's general official in England and was using the archbishop's counterseal (no. 356n.). The Crowland chronicler refers to the archbishop's action on the abbey's behalf in 1201 in terms which imply the use of a letter close to serve as envelope for another document (no. 425n.).

Baldwin's letter from Alençon exists in copy (no. 253), but nothing in it shows that the original was closed. And among the surviving letters of the four archbishops none can be positively proved to be a letter close. They formed a diplomatic category doomed to destruction, the ephemera: orders which demanded immediate compliance, private reports, personal expressions of regret or congratulation. If the seals must be broken before the letters were read, they were not likely to contain much of lasting legal interest, and the legal documents were the best preserved. Copies of letters close undoubtedly lurk in the collections of the famous letter-writers, as in the anthology of Lambeth ms. 415, but it is impossible to distinguish any of them. Nor do we fare much better with surviving original acta, of which most are grants and confirmations, settlements and judgments, and necessarily went out *patentes*. Eleven original mandates and occasional letters, which might have been closed by seal, have to be considered. The earliest (no. 178), from archbishop Richard to the vice-archdeacon of Oxford on behalf of Osney abbey, was preserved in the abbey. Its aspect does not seem compatible with its issue as a letter close. All other originals come from archbishop Hubert and show no physical features which settle their character, patent or close. Most of them are in the Canterbury archives (nos. 418, 474, 489, 532, 549, 649), while two probably come from the archives of the parties on whose behalf the letters were issued (nos. 414, 555), and two have come by uncertain ways into the public records (nos. 407, 507). Two acta (nos. 414, 474), besides the indication of a seal on the tongue, have a separate tie (without address) which militates against the idea that the seal closed the document,[61] and the placing of the seal on no. 555

---

[61] See Chaplais 10. No. 178 below has its seal lengthwise along the tongue, probably leaving no room for an address, and a tie may have been torn away.

suggests a letter patent. No. 532 might be a sealed letter close, were it not that it has a collective address to the bishops of the province and it remains in the Canterbury archives. Some of these survivors are almost certainly drafts (489, 550), others have been so mutilated as to conceal how, if at all, they were sealed (407, 418, 507, 549, 649). Dr Chaplais has described the pattern of letters close of the royal chancery (of which originals are excessively scarce), which inscribed the address on the tongue cut for carrying the seal between its loose end and the seal. While no archiepiscopal acta have been found which show whether or not this was the practice of the archbishops' clerks, there is evidence of a sort, short of compelling, in the letters close addressed to archbishop Hubert by his subordinates in the course of ordinary business. The deposit at Canterbury of judicial and administrative letters sent to archbishop Hubert includes many letters which, of their nature, would qualify for closure. As with the archbishop's mandates the evidence of method of sealing is usually lacking; all that remains is a vestigial stub at the bottom left-hand corner where the tongue, with or without tie, has been torn away. But on at least five letters from local officials and delegates of the archbishop a tongue does survive without a tie, and in these cases the tongue carries the address 'domino Cantuariensi' at its free end.[62] This conforms with the royal pattern of letters close.

THE SEALS

Turning to the seals, we find that the four archbishops all follow the general pattern set by their predecessors, Ralph, William and Theobald, although there are stylistic developments in the design of the effigies and style of script.[63] Their seals are pointed oval in shape, and the obverse depicts the archbishop vested for mass, holding his crosier, his right hand raised in blessing. The first three show the horns of the mitre at the sides, whereas Hubert wears his mitre with horns at front and back. In each case the matrix for the reverse of the seal is smaller; it was perhaps used independently as a signet, though surviving only in the acta as a counterseal. The wax was

---

[62] Canterbury, D. & C. C.A. C 1261 and Z 134 (cf. nos, 341, 588 below); ibid. Ch. Ch. letters II nos. 02, 226, 241. No. 02 is addressed on its tongue 'magistro Willelmo de Bosco', described in the letter as 'clericus domini Cant' '.

[63] For Theobald's seal see Saltman pp. 225–6 and W. de G. Birch, *Cat. of seals in the . . . Brit. Museum* i (1887). For stylistic changes see F. Saxl, *Engl. sculpture of the twelfth century* (1954) 18–22. Dr Chaplais tells me that the detached seal Bodl. ms. Ch. Kent 295 which has been attributed to Thomas, is unquestionably of archbishop Theobald.

coloured red (as in the only example of Thomas), green, brown or natural; seals of natural colour are often varnished brown.

THOMAS   No complete impression of both seal and counterseal survives among the four original acta (3, 16, 23, 34).

Obverse: casts exist in the BL and the Society of Antiquaries which closely resemble archbishop Theobald's seal (as seen, e.g. on BL Harl. ch. 83 C 26). BL Detached seal C II.1 a (a cast) measures approximately 90 × 55 mm. Inscr. on rim: + SIG TOME DEI GRATIA CANTVARIE (?) ARCHIEPISCOPVS (*sic*). The name 'Tome' is somewhat blurred, but the lombardic E is clear, as is also the VS at the end of 'archiepiscopus'. The crosier turns inward. Tancred Borenius reviewed the claims to authenticity of these casts (which cannot be linked with any known acta) in *Archaeologia* lxxix (1929) 29–30 and in his *St Thomas Becket in art* (1932) 12–13. One of them is certainly modern, and he found reasons for treating the others with reserve. One of them (source not stated) appears as pl. IV(d) in Fritz Saxl, *English sculpture of the twelfth century* (1954). Here the legend reads: SIGILLVM TOME DEI GRATIA AR-CHIEPISCOPI CANTVARIENSIS. Seals remained, in the eighteenth century, on the originals of two acta at St-Bertin, now lost (nos. 39, 40). Their description and the rough sketch by Dom Charles Dewitte correspond in general to the casts, but not entirely. His crude sketch depicts the archbishop on a square platform, and his crosier turns inward (as with his three next successors), whereas it turns outward on the Saxl cast, resembling archbishop Theobald's seal. The inscription on Dewitte's drawing is: TOMAS DEI GRATIA CANTVARIENSIS ARCHIEPISCOPVS, thus differ-ing from all others before Hubert in omitting SIGILLUM, using the nominative of the name and title, and transposing the last two words.

Reverse: an oval, approx. 29 × 24 mm., inscr. on rim: + SI-GILLVM TOME LVND', encloses a classical intaglio of Mercury standing beside a column. This survives in an impression in brown wax on no. 23, set in a larger oval of wax but lacking the face of the seal. It is also illustrated by Dewitte (no. 39). No. 23 is described by Joseph Burtt in *Archaeological Journal* xxvi (1869) 85–86, with an engraving opposite p. 84, whence later reproductions; see here, pl. I. The evidence of nos. 39–40 shows that Thomas had the use of seal and counterseal when he arrived in France in Nov. 1164 (cf. Foreville, 'Lettres "extravagantes" ' 235–6).

RICHARD   Substantial remains exist of twelve impressions of seal and counterseal, none perfect (80, 81*bis*, 85, 114, 136, 159–60, 177A, 178, 187, 215), with a drawing of no. 202 by Dom Charles Dewitte. Other acta have fragments, including two bags of bits (117, + 193).

Obverse: approx. 85 × 65 mm. Inscr. on rim: + SIGILLVM : RICARDI : DEI : GRATIA : CANTVARIENSIS : ARCHIEPISCOPI. In the impressions examined the field of the effigy is diapered in squares, although this is so delicate and so often badly worn that it is barely visible in some. No. 112 is reproduced in *Archaeologia Cant.* ii (1859) pl. facing p. 41 and in *Proc. Soc. Antiquaries* 2s. xi (1887) 273 from the same woodcut.

Reverse: approx. 40 × 24 mm. + a conical cavity of 8 mm. at the top which may indicate a fastening attached to the matrix.

Inscr. on rim: RICARDVS DEI GRATIA TOCIVS ANGLIE PRIMAS.[64] This surrounds a half-figure of the archbishop in mass vestments, with crosier in left hand, turned outward, his right hand raised in blessing. The figure rises above four wavy lines (? water or clouds). Above, a hand points downward between the horns of the mitre. No. 112 is reproduced in *Archaeologia Cant.* ii pl. facing p. 41 (and *Proc. Soc. Antiq.* 2s. xi 291); no. 114 is reproduced ibid. vi 195.
    The editor of no. 114 in *Archaeologia Cant.* vi observed (p. 195 n. 1) that 'this is not the seal used by the same archbishop and engraved in our Second Volume, p. 41 [no. 112], having no diapering on the groundwork. The counterseal is of a nearly identical design with the counterseal there given, though apparently from a different matrix.' This is not convincing. No. 112 is lost and the seal only recorded by the woodcuts of 1859; but these pictures conform in general with the better surviving impressions. The fragment attached to no. 114 is so imperfect that one cannot tell whether the background of the seal was originally diapered or plain, and the counterseal does not obviously differ from other examples. It must therefore remain doubtful whether archbishop Richard had a second seal.
    The legend of the counterseal introduces the primatial title for the first time on an archiepiscopal seal. Some twenty years earlier a seal of Christ Church, Canterbury, had borne the words: PRIME SEDIS BRITANNIE (Saltman p. 226).

---

[64] The inscription has ligatures for A–R and A–N.

BALDWIN Two fairly complete impressions survive (nos. 270, 298) of a seal and counterseal, with fragments of more seals on other acta.

Obverse: approx. 80 × 60 mm. Inscr. on rim: SIGILLVM BALDWINI DEI GRATIA CANTVARIENSIS ARCHIEPIS-COPI. The crosier turns inward.

Reverse: approx. 45 × 28 + a conical cavity of 8 mm. at the top, which may indicate a fastening attached to the matrix.

Inscr. on rim: SIGNVM SECRETVM, framing a full-length effigy of the archbishop in mass vestments, with horned mitre and pallium, holding crosier and blessing, as on obverse.

HUBERT Four fairly complete impressions survive (nos. 338, 345, 555, 597) of seal and counterseal. Eight more acta carry fragments.

Obverse: approx. 80 × 50 mm. Inscr. on rim: + HVBERTVS . DEI . GRATIA . CANTVARIENSIS . ARCHIEPISCOPVS.

Reverse: approx. 50 × 28 mm. A pointed oval. Inscr. on rim: + MARTIR ⁚ QUOD STILLAT ⁚ PRIMATIS ⁚ AB ⁚ ORE ⁚ SIGILLAT, framing the murder of St Thomas, depicted under an arcade of two arches, with (r.h.) Thomas kneeling and Grim standing behind, (l.h.) two murderers.

Reproductions of obverse of no. 597 in *EYC* xii pl. V and of reverse of same in W. de G. Birch, *Catalogue of seals in the British Museum* (1887–1900) no. 1187 and by T. Borenius in *Archaeologia* lxxix 44 pl. XVI(i) and *St Thomas Becket in art* pl. XXVII(i). Borenius notes reverse as 'the earliest more or less definitely datable representation of the murder' (*St Thomas* 74).

THE DIPLOMATIC OF THE ACTA: II. INTERNAL FEATURES

Copies of acta are far more numerous than originals, and these, when used carefully, can yield much information supplementary to the originals on matters of composition and style. They permit, in the first place, the generalization that the epistolary style predominates in all kinds of legal instruments and formal correspondence.

The impersonal form is occasionally used for solemn judicial settlements and injunctions after visitation, but even documents of this sort are sometimes cast as letters with *intitulatio* and general address.[65] In all his letters the archbishop speaks in the first person plural, except when addressing the pope.

The literary style shows nothing peculiar to the archbishops' secretariat. It reflects the usual development of ecclesiastical letter-writing in England, paying more attention than before to the customary *cursus*, and constantly pillaging the formulae of the papal and royal chanceries.[66] The draftsmen of beneficial acts probably depended less on formularies than on documents brought by the beneficiaries for inspection, so that some of the more elaborate confirmatory acta have an old-fashioned air (e.g. 92, 258, 397). Archbishop Theobald had provided some English monasteries with confirmations which have the full flavour of a papal privilege, and in a few cases this was taken over in later confirmations (e.g. no. 142). The language of privileges often recurs, though without exact copying, in the dispositive clauses of archbishop Richard's confirmations (e.g. nos. 176, 187), while other acta combine royal and papal wording with ingenious eclecticism (e.g. 23, 112, 200). A markedly royal writ-form appears in letters of institution given by archbishop Baldwin to the nephews of archbishop Thomas: 'Quare volumus et precipimus . . . ita quiete et pacifice possideat sicut . . . ' (nos. 248–9); and a mandate of archbishop Richard for St Albans reads 'ne . . . pro defectu iustitie iustam debeant ad nos querimoniam reportare'. (no. 200). The administrative acta of archbishop Hubert show another sort of papal influence: importation of the formulae coined in the court of Rome for its mandates to judges delegate: 'Quod si non omnes . . . ' (nos. 409, 524 cf. 481) 'Testes autem qui fuerint nominati . . . ' (nos. 409, 418, 649, 654).[67] In short, there were many stock words and phrases at hand and there was a tendency to use them capriciously and freely. Their very profusion warns us against reading significance into every variety of formula. The author of the twelfth-century *Ars dictandi Aurelianensis* makes a notable comment on papal formulae. He observes 'quod papa in suis literis *dei gracia* nec de sua nec de alia persona . . . apponit'. He asks: 'Ratio queritur, quare non apponit literis suis *dei gracia*?' and

---

[65] Cf. above, xliv–v. Later in the thirteenth century, under the influence of notarial practice, the impersonal form becomes more usual for certain sorts of record.

[66] *EBC* 77–81.

[67] Cf. merely formal phrases: 'Et quia nobis de rei veritate non consistit' (no. 404), 'Quia igitur de appellatione . . . nobis minime constat' (no. 407).

replies disarmingly: 'Forsitan nulla est racio, set sic est in usu apud curiam Romanam.'[68] This, of course, does not apply to clauses importing legal refinements.

Some diplomatic features of the acta must now be looked at more closely. Because beneficial acta are drafted with most formality, if not according to strict rules, they merit particular attention. They will be the main subject of the following pages.

INTITULATIO

None of the four archbishops used one invariable form, but for each of them a single style predominates and the evidence of originals is supported by many copies. One feature common to all is of particular importance because it affects the dating of the acta: each archbishop held the legatine office for a portion of his pontificate. Consequently, the style *apostolice sedis legatus* ought to be good evidence for narrowing the limits of date in undated acta.[69] This will receive further attention below (pp. lvii–viii).

THOMAS The archbishop's name occurs in the known four original acta as *Thom(as)* or *Tomas*. Although these are too few to allow us to affirm that the name, rather than the initial, was always used by the archbishop's clerks, the majority of copies supports the proposition. Since Thomas had succeeded Theobald, who most often used the simple *T.*, it would be a prudent rule for his clerks to distinguish their master's acta by writing the name in full.[70] It has been shown elsewhere that they also departed from the normal Canterbury practice to style Thomas usually *dei gratia Cantuariensis ecclesie minister humilis* (or *hum. min.*) and that they omitted the title of primate, used by Theobald after May 1145, although the pope confirmed this title for Thomas on 8 April 1166. All the texts edited here adopt this style, and all probably belong to the pre-legatine period. Letters preserved in the collected correspondence dated after Thomas was appointed legate show that in later years he sometimes used the style *dei gratia Cant. archiepiscopus et apostolice sedis legatus*.

Medieval copyists and commentators ascribed to Thomas many acta which in fact emanated from Theobald. The following selection is made on the basis of diplomatic tests for distinguishing the acta of

[68] Rockinger, *Briefsteller* i 105. cf. below, 56–61.
[69] C. R. Cheney, 'The deaths of popes and the expiry of legations in xii-cent. England', *Revue de Droit Canonique* xxviii (1978) 83–96.   [70] Saltman, *Theobald* 190.

the two archbishops proposed in the *Journal of the Society of Archivists*, 1981. Tests of this sort cannot, naturally, give absolute proof when applied to twelfth-century acta, and we might expect the troubled pontificate of Thomas Becket to be productive of aberrant forms. However, when copies in question can be tested by their contents and historical circumstances, the diplomatic distinction proves to be valid. These diplomatic criteria obviously cannot be applied to 'mentions' of texts now lost, which medieval clerks, claiming to have inspected them, attributed to Thomas. These, when acceptable on other grounds, are included here.

RICHARD   The archbishop's name is written in full in two original acta (nos. 165, 187) and in two it is reduced to an initial *R.*, but in the large majority of originals it appears as *Ric'*. Richard was consecrated at Rome by pope Alexander III on 7 April 1174, received confirmation of his primacy on 27 April,[71] and was appointed legate the next day. No acta are known to belong to the intervening weeks. Thereafter he usually appears as *dei gratia Cant. archiepiscopus totius Anglie primas* (with or without the title of legate) and this is common with his successors.[72] In view of the title adopted by Thomas — *dei gratia Cant. ecclesie minister humilis* — it is not surprising that a grant by archbishop Richard for Dover priory, in the same terms as one given by Thomas, should adopt the same title (nos. 9, 126). This title also appears in ten more of Richard's acta, which is hardly surprising, as it was common currency in other bishoprics of England and France. Three of them are in letters written by Peter of Blois, addressed to the pope and to the young king Henry, but the rest are to less important recipients, at dates both early and late in the pontificate.[73]

BALDWIN   This prelate's original acta are relatively scarce (fifteen) and this makes the evidence less compelling. However, it seems that the initial *B'* was usual, though scribes also wrote *Bald'* or *Baldewin'* in the title. Two originals have a new style: *divina miseratione (sancte) Cant. ecclesie minister,*[74] and copies of two letters in Peter of Blois' collection read respectively *divina permissione*

---

[71] *PUE* ii 325–7 no. 134.

[72] In two originals (nos. 55, 113) and many copies 'archiepiscopus' is followed by the conjunction 'et'.

[73] Nos. 121, 126, 134–5, 139, 166, 188, 222–4, 230. All are copies. All but no. 126 omit *dei gratia*, nos. 135 and 188 read *hum. min.*

[74] Nos. 235 and (without *sancte*) 311. Cf. nos. 316, 323 (copies), which add the titles of primate and legate.

Cant. ecclesie minister and *Cant. ecclesie minister humilis* (nos. 261, 322). Apart from these, both originals and copies conform to the usual style of archbishop Richard, i.e. *dei gratia Cant. archiepiscopus totius Anglie primas*, with the added legatine style, *et apostolice sedis legatus*, in thirty or so acta which may be dated in the years 1186–1187.

HUBERT As in the acta of his immediate predecessors, Hubert's acta normally describe him as *dei gratia Cant. archiepiscopus totius Anglie primas*, with the style *(et) apostolice sedis legatus* in the years when he exercised Celestine III's commission, that is, April 1195 — Feb. 1198. Variations on the usual titles are rare. They occur where they might be expected: in letters addressed to the pope. Five such letters give the title *divina permissione Cant. ecclesie minister humilis* (nos. 354, 383, 550 (*perm. div.* in a draft), 608, 611); four of these add *totius Anglie primas*. The fifth, which omits it, is a letter against Gerald of Wales, only preserved by Gerald, who perhaps omitted a title which was peculiarly offensive to him (no. 354). Hubert omits *dei gratia* in making his profession of obedience (no. 327). Other exceptional forms are few (nos. 486, 493, 695). The archbishop's writs as justiciar usually correspond in the title to letters issued in his capacity of archbishop or legate and, like the writs of other justiciars, do not give him the title of that office. An original (? draft) of a writ in favour of Margaret de Bretteville begins curtly: 'Archiepiscopus salutem vicecomiti Devonie' (App. no. 2) and the title of legate is absent from three more writs preserved only in copies (App. nos. 3–4, 6).

THE LEGATINE TITLE AND DATING OF ACTA

A legatine commission, if not withdrawn by the pope who issued it, expired with that pope, unless renewed by his successor. On this assumption, which seems to be well founded (see p. liv n. 69), the legatine office of a prelate may be a useful means (too often neglected) of narrowing the time-limits of undated acta. In the case of English legates we must reckon with a time-lag of about a month for the news to reach England from the Curia, both of the original commission and of the death of the pope. Between these limits we may expect the prelate to use the title except in letters to the pope.[75]

---

[75] To judge by copies, Thomas and Richard did not use it in addressing the pope, and the extant letters of Baldwin and Hubert to the pope were not written when they were legates.

But before we use the title as an instrument of dating, a warning must be sounded. The title, always in the form *et apostolice sedis legatus*, was only one element of an *intitulatio*. It might be inserted or dropped in the copy of a document without affecting the structure of the sentence or creating obvious absurdity. A careless copyist, accustomed to an *intitulatio* for an archbishop with or without the legatine style, might all too easily follow his usual practice rather than copy the title in front of him.[76] An example is seen in no. 442, a charter of archbishop Hubert for Dover priory. It is found in two cartularies of Dover and in the register of the see of Canterbury. The Dover copies give Hubert the title of legate; the Canterbury copy does not. There is an error here: is it of omission or commission? Without other means of dating, who shall say?

For our four archbishops the following approximate dates may be allotted to acta which declare them to be legates:

Thomas received the legation when in exile by a commission of 2 May 1166, which probably reached him towards the end of May at Pontigny or Soissons.[77] To judge by copies of Becket's letters in the collected correspondence, he only used the title when addressing ecclesiastics in England,[78] and he dropped it for parts of the years 1167–70 when his legatine powers were reduced.[79]

Richard received the legation when at the Curia on 28 April 1174, three weeks after consecration as archbishop;[80] and could have styled himself legate at once. He presumably dropped it on news reaching England of pope Alexander III's death on 30 August 1181, say, about the end of September 1181.

Baldwin, who received papal confirmation from Lucius III in mid-March 1185, did not receive from him the legation which king Henry II had asked for. He received it by letters of Urban III dated 17–18 Dec. 1185.[81] Urban III died on 28 Oct. 1187. The titles of Baldwin's acta are consistent with the view that he was styled legate between Jan. 1186 and Dec. 1187.

---

[76] For a scribal sin of commission — adding *dei gratia* to the style of king Henry I – see *EHR* xlii (1927) 81–2.

[77] *PUE* ii 311 no. 121. The pope announced it to the province by a letter dated 24 April.

[78] An exception is *MTB* vii 153 no. 602, to Mr Vivian, later cardinal.

[79] The evidence is complicated. See *Journal of Soc. of Archivists* 6 (1981) 473–4. *MTB* vi 555 no. 485, to the canons of Pentney, has the legatine title in ms. Cambridge, C.C.C. 134 fo. 1r, omitted from the printed text. Cf. below, no. 30n.

[80] *PUE* ii 327–8 no. 135.

[81] *EHR* ix (1894) 537–9, cf. *Rev. de Droit Canonique* xxviii 93 n. 41. Diceto gives the papal commission after the letter of Urban III (14 Jan. 1186) announcing his election (ii 39–40) and perhaps they were delivered together. He also suggests delay in delivery when he says that Baldwin visited Winchester on 1 May 'at the beginning of his legation' (ii 41); but this is hardly a reliable chronological pointer.

Hubert was appointed legate by a commission dated 18 March 1195, and may be presumed to have introduced the title into his acta by the end of April. The title was dropped when it became known that Innocent III had succeeded Celestine III on 8 Jan. 1198 and had not renewed the commission. This was probably during Feb. 1198.[82]

INSCRIPTIO

Acta with a particular, not a general, address are mostly mandates and letters on judicial or political or personal matters. The practice of addressing a beneficial letter to the beneficiary, which was still fairly common in archbishop Theobald's time,[83] is found once under Thomas in a charter for Fleury (no. 38), probably issued in France and possibly after the form of the lost charter of Theobald which it confirms. It occurs also once when Richard confirms the property of Newnham priory (no. 171A) and once when archbishop Hubert ratifies a grant of one of his staff to Peterborough abbey (no. 572). Apart from these instances, no beneficiary is addressed directly.

Sometimes under Thomas and Richard a grant of protection or a privilege is notified to local authorities: Thomas informs the bishop of Rochester and others that the nuns of Minster are exempted from the archdeacon's aid (no. 26, cf. 8, 9), and Richard addresses the archdeacons of Lincoln and other officials to announce the protection of the church of Canterbury for Bardney (no. 50). In this period too, when the archbishop admits a tenant of his lordship to an hereditary holding he may announce this to the reeves and hundred courts or his men French and English (nos. 5, 68–71). Such acta have nothing to distinguish them from private charters or letters patent involving property granted by a lay lord to his men. They follow traditional lines, in this resembling acta of archbishop Theobald by which he endowed the nuns of West Malling with lands of the see.[84]

As for the general address found in most beneficial documents, one need not dwell on the manifold divergences from the most common form of Thomas's time: *universis sancte matris ecclesie fidelibus*. Saltman set out in full the 'bewildering number of variations' and 'almost complete lack of common form' at one end of

---

[82] For an apparent exception see below, no. +594. Hubert's appointment in 1195 was apparently known in England by 30 April (*Ann. mon.* iv 388).

[83] Saltman 195–6.

[84] Ibid. 399, 402–4, nos. 176, 179–80. Cf. pope Gregory I's acts as a secular lord, JE 1222, 1391, 1623, cited by P. Classen, *Kaiserreskript u. Königsurkunde* (Byzantine Texts and Studies, Univ. of Thessaloniki. 1977) 211.

our period and Dr Major has done the same for Stephen Langton's time.[85] In the intervening pontificates the profusion of forms of Theobald's time was somewhat reduced, but no principle of choice is evident. To the formulae *Universis* (or *Omnibus*) . . . *fidelibus* (or *filiis*) is very often added (after Thomas's time, when it is still rare) some such phrase as *ad quos presentes littere pervenerint*. As alternatives to this phrase we find *ad quos presens scriptum* (or *scriptura* or *carta* or *pagina*) *pervenerit*. *Littere* is preferred by Richard's draftsmen; with Baldwin *scriptum* and *scriptura* enter into competition; with Hubert *scriptum* predominates.[86] The phrase is rarely replaced by a participial clause, but an indulgence of Richard for Dover priory is addressed *omnibus presentes litteras visuris vel audituris*, and there are similar examples from Hubert's time.[87]

The placing of the address in relation to the title need not detain us long. The custom approved by the writers on dictamen was observed: that is, letters addressed to persons of higher dignity (the pope, kings, and princes) and equals (such as another archbishop or the Cistercian general chapter) carry the addressee's name first; in letters to subordinates and persons of inferior dignity the archbishop's title comes first.

The prevalent habit of addressing beneficial letters to all the faithful, not to the beneficiary, allowed the *intitulatio* to be set first or second. During the last quarter of the century at Canterbury the choice seems to be at the whim of the draftsman. Under Theobald the archbishop's testament provides the only certain example of a general address preceding Theobald's name and title.[88] For Thomas we have no example; but under Richard, Baldwin, and Hubert the general address occurs before the *intitulatio* in a substantial minority of acta.[89] Surveying Langton's acta, Dr Major deduced that 'the custom of putting the archbishop's name first in an actum with a general address practically died out after 1215.'[90]

---

[85] Saltman 192–5, *Acta S. Langton* pp. xxv–vi; cf. Smith, *EEA* i p. liv.

[86] But see nos. 365 (*carta*) and 536, 579, 601 (*littere*), all originals.

[87] No. 124, and no. 91 ('presens scriptum . . . '); both are copies. Cf. Hubert's nos. 393, 473, 658–9.

[88] Saltman 190, 255. Saltman finds the same sequence in copies of two other acta (pp. 326–7, 341–2 nos. 105, 119); but another copy of no. 119 reverses the order and casts doubt on this example. For a like mixed tradition see no. 450 below.

[89] The calendar below indicates those acta which begin with general address; *EBC* exaggerates their rarity. The largest proportion is under Baldwin, the largest number under Hubert. Cf. *EEA* i pp. liii–iv.   [90] *Acta S. Langton* p. xxv.

SALUTATIO

So far as the evidence of these collected acta extends, Thomas followed
the practice of his predecessor and generally confined his greeting to
salutem. The only variant on this simple form is in the confirmation for
Dover priory which agrees in all respects, greeting included, with its
exemplar given by Theobald: *salutem et benedictionem*.[91] Letters in the
Becket collections are mostly of a different sort. They offer many
rhetorical elaborations of greeting, admonitory or subservient,
reminiscent of the dictaminal handbooks, which have no place in the
day-to-day mandates and confirmatory charters. There are a dozen
greetings to the pope, of which the less florid specimens resemble those
used by later archbishops in addressing the pope.[92]

    The successors of archbishop Thomas were seldom content to use
salutem alone in their official acta.[93] There are many varieties of
which none seems to be applied predominantly to one sort of
recipient or one sort of business, except for the formulae of humility
which adorn addresses to the pope. To particularize more than
twenty sorts would serve no useful purpose. *Eternam in domino
salutem* is by far the most common, and in Hubert's time appears in
fully a third of the acta which are preserved in full; but there is still
no uniformity. Copies of three inspeximus charters for St Nicholas'
priory, Exeter (nos. 457–9), all probably issued in the first few
months of Hubert's pontificate, possibly on the same occasion, have
three forms of greeting: *salutem in vero salutari, eternam in domino
salutem, salutem in domino*. A few forms, fairly common under
Richard and Baldwin (e.g. *illam que est in domino salutem*), are not
recorded under their successors. No rules were visibly applied.

    One greeting is of special interest: that composed by Peter of
Blois for archbishop Richard in the letter which threatens the young
king Henry with excommunication (no. 135); for it looks forward to

---

[91] No. 9, cf. Saltman 197, and cf. Foliot, *Letters* 23–4. This greeting, or *salutem et gratiam
et benedictionem*, is used fairly often by Richard and Baldwin and 36 times by Hubert,
especially when they address subordinate officials. Alberic of Monte Cassino and later
dictaminists regarded *benedictionem* as proper in greetings to subordinates (Rockinger,
Briefsteller i 14, cf. 62, 107, 198). For contemporary literary practice in general see Carol D.
Lanham, '*Salutatio' formulas in Latin letters to 1200* (Münchener Beiträge zur Mediaevistik-
und Renaissance-Forschung, 22. Munich 1975), especially 54–5.

[92] *MTB* v 48, 386, vi 154, 227, 293, 398, 486, 640, vii 17, 253, 326, 401, epp. 29, 195, 286,
322, 348, 407, 450, 530, 537, 646, 684, 723. Cf. below, nos. 166, 230, 322, 354, 383, 550, 608,
611, and *Acta S. Langton* p. xxxvii.

[93] With *salutem* alone: Richard nos. 153, 178 (originals), 46, 68, 75, 87–8, 111, 123, 185, 199
(copies). Baldwin and Hubert only yield examples in copies: nos. 245, 301, 319, 374, 393, 590.
Some of the copies show signs of abridgement elsewhere.

the formula of Innocent III's chancery for the address to excommunicates: 'spiritum consilii sanioris'.[94]

ARENGA

The practice of archbishops Theobald and Stephen in using the arenga (preamble, or harangue) in their acta has been analysed very thoroughly.[95] It is unnecessary here to list the many varieties used by the intervening archbishops, but some remarks on the use of the clause are called for.

Although the arenga is not confined to charters of confirmation, this category of instrument accounts for most of the examples. They present a whole series of related notions in a welter of words which embody one or more edifying thoughts: that it is a prelate's duty to guarantee the peace and quiet of the regular clergy or of the secular clergy, or the relief of the poor. A prelate should protect church property; it is good (or reasonable) for him to confirm the acts of charity of others, especially of those approved by his fellow-bishops. Nuns and lepers are singled out as particularly deserving classes. Indulgences are the occasion for urging the public to be free with alms. Stress is also laid on the fallibility of human memory and the modern prevalence of evil-doers, which require records to be made in writing. There is emphasis on 'memorialibus scriptis et testium numerositate' (no. 114). One early charter of archbishop Richard — perhaps the only one with an arenga in a grant to a secular clerk — confirms for Henry of Blackburn the church of Blackburn:

'Quoniam humane ambitionis exsecrabilis fames adeo in alienas possessiones exarsit ut exquisitis calumpniantium versutiis vix inveniatur qui sue possessionis quietem optineat, necesse est contra hec nequitie machinamenta remedium inveniri et beneficia que rationabiliter et canonice collata fuisse noscuntur auctoritatum patrociniis et instrumentorum testimoniis communiri.'[96]

[94] Cf. *SLI* 128 no. 44 and references in n.1.

[95] Saltman 197–208; Major, *Acta S. Langton* pp. xxviii–xxxiii. For the arenga in its earlier and broader setting see H. Fichtenau, *Arenga* (Mitteilungen des Inst. für Oesterreichische Gesch.-Forsch., Ergänzungsbd 18. Wien. 1957) and cf. P. Classen, op. cit. p. lviii n. 84, esp. 155–6, 205. For English bishoprics see *EBC* 69–77 and for German bishoprics P. Johanek, *Die Frühzeit der Siegelkunde in Bistum Würzburg* (Quellen u. Forsch. zur Gesch. des Bistums u. Hochstifts Würzburg. xx 1969) 284–7.

[96] No. 58 below (calendared). Similar collocations of words occur in others of Richard's arengas: nos. 54, 111, 131, 157. For arengas which stress the need for written title-deeds see also nos. 38, 46, 96, 108, 112, 114, 145, 176, 212, 215, 221, 228, 231, 326, 372, 494, 567, 601, 641. The sentiment often finds expression in the corroboration clause.

The arenga also appears from archbishop Richard's time onwards in a few records of judgments and settlements made in the archbishop's presence (nos. 85, 136, 153, 170, 196, 198, 337, 343, 392, etc.). Here one of the favourite themes is the need to publicize legal acts and commit them to writing. Ordinances and proclamations, like Roman imperial laws, naturally have sonorous preambles; but such documents are few.[97] A mandate of archbishop Hubert to the dean and chaplains of Dover on the duty of the parishioners to pay tithe has almost the character of a proclamation, which may account for an arenga dwelling upon the duties of the clergy to instruct and discipline their flocks (no. 438).

But the pious preamble was never an essential part of archiepiscopal acta of any type, and its use diminished as time went on — from about 40% in Theobald's time to less than half that proportion under Hubert. Dr Major calls it 'a dying element in archiepiscopal diplomatic' under Langton.[98] The decline is marked when a new form of confirmation, the inspeximus, becomes more common at the end of the twelfth century. The earliest examples of inspeximus, one under Richard and twenty-two under Baldwin, never use the arenga. In the 88 inspeximus charters of Hubert the arenga only occurs in nine, and it never appears in the numerous examples of the new form among Stephen's acta. Indeed, the choice between including or omitting an arenga seems to have been capricious. Two charters may have identical objects in view: one exhibits this embellishment, the other does not. This occurs at all periods and even in two grants made by the same archbishop for the same beneficiary. No legal differentiation between the two is discernible. Nor can it be said that by this time the themes and variations of arengas any longer offer noteworthy evidence for the student of social and political ideas. All we find are hackneyed expressions of a dying rhetorical custom, in sentiment and vocabulary redolent of old papal custom. The differences of one from another must be attributed either to the whims of the draftsmen or the wishes of the recipients. One suspects that it cost more to have a charter with an arenga: 'penny plain and tuppence coloured'.

The same sentiment might, however, be expressed without the elaborating of a separate preamble. Draftsmen sometimes achieve a more economical and simpler form by reducing the arenga to the

---

[97] The canons of Richard's council of Westminster (1175) have an eloquent preamble, but those issued by Hubert at councils of York (1195) and Westminster (1200), as transmitted to us, plunge *in medias res* without preliminaries. Cf. nos. 241, 389, 419, 656.

[98] *Acta S. Langton* p. xxxi. Cf. *EEA* i pp. lv–lvi.

status of a subordinate clause, introduced by some such word as
'quia', 'quoniam', or 'ut', which leads directly to the main narrative
or dispository clause, with or without words of notification. Thus
Richard's settlement of a suit concerning Dunstable priory (no. 128)
begins: 'Ut ea que pro bono pacis et utilitatis ecclesiastice facta sunt
perpetua gaudeant stabilitate, ad omnium volumus pervenire notitiam controversiam que vertebatur . . . terminatam esse et sopitam.'
His confirmation for the nuns of Westwood includes the beginning
of an arenga in standard style, which continues without break into
the dispository clause: 'Quoniam ea que domibus religiosis . . . sunt
concessa . . . debent stabilitate gaudere, ut . . . nulla . . . temeritate
divellantur, nos dilectis . . . monialibus de Westwude . . . '.[99]
Another practice involved omitting the arenga and introducing the
equivalent in the latter part of the text. This is exemplified by a
confirmation by Richard for St Frideswide's, Oxford, which inserts
the substance of an arenga between the *narratio* and the *dispositio*:
'Unde, quoniam ex officio suscepti regiminis nobis imminet ut
caritatis opera que a subditis nostris . . . facta esse noscuntur rata
habeamus et firma, . . . concessionem . . . ratam habemus et
firmam' (no. 180, cf. no. 154). Baldwin's confirmation of a settlement about tithes provides another example. He concludes: 'Hec
communi scripto duximus committenda, ne controversia hoc pacis
beneficio coram nobis semel terminata malignantium versutia in
recidivam futuris temporibus questionem deducatur.' (no. 297).
Drafts of Hubert's acta show that it might be in the choice of the
draftsman to insert these reflexions at the beginning, or in the
middle, or at the end of the text.[100]

As regards the substance of these effusions, they have little to
offer to the historian except as evidence of rhetorical fashion; but the
student of diplomatic should not on this account ignore arengas. For
the study of the archbishop's secretariat they are of interest when
comparison reveals identity — or near-identity — between arengas
of documents issued at different times for different beneficiaries.
The almost exact agreement of acta of Richard for Caen (no. 64) and
Newstead (no. 173) in their arengas seems to guarantee that they
were of 'internal' workmanship. Moreover, the 'ne malignantium
temeritate divellantur' of these charters compares with 'ne aliqua

[99] No. 228. Cf. no. 168 (Monks Kirby), which combines features of nos. 128 and 228. For a
briefer preamble to a notification see no. 225.
[100] Nos. 535–6. Other examples of the arenga swallowed by the notification are nos. 342,
427, 429, 434, 445, 473, 537, 618, 631. Dr Major notes the same happening later, *Acta S.
Langton* p. xxx.

temeritate divellantur' in a charter for Lilleshall (no. 157), 'ne aliquo temeritatis ausu divellantur' in charters for Belvoir and Holyrood, Edinburgh (nos. 56, 131), and 'nulla calumpnantium temeritate divellantur' for Westwood (no. 228). Further parallels can be seen in the Belvoir and Holyrood arengas. Other striking resemblances link Richard's acta for Thoby, Combwell, and Walden (nos. 215, 111, 220–2). Moreover, their common formulae reappear many years later in Hubert's confirmation charter for St-Victor-en-Caux (no. 601); but on this occasion Hubert explicitly renews his predecessor's grant (now lost), so that this points simply to one more example from Richard's secretariat.

If the witness-lists which accompany these arengas are examined, Mr Gerard appears in nine out of ten of them, Mr Peter of Blois in seven. Can it be inferred that either of these noted scholars — the most distinguished of all the archbishop's staff — fashioned the arengas? The question is worth asking, even if it only leads to the admission that we cannot answer it. Be that as it may, the recurrence of an arenga — not merely of a single favourite trope — points to the existence of formularies of a sort, or else to the practice of saving drafts or copies of acta as patterns to be repeated later. Such aids to composition were more likely to come into existence in this age as personal works of private enterprise than as official, systematic works of reference.[101]

NOTIFICATIO

The arenga is usually linked with the *narratio* and/or the *dispositio* by a conjunction, adverb, or adverbial phrase, the commonest being the 'Eapropter' familiar in papal privileges and letters of grace. Other link words are 'Unde', 'Hinc/Inde est quod', less often 'Considerantes' (nos. 102, 575), 'Attendentes' (nos. 223, 623), 'Hac igitur ratione' (no. 10).

Another pattern often occurs in those of Richard's acta which have an arenga. Here 'Eapropter' or 'Inde est quod' leads to words of notification. Thus, in a charter for Burton abbey (no. 63) an eloquent arenga on the archbishop's duty to make this provision is followed by: 'Eapropter ad universitatis vestre notitiam volumus pervenire nos monasterium Burthoniense . . . in protectione . . .

---

[101] *EBC* 122–30; J. E. Sayers, *Papal judges delegate in the province of Canterbury 1198–1254* (Oxford 1971) 47–54. For the rudiments of an early formulary in Bodl. ms. e Mus. 249, probably prepared in Gilbert Foliot's office, with forms used by his clerks, see Foliot, *Letters* 3–4, 516–9.

suscepisse et . . . confirmasse'. This combination of arenga with notification occurs in more than half the acta of Richard, Baldwin, and Hubert which open with an arenga.[102]

The arenga, it has been noted, does not appear in all letters with general address. Instead, the protocol may be followed at once by notificatory words which introduce the *dispositio*: 'Noverit universitas vestra', 'Ad universitatis vestre notitiam volumus pervenire', and the like. The verb 'scire', which occurs in royal and private charters in this context, is found in two acta of Thomas, but not later.[103]

There remain beneficial acta which have neither arenga or *notificatio*, and which plunge into their text with the *narratio* or *dispositio* (nos. 22, 213, 217, 306). Naturally, these include letters of a mandatory nature (nos. 17, 30, 169, 182, 524) and most letters with particular address.

NARRATIO AND DISPOSITIO

In the central part of the text we find a variety of treatment which defies easy classification and, at the same time, a general likeness to the forms adopted in other ecclesiastical and civil documents of the time. As elsewhere, the archbishops' acta sometimes give an extended story of past benefactions or legal disputes; but they may limit their narrative to a participial clause with a backward look: 'bone memorie Theobaldi decessoris nostri vestigiis inherentes' (no. 9, cf. 126) or dispense with the *narratio* altogether. A *narratio* may or may not lead on to a dispositive clause; memoranda framed to record uncompleted legal proceedings will omit it. But the most effective core of beneficial and judicial acta is normally the *dispositio*, and this uses the habitual formulae of grant, approval, confirmation, or prohibition. The substance of an act of confirmation may be restricted to a general statement, as exemplified in a charter of archbishop Thomas for Bardney (no. 1), which copies exactly a charter of Theobald in papal style; or it may rehearse all the rights and property involved, as in a solemn papal privilege: for example, 'possessiones . . . in quibus hec propriis duximus exprimenda vocabulis . . . ' (no. 56).

---

[102] Cf. *EEA* i p. lvi and nos. 212, 300, 321.

[103] 'Sciatis nos concessisse', nos. 1, 5. This corresponds to the practice at Lincoln, where Dr Smith notes that 'Scire' is in general used in connection with temporal property, not churches and tithes.

THE INSPEXIMUS

The last quarter of the twelfth century sees the evolution of a new method of confirmation: the enclosure in the text of a complete transcript of the earlier written grant or composition or judgment. It is prefaced with a brief notification and with the statement either that the beneficiary has presented to the archbishop a charter in the terms then repeated in full (e.g. nos. 240, 269–71, 273), or that the archbishop has inspected — and sometimes handled — the document (e.g. nos. 281, 290, 302, 323). The increasing use of the verb *inspicere*, which becomes usual with archbishop Hubert, has given rise to the description of this type of document as 'inspeximus' and its acceptance in the English royal chancery has naturalized the word as an English one.[104] The original charter having been recited, the disposition is completed with words of confirmation or approval by the archbishop's authority. There is much variety. A typical *dispositio* is seen in Baldwin's inspeximus for St James's priory, Exeter (nos. 270–1): 'Nos autem predicti episcopi confirmationem ratam habentes, eam quantum in nobis est presenti scripto et sigillo nostro confirmamus.'

This is the finished form of inspeximus. But before it evolved, it became increasingly common to cite earlier grants. Whereas under archbishops Theobald and Thomas a confirmation might silently copy the terms of earlier grants (e.g. no. 1), Richard and Baldwin often mention their forerunners when they copy them, with such words as 'ex tenore scripti sui oculata fide didicimus', or 'scriptis autenticis que oculis nostris perspeximus', or 'scriptis que nos vidimus et audivimus' (nos. 54, 156, 316). Many of Richard's charters give a circumstantial account of their exemplars, and reproduce their grants in similar terms, without reciting them in full (nos. 180–1, 217–8).

Words which emphasize personal examination (*vidisse, manibus nostris contrectasse*, etc.) are not uncommon in episcopal confirmations of the mid twelfth century;[105] but the practice of encasing the whole original grant in its confirmation only slowly takes hold, and not first at Canterbury. A charter of bishop Roger of Worcester,

---

[104] For the history of the inspeximus and related forms see A. Giry, *Manuel de diplomatique* (Paris 1894) 14–26, Bresslau, *Handbuch* ii 301–25, V. H. Galbraith in *EHR* lii (1937) 67–73, *EBC* 90–6, *Acta S. Langton* pp. xxxiii–iv. The papal practice of reciting a charter when confirming it is seen in *PUE* ii 468 no. 275 (1195) and *Letters of Innoc. III* nos. 51, 941, 962, 1004.

[105] They go back (as Prof. Brooke points out to me) to I John 1. 1: 'Quod audivimus, quod vidimus oculis nostris, quod perspeximus, et manus nostre contrectaverunt . . .'.

dated 1175, uses the word 'inspeximus', recites a private charter, and by implication approves it. The form is already taking shape and, at some time before bishop Roger's death in 1179, he inspects two charters of his predecessors, recites them, and then explicitly confirms them.[106] Other examples occur in the same decade in the dioceses of London, York, and Bath.[107]

The earliest known genuine inspeximus given by an archbishop of Canterbury is apparently no. 51 below, 1181 × 1184, which recites a charter of king Henry II for the church of Bath.[108] This is known only from a curtailed copy. Another confirmation by Richard, for Durford (no. 129), may be an earlier example abridged in the copying. The idea of reciting in full a document for confirmation was doubtless encouraged in this period by the increase in appellate litigation and the consequent need both to reproduce verbatim in English judicial records the mandates directed by the pope to judges delegate and to prepare authentic copies of title-deeds to be exhibited in the Curia (nos. 169, 276, 415, 560). With archbishop Baldwin the inspeximus-confirmation becomes popular, so that nearly half (22) of the total confirmations (46) take this form. During Hubert's pontificate the proportion gradually grows: of 120 confirmatory acta two-thirds are cast in the form of inspeximus.[109] The form is used more than once in Hubert's time for exemplification pure and simple, where all that is needed is an authentic copy of the original instrument.[110]

It will be evident that the inspeximus is often of great value to the historian in preserving a text of the earlier document when its original is lost. In general, a copy of this kind is more likely to be accurate than a copy in a cartulary, but carelessness or falsification is possible. A charter of archbishop Richard for Monks Kirby was inspected by Baldwin some twelve years later and originals of both survive (nos. 168, 296). Baldwin's confirmation not only omits the sanctions clause and witness-list of Richard's charter, but also a sentence of the *dispositio*; whether this was due to scribal oversight

---

[106] *Worcester cartulary* 90 no. 165 (pl. IX) and 34 no. 55; M. G. Cheney, *Roger of Worcester* 112.   [107] Foliot, *Letters* 456 no. 420a and *EBC* 95.

[108] The soi-disant inspeximus by Theobald for Rochester, 1145 (Saltman no. 222, cf. p. 228 and *EBC* 150–2) has not a good pedigree and is connected with obvious forgeries of later documents in inspeximus form.

[109] The form was less usual in the first years of Hubert. A series of seven confirmations for Strood (1194–5, nos. 623–9), which might have assumed this shape, do not do so; but this was perhaps because the Strood charters were all issued simultaneously with those of the diocesan and king Richard, which they confirm. Note that the word 'vidimus' is used in several cases instead of 'inspeximus'.

[110] In no. 520 an old private charter for Leeds is exemplified because 'sigillum . . . per vetustatem vidimus omnino fere consumptum'. Cf. no. 578.

or deliberate suppression one cannot say.[111] On the other hand, an inspeximus of Hubert for Fontevrault (no. 469) exists in the original along with the original of the inspected charter. Collation shows remarkable fidelity in the inspeximus, although the witness-list of the inspected charter is curtailed.

FINAL CLAUSES

The text in many acta of the beneficial sort concludes with one or more of various *clausulae*. They are seldom all found together, they may take diverse forms, and the sequence of clauses is not always the same.

INJUNCTIO

The first clause deserving mention is an injunctive clause which, as in the English royal charters of this time, may follow the *dispositio*. It restates the nature of the grant and orders its observance. Archbishop Thomas's charters provide four examples, of which the first reads 'Iccirco precipimus quod . . . teneant' (no. 1, cf. 3, 15, 23). In twelve such clauses in acta of archbishop Richard different formulae are used, including 'Quare volumus et precipimus', which recalls the 'Quare volo et firmiter precipio' of king Henry II's charters (no. 112, cf. 64, 67–70, 114, 144, 173). The 'Quare' incipit is used for the only three injunctive clauses in Baldwin's acta (nos. 253–4, 268). By Hubert's time the clause has disappeared, except in texts borrowed from earlier times.[112]

SANCTIO

Whether or not an injunctive clause is included in a confirmation charter, it may contain an admonition against disturbance of the grant. Already found in Archbishop Theobald's acta,[113] six examples of it occur under Thomas (nos. 15–17, 22–23, 29). As in Theobald's time, so under Thomas and Richard, simple prohibitions of this sort are greatly outnumbered by prohibitions supported by sanctions.[114]

---

[111] Cf. no. 270: both originals are extant and show minor divergences. Both were perhaps written by the beneficiary's scribe.

[112] No. 397, like Baldwin's no. 258, is copied from no. 92. For the 'Quare volumus' form in an act of bishop Seffrid II of Chichester see no. 452.

[113] Saltman 212.

[114] Papal privileges marked the subdivisions of the *sanctio* with large decorated initials: *admonitio*, 'Nulli ergo omnino hominum', *comminatio*, 'Si quis autem', *benedictio*, 'Cunctis autem eidem'. But these phrases do not follow a constant order.

Eight of Thomas go on to utter a curse on offenders (*anathema* or *maledictio*); only three (9, 24, 33) promise God's blessing on benefactors, and these may be following the acta of Theobald which they cite. The diction is not uniform. Archbishop Richard's acta include many more examples of the penal clause; blessings only occur in three: in a charter for Dover (no. 126) which follows verbatim those of Theobald and Thomas, in one for St James's, Northampton (no. 176) which goes beyond the curse which is taken over from Theobald's charter to add the 'Cunctis autem eidem' of papal privileges, and in one for Kenilworth (no. 142) which copies a charter of Theobald in reading 'Pax dei omnibus eis pacem conservantibus'. Under Richard there are a few unique forms, but most conform roughly to a single pattern: 'Statuimus quoque et sub interminatione anathematis prohibemus ne quis hanc nostre protectionis et confirmationis paginam infringere vel ei aliquatenus temere contraire presumat' (no. 63, cf. 64, 80, 85, 87–8, 95, 112, 125, 128, 160, 162, 173, 228).

The draftsmen of Baldwin's acta were less disposed to use a sanctions clause. One charter of Baldwin for Combwell adds a curse to the simple prohibition pronounced in its exemplar (nos. 111, 224); but the only other sanction (no. 258) comes from a charter of Richard, apart from two elaborate curses in *spuria* from Rochester (nos. +304–5, cf. +194–5). The more abundant evidence from Hubert's time points the same way. Out of ten sanctions clauses four were modelled on existing exemplars (nos. 397, 412, 446, 512), one probably came from a lost exemplar (no. 601), two occur in *spuria* from Goldcliff and Rochester (nos. +484, +594). Three more acta with sanctions are probably genuine but they may be of 'external' composition (nos. 471, 585–6). Two of these three (nos. 585–6) for Reading are the only acta to utter blessings. This trend to dispense with sanctions continues under archbishop Stephen.[115]

CORROBORATIO

During this period, when injunctive and sanctions clauses are passing out of fashion, in certain classes of acta another final clause comes into common use: the corroboration. This supplements the *dispositio*, which records the archbishop's grant or judgment, or confirmation of a grant or judgment or compromise. It spells out the nature of his validation of a lawful gift or agreement on ecclesiastical

---

[115] *Acta S. Langton* pp. xli–ii: only two examples.

rights or property, even though the word 'confirmamus' or the like
has already appeared in the *dispositio*. In its developed form the
corroboratio opens with a subordinate clause (*ut, quia,* or *ne*) which
states the need to strengthen the legal act, and goes on to describe
the method, with reference to 'the present writing/charter' or to 'our
seal' or to 'the subscriptions of witnesses', or to all or any of these.
The main verb may be 'roboramus' or 'corroboramus', but equally
often it is 'confirmamus' or 'communimus'. So a charter of
archbishop Hubert which confirms the English possessions of a
Breton abbey (no. 334) reads:

Unde et eadem ordinatio pia prescripti nobilis viri futuris temporibus firmior perseveret, eam prout rationabiliter facta est . . .
auctoritate qua fungimur confirmamus et tam presenti scripto quam
sigilli nostri appositione communimus.

This sort of clause already had a long history, but was used far
more extensively on the continent than in England in the acts of
princes, prelates, and lay nobles. In England the royal charters and
letters patent seldom used it until a fairly fixed formula was
introduced into some categories of letters patent in king John's
reign.[116] In twelfth-century English baronial charters the clause is
rare, becoming a little commoner as the century advances. In
English episcopal acta the developments in some dioceses is in
advance of the trend at Canterbury.[117] It never became an indispens-
able and distinct part of the archbishops' acta, for other ways were
found of achieving its object. First, draftsmen might announce
validation economically by prefacing the *dispositio* with a few words.
Archbishop Thomas precedes the details of a confirmation with
'Noverit universitas vestra nos sigilli nostri atestatione corroborasse
et confirmasse . . . ' (no. 3). In other cases the dispositive words are
followed immediately by reference to the seal. Thus Baldwin writes:
'cuius concessionem et donationem nos ratam habentes, eandem
sicut canonice et rationabiliter facta est, auctoritate qua fungimur
confirmamus et sigilli nostri appositione communimus' (no. 315).
When the inspeximus is used for confirmations, draftsmen evolve a

[116] For earlier royal *corroboratio* see, e.g. *Reg. regum* iii nos. 24, 34, 36, 74, 76, 112, 116,
280–1 (King Stephen and Matilda, mainly for Norman beneficiaries, cf. Bishop, *Scriptores
regis* 20); *Recueil des actes d'Henri II* Intro. 224 (citing eight, including *dubia*); *Foedera* (Rec.
Com.) I i 50, 63, 67 (Richard I).

[117] Theobald's clerks rarely use such a clause (Saltman 210–1). Cf. *Chichester acta* 31,
Foliot, *Letters* 25, *EEA* i p. lviii. A clerk in Foliot's office includes a short *corroboratio* in the
formulas in Bodl. ms. e Musaeo 249 (Foliot, *Letters* 518 no. 16).

standard dispositive clause to follow the text of the inspected document. This may be cast in the terms of a corroboration clause, and so may easily be taken to be one,[118] but in fact it is the sole dispositive part of the inspeximus, which shows it to be a confirmation as opposed to a mere authenticated copy or exemplification. It often begins with the characteristic opening of a *corroboratio*: 'Ut igitur quod . . . ' or 'Ne inposterum . . . '.

A few observations may be made about the use of the *corroboratio* under successive archbishops.

THOMAS Out of twenty-six grants and confirmations of property and ratifications of settlements in the name of archbishop Thomas, fourteen mention validation by the testimony of 'the present writing' or 'our charter' or 'our seal', and four of them use the verb 'roborare' or 'corroborare'. But in most cases these phrases are added to the main dispositive words (e.g. no. 3). In four cases only the validation is distinguishable as a separate clause (nos. 21, 24, 33, 38).

RICHARD Mentions of validation are now far commoner than in Thomas's day and the vocabulary is richer. 'Presentis scripti patrocinio' occurs often, as well as the customary 'attestatione/munimine/testimonio/auctoritate'. 'Pagina' is used as well as the 'scriptum/carta' of Thomas's acta. The verb 'communire' is more usual than before, and 'commendare' (no. 86) and 'indulgere' (no. 102) are alternatives. These are minor stylistic points. Another element is added in a few cases, namely, reference to witnesses (nos. 113, 136, 138, 175, 183, 199, 217). Although the validatory words are still sometimes inserted in the *dispositio*, the draftsmen far more often make a separate corroborative clause — there are some forty in all — marked by a clear beginning such as 'Quod ne forte', 'Et ut nostre', 'Quod ne revocari', 'Et ut hec donatio' (nos. 66, 68, 84, 87). Two short business-like formulae point to the future: 'In cuius rei testimonium presenti (huic) scripto sigillum nostrum fecimus apponi (apponi dignum duximus)' (nos. 91, 151).

BALDWIN By this time beneficial documents and records of judicial settlements nearly always mention *scriptum* and/or *sigillum*, and Baldwin's clerks refer more often than Richard's to the seal. But

---

[118] Cf. *Acta S. Langton* pp. xxxix–xl; *Chichester acta* 31.

witnesses only appear once.[119] Diction is more uniform than before. A recurrent formula is 'auctoritate qua fungimur confirmamus et sigilli nostri appositione communimus'. But the use of a separate *corroboratio* is no more common than before. Increase was checked, maybe, by the development in this pontificate of the inspeximus. This economical form, which blended *dispositio* and *corroboratio*, could be adapted to other confirmatory charters of Baldwin which do not inspect verbatim, but repeat the substance of, the previous acts.[120] Finally, it should be noted that the short form which appears twice in Richard's later years occurs only once at the outset of Baldwin's pontificate, for one of the same beneficiaries: 'In cuius rei testimonium presentibus literis sigillum nostrum apponi fecimus' (no. 282).

HUBERT The grants, confirmations, and ratifications of Hubert's time amount to more than all the preceding ones. Apart from inspeximus charters, relatively few lack a separate clause of corroboration. It still shows great variety of wording. The word 'corroborare' is rather rare, and mention of the witnesses is exceptional (nos. 335, 505, 522, 621). In this period, when the arenga is passing out of fashion, its highflown sentiments are occasionally transplanted to embellish the *corroboratio*. The ratification of an agreement reached in the archbishop's court ends: 'Ne igitur ea que in hac parte coram nobis sollempniter acta sunt in recidive contentionis scrupulum processu temporis redeant, in rei geste testimonium presenti pagine sigillum nostrum duximus apponendum' (no. 535, cf. 536). In Hubert's pontificate, as in Baldwin's, we find only one example of the short form: 'in huius rei testimonium . . . ' (no. 647, a copy). Its rarity is remarkable because at this time, when the archbishop was the king's chancellor, the royal chancery brought into regular use a similarly worded *corroboratio*. In the latter part of Stephen Langton's pontificate the variations on this short form almost drive the longer forms out of use in his acta.[121]

APPRECATIO

As a tailpiece to the text beneficial documents may add 'Amen',

---

[119] No. 264 for Combwell perhaps copied no. 113 of archbishop Richard. No. 264 refers to the seal in the *dispositio*, to the witnesses in the *corroboratio*; the latter here follows the *sanctio*.
[120] No. 287 is a simple example, no. 236 a more elaborate one.
[121] *Acta S. Langton* pp. xxxix–xli.

reminiscent of the three-fold *apprecatio* of the papal privilege.[122] Acta which end with 'Amen' are, however, very scarce (nos. 6, 9, 15, 126, 176, 585–6), and there is no authentic original in the whole collection.

ESCHATOCOL

It is hard to discover rhyme or reason in the changing forms of eschatocols. They may include any of three elements: witness-list, final greeting, and date; but since these were not of permanent legal importance, those who make copies of original charters may omit all or any of these sections without impairing the validity of the texts. Sometimes a copyist may indicate an omission with an *etc.*: 'Hiis testibus etc.', 'Valete etc.', or 'Datum etc.'. More often he does not. Given the preponderance of copies over originals in this collection, one can only venture a few general remarks on the prevailing practice at Canterbury in this period. No original contains all three elements. Witnesses and final greetings are alternative. A date is a relatively rare addition, and may be appended to documents with witnesses or valediction or neither.

Witnesses occur only in acta which grant or confirm property and rights or ratify judicial settlements and compromises. The originals number seventy-four. Besides these, twenty-one acta of the same sorts have no witnesses. Moreover, fifteen of the unwitnessed acta have no valediction, but end with the *corroboratio* or a date.[123] Maybe in this group an eschatocol was intended, left to the last minute and never added to the engrossment; but it would be rash to assume that negligence explains all these cases.

The pattern of witness-lists does not change markedly during the period. The sequence of the witnesses (as noted above, p. xxxi) shows regard for precedence and seniority, but the scribes are not always consistent in their placing of individuals, especially towards the lower end of the list. Witness-lists in Thomas's acta are introduced in various ways and, although with Richard *Hiis testibus* predominates in originals, *Testibus* and and *Testibus hiis* occur as well. Greater uniformity comes (as elsewhere in acta) with Baldwin and Hubert. *Hiis testibus* is now the rule, only occasionally breached. Witness-lists commonly conclude with 'et aliis', 'et multis

[122] I follow R. L. Poole, *Papal chancery* 47, in treating the *apprecatio* as the last of the final clauses, rather than the beginning of the eschatocol, as Bresslau, *Handbuch* i 48 and Boüard, *Manuel* i 257.

[123] Nos. 153, 187, 235, 315, 334, 337, 345, 370–1, 428, 512, 524, 526, 535, 578.

aliis', and the like, and the variety suggests that no importance attaches to the words.

In contrast to beneficial acta, mandates never have witnesses but usually include a simple valediction, *Vale* or *Valete*. No. 489, a draft mandate, has no valediction, but may have been intended to receive the addition of *Valete*.[124] Letters of a more personal nature and letters to the pope (nos. 322, 383) omit witnesses and may employ valedictory formulae more ornate than usual (e.g. no. 550).

As regards date, it may be said that dated acta are still highly unusual: so unusual, indeed, in any but spurious documents, that dated acta prompt questions about their authenticity.[125] While a few English bishops closely associated with royal administration are beginning, in the 1190s, to date their deeds, the archbishops of Canterbury do not follow suit. Even archbishop Hubert, justiciar and chancellor of the Angevin kings, does not make dating a rule in his secretariat. Dated original acta remain exceptional: for Thomas one (no. 34), Richard two (nos. 85, 215 cf. no. †194), Baldwin none (cf. no. †304), and Hubert six (nos. 334, 337, 370, 383, 428, 598 cf. no. †593). Most of these have peculiar features, and are the outcome of negotiations between important parties; no. 428 is a somewhat dubious indulgence. If we look beyond originals to dated copies of acta, they comprise a few judicial or quasi-judicial acta (78, 262, 447, 576), with a few beneficial documents (282, 383, 538), including some of the indulgences (124, 486, 575, 615).

One feature common to many dated acta which record settlements of lawsuits and amicable exchanges may throw a little light on the reason why dates were assigned to certain documents of this sort, though not to all. In most of the dated acta one of the parties to the transaction is a religious house and the other an individual prelate or lay magnate. Was it considered especially desirable, in an agreement made by an undying corporation with a mere mortal, to spell out clearly the historical facts?

The date is usually announced with the words 'Acta est' or 'Facta est', followed sometimes by a place-date and usually by a description of the act: *commutatio, compositio, concessio, confirmatio, conventio, indulgentia, relaxatio, renunciatio, sententia, transactio*. Only three dated acta begin with the word 'Dat' ' (nos. 124, 182, 282).

A few dated acta only record the year: the year of grace or incarnation (reckoned from the Annunciation), or the regnal year,

---

[124] Hubert's writs as justiciar follow the pattern of such writs of civil government: see the appendix to Hubert's acta below, and H. G. Richardson in *Memoranda roll 1 John* (PRS n.s. 21 1943) pp. lxxii–lxxv.   [125] *EBC* 81–90; *Acta S. Langton* xlii–xlv.

or the archbishop's pontifical year, or more than one of these methods.[126] Acta which give more detail use the Roman calendar or the feasts of the Church. No. 598 is peculiar in being dated by a bishop's consecration (cf. no. †304). These manifold forms of expressing dates emphasize the unfamiliarity of the procedure at Canterbury.

EDITORIAL METHOD

The acta in these two volumes have been prepared on the lines of D. M. Smith's edition of the Lincoln acta, published in 1980 as the first of this series of English Episcopal Acta. The principles of selection and the method of presentation are those set out in Dr Smith's introduction (pp. lxi–lxiv). Here it may suffice to recall a few salient features and to refer the reader to volume I for more details.

The text of every original actum is printed (and given the siglum A, or A^1 and A^2 in the case of duplicates). Under 'Original' is included not only engrossments for despatch to addressees or beneficiaries, but also single-sheet texts with or without sign of sealing, which may be drafts or file-copies retained in the archives of the issuing authority (e.g. no. 383 cf. above, p. xxxix). When the originals are lost and copies survive, provided that reasonably accurate editions are accessible, the acta are calendared in English, witness-lists being reproduced in the Latin form. Texts only surviving in copies which are hitherto unprinted, or inadequately printed, are given *in extenso*. All texts have been fully collated, but only selected variants are noted; and in matters of orthography unusual spellings have been allowed to stand without annotation, if they are not misleading. Any actum of which the text is totally lost, but of which the former existence is assured, is noted as a 'mention' and is included in the main series with an asterisk preceding its number. Uncertain cases in which the archbishop may have issued mere verbal instructions or acted through his clerks and proctors are excluded.[127] A cross before a number warns the reader that the

[126] Evidence for the use of the Annunciation style is slight but seems decisive: nos. 124, 486. Gervas. Cant. preferred the Nativity style in his chronicle (i 88). Two acta of Richard (nos. 94, 215), dated a.d. 1175, are also 'ordinationis nostre secundo' (therefore after 7 Apr. 1175). Copies of an actum of Baldwin, dated in 1185, add 'consecrationis nostre anno secundo', which is impossible (no. 282): he was consecrated in 1180. No. 389 is dated a.d. 1203 and the tenth pontifical year of Hubert; he was consecrated in 1189, but succeeded to Canterbury in 1193.

[127] Disputes over a pension from a chapel, between Lewes priory and the college of South Malling, came before archbps Richard and Hubert, who both authorized agreements. But the record by the dean of Malling, *c*.1200, does not say that the settlements were cast in the form of archiepiscopal acta (*Lewes chartulary* ii 131–2). Cf. above, pp. xxxix–xl.

actum, at least in its surviving form, is not believed to be an authentic document which was approved and sealed by the archbishop's clerks. Besides downright forgeries such as nos. 6 and 595, there are *spuria* of various sorts; a few others have been given the warning cross to show that they are suspect.

In each pontificate the acta are printed in one alphabetical sequence: beneficial documents under beneficiaries, mandates and judicial decisions under the persons or institutions primarily affected by the orders. Few letters do not fall in one or other of these categories. Letters relating to churches and tenants of the archbishops appear *s.v.* Canterbury see, likewise a tenant of Salisbury under that see. Letters of a diplomatic or personal nature (cf. pp. xxxv–vi) are placed under the names of the addressees.

The editorial method adopted for calculating and expressing limits of date in undated acta requires somewhat more explicit explanation, and notes on criteria for dating follow.

CRITERIA FOR DATING

Relatively few acta are dated. For the rest, the dates which are given below, following the captions, between square brackets, are drawn from internal evidence or from other documents or literary sources. It is usually only possible to state limiting dates within which an actum can be placed (thus, no. 129: [28 Apr. 1174 × 26 Apr. 1180]). Since no archbishop enjoyed the office of legate throughout his pontificate, the legatine title provides a useful limiting factor, except for archbishop Thomas, who seems to have used it seldom. These dates have been set out above on pp. lvi–viii.[128] Some letters can be placed by reference to dated papal mandates which they cite or dateable charters which they confirm or by consequential action. Acta with witness-lists often give the means of establishing narrower limits than the length of a pontificate or legation, if the tenure of offices held by witnesses can be dated or if, as occasionally happens, their absence from the archbishop at certain periods can be proved. Dating of particular acta is discussed in the notes appended to them, and throughout this volume and the next the reader may assume that the usual aids to chronology have been used: e.g. Le Neve's *Fasti* (especially the new edition), *Heads of*

---

[128] We have no examples of acta given by an archbishop elect, only the personal letter printed in this volume as App. I; and there is only one 'mention' (no. 52). Baldwin attests a royal charter which Eyton dates March 1185 as 'Cantuariensis electus' (*Leiston cart.* 132 no. 121, cf. Eyton 262).

religious houses, compiled by D. Knowles, C. N. L. Brooke, and
V. C. M. London, and other works listed in the bibliography of the
Handbook of dates (Royal Hist. Soc., 1981). The notes which follow
here call attention to some considerations which bear on the acta of
each of the four archbishops.

THOMAS After the archbishop's flight from England in October
1164, his secretariat probably issued few beneficial documents for
recipients in England and few cases came for judgment in his court;
hence the conjectural dating of most of the surviving texts. The
absence of the legatine style from the acta has been noted above (p.
lvii) and supports the view that most of the documents edited here
were issued in England, or at least precede the grant of the legatine
office in May 1166. The meagre eight witness-lists are not utterly
useless for dating, since we know some of his household who joined
the archbishop abroad and some who stayed at home.

RICHARD Richard was consecrated in the Curia on 7 April, and
was able to style himself primate and legate by 28 April 1174. He
used the legatine title until the death of pope Alexander III in 1181.
He perhaps arrived in England in August 1174, so that the end of
August is probably the earliest possible date for acta which imply an
antecedent hearing in his court (e.g. nos. 140–1, 153). Numerous
witness-lists permit closer dating than can be inferred from the
presence or absence of the legatine title. For Benedict the chancellor
and Peter of Blois see above, p. xxvi. The most distinguished of
Richard's other witnesses are Mr Gerard Pucella, elected bishop of
Coventry May × June 1183, Waleran archdeacon of Bayeux, elected
bishop of Rochester 9 × 10 Oct. 1182, and William of Northolt, who
became archdeacon of Gloucester May × Dec. 1177. These continued to witness acta with their new titles.

BALDWIN The short period of Baldwin's legation (Jan. 1186 ×
Dec. 1187) provides convenient means of narrowing limits of date.
Members of his household who habitually attest his acta did not
change in status during the pontificate, unless we count William,
archdeacon of Gloucester, who was elected bishop of Worcester in
May 1186.[129] On the other hand, extraneous witnesses are more
common in surviving acta than in archbishop Richard's time.

---

[129] But Mr Peter of Blois (cf. above, p. xxvi) was absent on a mission to the Curia from
Feb. to Dec. 1187 (J. A. Robinson, *Somerset historical essays* 119–21).

Narrow limits can be set to acta in which appear Hubert, elect of Salisbury (no. 281), and Godfrey, bishop of Winchester (no. 319), and the notorious Roger Norreys as prior of Canterbury (no. 298). Moreover the deaths of king Henry II, Baldwin de Redvers, bishop Gilbert Foliot, and other celebrities constitute fixed points for dating acta which name them as alive or dead. Other sources help. The letters concerning Baldwin's relations with Christ Church can be set in the context of the collection in Lambeth ms. 415. Beneficial acta for Brecon and Gloucester fit into the itinerary provided by Gerald of Wales for Spring 1188; others for churches in the march can be associated with Baldwin's known journey to Chester in 1187 (nos. 260, 278, 313–4, 325).

HUBERT   Making allowance for time taken in the transmission of orders and news from Rome, we may date Hubert's legatine acta Apr. 1195 × Feb. 1198. Witness-lists yield names and titles useful for dating. While the archbishop was justiciar (Dec. 1193 — July 1198) he was often attended by men we know as exchequer officials and judges of the king's court, e.g. William of Necton, Geoffrey of Buckland, Godfrey de Insula. These seldom appear in later years, so that their appearance offers a presumption (though no more) of a date before July 1198. The same presumption applies to several men who had connections with Salisbury and had served Hubert as bishop. We meet with Ranulf (? of Gedding) treasurer of Salisbury, Thomas of Hurstbourne, Mr Simon de Scales, and Robert of Rudby — but not in later years. Two men who gained important preferment provide fixed points. Mr Simon of Sywell is prominent as a witness both with and without the title of treasurer of Lichfield. He attests with the title no. 491, which precedes the death of bishop William of Hereford on 24 Dec. 1198; and he appears without the title in no. 568, which may be assigned to the vacancy at Worcester caused by the death of bishop John of Coutances on 24 Sept. 1198. Simon FitzRobert, or de Camera, became archdeacon of Wells c. June 1198 and was bishop-elect of Chichester by 9 Apr. 1204. Two major disputes are illuminated, and the approximate dates of the relevant letters of the archbishop are established, by the Christ Church collection in Lambeth ms. 415 and in the writings of Gerald of Wales. The itinerary, by showing with a fair degree of accuracy when Hubert was in France, sets limits to the possible dates of certain undated acta.

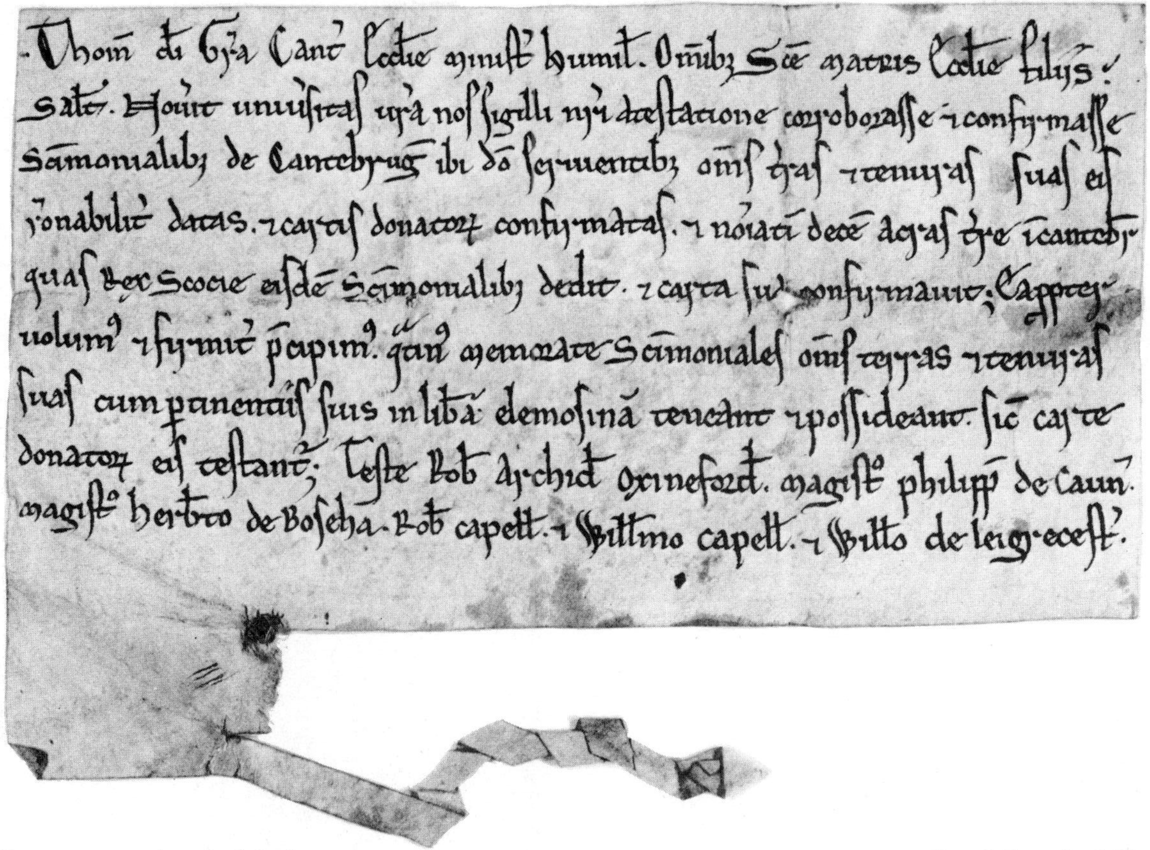

Jesus College, Cambridge

No. 3, approx. size of original

PLATE I

ACTA OF ARCHBISHOP RICHARD

(i) No. 77 (Scribe III), much enlarged

Dean and Chapter of Canterbury

(ii) No. 80 (Scribe II), much enlarged

Dean and Chapter of Canterbury

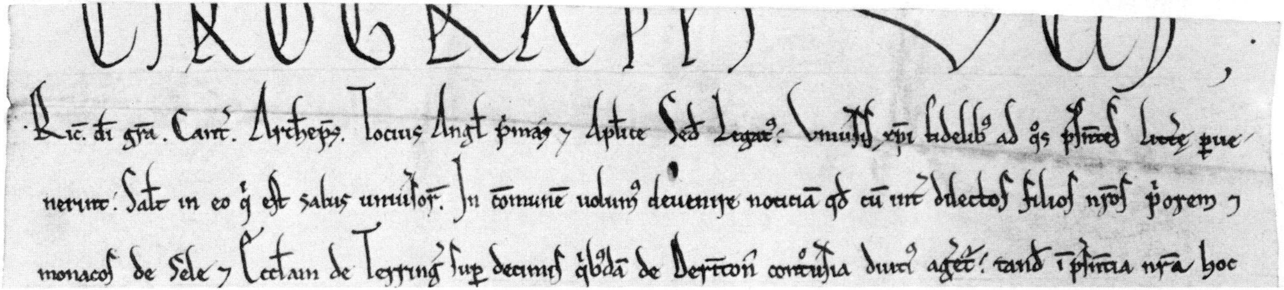

(iii) No. 211 (Scribe IV), approx. size of original

Magdalen College, Oxford

PLATE II

ACTA OF ARCHBISHOP BALDWIN

College of Arms

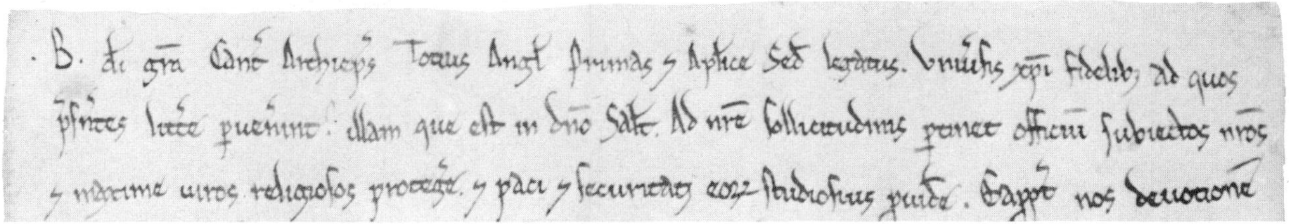

(i) No. 264, approx. size of original

Archives Nationales, Paris

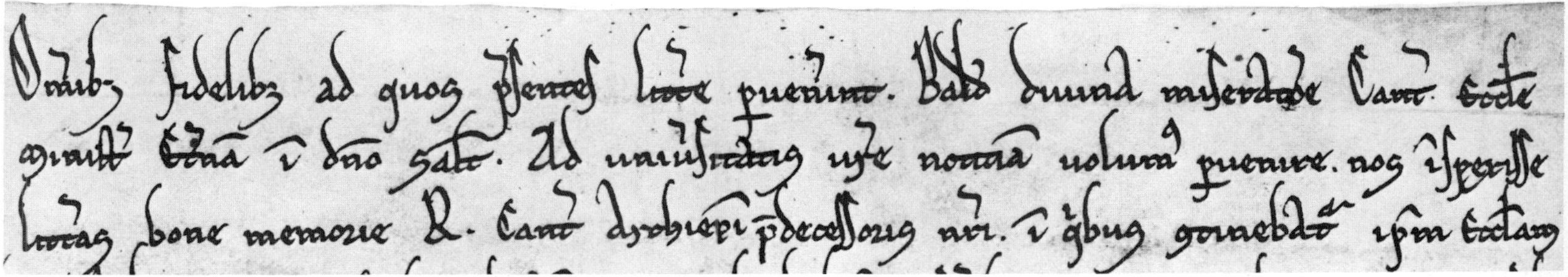

(ii) No. 311, much enlarged

Staffordshire Record Office

(iii) No. 312, approx. size of original

PLATE III

(*i*) Counterseal of Archbishop Thomas (actum no. 23), much enlarged

Crown copyright

(*ii*) Seal and counterseal of Archbishop Richard (actum no. 215), reduced

Lord Petre

PLATE IV

No. 489 (Scribe III), much reduced

PLATE V

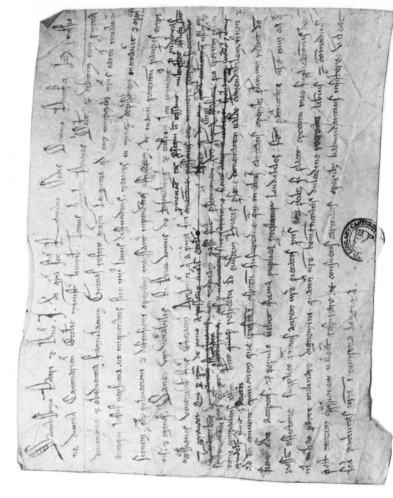

No. 550 (Scribe V), *much reduced*

Dean and Chapter of Canterbury

PLATE VI

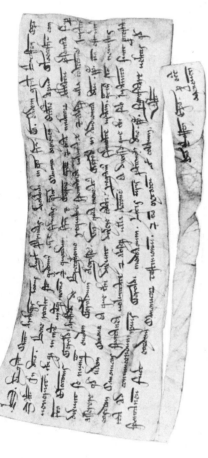

Dean and Chapter of Canterbury

(i) No. 355 (Scribe IV), reduced

Dean and Chapter of Canterbury

(ii) No. 387 (Scribe IV), much reduced

PLATE VII

ACTA OF ARCHBISHOP HUBERT

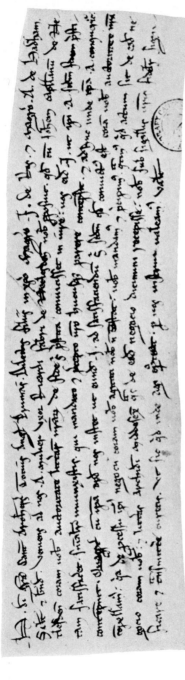

Dean and Chapter of Canterbury

(*i*) No. 549 (Scribe I), slightly reduced

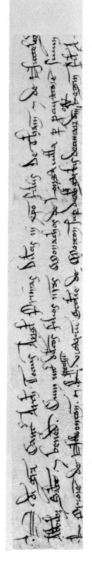

New College, Oxford

(*ii*) No. 555 (Scribe VI), slightly reduced

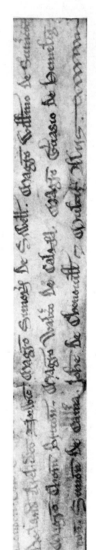

Norfolk Record Office

(*iii*) No. 558 (Scribe II), slightly reduced

PLATE VIII

THOMAS BECKET, 1162—1170

1. Bardney abbey

Confirmation for abbot Walter and the monks of Bardney of all their churches, lands, and possessions, as confirmed and enumerated by their diocesan.   [? 3 June 1162 × Oct. 1164]

B = BL ms. Cotton Vesp. E xx (Bardney cartulary) fo. 29r (25r). s. xiii ex.

T. dei gratia Cantuariensis ecclesie humilis minister omnibus sancte ecclesie fidelibus per Angliam*a* constitutis salutem. Sciatis nos concessisse et confirmasse monasterio sancti Oswaldi de Bard' et abbati Waltero monachisque ibidem deo ministrantibus omnes ecclesias, terras, possessiones quas canonice possident sive principum sive clericorum sive laicorum quorumcumque*b* largitione eas adepti sunt, sicut eorum diocesanus episcopus easdem possessiones illis carta sua concessit, confirmavit, et nominatim distinxit. Iccirco precipimus quod eas bene et in pace et libere teneant, prohibentes ne quis eos vel sua inquietare presumat. Quod siquis presumpserit, se vinculo anathematis innodandum cognoscat. Valete.

a per Angliam: *om.* B   *b* quorumcumque: quorum B

A charter of archbp Theobald in similar terms precedes this in the cartulary (pd Saltman, *Theobald* 237 no. 4). The title of the earlier charter runs: 'T. dei gratia Cantuariensis archiepiscopus et Anglorum primas', the abbot is named John. For other minor variants see Saltman no. 4. For the charter of the bp of Lincoln see *EEA* i no. 72. Walter had succeeded abbot John of Bardney by 22 Jan. 1155.

2. Bruton priory

Confirmation for the prior and convent of Bruton of the grant by bishop Robert of Bath of the church of Banwell and all its appurtenances.
                                          [? Woodstock. Early June 1163]

B = lost: in the part now missing (fos. 1–72) of BL ms. Egerton 3772 (Bruton cartulary), formerly on fo. 59r. s. xiii ex. C = Oxford, David Rogers, Esq., c/o Bodl. Libr. (formerly Phillipps ms. 4808) p. 90, abstract only, with curtailed witness-list, made by Rev. G. Harbin in 1719 from B, when the cartulary was complete. D = BL ms. Egerton 3772 encloses a transcript of C. s. xix med.

Pd (calendar) from D in *Bruton cartulary* 29 no. 124 (i).

Testibus: Henrico filio regis, Ricardo Pictaviensi archidiacono, Roberto de Belfou.

The charter was apparently given at the royal court when king Henry II made his grant of the same church, witnessed by the archbp. It can be dated with a fair degree of certainty (*Cal. Ch. Rolls* iii 270, cf. Eyton, *Itinerary* 63; a faulty abstract is in *Bruton cart.* 29 no. 124 (ii)). The ms. also contained the charters of bps Robert and Reginald of Bath (ibid. nos. 122, 123).

The placing of the king's son at the head of the witness-list is an early appearance of the prince in public affairs. He was eight years old, and had been present at the Treaty of Dover in March 1163.

3. Cambridge: priory of St Radegund

Confirmation for the nuns of Cambridge of all their lands and holdings, according to the donors' charters, to hold in free alms, especially ten acres of land in Cambridge given them by the king of Scotland.

[3 June 1162 × Oct. 1164]

A = Cambridge, Jesus College Archives A. 2 (Caryl), 4c (Gray). Endorsed, s. xiii: Thomas archiepiscopus Cantuariensis, with additions s. xvi ex.: confirmat monialibus terras suas, and s. xviii in. (? Charles Ashton): datas per Malcolmum R. Scotorum viz. 10 acras terrae; s. xiv in.: G. Secheford' .;.; s. xvii med. (? John Sherman): sance date. 8. Approx. 151 × 83 + 20 mm. step. Sealing s.q.; tongue and seal lost, tie intact. The hand is that of nos. 34, 136 below.

Pd from A by A. Gray, *The priory of St Radegund, Cambridge* (Cambridge Antiquarian Soc. 8vo publ. xxxi. 1898) 77.

Thom(as) dei gratia Cantuariensis ecclesie minister humilis . omnibus sancte matris ecclesie filiis .*¹* salutem. Noverit universitas vestra nos sigilli nostri atestatione corroborasse et confirmasse sanctimonialibus de Cantebrug' ibi deo servientibus omnes terras et tenuras suas eis rationabiliter datas . et cartis donatorum confirmatas . et nominatim decem acras terre in Cantebr' quas rex Scocie eisdem sanctimonialibus dedit et carta sua confirmavit. Eapropter volumus et firmiter precipimus quatinus memorate sanctimoniales omnes terras et tenuras suas cum pertinentiis suis in liberam elemosinam teneant et possideant sicut carte donatorum eis testantur. Testibus*ᵃ* Roberto archidiacono Oxineford' . magistro Philippo de Caun' . magistro Herberto de Boseham . Roberto capellano . et Willelmo capellano . et Willelmo de Leigrecest'.

ᵃ Teste A

The grant of ten acres 'iuxta Grenecroft' for the building of the nuns' church is the subject of two charters of king Malcolm IV (1157 × 1162 and 1161 × 20 Sept. 1164), printed by Gray, op. cit. 76–77 and (better) in *Acts of Malcolm IV* (Regesta regum Scottorum I. 1960) 203, 240 nos. 147, 207. Gray prints other early charters of gift and confirmations, 74–78. The second charter of king Malcolm is the only one of these documents to speak of the nuns' church as of 'St Mary and St Radegund'. As Robert Foliot, archdn of Oxford, did not go into exile in 1164, this is dated before the archbp left England.

The notary public who endorses this (and archbp Stephen's charter, *Acta S. Langton* 152 no. 138) with his flourished sign-manual is Gilbertus Iohannis dictus Hamergold de Secheford (for whom see Cheney, *Notaries public in England* 114–5, 129 n. 1, cf. 57–58). He also signed seven other charters (s. xii–xiii) relating to appropriated churches of St Radegund's. Other of his acts are dated 1305–1314.[1]

*4. Canterbury: churches of the see

Grant and confirmation for William, priest of Chiddingstone, of the chapel of Penshurst, with the threat of excommunication against any who should presume to deprive him of it.   [26 × 28 Dec. 1170]

> Mentioned only, in the *Vita S. Thome* of William FitzStephen. Shortly before this, the priest had persuaded the archbp that in a vision St Laurence had apprised him of a miracle which had happened to, and was only known to, the archbp. In his last days the archbp caused the grant to be drawn up in writing and ordered William Beivin to search out the priest and hand over the charter; thanks to this, the priest was left in possession of his chapelry by the young king, who feared the archbp's anathema. (*MTB* iii 131 (c. 131), cf. iii 124–5 (c. 123)).

5. Canterbury: lands of the see

Notification to the reeves and hundred-courts of Pagham and Lavant that the archbishop has granted to Wulnoth son of Seman his father's land in inheritance in return for an annual payment of one hundred cuttle-fish.   Lavant [mid-June 1162 × early Sept. 1164]

B = BL ms. Cotton Claud. A vi (Boxgrove cartulary) fo. 150v (145v) s. xiii.

Pd (calendar) from B in *Boxgrove chartulary* 171 no. 397.

Thomas dei gratia Cantuariensis ecclesie minister humilis preposito de Pagaham quicumque fuerit et toti hundredo et preposito de Lovetona et toti hundredo salutem. Sciatis nos concessisse Wulnodo filio Semanni terram patris sui libere et hereditarie bene et in pace et integre et honorifice de nobis et de sucessoribus nostris tenendam sicut ipse Semannus eam melius et liberius tenuit de Lanfranco et de Anselmo et aliis antecessoribus nostris et idem Wulnodus filius eius post eum. Et ad recognitionem quod libere teneat omni anno dabit nobis et sucessoribus nostris centum sepias. Testibus hiis: W. capellano, Alveredo de Watamestede, Gervasio Cicestrensi, Godardo presbitero de Loveton', Henrico de Andevill',

---

[1] For help with the endorsements, as well as for facilities in handling the charter, I am indebted to the archivist of Jesus College, Mrs Freda Jones.

Alveredo de Wico, Gifardo de Pagaham, W. filio Herefredi, Gervasio de Coleuurda, et pluribus aliis apud Loventonam.

> Followed on the same page by a similar notification of grant to Wulnoth by archbp T. dated at Pagham, probably of Theobald (not in Saltman), calendared in *Chartulary* 172 no. 398. This is followed (*Chartulary* 172 no. 399) by a charter of 'R. archiepiscopus' for Wulnoth son of Seman addressed to the same hundred courts and partly in the same terms, but referring to Seman's tenure only under archbp Lanfranc. The use of first person singular and the appearance of Robert de Ceresio as the first witness (cf. Round, *Ancient Charters* 17 no. 9) show that 'R.' stands for archbp Ralph, i.e., before 20 Oct. 1122. After this document the page and quire end with the beginning of a charter: 'Ricardus dei gratia Cantuariensis archiepiscopus totius Anglie primas et apostolice sedis legatus omnibus hominibus suis francis et anglis tam presentibus'. This may have referred to the same property but not necessarily to Wulnoth. See below, no. 71. By the time he received this charter from Thomas, Wulnoth had held his land for at least forty years.

†6. Canterbury: Christ Church (*spurious*)

Grant to the church of Canterbury, which has been labouring under many oppressions on the archbishop's account for the last seven years. I. The archbishop places the church, its persons, lands, revenues, and rights under the protection of God, the Roman Curia, and himself, forbidding alienations without consent of the whole chapter of monks. II. He anathematizes those who harm the possessions or rights of the church or maliciously reveal the chapter's secrets. III. No person of other profession or order may be admitted to the chapter's secrets. IV. Manors and possessions of the monks and the churches on them, with the exennia, are confirmed. V. The monks are confirmed in their right to appoint and remove their officials and servants. VI. They may utter ecclesiastical censures against all malefactors. VII. They may appeal to the apostolic see 'contra omnia gravamina'. VIII. The archbishop anathematizes anyone who attempts to transfer the metropolitan see or the primacy elsewhere. IX. Suffragan bishops of the church of Canterbury are not to be consecrated elsewhere than in the church of Canterbury, except by common consent of the whole chapter. X. Chrism and oil for the province of Canterbury shall be distributed only from the cathedral church. XI. The archbishop wishes and implores the monks to show all reverence and honour to the suffragan bishops and the abbots of the province, and the bishops to show their sincere love for the monks. XII. He confirms the rights, revenues, and churches of his fellow-exiles and implores all to refrain from harming them.   [Supposedly Dec. 1170]

> B = Lambeth Palace, Cartae misc. XIII. 6 (ii). s. xiii ex. and other texts listed in Cheney, 'Magna Carta' (see below).

> Pd in Wilkins, *Concilia* i 427–8, *MTB* vii 60–63 ep. 555, Cheney, 'Magna Carta', etc.

This document, known in Canterbury in the later Middle Ages as 'Magna Carta beati Thome', is a gross forgery produced at Christ Church, Canterbury, in 1235 or 1236 and exposed in the following years. The monks of Canterbury continued to copy and cite it in later centuries (cf. above, p. xli). The proof of its spuriousness and the circumstances of its manufacture are set out in C. R. Cheney, 'Magna Carta beati Thome: another Canterbury forgery', *BIHR* xxxvi (1963) 1–26 (repd in Cheney, *Medieval texts and studies* (Oxford 1973) 78–110), with a text of the charter based on the collation of twelve mss.

The archbp is styled 'Thomas dei gratia Cantuariensis archiepiscopus et apostolice sedis legatus'. The charter ends with a sanctions clause followed by the *apprecatio* 'Amen' but no final greeting.

*7. Canterbury: Hospital of St John the baptist, Northgate

Grant of indulgence of forty days to benefactors of the brethren and sisters of Northgate hospital, Canterbury.

[3 June 1162 × 29 Dec. 1170]

Mentioned only, in a list of indulgences granted by archbps Lanfranc, Thomas, Stephen, Theobald, Richard, and Edmund (in that order), contained in letters patent prepared for the hospital's questor to publicize, 29 June 1375. Pd in J. Duncombe and N. Battely, *Hist. and antiquities of the three archiepiscopal hospitals and other charitable foundations at and near Canterbury*, London 1785, 254 (in Nichols, *Bibliotheca* no. XXX), from the muniments of Northgate hospital, destroyed in June 1942.

All the indulgences, including that of the founder, archbp Lanfranc, are said to be for forty days; this is greatly in excess of indulgences granted elsewhere by the archbps before the thirteenth century.

8. Cirencester abbey

Notification to Matthew archdeacon of Gloucester and the (rural) chapter of Cheltenham that the controversy between the canons of Cirencester and Henry priest of Leckhampton has been settled in the archbishop's presence (audientia nostra). *Henry admits that the chapel of Leckhampton with all its appurtenances belongs to the church of Cheltenham, and that tithes of the land which Geoffrey Cook* (Cocus) *and Oliver de la Mara hold in the land of Cheltenham belong rightfully to the mother church, and he undertakes to pay to the canons of Cirencester, who have the church of Cheltenham, two shillings yearly for the chapel and for the tithe of Geoffrey Cook, which he, Henry, will hold during his lifetime.*

[3 June 1162 × Oct. 1164]

B = Bodl., loan from Lord Vestey, Stowell Park, Cirencester Reg. A fo. 120v. s. xiii med. C = Bodl. (as above), Cirencester Reg. B fo. 109v. s. xiv ex.

Pd from B and C in *Cirencester cartulary* ii 371 no. 412/443.

The archbp is styled 'T. dei gratia Cantuariensis ecclesie minister humilis'. Concludes with 'Valete'.

9. Dover priory

Confirmation, following a grant by archbishop Theobald, for the monastery of St Martin of Dover of the tithe of all fishing of the burgesses of Dover.   [3 June 1162 × 29 Dec. 1170]

B = Lambeth Palace ms. 241 (Dover cartulary) fo. 36v (35v). s. xiv ex.

Thomas dei gratia Cantuariensis ecclesie minister humilis venerabili fratri et amico Walterio Rofensi episcopo et universo clero et populo totius Cantie salutem et benedictionem. Que deo auctore semel divinis prestita sunt usibus, irrevocabiliter firmare et firmata inviolabiliter conservare debemus. Inde est quod bone memorie Theobaldi decessoris nostri vestigiis inherentes, decimam totius anni de omni genere piscationis burgensium Dovorr' quam dederunt deo et monasterio beati Martini in usum monachorum et pauperum perpetualiter, preter illam communem decimam allecis inter festum beati Michaelis et Passionem beati Andree apostoli ab antiquo tempore datam, sicut communi assensu pro salute animarum suarum et omnium successorum incolumitate eam dederunt, ita eam ad opus monachorum sancti Martini de Dovorr' confirmamus et ratam huius elemosine donationem et a monachis orationum promissam burgensibus recompensationem cum monasterii fraternitate firmam esse volumus. Hanc itaque elemosinam a nobis confirmatam conservantes eterne retributionis gloriam consequantur, diminuere seu aliquatenus inquietare presumentes dei et nostram incurrant maledictionem. Amen. Valete.

Probably, though not certainly, from the first years of the pontificate. Thomas was at Dover with the king on 19 March 1163 (Eyton, *Itinerary* 61). Apart from the reference to the archbp's predecessor, which establishes the ascription, and the archbp's name and style, the charter agrees exactly in wording with a charter of archbp Theobald which precedes it in the cartulary (Saltman, *Theobald* 314 no. 91). It is followed (fo. 37r) by another charter on the same subject in which 'Thomas dei gratia archiep. Cant., totius Anglie primas, et apost. sedis legatus' addresses Richard prior of Dover (1157–74) etc. This agrees in all details except for the two names with an earlier charter of Theobald addressed to prior Hugh (1149–57) on fo. 36r, pd by Saltman 313 no. 90: its content suggests that it preceded no. 91. The charter addressed to Richard should probably be likewise assigned to Theobald (not pd by Saltman). In a renewal by archbp Thomas we should expect the same distinguishing marks as those in the confirmation pd above. Archbp Richard renewed the charter, adopting for the occasion archbp Thomas's style (below, no. 126).

10. Drax priory

Confirmation for the canons of Drax of the churches of Saltby, with the chapels of Bescaby and Garthorpe, and of Swinstead, and of land in Saltby and Roxby, granted by bishop Robert II of Lincoln.

[3 June 1162 × 27 Dec. 1166]

B = Bodl. ms. Top. Yorks. c. 72 (Drax cartulary) fo. 6v. s. xiv med. C = Ibid. fo. 7r, in inspeximus by archbp Hubert (*EEA* iii no. 448).

Pd (in translation) in *Memoirs illustrative of the history and antiquities of the County and City of York, ... meeting of the Archaeological Institute ... at York, July 1846* (London 1848) 41.

Thomas dei gratia Cantuariensis ecclesie minister humilis omnibus sancte matris ecclesie fidelibus*a* salutem. Equum est et rationabile ut quod a venerabili fratre nostro Roberto Lincolniensi episcopo statuitur, id [fo. 7r] merito nostre auctoritatis munimine confirmatur. Hac igitur ratione canonicis regularibus de Drax quos fama religionis multum commendat ecclesiam de Salteby cum duabus capellis de Barscaldeby et de Garthorp' et ecclesiam de Swynhamested' cum omnibus pertinentiis canonice adeptis et duas carucatas terre in Salteby et terram de Roxeby rationabiliter adeptam in perpetuam elemosinam confirmamus et sigilli nostri attestatione corroboramus, sicut carte donatorum testantur et episcopi Lincolniensis et capituli Lincolniensis.

a fidelibus B; filiis C

Probably before the archbp's exile, and certainly before he had news of the death of bp Robert of Lincoln in Dec. 1166. For the charter of Robert see *EEA* i no. 106.

*11. Dunstable priory

Grants and confirmations for the canons of Dunstable.

[3 June 1162 × 29 Dec. 1170]

Mentioned only in an inventory of the priory's muniments: B = BL ms. Harl. 1885 (Dunstable cartulary) s. xiii in. fo. 4rb (3rb) *Concessiones et confirmationes archiepiscoporum....* Item Thome confirmatio et sententia generalis. Item Thome sententia de pace fori nostri. fo. 5va (4va) *De Asspeleia.....* Thome archiepiscopi et Ricardi confirmatio. fo. 6va (5va) *Confirmationes episcoporum....* Confirmatio generalis beati Thome martiris.

These items in classified lists may represent different documents, but may include more than one reference to a single document. Each section of the inventory has preceding entries under the name of Theobald: this adds colour to these attributions to Thomas.

*12. Dunstable priory

Confirmation for the canons of Dunstable of the church of Totternhoe.
[3 June 1162 × 29 Dec. 1170]

B = BL ms. Harl. 1885 (Dunstable cartulary) fo. 67v. s. xiii in.

Pd from B in *Dunstable cartulary* 206 nos. 767–8.

Mentioned only, in a letter of pope Honorius III. This may refer to a general
confirmation which enumerated possessions, rather than a particular confirmation of Totternhoe; see the entry for Aspley in the inventory in no. 11.

13. Edinburgh: abbey of Holyrood

*Confirmation for the canons of Holyrood, Edinburgh, of the gift of the
church of (Great) Paxton in free alms by king Malcolm (IV) of
Scotland, saving the dignity of the church and bishop of Lincoln. The
grant was made in the presence of bishop Robert (II) of Lincoln and
confirmed by his charter.*   [Oct. 1162 × early 1163]

B = Lincoln, Lincs. Archives Office, Lincoln D. & C. Mun. A/1/6 ('Registrum')
no. 291. s. xiv med.

Pd from B in *Lincoln reg. ant.* iii 156 no. 808.

Testibus: A. Rievall' abbate, Gaufrido Ridel', Iohanne de Sar',
Roberto Oxineford', Ricardo capellano regis Scotie.

The archbp is styled 'Thomas dei gratia Cantuariensis ecclesie minister humilis'.
King Malcolm's charter (*Lincoln reg. ant.* iii 153 no. 804) is dated by G. W. S.
Barrow 'probably late 1161 × 24 Jan. 1162' (*Regesta regum Scottorum* i 233 no. 197).
Henry II confirmed the gift at Andely, although he is apparently not otherwise
recorded there later than early 1161 (*Cartae antiquae 1–10* (PRS n.s. 17) no. 303 and
Recueil des actes i 339, 341). Bp Robert's charter is dated Oct. 1162 (*Lincoln reg. ant.*
iii 155 no. 807; *EEA* i no. 111). The present confirmation may have been given at
London early in March 1163 when abbot Ailred of Rievaulx was present at king
Henry's court with archbp Thomas and bp Robert (*Lincoln reg. ant.* i 65 no. 104);
but the king of Scotland's chaplain, Richard, who witnesses it, was elected to the see
of St Andrews apparently at the beginning of 1163 (D. E. R. Watt, *Fasti eccl. Scot.*
(1969) 291) and is styled elect of St Andrews in witness-lists of later charters of king
Malcolm. Geoffrey Ridel witnesses without the title of archdn of Canterbury, a title
which he bore by 8 March 1163. The evidence is not conclusive, for the copyist is
probably guilty of an omission elsewhere: 'Roberto Oxineford' ' probably is Robert
Foliot, archdn of Oxford, one of Becket's *eruditi*. The wording of archbp Thomas's
charter was repeated by archbp Richard (below, no. 131).

†14. Exeter: priory of St Nicholas (*spurious*)

*Confirmation for the church of St Nicholas, Exeter, of the church of
Cadbury given by William FitzRalph and Albreda, his wife, and of the
church of Butterleigh.*   [Dec. 1170]

B = BL ms. Cotton Vit. D ix (cartulary of the priory of St Nicholas) fo. 32v.
Badly stained. s. xiii med.

Pd from B by Morey, *Bartholomew of Exeter* 154 no. 35.

The opening formula 'Ego Thomas Cantuariensis archiepiscopus mea auctoritate et sigillo confirmo ... ', the use of the first person singular throughout, and the clumsy blending of the two separate grants mark this as spurious. For the supposed date see Morey, op. cit. 122.

15. Glastonbury abbey

Confirmation for the monastery of Glastonbury of the church of Winfrith Newburgh and its chapels, lands, tithes, etc., given by bishop Jocelin of Salisbury. [? 3 June 1162 × Oct. 1164]

B = Bodl. ms. Ashmole 790 fo. 190r. s. xv ex.

Thomas dei gratia Cantuariensis ecclesie minister humilis universis sancte matris ecclesie fidelibus salutem. Que a venerabilibus fratribus nostris et episcopis canonice data et concessa sunt, ea firma permanere volumus et rata habemus. Inde est quod ecclesiam de Wynford' quam venerabilis frater noster Iocelinus Saresberiensis[a] episcopus sacro conventui Glastonie cum capellis, terris, decimis, aliisque pertinentiis in elemosinam canonice dedit et carta sua confirmavit, eidem sacro conventui Glastonie concedimus et auctoritate nostra confirmamus, precipientes ut libere et quiete ipsam ecclesiam cum pertinentiis suis possideant. Ne quis predictum conventum a predicta ecclesia inde molestare presumat, ex parte [fo. 190v] dei omnipotentis patris et filii et spiritus sancti necnon beatissime Marie matris redemptoris nostri firmiter inhibemus. Amen.

[a] Sarum B

In a short collection of Glastonbury deeds relating to Winfrith Newburgh, written by prior Thomas Wason after a copy of John of Glastonbury's *Historia*. Preceded on the same page by the grant of the church by Walkelin le Warreer to abbot Herlewin (1100–18) and the convent of Glastonbury, and by the confirmation by bp Jocelin of the recognition of the same gift by the donor's nephew, William of Glastonbury, at Sherborne.

16. Ivinghoe priory

Grant of protection and confirmation of possessions for the nuns of Ivinghoe. [? 3 June 1162 × Oct. 1164]

A = Bodl. ms. ch. Bucks. a 4. Endorsement illegible, s. xiv; ? Carta Thome archiepiscopi Cant' .... Approx. 159 × 82 mm. without trace of fold at foot. A rough edge on the left perhaps indicates sealing simple queue: no tongue, tie, or seal. Identified by Mr Bishop as royal scribe **xxvii** (*Scriptores regis* pl. XXVIa and *Lincoln reg. ant.* ii pl. XIII(a)).

Pd 'ex autog. olim penes Ric. Rawlinson', *Mon. Ang.* iv 269–70.

Thom(as) dei gratia Cantuariensis ecclesie minister humilis . universis sancte matris ecclesie filiis ⸴ salutem. Karitatis officium est Christi servos et ancillas fovere et tueri . eos maxime quos urget cotidie rei familiaris inopia. Eapropter dilectas filias nostras sanctimoniales de bosco de Ivingehou sub dei et nostra protectione suscepimus . et omnes possessiones suas quas venerabilis frater Willelmus quondam Wintoniensis episcopus eis dedit et postea Henricus successor ipsius concessit . et carta sua confirmavit ⸴ et omnes illas quas ex dono Milonis Neirenuit eiusdem carta confirmatas adepte sunt ⸴ terram quoque quam ex dono Willelmi de Pichenestorre consecute sunt . necnon et alias omnes possessiones suas quas canonice adquisiverunt vel in futurum adquisiturę sunt ⸴ eisdem sanctimonialibus confirmamus . et presentis sigilli munimine roboramus ⸴ statuentes nequis eas subtrahere aut diminuere ius suum presumat . nisi iram dei et nostram maledictionem incurrere contempnat. Valete.

The charter of bp Henry of Winchester is Greater London Record Office Acc. 312/214 (formerly property of Mrs Tarleton of Harefield).

17. Kenilworth priory

Mandate to the bishops of Lincoln, Coventry, and Worcester, in pursuance of a papal mandate, to protect the church of Kenilworth from damage to possessions or diminution of privileges.

[? 23 Aug. × Oct. 1164]

B = BL ms. Harl. 3650 (Kenilworth cartulary) fo. 54v (p. 108). s. xiii in. C = BL ms. 47677 (Kenilworth cartulary) fo. 94v (89v). s. xvi in.

T. dei gratia Cantuariensis ecclesie minister humilis venerabilibus fratribus Lincolniensi et Coventrensi et Wigornensi episcopis salutem. Mandatum domini pape accepimus pro ecclesia de Kenill'[a] ut eam et omnes eius possessiones quas iuste et canonice adquisivit, sicut ipse dominus papa eas sub sua protectione recepit, ita et nos sub nostra tuitione suscipientes eandem ecclesiam vestre commendemus fraternitati tuendam [fo. 55r] et conservandam, ne secundum quod vestra interest aliquod[b] iuris sui dispendium patiatur. Volumus enim et ex parte dei et domini pape et nostra auctoritate precipimus nequis eiusdem ecclesie possessiones diripere aut libertates diminuere temere presumat. Valete.[c]

a Kenell' C   *b* aliquid C   *c* Valete B, *om.* C

The see of Worcester was filled by the consecration of bp Roger, 23 Aug. 1164. Even if this mandate was issued by the archbp when he was in France, it must have been before he had news of the death of bp Robert II of Lincoln in Dec. 1166. The papal mandate was probably impetrated with one of the undated letters and privileges for the prior and canons of Kenilworth granted by Alexander III (*PUE* iii 412–5 nos. 289, 291–2).

18. Leeds priory

Confirmation for the canons of Leeds of the churches of Goudhurst and Boughton (Monchelsea), granted by their patrons (advocati), Daniel de Crevequer and Henry of Boughton, and conferred by the hand of the archbishop. Maidstone [3 June 1162 × Oct. 1164]

A = Original lost, probable mention in Lambeth Palace, Carte misc. V/111 (inventory of Leeds muniments): 'Carte sancti Tome Cant' archiepiscopi et confirmatio de ecclesiis Gutherste et Botune.' s. xiii in.

B = Lambeth Palace, Reg. W. Warham fo. 97v (99v) in copy of inspeximus, 1278, by archbp Robert. s. xvi in. C = Ibid. fo. 104r (106r) in copy of inspeximus, 1314, by p. and c., Ch. Ch., Canterbury. D = Cambridge UL ms. Ee 5.31 (register of prior Henry of Ch. Ch.) fo. 151v (153v no. ix) in copy of same inspeximus. s. xiv in. E = Maidstone, Kent Archives Office ms. U/120 Q/13 (Leeds cartulary) fo. 4r in copy of inspeximus, 1278, by archbp Robert. s. xiv med.

Thomas dei gratia Cantuariensis ecclesie minister humilis omnibus sancte matris ecclesie filiis ad quos littere iste pervenerint salutem. Ex officio nobis iniuncto locis venerabilibus omni debemus sollicitudine consulere et eorum utilitati quantum possumus salubriter[a] providere. Inde est quod ecclesias de Gouthersta et de Boctona ab advocatis earundem, Daniele scilicet de Crevequer et Henrico de Boctona, canonicis regularibus apud Ledes Christo militantibus concessas, et eisdem fratribus per manum nostram collatas[b] confirmamus et presentis scripti testimonio cum earum pertinentiis omnibus communimus, statuentes ne quis ausu temerario earundem possessionem perturbare presumat. Hiis testibus: magistro Arnaldo de Otteford', magistro Iohanne de Tylbery, Hereberto[c] de Boseham, Ricardo capellano, Alexandro, Hugone de Aura, Willelmo de Eynesford', Radulpho de Aldeham.[d]

[a] salubriter CDE, *om.* B   [b] per m. n. collatas CDE; ecclesiam n. colat' B   [c] Heberto BC   [d] Aldeham BCE; Adham D

The grant by Henry of Boughton (Reg. W. Warham fo. 104r) provides the place-date for the transaction, if not for the writing of the charter: coram domino Thoma archiepiscopo in cuius manu eam posui et ille in manu Alexandri prioris apud Maydestan'. The witnesses to Henry's charter include Mr John of Tilbury, Herbert of Bosham, and Alexander priest of Boughton, who is possibly the Alexander who witnesses the archbp's charter (though the latter may be Alexander Walensis). Another witness, 'Alanus filius Renberti', may be the 'Alanus' of no. 26.

*19. Leeds priory

*Confirmation of an agreement made between the prior and convent of
Leeds and Robert FitzGerold about a chapel of the church of Rainham.*
[3 June 1162 × 29 Dec. 1170]

> Mentioned only, in Lambeth Palace, Carte misc. V/111 (inventory of Leeds
> muniments): 'Confirmatio [sancti Thome] de conventione facta inter conventum
> et priorem de Ledes et Robertum filium Geroldi de amministratione capelle
> matricis ecclesie de Renham.' s. xiii in. Follows mention of no. 18 above.

*20. Leicester abbey

*Confirmation for the abbot and convent of St Mary de Pré, Leicester,
that the chapels of Ansty and Shilton appertain to the mother church of
Bulkington.*   [? 3 June 1162 × Oct. 1164]

> B = Bodl. ms. Laud misc. 625 (Leicester register) fo. 182r (185r). s. xvi in.
> Mentioned only, in an inventory of '(Littere) archiepiscoporum Cantuarien-
> sium'.

Littera sancti Thome archiepiscopi Cantuariensis pro abbate et
conventu Leycestrie super capellis de Ansty et Scheltona quod
pertineant ad matricem ecclesiam de Bulkyngton'.

> Elsewhere in the inventory, under the heading of Knighton, is the entry:
> 'Habemus confirmationem T. Cantuariensis episcopi etc. ut in carta vii^a. Item
> habemus aliam cartam T. etc. de eisdem.' (fo. 81r (85r), pd. by J. Nichols,
> *History of Leicestershire* IV i 235). Many of the abbey's endowments date from
> Theobald's time and Nichols extended 'T' to 'Theobaldi'. The scribe's contrast-
> ing use here of the name 'Thomas' instead of 'T' is a point in favour of his
> ascription.

21. Lilleshall abbey

*Confirmation for the canons of Lilleshall of their assignment of the
church of Atcham to the purposes of hospitality.*
[? 3 June 1162 × Oct. 1164]

> B = BL ms. Add 50121 (Lilleshall cartulary) fo. 24r (p. 46). s. xiii med.

Thomas dei gratia Cantuariensis ecclesie minister humilis universis
sancte matris ecclesie fidelibus salutem. Operibus karitatis facilem
debemus adhibere assensum, quocirca universitati vestre manifestum esse volumus nos auctoritate nostra ratum habere quod
canonici de Lilleshull' communi assensu super ecclesia de Ettin-
gham canonice statuerunt, videlicet ut ipsa cum omnibus pertinentiis suis de cetero ad officium hospitalitatis^a domus sue de Lilleshull'
deputata sit. Decernimus itaque et presentis scripti auctoritate

communimus ut ad dictum domus obsequium ecclesia illa inperpetuum assignata permaneat, et nullus omnino fidelium eam inde
avellere presumat si dei omnipotentis iram et nostram veretur
incurrere maledictionem. Valete.

a hospitalitem B

22. London: priory of Holy Trinity, Aldgate

*Confirmation for the prior and canons of Holy Trinity, London,
following the example of archbishop Theobald, of the church of Lessness
with its appurtenances, as granted and confirmed by bishop Walter of
Rochester.* [? 3 June 1162 × Oct. 1164]

> B = Maidstone, Kent Archives Office, Rochester Muniments DRc/R7 (Reg.
> John Fisher) fo. 95v. s. xvi in. C = Bodl. ms. Rawl. B 461 fo. 56r (extract by
> John Blackbourne from lost cartulary of Lessness). s. xviii in.
>
> Pd from B in *Reg. Roff*. 328; Foreville, 'Lettres "extravagantes" ' 229 no. 3.
>
> The archbp is styled 'T. dei gratia Cantuariensis ecclesie minister humilis'.
> Concludes with 'Valete'. The charters of bp Walter and archbp Theobald, with
> the original grant by Richard de Lucy and related documents, are printed from
> Reg. John Fisher in *Reg. Roff*. 325–8 (cf. ms. Rawl. B 461 fos. 55r—57r). For the
> date of the original grant (? *c.*1148) see *Facs. of royal and other charters in the
> British Museum* ed. G. F. Warner and H. J. Ellis (1903) no. 34; also pd from
> Cartae antiquae roll N 19 in *Cartae antiquae rolls 11–20* (PRS n.s. 33) no. 403.
> Theobald's confirmation (also pd by Saltman, *Theobald* 389 no. 166) is probably
> not later than 1150.

23. London: priory of Holy Trinity, Aldgate

*Confirmation for the canons of Holy Trinity, London, of the church of
St Mary of Bexley, granted to them in perpetual alms by archbishop
William and confirmed by archbishop Theobald. The grant includes
lands pertaining to the church and tithes and specified rights of grazing.*
[? 3 June 1162 × Oct. 1164]

> A = PRO E 40/4913. Endorsed, s. xii: Bixle. Sanctus Thomas archiepiscopus de
> ecclesia de Bixle . et de .x. animalibus in dominico herbagio . et de .x. porcis
> sine pannagio . et de decima pannagii. Approx. 140 × 160 + 22 mm. Sealing
> d.q. 2; face of seal lost, counterseal (brown wax) inscribed: + Sigillum Tome
> Lund', set in large oval lump of modern wax, attached to tag. Fine gold-
> embroidered red-lined seal case, described by J. Burtt (*ut inf.*)
> B = BL ms. Lansdowne 448 (cartulary of Holy Trinity) fo. 11v (12v). s. xv in.
> C = Lambeth Palace, Reg. W. Warham fo. 147v (151v). s. xvi in.
>
> Pd from A by J. Burtt in *Archaeol. Journal* xxix (1869) reproducing counterseal,
> facing p. 84; by Foreville, 'Lettres "extravagantes" ' 228 no. 2.

Tomas dei gratia Cantuariensis ęcclesię minister humilis . venerabili
fratri Waltero Rofensi episcopo . et universis sancte matris ęcclesię
filiis salutem. Quod ad multorum noticiam pervenire congruum

duximus ⸴ litterarum monimentis commendare decrevimus. Noscat igitur presens etas . et secutura posteritas . nos concessisse et presenti carta confirmasse . dilectis filiis nostris canonicis Sancte Trinitatis Lond' . tam presentibus quam futuris . ęcclesiam sancte Marie de Bixle . quiete habendam et perpetuo possidendam . quam bone memorię Willelmus predecessor noster illis in elemosinam perpetuam contulit . et pie recordationis Teobaldus successor illius . noster vero predecessor ⸴ eisdem perpetuo concessit et confirmavit. Unde et nos quoque memoratorum patrum sequentes vestigia . caritatis intuitu hanc eandem ęcclesiam predictis fratribus sicut nostram propriam elemosinam perpetuo confirmamus et auctoritate qua fungimur corroboramus . cum terris ad eam pertinentibus . et decimis omnium rerum que decimari debent . et nominatim de pannagio . de porcis . et de denariis . et concedimus eis habere .x. animalia in dominico herbagio nostro . et .x. porcos in bosco nostro sine pannagio. Volumus itaque et precipimus . ut predicti fratres hanc elemosinam nostram bene . et in pace . libere . et quiete . et honorifice teneant ⸴ sicut melius et quietius tenuerunt aliquo tempore . prohibentes ne ulli omnino hominum temere inde eos liceat perturbare . aut aliquibus vexationibus fatigare.

Probably issued before the archbp's departure from England. For the original grant by archbp William (1128 × 1133) see F. R. H. Du Boulay, 'Bexley church: some early documents', *Archaeologia Cantiana* lxxii (1958) 41–53. It was confirmed in similar terms by archbp Theobald, 1139 × 1140 (Saltman, *Theobald* 384–5 no. 161). The address to the bp of Rochester indicates the need to secure the concurrence of the diocesan of Bexley, recorded in a charter of bp John. The prior and convent of Christ Church, Canterbury, also confirmed the grant (ibid. 51–52).

For the script see Introduction, p. xliii n. 45.

24. London: priory of St Bartholomew, Smithfield

Protection for the church of St Bartholomew, London, and of the canons regular there serving God. Confirmation of the site, Smithfield, where their church is built, and the hospital and lands and tenements and liberties, etc., as king Henry I granted them the site in perpetual and free alms; also confirmation of all the canons' churches and lawful possessions present and future, and their liberties and dignities.

[? 3 June 1162 × Oct. 1164]

B = London, St Bartholomew's Hospital Archives, 'Cok's cartulary' fo. 39v. s. xv ex.

Pd from B by Norman Moore, *History of St Bartholomew's Hospital* (1918) i 57 n. 2; calendared in *Cartulary of St Bartholomew's Hospital: a calendar* ed. N. J. M. Kerling (1973) 18 no. 17.

The archbp is styled 'Thomas dei gratia Cant. ecclesie humilis minister'. The charter concludes with a sanctions clause.

25. Walter Mansellus

Fragment of a letter to the prior and convent of Worcester on behalf of Walter Mansellus. [3 June 1162 × 29 Dec. 1170]

B = Bodl. ms. Hatton 23 fo. 1r. s. xii ex.

Thomas dei gratia Cantuariensis ecclesie minister humilis priori et conventui Wigornensis*a* ecclesie dilectis filiis in Christo salutem. Presentium lator Walterus Mansellus in auditorio nostro lacrimabi-lem*b*.

a Wigornensis *erased*, Malvernensis *written over it in a clumsy hand, s. xv* B
b lac *repeated in fainter ink* B

The fragment is written on three lines at the head of the first page, otherwise blank save for the bottom three lines on which begins a fine Cassian ms. (s. xi ex.) from Worcester cathedral library. For the ms. see Bodleian *Summary catalogue of western mss.* no. 4115 and N. R. Ker, *English mss. in the century after the Norman Conquest* (Oxford 1960) 20, 22 and *Medieval libraries of Great Britain* (2nd ed. Royal Hist. Soc. 1964) 209.

Walter Mansellus has not been identified. One of this name held a knight's fee in Staffordshire of Gervase Paynel in 1166 and, like his lord, was a benefactor of Newport priory at an earlier date (*EEA* i no. 183).

26. Minster-in-Sheppey priory

Grant for the nuns of St Mary and St Sexburga of Sheppey (Minster) of exemption from payment of the archdeacon's aid.
[1163 × Sept. 1167]

B = Lambeth Palace, Reg. W. Warham fo. 136r (140r). s. xvi in.

Thomas dei gratia Cantuariensis ecclesie minister humilis venera-bili fratri W. eadem gratia Rofensi episcopo, Gwiberto priori Cantuariensis ecclesie, Gaufrido eiusdem ecclesie archidiacono, omnibusque sancte matris ecclesie filiis ad quos litere iste pervener-int salutem. Noverit universitas vestra quod nos ecclesiam beate Marie et beate Sexburge de Scapeya, compatientes inopie sanctimo-nialium ibidem deo militantium, ab auxilio annuo quod archidiaco-nus ab eadem ecclesia exigere solebat et exactione liberam et quietam constituimus, prohibentes sub anathemate ne quis de cetero seu archidiaconus seu alius pretaxatum*a* auxilium ab ipsis sanctimonialibus vel a monasterio suo exigere presumant. Testi-bus*b*: Roberto capellano, Gilberto capellano, magistro Lumbardo, magistro Guntero, Rogero cancellario, Alano, et aliis.

a pretaxant (?) B   *b* Teste B

The approximate limits of date are fixed by the third and second addressees respectively. The witnesses include several who attended the archbishop during his exile. Lumbardus and Gunterus were at St-Bertin in 1164, the chaplains Robert and Gilbert, Lumbardus 'de Placentia' (Piacenza), and Alan were at the meeting with the cardinals at Trie, 18 Nov. 1167 (*MTB* vi 262).

27. Nostell priory

Confirmation for the prior and canons of Nostell of the grant by bishop Robert (II) of Lincoln of the churches of Cheddington, (King's) Langley, and Charwelton. [? 3 June 1162 × Oct. 1164]

B = BL ms. Cotton Vesp. E xix (Nostell cartulary) fo. 112r (p. 171). s. xiii ex.

Thomas dei gratia Cantuariensis ecclesie minister humilis omnibus sancte matris ecclesie fidelibus salutem. Quod a venerabilibus fratribus nostris coepiscopis canonice factum esse dinoscitur, benigno favore prosequi dignum reputamus, presertim cum religiosorum res agitur quos vita commendat et honestatis propositum. Inde est quod dilecti filii A. prioris beati Osuualdi probabili desiderio prompto faventes animo, concessioni et confirmationi quam venerabilis frater noster R. Lincolniensis episcopus eidem priori et canonicis suis canonice indulsit auctoritatis qua fungimur corroborationem et scripti nostri communitionem adiungimus, nominatim de ecclesia de Chedendona et de ecclesia de Langel' et de ecclesia de Chereweltona. Valete.

Anketil was already prior when Thomas became archbp, and died in 1196. The charter must be dated at latest before news of bp Robert's death in Dec. 1166 reached the archbp in France. The churches were granted to the canons by Adeliza, widow of Ralph Chesney, and her son Simon (died *c.*1130). In the cartulary there follow confirmations by bp Robert II of Lincoln (*EEA* i no. 202), William d'Aubigny Brito, and king Henry I (*Regesta regum* ii 371 no. CCXLV).

*28. Notley abbey

Confirmation of the foundation of the abbey of Notley (or St Mary de Parco, Long Crendon) by Walter Giffard, earl of Buckingham, and Ermengarde his wife. [3 June × 18 Dec. 1162]

Mentioned only, in the extract of a 'historia fundationis' of the abbey contained in a lost cartulary. The extract was made by Sir Richard Grenville, in San Marino (Calif.) Huntington Libr. ms. Stowe 1 (s. xvii in.). It states that the foundation was made in the year 1162, the eighth year of Henry II, with the assent of the blessed martyr Thomas, archbp of Canterbury, who laid the first stone of the church and confirmed the foundation with his seal to abbot Osbert. See J. G. Jenkins, *Huntington Libr. Quarterly* (1953–4) 379–96. The reference to the archbp's act is explicit; although the source is not a very reliable one, it squares with other evidence for the date of foundation. The founders' charter is in *Mon. Ang.* vi 278. See W. A. Pantin, 'Notley abbey' *Oxoniensia* vi (1941) 22–23 and L. Milis, *L'ordre des chanoines réguliers d'Arrouaise* (Rijksuniversiteit te Gent. Werken uitgegeven door de Faculteit van de Letteren en Wijsbegeerte no. 147. Brugge 1969) 286–7.

29. Oxford: priory of St Frideswide

Confirmation for the canons of St Frideswide's, Oxford, of the manor of Piddington, granted by Malcolm (IV) king of the Scots, referring also to the charter of Henry (II) king of England.

[? 3 June 1162 × Oct. 1164]

B = Oxford, Christ Church Chapter Libr. ms. 224 (Register A of St Frideswide's) p. 117b. s. xv.

Pd from B by Kennett, *Paroch. antiquities* i 549 and in *St Frideswide's cartulary* ii 93–4 no. 789 (omitting the final words: 'Valete etc.').

The charter was probably issued before Thomas left England and certainly before he heard of the death of kg Malcolm (9 Dec. 1165). Malcolm's charters are printed by Kennett i 460, *Mon. Ang.* ii 147, *Cart. St Frideswide's* ii 92, and G. W. S. Barrow, *Regesta regum Scottorum* i 249–50 nos. 224–5, dated 1157 × 1165. Henry II's charter is in Kennett i 548, *Mon. Ang.* ii 147, and *Cartulary* ii 93 no. 788, and the charter of earl Simon of Huntingdon in Kennett i 100, 549, *Mon. Ang.* ii 148, and *Cartulary* ii 94 no. 790. For two bulls of Alexander III see (i) 1171 × 1172, May: *PUE* iii 324 no. 188, Kennett i 161, and *Cartulary* ii 95–6 no. 792; (ii) ? Oct. 1174 × 1175: Kennett i 550, *Mon. Ang* ii 147, *Cartulary* ii 94–5 no. 791, JL 12428. The archbp is styled 'Thomas dei gratia Cantuariensis ecclesie minister humilis'. Concludes with 'Valete etc.'.

30. Pentney priory

Mandate to bishop Gilbert of London and all the other suffragans of Canterbury. The archbishop has received a papal letter addressed to him and the suffragans and has accordingly excommunicated earl Hugh of Norfolk and William de Vals, who had attacked the property and possessions of the church of Pentney. He orders the addressees to pronounce the sentence and enforce it throughout their dioceses. The archbishop has also excommunicated Alan de Nevill who laid violent hands on the archbishop's chaplain, William, and orders them to pronounce the sentence throughout their dioceses. He orders the bishop of London to show all his brother bishops the letter in which the archbishop replies to the letter which they sent him by Nicholas archdeacon of London and Richard de Amari. [? late 1166]

B = Bodl. ms. Bodley 509 (SC 2672) fo. 109r, no. 84 (and last) in a collection of Becket correspondence, followed by other material relating to the life and passion of St Thomas. s. xii ex.

Thomas dei gratia Cantuariensis ecclesie humilis minister venerabilibus fratribus G. Lundoniensi episcopo ceterisque omnibus eiusdem ecclesie Cantuariensis suffraganeis salutem. Literas domini pape tam nobis quam vobis destinatas accepimus, et iamque iuxta tenorem earum comitem H. et W. de Vals qui bona et possessiones ecclesie de Panteneia*a* invadere presumpserunt excommunicavimus et excommunicatos denuntiamus vobis, et in virtute obedientie precipiendo mandamus ut eosdem iuxta mandatum domini pape anathematis gladio innodatos accensis candelis publice nuntietis, et sicut excommunicatos per dioceses vestras faciatis ab omnibus evitari, donec ecclesie predicte ablata universa restituant et de iniuriis illatis condignam sibi satisfactionem exibeant. Alanum quoque de 'Nova' villa qui violentas in W. cappellanum nostrum manus iniecit excommunicavimus, et ut eum excom-[fo. 109v]municatum per parrochias vestras publice nuntietis in vi obedientie vobis precipimus. Tibi etiam frater Lundon' damus in mandatis quatinus literas nostras quibus respondemus literis vestris quas tu et alii fratres nostri per Nicholaum archidiaconum Lundoniensem et per Ricardum de Amari nobis misisti ipsis fratribus omnibus ostendas. Val'.

a Pantu B

The history of the dispute of the earl of Norfolk and William de Vals (Vaux) with the Austin canons of Pentney and its consequences is well set out by Foreville, *L'Église et la royauté* 206–9; cf. *VCH Norfolk* ii 389 and Foliot, *Letters* 210–4. This letter is pd here because, although it occurs in a contemporary epistolary collection, it was not printed in *MTB*. Other documents in this case (pd from the Becket collections in *MTB* vi 543–61 and vii 250, 363–4, 414–8) include six more from the archbp: *MTB* vi 551–3, 560–1, vii 245–52, 414–7, epp. 485, 489, 644, 725–7. Ep. 485 occurs with full archiepiscopal style ('Thomas dei gratia Cantuariensis archiepiscopus et apostolice sedis legatus') in Cambridge ms. C. C. C. 134 fo. 1r (s. xii ex.); on the same page of this ms., a blank page preceding 'Berengaldus super Apocalypsin' (s. xii), is a letter of archbp Thomas to bp William of Norwich (*MTB* vi 560–1 ep. 489).

The papal letter which the archbp cites, and of which he repeats much of the wording, immediately precedes the above letter in ms. Bodley 509 fo. 108v (JL 11285: *MTB* vi 550 ep. 484, dated 7 July [1166]).

On the misfortunes of William the chaplain see *MTB* v 169 ep. 88. He was probably the William of Salisbury who, according to William Fitz-Stephen, was imprisoned for half a year in Corfe castle (*MTB* iii 78). Alan de Nevill was a royal judge. According to Diceto (but not other sources) he was excommunicated in June 1166 at Vézelay and absolved by the bp of London; Diceto again records his excommunication by the archbp for imprisoning William the chaplain s. a. 1168 (*Opp.* i 318–9, 332). The failure of Jocelin of Salisbury to secure the chaplain's release was one of the grounds for the bp's suspension by the archbp (Foliot *Letters* 243–4 ep. 171, cf. p. 227 n. 1).

The letter delivered by Nicholas archdn of London and the archbp's reply cannot be certainly identified. The reference here may be to *MTB* v 408–13 ep. 205 (Foliot, *Letters* 222–5 ep. 167) and *MTB* v 512–20 ep. 224, which appear together in that sequence in Diceto, *Opp.* i. 321–5. If Richard de Amari was Mr

Richard de Almaria, precentor of Lincoln and archdn of Stow (*Fasti 1066–1300* vol. 3), it is strange that his title and dignity should be omitted.

Cf. the final sentence with admonitions in other letters of the archbp addressed to his suffragans (*MTB* v 359, 397, vi 37, epp. 183, 198, 239).

*31. Pershore abbey

Confirmation for the church of Pershore of its rights and customs as confirmed by archbishop Theobald. [? 3 June 1162 × Oct. 1164]

> Mentioned only, in confirmation by archbp Richard (below, no. 181). In the cartulary Richard's confirmation is followed by 'Confirmatio S. Thome Cantuariensis archiepiscopi ... ', but this is in fact Theobald's (Saltman, *Theobald* 420–1 no. 199). Since Richard claimed to have inspected two charters, of both Theobald and Thomas, a confirmation by Thomas was probably omitted from the cartulary through oversight.

*32. Pont-Audemer: hospital of St-Gilles

Confirmation of an agreement, made in the presence of the archbishop and of Jocelin bishop of Salisbury, between Walter clerk of the church of Sturminster and the proctors of the leper hospital of St-Gilles of Pont-Audemer, whereby the clerks of the church were to pay sixty shillings a year to the hospital. [3 June 1162 × Oct. 1164]

> Mentioned only, in a confirmation of the agreement by bp Jocelin (*CDF* 85 no. 246) and in the confirmation by archbp Baldwin of the grant of the church and of the above agreement (below, no. 299).

> The archbp and the bp of Salisbury can only have heard this case before Thomas's exile. Waleran, count of Meulan and earl of Worcester, donor of the church, was still alive then; and he died in April 1166.

33. Prittlewell priory

Confirmation for the monks of Prittlewell, following a charter of archbishop Theobald, granting them general protection and specifying their churches of Prittlewell with its chapels of Sutton (Magna) and Eastwood and all the tithes of Middleton, and the churches of Rayleigh, Rawreth, Thundersley, North and South Shoebury, Canewdon, Wickford, Stoke (by Nayland), Clavering, and Langley, and their appurtenances. [? 3 June 1162 × Oct. 1164]

> B = London, Guildhall Libr. ms. 9531/6 (register of bp Robert Gilbert) fo. 209r (187r) in copy of inspeximus by archbp Hubert. s. xv med.

> Pd (abridged) from B by Newcourt, *Repertorium* ii 472–3, whence *Mon. Ang.* v 21; transl. by John Stevens, *History of the antient abbeys ...* (1723) ii 17.

Thomas dei gratia Cantuariensis ecclesie minister humilis universis sancte ecclesie filiis ad quod presentes litere pervenerint salutem. Suscepti nos officii solicitudo admonet servorum dei paci et tranquillitati cura providere pervigili. Inde est quod monasterium beate Marie de Pritewell' et monachos[a] ibidem deo servientes et quecumque bona et possessiones quascumque inpresentiarum possident vel infuturum prestante domino canonice adipisci poterunt, sub dei et nostra protectione suscepimus, videlicet ipsam matricem ecclesiam de Prytewell' cum capellis suis de Sutton et de Estwode et cum omnibus decimis ville de Middelton' et omni parochiali iure eiusdem ville, ecclesias etiam de Raylegh' et Ragele et Thundrisle et de utraque Shoberya et Canewenden', Wykford', Stoke, Claveryng, Langeley, cum omnibus pertinentiis earum. Hec omnia sicut in auctentica carta felicis memorie Theobaldi archiepiscopi predecessoris nostri continentur expressa presentis carte munimine memoratis fratribus confirmamus auctoritate dei et nostra qua fungimur, anathematis interpositione prohibentes ne quis eos super prenominatis possessionibus vexare vel ea auferre, diminuere, vel quomodolibet male alienare presumat. Bona vero eidem loco facientibus et iusta conservantibus sit pax et misericordia et benedictio hic et ineternum.

[a] monachis B

34. Ramsey abbey

Notification of the amends promised by earl Geoffrey of Essex to the abbot and monks of Ramsey abbey for the harm done by his father, Geoffrey de Mandeville, to the monastery in time of war.

Windsor, 6 April 1163.

A = PRO E 40/14414. Approx. 183 × 114 mm., including tongue and tie. Sealing s.q.; remains of tongue and tie, seal lost. The hand is that of nos. 3 and 136.

B = PRO E 164/28 (Ramsey cartulary) fo. 167r. s. xiv. C = Bodl. ms. Rawl. B 333 (Ramsey 'Historia abbatiae') fo. 50v no. 380. s. xiv in.

Pd from A by Cheney, *English bishops' chanceries* 154 and pl. IV and by Foreville, 'Lettres "extravagantes" ' 227–8 no. 1; from B in *Ramsey cartulary* ii 197; from C in *Chronicon abbatiae Rameseiensis* (RS) 306 no. 380; transl. from *Eng. bps' chanceries* in *English historical documents 1042–1189*, ed. D. C. Douglas and G. W. Greenaway (1953) 783.

Thom(as) dei gratia Cantuariensis ecclesie minister humilis . universis sancte matris ecclesie fidelibus salutem. Publice notum est . Gaufridum de Mandevill' multa dampna monasterio de Rameseia tempore hostilitatis irrogasse. Quapropter comes Gaufridus filius eius pro patre suo satisfacere desiderans ⁚ cum Willelmo abbate monachisque cenobii de Rameseia in hunc modum composuit . Triennio isto solvet prefatus comes monachis annuos centum solidos medietatem ad festum sancti Micaelis . medietatem ad Pasca . et antequam compleatur hoc triennium ·' assignabit comes Gaufridus cenobio de Rameseia redditum centum solidorum . loco oportuno et commodo in terris vel in ecclesiis . Quod se facturum sub fidei religione in nostra manu promisit . presente venerabili fratre nostro Hylario . Cicestrensi episcopo . et assidentibus nobis clericis nostris Roberto archidiacono de Oxineford' . Iohanne de Tyleb(eri) . Roberto de Bellafago . Stephano de Echetona . Willelmo de Leigr(e)c(estre). Hec conventio facta est . apud Winlesoveram anno ab incarnatione domini . m . c . lxiii . primo Sabbato post octabas Pasce.

For the misdeeds of Geoffrey de Mandeville, earl of Essex 1140–1144, his death at Burwell in Sept. 1144 when excommunicate, and his burial after absolution in the cemetery of the New Temple, London, see *Mon. Ang.* iv 142 and *GEC* v 116. Geoffrey de Mandeville, second earl of Essex (1156–1166), confirmed his agreement with Ramsey in a written notification 'omnibus amicis suis et hominibus et universis sancte ecclesie filiis', partly in the same terms as the above document (*Ramsey cartulary* ii 196–7). In it he specifies the nature of his father's misdeeds ('constat patrem meum ... bona thesauri in cappis et textis et huiusmodi plurimum delapidasse'); he has made amends by offering this rent on the altar of the church of Ramsey in the presence of the whole convent. He states that king Henry was present at Windsor on the Saturday after the octave of Easter when the archbp of Canterbury and the bp of Chichester gave their assent.

35. Reading abbey

Grant of indulgence of twenty days for visitors to Reading abbey on the feast of St James and within the octave.

[? Reading. 19 April 1164]

B = BL ms. Egerton 3031 (Reading cartulary) fo. 57v (44v). s. xii/xiii.

Thomas dei gratia Cantuariensis ecclesie minister humilis universis sancte matris ecclesie fidelibus salutem. Domini et patris nostri pie memorie T. archiepiscopi vestigiis inherentes, ad honorem dei et reverentiam beati Iacobi cuius manus in ecclesia sancte virginis Marie apud Rading' habetur, omnibus Christi fidelibus qui in eiusdem apostoli sollemnitate vel infra sollemnitatis octavas eandem ecclesiam de Rading' ob gloriosi apostoli venerationem pio affectu visitaverint, de penitentia sibi iniuncta viginti dies indulgemus. Valete.

The archbp dedicated Reading abbey church on 19 April 1164 with many bps of the province and in the presence of king Henry II; and it was probably then that this indulgence with others was announced, if not at once put in writing. See

Chichester acta 31–2, 129 and K. Leyser in *EHR* xc (1975) 498. The earlier indulgence by archbp Theobald (for forty days) is in Saltman, *Theobald* 435–6 no. 213, with an arenga; an arenga may have been omitted by the copyist of Thomas's indulgence. For the indulgence of twenty days given by bp Robert II of Lincoln see *EEA* i no. 231.

*36. Rouen: hospital of St James

Confirmation for the brethren and infirm of the church of St James supra montem *at Rouen of the church of Vange, granted to them by Cecilia Talbot and confirmed by a charter of bishop Gilbert of London.*
[3 June 1162 × 29 Dec. 1170]

Mentioned only, in a notification by bp Gilbert (after 1173), who had instituted, in the name of the church of St James, its prior Herbert to be parson of Vange (*Epistolae G. Foliot* ed. J. A. Giles (Oxford 1846) no. 326; Foliot, *Letters* 472 no. 436). Archbp Thomas and his companions in exile were in correspondence with Nicholas, probably prior of the hospital of St James, from 1164 onwards (*MTB* vols. v and vi, and John of Salisbury *Letters* ii 64–65). Herbert apparently was the next prior. King Henry had patronized the house from the beginning of his reign (*Recueil des actes* i 93, 548, ii 281, and see *Regesta regum* iii 269 no. 730). Cf. P. Langlois, *Hist. du prieuré du Mont-aux-Malades-lès-Rouen* (Rouen 1851) and E. M. Hallam in *Journal of Eccl. Hist.* xxviii (1977) 128. A new church was built for the hospital in 1174 and dedicated to St Thomas the martyr, perhaps at the king's request. Cf. Alexander III's letter addressed with this dedication in July 1181 (Langlois, *op. cit.* 425, JL 14090, date as corrected in *PU Frankreich* 2: *Normandie* 14) and Henry II's charter of uncertain date (*Recueil des actes* ii 311 no. 686).

*37. Abbey of St Albans

Confirmation of a composition reached in the king's court at Westminster between bishop Robert (II) of Lincoln and abbot Robert of St Albans, on behalf of their respective churches.   [March 1163]

Mentioned only, in the confirmation of this transaction by archbp Richard (below, no. 198) and in the account of the proceedings in *Gesta abbatum S. Albani* (RS) i 150–8, which gives (i 156) the following abstract of the archbp's charter:

Decisiones causarum etc. nihil ergo amodo monachis Beati Albani et episcopo Lincolniensi. Ille predicti predii commodis utatur, isti libertate indubia fruantur securaque et inconcussa. Non eum agnoscant diocesanum suum vel episcopum magis quam Wintoniensem sive Exoniensem. Sed neque sic, quia magis iste cavetur.

The royal charter announcing the *compositio* names the very numerous prelates and magnates present at Westminster, 3 March 1163 (*Lincoln reg. ant.* i 64–6 no. 104). It shows that Lincoln renounced diocesan rights over St Albans, and the abbey made over to the bp the church and manor of Fingest. The abbey recovered the tithe of Wakerley, which it had surrendered to the church of Lincoln. All the parish churches belonging to St Albans other than the fifteen within the peculiar of the abbey were to be obedient to the bp of Lincoln and his archdns, like other churches of the diocese. The record drawn up in the name of the abbot and convent of St Albans is in *Lincoln reg. ant.* ii 11–13 no. 321, bp Robert's charter is *EEA* i no. 231. Cf. J. E. Sayers in *The study of medieval records: essays in honour of Kathleen Major* (Oxford 1971) 64–5.

38. Abbey of St-Benoît-sur-Loire

Confirmation for Arraud, abbot, and the monks of St-Benoît-sur-Loire (Fleury) of the grant of the churches of St Andrew, Minting, and All Saints, Gautby, made by Ranulf (II) earl of Chester and confirmed by archbishop Theobald and Robert (II) bishop of Lincoln.

[3 June 1162 × Dec. 1166 (? c.25 April 1165)]

B = Cartulary of St-Benoît fo. 178r. s. xiv–xv. Now lost. C = Orléans, Bibl. de la ville mss. 490–1 (copied from B by Dom Chazal, 1725) p. 793. D = Paris, BN ms. lat. 12775 (copied from B by Dom Estiennot, s. xvii) p. 113.

Pd from C and D in *Recueil des chartes de l'abbaye de S.-Benoit-sur-Loire*, ed. M. Prou and A. Vidier, 2 vols. 1907–37 (Documents publiés par la Société historique et archéologique du Gâtinais) ii 7–8, whence pd here.

Thomas dei gratia Cantuariensis ecclesie minister humilis Arraudo abbati et fratribus S. Benedicti super Ligerim salutem. Que semel recte facta esse noscuntur ideo scripto committuntur ne tractu temporis in irritum revocentur[a] vel iniustis quoquo modo concussionibus perturbentur. Eapropter, carissimi in domino fratres, vestris iustis postulationibus[b] gratum prebentes assensum, ecclesiam beati Andree de Mintingues[c] cum villa eiusdem loci et ecclesiam omnium sanctorum de Gottebi[d] cum omnibus que donatione nobilis viri Ranulfi comitis Cestrie in illis partibus rationabiliter possidetis, quemadmodum a bone memorie Theobaldo predecessore nostro[e] et a venerabili fratre nostro Roberto Lincolniensi episcopo cum assensu eiusdem comitis monasterio vestro concessa sunt et confirmata, ut scripta eorum testantur, vobis et per vos monasterio vestro auctoritate nostra confirmamus. Et ut hec confirmatio nostra rata et illibata permaneat, presentis eam scripti attestatione et sigilli nostri munimine roboramus, salva in omnibus Lincolniensis ecclesie reverentia et illius episcopi debita reverentia. Valete.

   [a] revocentur D; devocentur C   [b] postulationibus D; petitionibus C
[c] Mintingues C; Mentinghes D   [d] Gottebi C; Goltebi D   [e] nostro D; meo C
[f] eam scripti C, *trs.* D

For earl Ranulf's charter (1147 × 1153) see *Cal. Ch. Rolls* iv 378 and *Mon. Ang.* vii 1024, cf. W. Farrer, *Honors and knights' fees* (Manchester 1923–5) ii 172–3. The confirmations by archbp Theobald and bp Robert (*EEA* i no. 235) are not otherwise known. The date is before news of the death of bp Robert of Lincoln in Dec. 1166 reached the archbp. Thomas accompanied pope Alexander III, on his departure from France in 1165, as far as Bourges, and the pope was at St-Benoît on 25 April (JL 11183).

39. Abbey of St-Bertin

Confirmation for the monastery of St-Bertin of the church of Throw-
ley, with its lands, tithes, chapels and all appurtenances (accessionibus),
granted in alms by William of Ypres, then patron (advocatus fundi),
and confirmed by archbishop Theobald in his charter which archbishop
Thomas has seen.   [? St-Bertin. 5 × 10 Nov. 1164]

A = Original lost, from abbey of St-Bertin, St-Omer.

B = St-Omer, Bibliothèque municipale, ms. 803 (Grand cartulaire de St-Bertin)
vol. i pp. 332–3 no. 224, with description: 'Ex originali in Theca Angleterre
no. 3. Cet original a 2 pouces et un quart d'hauteur et 6 pouces de largeur', and
with a rough sketch of the archbp's seal and counterseal. Transcript of A by
Dom C. J. Dewitte. s. xviii ex. C = PRO, P. R. O. 31/8/144 (part 6) fo. 71r no.
7: transcript of B. s. xix med.

Pd from B in *Chartes de St-Bertin* i 110 no. 242, whence Foreville 'Lettres
"extravagantes" ' 231–2 no. 7. Calendared from B in *Archaeologia Cantiana* iv
(1861) 209, and from C in *CDF* 486 no. 1337.

Testibus: Baldewino de Bolonia Norwicensi[a] archidiacono, Silvestro thesaurario Lixoviensi, Theoldo canonico Sancti Martini,
Roberto canonico Meritonę, magistro Herberto, magistro Lumbardo, magistro Ernulfo, Gunterio, Ricardo de Sar' capellano,
Alexandro Walensi, et pluribus aliis.

  [a] Norwicensi: Norwico B

The archbp is styled 'Thomas dei gratia Cantuariensis ecclesie humilis minister'.
Theobald's charter is in *Chartes de St-Bertin* i 97 and Saltman, *Theobald* 464 no.
239. The charter of William of Ypres (d. 1162) and related documents are in
Chartes (cf. *CDF* pp. 484–9). For the witnesses of Thomas's charter see Foreville
235–6, who shows that they probably represent members of the archbp's *familia*
who stayed with him at St-Bertin immediately after his flight from England. In
1310 this charter and the next were produced before the archbp of Canterbury's
chancellor by the proctor of St-Bertin's, being described as 'appropriationes
ipsarum ecclesiarum predicto monasterio factas per gloriosissimum martirem
beatum Thomam ... sub originalibus litteris eiusdem martiris sigillo eiusdem
signatis ... ' (St-Omer, Bibliothèque municipale ms. 746 fo. 247v).

40. Abbey of St-Bertin

Confirmation for the abbey of St-Bertin of the church of Chilham, with
its lands, tithes, chapels, and all appurtenances, granted in alms by the
patron and confirmed by archbishop Theobald in his charter which
archbishop Thomas has seen.   [? St-Bertin. 5 × 10 Nov. 1164]

A = Original lost, from abbey of St-Bertin, St-Omer.

B = St-Omer, Bibliothèque municipale, ms. 803 (Grand cartulaire de St-Bertin)
vol. i pp. 333–4 no. 225, with description: 'Ex originali in Theca Angleterre
no. 4. 1° loco. Cet original a un pouce et trois quarts d'hauteur sur 8 p. et 3 q.
de largeur', and with note that seal and counterseal correspond to those on the

preceding page (cf. no. 39). Transcript of A by Dom C. J. Dewitte. s. xviii ex.
C = Ibid. ms. 746 (fragment of a cartulary) fo. 204v. s. xv in. D = Ibid. ms.
746 fo. 212r, in copy of a vidimus. E = PRO, P. R. O. 31/8/144 (part 6) fo. 71v
no. 8: transcript of B. s. xix med.

Pd (much abridged) from B in *Chartes de St-Bertin* i 110 no. 243, whence
Foreville 'Lettres "extravagantes" ' 232 no. 8. Calendared from E in *CDF* 486
no. 1338, and noted from B in *Archaeologia Cantiana* iv (1861) 209. Pd here
from B.

Thomas dei gratia Cantuariensis ecclesię humilis minister omnibus
catholicę matris ecclesię fidelibus salutem. Favorabile est locis
religiosis pertinentias et bona sua confirmare [p. 334] quę eis
canonice collata fuisse noscuntur. Inde est quod*a* monasterio Sancti
Bertini ecclesiam de Chilleham in Cantia cum omnibus accessionibus suis iuste et canonice possidendam concedimus et presenti
pagina communimus sicut eam sibi ab advocato fundi in elemosinam*b* collatam venerabilis memorię predecessor et dominus noster
archiepiscopus Theobaldus concessit et carta sua quam vidimus
confirmavit. Testibus hiis: Silvestro thesaurario Lixoviensi, Theoldo*c* canonico Sancti Martini*d*, Roberto canonico Meritonę*e*, magistro Herberto, magistro Lumbardo, magistro Ernulf, Gunterio*f*,
Ricardo de Sar' capellano, Alexandro Walensi, et pluribus aliis.

a add in BE   *b* elemosina BE   *c* Theoldo BE; Theobaldo CD   *d* add etc. and om.
rest D   *e* Meritonę BE; om. (space) C   *f* Gunterio BE; magistro C

For the date and circumstances see no. 39 above, in closely similar terms.
Theobald's charter is in *Chartes de St-Bertin* i 97 and Saltman *Theobald* 464–5 no.
240. It supplies the name of the donor: 'quod Hugo filius Fulberti dedit et concessit.'
For Hugh son of Fulbert of Dover see John of Salisbury, *Letters* i 259–60.

41. Stoke by Clare priory

*Notification that after long dispute over the church of Ashen between
the prior of Stoke and Abraham, it has been settled by an agreement
before the archbishop. The archbishop has confirmed the settlement.
Abraham has surrendered the church and renounced all right in it; for
his withdrawal the prior has paid him three marks of silver and a
pellice.*   [? 3 June 1162 × Oct. 1164]

B = BL ms. Cotton Appendix xxi (register of Stoke Priory) fo. 62r (63r, 52r). s.
xiii ex.

Pd from B in *Stoke by Clare cartulary* ed. C. Harper-Bill and R. Mortimer
(Suffolk Records Soc.: Suffolk charters) part 1 (1982) pp. 105–6 no. 132.

Thomas dei gratia Cantuariensis ecclesie minister humilis universis
sancte matris ecclesie fidelibus salutem. Noverit universitas vestra
causam que inter priorem de Stok' et Abraham super ecclesia de

Essa diutius agitata est in presentia nostra transactione decisam esse. Que quoniam de iure nitebatur eam confirmavimus, et ne aliquo casu in posterum rescindatur presentis scripti testimonio communivimus. Porro Abraham predicte ecclesie et omni iuri quod in ea habebat in manu nostra inperpetuum renuntiavit, et ut recederet a lite memoratus prior iii marcas argenti donavit et pellicium.

Followed by a mandate of archbp Theobald to the archdn of Middlesex which shows that the church of Ashen had been in dispute probably 1145 × 1150 and that the monks had been awarded possession, pending a further hearing on the question of right (Saltman, *Theobald* 491–2 no. 258, where dated 1139 × 1152). Ashen appears among the possessions of Stoke in Alexander III's privilege of 30 June 1174 (*Mon. Ang.* viii 1661).

42. Order of the Temple: London, New Temple

Grant to all who visit the house of the Temple at London on the Thames on the day of its dedication, and give alms to it, of an indulgence of twenty days and a share in all the spiritual benefits of the church of Canterbury.   [? 3 June 1162 × Oct. 1164]

B = BL ms. Cotton Nero E vi (Hospitallers' cartulary) fo. 24r. s. xv med.

Pd from B in *Records of the Templars in England* ed. B. A. Lees (Records of Social and Econ. Hist. IX. British Academy 1935) 162–3 no. 7.

A like indulgence of twenty days had been assigned by archbp Theobald to the Temple 'extra London' ' (i.e. the Old Temple in the parish of St Andrew's, Holborn) for those who visited and gave alms in Whit week (Lees, *Records* 162 no. 6 and Saltman, *Theobald* 494 no. 261). That site was granted by the Templars to the bps of Lincoln according to an act given at the New Temple in May 1161 (*Lincoln reg. ant.* ii 15–16 no. 323). Their new 'locus' on the Thames received an indulgence from bp Robert II of Lincoln in terms so similar to that of archbp Thomas as to suggest one occasion, probably before the archbp left England and certainly before bp Robert's death, 27 Dec. 1166 (*EEA* i no. 258). Presumably the unfinished church on the new site, or an altar in it, was dedicated by then, and at Easter 1163 the body of earl Geoffrey de Mandeville received christian burial in its humble cemetery (*Mon. Ang.* iv 142b, cf. above, no. 34n.). The church was probably not completed until much later; it was ceremoniously dedicated by the patriarch of Jerusalem on 10 Feb. 1185, and again when a new chancel was completed in 1240 (Paris, *Chron. maj.* iv 11 and Lees, *Records* p. lvi n. 10).

The archbp is styled 'Thomas dei gratia Cantuariensis ecclesie minister humilis'; no witnesses; ending 'Valete'.

43. Wintney Priory

Protection for the nuns of Wintney and their possessions, with confirmation of their possessions present and future in accordance with the charter of bishop Henry of Winchester and the confirmation by archbishop Theobald.   [? 3 June 1162 × Oct. 1164]

B = PRO C 53/124 (Charter roll 11 Edw. III) m. 31.
Pd. from B in *Cal. Ch. Rolls* iv 395.

The charter of archbp Theobald was inspected at the same time (18 March 1337), at which time was also inspected an inspeximus (7 June 1287) of bp Henry's letters of protection (*Cal. Ch. Rolls* iv 395, 394 and Saltman, *Theobald* 510 no. 280). Theobald's charter uses the legatine style. The inspeximus of 1337, which includes a charter purporting to be of king Henry II (1161 × 1174) in somewhat unusual form, does not seem to have been used in the chief reference books, from *VCH Hants* onwards, and the foundation of the house is generally stated as 'before 1200'. It must have occurred before Theobald died, 18 April 1161, and probably not later than 1159. The archbp is styled 'Thomas dei gratia Cantuariensis ecclesie minister humilis'. The charter ends with 'Valete'.

*44. York: priory of Holy Trinity

Confirmation for the monks of Holy Trinity, York, of the grant of the church of All Saints, Great Rasen (West Rasen), recorded in charters of Hugh (I) and Fulk Paynel and confirmed by bishop Robert II of Lincoln. [? 3 June 1162 × Oct. 1164]

Mentioned only, as having been produced in the king's court in 1220, together with the other charters, for an assize of darrein presentment brought by Hugh Paynel II against Holy Trinity priory (*CRR* ix 100 (*Bracton's note book* ed. F. W. Maitland iii 368 no. 1415). Cf. Clay, *EYC* vi 7, 132). Possibly the charters of Hugh and Fulk Paynel were of much earlier date; if so, the confirmation accepted in court in 1220 as Thomas's may have been Theobald's.

45. York: hospital of St Peter

Grant of an indulgence of fifteen days and participation in the spiritual benefits of the church of Canterbury for those who subscribe to the relief of the inmates of the hospital of St Peter at York. Those who come begging for the hospital within the archbishop's jurisdiction are to be received to preach, in the customary way.

[? 3 June 1162 × Oct. 1164]

B = BL ms. Cotton Nero D iii (cartulary of St Leonard's hospital, York) fo. 10r. s. xiv ex.

Pd in *EYC* i 151 no. 180 and Saltman, *Theobald* 517–8 no. 288, both from B. Both ascribe to Theobald (Saltman with some hesitation: cf. his dating on p. 518 and p. 192 n. 3 'very doubtful'). There seems no reason for not extending the title T. to Thomas. The style is normal for Thomas, highly exceptional for Theobald: 'T. dei gratia Cantuariensis ecclesie minister humilis'. There is neither witness-list nor final greeting.

RICHARD OF DOVER, 1173/4—1184

46. Abingdon abbey

Confirmation for the monks of Abingdon of their possessions, particularly the church of Wickham, of which the revenue is assigned to the altar of the church of Abingdon. [28 April 1174 × Sept. 1181]

> B = Bodl. ms. Lyell 15 (Abingdon cartulary) fo. 56r: Particula III (de decretis confirmationibus ordinationibus vicariarum et aliis factis episcopalibus et capitul') xiii. s. xiv med.

Ricardus dei gratia Cantuariensis archiepiscopus totius Anglie primas et apostolice sedis legatus omnibus sancte matris ecclesie filiis salutem. Que in posterum profutura sunt eo solidius subsistunt quo magis memorie mandantur et quo maiori instrumentorum auctoritate roborantur. Inde est quod iuste adquisitas possessiones ecclesie de Abbendona, specialiter ecclesiam de Wikham altari prescripte ecclesie canonice assignatam, sicut scriptis Romanorum pontificum confirmata est, confirmamus et presentis scripti munimine roboramus. Valete.

> This is Wickham, a chapelry of Welford, Berks: cf. *Book of fees* (HMSO 1920–31) i 301 and *Chron. mon. de Abingdon* ed. Joseph Stevenson (2 vols. RS 1858). The church is among those listed 'de redditibus altaris' in a privilege of Eugenius III, 7 Apr. 1152 (*Chron.* ii 196; JL 9567).

*47. Pope Alexander III

Report to pope Alexander III on a case concerning a youth, R., and Mary daughter of Gilbert of St Leger, who were said to be married per verba de praesenti *but (because they contracted during Lent) without solemnization in church. The archbishop was later informed that R. wished to marry another woman and forbade a second marriage pending investigation of the first contract. R., however, in defiance married solemnly Matilda daughter of Hugh of Polstead. In the presence of the archbishop and both women, he admitted both marriages. Mary denied more than betrothal, and Matilda claimed R. as her husband. When the archbishop wished to enquire into the former marriage, especially since there was some question of consanguinity between the two women, Mary appealed to the pope. The archbishop then ordered her under pain of anathema to refrain from re-marriage before the case was heard by the*

*pope or his delegates. She, relying on her appeal, married a certain W.
Being summoned before the archbishop on this account, she would not
appear because of the appeal.* [late 1174 × 1178]

> Mentioned only, in the pope's response to the archbp and, with more detail, in
> his commission to the bps of Winchester, Bath, and Hereford to settle the case,
> which probably reproduces much of the archbp's report (JL 13793, 14300;
> *Extra* 4 1 7 and 4 16 2). The decretals were probably sent simultaneously; the
> latter is dated 5 Feb. and is cited by Simon of Bisignano (*Traditio* xviii (1962)
> 450); both may therefore be dated 5 Feb. [1175 × 1179]. The importance of the
> case is discussed by J. Dauvillier, *Le mariage dans le droit classique de l'église*
> (Paris 1933) 23–26.

*47A. Pope Alexander III

*Report to the pope on a matrimonial case which he has heard in his
synod. A. and A. had been married in church after banns were
published three times, without any objection; but rumour later grew that
they were related* proxima linea consanguinitatis. *Reliable witnesses,
summoned to give testimony in synod on oath, stated that they believed
the couple to be related in the fourth and fifth degrees of consanguinity.
A., fearing a divorce, has appealed to the pope and, being himself too ill
to travel, sends his messenger to the Curia with the archbishop's letter.*
[Sept. 1174 × early 1181]

> Mentioned only, in a papal commission to the bp of Worcester (Roger or
> Baldwin): 'Accepimus litteras venerabilis f. n. R. Cant.'. The case cannot have
> been heard before the archbp arrived in England and this report reached the
> Curia in time for Alexander III to reply. He instructs the bp to investigate
> and, if the matter is as reported, to impose silence on the witnesses and absolve
> the couple of the charge. This decretal is only known from 'Collectio
> Wigorniensis' 1 48, pd in *Zeitschrift der Savigny-Stiftung für Rechtsgesch.* kan.
> Abt. 22 (1933) 88, and calendared by M. G. Cheney, *Roger of Worcester* 318
> App. II no. 3.

*47B. Pope Alexander III

*Report to the pope on the case of M., a noble lady married when a child
to R. knight, son of R. Her relatives had later caused her and her
husband to be summoned before the bishop of Lincoln to investigate the
degree of their consanguinity, and the wife, now pregnant, left her
husband. He appealed to the archbishop, asking that she should be
restored to him. After dispute between the parties before delegates and
the archbishop in person, the husband appealed to the pope. While
awaiting the appeal, the wife took refuge in the church of St Margaret,
Lincoln, was pursued and forced to agree that four arbitrators should
settle the dispute.* [1175 × early 1181]

Mentioned only, in a papal commission ('Veniens ad apostolice') to bp Adam of
St Asaph and another, to enquire whether violence was used against the wife
after the appeal in order to secure her acceptance of arbitration and, if so, to
release her from her oath, and then to hear and settle the case about
consanguinity: in two decretal collections, *Sangermanensis* and *Abrincensis
prima*. Pd by H. Singer, *SB Akad. Wien* 171. 2 (1914) 344–6 and
W. Holtzmann and E. W. Kemp, *Papal decretals relating to the diocese of
Lincoln in the twelfth century* (Lincoln Rec. Soc. 1954) pp. 44–7 no. 18 (with
translation).

The archbp had proceeded some way with the case before writing to the pope,
therefore in 1175 or after, and in time for Alexander III to reply.

*48.   Pope Alexander III

*Consultation addressed to pope Alexander III concerning clerks who
receive churches and ecclesiastical benefices without the consent of the
diocesan or his officials. The archbishop has pronounced a general
sentence of excommunication on clerks who occupy benefices in this way.*

[? May × June 1175]

Mentioned only (' ... sicut ex litteris tuis intelleximus') in a decretal letter of the
pope addressed to the archbp and his suffragans, which confirms the archbp's
sentence (JL 13817; *Extra* 3 7 3, 'Ex frequentibus querelis'). The date can be
approximately fixed by the occurrence of this topic in the agenda of the
Council of Westminster, May 1175 (see M. G. Cheney in *Studies in Church
History* xi (1975) ed. Derek Baker, 64–65).

*48A.   Pope Alexander III

*Report to the pope on a case committed to him by the pope to hear and
terminate, between H. and A., clerks, about the church of Lega, of
which A. claimed to be unjustly despoiled. The archbishop's investigation shows that H. was parson, properly instituted during the bishop of
London's absence abroad by R., his archdeacon. Upon a false report
from the late Richard de Lucy that H. was dead, the bishop later
instituted Richard's clerk, A., but his corporal induction was obstructed
by an appeal from H. until A. got papal letters to the late bishop of
Worcester and the abbot of St Albans against H., by which A. got
possession* causa rei servande. *The archbishop asks the pope for
direction* (formam observandam) *on how to proceed* in possessorio
ipsius H.   [Sept. 1179 × early 1181]

Mentioned only, in the pope's reply: 'Ex litteris fraternitatis tue'. The decretal is
found in several collections, pd in *Collectio Sangermanensis* (ed. H. Singer, *SB
Akad. Wien* 171. 2 (1914) 248–9) VI. 1. 15, and calendared by M. G. Cheney,
Roger of Worcester 340 App. II no. 48. The archbp's letter was written after
the death of bp Roger and reached the Curia in time for Alexander III to reply.

49. Bardney abbey

Notification, as papal judge delegate, of his judgment in the dispute between Mr Ralph of Kyme and William the priest over the church of Sotby. Confirmation of Mr Ralph's possession of the church, subject to a yearly pension of thirty shillings to the monks of Bardney, who had granted him the church. [May 1177 × Sept. 1181]

B = BL ms. Cotton Vesp. E xx (Bardney cartulary) fo. 91v (86v). s. xiii ex.
C = Ibid. fo. 92r (87r) in confirmation by R. of Kyme, canon of York, in form of an inspeximus.

Ricardus dei gratia Cantuariensis archiepiscopus totius Anglie primas et apostolice sedis legatus universis Christi fidelibus ad quos presentes littere pervenerint eternam in domino salutem. Ad universitatis vestre notitiam volumus pervenire quod cum dilectus noster filius magister Radulfus de Kyme et Willelmus presbiter in nostra fuissent presentia constituti, ad sequendam causam inter eos super ecclesia de Sottebi motam, quam de mandato apostolico susceperamus audiendam et fine debito terminandam,[a] predictus W. publice in iure confessus est se in eadem ecclesia nichil iuris omnino sibi vendicare et nos eam eidem Willelmo inperpetuum abiudicavimus. Cumque postmodum ex autentico instrumento abbatis et conventus de Bardeneia evidenter intelligeremus quod ecclesiam predictam memorato Radulfo sub annua pensione triginta solidorum in liberam et perpetuam concesserant elemosinam, nos eidem Radulfo eandem ecclesiam auctoritate domini pape adiudicantes, sub prelibata pensione eam sibi confirmavimus. Testibus: magistro Gerardo, Walerano[b] de Bayoc', Willelmo Gloc' archdiaconis, magistro H.[c] de Norhamton', magistro Rogero[d] de Norwico,[e] etc.

[a] audiendam ... terminandam C; audientiam ... determinandam B
[b] Waler' C; W. B   [c] H.: R. B   [d] Rogero: Roberto B   [e] Bayoc' ... Norwico B; Bagot' C

After William of Northolt became archdn of Gloucester, May × Dec. 1177. Mr Ralph of Kyme is later recorded as a canon of York and was archbp Geoffrey's candidate for the archdnry of Cleveland in 1201 (C. T. Clay in *Yorks. Archaeol. Journal* xxxvi (1941) 429 and *York minster fasti* passim).

50. Bardney abbey

Notification to the archdeacons, vice-archdeacons, deans, and all officials of the church of Lincoln that the archbishop has granted to the abbot and monks of Bardney the protection of the church of Canterbury for themselves and their possessions. [? Oct. 1181 × June 1183]

B = BL ms. Cotton Vesp. E xx (Bardney cartulary) fo. 29r (25r). s. xiii ex.

Ricardus dei gratia Cantuariensis archiepiscopus totius Anglie primas dilectis filiis archidiaconis, vicearchidiaconis, decanis, et universis officialibus ecclesie Lincolniensis [fo. 29v] salutem in Christo. Ad notitiam vestram pervenire volumus nos sub speciali protectione Cantuariensis ecclesie et nostra ecclesiam de Bard' suscepisse et personas ac possessiones universas ad eandem ecclesiam pertinentes, salvo quidem iure Lincolniensis ecclesie. Prohibemus igitur ex parte dei et ecclesie Cantuariensis ac nostra ne quis vestrum in abbatem eiusdem ecclesie vel monachos suos aut in ipsam ecclesiam sive in alias ecclesias parochiales ad eam pertinentes vel in capellanos earum aut in alias personas sibi servientes citra cause legitimam cognitionem et iuris ordinem interdicti vel suspensionis aut excommunicationis sententiam ferre presumat. Si contra hanc prohibitionem nostram factum fuerit, profecto sciatis quod ex quo ad nostram notitiam querela pervenerit, quod a vobis citra iuris ordinem ad iniuriam ecclesie Cantuariensis et nostram factum fuerit irritabimus et pena sequente docebimus qualiter debueritis nostris prohibitionibus obedire. Valete.

The address points to the vacancy of the see before the consecration of bp Walter of Lincoln.

51.   Bath: lands of the see

Inspeximus of a charter of king Henry II confirming a final concord in his court between bishop Reginald of Bath and Henry de Tilli concerning the manor of Dogmersfield and the fee of Dinder. The bishop was awarded Dogmersfield to hold in free alms in demesne and the fee of Dinder for Godfrey of Dinder and his heirs to hold from the bishop for the service of one knight. The bishop paid Henry de Tilli one hundred pounds. [Oct. 1181 × 16 Feb. 1184]

B = Wells, D. & C. Libr. Liber albus I (Reg. I) fo. 46v. s. xiii med.

Pd (calendar, including the inspected royal charter) from B in *HMCR Wells* i (1907) 54 no. clxxxi; the inspected charter only (with the first three witnesses) in copy of a royal inspeximus of 26 Nov. 1189, calendared ibid. i 15 no. xxxviii, and pd in full in *Cal. Ch. Rolls* iii 471–2.

Ricardus dei gratia Cantuariensis archiepiscopus totius Anglie primas universis Christi fidelibus ad quos presentes littere pervenerint salutem in vero salutari. Ad omnium notitiam volumus pervenire nos cartam domini nostri illustrissimi Anglorum regis

Henrici secundi inspexisse, legisse, et manibus propriis contrectasse in hac forma conceptam: Henricus dei gratia rex ... [fo. 47r] .... Testes Rogerus archiepiscopus Eboracensis etc.

The charter roll omits the words 'in capite' at the end of the royal charter, but gives the full list of witnesses and datary. The attestations of earl Hugh of Chester and of Wido dean of Waltham give limits of date Jan. 1174 × Jan. 1177, and a probable date is Feb. 1176 (Eyton, *Itinerary* 200). The absence of any final clause makes it uncertain whether the archbp formally added his confirmation to the king's. A papal privilege for the bps of Bath, 22 April 1179, confirms the fine and the royal charter (*PUE* ii 386 no. 189).

*52. Battle abbey: church of Wye

Letters of institution for Godfrey de Lucy in the church of Wye, at the presentation of king Henry II.   [3 June × Nov. 1173]

Mentioned only, in *Chron. mon. de Bello* (Anglia Christiana Soc.) 141, 175, 177, (ed. Searle) 278, 328, 330–2. Granted during the vacancy in Battle abbey after abbot Walter de Lucy died (22 Jan. 1171). His brother, Richard de Lucy, persuaded king Henry II to present Richard's son Godfrey to Wye and the archbp-elect to institute him. These letters of institution were granted before the elect left England (by Nov. 1173) to get confirmation in his office; when confirmed, the archbp renewed his institution of Godfrey (below, no. 53).

For the litigation which ensued see *Chron. mon. de Bello* (ACS) 170–9, (ed. Searle) 320–34, and cf. no. 54 below. The prior and convent armed themselves in 1173 and 1174 with papal letters and a privilege to protect their rights in Wye and other parish churches (*PUE* iii 342–6 nos. 209–12). Mr Ivo of Cornwall is said to have produced the two letters of institution in court in March 1176, in support of Godfrey de Lucy's claim. Mr Gerard Pucella, for Battle abbey, replied that the presentation was invalid, and the institution was invalid both for this reason and because the archbp, whose election was not yet confirmed by the pope, had not the power to admit or institute. Cf. *Chron.* (ACS) 141, (ed. Searle) 270: 'Quantula tamen potuit illum auctoritate instituit, quali etiam carta potuit institutionem confirmavit.' Richard was confirmed by the pope on 2 April, consecrated 7 April, 1174.

*53. Battle abbey: church of Wye

Confirmation for Godfrey de Lucy of his former institution (by the archbishop as elect of Canterbury) in the church of Wye at the presentation of king Henry II.   [Aug. 1174 × 1175]

Mentioned only, in *Chron. mon. de Bello*, as above, no. 52. The chronicler says: 'Dicitur tamen eum conditionaliter instituisse, salvo scilicet omnium hominum iure' (p. 141).

*53A. Battle abbey

Notice to the abbot and convent of Battle that the archbishop intends to visit the abbey by legatine authority.   [Oct. 1175]

Mentioned only in *Chron. mon. de Bello* (ACS) 167, (ed. Searle) 314, implying that this was a formal summons to a canonical visitation. It was written a few days after abbot Odo was received in his monastery (29 Sept. 1175. ibid. (ACS) 162, (ed. Searle) 305). The chronicler does not say whether the visit took place.

A little earlier the abbot of another exempt house — St Edmunds — heard a rumour that the archbp wished to come 'ad scrutinium faciendum in ecclesia nostra, auctoritate legatie sue' (*Chron. of Jocelin of Brakelond*, ed. H. E. Butler (Nelson's Medieval Classics. 1949) 5, and armed himself against visitation with a papal mandate to archbp Richard, 23 April 1175, which supplemented the abbey's privileges of 7 April 1172 and 13 April 1175 (*PUE* iii 352 no. 218; cf. ibid. 322–3, 350–1, nos. 187, 216).

54. Battle abbey: church of Wye

Confirmation for the abbot and monks of Battle of the church of Wye and its appurtenances as confirmed in the writing of pope Alexander III which the archbishop has handled and examined.

[25 Sept. 1183 × 16 Feb. 1184]

B = San Marino (Calif.) Huntington Libr. ms. B. A. 29 (Battle cartulary) fo. 59r (48r). s. xiii ex. C = Ibid. ms. B. A. 29 fo. 59r (48r) in inspeximus by archbp Hubert which, like all other texts of the inspeximus, omits the last eight witnesses of Richard's charter. D = Ibid. ms. B. A. 29 fo. 60r (49r) in inspeximus of Hubert's charter by archbp Edmund. E = Ibid. ms. B. A. 29 fo. 60v (49v) in inspeximus by archbp Baldwin, omitting last eight witnesses of Richard's charter. F = Ibid. ms. B. A. 29 fo. 61v (50v) in inspeximus of Hubert's charter by John prior and convent of Ch. Ch. Canterbury. G = Ibid. ms. B. A. 30 (Battle cartulary) fo. 107v. s. xv in. H = London, Lincoln's Inn ms. Hale 87 (Battle cartulary) fo. 25r. s. xiii med. Only first two witnesses' names. J = PRO E 315 (Augm. Office misc. bks)/45 fo. 35r no. 139, in inspeximus of Hubert's charter by archbp Edmund. s. xiii in. K = Ibid. E 315/46 fo. 15r no. 68 in inspeximus of Hubert's charter by John prior and convent of Ch. Ch. s. xiii ex. L = Lambeth Palace, Reg. W. Warham fo. 124r. s. xvi in. M = Ibid. fo. 124r, in inspeximus by archbp Hubert. N = Ibid. fo. 124v in inspeximus of Hubert's charter by John prior and convent of Ch. Ch.

Ricardus dei gratia Cantuariensis archiepiscopus totius Anglie primas universis Christi fidelibus ad quos presens scriptum pervenerit eternam in Christo salutem. Quoniam exquisitis calumpniantium versutiis ecclesiastica libertas modernorum temporibus multipliciter solet impugnari, necesse est ea bona que religiosis maxime locis caritatis intuitu sunt collata scriptis autenticis annotari et eorum perpetuo patrocinio communiri. Eapropter felicis memorie pape Alexandri auctoritatem sequentes,[a] dilectis filiis nostris abbati et monachis de Bello ecclesiam de Wy cum terris et decimis et omnibus pertinentiis suis, sicut ad opera monasterii rationabiliter deputata et assignata esse noscuntur, et autentico scripto prefati patris nostri quod oculis nostris vidimus et manibus contrectavimus confirmata, nostra quoque auctoritate confirmamus et presentis scripti pagina communimus, statuentes et sub interminatione anathematis prohibentes ne quis hanc nostre confirmationis paginam presumat infringere vel ei aliquatenus temere contraire. Testibus: venerabilibus fratribus nostris Walerano Rofensi et G. Coventrensi episcopis, Alano Cantuariensi et Moyse Coventrensi prioribus, magistro Petro Blesensi cancellario nostro archidiacono Bathoniensi, W. archidiacono Gloecestrie, magistro Roberto de Inglesham, magistro Rogero de Rolveston, magistro Aimerico, Willelmo de Sotindon,[b] magistro Rogero Norewicensi et Gaufrido clericis, Rogero decano de Cranebroc, et aliis.

[a] Eapropter felicis ... sequentes *oblit. in* BCDEF; pape Alexandri *oblit. in* J
[b] Stotind' B

After Gerard's consecration as bp, 25 Sept. 1183. The church of Wye had been subject of a claim by Godfrey de Lucy (above, nos. 52–3). The bps of Rochester and Coventry suitably head this witness-list for it was this pair, when they were clerks in the archbp's household in March 1176, who alone dared to argue in court that the archbp's institution of Godfrey de Lucy was invalid (*Chron. mon. de Bello* (ACS) 176, (ed. Searle) 328–30.)

55. Abbey of Le Bec-Hellouin

Confirmation of the composition formerly made between Ralph Loharing' and Gilbert de Cornelai, monk of Le Bec, concerning the chapel of Compton, which was confirmed by archbishop Theobald.

[Oct. 1181 × Oct. 1182]

A = Windsor, St George's Chapel Mun. XI G 13. Endorsed, s. xiii med.: Testimonium Ricardi Cantuariensis archiepiscopi de transactione facta inter nos et Radulfum Loharang' super capella de Compton'; s. xiii: Chesinberi de capella de Compton'. Approx. 162 × 50 + 12 mm. for tongue and + 6 mm. for tie. Sealing s.q.; tongue and tie remain, seal lost. Scribe V.

Pd (calendar) from A in *MSS. of St George's Chapel, Windsor Castle* ed. J. N. Dalton and M. F. Bond (1957) 49, ascribed to archbp Richard le Grant.

Ric(ardus) dei gratia Cantuariensis archiepiscopus et totius Anglie primas ∴ omnibus Christi fidelibus ad quos presentes littere[a] pervenerint ∴ salutem in domino. Ad universitatis vestre noticiam volumus pervenire . quod nos compositionem illam que olim inter Radulfum Loharing' . et Gilebertum de Cornelai monachum Becci super capella de Comton facta est ∴ et auctoritate felicis recordationis Teobaldi predecessoris nostri confirmata ∴ ratam habemus et acceptam . et eam auctoritatis nostre munimine sicut rationabiliter facta ∴ est ∴ communimus. Hiis testibus . magistro . Girardo .

Walerano Baiocensi archidiacono magistro . Roberto . de Inglesham
. magistro . Rogerio de Rulveston' . Willelmo de Sotindon' . Thoma
de Niwesol' . Ricardo . Lond' . Iohanne de Riveria . Gaufrido .
clericis et aliis multis.

^a litteræ A

Waleran was elected bp of Rochester in Oct. 1182. Theobald's confirmation of
the agreement is not known to exist. The grant to Le Bec by Robert count of
Meulan 'de capella sua de Cumton cum omnibus pertinenciis que est in
Wyltescira' is recorded in an inspeximus charter for Le Bec by king Edward III,
28 Jan. 1332 (A. A. Porée, *Hist. de l'abbaye du Bec* (Évreux 1901) ii 578; *Cal. Ch.
Rolls* iv 261). By the time of archbp Richard the church of Enford and its chapel
of Compton were included in the possessions of St Swithun's, Winchester (see
bp Henry's charter of 1171 in *Winchester chartulary* 2–3 no. 3). The thirteenth-
century custumal of Le Bec for Chisenbury records a yearly pension of a mark
from Enford in respect of the chapel (M. Morgan, *Engl. lands of the abbey of Bec*
(Oxford, 1946) 140, *Bec docts.* 57).

56. Belvoir priory

*Confirmation for the monks of Belvoir of all their present possessions,
the churches being enumerated, and all else they may justly acquire in
future.*   [28 April 1174 × autumn 1177]

A = Belvoir Castle, original charter 106 (cupboard 3 box 43). Endorsed, at left of
    seal tag, s. xii ex.: Confirmatio Ricardi episcopi (*sic*) Cantuarie ecclesiarum
    nostrarum; lower centre, s. xv: Confirmatio episcopi (*sic*) Cant' fact' priori de
    Bevere de ecclesia (*sic*) de Plungar, Barston, Redmile, Norton, Wolstrop,
    Hornyngwold, Claxton, Howes, Talington, and Uffyngton'. Approx.
    179 × 192 + 32 mm. Sealing d.q. 2; tag cut short, seal lost.

B = Ibid. ms. Add. 105 (Belvoir cartulary) fo. 15v. s. xv in.

Pd (calendar) from A in *HMCR Rutland* iv (1905) 111.

.R. dei gratia Cantuariensis archiepiscopus tocius Anglie primas et
apostolice sedis legatus . universis sancte matris ecclesie filiis^a ad
quos presentes littere pervenerint ⫽ eternam in domino salutem. Ęa
que religiosis personis canonice collata esse noscuntur ut debita
gaudeant tranquillitate ne in posterum aliquo temeritatis ausu
divellantur ⫽ nostri officii est modis omnibus procurare. Eapropter
ad universitatis vestre noticiam volumus devenire . nos intuitu
pietatis presenti carta confirmasse . ecclesie beate virginis Marie de
Bealver ⫽ et monachis ibidem deo militantibus ⫽ universas
possessiones quas in presentiarum iuste et canonice adeptas possident . aut de cetero iustis modis poterunt adipisci . in quibus hec
propriis duximus exprimenda vocabulis . ecclesiam de Hor-
ningwald' . ecclesiam de Norton . ecclesiam de Clacston' . ecclesiam
de Hous . ecclesiam de Plungard . ecclesiam de Barcheston^b.

ecclesiam de Talintona*c*. ecclesiam de Wlestorp . ecclesiam de Redmella*d*. ecclesiam de Offinton' . et terram de Talinton' . et dominicum masuagium . iuxta ecclesiam de Talinton . quod Willelmus de Albeni iunior eis dedit . et terram in Denton' . quam eis donavit Ursellus*e* de Crasmeinil et Lucas confirmavit. Volumus igitur et precipimus . ut prelibati monachi . prescriptas possessiones sicut eas iuste et canonice adepti sunt integre et pacifice possideant . statuentes et sub interminatione anathematis prohibentes . ne quis hanc nostre confirmationis paginam imfringere vel ei aliquatenus temere contraire presumat. Hiis testibus . magistro Gerardo . Waleranno Baiocensi archidiacono . magistro Petro Blesensi . Willelmo de Norhalle . Radulfo de Wingheham . Henrico Baiocensi canonico . Radulfo de Sancto Martino . Rogero Norwic' . Amicio . Willelmo de Sotindon' . Rogerio decano . et aliis pluribus.

a filii AB   *b* Barcheston B; Barchestonei A   *c* Taintona B   *d* Redmilla B
e Vicellus B

Mr Gerard and Mr Peter of Blois left England for Rome in autumn 1177 and William of Northolt became archdn of Gloucester May × Dec. 1177. The charter was inspected soon after the archbp's death by bp Walter of Lincoln (*EEA* i no. 298).

57. Belvoir priory

Notification that Ralph d'Aubigny has, in the archbishop's presence, granted his rights in the church of Aubourn with six bovates of land in frankalmoin to the monks of Belvoir.

[28 April 1174 × May 1177]

B = Belvoir Castle ms. Add. 105 (Belvoir priory cartulary) fo. 26v.

Pd (calendar) from B in *HMCR Rutland* iv (1905) 113.

Universis sancte matris ecclesie filiis ad quos presentes littere pervenerint Ricardus dei gratia Cantuariensis archiepiscopus totius Anglie primas et apostolice sedis legatus eternam in domino salutem. Ad universitatis vestre notitiam volumus devenire dilectum filium nostrum Radulfum de Albeny in presentia nostra quicquid iuris habebat in ecclesia de Aburna cum sex bovatis terre filiis nostris monachis de Belver in liberam et perpetuam elemosinam contulisse, cuius donationis coram nobis facte testes sumus eamque ne processu temporis super hoc dubitetur presenti scripto duximus commendare. Testibus: Walerano Baiocensi archidiacono, magistro Petro Blesensi, magistro Hugone de Suwell cum ceteris aliis.

Cf. below, no. 104n. for the final date. See also no. 234. Bp Walter of Lincoln appropriated the church to Belvoir 1184 × 1185 (*EEA* i no. 299).

58. Blackburn church

Confirmation for Henry of Blackburn (Blak'), clerk, of the church of Blackburn with all its appurtenances, including the chapel of Walton-le-Dale, granted to him on the presentation of the lord of the fee, Henry de Lascy, and collated to him canonically and confirmed by bishop Richard of Coventry.   [Aug. 1174 × autumn 1177]

> B = BL ms. Egerton 3126 (Whalley cartulary) fo. 57r. s. xiv med.
>
> Pd from B in *The coucher book or chartulary of Whalley abbey*, ed. W. A. Hulton (Chetham Soc. x 1847) i 79–80 no. ix.

Testibus: Herlewyno et Radulfo monachis Cantuariensis ecclesie, dompno Roberto de Novoburgo, magistro Gerardo, Walerrano archidiacono Baiocensi, magistro Petro Blesensi, Willelmo de Northall', Radulpho de Sancto Martino, magistro Michaele, Amico, Willelmo, Rogero, clericis, et aliis multis.

> Herlewyn became prior of Christ Church, Canterbury, in 1177, Mr Gerard and Mr Peter of Blois left England for Rome in autumn, and William of Northolt became archdn of Gloucester in the same year. The church of Blackburn was appropriated in 1259 to Stanlow abbey, which later migrated to Whalley (*VCH Lancs* ii 132). The charters of Henry de Lascy and bp Richard of Coventry were also copied in the Whalley coucher (i 75, 78 nos. iv, vii).

59. Boxgrove priory

Confirmation for the monks of Boxgrove priory of all the grants confirmed by bishop John of Chichester, specifying gifts of Robert de Haia and Roger and William St John. The third part of the tithes and offerings of churches and cemeteries in appropriated churches is to be assigned to the vicars.   [1176 × 26 April 1180]

> B = BL ms. Cotton Claud. A vi (Boxgrove cartulary) fo. 62r (59r). s. xiii med.
> Pd (transl.) from B in *Boxgrove chartulary* 57–58 no. 67.

Ricardus dei gratia Cantuariensis archiepiscopus totius Anglie primas et apostolice sedis legatus universis sancte matris ecclesie filiis salutem in vero salutari. Religiosorum virorum pax et quies in hoc maxime procuratur si ea que a fidelibus dei in perpetuam collata sunt elemosinam tantis fuerint vallata presidiis et auctoritatibus communita ut malorum improbitas attemptare non audeat eorum tranquillitatem perturbare et collata sibi beneficia diminuere. Ut igitur dilecti filii nostri monachi de Boxgrava universas ecclesias et decimas et terras et possessiones quas impresentiarum rationabiliter adepti sunt auctore domino inperpetuum pacifice et quiete libere teneant et inconcusse, sicut eis a venerabili fratre*a* nostro Johanne

Cicestrensi episcopo diocesano concesse sunt et scripto suo autentico quod nos ibi vidimus et legimus confirmate, ita scripti nostri munimine duximus eis auctoritate qua fungimur communire, videlicet omnia [fo. 62v (59v)] illa que Robertus de Haia et Rogerus et Willelmus de Sancto Iohanne dederunt in elemosinam, ecclesiam de Boxgrava cum toto territorio de Boxgrava cum decimis et obventionibus omnimodis et pertinentiis, ecclesiam sancte Marie de Walburg-*etona*, ecclesiam de Berneham, ecclesiam sancti Petri de Hamton', ecclesiam sancti Leodegarii de Hunesta*n*, ecclesiam de Mundeham, in quibus due portiones tam de terris quam decimis frugum et fructuum ad ipsos monachos specialiter pertinent. Tertia vero portio assignata est vicariis earundem ecclesiarum qui cum assensu eorundem monachorum iam instituti sunt aut qui de cetero per priorem et conventum de Boxgrava diocesano episcopo representabuntur instituendi, sicut carta predicti fratris nostri Cicestrensis episcopi quam inspeximus testatur. Nichilominus etiam idem vicarii preter tertiam portionem prescriptam sibi assignatam, omnes obventiones altarium et cimiteriorum illarum ecclesiarum quibus preerunt licite percipient. De ecclesia quoque de Brideham memorati monachi vi solidos et de ecclesia de Ikenora iiii solidos percipient annuatim, secundum formam*b* in carta prelibati episcopi comprehensam, decimam quoque de Tadeham et decimam de Kinora et decimam de Liperinges et tertiam partem de Mundeham et terram illam que vocatur Wurda, et apud Butenhillam terram illam quam tenuit Rogerus, et molendinum cum pertinentiis que dedit eis Willelmus de Kaisneto [fo. 63r (60r)], et unam hydam terre in Herting' ex dono Emme de Falesia, et unam virgatam terre in Abbitona de dono Hunfridi de Sartilleio, et unam virgatam terre et dimidiam de dono Gisleberti de Sartilleio, et dimidiam hydam terre in Mildenton', et quandam partem nemoris de Bessesola cum Wigingiis, et xl acras terre in manerio de Stochton' cum quodam masuagio de dono Willelmi comitis Arundelli, molendinum etiam de Feningetrow' de donatione Willelmi de Sancto Iohanne, prescripta auctoritate in perpetuum eisdem monachis confirmamus, sicut sepedicta carta venerabilis fratris nostri Cicestrensis episcopi testatur et sicut in cartis donatorum continetur. Has itaque possessiones et si quas futuris temporibus prestante domino rationabiliter poterunt adipisci, sepedictis monachis auctoritate qua fungimur inperpetuum confirmamus et sigilli nostri munimine roboramus. Testibus: Waleranno archidiacono Baiocensi, magistro Petro Blesensi, magistro Radulpho de Sancto Martino, Nicholao decano, magistro Willelmo de Sottindona, Rogero Norwicensi, Gerardo camerario, et aliis multis.

a fratro B   *b* forma B

The limits of date are determined by the dependence of the text on the charter (1176) of bp John of Chichester and by the reference to him as living. Much of the text repeats bp John's charter, printed from the cartulary (fo. 50r) in *Chichester acta* 116–8 no. 58, transl. in *Boxgrove chartulary* no. 59. The archbp's confirmation is no. 10 in the list on fo. 4r (1r) of the cartulary and is no. 11 in the list on fo. 15r (12r): 'confirmatio generalis'. The number *xi* is beside the text.

60.   Bruton priory

Confirmation for the prior and canons of Bruton of the church of South Petherton.   [1182 × 16 Feb. 1184]

> B = lost: in the part now missing (fos. 1–72) of BL ms. Egerton 3772 (Bruton cartulary) fo. 59r. s. xiii ex. C = Oxford, David Rogers, Esq. c/o Bodl. Libr. (formerly Phillipps ms. 4808) p. 103, a note made in 1719 by Rev. G. Harbin from B, when the cartulary was complete. D = BL ms. Egerton 3772 encloses a transcript of C. s. xix med.
>
> Pd (calendar) from D in *Bruton cartulary* 34 no. 147.

The archbp is not styled legate. The church was given and confirmed to the priory in free and perpetual alms, probably in Dec. 1181, by kg Henry II (*Cal. Ch. Rolls* iii 270, cf. Eyton, *Itinerary* 245); a faulty abstract is in *Bruton cartulary* 34 no. 144. It was also confirmed to the priory by bp Reginald of Bath (ibid. 34 nos. 145–6).

61.   Bruton priory

Confirmation for the prior and canons of Bruton of all the gifts made to them of the churches of South Petherton, Banwell, Westbury, Shepton Montague, Charlton Adam, Milton Clevedon.[1182 × 16 Feb. 1184]

> B = lost: in the part now missing (fos. 1–72) of BL ms. Egerton 3772 (Bruton cartulary) fo. 51r. s. xiii ex. C = Oxford, David Rogers, Esq. c/o Bodl. Libr. (formerly Phillipps ms. 4808) p. 90, abstract only, made by Rev. G. Harbin in 1719 from B, when the cartulary was complete. D = BL ms. Egerton 3772 encloses a transcript of C. s. xix med.
>
> Pd (calendar) from D in *Bruton cartulary* 30 no. 125.

The archbp is not styled legate. A like confirmation by bp Reginald of Bath followed this in the cartulary (*Bruton cartulary* 30 no. 126). For the grant of South Petherton, probably in Dec. 1181, see above, no. 60; that may have been the occasion for this general confirmation. Banwell was given as early as 1163 (above, no. 2), and by June 1176 the canons owed the chapter of Wells a yearly pension of three marks for wax, in respect of the churches of Banwell and Westbury (*HMCR Wells* i 534; *PUE* ii 348–9 no. 159). The cartulary contains many deeds relating to these and the other churches.

62. Churches of Bulmer and Brundon

Confirmation of the composition made in the presence of bishop Gilbert
of London in the dispute concerning the churches of Bulmer and
Brundon.   [2 Dec. 1178 × 1180]

A = PRO DL 36/3 no. 210. Endorsed, s. xiii ex.: 'Brandone'. Approx. 166 ×
   85 + 15 mm. Sealing d.q. 1; tag and seal lost.

Pd from A in *Ancient charters, royal and private, prior to 1200* ed. J. H. Round
   (PRS 10. 1888) 77–78 no. 47.

Ric(ardus) dei gratia Cantuariensis archiepiscopus totius Anglie
primas et apostolice sedis legatus .· universis ad quos presentes littere
pervenerint .· eternam in domino salutem. Compositionem factam
inter ecclesias de Bulemera et de Brandona . et clericos qui in ipsa
ecclesia de Bulemara aliquid iuris sibi vendicabant .· Radulfum
videlicet de Disci archidiaconum ecclesie Lundoniensis . et Gilleber-
tum de Geldham decanum . et Walterum de Bulemera .· magistrum
quoque Radulfum de Altaripa pro ecclesia de Brandona . et Iohannem
Le Manant militem . eiusdem ecclesie de*a* Brandona patronum .· coram
venerabili fratre nostro Gilleberto Londoniensi episcopo diocesano*b* .·
et aliis viris prudentibus ac discretis sollempniter tractatam .· et sub
certa forma quam ex tenore litterarum eiusdem fratris nostri
Londoniensis episcopi perspeximus comprehensam .· et fide
predictorum clericorum interposita utrimque firmatam .· auctoritate
insuper prelibati fratris nostri confirmatam cognovimus . atque sigilli
ipsius testimonio roboratam. Nos igitur eandem compositionem
futuris temporibus ratam manere et perpetuum robur decernentes
obtinere .· ea qua fungimur auctoritate eam confirmamus . et presentis
scripti atque sigilli nostri patrocinio communimus. Testibus . magistro Gerardo . Willelmo archidiacono Glouecestr' . magistro Roberto
de Inglesham . Henrico Baiocensi . Willelmo de Sottindon' . Rogero
Norwicensi . Ricardo de Windeshor' . Galfrido clerico . et aliis multis.

a da A   *b* diocesanio A

The date is fixed by the description of Ralph de Diceto as archdn (of Middlesex)
and by the date of the settlement in the notification by bp Foliot (2 Dec. 1178)
which the archbp confirms (printed in *Ancient charters* 74–76 no. 46 and Foliot,
Letters 448–9 no. 410).

63. Burton abbey

Grant to the monastery and monks of Burton of the protection of the
church of Canterbury, with confirmation of their liberties and

possessions (churches enumerated), citing charters of archbishops Theobald and Thomas and of bishops of Coventry.

[May 1177 × Sept. 1181]

B = BL ms. Loan 30 (Burton cartulary) fo. 23r (12ra). s. xiii in. C = Ibid. fo. 23v (12va) in copy of inspeximus by archbp Baldwin. D = Ibid. fo. 24ra (13ra) in copy of inspeximus by archbp Hubert. E = Burton-upon-Trent Libr. D 27/42 in original of inspeximus by archbp Hubert (below, no. 360). F = Ibid. D 27/164 in inspeximus (including other charters) in Benedictine General Chapter, Gloucester 26 March 1260.

Pd (brief calendar) from B in *Burton chartulary* 17.

Ricardus dei gratia Cantuariensis archiepiscopus totius Anglie primas et apostolice sedis legatus universis sancte matris ecclesie filiis ad quos presentes littere pervenerint eternam in domino salutem. Libertates et possessiones que religiosis personis canonice collate esse nos-[fo. 23rb]cuntur firma debent stabilitate gaudere et ne malignantium versutiis contra iuris ordinem aliquatenus inquietentur, ex iniuncto nobis cure pastoralis officio tenemur cum ea qua possumus diligentia et sollicitudine providere. Eapropter ad universitatis vestre notitiam volumus pervenire nos monasterium Burthoniense et fratres ibidem divino mancipatos servitio in protectione dei et ecclesie Cantuariensis et nostra suscepisse, et eidem monasterio omnes libertates et possessiones quas in presentiarum iuste possidet vel in posterum iustis modis poterit adipisci concessisse et hac carta nostra confirmasse imperpetuum has propriis duximus exprimendas vocabulis: ecclesiam videlicet de Stapenhell',[a] ecclesiam de Ufra,[b] ecclesiam de Wilenton',[c] ecclesiam de Lega, ecclesiam de Bromlega,[d] ecclesiam de Ylum. Sequentes etiam vestigia pie recordationis Theodbaldi et beati martiris Thome predecessorum nostrorum, iuxta tenorem quoque cartarum sancte memorie Roberti, Rogeri, Walteri, Ricardi episcoporum Conventrensium, quasdam predicti monasterii Burtoniensis libertates duximus manifeste designandas, scilicet ut nullam reddat consuetudinem pro crismate vel oleo sancto, neque pro aliqua re parrochiali de parrochia Burtonie nec mittat hominem vel feminam de tota terra sua nec capellanum ecclesie Burthonie ad capitula vel synodos, set in omni causa iustitiam teneat in curia sua quamdiu in exhibitione iustitie non defecerit. Capellanus quoque nullam solvat consuetudinem vel exactionem episcopo Conventrensi vel archidiacono Staffordie[e] aut eorum officialibus. Quinque etiam solidos de denario beati• Petri predicto Conventrensi episcopo sicut ab antiquo consuevit persolvat nec aliquid ulterius exigatur. Prelibatas igitur possessiones et libertates sepedicto monasterio Burthoniensi, sicut ei sive a memoratis predecessoribus nostris sive a predictis episcopis Conventrensibus concesse sunt et confirmate, nos quoque concedimus et [fo. 23va] confirmamus, statuentes et sub interminatione anathematis prohibentes ne quis hanc nostre protectionis et confirmationis paginam infringere vel ei aliquatenus temere contraire presumat.*f* Testibus hiis: magistro Gerardo, Willelmo archidiacono Gloucestriensi, magistro Roberto de Inglesham, magistro R. Norwicensi, Henrico Baiocensi, R. clerico magistri Gerardi, Rogero elemosinario, Galfrido clerico, Willelmo de Sotindon',*g* et pluribus aliis.

a Stapenhell' BD; Stapenhull' CE; Stap' F   *b* Ufra BCDE; Overa F
c Wilenton' BCD; Wilinton' E; Wylint' F   *d* Lega ... Bromlega BCDF; Legha ...
Bramlega E   *e* *add* vel archid. Derbeye C   *f* E *ends here*   *g* hiis: magistro Gerardo
... Sotindon' (*reading* Stodin') BDF; magistro Gerardo etc. C

William of Northolt became archdn of Gloucester May × Dec. 1177. The reference to charters by archbps Theobald and Thomas leads us to a charter of Theobald printed from the same page of the cartulary by Saltman, *Theobald* 250–1 no. 23; an inspeximus by archbp Stephen ascribes the same charter to Thomas (*Acta S. Langton* 26–27 no. 19) and the inspeximus of 1260 (Burton-upon-Trent Libr. D 27/164) ascribes it to Theobald. The original of this (Burton Libr. D 27/16) has a s. xii/xiii endorsement ascribing it to Theobald. It is very well written in a sophisticated informal cursive, probably by Petrus scriba (for whom see Bishop, *Scriptores regis* pp. 24–25; *Regesta regum* iii pp. xiv–xv). Burton D 27/15 is another original, in a more formal hand on irregularly shaped parchment, which agrees almost exactly with D 27/16 in text. It is ascribed on the dorse (by the same hand as on D 27/15) to 'Sanctus' Thomas; but it is not the exemplar of the Langton inspeximus, and is probably a duplicate prepared from D 27/16 at about the time of issue. Both originals describe the grantor as: T. dei gratia Cantuariensis archiepiscopus Anglorum primas et apostolice sedis legatus: archbp Theobald's style. It seems likely that Richard was shown both D 27/15 and D 27/16 and supposed one of them to emanate from Thomas.

64. Caen: abbey of St Stephen

Confirmation for the monks of St Stephen, Caen, of their possessions in the province of Canterbury, granted to them by various benefactors whose charters the archbishop has inspected.

[19 Dec. 1182 × May 1183]

A = Caen, Archives dép. du Calvados, H 1884. Endorsed, s. xii ex. (? same hand as text): Carta Cant' archiepiscopi *and* .K. Also post-medieval endorsements. Approx. 333 × 231 + 32 mm. Two holes in fold for cord, cord and seal lost.

B = PRO, P. R. O. 31/8/140B/1 p. 181, transcript of A. s. xix in.

Pd (calendar) from B in *CDF* 162 no. 459.

Ric(ardus) dei gratia Cantuariensis archiepiscopus . totius Anglie primas *:* universis sancte matris ecclesie filiis ad quos littere iste pervenerint *:* eternam in domino salutem. Ea que religiosis personis

et locis iuste collata esse noscuntur . firma debent stabilitate gaudere
. et ne aliqua malignantium temeritate divellantur ·/ prelatorum
interest sollicite providere. Eapropter ad omnium noticiam volumus
pervenire . nos attendentes honestam sancti conventus monasterii
sancti Stephani de Cadomo conversationem et religionem que se
longe lateque diffundit ·/ universas possessiones quas predictum
monasterium et fratres eiusdem . tam in ecclesiis quam in decimis .
pratis . silvis . aquis . pascuis . molendinis . domibus . terris et
earum habitatoribus . largitione regum . donatione pontificum . seu
quorumque fidelium . in provincia Cantuariensi iuste possidere
noscuntur ·/ sub protectione dei et sancte Cantuariensis ecclesie et
nostra ·/ suscepisse et eidem monasterio ac fratribus ibidem divino
mancipatis servicio ·/ carta presenti confirmasse . quas quidem
possessiones ·/ propriis duximus exprimendas vocabulis . manerium
scilicet de Northam . et ecclesiam eiusdem loci . cum Aisserugia
membro eiusdem manerii . cum libertatibus . et consuetudinibus et
omnimodis tam ipsius manerii quam predicte ecclesie pertinentiis .
in Dorsetha ·/ Frontonam cum omnibus membris et appenditiis suis
·/ in boscho et plano . Biencommam ·/ cum ecclesia eiusdem ville . et
omnibus pertinentiis suis . in Berchesira apud Henreth' ·/ vii. hidas
terre . in Dorsetha ·/ Bridetonam cum libertatibus et consuetudinibus . et omnibus aliis ad idem manerium pertinentibus . in Essessa ·/
Penfeldam cum boscho et lundis et omnibus aliis pertinentiis suis .
quod manerium ·/ Walerannus filius Rannulfi dedit predicto monasterio cum tota decima de Tiedesham . de Elesingeham . de Foleborna
. de Ævialeio . de Buris . cum mansione terre infra London' in
Wedestr' . ecclesiam quoque de Mortona cum virgulto et terra . et
decima de dominio Willelmi de Abrincis . de molendino suo . de
pasnagio . caseo . vitulis . pullis . pomis . nucibus . et aliis decimis ad
eandem ecclesiam pertinentibus . sicut carta ipsius Willelmi
determinat . masagium etiam Iohannis cappellani iuxta cimiterium .
cum linaria que iacet iuxta idem masagium . quod dedit sancto
Stephano predictus Willelmus . in Norfolchia quoque ·/ manerium
quod vocatur Welles . et ecclesiam sancti Nicholai de Gaiton' . cum
terris et pratis . et decimis . et hominibus . et omnimodis tam ipsius
manerii quam predicte ecclesie pertinentiis. Ad hec etiam ·/ ecclesiam de Fronton' . ecclesiam de Biencomb' . ecclesiam de Wintre-
burn' . ecclesiam de Abetescomb' . salvis episcopalibus consuetudinibus sicut carta venerabilis fratris nostri Ioscelini Saresberiensis
episcopi ·/ determinat et distinguit. Volumus igitur . et ea qua
fungimur auctoritate precipimus ut predictum monasterium et
fratres in eodem deo famulantes . habeant et teneant prelibatas

possessiones et ecclesias universas et singulas ∴ integre . libere . et
pacifice . sicut eis iuste collate esse noscuntur . et sicut in cartis
donatorum quas vidimus et propriis manibus contrectavimus ∴
dinoscitur contineri. Statuimus quoque et sub interminatione anathematis prohibemus ∴ ne quis hanc nostre protectionis et confirmationis paginam infringere . vel ei aliquatenus temere contraire
presumat. Testibus Walerano Rofensi episcopo . magistro Petro
Blesensi . archidiacono Bathon*iensi* . Moyse capellano . magistro
Rogero de Roulvest' . Henrico Baiocensi . Iohanne capellano .
Roberto de Bathvento . Willelmo de Sotewaine . et aliis multis.

> After the consecration of bp Waleran at Lisieux, 19 Dec. 1182, and before the
> monk Moses, the archbp's chaplain, was chosen prior of Coventry at Caen, about
> the end of May 1183. Mr Peter of Blois was absent in England for a time in
> April × May (see below, no. 156 note). Many of the possessions enumerated were
> confirmed by kg Henry II in a charter, 1156 × 1161, of unusual form, which also
> includes much other property (*Recueil des actes* i 261–4 no. 152). Cf. the arenga
> and other formal parts with no. 173 below.

65. Canterbury: churches of the see

*Confirmation of the grant by the archbishop's clerk, Mr Gerard, when
parson of Teynham, at the request of Hugh son of Hervey, of tithes
from the assart of 'Pidinge' to the use of the chapel of Doddington. The
revenue is to be expended on the fabric and necessary books, vestments,
and ornaments for the chapel, by the chaplain and two or three reliable
parishioners.* [May 1177 × Sept. 1181]

> A = Canterbury, D. & C. C.A. D 113. Approx. 192 × 162 + 21 mm. Sealing d.q.
> 2; tag and seal lost. Damp-stained at foot.

Ric(ardus) dei gracia Cantuariensis archiepiscopus tocius Anglie
primas et apostolice sedis legatus universis Christi fidelibus ad quos
littere presentes pervenerint ∴ eternam in domino salutem. Ad
universorum volumus noticiam pervenire quod dilectus filius et
clericus noster magister Girardus cum esset persona ecclesie de
Tenham et eam cum omnibus pertinenciis suis ex institutione
nostra quiete possideret ∴ ad preces Hugonis filii Herevici concessit
capelle de Dudintunia ut decime .xx^{ti}. acrarum de essarto de Pidinge
ad usum capelle in perpetuum recipiantur . et per dispositionem
capellani et duorum aut trium parrochianorum fidelium expendan-
tur . ad sarta tecta . ad libros . ad vestimenta . seu ornamenta . que
eidem capelle necessaria fuerint ∴ procuranda . ita tamen quod si
plures acre quam .xx. infra essartum illud contineantur . decima de
superhabundanti^{a} proveniens ∴ matrici ecclesie de Tenham annuatim persolvatur. Nos autem ad ipsius magistri Girardi instantiam et

devotionem prefati Hugonis quod a magistro Girardo concessum est ·² ratum habemus . et auctoritate qua fungimur confirmamus . sub interminatione anathematis districtius inhibentes ne quis in posterum contra presentem confirmationem nostram venire presumat. Indignationem quoque dei omnipotentis et sancti Iohannis baptiste . necnon apostolorum Petri et Pauli omniumque sanctorum et nostram incurrat ·² quicumque contra presentis confirmationis nostre paginam aliquo tempore presumpserit venire. Hiis testibus . Willelmo archidiacono Gloecestriensi . Willelmo et Moyse*b* capellanis . magistro Rogero de Rolveston' . magistro Rogero de Norwico . Willelmo de Sotindon . magistro Rogero Walensi . Galfrido et Ricardo clericis . et multis aliis.*c*

a superhubundanti A   *b* Mayse A   *c* aliis *oblit.* A

William of Northolt became archdn of Gloucester May × Dec. 1177. The church of Teynham (an archiepiscopal manor) was in the archbp's gift, and Doddington was a chapel in Teynham. Pidinge, or Peddynge, was in Doddington (J. K. Wallenberg, *Place names of Kent* (Uppsala 1934) 275; Du Boulay, *Lordship of Canterbury* 377–8). Master Gerard, the archbp's clerk, was almost certainly Gerard Pucella.

66.   Canterbury: churches of the see

Grant, at the request of the archbishop's clerk, William of Shottenden, parson of the church of Orpington, to Justinus de Burn', of a perpetual vicarage in that church. The perpetual vicar shall pay the parson of the church a yearly pension of two marks.   [1182 × 16 Feb. 1184]

A = lost original listed (in 'vas xix') in inventory of archbpric deeds, 1330, PRO E 36/137 p. 12a, pd in 'Canterbury archbpric charters' 13.

B = Lambeth Palace ms. 1212 (register of the see of Canterbury) fo. 52r (fo. 37r, p. 99) no. l. s. xiii ex. C = Bodl. ms. Tanner 223 (register of the see) fo. 58v (p. 112). s. xvi in., copied from B. D = Canterbury, D. & C. Black book of the archdnry fo. 66v. s. xvi ex.

Ricardus dei gratia Cantuariensis archiepiscopus totius Anglie primas universis Christi fidelibus ad quos littere iste pervenerint eternam in domino salutem. Nosse volumus universitatem vestram nos de voluntate et petitione dilecti filii nostri et clerici Willelmi de Sottindon' persone ecclesie de Orpinton' sollempniter et canonice concessisse ac dedisse dilecto filio nostro I. de Burn' perpetuam vicariam in prescripta ecclesia de Orpinton', ita quod prefatus Iustinus omnia bona et omnes obventiones eiusdem ecclesie tam in temporalibus quam in spiritualibus toto tempore vite sue cum omni integritate percipiet et pacifice possidebit, solvendo de eadem ecclesia prefato Willelmo vel alie persone, si aliam diebus Iustini forte contigerit, nomine perpetue vicarie duas marcas argenti, scilicet ad Pascha unam marcam et alteram ad festum sancti Michaelis. Quod ne forte temporis processu revocari possit*a* in dubium, presenti scripto nostro duximus annotare et confirmare et sigilli nostri munimine roborare. Testibus: magistro P. Blesensi archidiacono Bathoniensi cancellario nostro, Willelmo Gloecestriensi archidiacono, magistro H. de Northanton, magistro Roberto de Inglesham, magistro Aimero de Partim', magistro Rogero Norwycensi, Ricardo et Gaufrido et Rogero decano clericis nostris, et preterea Radulfo pincerna et Roberto de Hese, et aliis multis tam clericis quam laicis.

a possint BCD

Peter of Blois became archdn of Bath in 1182. The fifth witness, named Aimericus de Partimacho, was a clerk to Cardinal Hugh Pierleone of St Angelo and received a pension of 60 shillings from Merton Priory in 1178 'ad mandatum domini pape et ad preces domini regis' (*PUE* i. 424–5 no. 153). The witness-list agrees very closely with no. 167 for Missenden (May × 25 Sept. 1183), and cf. no. 96 for Canterbury, St Nicholas (25 Sept. 1183 × 16 Feb. 1184).

67. Canterbury: lands of the see

Grant to Adam of Charing, son of Ivo, and after his death to his son, of the manor of Charing on the conditions on which Adam's father Ivo held it in the time of archbishops Ralph, William, and Theobald, and as Adam held it in the time of archbishops Theobald and Thomas.

[28 April 1174 × Sept. 1181]

B = Lambeth Palace ms. 1212 (register of the see of Canterbury) fo. 110r (97r, p. 212). s. xiii med.

Ricardus dei gratia Cantuariensis archiepiscopus totius Anglie primas et apostolice sedis legatus venerabili fratri Waltero eadem gratia Roffensi episcopo et omnibus Francis et Anglis in archiepiscopatu Cantuariensi constitutis salutem et benedictionem. Sciatis nos concessisse dilecto filio nostro Ade de Cerring' filio Yvonis et filio eius post mortem patris eius manerium de Cerring', tenendum ad firmam cum omnibus pertinentiis eius, pro triginta et duabus libris argenti annuatim inde reddendis, ita tamen quod si nos ad idem manerium divertere volumus ipse Adam vel filius eius firmam duarum septimanarum nobis preparabit secundum comparationem archiepiscopatus, et ipsa firma in predictis triginta et duabus libris computabitur. Et preterea dictus Adam vel filius eius reddet annuatim quatuor libras argenti et sex solidos et i denarium et obolum camere nostre de gabulo media quadragesima. Volumus ergo et precipimus ut ipse Adam et filius eius predictum manerium cum omnibus pertinentiis suis ita bene et libere teneant sicut Yvo pater ipsius Ade illud tenuit temporibus predecessorum nostrorum felicis memorie Radulfi et Willelmi et Theobaldi archiepiscoporum Cantuariensium et sicut prefatus Adam temporibus Theobaldi et beati Thome martiris gloriosi cognoscitur tenuisse, ita quod ipse et filius eius prenominatus manerium teneant liberum et quietum quamdiu vixerint. Testibus etc.

For this charter and for the family of Adam son of Ivo see Du Boulay, *Lordship of Canterbury* 201–3, and Urry, *Canterbury* 13, 180–1. Adam died *c*.1206–7, his son having predeceased him.

68. Canterbury: lands of the see

Confirmation for William son of Richard and his heirs of one hide of land in Cranesham (or Crimsham) which William bought from Giffard of Tangmere in the hundred court of Pagham, rendering to the archbishop a yearly rent of twenty-eight shillings for all service.

[28 April 1174 × autumn 1177]

B = Lambeth Palace ms. 1212 (register of the see of Canterbury) fo. 107r (fo. 94r, p. 206). s. xiii med.

Ricardus dei gratia Cantuariensis archiepiscopus totius Anglie primas et apostolice sedis legatus omnibus hominibus suis Francis et Anglis salutem. Ad universitatis vestre notitiam volumus pervenire nos concessisse et presenti carta nostra confirmasse dilecto filio nostro Willelmo filio Ricardi unam hidam terre in Cranesham que vocatur Hyda, et quam idem Willelmus emit coram hundredo de Pageham de Giffardo de Tangemere hereditabiliter de nobis tenendam, reddendo inde annuatim viginti octo solidos pro omni servitio. Quare volumus et precipimus ut predictus Willelmus habeat et teneat predictam hydam et heredes sui post eum hereditabiliter per predictum servitium, ita libere et integre et pacifice sicut aliquis predecessorum eiusdem Willelmi eandem hidam melius et liberius tenuisse dinoscitur. Et ut nostre confirmationis pagina perpetuam optineat firmitatem, eam sigilli nostri appositione roboramus. Hiis testibus: Walerano Baiocensi archidiacono, magistro P. Blesensi, Willelmo de Norhall', magistro Roberto de Inglesham, Henrico Baiocensi. Rogero decano, Radulfo pincerna, Roberto de Hesa, Ebrewino dispensatore, Goldewino coco, Willelmo Scardevill', Willelmo capellano, Hamone de Cramesham', Rogero clerico, Ger-

vasio de Colewerda, Andrea de Boghenhore, Eadwardo de Eal-
dewyk', Willelmo de Sotindun', et pluribus aliis tam clericis quam
laicis.

Mr Peter of Blois left England for Rome in autumn 1177. William of Northolt
became archdn of Gloucester May × Dec. 1177. Between 1197 and 1204 Roger
son of William of 'Cremesham' granted this hide to archbp Hubert in exchange
for three messuages 'in vico que vocatur Palente' in Chichester and for 15 silver
marks (ms. 1212 fo. 112r (99r, p. 216)). The north, south, east and west Pallants
traverse the archbp's peculiar within the city.

69. Canterbury: lands of the see

*Grant to Simon son of Osmar of the land which his father held in the
archbishop's manor of Harrow: one and a half hides with pannage, at a
yearly rent of five shillings.* [May 1177 × Sept. 1181]

B = Westminster Abbey, muniment book 11 ('Domesday') fo. 502r (526r). s. xiv in.

Ricardus dei gratia Cantuariensis archiepiscopus totius Anglie
primas et apostolice sedis legatus universis hominibus suis Francis
et Anglis de Herghes salutem, gratiam, et benedictionem. Sciatis
nos concessisse et hac carta nostra confirmasse dilecto filio nostro
Simoni filio Osmari terram patris sui quam pater suus tenuit in
manerio nostro de Herges, scilicet hidam unam et dimidiam faciendo servitium quod ad ipsam terram pertinet, scilicet quinque
solidos pro omni servitio annuatim. Quare volumus et precipimus
ut predictus S. et heredes sui post eum habeant et teneant eandem
terram honorabiliter et libere in bosco et plano et prato et pascuis
cum pasnagio suo sicut pater suus illud dirationavit. Testibus hiis:
Willelmo Glocestriensi archidiacono, magistro Roberto de Inglesham, Willelmo et Moyse capellanis, magistro Rogero Norwicensi, Ricardo et Galfrido clericis, Willelmo de Sotindon', et
pluribus aliis.

William of Northolt became archdn of Gloucester May × Dec. 1177. Archbp
Theobald had previously (1150 × 1152) granted the land of Osmar *medicus* to his
son and heir Edmund on the same terms and in similar wording (Saltman,
Theobald 346 no. 124).

70. Canterbury: lands of the see

*Grant to Matilda, daughter of Simon son of Osmar, of the land which
her father held in the archbishop's manor of Harrow: one and a half
hides with pannage, at a yearly rent of five shillings.*

[1182 × May 1183]

B = Westminster Abbey, muniment book 11 ('Domesday') fo. 502r (526r). s. xiv in.

Ricardus dei gratia Cantuariensis archiepiscopus totius Anglie primas universis hominibus suis Francis et Anglis de Herges salutem et benedictionem. Sciatis nos concessisse et hac carta nostra confirmasse Matilde filie Simonis filii Osmari terram patris sui quam pater suus tenuit in manerio nostro de Herges', scilicet hidam unam et dimidiam, faciendo servitium quod ad ipsam terram pertinet, scilicet quinque solidos pro omni servitio annuatim. Quare volumus et precipimus ut predicta Matilda et heredes sui post eam habeant et teneant eandem terram honorabiliter et libere in bosco et plano et prato et pascuis cum pasnagio suo sicut pater prefati S. illud dirationavit. Testibus hiis: magistro Petro Blesensi Bathoniensi*a*, Willelmo Gloecestriensi archidiaconis, magistro Roberto de Inglesham, Willelmo et Moyse capellanis, magistro Rogero de Rolveston', Rogero decano, Thoma de Newesol', Galfrido et Iohanne clericis, Ricardo de London', et aliis.

a Bathoniensi: *om.* B

The emendation 'Bathoniensi' is suggested by 'archidiaconis'. If it is correct, the grant cannot be earlier than 1182, when Peter of Blois became archdn of Bath. Although Peter was junior to William of Northolt as archdn, he precedes William in the witness-lists of archbp Richard's acta both before and after they were archdns. Perhaps Peter was accorded precedence because of his position in the secretariat, although he is only styled *cancellarius* in three acta (nos. 54, 66, 167) of 1182 to 1184. Under archbp Baldwin the two archdns attest together nine times, and William always precedes Peter. Moses became prior of Coventry late in May 1183. The grant is followed (fo. 502rv) by two charters of Matilda (described as Matilda of Paris), granting the land to the church of Westminster, subject to payment by the abbey to the archbp of five shillings yearly.

71. Canterbury: lands of the see

Part of a protocol (remainder of charter lost) of a notification to the archbishop's men, French and English, present and future, ... probably concerning land of Wulnoth son of Seman in Pagham.

[28 April 1174 × Sept. 1181]

B = BL ms. Cotton Claud. A vi (Boxgrove cartulary) fo. 150v (145v). s. xiii med.

Pd (calendar) in *Boxgrove chartulary* 172 no. 400.

All that remains at the end of a leaf is: 'Ricardus dei gratia Cantuariensis archiepiscopus totius Anglie primas et apostolice sedis legatus omnibus hominibus suis francis et anglis tam presentibus'. This follows a group of earlier letters (of archbps Thomas, Theobald, and Ralph — in that order) about the land of Wulnoth, each with a local address. Since this letter also is addressed to tenants of the archbp, it may well concern the same subject. When the property came into the hands of Boxgrove is unknown. This document may have recorded a grant of Wulnoth's land to Boxgrove. Cf. no. 5, above.

72. Canterbury: lands of the see

Confirmation for Godard rector of Slindon of the temporal rights of the church in the manor of Slindon after complaint by Godard and Alexander, priest, vicar of the church, about exactions by the officers of the archbishop. These rights have been established by an inquest of clerks and laymen. The archbishop grants an indulgence of ten days for visitors on the anniversary of his dedication of the church.

[11 July 1176 × Sept. 1181]

B = Canterbury, D. & C. C.A. S 354 (S 270, S 387). Single sheet copy, s. xiv ex. Approx. 314 × 121 mm. Written on face and dorse.

Ricardus dei gratia Cantuariensis archiepiscopus totius Anglie primas et apostolice sedis legatus universis sancte matris ecclesie filiis ad quos presentes litere pervenerint salutem in domino. Universitati vestre notum fieri volumus quod cum querimonia*a* dilectorum filiorum nostrorum Godardi rectoris ecclesie de Slyndon' et Alexandri capellani eiusdem ecclesie vicarii ad nos pervenisset*b* de eo quod ministri nostri ecclesie libertatem et iura in bosco et in pasturis et in aliis coartarent et eis que solebant habere denegarent, quia nobis per cartam Teobaldi Cantuariensis archiepiscopi ipsi Godardo cum antedicta ecclesia datam de iure et libertatibus ecclesie plene non constabat, diligenti examinatione fidelium et proborum virorum tam clericorum quam laicorum didicimus quod temporibus militum qui villam de Slyndon' tenuerunt, ante prenominatum Teobaldum et gloriosum martirem Thomam, habuit predicta ecclesia sine aliqua contradictione quando voluit de bosco eiusdem ville omnia que fuerant ei necessaria et ubique in pasturis ad eandem pertinentibus cum instauro dominorum libere, quiete, et sine contradictione de iure ecclesie duos equos, octo boves, sexaginta oves, agnos in bladis, porcos quotquot habebat in stipulis, et in tempore pannagii decem porcos, liberos et quietos in illa villa et in walda quinque similiter liberos et quietos. De bosco vero infra septa*c* camporum parochianorum rectores dicti monasterii ad dilatandam terram dicte ecclesie quantum voluerint assartare ubique poterint. Et in villa per domos et conduticias in fundo ecclesiastico erectas et omnibus aliis iustis modis quibus possunt redditus suos eis licuit ampliare dum tamen emolumentum proveniens propriis ecclesie usibus accresceret. Et si quid animal adventivum vel aliqua alia res super terram ecclesie primo fuisset inventa, nisi aliquis suam esse coram rectore dicti monasterii legitime probaret, domini fundi nichil sibi vendicantes eam rectoris ecclesie memorate esse iudicabant. Homines vero de ecclesia tenentes sibi necessaria de communi bosco eiusdem ville capientes et communam pasture cum aliis hominibus de villa habentes nec ad curiam dominorum fundi veniebant aut aliquod servitium ex toto anno eis faciebant nec in aliquo eis respondebant. Nos siquidem in preiudicium iuris et libertatum dicte ecclesie nichil facere cupientes set illesas per omnia custodire volentes, paupertati eius compatiendo, salvo iure Cantuariensis ecclesie necessitati sue inperpetuum subvenire desiderantes eas potius augere quam diminuere sudavimus[d]. Et quia multi sunt deo et ecclesie Christi ministrantium inpugnatores ecclesiasticique iuris multi inveniuntur oppressores, ne iura et libertates ecclesie que ecclesie Christi a Christi fidelibus in perpetuam elemosinam divine pietatis intuitu canonice sunt concesse et ab ea longa antiquorum temporum diuturnitate possesse calumniantium versutiis possint in irritum revocari, necessarium duximus eas scriptorum autenticorum patrocinio testium subscriptione communire. Eapropter volumus in communem notitiam devenire nos concessisse et presenti scripto confirmasse ecclesie de Slyndon' curiam et duas virgatas terre quas ab antiquis temporibus possedit cum omnibus pertinentiis suis et iura et libertates eius prenominatas quibus gavisa est per maxima preteritorum temporum curricula, cum decimis assartorum que de cetero in illa fient parochia et cum decimis predicti pannagii cuiuslibet venditionis bosci, cuiuslibet herbagii venditi, et omnium provenientium et omnium emolumentorum que nostris et successorum nostrorum temporibus poterunt evenire unde decima magna vel parva possit surgere sine omni contradictione, de bosco, de pasturis, et omnibus aliis rebus habendas et inconcusse perpetuo iure possidendas.[e][*dorse*:] Et quoniam ea que ad honorem dei et augmentum iuris et libertatum ecclesiarum canonice fieri dinoscuntur firma debent permanere et inconcussa stabilitate roborari, volumus et firmiter statuimus ut omnes rectores ecclesie de Slyndon' inperpetuum bene, libere, quiete, pacifice, et cum omni integritate omnia predicta sicut antiquitus habuit ecclesia teneant[f] et nulla interruptione seu contradictione interveniente possideant, sub anathemate prohibentes ne quis prefate ecclesie rectores vel homines suos super ulla possessione sua et iure et libertatibus ecclesie diu ante tempora nostra iuste collatis bona fide canoniceque possessis vel aliis eidem ecclesie a nobis de novo recte ac pie datis iniuste et temere presumpserit inquietare. Hanc autem concessionis et confirmationis nostre paginam ut firma et inconcussa permaneat sigilli nostri appositione communivimus in die Translationis sancti Benedicti [11 July] quo memoratam ecclesiam dedicavimus, et crofta^g quam Sefridus^h surdus tenuit ei in dotem quiete et libere inperpetuum dotavimus. De dei igitur misericordia confisi omnibus qui ad predictam ecclesiam dicto die oraturi devote advenerint et ei aliquod beneficium caritative impenderint vere confessis et penitentibus de iniuncta sibi penitentia singulis annis decem^j dies relaxamus.^{k} Hiis testibus: magistro Gerardo Pucella et aliis, etc.

^{a} querimoniam B ^{b} pervenisse B ^{c} infra septa: infrascripta B ^{d} suduimus B
^{e}Verte — etc. B ^{f} word partly oblit. B ^{g} croftam B ^{h} Sefridus after Alfridus
del. B ^{j} decem after x del. B ^{k} rellaxamus B

The archbp's itinerary shows that he cannot have dedicated the church on 11 July before the year 1176. The record of this dedication must be compared with a charter by which archbp Theobald grants a curtilage to the church when *he* dedicates it (Saltman, *Theobald* 474 no. 250, Bishop, *Scriptores regis* pl. XVII(b)). Perhaps that grant was in view of a prospective dedication which was never solemnized, or new building called for a fresh ceremony in archbp Richard's time.

The construction of the present charter, only preserved in a late and careless copy, is diffuse and repetitive. The style is unusual; but this could be explained by the external drafting of a document which was not in the normal course of business. Possibly it is copied from an uncorrected draft. The use of *monasterium* as an alternative description of the *ecclesia* of Slindon (Dr Major kindly suggests to me) may point to the status of the church as an old minster on a one-time royal portion of the archiepiscopal estates (cf. *Regesta regum* ii no. 756).

Neither this actum nor the record of Theobald's dedication of the church (1150 × 1154) describes it as in monastic hands. But a series of grants which must be treated with deep suspicion assign it to Lewes or her dependent priory of Horton. An original actum of Theobald, which must — if genuine — come from the time before he styled himself primate (i.e. before 1145: Saltman, 374–5 no. 151), grants Lewes the church. It is written in a book hand unlike most acta of Theobald (*EBC* 52–3) and is open to doubt. The grant is also recorded in a spurious Lewes charter attributed to bp Hilary of Chichester (*Chichester acta* 194 no. 40). Moreover, no. 497 below (= Saltman 376–8 no. 153) includes Slindon in a comprehensive confirmation by Theobald for the monks of Lewes at Horton, 1154 × 1158, which the prior of Lewes produced for archbp Hubert's inspection (1195 × 1198). If these documents from Lewes are not sufficient to discredit any idea of a grant made to Lewes or Horton, then the possibility suggested by L. F. Salzman may be accepted that Theobald's gift, 'because it had not been ratified by the chapter of Canterbury, did not take effect' (*VCH Sussex* iv (1953) 237). In any case, Slindon remained a rectory within the peculiar jurisdiction, and in the gift, of the archbishops in the later Middle Ages.

*73. Canterbury: suffragans of the province

Mandate to bishop Gilbert of London to summon the bishops of the province and other prelates of churches to attend a council at London under his presidency, according to the ancient custom of the fathers, on the Sunday on which is sung Cantate domino canticum novum.

[early 1175]

Mentioned only, in the summons as transmitted by the bp of London (dean of the province) to bp Jocelin of Salisbury ('ab ipso ut id faciamus in mandatis accepimus'): Foliot, *Letters* 306 no. 234. The editors identify the council, which the archbp summoned as primate and legate, as the Council of Westminster which met in May 1175. Cf. *Councils and synods* i 965–93. *Cantate domino* fell on 11 May in 1175.

74. Canterbury: suffragans of the province

Admonition to the archbishop's fellow-bishops in the province of Canterbury to be on their guard against pseudo-bishops who claim to be of Irish or Scottish tongue and who administer episcopal rites to the people without being properly ordained, dedicating churches, consecrating altars, and blessing abbots. These have caused scandal in the English church. Those whose consecration is not verified must not be received as bishops. Forgers of papal bulle *and of the seals of the archbishop and bishops, with their accomplices, are to be solemnly denounced as excommunicate on every festival of the church.*

[? Oct. 1181 × Feb. 1184]

Petri Blesensis opp. i 160–2 ep. 53.

The archbp is styled 'Ricardus dei gratia Cantuariensis archiepiscopus totius Anglie primas'. If this is correct, his legation had expired and Giles's date 'a.d. 1178?' is too early.

75. Canterbury: Herbert the archdeacon

Letters patent defining the rights which archdeacon Herbert claims to pertain to the office of archdeacon of Canterbury, and which the archbishop has granted to him personally. The grant is made without prejudice to the church of Canterbury or the archbishop's successors.

[28 April 1174 × Sept. 1181]

B = Lambeth Palace ms. 1212 (register of the see of Canterbury) fo. 51v (36v, p. 98) no. xlvii. s. xiii ex. C = Bodl. ms. Tanner 223 (register of the see) fo. 57v (p. 110). s. xvi in., copied from B. D = Canterbury D. & C. Black book of the archdnry fo. 63v (addition). s. xvi ex.

Pd from D by Somner, *Canterbury* (1640) 306–7 and ed. Battely (1703) pt. 1 appendix 65 no. lix, omitting names of last eight witnesses.

Ricardus dei gratia Cantuariensis archiepiscopus totius Anglie primas et apostolice sedis legatus universis Christi fidelibus ad quos presentes littere pervenerint salutem. Cum dilectus filius Herbertus archidiaconus noster plura ad archidiaconatum suum de iure debere pertinere vendicaret, de quibus nobis non constabat, intuitu probitatis sue et sincera affectione quam circa personam ipsius gerimus, hec ei personaliter concessimus sine omni preiudicio Cantuariensis

ecclesie et successorum nostrorum : institutiones videlicet et desti-
tutiones decanorum prehabito consilio nostro, custodiam vacantium
ecclesiarum ad nostram donationem non pertinentium et omnes
fructus dum vacaverint inde provenientes libere et absolute, placita
etiam ecclesiastica et omnia emolumenta inde provenientia tam de
dominiis nostris quam monachorum ecclesie Cantuariensis in archidiaconatu Cantuariensi constitutis, omnia etiam emolumenta de
placitis archidiaconatus sui ubicumque agitentur, ita tamen quod si
modum circa homines nostros[a] vel monachorum excesserit, nobis
excessus correctionem reservavimus, cognitionem etiam de causis
matrimoniorum cum accusantur usque ad definitivum calculum, et
si dirimendum fuerit matrimonium id nobis reservavimus, institutiones[b] personarum in ecclesiis vacantibus que ad nostram specialiter non pertineant donationem cum extra provinciam fuerimus,
cum autem presentes fuerimus et persona aliqua instituenda prius
oblata fuerit archidiacono, dummodo hoc non fuerit procuratum,
cum eam ad nos introduxerit honorem ei in facto suo conservabi-
mus. Omnes autem per nos instituti, tam in ecclesiis de dominio
nostro[c] et monachorum quam in aliis per archidiaconum vel eius
officialem introducentur in corporalem possessionem ecclesiarum in
quibus fuerint instituti. Hec autem omnia prescripta sub presentis
scripti et sigilli nostri testimonio duximus redigenda, ut sicut ea
prefato archidiacono nostro sunt a nobis personaliter concessa, ita
eius persone illibata conserventur. Hiis testibus : magistro Gerardo,
Waleranno archidiacono Baiocensi, magistro Petro Blesensi, magistro Waltero de Cant[d], magistro Matheo Cicestrensi, magistro Hugone de Gaherst', Philippo de Hasting', magistro Radulfo de Sancto
Martino, Amicio et Rogero et Willelmo clericis et aliis.

[a] nostros BC; episcopos D   [b] *add* etiam D   [c] nostro D; meo BC
[d] Cant' BC; Gant D

For the rights and customs attached to the office of archdn of Canterbury see
Churchill, *Canterbury administration* i 43–53 and B. L. Woodcock, *Med. eccles.
courts in the diocese of Canterbury* (Oxford 1952) 19–21. Herbert le Poer was
appointed archdn by archbp Richard in 1175 or 1176. If for a short time he was
one of three archdns in the diocese (Diceto i 403), the older practice of
appointing only a single archdn was soon resumed. In 1202 archbp Hubert asked
for a papal indult to have two additional archdns for the archiepiscopal peculiars,
but this was never put into effect (*Letters of Innocent III* no. 413).

76. Canterbury: Christ Church

*Mandate to rural deans and their chapters in the archdeaconry of
Canterbury, revoking the mandate given to the deans in a recent synod*

about the collection of synodal pennies, lest it should be prejudicial to the church of Canterbury and the prior and convent. He wishes the prior to collect the synodal pennies, with the archbishop's authority to pronounce sentence on defaulters. [Oct. 1181 × 16 Feb. 1184]

B = Canterbury, D. & C. Reg. H fo. 26r. s. xiii in.

Ricardus dei gratia Cantuariensis archiepiscopus totius Anglie primas dilectis in domino filiis decanis et capitulis per archidiaconatum Cantuariensem constitutis eternam in domino salutem. Mandatum quod vobis, filii decani, super denariis sinodalibus colligendis in sinodo nostra nuper celebrata iniunximus, quia timemus ne processu temporis in preiudicium ecclesie Cantuariensis et detrimentum prioris et conventus eiusdem loci debeat redundare, saniori usi consilio omnino revocamus. Volumus enim ut predictus prior prelibatos denarios sinodales colligat et si pro detentione eorumdem denariorum iustam in aliquem nostrum tulerit sententiam, nos eam ratam habebimus et firmiter faciemus observari. Valete.

Preceded in the register by archbp Theobald's synodal order for all priests to pay synodal pence to the prior: it laid under interdict the churches of defaulters (Saltman, *Theobald* 276 no. 49).

77. Canterbury: Christ Church

Notification that the prior and convent of Christ Church, at the request of the king and the archbishop and out of respect for St Thomas, have granted the corrody of a monk to William Capes, their ianitor curie, *for life. The archbishop forbids any claim to be made for this grant for the janitor after William's death.* [28 April 1174 × Sept. 1181]

A = Canterbury, D. & C. C.A. C 179 (C 461 (*del.*), C 178). Endorsed, s. xii/xiii: De Willelmo de Capes. Ric' arch'; s. xiii: quod W. de Capes ianitori curie nostre ad vitam suam dabatur corrodium unius monachi et quod ratione istius doni alii successores sui hoc ipsum non debent habere. Approx. 188 × 58 mm., trimmed, without fold or step or trace of seal; but the bottom edge suggests sealing simple queue. Scribe **III**.

.Ric(ardus). dei gracia Cantuariensis archiepiscopus . tocius Anglie primas et apostolice sedis legatus ⸴ universis sancte matris ecclesie filiis ⸴ ad quos littere iste pervenerint ⸴ eternam in domino salutem. Ad omnium noticiam volumus pervenire ⸴ dilectos in Christo filios nostros priorem et conventum ecclesie Christi Cantuariensis ad preces domini regis Anglie et nostras necnon ob honorem et reverentiam gloriosi martiris Thome concessisse et assignasse dilecto filio nostro Willelmo de Capes ianitori curie predictorum monachorum ⸴ conredium unius monachi . quoad idem Willelmus vixerit ∴ libere possidendum ∴ Unde ne hoc beneficium quod personale tantum est ∴ post decessum ipsius Willelmi . quasi ministerii ianue . accessorium ∴ ab aliquo possit repeti ∴ nos idem beneficium personale tantum esse presenti scripto testificamur . et ne post obitum predicti Willelmi racione porte ab aliquo in posterum exigatur ∴ ea qua fungimur auctoritate prohibemus. Valete.

HMCR v (1876) 429a gives a faulty description. For William's services to archbp Thomas and the monks see Urry, *Canterbury* 183. He was still alive in 1191, or later (ibid. 434–5).

78. Canterbury: Christ Church˙

Confirmation of the agreement for exchange of city property made by Benedict prior and the convent of Christ Church with Roger abbot elect and the convent of St Augustine's, Canterbury. At the request of Henry II and archbishop Richard, St Augustine's has surrendered to Christ Church land with a rental of 20s. 11d. a year, lying on the south side of the cathedral bell-tower, because the property presents serious risks of fire. In return, Christ Church has granted to the abbey other land in Canterbury with a rental of 22s. 2d. and Christ Church will in future pay 20d. a year charged on a tenement surrendered by the abbey in respect of royal farm. The properties and their tenants are enumerated. 'Facta est autem hec commutatio anno incarnationis dominice *[fo. 73r]* millesimo centesimo septuagesimo septimo, regnante illustrissimo Anglorum rege Henrico secundo.'

[25 March × 29 May 1177]

B = BL ms. Cotton Claud. D x (Red book of St Augustine's) fo. 72v. s. xiii/xiv.

Pd, imperfectly and abridged, by Somner, *Canterbury* (1640) 415–6, App. no. X; and ed. Battely (1703), Part 1 App. 23–24 no. XXVIII. Full text from B in Urry, *Canterbury* 407–8 no. XXVII.

Prior Benedict was elected abbot of Peterborough 29 May 1177. A charter of similar substance, made by the abbot-elect and convent of St Augustine's, is printed from the original (C. A. C 1112) by Urry, *Canterbury* 405–6 no. XXVI; its counterpart, made by Christ Church, precedes the archbp's confirmation in the Red book (fo. 72r) and kg Henry II's charter follows (fo. 73r). The former is found abridged in William Thorne's chronicle (Twysden, 1820); the latter is printed in Elmham, *Historia mon. S. Augustini* 461, and from the original by Urry, *Canterbury* 408–9 no. XXVIII. Much fresh light is thrown on the properties and tenants named in the agreement by Urry's book (and see Paul Bennett in *Archaeologia Cantiana* xcvi (1980) 399–402). The agreement followed soon after the fire of Sept. 1174, and the re-building of the choir was still in progress. The fire had spread to the roof of the cathedral from blazing cottages nearby. (Gervas. Cant. i 3–29, transl. R. Willis, *Architectural hist. of Canterbury cathedral.* 1845).

79. Canterbury: Christ Church

Mandate to the chaplains of the churches of 'Bernchi ... ', 'Wede', *and Eastry, and the chapel of* 'Werde', *to take oath of fealty to the prior and monks of Christ Church, Canterbury, or to appear before the archbishop without fail next Sunday to show why they should not do so.*

[Aug. 1174 × Sept. 1181]

> A = Canterbury, D. & C. C.A. A 27 (A 128). Endorsed, s. xiii: Ricardus archiepiscopus de ecclesiis; s. xiv: Ricardus archiepiscopus precipit quibusdam capellanis promotis per nos quod sacramentum nobis prestent de fidelitate. Approx. 168 × 41 + 20 (step) mm. Sealing s.q.; only stubs of tongue and tie remain, seal lost. Scribe **III**.

.Ric(ardus). dei gracia Cantuariensis archiepiscopus ⁃ tocius Anglie primas et apostolice sedis legatus ⁃ dilectis in domino filiis ⁃ Roberto ecclesie de Bernchi ... Walterio ecclesie de Wede ⁃ Ioseph' capelle de Werde ⁃ Willelmo ecclesie de Ætreya ⁃ capellanis . salutem . in domino. Mandamus vobis et districte precipimus ⁃ quatinus dilectis filiis nostris priori et monachis ecclesie Christi Cantuariensis ⁃ de quorum munificencia et liberalitate ⁃ beneficia habetis ecclesiastica ⁃ super exhibenda eis fidelitate ⁃ sacramentum prestetis et securitatem . aut hac die dominica proxima futura ⁃ omni occasione cessante ⁃ coram nobis appareatis . ostensuri quare hoc non feceritis . aut facere non debeatis. Valete.

> Of these churches only Eastry has been identified. If 'Bernchi ... ', of which the ending is damaged and torn, is 'Bernchisleia', this might be 'Brenchesleia' or Brenchley (Kent); but by 1192 Brenchley was a chapel of Yalding church, appropriated to Tonbridge priory (*PUE* ii 458 no. 266).

80. Canterbury: Christ Church

Confirmation for the monks of Christ Church of the grant by bishop William of Norwich of the church of Deopham.

[May 1177 × Sept. 1181]

> A = Canterbury, D. & C. C.A. D 19 (C 176 *del.*). Endorsed, s. xii/xiii: Carta de ecclesia de Diepeham; s. xiii: Confirmatio ecclesie de diepeham et pertinentiis suis *and* .IX. *del.*; s. xiv in.: Registratur. Diepeham. Approx. 180 × 76 + 18 (step) mm. Sealing s.q., step at lefthand; seal (red wax) lengthwise on step; inscription much damaged, seal and counterseal badly rubbed. Scribe **II**.
>
> B = Ibid. Reg. I fo. 90r (131r, 103r). s. xiii ex. C = Ibid. Reg. B fo. 220r (438r (in red), 224r). s. xiii ex. D = Ibid. Reg. E fo. 392r (390 *del.*). s. xiii ex.

.Ric(ardus). dei gracia Cantuariensis archiepiscopus . tocius Anglie primas et apostolice sedis legatus ⁃ universis sancte matris ecclesie filiis ad quos presentes littere pervenerint ⁃ eternam in domino salutem. Que a fratribus et coepiscopis nostris racionabiliter facta esse noscuntur ." sua debent stabilitate gaudere . et ut firmioris robur pacis optineant ." nostra interest sollicite providere. Eapropter dilectis in domino filiis nostris monachis in sancta Cantuariensi ecclesia divino mancipatis servicio ." ecclesiam de Diepeham*a* cum liberis terris et decimis et oblacionibus et omnibus ad ius eiusdem ecclesie pertinentibus ." sicut eis a pie memorie Willelmo quondam Norwicensi episcopo concessa est et confirmata ." nos quoque concedimus et carta presenti confirmamus . statuentes et sub interminatione anathematis prohibentes . nequis hanc nostre confirmacionis paginam infringere ." vel ei aliquatenus temere contraire presumat. Testibus . Willelmo Gloecestriensi archidiacono . Henrico Baiocensi . magistro Rogerio Norwicensi . Willelmo de Sotindon' . et aliis pluribus. ".'

a Diepeham A; Diepham B; Depeham C; Dyepeham D

William of Northolt became archdn of Gloucester May × Dec. 1177. The grant by bp William of Norwich is in Reg. E (fo. 391v) and Reg. B (fo. 219v).

81. Canterbury: Christ Church

Confirmation of the settlement in the archbishop's presence of a dispute between Christ Church, Canterbury, and Robert the priest about the church of Deopham. Robert admitted that the church was given in perpetual alms to Christ Church by bishop William of Norwich at the presentation of Henry de Ria, and that he, Robert, held it as vicar of Christ Church, subject to a yearly pension of two marks, which he had withheld for about ten years. As he has now paid part of these arrears, the prior and convent have agreed to take no further action against him, and have confirmed him in the vicarage, subject to the pension of two marks. Robert has sworn that he will pay the pension and has done fealty to the prior and convent who, in turn, have promised to safeguard his possession of the church during good behaviour.

[May 1177 × Sept. 1181]

A¹ = Canterbury, D. & C. C.A. D 7 (D 124 (*del.*), 2, and D 1). Endorsed. s. xii/xiii: de ecclesia de Diepeham; s. xiii: .Ric' arch'.; s. xiii/xiv: vacat *and* .xxxiiii. Approx. 200 × 161 + 31 mm. Sealing d.q. 2: fine seal and counterseal (brownish white wax). Top half of chirograph, inverted, divided by a straight cut.

A² = Ibid. C.A. D 8 (D 122 (*del.*), 3, and D 2). Endorsed, s. xii ex.: Cyrografum inter nos et Rodbertum de Diepeham; s. xiii : Ric' archiepiscopus de ecclesia de Depeham; s. xiii/xiv: duplicata est. Approx. 200 × 165 + 33 mm. Sealing d.q. 2; seal and counterseal (brown wax). Bottom half of chirograph, in the same hand as A¹, displaying marvellous consistency.

B = Ibid. Reg. B fo. 215v (217v). s. xiv/xv.

CYROGRAPHUM

Ric(ardus) dei gratia Cantuariensis archiepiscopus totius Anglie primas et apostolice sedis legatus . universis Christi fidelibus ad quos presentes littere pervenerint eternam in domino salutem. Causa que vertebatur inter ecclesiam Christi Cantuariensem et Robertum presbiterum de Diepham[a] super ecclesia de Depham . in presentia nostra et multorum fide dignorum tali fine conquievit. Robertus siquidem recognovit se fuisse et esse vicarium ecclesie Christi Cantuariensis in ecclesia de Depham que a pie recordationis Willelmo quondam Norwicensi episcopo eidem ecclesie Christi Cantuariensi ad presentationem et donationem bone memorie Henrici de Ria ⁒ in perpetuam elemosinam concessa fuerat et collata. Recognovit etiam quod a multis retro temporibus annuam inde debuit pensionem duarum marcarum quam quia per aliquot circiter .X. annos detinuerat ⁒ prestita competenti satisfactione et parte reddita detentorum ⁒ misericorditer obtinuit ut quamdiu se erga ecclesiam Cantuariensem fideliter habebit ⁒ super detentis nullam sentiet exactionem. Prior igitur et conventus eiusdem ecclesie Christi Cantuariensis concessit et carta sua confirmavit ipsi Roberto predictam ecclesiam de Depham in perpetuam vicariam de eis tenendam . reddendo inde .II. marcas annuatim nomine pensionis iampridem constitute. Robertus vero tactis sacrosanctis ewangeliis iuravit quod pensionem illam annuatim fideliter et absque difficultate priori et conventui ecclesie Christi Cantuariensis de cetero persolvet . et modis omnibus fidelitatem eis servabit de eadem ecclesia et aliis omnibus que ad ecclesiam Cantuariensem noscuntur pertinere. Prior etiam et conventus fideliter promisit quod omnimodam auctoritatem ei prestabunt et parabunt securitatem possidendi . quamdiu idem Robertus erga eos fideliter se habebit. Ut igitur ea que coram nobis facta sunt perpetuam optineant firmitatem . ea qua fungimur auctoritate confirmamus et sigilli nostri patrocinio communimus. Testibus . Herberto archidiacono . Cantuariensi . Walerano archidiacono Baiocensi . Willelmo archidiacono Glouecestriensi . magistro Waltero de Augo . magistro Roberto de Inglesham . Henrico Baiocensi . magistro Petro Gaio . Willelmo de Sottind(on) . Rogero Norwicensi[b]. Roberto de Wimundham . Roberto de Wiclewd' . clericis.

[a] Diepham A¹; Depham A²   [b] Rogero Norwicensi A², *trsp.* A¹B

William of Northolt became archdn of Gloucester May × Dec. 1177. Henry de Ria granted the manor of Deopham to Christ Church, Canterbury, in 1146 in exchange for the manor of Mulbarton, which his father Hubert had given to the monks and of which they had been despoiled. For the transaction see Saltman, *Theobald* 536–8 and for king Stephen's confirmation, *Reg. regum* iii 55–6 no. 150.

82. Canterbury: Christ Church

Grant to the monks of Christ Church of the churches of Eastry and Monkton with their dependent chapels and other appurtenances, to be assigned to the use of the almonry. [? 28 April 1174 × 6 April 1175]

B = Canterbury, D. & C. Reg. I fo. 90v (131v, 103v). s. xiii ex. C = BL ms. Add. 6159 (register of Ch. Ch.) fo. 287v (285v, 289v), omitting witness-list. s. xiii/xiv. D = Lambeth Palace Libr. Cart. misc. XIII/15 (Ch. Ch. almonry cartulary, fragm.) fo. 10v. s. xiv in. E = Ibid. fo. 10v. F = Canterbury, D. & C. Reg. C fo. 140r. s. xiv. G = Bodl. ms. Tanner 18 (Ch. Ch. almonry cartulary) fo. 8r (p. 15). s. xv in.

Ricardus dei gratia Cantuariensis archiepiscopus totius Anglie primas et apostolice sedis legatus universis sancte matris ecclesie filiis salutem in domino*a*. Ad officii nostri sollicitudinem pertinere dinoscitur pauperibus Christi opus misericordie et pietatis*b* impendere et eorum*c* sustentationi que perpetuitatem inposterum optineat cura propensiori providere. Eapropter in communem Christi fidelium notitiam volumus devenire nos concessisse et canonice dedisse conventui ecclesie Christi Cantuariensis in puram et perpetuam elemosinam ecclesias de Estreya et Moneketon' cum capellis et aliis universis ad easdem ecclesias pertinentibus, ita bene, libere, et quiete tenendas sicut umquam aliquis predecessorum suorum melius et liberius eas tenuit, ita tamen quod eedem ecclesie cum omnibus suis pertinentibus elemosinarie specialiter de cetero*d* sint assignate et in perpetuos usus*e* pauperum deputate. Et ut hec nostra donatio perpetuum robur optineat, presentis scripti patrocinio eam confirmamus et sigilli nostri munimine roboramus, statuentes et sub interminatione anathematis prohibentes ne quis hanc nostre donationis et confirmationis paginam infringere vel ei aliquatenus contraire presumat. Hiis testibus: magistro Gerardo, Waleranno archidiacono Baiocensi, [fo. 91r] magistro Petro Blesensi, Willelmo de Norhal', Radulfo de Wingeham, magistro Hugone de Sutwelle, magistro Ricardo de Saloppesberi, magistro Roberto de Ynglesham, Radulfo de Sancto Martino, Rogerio Norwicensi, Henrico Baiocensi, Amico clerico, Rogero elemosinario, Roberto de Batwento, Willelmo de Sotindon', et aliis.

a in domino CDEFG, *om.* B   *b* misericordie et pietatis BCDG, *trsp.* EF
c eorum BCG; suorum DEF   *d* decetero CDEFG, *om.* B   *e* perpetuos usus BDE; perpetuis usibus CFG

Gervase of Canterbury praises the archbp for restoring to the monks in the first year of his election all the churches of their manors 'quas confessus est in audientia multorum de iure et donatione eorum fuisse' (*Opp.* ii 399). The grant of Eastry and Monkton to the almonry was confirmed by Alexander III, 29 May

1178 and 16 Feb. 1179, and by Lucius III, 26 May 1184 (*PUE* ii 364, 370, 417–8 nos. 172, 179, 224). The efforts of archbp Richard's successors to resume alienated property for the archiepiscopal *mensa* (*Letters of Innocent III* no. 52) led to later disputes over these and other churches. See below, no. 382. Eastry and Monkton churches ultimately reverted to the prior and convent by settlement with archbp Simon Islip, 1365. The archbp received in exchange the London churches of All Hallows, Bread Street, St Dunstan in the East, and St Pancras, which were henceforth archiepiscopal peculiars (Canterbury, D. & C. C.A. E 176 and 178, *HMCR* v (1876) 440*a*, 442*a*).

83. Canterbury: Christ Church

Mandate to Herbert archdeacon of Canterbury and his officials. If any chaplain of the churches of Eastry or Monkton or their chapels should die, or resign or surrender his vicarage, they are to admit to the church the chaplain or chaplains presented by the prior and convent of Canterbury and allow them to minister in the name of the monks.

[Oct. 1181 × 16 Feb. 1184]

B = Lambeth Palace, Cart. misc. XIII/15 (Ch. Ch. almonry cartulary, fragm.) fo. 11r. s. xiv in.

Ricardus dei gratia Cantuariensis archiepiscopus totius Anglie primas dilectis filiis H. Cantuariensi archidiacono*a* et officialibus suis salutem, gratiam, et benedictionem. Mandamus vobis et precipimus quatinus si aliquem de capellanis ecclesiarum de Munketone et de Estria vel capellarum ad easdem ecclesias pertinentium mori vel vicariam suam resignare vel quomodolibet cedere contigerit, capellanum seu capellanos quos dilecti filii nostri prior et conventus noster Cantuariensis ad*b* ecclesias illas vel capellas vobis vel alicui vestrum presentaverint sine molestia qualibet recipiatis et nomine monachorum ministrare permittatis. Valete.

a archideacono B   *b* ad: vobis ad B

84. Canterbury: Christ Church

Notification that when the archbishop was a claustral monk at Christ Church, he witnessed the grant to the prior and convent of the church of Eynsford by William of Eynsford, when he took the monastic habit, with the assent of his son and heir, William Guram. Confirmation for the prior and convent of their right of patronage in the church.

[May 1177 × Sept. 1181]

A = Canterbury, D. & C. C.A. E 189*b* (E 6, E 191). endorsed, s. xiii: Confirmacio ecclesie de Einesford. .v.; s. xiv: Ric' archiepiscopus confirmat cartam W. de Eynesford per quam nobis dedit ecclesiam de Eyneford. Approx. 175 × 129 + 23 mm. Sealing d.q. 2; tag and seal lost. Scribe **IV**.

B = Ibid. Reg. I fo. 88r (129r, 101r). s. xiii ex. C = BL ms. Add. 6159 (register of Ch. Ch.) fo. 287r (285r, 289r), witnesses omitted. s. xiii/xiv. D = Canterbury, D. & C. Reg. B fo. 4r. s. xiv/xv. E = Bodl. ms. Tanner 18 (Ch. Ch. almonry cartulary) fo. 75r (p. 149). s. xv in.

.Ric(ardus). dei gratia Cantuariensis archiepiscopus . tocius . Anglie . primas et apostolice sedis legatus .' universis sancte matris ecclesie filiis ad quos presentes littere pervenerint .' eternam in Christo salutem. Ad omnium volumus devenire noticiam . quod cum olim in ecclesia . Cantuariensi . cui deo presidemus autore . claustralis monachus essemus .' Willelmus de Einesford' pater Willelmi .ᵃGuram . volens in eadem ecclesia monachari .' in presentia nostra necnon et aliorum multorum fidedignorum quicquid iuris habuit in ecclesia de Einesford in fundo suo sita . et in omnibus eiusdem ecclesie pertinentiis .' priori et conventui prefate ecclesie nostre in perpetuam contulit elemosinam . et nobis et aliis multis intuentibus .' propria manu per quendam cultellum sicut moris est complicatum . et quoddamᵇ bacchile argenteum .' super altare Christi obtulit . presente filio suo et herede Willelmoᶜ Guram patrisque sui donationi gratum impertiente favorem et consensum. Et quoniam divina gratia permittente eo loci constituti sumus . ut prefate ecclesie nostre libertatibus et conventus nostri possessionibus universis .' attentius providere debeamus .' prefati militis Willelmi donationem in iamdicta ecclesia de Einesford ratam habentes et firmam . utpote quam oculis nostris perspeximus et auribus nostris audivimus .' priori et conventui eiusdem ecclesie nostre autoritate qua fungimur confirmamus . ita ut ipsi ius patronatus eiusdem ecclesie quiete et libere possideant in perpetuum. Quod ne revocari de cetero possit in dubium .' presenti scripto nostro duximus commendandum . et sigilli nostri munimine roborandum. Testibus hiis . magistro Girardo . Willelmo Gloecestriensi . archidiacono . magistro Rogerio de Rulveston' . Willelmo et Moyse capellanis . magistro Rogerio Norwicensi . magistro Rogerio Walensi . Ricardo clerico . Rogerio decano . et aliis multis clericis et laicis.

ᵃ de *erased* A   ᵇ quodam A   ᶜ de *erased* A

William of Northolt became archdn of Gloucester May × Dec. 1177.

This document and the next illustrate the problems arising in this period about grants made in an earlier generation without written record. For the family of Eynsford see D. C. Douglas, *Domesday monachorum of Canterbury* (R. Hist. Soc. 1944) 44–47, Du Boulay, *Lordship of Canterbury* 108–110, Urry, *Canterbury* 54–55. William son of Ralph, a knight of the see, became a monk *c.*1130. His grandson William (son of William Goram, or Guram) went surety for archbp Thomas in 1164, was mulcted 100 marks when the archbp fled, and eventually recovered the money from the monks of Canterbury out of the offerings at St Thomas's shrine. He died 1183 × 1185.

There is no sign how Eynsford church was served under archbps Theobald and Thomas: whether its incumbent was regarded as rector or vicar, or what part of its revenues reached the almonry of Christ Church. But the next letter, and a letter of the donor's grandson (*Domesday monachorum* 109–10) show that the family blamed the archbps for misapplying the gift. Further light is thrown on this by William FitzStephen. In his account of archbp Thomas's collation of the church to a clerk named Laurence and of the trouble which ensued with William of Eynsford and the king, he states that the archbp had the gift of vacant churches in the manors of his barons and of the monks of Canterbury (*MTB* iii 43). This may explain the present confirmation and the proceedings recounted in no. 85; their immediate cause was probably that archbp Richard, yielding to the pope's pressure, had collated the rectory to Alexander III's nephew, Gentilis. A comparable situation arose at Meopham (nos. 87–88).

85. Canterbury: Christ Church

Notification of a settlement in the dispute over the church of Eynsford, between William of Eynsford (III), the donor's grandson, and the church and archbishop of Canterbury. The archbishop recalls the circumstances of the original gift (see above, no. 84). William III's claim to the manor of Ruckinge, arising from this gift, came to the hearing of king Henry II, who authorized an enquiry in the presence of his envoys. On the evidence given, the archbishop confirms the original grant (not confirmed by his predecessors) of the church of Eynsford and its chapels in free and perpetual alms for the almonry of Christ Church. He reserves the rights of Gentilis, nephew of pope Alexander III, to whom he had given the church. When Gentilis vacates the church, it and its chapels shall be served by vicars to be presented by the prior and convent for institution to the archbishop or, sede vacante, *to the rural dean.*   [1182]

A = Canterbury, D. & C. C.A. F 4 (A 83 *del.*). Endorsed, s. xii/xiii: De ecclesia de Einesford' qualiter ecclesie Christi adiudicata fuit in capitulo; *before and after this*, s. xiv: Confirmacio Ric' archiepiscopi, *and*: cum capellis de Stanes et de Freningham. Approx. 250 × 297 + 23 mm. Sealing d.q. 2; seal and counterseal (red wax). Scribe **III**.

B = Canterbury, D. & C. Libr. ms. Lit. E 28 (Domesday monachorum) fo. 8r. s. xii ex. C = Ibid. Reg. I fo. 86v (127v, 99v). s. xiii ex. D = BL ms. Add. 6159 (register of Ch. Ch.) fo. 286r (284r, 288r). s. xiii/xiv. E = Lambeth Palace Libr. Carte misc. XIII/15 (Ch. Ch. almonry cartulary, fragm.) fo. 8r. s. xiv in. F = Canterbury, D. & C. Reg. B fo. 4r. s. xiv/xv. G = Bodl. ms. Tanner 18 (Ch. Ch. almonry cartulary) fo. 75v (p. 150). s. xv in.

Pd from B in *Domesday monachorum of Christ Church* 108–9.

.Ric(ardus). dei gratia Cantuariensis archiepiscopus . tocius Anglie primas ⠒ universis Christi fidelibus ad quos littere iste pervenerint ⠒ eternam in domino ⠒ salutem. Res gesta scripto provide commendatur . ne vel a memoria hominum possit elabi ⠒ vel si forte tractu

temporis oblivionem incurrerit ⸴ suffragante litterarum testimonio ⸴
ad memorie certitudinem reparetur . Eapropter ad omnium notitiam volumus pervenire ⸴ quod cum in ecclesia Cantuariensi simpli-
cem adhuc claustralis monachi vitam ageremus ⸴ Willelmus filius
Radulfi dominus fundi de Einesford' in pretaxata Cantuariensi
ecclesia ⸴ habitum monachilem suscepturus . presente et assensum
prebente per omnia Willelmo de Einesford' filio et herede suo ⸴
cognomento Gurham ⸴ nobis et multis aliis videntibus ⸴ ecclesiam
sancti Martini de Einesford' cum omnibus ad eam pertinentibus per
scutellam argenteam et cultellum unum ⸴ super altare ecclesie
Christi Cantuariensis ⸴ optulit et in perpetuam concessit atque
donavit elemosinam. Unde cum processu temporis super eadem
donatione inter ecclesiam Cantuariensem et nos . et Willelmum de
Einesford' nepotem predicti Willelmi filii Radulfi ⸴ orta fuisset
controversia . et ad audientiam domini .H. illustris Anglorum regis .
tandem deducta ⸴ ita de assensu eiusdem regis inter dilectos filios
nostros monachos Cantuarienses . et nos . et memoratum Willelmum nepotem prelibati Willelmi filii Radulfi ⸴ qui ecclesiam de
Einesford' ecclesie Cantuariensi sub hac condicione datam fuisse
asserebat ⸴ ut cum eandem ecclesiam de Einesford' vacare contin-
geret ⸴ manerium de Roching' ad liberum dominium domini de
Einesford' redire deberet ⸴ convenit ⸴ ut presentibus nunciis domini
regis ⸴ de predicta donatione sed et condicione prelibata si forte
inserta fuit ⸴ in capitulo Cantuariensi per fratres eiusdem capituli
sub anathematis periculo veritas eliceretur. Unde presentibus tandem in eodem capitulo ⸴ nunciis domini regis ad hoc specialiter
destinatis ⸴ videlicet Gilleberto de Colevill' et Willelmo Malduit
domini regis camerario . et Willelmo filio Nigelli ⸴ presentibus
nichilominus Willelmo de Einesford' nepote Willelmi filii Radulfi et
Willelmo eiusdem Willelmi filio ac herede ⸴ Roberto quoque filio
Bernardi ⸴ et multis aliis ⸴ super veritate dicenda ⸴ excommunicacionis sententiam expresse protulimus . qua prolata ⸴ tam a nobis
quam ab aliis omnibus ⸴ acclamatum est unanimiter et publice
protestatum ⸴ quod de predicta condicione nichil omnino sciebant
vel eciam audierant. Plures quoque eorumdem fratrum una nobis-
cum sollempniter protestati sunt ⸴ sepedictam ecclesiam de Einesford' pure et sine condicione qualibet ecclesie Cantuariensi fuisse
collatam. Quoniam ergo eadem ecclesia de Einesford' ecclesie
Cantuariensi a nullo predecessorum nostrorum hactenus confirmata
est ⸴ sed tantum simplex a laico facta fuit inde donacio . volentes
quod minus actum est ⸴ ad perfectionis plenitudinem ⸴ deduci ⸴
prescriptam ecclesiam de Einesford' cum capellis de Stanes et de

Freningham ⸴ et terris . decimis . et omnimodis possessionibus ad ecclesiam ipsam vel capellas pertinentibus ⸴ ecclesie Cantuariensi ad usus pauperum elemosinarie in liberam et perpetuam elemosinam concedimus et confirmamus . ita quidem ut cum eandem ecclesiam de Einesford' vacare contigerit ⸴ decime . oblationes . et omnimode obventiones ⸴ de ea provenientes ⸴ in usus pauperum elemosinarie ⸴ libere convertantur . salva nobis et successoribus nostris in iamdictis ecclesia et capellis ⸴ canonica iustitia . quatinus in eisdem scilicet divina exhibeantur obsequia per idoneos vicarios a dilectis filiis nostris monachis ecclesie Cantuariensis ⸴ nobis vel successoribus nostris presentandos et instituendos . salva eciam dilecto filio nostro Gentili nepoti sancte memorie .A. quondam summi pontificis donacione quam eidem .G. fecimus de predicta ecclesia quamdiu eam tenuerit. Hoc quoque duximus adiciendum ⸴ quatinus si forte vacante sede cui ad presens disponente domino presidemus ⸴ antefatam ecclesiam de Einesford' vacare contigerit ⸴ prelibati monachi nichilominus eam libere ingredientur . et decano loci ad exhibenda divina officia idoneum vicarium presentabunt . quem ab ipso decano sine molestia qualibet recipi volumus atque precipimus. Ut ergo hec nostra concessio firma et inconvulsa permaneat ⸴ eam presenti scripto confirmamus et sigilli nostri apposicione roboramus . statuentes et sub interminacione anathematis prohibentes ⸴ nequis hanc nostre confirmationis seu concessionis paginam infringere vel ei aliquatenus temere contraire presumat. Testibus his . magistro Gerardo . Walerano Baiocensi ⸴ P. Batthoniensi ⸴ et Willelmo Gloecestriensi ⸴ archidiaconis . magistro Roberto de Inglesham . Henrico Baiocensi . magistro Rogerio de Roulvest(on) . Gilleberto de Piris . Galfrido clerico . magistro Rogerio Walensi . Willelmo de Sotindona . et multis aliis tam clericis quam laicis.

Not before 1182 when Peter of Blois became archdn of Bath. Nov. × early Dec., suggested as the date by D. C. Douglas on the grounds that many of the witnesses were found with the archbp in France three months later, is too late; for Waleran was elected bp of Rochester 9 × 10 Oct. 1182.

Although this settlement gave Christ Church a larger claim in Eynsford church than the archbp's earlier confirmation allowed (no. 84), the convent did not benefit much. The death of Gentilis in 1182 or 1183 resulted in the institution of another papal nominee before 1186, if we interpret correctly a letter of prior Alan of Canterbury (PL cxc 1485-7 ep. XI). This was John Bellesmains (John of Canterbury), archbp of Lyon, once a familiar of archbp Theobald with Thomas Becket. The prior's reproaches to John (1182 × 1186), with the proposition that he should restore the rectory to the church of which he was a son and alumnus in return for a pension of a hundred shillings to one of his clerks, were fruitless. A second letter (ep. XII) declared that the tenure of this rectory by an alien bp caused scandal and that the king had said he would not stand it ('in vita sua non sustinebit quod Lugdunensis archiepiscopus ecclesiam de Einesford quoquo modo possideat'). Alan's letters may explain why a royal clerk, William of Ste-Mère-Église, claimed the church in 1191. When a writ of prohibition was issued against judges delegate in the case of the monks of Canterbury v. William of Ste-Mère-Église about his church of Eynsford and the chapel of Farningham, it stated that he was a crusader, that he held the church by the gift of the late archbp, and that the status of the church should not be changed *sede vacante* (*Ep. Cant.* 343 no. 369). But the former archbp of Lyon still held the church in Jan. 1199, when the monks tried to oust him (ibid. 472 no. 505). His rights were reserved by the award of November 1200. When he died a third of the revenues was to go to the monks' almonry, but the rest was to remain in the gift of the archbp (below, no. 383). A later settlement after dispute in 1225 left the rector in complete possession of Eynsford church and allocated to the almonry much of the revenues of Farningham, but its vicarage was to be in the gift of the rector (*Acta S. Langton* 97–8 no. 78).

For the family of Eynsford see above, no. 84n. Gilbert de Colevill, William Malduit, and William son of Nigel were well-known royal servants. Robert FitzBernard was sheriff of Kent 1174–83, and William son of Nigel succeeded him.

Gentilis was still a young man when he died in France in 1182 or 1183. He had been given a prebend of Lincoln by Geoffrey, bp-elect, and his obit was celebrated there on 23 Oct. (*Fasti eccl. angl. 1066–1300: Lincoln* 122–3). He was commemorated on 22 Nov. at the abbey of Ste-Geneviève, Paris, whose abbot, Stephen of Tournai, wrote to king Henry II to ask that the English property of Gentilis should be handed over to his executor to be distributed in alms, according to his testament (*PL* ccxi 380).

86. Canterbury: Christ Church

Notification that the priest Jocelin detained the key of the church of St Dunstan in the East, London, after the death of William son of Marewen, who had held the church for many years at a yearly pension of ten shillings from the monks of Canterbury. Jocelin has relinquished the key and his claim to the church and the archbp has instituted his clerk, Master Ralph de S. Martino, as perpetual vicar, on the presentation of the monks, paying a pension of twelve shillings yearly to the monks. Ralph has granted the church to Jocelin who has sworn to pay him a pension of twenty shillings a year.

[May 1177 × 21 Sept. 1180]

B = Canterbury, D. & C. Reg. A fo. 165r (187r). s. xiii ex. C = Ibid. Reg. E fo. 61v (31v). s. xiii ex.

R. dei gratia Cantuariensis archiepiscopus totius Anglie primas et apostolice sedis legatus omnibus Christi fidelibus ad quos presentes littere pervenerint eternam in domino salutem. Ad universitatis vestre notitiam volumus pervenire quod cum, defuncto Willelmo filio Marewen qui ecclesiam beati Dunstani Londoniensis sub annua pensione decem solidorum de dilectis filiis nostris monachis Cantuariensibus annis pluribus tenuerat, Iocelinus sacerdos clavem eiusdem ecclesie iniuste detineret, vocatus super hoc in ius ante presentiam nostram idem Iocelinus tandem sponte et sine omni coactione clavem predicte ecclesie et quicquid iuris in eadem ecclesia sibi vendicabat in manu nostra resignavit. Nos ergo prelibatam ecclesiam prescriptis monachis nostris qui ipsius ecclesie personatum a multis retro temporibus possiderant libere et integre restituimus, et ad petitionem et presentationem eorumdem monachorum sepedictam ecclesiam cum universis pertinentiis eius dilecto filio et clerico nostro magistro Radulfo de Sancto Martino sub annuo canone xii solidorum monachis ipsis ad Pentecosten annuatim solvendorum in liberam et perpetuam contulimus elemosinam, ipsumque Radulfum in eadem ecclesia perpetuum vicarium canonice instituimus. Radulfus vero pietate motus et prece nostra inductus eandem ecclesiam prenominato Iocelino sub annua pensione xl solidorum, ipsi Radulfo duobus terminis annuatim solvendorum, xx solidos scilicet ad Pentecosten et xx solidos ad festum sancti Martini, quoad uterque eorum vixerit tenendam concessit. Iocelinus autem de fidelitate eidem Radulfo servanda et predicta pensione statutis terminis annuatim solvenda fidei religionem in presentia nostra interposuit. Quare ne posteris temporibus alicui veniat in dubium, presenti scripto sub sigilli nostri appositione duximus commendare. Hiis testibus: Willelmo archidiacono Gloecestriensi, Warino priore Dovur', magistro Roberto de Inglesham, magistro Iohanne Planeta, magistro Rogero Norwicensi, Rogero elemosinario, Galfrido clerico, Willelmo filio Heltonis, Iohanne de Hastingleg', Willelmo de Sothindon', et pluribus aliis tam clericis quam laicis.

William of Northolt became archdn of Gloucester May × Dec. 1177. Despite the statement that the prior and convent of Christ Church held the parsonage and that Mr Ralph de S. Martino was presented to a perpetual vicarage by them, archbp Stephen appropriated the church afresh, to the fabric of Christ Church, and ordained a vicarage, 1225 × 1228. *Acta S. Langton* 143–4 no. 128.

Mr Ralph de Sancto Martino had a career of royal and archiepiscopal service ahead of him. He is last heard of in 1208, concerned in the royal custody of the vacant see of Canterbury. His life-interest in the rectory of Eastry had been safeguarded in Nov. 1200 (below, no. 383).

87. Canterbury: Christ Church

Grant to the monks of Christ Church of the church of Meopham for the almonry, the archbishop's former gift of the churches of Eastry and Monkton having proved insufficient. Virgil is to hold the church of Meopham of the monks for his life as parson, and shall pay a bezant yearly to the almonry. [June × Dec. 1177]

B = Lambeth Palace, Cart. misc. XIII/15 (Ch. Ch. almonry cartulary fragm.) fo. 10r. s. xiv in. C = Ibid. fo. 10r. D = Bodl. ms. Tanner 18 (Ch. Ch. almonry cartulary) fo. 95ᵗ (p. 187). s. xv in.

Ricardus dei gratia Cantuariensis archiepiscopus totius Anglie primas et apostolice sedis legatus universis sancte[a] matris ecclesie filiis salutem. Ad universitatis vestre notitiam volumus pervenire quod ex debito nobis iniuncti officii egentium necessitati volentes consulere[b] ecclesias de Eastreia et Muneketune cum capellis et ceteris pertinentiis suis conventui ecclesie Christi Cantuariensis in perpetuam elemosinam concessimus, dedimus, et assignavimus, ad usus tamen pauperum elemosinarie ipsius ecclesie cum suis fructibus specialiter deputatas. Verunptamen quia has ad hoc minus sufficere advertimus, ideo ecclesiam de Meapeham cum omni suo iure et integritate prescriptis ecclesiis adiecimus, ut ipsa ecclesia de Meapeham usui et sustentationi pauperum sicut et cetere due perpetuo cedat, Virgilio persona predicte ecclesie de Meapeham prebente assensum, cui ad preces et postulationes domini pape Alexandri eandem ecclesiam dedimus et confirmavimus. Ad hoc tamen idem Virgilius ita consensit quod debeat in ipsa ecclesie cum integritate sui iuris in vita sua persona permanere, tenebitque eam de priore et conventu Cantuariensis ecclesie, solvendo annuatim unum bizantium elemosinarie ipsius ecclesie. Post eius vero obitum ipsa ecclesia de Meapeham cum omnibus his que ad eam pertinent quiete, integre, et inconcusse remanebit usibus pauperum, sicut dictum est, in perpetuum deputata. Et ut hec donatio nostra perpetue firmitatis robur obtineat, eam sigilli nostri munimine confirmamus, sub interminatione anathematis prohibentes nequis id quod tam pie et misericorditer actum est temerario ausu debeat perturbare. Qui autem hoc egerit, noverit se iram et indignationem omnipotentis dei gravius incursurum.

[a] sancte CD; sante B   [b] *add* Unde est C

The date of this and the next act is probably fixed by the related deed of prior Herlewin, not earlier than June 1177 (cf. below, no. 88n.).

88. Canterbury: Christ Church

Protection for Virgil, parson of Meopham, in his incumbency of the church, subject to conditions made when the archbishop granted the church to Christ Church, Canterbury, to be assigned to the almonry after Virgil's death. [June × Dec. 1177]

B = Lambeth Palace, Cart. misc. XIII/15 (Ch. Ch. almonry cartulary, fragm.) fo. 10r. s. xiv in.

Ricardus dei gratia Cantuariensis archiepiscopus totius Anglie primas et apostolice sedis legatus universis sancte matris ecclesie filiis salutem. Noverit universitas vestra quod cum ecclesiam de Meapeham, Virgilio eiusdem ecclesie persona prebente assensum, ad elemosinariam Cantuariensis ecclesie post ipsius Virgilii decessum deputaverimus et eandem elemosinario pensionariam fecerimus, in nullo volumus predicti Virgilii iura diminui sed ea illi omnia integra et illibata conservari. Ita quidem prebuit idem Virgilius assensum quod in predicta ecclesia de Meapeham perpetua persona permaneat et salvo personatu suo et salva confirmatione quam inde vel a nobis habet vel a domino papa Alexandro, elemosinario Cantuariensis ecclesie bisantium unum annuatim persolvat. Licet igitur predictam ecclesiam de Meapeham non resignaverit, tamen propter exquisitas malignantium versutias eandem ei cum omnibus decimis et omnimodis obventionibus, tam curie monachorum quam etiam totius parrochie, tam in blado quam etiam de nutrimentis animalium et omnium aliarum rerum obventionibus, iterato confirmamus et sigilli nostri munimine roboramus, sub interminatione anathematis inhibentes nequis eidem Virgilio quicquam de predicte ecclesie obventionibus subtrahat vel in aliquo illius iura minuere vel eum in aliquo iniuste molestare presumat. Testibus: Walerano archidiacono,[a] Willelmo de Norhalle, Willelmo de Sotindune, Rogero de Norwico, magistro Amicio,[b] et aliis multis.

[a] Testes Waleranus archidiaconus B   [b] Amico B

In a complementary deed H(erlewinus) prior and the convent of Christ Church announce that at the prayers and demands of pope Alexander III the archbp instituted Virgil the clerk as parson, and they confirm his tenure of the church on the conditions stated above. Virgil has sworn fealty to the prior and convent and they have taken him under their protection as their clerk (Canterbury, D. & C. C.A. M 124). Virgil's life-interest was safeguarded in the composition between archbp Hubert and the convent in Nov. 1200, but the eventual rights of the almonry in the church were then reduced to a third of the tithes and other appurtenances (below, no. 383).

The archbp's act can probably be dated by the tenure of the prior, and the witness of William of Northolt, not yet archdn.

89. Canterbury: Christ Church

Confirmation for Christ Church, Canterbury, of the grant of the church of (Bircham) Tofts made by Roger of Tofts and confirmed by bishop William of Norwich, whose charter the archbishop has inspected.

[? June 1177 × Aug. 1179]

B = Canterbury, D. & C. Reg. E fo. 398r (406r (in red), 405r, 340r). s. xiii ex. C = Ibid. Reg. B fo. 217r (219r). s. xiv/xv. D = Ibid. Reg. B fo. 399v (402v, 407v). s. xiv/xv. E = Ibid. Reg. D fo. 505r, very imperfect text, margins lost. s. xv.

Ricardus dei gratia Cantuariensis archiepiscopus totius Anglie primas et apostolice sedis legatus universis sancte matris ecclesie filiis ad quos presentes littere pervenerint eternam in domino salutem. Ex scripto autentico W. pie recordationis quondam Norwicensis episcopi cognovimus Rogerum[a] de Thoftes[b] quantum iuris habebat in ecclesia eiusdem ville liberum et ab omni reclamatione absolutum in manu eiusdem episcopi reliquisse, ipsumque episcopum eandem ecclesiam sancte Cantuariensi ecclesie, salvo iure Norwicensis ecclesie ac consuetudinibus ab eadem annuatim ei prestandis indempniter observatis, cum omnibus pertinentiis suis perpetuo possidendam concessisse et confirmasse. Nos itaque eandem concessionem et confirmationem canonice factam ea qua fungimur auctoritate confirmamus et presenti carta cum sigilli nostri appositione roboramus. Testibus: Walerano Baiocensi et Willelmo Glocestriensi archidiaconis, Henrico Baiocensi, Rogero Norwicensi, Willelmo de Sotindun' et aliis.

[a] Rogerum C; Reginaldum BDE   [b] Thoftes B; Toftes CDE

The similarity of witness-lists in nos. 89 and 90 suggests that both were prepared at the same time, and the priorate of Herlewin gives limits of date for no. 90. The church is that of St Andrew, Bircham Tofts, deanery of Heacham. The pension to Christ Church is recorded in 1254 in *The valuation of Norwich*, ed. W. E. Lunt (1926) 407 and in 1291 in *Taxatio pp. Nicholai IV* (Record Comm. 1802) 89a. The charter of bp William which confirmed the churches of Deopham and Tofts to Christ Church (see above, no. 80 n.) was confirmed by bp John I in 1181 (Reg. E fo. 398r, B fo. 216v and 399v, D fo. 505r).

90. Canterbury: Christ Church

Confirmation of the settlement in the archbishop's presence of a dispute between the prior and convent of Christ Church and Roger of Tofts about the church of (Bircham) Tofts. Roger has admitted that the church was given in perpetual alms to Christ Church. Prior Herlewin with the assent of his convent has granted that Roger shall have the right to present to them a vicar whom they will present to the bishop of Norwich for institution, and the vicar shall pay a pension of four shillings yearly to Christ Church.   [June 1177 × Aug. 1179]

A = Canterbury, D. & C. C.A. T 35 (A 88). Endorsed, s. xii/xiii: XII (*del.*); s. xiii in.: Cirografum inter nos et Rogerum de Toftes; s. xiii/xiv: Confirmacio Ric' archiepiscopi *and* De presentacione vicarie ecclesie de Toftes (all in middle of dorse). Approx. 194 × 180 + 15 mm. Sealing d.q. 2; tag and seal lost. Scribe **II**. Top half of chirograph, inverted, divided by a straight cut.

B = Ibid. Reg. E fo. 398r (406r, 405r, 340r). s. xiii ex. C = Ibid. Reg. B fo. 217r (219r). s. xiv/xv. D = Ibid. Reg. B fo. 400r (403r, 408r). s. xiv/xv. E = Ibid. Reg. D fo. 505v, badly damaged, margins lost, breaks off incomplete at foot of folio. s. xv.

CYROGRAPHUM

Ric(ardus) dei gratia Cantuariensis archiepiscopus totius Anglie primas et apostolice sedis legatus . universis Christi fidelibus . eternam in domino salutem. Notum sit omnibus tam presentibus quam posteris . quod causa que vertebatur inter conventum ecclesie Christi Cantuariensis et Rogerum de Toftes . super ecclesia de Toftes ⁒ hoc fine conquievit. Predictus siquidem Rogerus in presentia nostra constitutus ⁒ coram pluribus viris honestis et discretis confessus est . quod bone memorie Willelmus quondam Norwicensis episcopus ad representationem ipsius Rogeri concesserat ipsam ecclesiam de Toftes ecclesie Christi Cantuariensi et fratribus monachis ibidem deo famulantibus in perpetuam elemosinam . et carta sua quam oculis nostris perspeximus confirmaverat. Prior vero ecclesie Cantuariensis Herlewinus . de assensu conventus ⁒ propter bonum pacis et ut omnis controversia inter conventum ecclesie Christi Cantuariensis et ipsum Rogerum et heredes suos sopiretur ⁒ eidem Rogero concessit . quod vicarium quem ipse Rogerus et heredes sui prefato priori Cantuariensis ecclesie et conventui idoneum presentaverint ⁒ sine dolo et malo ingenio recipient . et eum Norwicensi episcopo instituendum in perpetuum vicarium eiusdem ecclesie de Toftes presentabunt . qui vicarius .IIII. solidos annuatim conventui ecclesie Christi Cantuariensis fideliter in festo beati Iohannis baptiste vel infra octavas perpetua pensione persolvet . ita ut de eadem ecclesia nunquam amplius exiget conventus ecclesie Christi Cantuariensis ⁒ preter hanc statutam pensionem . neque eosdem .IIII. solidos alicui persone extra ecclesiam Cantuariensem assignabunt . neque alium vicarium presentabunt episcopo Norwicensi ad eam ecclesiam instituendum ⁒ nisi illum quem sepedictus Rogerus vel heredes sui eis idoneum presentaverint . neque Rogerus vel heredes sui alium nisi quem prior et conventus ecclesie Cantuariensis ad eorum representationem idoneum receperint ⁒ ad eandem ecclesiam de Toftes in vicarium vel personam aliquatenus presentabunt. Hanc quoque conventionem sine dolo et malo ingenio tenendam memoratus Rogerus fide interposita firmavit firmiter et inviolabiliter observandam. Et ut ipsa futuris temporibus perpetuam obtineat firmitatem ⁒ presenti scripto eam confirmamus et sigilli nostri patrocinio communimus. Testibus . Walerano archidiacono Baiocensi . Willelmo archidiacono Glouecestriensi . Henrico Baiocensi . Willelmo de Sottindon' . Rogero elemosinario . Rogero Norwicensi . et aliis multis.

C. A. T 34 is the original of a notification by prior Herlewin and the convent of Christ Church of this settlement with Roger of Tofts, probably issued at the same time as no. 90. Both T 34 and T 35 show the donor's name to have been Roger, not Reginald, as in some of the cartulary copies of nos. 89 and 90. For a charter of bp William of Norwich, including both Deopham and Tofts, see above, no. 80n.

91. Canterbury: abbey of St Augustine

Confirmation for the monks of St Augustine's, Canterbury, of the churches of Minster in Thanet, Northbourne, and Chislet, appropriated of old to various uses of the monastery and confirmed to those uses by various popes. [? Poitiers. *c*.8 March 1183]

> B = BL ms. Cotton Claud. D x (Red book of St Augustine's) fo. 264r (267r). s. xiii/xiv. C = BL ms. Cotton Julius D ii (register of St Augustine's) fo. 76v (69v) no. 130. s. xiii med. D = Lambeth Palace, Reg. W. Warham fo. 94r (96r). s. xvi in. E = ibid. fo. 96v (98v), only first name of witness-list copied.

Ricardus dei gratia Cantuariensis archiepiscopus totius Anglie primas universis sancte matris ecclesie filiis presens scriptum visuris vel audituris salutem in domino. Ea que pietatem continent misericordie visceribus amplexari volumus ut debemus, et que ad virorum religiosorum sustentationem provide statuuntur nos qui sancte religionis sumus professores omnimodam volumus habere firmitatem. Cum igitur in monasterio sancti Augustini Cantuarie ecclesie de Menstre et de Northburn' et de Cistelet ob evidentes necessitates ad diversos usus eiusdem monasterii ab antiquo fuerint assignate et a diversis Romanis pontificibus ad eosdem usus pure confirmate, nos dilectorum filiorum abbatis et conventus prefati monasterii precibus inclinati divine caritatis intuitu et sancte religionis, quam in prefato loco vigere novimus et credimus in futuro, ad prefatos usus dictas ecclesias cum omnibus pertinentiis suis deo et beato Augustino confirmamus. In cuius rei testimonium presenti [fo. 264v] scripto sigillum nostrum fecimus apponi. Hiis testibus: domino W. Rofensi episcopo, magistro G. Pucella, magistro Rogero de Rolveston*ᵃ*, magistro R. Blundo, magistro Radulfo de Forda, et multis aliis.

ᵃ Rolveston: Ramstone B; Fulvistun C; Ravistun D

The churches of Minster and Northbourne were already confirmed to St Augustine's in several bulls (JL 10129, 12436, 12711, 13535), but no earlier confirmation for Chislet is among the abbey's papalia; Chislet was confirmed by Celestine III in 1195 (*PUE* i 626–7 no. 326). Limits of date are set by the absence of the legatine title and the presence of Gerard Pucella, not yet elected to the bpric of Coventry. If W. bp of Rochester is Waleran the charter is later than 19 Dec. 1182. In fact, the witness-list suggests the same occasion as the 'pax et concordia' reached in the royal court at Poitiers 8 March 1183 between archbp

Richard and abbot Roger of St Augustine's. (The abbey chronicler says that the archbp's confirmation of the three churches was in the same year as the composition: Twysden 1837). According to the composition the archbp undertook not to impugn the authenticity of the ancient privileges of the abbey and renounced a claim to profession of obedience by the abbot; and the abbot recognized the rights of the archbp and archdn in churches belonging to the abbey, except for Minster, Northbourne, Chislet, Milton and Faversham. While this composition — dated 'anno ab incarn. domini mclxxxii oct. id. Martii apud Pictaviam' — is framed within an inspeximus charter of kg Henry II, the thirteen witnesses are all clerics, mostly of the archbp's circle: bps Henry of Bayeux and Waleran of Rochester, Mr Gerard Pucella, Mr Peter and Henry archdns of Bath and Bayeux, Mr Stephen Remensis, Mr Robert Blund, Mr Roger of Rolleston, Mr Peter Gay, Mr Ralph de Forde, Mr Ralph de Esseburn, Henry of Bayeux, William of Shottenden (Elmham 449–52 and — without witnesses — Twysden 1836–7. Other abbey registers contain the text: PRO E 164/27 fo. 141r (145r), BL ms. Cotton Julius D ii fo. 74r (67r) no. 122, and Cambridge, Gonv. and Caius Coll. ms. 238(124) fo. 147r. It was kept in the archbp's archives among *Tituli compositionum* 'in vase x°' no. I (see the list in Lambeth Palace ms. 1212 fo.6r (p.11). For the circumstances and results of the composition see E. John, *BJRL* xxxix (1957) 395–7.

92. Canterbury: priory of St Gregory

Confirmation for the prior and canons of St Gregory, Canterbury, which specially pertains to the archbishop's lordship, of the possessions which they now lawfully hold or may acquire in future. There are specified the twelve daily prebends due to them from the hospital of Northgate, and the churches, tithes, lands, and other possessions are enumerated. [28 April 1174 × Sept. 1181]

B = Cambridge UL ms. Ll 2 15 (cartulary of St Gregory's) fo. 9rb. s. xiii med.
Pd from B in *St Gregory's cartulary* 11–12 no. 15.

Hiis testibus: Walerano Baiocensi archidiacono, magistro Roberto de Inglesham, Henrico Baiocensi, Moysi capellano, Iohanne capellano, Ricardo et Galfrido capellanis, Willelmo de Sotindon', et aliis.

The archbp is styled legate. For description of the priory's possessions see *Cart.* pp. ix–xix, 177–80 and Urry, *Canterbury*. The charter lists the possessions which had been confirmed by archbp Theobald in 1145 × 1146 in the same order and words, and its arenga is reminiscent of Theobald's charter (*Cart.* 10 no. 14, Saltman, *Theobald* 285–6 no. 59). In the copy of Theobald's charter 'decima de Goldstanestone' is missing before 'decima de Gosehale' (Goss Hall), probably omitted in error, since it appears in the privilege of pope Eugenius III, 10 Dec. 1146, based on Theobald's act (*Cart.* 19–20 no. 25; *PUE* iii 184 no. 59). Richard's charter may have used both Theobald's and the papal privilege in its drafting; and it adds at the end of the possessions listed by Theobald and Eugenius the churches of Bekesbourne, Nackington, and Stalisfield. These additions do not appear in the undated privilege of Alexander III (*Cart.* 20–22 no. 26; *PUE* iii 497–8 no. 282). That privilege adds to the entry for St Bartholomew of Waltham 'et cum capella S. Iacobi de Elmstede', which had already been confirmed to the canons by archbp Theobald in or after 1150 (*Cart.* 4 no. 4; Saltman, *Theobald* 288 no. 62). The claim that the priory was under the direct lordship of the archbp had been stated by Theobald (loc. cit.) and was later included in a privilege of Innocent III (1199) for the see of Canterbury (*Letters of Innocent III* 205–6 no. 160). The two witnesses, Richard and Geoffrey, appear in no other acta of archbp Richard as chaplains, but very often as clerks.

93. Canterbury: priory of St Gregory

Notification that Eustace de Burnes has resigned to the archbishop his right to the patronage of the church of St Peter, Bekesbourne, and Michael, his brother, whom the archbishop had instituted as its parson, has resigned his parsonage. At their request the archbishop has confirmed the patronage and parsonage of the church to the prior and canons of St Gregory, Canterbury. [28 April 1174 × 9 Oct. 1182]

B = BL ms. Harl. 7048 (Thomas Baker's transcripts) fo. 176r. s. xviii in., abridged copy of lost leaf of Cambridge, UL ms. Ll 2 15 (cartulary of St Gregory's).

Pd from B in *St Gregory's cartulary* 28 no. 37 note.

Testibus: Walerano Baiocensi archidiacono, magistro Petro Blesensi, etc.

An abbreviated title, which does not show the archbp's style, follows a general address.

Archdn Waleran was elected to the see of Rochester 9 or 10 Oct. 1182. Eustace's charter, given with Michael's consent, records the grant as being made by him directly to the prior and canons, in their chapter-house; it does not mention the archbp (*St Gregory's cartulary* 28–29 no. 37). The advowson of Bekesbourne was the subject of a case in the kg's court in 1190 between Eustace de Burnes and William del Bec, who jointly held land in Bekesbourne (otherwise Livingeburne) by serjeanty. The latter quit-claimed the advowson to Eustace and by a separate deed annulled charters by which his father and he had given the church to the church of Holy Trinity, Hastings or to the Hospitallers or others, and recognized the previous gift of the church by Eustace to St Gregory's (ibid. 29–30 nos. 38–9). Holy Trinity, Hastings likewise relinquished all claim on the church to St Gregory's (ibid. 121 no. 164, cf. 157, 160 nos. 218, 222).

94. Canterbury: priory of St Gregory

Notification that Ailgar priest of Wootton has made a composition with Richard prior and the canons of St Gregory, Canterbury, about the tithes of Wootton. Ailgar shall hold them for his lifetime, giving to the canons one mark of silver yearly. [7 April 1175 × 24 March 1176]

B = BL ms. Harl. 7048 (Thomas Baker's transcripts) fo. 176r. s. xviii in. Abridged copy of lost leaf of Cambridge UL ms. Ll 2 15 (cartulary of St Gregory's).

Pd from B in *St Gregory's cartulary* 11 n.1.

Facta est autem haec compositio apud Cantuariam anno ab incarnatione domini MCLXXV ordinationis autem nostrae secundo. Hiis testibus: magistro Gerardo, Walerano Baiocensi archidiacono, magistro Petro Blesensi.

With an abbreviated title, which does not show the archbp's style.

95.   Canterbury: priory of the Holy Sepulchre

Confirmation for the nuns of St Sepulchre's priory, Canterbury, of the church of St Edmund Ridingate, Canterbury, of which Hamo of Stourmouth has resigned his right as patron into the archbishop's hand, requesting him to transfer the patronage to the nuns.

[6 Aug. 1179 × Sept. 1181]

B = Lambeth Palace, Reg. W. Warham fo. 132v (136v). s. xvi in.

Ricardus dei gratia Cantuariensis archiepiscopus totius Anglie primas et apostolice sedis legatus universis sancte matris ecclesie filiis ad quos presentes littere pervenerint eternam in domino salutem. Notum fieri volumus universitati vestre quod Hamo miles de Sturmue in nostra presentia constitutus quicquid iure patronatus in ecclesia sancti Edmundi de Radingat' Cant' possidebat spontanea voluntate in manu nostra resignavit, postulans a nobis humiliter ut pietatis*a* intuitu ius patronatus*b* prelibate ecclesie in ecclesiam sancti Sepulcri Cant' transferremus. Nos itaque ipsius petitioni annuentes universum ius advocationis quod prefatus miles Hamo de Sturmue in*c* iamdicta habebat ecclesia memorate ecclesie sancti Sepulcri in subsidium monialium ibidem deo iugiter famulantium in perpetuam contulimus elemosinam, ita libere, plenarie, et honorifice possidendum sicut unquam idem Hamo vel eius antecessores plenius et melius possedisse dinoscitur. Ut igitur hec nostra donatio firma in perpetuum et inconvulsa permaneat, presentis eam scripti patrocinio communimus et sigilli nostri appositione roboramus, sub interminatione anathematis districtius inhibentes nequis prefatas moniales in iure suo in prescripta ecclesia temere perturbare presumat. Hiis testibus : Benedicto abbate Burgi, Alano priore Cantuariensi, Willelmo Glouecestriensi archidiacono, magistro Radulpho de Sancto Martino, magistro Roberto de Inglesham, Willelmo de Sotindon, Ricardo clerico de Lund', Hamone clerico, Alexandro, Rogerio sacerdote, Ivone de Mares, Godefrido de Tannit', Radulpho pincerna, Willelmo de Yfeld', Ricardo camerario prioris, Helia de Siling', Iohanne Haringod et fratribus eius, Alexandro Walensi, Rogerio decano et aliis.

a pietatis: pietatus B   *b* ius patronatus: patronatus patronat' B   *c om.* in B

Prior Alan of Christ Church was elected 6 Aug. 1179. For this Hamo de Stourmouth and his family see Urry, *Canterbury* 51–53, cf. 211–2. The church of St Edmund was founded by his grandfather, Hamo. A charter of abbot Roger of St Augustine's, Canterbury, states that Hamo son of William of Stourmouth has abandoned *to the abbey* any right he claimed in the church of St Edmund Ridingate (*Black Book of St Augustine's, Canterbury* ed. G. J. Turner and H. E. Salter (Brit. Acad. Records of Social and Economic History, 1915, 1924) ii 542). This can be dated during the vacancy of the see of Canterbury, in or after mid-June 1184, by the attestation of Vincent, a clerk of the duchess of Saxony, who arrived with her father, king Henry II, and came to Canterbury *c.*13 June (Eyton, *Itinerary* 256). A second charter of the abbot, dated in the year of incarnation 1184, granted the church of St Edmund in perpetual and free alms to the nuns of St Sepulchre's (*Black Book* ii 542–3).

96. Canterbury: Hospitals of Harbledown and Northgate

Grant to the hospitals of St Nicholas, Harbledown, and St John the baptist, Northgate, Canterbury, of twenty pounds yearly from the church of Reculver which Hugh the parson has resigned, to supplement their original endowment of one hundred and forty pounds from the manors of Reculver and Boughton under Blean.

[25 Sept. 1183 × 16 Feb. 1184]

A = Original, now lost, in 1760 belonged to Rev. Henry Hall, rector of Harbledown (cf. his letter in J. Duncombe, *Hist. and antiquities of Reculver and Herne* (1784) 188–9 in Nichols, *Bibliotheca* vol. I no. xviii). Endorsed, according to B: Donatio xx librarum ex ecclesia de Raculver ultra cxl libras prius concessas ex maneriis de Raculfe et Boctun.

B = Lambeth Palace ms. 1131 pp. 23–24 no. 29.1, copy of A among deeds of Canterbury hospitals copied from originals by Henry Hall, 1763. C = Ibid. ms. 582 p. 53 no. 9. Extracts from A by Henry Wharton. s. xvii ex. D = Canterbury, D. & C. Lit. ms. E 30(i), single sheet. s. xv.

Pd from A by Duncombe, as above and, probably from D, a very inaccurate and abridged copy, in Somner, *Canterbury* App. to suppl. 61 no. xxxv. Pd here from B with selected variants of C and D.

Ricardus dei gratia Cantuariensis archiepiscopus totius Anglie primas universis sancte matris ecclesie filiis ad quos littere iste pervenerint eternam in domino salutem. Res gesta scripto provide commendatur ne processu temporis aut a memoria decedat*a* aut aliqua malignantium versutia infirmetur. Eapropter ad omnium notitiam volumus pervenire quod cum olim bone memorie Lanfrancus predecessor noster duo hospitalia, unum scilicet apud Herbaldowne*b* et aliud apud Cantuariam extra Norgate*c* instituisset et ad sustentationem fratrum, hinc leprosorum illinc claudorum, cecorum, et debilium, septies viginti libras sterlingorum de duobus maneriis videlicet de Racolvere*d* et Boctun' annuatim percipiendas assignasset,[e] tandem ad curam et regimen sancte Cantuariensis ecclesie licet indigni domino tamen disponente vocati, cum predictas septies viginti libras ad sustentationem hospitalium minime sufficere et fratres eorumdem hospitalium gravissima paupertate et inedia videremus laborare, desiderio desideravimus eorum paupertati et insufficientie subvenire. Quod quidem diu in animo volventes et revolventes, commodius et plenius adimpleri posse non credidimus alibi quam in ecclesia de Raculve[f] que in manerio de Raculve fundata est, de quo ex parte maxima redditus predictarum septies xx librarum annuatim provenire debebat. Cum ergo dilectus filius noster Hugo persona eiusdem ecclesie, super hoc diligenter ammonitus, reverenter et devote divina preveniente gratia ammonitionibus nostris obtemperando ecclesiam ipsam libere nobis resignasset, predictis hospitalibus et fratribus eorumdem hospitalium in sepedicta ecclesia viginti libras sterlingorum in festo sancti Iohannis baptiste annuatim percipiendas in liberam et perpetuam elemosinam concessimus[g] et assignavimus, ita quidem quod residuum fructuum ipsius ecclesie in nostra et successorum nostrorum manu et potestate residebit [p. 24] secundum deum sicut nobis placuerit disponendum. Unde volumus et ea qua fungimur auctoritate precipimus quod predicta hospitalia et fratres in eis degentes habeant et percipiant annuatim sicut diximus in prenominata ecclesia xx libras sterlingorum. Et ut hec nostra donatio firma et inconvulsa permaneat, eam presenti scripto et sigilli nostri appositione decrevimus confirmare, statuentes et sub interminatione anathematis prohibentes ne quis hanc nostre confirmationis paginam infringere vel ei aliquatenus temere contraire presumat. Testibus his: Gerardo episcopo et Moyse priore Coventr', magistro Petro Blesensi Batthoniensi, Willelmo Gloecestriensi archidiaconis, magistro Henrico Northamton', Willelmo et Honorio capellanis, magistro Roberto de Inglesham,[h] magistro R. de Rulvestun', magistro Radulfo de Sancto Martino, magistro Rogero Norwicensi, Rogero decano, magistro Aimerico, Thoma de Niwesole, Ricardo Lundoniensi, Galfrido Forti, Eustachio elemosinario, Michaele[j] de Burnes, Willelmo Sotewaine,[k] et pluribus aliis.

[a] decedat B; decidat D   [b] Herbaldowne CD; Herebald' B   [c] Norgate BC; Northgate D   [d] Racolvere CD; Raculve B   [e] add nos. and om. all before predictis hospitalibus C   [f] Racolvere D; Raculve B   [g] concessimus B; contulimus D   [h] Inglesham D; Ingleham B   [j] Michaele D; Michale B   [k] Sotewaine B; de Nonynton D

Gerard Pucella was consecrated bp of Coventry 25 Sept. 1183.

A table of contents in Lambeth Palace ms. 1212 (s. xiii), which refers to texts no longer in this register, includes: 'Ordinatio eiusdem R. archiepiscopi de pensione C marcarum assignata hospitali de Northgate de ecclesia de Raculvere' (fo. 4r (p. 7) no. lxxv). This is hard to square with the above grant, unless 100 marks represented the share of Northgate hospital in the benefaction.

*97. Canterbury: Hospital of St John, Northgate

Grant of indulgence of forty days to benefactors of the brethren and sisters of Northgate hospital, Canterbury.

[? 7 April 1174 × 16 Feb. 1184]

Mentioned only, in a list of indulgences granted by archbps Lanfranc, Thomas, Stephen, Theobald, Richard, and Edmund (in that order), contained in letters patent prepared for the hospital's questor to publicize, 29 June 1375.

Pd in J. Duncombe and N. Battely, *Hist. and antiquities of the three archiepiscopal hospitals and other charitable foundations at and near Canterbury* (1785) 254 (in Nichols, *Bibliotheca* vol. i no. XXX), from the muniments of Northgate hospital, destroyed in June 1942.

All the indulgences, including that of the founder, archbp Lanfranc, are said to be for forty days; this is greatly in excess of indulgences granted elsewhere by the archbps before the thirteenth century. It is possible that the Richard here listed was archbp Richard (II) le Grant (1229–31).

98. Castle Acre priory

Notification that Richard son of Jocelin of Fleet confirmed in the archbishop's presence his father's gift of the church of Fleet to the monks of Acre, and presented one of the monks to the archbishop to receive it in perpetual possession in the name of the church of Acre. The archbishop confirmed the church to the monks of Acre in perpetuity.

[May 1177 × Sept. 1181]

B = BL ms. Harl. 2110 (Castle Acre cartulary) fo. 119r (113r). s. xiii in.

Ricardus dei gratia Cantuariensis archiepiscopus totius Anglie primas et apostolice sedis legatus*a* 'universis' Christi fidelibus ad quos presentes littere pervenerint eternam in domino salutem. Ad universitatis vestre notitiam volumus pervenire quod Ricardus filius Iocelini ad nos accedens publice confessus est quod pater eius Iocelinus de Fleta concesserat et dederat atque carta sua confirmaverat monachis de Acra ecclesiam de Flete cum universis pertinentiis suis in perpetuam elemosinam, quodque ipse Ricardus eandem concessionem et donationem atque confirmationem patris sui ratam habebit et firmam et eam voluit robur perpetuum obtinere. Set et ipse Ricardus quemdam monachum de Acra in manu nostra posuit, ut nomine ecclesie de Acre perpetuam eiusdem ecclesie de Flete possessionem retineret. Nos igitur ipsius devotionem approbantes, ipsam ecclesiam de Fleta memoratis monachis de Acra duximus auctoritate qua fungimur in perpetuum confirmandam. Testibus: magistro Gerardo*b*, Walerano archidiacono Baiocensi, Willelmo archidiacono Gloucestriensi, magistro Roberto de Inglesham, Henrico Baiocensi, Willelmo de Sottindon, Rogero decano, Rogero Norwic', Ricardo et Gaufrido clericis, et multis aliis.

a et ap. sed. legatus *roughly erased in* B (*as elsewhere in this cartulary*)
b Gerad' B

> After William of Northolt became archdn of Gloucester, May × Dec. 1177; probably at a time when the bp-elect of Lincoln (Geoffrey) was absent from his diocese. Jocelin's grant of the church to Castle Acre is in the cartulary (fo. 76v (70v)), also successive confirmations by bp Robert II of Lincoln (*EEA* i no. 94) and archbp Theobald (Saltman, *Theobald* 290–1 nos. 64–65).

99. Chester abbey

Confirmation for St Werburgh's abbey, Chester, of the church of Bebington, given by Robert Launcelyn with four bovates of land, half of the church of Wallasey given by William de Waley, an annual rent of eight shillings from the church of Handley given by Helto de Boydel, the church of Astbury given by William de Venables, and the church of Prestbury given by earl Hugh of Chester.

[7 April 1174 × 15 Feb. 1184]

> Abstract only.
> B = BL ms. Harl. 1965 (Chester cartulary) fo. 10r. s. xiv in.
> Pd from B in *Chester chartulary* i 127–8 no. 96.

100. Chester abbey

Confirmation for the chapel of the blessed martyr Thomas in Wirral of all its possessions, specially one carucate of land and half of the site (loci) of a mill, a fishery, and part of a wood which Randulf Walensis and Bernard his brother gave to the chapel, saving the right of the mother church of Bebington.   [7 April 1174 × 15 Feb. 1184]

> Abstract only.
> B = BL ms. Harl. 1965 (Chester cartulary) fo. 10r. s. xiv in.
> Pd from B in *Chester chartulary* i 126 no. 91.

101. Chester abbey

Grant for St Werburgh's abbey, Chester, of the protection of the church of Canterbury for all its possessions, forbidding unjust interference with

the church or its monks and ordering payment of its rents at their stated
terms.   [7 April 1174 × 15 Feb. 1184]

Abstract only.

B = BL ms. Harl. 1965 (Chester cartulary) fo. 10r. s. xiv in.

Pd from B in *Chester chartulary* i 127 no. 94.

102. Chester abbey

Confirmation for St Werburgh's abbey, Chester, of the church of
Neston with the right of patronage thereof acquired by the gift and
presentation of Ralph of Mold, as confirmed by bishop Richard of
Coventry.   [Oct. 1181 × Oct. 1182]

B = BL ms. Harl. 2071 (fragment of Chester cartulary) fo. 38r (24r). s. xiii ex.

Pd from B in *Chester chartulary* i 121 no. 81.

Testibus: magistro Girardo, Willelmo archidiacono Gloecestriensi,
magistro Roberto de Inglesham, magistro Rogero de Rovelveston',
Willelmo de Sottendon', Rogero decano, Galfrido clerico, Iohanne
de River', Ricardo de London'.

The archbp is not styled legate. Bp Richard of Coventry is alive.

103. The church of Chichester

Grant of an indulgence of forty days for those who visit the church of
Chichester with contrite hearts and with performance of good works, on
the feast of St Denis, which is the feast of relics, or within the octave.
Visitors shall share the benefit of prayers said in the church of
Canterbury.   [28 April 1174 × Sept. 1181]

B = Chichester, West Sussex Record Office, Diocesan archives, Ep. vi/1/6
('Liber Y') fo. 80r (24r). s. xiii med.

Pd (calendar) from B in *Chichester chartulary* 19 no. 74.

R. dei gratia Cantuariensis archiepiscopus totius Anglie primas et
apostolice sedis legatus universis Christi fidelibus ad quos presentes
littere pervenerint eternam in domino salutem. Ad eorum gratiam
nobis conciliandam tota mentis devotione debemus aspirare quorum meritis et precibus ad illa permansura lucis eterne gaudia
speramus pervenire, ut quod nostra non valet infirmitas eorum
intercessionibus de meritorum nostrorum exigentia consequamur.
Hii sunt viri sancti quos elegit dominus in caritate non ficta, quos
constituit in circuitu suo in splendore luminis quod nunquam
deficiet, ubi sunt lucidissime mansiones, ubi requiescunt sanctorum

anime, de quibus scriptum est: Pro Christo certamen habuerunt in seculo, mercedem laborum suorum retribuam, dicit dominus. Hii sunt quos dominus in terris voluit coruscare miraculis ut in eis ad laudem et honorem nominis sui cresceret ecclesia et fidelium multitudo, et qui in fide vacillantes invenirentur infirmi certis fidei argumentis spe quoque illius celestis [fo. 80v] glorie in constantia fidei roborarentur. Horum quasdam reliquias transtulit devotio fidelium ad ecclesias per orbem terrarum diffusas ut in singulis ecclesiis singule fidelium congregationes aliquod memoriale sanctorum haberent, in quorum veneratione corda fidelium ad ignem divine amoris accenderentur et caritas incensa magis ac magis in eis habundaret. Inter quas ecclesia Cycestrensis, in nomine sancte et individue Trinitatis fundata, plurimorum sanctorum illustrata reliquiis in earum dulcedine interius affluens delictis ad earumdem prout decet exaltationem et summam venerationem iugi desiderio invigilat et studiosius intendit. In votis siquidem habent et in proposito dilecti filii nostri eiusdem ecclesie canonici quod ad honorem et gloriam nominis Christiani in festo sancti Dionisii [9 Oct.] sanctorum reliquias que in Cycestrensi continentur ecclesia cum debita sollempnitate publicabunt, ut ex publicatione[a] facta in communem veniat notitiam quibus et quantis eadem ecclesia gaudeat patronis, et exinde tam mentes eorum qui in eadem ecclesia iugiter deo deserviunt quam aliorum Christi fidelium ad ampliorem eiusdem loci venerationem excitentur. Attendendum est itaque, filii dilectissimi, nos qui Christiane professionis nomine censemur[b], quod cum non habeamus hic manentem civitatem, expedit nobis summo opere salutis nostre auctorem in venerationem sanctorum suorum in elemosinis, vigiliis, ieiuniis et orationibus nobis efficere propitium, ut nostre misertus captivitatis ad illam celestem Ierusalem nos perducere dignetur, ubi in domo patris sui mansiones multe sunt, ubi perpetue sunt lucis et temporum eternitates. Universitatem igitur vestram ex officii nostri debito rogamus, monemus et ad salutem animarum vestrarum exhortamur attentius ut ad prenominatum diem sancti Dionisii in spiritu humiliato et corde contrito ecclesiam Cycestrensem ad honorem sancte et individue Trinitatis cum ea que decet reverentia visitare studeatis et auxilium eorum quorum reliquiarum sollempnia in eadem ecclesia publicabuntur bonis operibus et votivis orationibus vobis inplorare satagatis quatinus, intercedentibus sanctis quorum reliquiarum sollempnia celebrabuntur, indulgeat deus vobis veniam delictorum et eam in vobis augeat devotionem, ut meritis eorum ad celestem valeatis pervenire societatem. Nos autem de divina misericordia et meritis

sanctorum quorum reliquiarum sollempnia in prefata ecclesia co-
lentur in Christo confidentes, omnibus qui prescripta sollempni die
vel in octavis et infra ecclesiam Cycestrensem in ea que decet cordis
contritione et bonorum operum exhibitione visitaverint, confessis
videlicet et vere penitentibus, de iniuncta sibi penitentia XL dies
relaxamus et orationum que fiunt in ecclesia Cantuariensi participes
esse concedimus. Valete.

a ex publicatione: exp^catione B   *b* censemur: censemini B

104. Cirencester abbey

Confirmation for the canons of Cirencester in free and perpetual alms of
the church of Marston (Bigot) with all its appurtenances, as granted to
them by bishop Reginald of Bath and Richard son of Odo, patron
(advocatus) of the church.   [23 June 1174 × May 1177]

> B = Bodl., loan from Lord Vestey, Stowell Park, Cirencester Reg. A fo. 158r. s.
> xiii med.
>
> Pd from B in *Cirencester cartulary* ii 519 no. 606.

Hiis testibus: magistro Gerardo, Walerano archidiacono Baiocensi,
magistro P. Blesensi, magistro Hugone de Suwell'*a*, magistro R. de
Inglesham, magistro Radulfo de Sancto Martino, magistro Rogero
Norwicensi, Amicio et Willelmo clericis, et multis aliis.

> *a* Duwell' B

> The archbp is styled legate. Bp Reginald was consecrated by the archbp 23 June
> 1174 at St-Jean-de-Maurienne. The donor of the church had died by 1173. His
> charter (*c.*1160 × 1173) and the confirmation by bp Reginald are in the cartulary
> (ii 519–20 nos. 605, 607). Mr Hugh de Suwell was unlikely to appear in this
> company after a papal mandate, *c.*April 1177, was received by the archbp of York
> and bp of Durham, which ordered the deprivation and imprisonment of Mr
> Hugh 'de Suellis' for forgery (G. V. Scammell, *Hugh du Puiset, bishop of Durham*
> (Cambridge 1956) 251).

105. Cirencester abbey

Notification of proceedings in a case between Reginald and Randulf,
priests of Cheltenham. Randulf produced a papal mandate to the
archbishop to hear without appeal his claim against Reginald over
unjust spoliation of a certain benefice and failure to observe an
agreement (transactio). *The archbishop summoned the parties before*
him, took evidence for Reginald, and appointed a day for a second
production of Reginald's witnesses. At the second hearing Reginald
appeared but Randulf neither came nor sent excuse. The archbishop has
therefore proceeded no further in execution of the mandate.

[late 1174 × Sept. 1181]

B = Bodl., loan by Lord Vestey, Stowell Park, Reg. A fo. 122r. s. xiii med.
C = Ibid., Reg. B fo. 112r. s. xiv ex.

Pd from B and C in *Cirencester cartulary* ii 381 no. 424/455.

The archbp is styled legate.

The dispute concerned a portion or vicarage in the church of Cheltenham. Before or after this episode (probably earlier) Randulf got a papal mandate to bp John of Chichester as judge delegate which resulted in his surrendering any claim on the vicarage in return for payment of four marks by Reginald (*Cirencester cartulary* ii 380–1 no. 423/454). Later litigation over the church before judges delegate between Reginald and Cirencester, which had longstanding claims on the church, is recorded in the cartulary.

106. Abbey of Cîteaux

Complaint to the abbot and convent of Cîteaux that their admirable religious Order has a bad reputation for greed. Everyone blames them for grasping the property of others and for taking away tithes due to monks and clerks. Why do they get exemption from tithe-paying on land which previously was liable to tithe? Why should others suffer this loss because land has come into their possession? In France the knightly class usurp tithes and disregard Cistercian privilege. It is against such usurpers as these, not against the clergy and their churches, that the monks should be up in arms. The archbishop does not 'set his mouth against the heavens' nor dispute the lord pope's action; but a privilege which the pope once gave them when their Order was poor could then be tolerated as a matter of necessity; it should not apply now that they are richly endowed with possessions. By making restitution they will gain a better reputation and attract more endowments. If they are inflexible the archbishop will excommunicate all who grant them or sell them titheable property. He has the favour of lay princes, so that the spiritual sword may be supported by the lay arm. If, as pope Adrian IV provided, their exemption were confined to newly-cultivated lands, it would be more tolerable because clergy had not derived profit from them in the past.   [Aug. 1174 × Sept. 1181]

Petri Blesensis opera i 247–51 ep. 82; *PL* ccvii 252–55.

The archbp is styled legate.

See the extracts from and comments on this letter by Giles Constable, *Monastic tithes from their origins to the twelfth century* (Cambridge 1964) 292–4, who notes textual similarities in John of Salisbury's *Policraticus* lib. 7 c.21. For Alexander III's attitude see Constable, 294–303. English prelates preparing agenda for the provincial council of Westminster, 1175, seem to have put down this topic: 'Monachi albi non presumant amodo detinere decimas quas colunt in parochiis ecclesiarum quas eedem habere solebant' (Wilkins, *Concilia* i 474 c.2, cf. M. G. Cheney in *Studies in church history* xi (1975) 61–63). In 1180 the

General Chapter admitted that the Cistercian retention of tithes was a cause of scandal (Constable, 303). Cf. the archbp's confirmation of a composition over tithe made between Boxley abbey and the monks of Rochester, patrons of Boxley parish church, in 1180 (below, no. 196).

107. Colchester abbey

Mandate addressed to the archbishop's suffragans in whose dioceses the monks of St John the baptist, Colchester, have possessions, and to their archdeacons, rural deans, and other officials (ministeriales). *Orders them to protect the monks in possession of tithes due to them and do justice for them against persons who abstract their tithe or disturb their possessions.* [28 April 1174 × Sept. 1181]

B = Colchester, Colchester and Essex Museum, St John's abbey cartulary p. 63a. s. xiii ex.

Pd from B in *Colchester cartulary* i 109.

Ricardus dei gratia Cantuariensis archiepiscopus totius Anglie primas et apostolice sedis legatus venerabilibus fratribus et amicis Anglorum episcopis suffraganeis suis, archidiaconis quoque et decanis et ceteris ecclesie ministerialibus in quorum ministeriis ecclesia sancti Iohannis Colecestrie redditus habere dinoscitur eternam in domino salutem. Ideo ad regimen ecclesiarum domino disponente sumus constituti ut ecclesiis et ecclesiasticis personis precipue autem viris religiosis iura sua integra servemus et illibata. Hinc est quod fraternitati vestre presentium auctoritate mandamus atque precipimus quatinus dilectis filiis nostris monachis Colec' quorumcumque dominiorum decimas per bailivas vestras ex antiqua vel nova donatione fidelium canonice sunt adepti, ipsas eis habere et pacifice tenere, et decimas iniuste subtractas vel ablatas iustitia mediante restitui faciatis, ad quoscunque colonos ipsa dominia fuerint conversa, ne propter transmutationem vel translationem dominiorum ius ipsorum in aliquo diminuatur. Similiter et de nemoribus et pascuis dominiorum in agros*a* arabiles et in novalia conversis, ius eorum integrum precipimus eis conservari et illibatum. Quicumque ergo de hiis que ad ipsos de iure pertinent aliqua eis detinere presumpserint, seu eorumdem beneficiorum perceptionem vel quamcumque eorum possessionem inquietaverint seu perturbaverint, de ipsis perturbatoribus absque dilatione iustitiam eis ecclesiasticam exhibeatis. Inhibemus quoque sub interminatione anathematis ne quis eos vel possessiones eorum temere inquietet aut conturbet. Valete in domino.

a agros: agris B

108. Colchester abbey

Confirmation for the monks of St John the baptist, Colchester, of all their churches and other possessions. Mandate to all to preserve the customs and liberties granted to the monastery by king Henry (I) and confirmed by pope Calixtus (II), and to enforce the sentence upon disturbers of the monks imposed by pope Calixtus and the archbishop's predecessors. Sentence upon those who infringe this confirmation.

[28 April 1174 × Sept. 1181]

B = Colchester, Colchester and Essex Museum, St John's abbey cartulary p. 63b. s. xiii ex.

Pd from B in *Colchester cartulary* i 110.

Ricardus dei gratia Cantuariensis archiepiscopus totius Anglie primas et apostolice sedis legatus omnibus sancte ecclesie fidelibus ad quos presentes littere pervenerint salutem in domino. Quoniam veritas adeo multipliciter impugnatur ut vix aliquis hodie possessionis sue quietem optineat, necesse est ea que ex aliquorum munificentia aliquibus intuitu pietatis sunt collata scriptorum autenticorum et testium patrocinio communiri. Ea propter in communem volumus devenire notitiam nos dilectis filiis nostris monachis sancti Iohannis baptiste de Colecestr' presentis scripti munimine confirmasse omnes possessiones et elemosinas quas canonice sunt adepti, vel in posterum adipiscentur, in ecclesiis, terris, et decimis, et aliis quibuscumque possessionibus. Consuetudines etiam et libertates quas rex Henricus eidem monasterio concessit sicut eas dompnus papa Kalixtus confirmavit intemeratas conservari precipimus, et sententiam quam in perturbatores eiusdem monasterii vel antecessores nostri archiepiscopi vel dompnus papa Kalixtus imposuit nos etiam corroboramus. Statuimus quoque et sub anathematis interminatione inhibemus ne quis hanc nostre confirmationis paginam infringere vel ei aliquatenus contraire presumat. Valete in domino.

The cartulary contains the bull of Calixtus II (i 11, 70, whence *PUE* iii 131 no. 7) and archbp Theobald's confirmation (ibid. i 107, whence Saltman, *Theobald* 298 no. 73), of which much of the wording is followed here. Theobald refers to the sentence imposed by archbp Ralph, and in two other mandates orders the excommunication of transgressors (*Cartulary* i 108, 111, Saltman, *Theobald* 298–300 nos. 74–75).

109. Colchester abbey

Mandate to Ralph dean of St Paul's and Nicholas archdeacon of London to induct Martin, clerk of Colchester, into full corporal

*possession of the church of Barkway, and to protect his incumbency. In
hearings before the archbishop, Martin has proved that he was
canonically instituted after Walter, clerk of Barkway, had resigned the
church. Walter later intruded himself into the church and displaced
Martin's vicar, Henry, a priest. The church has been adjudicated to
Martin, to whom the fruits since* litis contestatio *are to be restored.*

[Oct. 1181 × 16 Feb. 1184]

A = BL Harl. ch. 75 A 13. No endorsement. Approx. 176 × 172 + 25 mm. Sealing
d.q. 2; remains of seal (brown wax). Scribe **III**.

.Ric(ardus). dei gratia Cantuariensis archiepiscopus . totius Anglie
primas ּ dilectis in domino filiis R. decano . et N. archidiacono ּ
Lundon' ּ salutem . gratiam . et benedictionem. Accessit ad nos iam
a multis retroactis diebus ּ dilectus filius noster Martinus clericus de
Colecestr' . et oblata nobis conquestione monstravit ּ quod cum ad
cessionem Walteri clerici de Bercheweie in ecclesia de Bercheweie
canonice fuisset institutus ּ et in eadem ecclesia vicarium quendam
constituisset ּ defunctoque eodem vicario idem .M. alium ibidem
posuisset ּ prefatus .W. postmodum prefatam ecclesiam sua auctoritate ingressus ּ illicite detinere presumebat . et .H. presbitero[a] .
secundo vicario violenter eiecto ּ vicarie sepedicte ecclesie ּ incum-
bere non metuebat. Partes itaque ante presentiam nostram convo-
cavimus . quibus quandoque comparentibus . quandoque vero
memoratis W. et .H. absentiam suam excusantibus ּ cum tandem de
continua possessione sepedicti .W. qui per prescriptionem longi
temporis ius suum tueri nitebatur ּ de cessione quoque eiusdem .W.
et canonica institutione antefati .M. econtra fuisset allegatum ּ eo
usque processimus ּ quod super assertione utriusque partis testes
recepimus . et sicut convenit adiuratos ּ diligenter examinavimus .
et eorumdem attestationes conscribi fecimus . quibus postmodum
cum productioni testium fuisset renuntiatum . publicatis ּ data
utrique parti et in testes et in dicta testium dicendi copia ּ tandem ad
suscipiendum diffinitive sententie calculum ּ diem peremptorio
constituimus edicto . ad quem ּ cum antefatus .M. copiam sui nobis
exhiberet ּ pars vero adversa nec veniret nec pro se responsalem aut
excusatorem mitteret sufficientem ּ nos ordine iudiciario proce-
dentes ּ cum de cessione pretaxati .W. et canonica institutione
prelibati .M. ad presentationem monachorum Colecestr' ּ tum ex
legitimo testium testimonio ּ tum et ex tuis fili decane qui tunc
temporis archidiaconus Middelsessie nosceris extitisse ּ necnon et
litteris venerabilis fratris nostri .G. Lundoniensis episcopi fides
nobis facta fuisset ad plenum ּ sepedicto .M. prenominatam eccle-

siam adiudicavimus . presertim .ᵃ cum testes partis adverse nichil
assertive sed omnia negative protestati fuissent .ᵃ videlicet quod
nichil aliquando de cessione .W. aut de institutione ipsius .M.
viderant vel audierant . sed nec prefatus .H. capellanus super
canonico ingressu suo in iamdictam ecclesiam quem ostendere
debuerat et probare .ᵃ aliquam nobis fidem fecit. Hinc est quod
dilectioni vestre presentium auctoritate mandamus atque precipimus . quatinus memoratum .M. in corporalem sepedicte ecclesie
possessionem .ᵃ induci . et ecclesiam ipsam eidem .M. in pace dimitti
.ᵃ faciatis . ita quidem quod siquos quo minus mandatum nostrum
exsequi valeatis temere resistentes inveneritis .ᵃ ipsos sententia
excommunicationis involvere . et excommunicatos publice denunti-
are non omittatis . provisuri attentius .ᵃ ut fructus pretaxate ecclesie a
tempore litis coram nobis contestate perceptos .ᵃ eidem .M. iustitia
mediante restitui faciatis. Valete semper in domino.

ᵃ presbiter A

Ralph de Diceto, the dean, was archdn of Middlesex from 1152 × 1153 to
1180 × Jan. 1181.
Bp Gilbert of London appropriated the church of Barkway to its patron, St
John's abbey, Colchester, at a date unknown, safeguarding a vicarage for 'Martin
our clerk' and reasonable sustenance ('de proventibus altaris ... non annua set
perpetua') for a priest serving the church. (*Colchester cartulary* i 83–4; Foliot,
Letters and charters 410 no. 361). On 18 March 1179 Alexander III granted the
appropriation of Barkway to the abbey (*Colchester cartulary* i 71; *PUE* iii 392 no.
262). The vicarage was taxed by episcopal authority in 1237, and Newcourt
treats this as its first ordination (*Repertorium* i 800–1, quoting London Guildhall
Libr. ms. 9531/6 (register of bp Robert Gilbert) fo. 224v (200v)).

*110. Combwell abbey

Grant for the canons of Combwell of the church of Benenden.
[7 April 1174 × 16 Feb. 1184]

Mentioned only, in a confirmation of four churches by the P. & C. of Christ
Church, Canterbury, 1222 × 1228: London, College of Arms, Combwell
charters 103, whence pd in *Archaeologia Cantiana* vi (1864) 196 no. XXX.
Apart from Benenden, the churches named are subjects of separate existing
grants (below, nos. 112–4). Since the charter of the P. & C. refers indiscrimi-
nately to charters of archbps Richard, Hubert, and Stephen, the church of
Benenden may have been confirmed first by one of Richard's successors.

111. Combwell abbey

*Confirmation for the canons of Combwell of the donations of their
founder, Robert of Thurnham and of his son Stephen, according to their
charters and of other possessions hereafter lawfully acquired.*
[? Aug. 1174 × Sept. 1175]

B = Lambeth Palace, Reg. W. Warham fo. 138v (142v) in copy of an inspeximus (1287) of archbp John. s. xvi in.

Universis sancte matris ecclesie filiis Ricardus dei gratia Cantuariensis archiepiscopus totius Anglie primas et apostolice sedis legatus salutem. Quoniam exquisitis calumpniantium versutiis veritas multipliciter impugnatur, ut vix inveniatur hodie qui sue possessionis quietem obtineat, necesse est instrumentis autenticis ea roborari que ex aliquorum munificentia rationabiliter fuisse collata noscuntur. Eapropter dilectos filios nostros abbatem de Cumbewell et fratres ibidem deo et sancte Marie Magdalene canonice servientes caritatis sincere brachiis amplectentes in Christo, omnia que ipsis sub nostra iurisdictione rationabiliter donata sunt integra eis et illibata servare volentes, confirmamus eis omnia que Robertus de Thorneham eisdem fratribus rationabiliter dedit in liberam et perpetuam elemosinam, scilicet Henle, que est sedes ecclesie et ecclesiam sancte Marie de Torneham et ecclesiam sancte Marie de Brichelle cum omnibus earumdem ecclesiarum pertinentiis, et in Torneham quandam terram que vocatur Hoc, et Eastheye, et super montes de Torneham viginti acras. Preterea ex propria donatione Stephani filii predicti Roberti, quam ipse concessit et dedit predicte ecclesie et fratribus ibidem deo servientibus in liberam et perpetuam elemosinam, decem acras in Brichelle de proprio dominio suo et in Torneham super montes duas acras. Hec autem omnia sicut eis concessa sunt et donata a predictis dominis fundi et cartis eorum rationabiliter confirmata, sicut carte eorumdem testantur, ita ea nostre auctoritatis munimine roboramus quatinus sepedicte ecclesie et memoratorum fratrum possessio tot instrumentorum vallata presidiis nulla inposterum calumpniatorum malitia divellatur. Quecumque etiam inposterum prefata ecclesia iuste et canonice poterit adipisci sub protectione dei et sancte Cantuariensis ecclesie et nostra suscipimus, prohibentes ne quis eis vel possessionibus suis iniuriam aliquam seu molestiam inferre presumat. Testibus: Waltero abbate de Boxle, Roberto de Novo Burgo, Benedicto cancellario, magistro Gerardo, Herlewyno et Radulfo monachis, Amicio archidiacono Rothomagensi, magistro Thoma Ebroycensi, magistro Petro Blesensi, Radulfo de Wyngeham, Willelmo de Northal', Herberto elemosinario, Willelmo Wynt', Willelmo Cadomensi, Amicio et Rogero clericis, Stephano de Torneham, Michaele de Torneham.

Benedict, a monk of Christ Church, was presumably appointed the archbp's chancellor as a result of the papal mandate of 11 May 1174. If he had gone with the archbp-elect to Rome he could have acted as chancellor before the archbp returned to England in Aug. but the witness-list suggests a date after his return.

He was elected prior of Canterbury July × Sept. 1175. The charter cited by Cheney, *EBC* 32 as evidence of Benedict as chancellor 15 May 1177 is probably spurious (below, no. + 194).

A charter of Stephen of Thurnham, which confirms his father's gifts, adds to them more land than is given here. This is contained in a royal inspeximus of 1227 (*Cal. Ch. Rolls* i 48, *Mon. Ang.* vi 413).

The archbp is probably confirming an earlier grant, using much of the same wording. *Henle* is an alternative name for Combwell. The land here described as *Hoc* and *Eastheye* appears as *Hoch* and *Castreye* in the royal inspeximus.

112. Combwell abbey

Grant to the canons of Combwell of the church of St Peter of Aldington, at the request and presentation of William son of Helto.

[May 1177 × 1180]

A = Lost, formerly in the Surrenden deeds owned by the Dering family, described by L. B. Larking in *Archaeologia Cantiana* ii (1859) 40–2, with woodcut plates of seal and counterseal suspended on cord. Described as damaged by S. C. Ratcliff in *HMCR* 79 *Suppl. report on mss. of the earl of Lindsey* (1942) p. xi. Not now (1980) in this collection, deposited in Kent Archives Office (U 512) in 1955.

B = Lambeth Palace, Reg. W. Warham fo. 138v (142v). s. xvi in.

Ricardus dei gratia Cantuariensis archiepiscopus totius Anglie primas et apostolice sedis legatus universis sancte matris ecclesie filiis ad quos presentes littere pervenerint eternam in domino salutem. Que a nobis canonice gesta sunt, ne posteris temporibus in dubium revocentur, presentis scripti memorie duximus commendare. Ea propter ad omnium notitiam volumus pervenire nos ad petitionem et presentationem Willelmi filii Heltonis concessisse et dedisse in liberam et perpetuam elemosinam ecclesie beate Marie Magdalene de Cumbewell et fratribus ibidem divino mancipatis servitio ecclesiam beati Petri de Aldington cum omnibus ad eandem ecclesiam pertinentibus. Quare volumus et ea qua fungimur auctoritate precipimus ut predicta ecclesia de Cumbewell et fratres eiusdem loci prelibatam ecclesiam de Aldington' cum universis pertinentiis in liberam et perpetuam possideant elemosinam. Et ut hec donatio firma et inconcussa permaneat, eam presenti carta confirmamus, statuentes et sub interminatione anathematis prohibentes ne quis hanc nostre confirmationis paginam infringere vel ei aliquatenus temere et contra iuris ordinem obviare presumat. Testibus hiis: Walerano Baiocensi Willelmo Gloecestrensi archidiaconis, Willelmo et Moyse capellanis, Henrico Baiocensi, magistro Rogero Norwicensi, Ricardo et Galfrido clericis, Willelmo Sotewayne, Benedicto, Iohanne, Willelmo Beivino, et aliis pluribus clericis et laicis.

William of Northolt became archdn of Gloucester May × Dec. 1177. William son of Helto is recorded as dead in *PR 26 Henr. II* (PRS 29, 1908) 147; cf. I. J. Sanders, *Eng. baronies* 1. William's charter is pd in *Archaeol. Cantiana* ii 29, and plate.

113. Combwell abbey

Grant to the canons of Combwell of the church of Thurnham, at the request and presentation of Stephen of Thurnham, to hold in usus suos after the death of Robert, chaplain of the church. Future chaplains serving the church on behalf of the canons shall be presented to the bishop. The archbishop has settled a dispute between Stephen of Thurnham and Robert the chaplain over lands of the church and the service of Stephen's chapel. [1182 × May 1183]

A = London, College of Arms, Combwell charters no. 96. Endorsed, s. xiii: R. Cant' arch' super ecclesia de Torneham; s. xvii/xviii: description by Peter Le Neve. Approx. 183 × 210 + 24 mm. Sealing d.q. 2; tag remains, seal lost. Scribe V.
Pd from A in *Archaeologia Cantiana* v (1862) 201–2 no. V.

Ric(ardus) dei gratia Cantuariensis archiepiscopus et totius Anglie primas ፡ omnibus Christi fidelibus ad quos presentes littere pervenerint ፡ illam que est in domino salutem. Ad universitatis vestre noticiam volumus pervenire nos ad petitionem et presentationem dilecti filii nostri Stephani de Thorneham domini fundi dedisse et concessisse dilectis filiis canonicis*a* de Cumbwell' . ecclesiam de Thorneham cum universis pertinentiis suis libere et quiete post decessum Roberti eiusdem ecclesie capellani possidendam . ita quidem ut fructus et obventiones quaslibet de ea provenientes . salvo episcopali iure quod de ea debetur in usus suos convertant. Capellanus tamen qui in eadem ecclesia nomine canonicorum divina officia celebrabit ad eorum presentationem ab episcopo recipietur . qui eidem episcopo de hiis que sibi debentur respondeat et canonicis prout ab eis ordinatum fuerit . de temporalibus respondeat et satisfaciat. Hoc quoque ad communem omnium volumus devenire noticiam quod cum controversia inter predictum Stephanum et Robertum eiusdem presbiterum super quadam terra ad ecclesiam de Thorneham pertinente mota ad nostram audienciam fuisset delata ፡ tandem eandem questionem sub tali compositionis forma ad pacem reduximus et concordie unitatem reformavimus. Prefatus Stephanus dedit et concessit ecclesie de Thorneham in liberam et perpetuam elemosinam sex acras . et tres virgatas terre in bosco suo versus orientalem plagam . partem videlicet in bosco . partem in plano . liberas et quietas*b* ab omni seculari servitio in concambium illius terre quam idem .S. habet in parco suo versus occidentem . que olim ad ecclesiam de Thorneham pertinebat. Preterea idem .S. concessit tres acras terre que iacent iuxta Dunstrat' ecclesie de Thorneham quas pater eiusdem Stephani olim eidem ecclesie pietatis intuitu in liberam contulerat elemosinam. Robertus vero capellanus ecclesie de Thorneham . facto concambio et controversia inter ipsum et Stephanum sopita *:* concessit et firmiter promisit . quod in capella Stephani de Thorneham quam habet in curia sua fundatam . si idem .S. cum familia sua ibi moram fecerit tribus diebus in septimana videlicet feria . quarta . et sexta nisi festus dies qui preferri debeat intervenerit . et die dominica per se vel per capellanum suum divina faciet celebrari. Quod si idem .S. residentiam ibi non fecerit *:* per unum diem tantum in septimana pro fidelibus defunctis per eundem Robertum . vel capellanum eius divina in eadem capella celebrabuntur . ita quidem quod memoratus .S. in libris in vestimentis et ceteris quibuslibet divinorum celebrationi necessariis *:* in capella sua faciet exhiberi. Id ipsum quoque abbas et canonici Cumbwell' temporibus suis cum liberam eiusdem ecclesie de Thorneham habuerint dispositionem eidem militi se exhibituros promiserunt. Et quia ea que coram nobis et a nobis rationabiliter ordinata sunt volumus perpetua stabilitate gaudere *:* eadem presentis scripti patrocinio . et testium subscriptione communimus. Hiis testibus . magistro Girardo . magistro .P. Blesensi . archidiacono Bathoniensi . magistro Roberto de Inglesham . magistro Rogerio de Rulveston' . Willelmo de Sotindon' . Henrico Baiocensi . Thoma de Niwesol' . Micahele de Burn' . magistro Rogerio Herefordensi . Hereberto elemosinario . Gaufrido de Mildehal' . et multis aliis clericis et laicis.

a canoncis A   *b* quetas A

Peter of Blois became archdn of Bath in 1182. Gerard Pucella was elected bp of Coventry ? late May 1183.

114. Combwell abbey

Notification that at the presentation of Denise, patron (advocata) of the church of Whitfield, or Beauxfield, and after resignation of the church in the archbishop's hand by her son and heir Thomas, the last parson, the archbishop has admitted the abbot and canons of Combwell and instituted them canonically in the vacant church.

[1182 × 16 Feb. 1184]

A = London, College of Arms, Combwell charters no. 20. Endorsed, s. xiii: R. Cant' arch' super ecclesia de Beasfeld'; s. xvii/xviii: description by Peter Le

Neve. Approx. 176 × 108 + 18 mm. Sealing d.q. 2; half of damaged seal and counterseal (natural wax, brown varnish). Scribe **IV**.

B = Lambeth Palace, Reg. W. Warham fo. 138v (142v), in copy of inspeximus (1287) by archbp John. s. xvi in.

Pd from A in *Archaeologia Cantiana* vi (1864) 192–5 no. XXIX, with engraving of counterseal on p. 195.

.Ric(ardus). dei gracia Cantuariensis . archiepiscopus . tocius Anglie primas ⸴ universis sancte matris ecclesie filiis ad quos littere iste pervenerint ⸴ eternam in Christo salutem. Adeo modernorum temporibus execrabilis ardor ambitionis invaluit . ut ea que canonice acta sunt calumpniantium versutias vitare non possint ⸴ nisi memorialibus scriptis et testium numerositate muniantur. Eapropter ad omnium volumus pervenire noticiam . quod cum Dionisia advocata ęcclesię de Biausfeld dilectos filios nostros abbatem et canonicos de Cumbwell' nobis ad eandem ecclesiam de Biausfeld presentasset ⸴ nos de concessione et plena voluntate dilecti filii nostri Tomę clerici filii et heredis memorate Dionisie . qui ultima eiusdem ecclesie persona fuerat ⸴ facta prius resignatione eiusdem ecclesie per prefatum Tomam in manu nostra ⸴ predictos abbatem et canonicos de Cumbwell' ad supradictam ecclesiam liberam et vacantem admisimus . et eos in ea canonice sine omni contradictione instituimus. Volumus itaque et ea qua fungimur autoritate precipimus . quod idem canonici prescriptam ecclesiam cum omnibus ad eam pertinentibus ita bene et plene . libere et in pace possideant in perpetuum ⸴ sicut eam aliquis unquam ante illos melius et plenius ac liberius possedisse dinoscitur. Et ut hec nostra institutio firma in posterum et inconvulsa permaneat ⸴ nos eam presentis scripti nostri annotatione et sigilli nostri munimine duximus roborare. Hiis testibus . magistro Petro Blesensi . archidiacono Bathoniensi . Willelmo archidiacono Gloecestriensi . magistro Henrico de Norhamton . magistro Roberto de Inglesham . magistro Rogero de Roulveston . magistro Rogero Norwicensi . Willelmo de Sotindon . Ricardo de Lundonia . Gaufrido Forti . Rogero decano de Cranebr' et aliis;

Mr Peter of Blois became archdn of Bath between January and October 1182: cf. nos. 227 and 206 below.

115. Coventry: archdeacons of the diocese

Mandate to the archdeacons of the diocese of Coventry (or to the archdeacons of Coventry and Stafford), reciting a mandate of pope Alexander III to the archbishop which orders that certain financial exactions by the archdeacons cease. [Aug. 1174 × Sept. 1181]

B = BL ms. Harl. 3650 (Kenilworth cartulary) fo. 52v (p. 104). s. xiii in.
C = Ibid. fo. 54r (p. 107). D = Ibid. ms. Add. 47677 (Kenilworth cartulary) fo.
95r (90r). s. xvi in.

*a*R. dei gratia Cantuariensis archiepiscopus totius Anglie primas et*b*
apostolice sedis legatus dilectis filiis archidiaconis per Coventrensem episcopatum constitutis*c* salutem. Mandatum domini pape*d*
suscepimus in hec verba: Alexander episcopus servus servorum dei
venerabili fratri R. Cantuariensi archiepiscopo apostolice sedis
legato salutem et apostolicam benedictionem. Licet iuxta apostolum
arguere, obsecrare, et increpare debeamus, sic tamen debemus
excessus corrigere singulorum ut probemur non que nostra set que
Iesu Christi sunt querere et in correctione facienda videamur*e*
modestiam et maturitatem servare. Accepimus autem quod archidiaconi Coventrensis episcopatus pro excessibus et criminibus puniendis a clericis et laicis penam pecuniariam exigunt, in examinatione
ignis et aque xxx^ta denarios a viro et muliere querere presumunt et
pro annua exactione pecunie personas quandoque suspendunt et
ecclesias interdicunt. A vicariis quoque xx denarios ut in ecclesiis
eos cantare permittant exigere non formidant, et alia agunt que
canonum obviant institutis et de radice cupiditatis et avaritie
videntur prodire. Quia igitur sollicitudini nostre incumbit pastorali
diligentia providere ne ab ecclesiasticis personis provincie tue
aliquid agatur quod reprehensioni subiaceat vel ecclesiasticam honestatem denigret, fraternitati tue per apostolica scripta precipiendo
mandamus et mandando precipimus quatinus archidiaconis predicti
episcopatus ex parte nostra et tua districte inhibeas ne pro excessibus corrigendis aut criminibus puniendis a clericis [fo. 53r] vel
laicis penam pecuniariam nec in examinatione ignis vel aque denarios amplius exigere audeant, vel alia que dicta sunt quomodolibet
excercere.*f* Si autem contra prohibitionem tuam ausu temerario
venire presumpserint, eos omni occasione et appellatione remota
ecclesiastica censura percellas et sententiam ipsam usque ad dignam
satisfactionem facias inviolabiliter observari. Dat' Anagnie vi kal.
Iulii [26 June 1174 × 1176]. Apostolica igitur auctoritate et nostra in
virtute obedientie et sub periculo ordinis et honoris districte vobis
inhibemus ne quis vestrum in archidiaconatu suo aliquid eorum que
predicta sunt ulterius exigere vel excercere presumat vel apostolicis
in aliquo contraire statutis. Siquis autem vestrum contra hoc venire
temptaverit, nos eius inobedientiam sic iuxta domini pape*d* mandatum ecclesiastica censura puniemus quod pena docente cognoscet
quam periculosum sit apostolicis obviare preceptis. Valete.*g*

     a in margin: Ne pena pecuniaria exigatur pro excessibus etc. B; De pena pecuniaria predicta inhibend' CD ^{b} et CD, *om.* B ^{c} archid..... constitutis B; Coventreie et Stafford archidiaconis CD ^{d} pape *erased and roughly re-written in s. xvi ?* B ^{e} videamur CD; iudicamur B ^{f} add *etc. and om. rest* D ^{g} Valete C, *om.* B

The date of the pope's mandate probably narrows the dating of the archbp's to 1174 × 1176. The papal mandate (JL 14315) is found in decretal collections, eventually (abridged) in *Extra* 5. 37. 3. Part of another (abridged) mandate of Alexander III about extortions by the archdn of Chester, found in decretal collections addressed to the bp of Coventry and the abbot of Chester, is in like terms. JL 13857, *Extra* 1. 23. 6.

116. Coventry: hospital of St John the baptist

Confirmation for the hospital of St John the baptist, Coventry, of the site of the hospital and its lands and buildings and other possessions, which were granted and confirmed to the house for the use of the poor by Laurence, formerly prior, and the convent of Coventry, at the request of Edmund archdeacon of Coventry.   [30 Jan. 1179 × Sept. 1181]

> B = Register of the hospital, now lost, in possession of John Hales, esq. of
>   Coventry a.d. 1653.
> Pd from B by Dugdale, *Mon. Ang.* vii 659a no. III.

Testibus: magistro Gerardo, Willielmo archidiacono Gloucestriae, et aliis.

> The archbp is styled legate. From the same source Dugdale printed the charters
> of prior Laurence and archdn Edmund. Laurence d. 29 Jan. 1179; the date of
> Edmund's death (in 1179 if not earlier) is not known.

117. Chapel of St Michael of Croughton

Confirmation of agreement after prolonged dispute between Laurence priest of Croughton and R. clerk of Waure, concerning the chapel of St Michael of Croughton, detailing the division of tithes, etc. between the chapel and the mother church. Richard may have divine office cele-brated in the chapel without leave of the parson of Croughton. The agreement of the parties has the concurrence of Geoffrey de Waure and Osbert son of Richard and of the patrons of the church of Croughton, Richard Neirenuit and Henry Pirun.   [May 1177 × Sept. 1181]

> A = Oxford, Magdalen College deeds: Brackley 76a. Endorsed, s. xiii: Carta de
>   decimis capelle de Crolton'; s. xiv: Cyrencestr' (with notary's signs ?). Approx.
>   188 × 110 + 20 mm. Sealing d.q. 2; tag with fragments of seal sewn in patterned
>   canvas bag. Scribe **III**.
> B = Ibid. Estate paper 137/1 (Aynho cartulary roll) m. 6, omitting witness-list. s.
>   xiii.
> Pd (calendar) from A in *The collection of Brackley deeds at Magdalen College,
>   Oxford* ed. W. D. Macray (1910).

.Ric(ardus) dei gratia Cantuariensis archiepiscopus . tocius Anglie primas et apostolice sedis legatus ∴ universis Christi fidelibus ad quos littere iste pervenerint ∴ eternam in domino salutem. Ad omnium noticiam volumus pervenire ∴ controversiam inter dilectos filios nostros Laurencium presbiterum de Creulton' . et R. clericum de Waure . super capella sancti Michaelis de Creult' . et pertinenciis eius motam . et aliquandiu agitatam ∴ tandem sub hac transactionis forma conquievisse. Predictus .R. percipiet omnes decimas tocius dominii Galfridi de Waure . et Osberti filii Ricardi . quod est de feodo comitis Willelmi de Mandevill' ∴ in villa de Creult' . a quocunque culti . et omnes decimas de garbis molendinarii et firma molendini . minute autem decime molendinarii et oblationes ∴ apud matricem ecclesiam de Creult' ∴ residebunt . ubi idem molendinarius et sui ∴ spiritualia percipient. Preter hec autem percipiet ecclesia de Creult' ∴ in autumpno ∴ omnes fructus unius acre . et unum . agnum . et unum porcellum . et unum vellus . et unum caseum . annuatim ∴ si forte de dominio predicti .G. talia provenerint. Omnia vero alia inde proveniencia ∴ ad predictam capellam pertinebunt. Preterea habebit matrix ecclesia ∴ decimas provenientes de quarta parte virgate terre . ad prelibatam capellam pertinente. Prescriptus quoque .R. absque licencia persone ecclesie de Creult' ∴ libere et sine contradictione ∴ in pretaxata capella divina faciet celebrari officia. Unde ut eadem transactio ∴ que de voluntate et beneplacito . predictorum .G. et .O. et Ricardi Nigrenoctis . et .H. Pirun ∴ advocatorum ecclesie de Creult' ∴ sicut prefati .L. presbiter . et .R. clericus constanter nobis proposuerunt ∴ facta est ∴ permaneat in posterum inconvulsa ∴ eam presenti scripto confirmamus . et sigilli nostri apposicione roboramus. His testibus . magistro Gerardo . Willelmo archidiacono Gloecestriensi . magistro .R. de Sancto Martino . magistro .R. de Roulvest' . Nicholao Walensi . magistro .R. Norwicensi . magistro .R. Walensi . Henrico Baiocensi . Ricardo et Galfrido clericis . Willelmo de Sotindon' .

William of Northolt became archdn of Gloucester May × Dec. 1177. The chapel of Croughton apparently passed to the hospital of Aynho about 1215 (*Liber antiquus H. Wells* ed. A. Gibbons (Lincoln 1888) 73–4). The hospital, like that of Brackley, passed into the hands of Magdalen College in 1485. The families of Neirenuit and Pirun were still joint patrons of Croughton parish church when bp Robert Grosseteste instituted Richard Neyrenut in the rectory, 1247 × 1248 (*Rot. R. Grosseteste* (CYS x. 1913) 232).

118. Crowland abbey

Confirmation for the monks of Crowland of the grant of the churches of Gedney and Whaplode by the patron, Fulk de Oyri, as granted and confirmed by bishop Robert of Lincoln and archbishop Theobald of Canterbury, saving episcopal rights and the agreement made between the monks and Baldwin de Oyri, clerk, for the duration of his tenure of the churches. After his death the monks shall have the churches for their own uses. [28 April 1174 × Sept. 1181]

B = Spalding, Gentlemen's Society, Crowland cartulary fo. 76v. s. xiv med.
C = Ibid. fo. 106r (protocol and incipit only).

Ricardus dei gratia Cantuariensis archiepiscopus totius Anglie primas et apostolice sedis legatus universis Christi fidelibus ad quos presentes littere pervenerint salutem in domino. Fraterne caritatis unitas hortatur et officii nostri debitum*a* exposcit virorum religiosorum qui divinis insistunt obsequiis iustis desideriis clementer imminere et rationabilibus eorum petitionibus assensum libenti animo prebere. Inde est quod dilectorum filiorum nostrorum monachorum Croiland' iustis postulationibus clementer annuentes, concessionem ecclesiarum de Gedeneye et Quappelade a Fulcone de Oyri ad quem ius patronatus earundem ecclesiarum pertinere dicitur monasterio de Croiland' factam et donatione et confirmatione bone memorie Roberti Lincolniensis episcopi necnon pie et felicis memorie predecessoris nostri Theobaldi Cantuariensis archiepiscopi prefatis monachis collatis et diligentius inspectis et cognitis nostra auctoritate interveniente sicut rationabiliter facta est perpetuum robur habere decernimus et presentis scripti nostri munimine corroboramus et confirmamus, salvis nimirum diocesani per omnia episcopi dignitatibus et pactionibus que inter memoratos monachos et Baldewynum de Oyri clericum super iamdictis ecclesiis dum eas tenuerit intervenerunt. Post cuius decessum sepedicte ecclesie ad usus et proprietates intendent supramemoratorum monachorum.

a debitum etc. C *ends here with marginal note*: Sicut inter illas de Quappelad'.

Thirteenth-century records show that Crowland's patronal rights were not accepted fully in either church without trouble, and that in each church not only did the abbey have to present a rector but that a perpetual vicarage was also ordained. (*Rot. H. Welles* (CYS) iii 144, 187–8, 214, *Rot. R. Grosseteste* (CYS) 83, 113, 122, 125). Only in Jan. 1269 was Whaplode appropriated to Crowland and a perpetual vicarage newly ordained (*Rot. R. Gravesend* (CYS) 33–34). In a suit over Whaplode in the king's court in 1230 Fulk son of Fulk de Oyri declared that 'a certain Hubert Walter, later archbishop of Canterbury' had been admitted at his presentation, presumably in succession to Baldwin de Oyri (*CRR* xiv 33

no. 169, xiv 238 no. 1131). For the agreement between Fulk de Oyri and
Crowland over the church of Gedney see below, no. 424. For the confirmations
of the churches of Gedney and Whaplode to Crowland by bp Robert II and
archbp Theobald see *EEA* i no. 102.

119. Crowland abbey

*Confirmation of the agreement made between Baldwin de Oyri and the
monks of Crowland by which he held the churches of Gedney and
Whaplode from them, paying a yearly pension of one mark, instead of
his former payment of two shillings. After his death the monks shall
have the churches for their own uses.*

[28 April 1174 × Sept. 1181]

B = Spalding, Gentlemen's Society, Crowland cartulary fo. 106r. s. xiv med.

Ricardus dei gratia Cantuariensis archiepiscopus totius Anglie
primas et apostolice sedis legatus uni-[fo. 106v]versis Christi fidelibus ad quos presentes littere pervenerint salutem in domino. Sicut
ex testimonio litterarum dilecti filii nostri Rogeri de Derby cognovimus eo tempore quo idem Rogerus custos fuit archidiaconatus
Lincolniensis Baldewynus de Oyri in presentia ipsius Rogeri et
aliorum plurimorum recognovit se tenuisse et tenere debere ecclesias de Gedeneye et de Quappelad' de monachis de Croyland',
quarum nomine reddet eis annua pensione unam marcam ad festum
sancti Bartholomei pro quibus reddebat eis prius duos solidos.
Securos etiam eos fecit fidei interpositione quod neque per se neque
per aliam personam queret eis dampnum vel impedimentum de
eisdem ecclesiis, quod et illi ei fecerunt. Post cuius decessum libere
et quiete cedent in usus et proprietates monachorum. Facta sunt
autem hec sicut ex predictis litteris sepedicti Rogeri accepimus sub
testimonio magistri Clementis etc. Nos igitur super eisdem ecclesiis, concessionibus eorum ad quos ius patronatus earundem ecclesiarum pertinebat memorate ecclesie de Croiland' factis et donatione
et confirmatione bone memorie Roberti Lincolniensis episcopi sed
et confirmatione predecessoris nostri pie et felicis memorie Theobaldi Cantuariensis archiepiscopi eisdem monachis collatis diligentius inspectis et cognitis, prescriptam recognitionem sub cirograffo
inter sepedictos monachos et prefatum Baldewynum factam et
conscriptam et fide interposita firmatam nostra auctoritate interveniente sicut rationabiliter facta est perpetuum robur optinere decernimus. Valete.

120. Daventry priory

Confirmation for the monks of La Charité serving God in the church of St Augustine, Daventry, of this church and all the other churches granted to them.

[? 28 April 1174 × autumn 1177 or Oct. 1181 × 1182]

B = BL ms. Cotton Claud. D xii (Daventry cartulary) fo. 166r (162r). s. xiv ex.
C = Ibid. fo. 166v (162v) in inspeximus by archbp Boniface, 7 Nov. 1260.
D = Ibid. fo. 167r (163r) in inspeximus of archbp Boniface's charter by archbp Robert, 2 May 1277.

Ricardus dei gratia Cantuariensis archiepiscopus et totius Anglie primas universis sancte ecclesie filiis tam laicis quam clericis per Angliam constitutis salutem et paternam benedictionem. Noverint tam presentes quam futuri quod fratribus et monachis de Caritate apud Daventre in ecclesia sancti Augustini deo servientibus concedimus, confirmamus, et auctoritate scripti nostri corroboramus, specialiter prefatam ecclesiam sancti Augustini in qua iidem*a* monachi divino mancipati sunt officio cum universis pertinentiis suis sicut eam rationabiliter sunt adepti. Alia etiam beneficia eisdem confirmamus sicut ex largitione fidelium eis pie et canonice sunt collata, ea specialiter que propriis vocabulis duximus designanda, capellam videlicet de Welton' que ad eandem ecclesiam spectat cum pertinentiis suis, ecclesiam de Staverton' cum pertinentiis suis, ecclesiam de Throp*b* cum pertinentiis suis, ecclesiam de Falwesley cum pertinentiis suis, ecclesiam de Norton' cum pertinentiis suis, ecclesiam de Haddon' cum pertinentiis suis, ecclesiam de Eltendon'*c* cum pertinentiis suis, ecclesiam de Lobenho cum pertinentiis suis, ecclesiam de Foxton' cum pertinentiis suis, ecclesiam de Guthmundele*d* cum pertinentiis suis, ecclesiam de Scaldeford' cum pertinentiis suis, ecclesiam de Braybroc cum pertinentiis suis, ecclesiam de Bitlesbroc cum pertinentiis suis, ecclesiam de Esseby cum pertinentiis suis. Ut autem hec nostra confirmatio perpetuum et inviolabile robur optineat, eam scripti et sigilli nostri munimine roboramus. Hiis testibus: magistro Gerardo, Walerano archidiacono Baiocensi*e*, magistro Petro Blesensi, Willelmo de Northal', Radulfo de Wingham, et pluribus*f* aliis.

a iidem CD; idem B   *b* Throp CD; Trohp B   *c* Eltendon' B; Eltindon' CD
*d*Guthmundele B; Gothmundele C; Gomundele D   *e* Walerano archid. Baioc. CD;
Waltero archid. B   *f* Radulfo ... pluribus B; et CD

Mr Gerard and Mr Peter of Blois left England for Rome in autumn 1177. The latter became archdn of Bath during 1182. The absence of the legatine title is incompatible with the appearance of William of Northolt without the title of archdn of Gloucester. Both address and salutation are in unusual forms and point to external writing, which might account for an error in the intitulatio or the omission of the archdn's office in the original from which both B and C were taken.

121. Davington priory

Confirmation for the nuns of Davington of the church of Newnham, granted to them by William son of Philip and Juliana, William's wife.
[Oct. 1181 × 16 Feb. 1184]

> B = Lambeth Palace, Reg. W. Warham fo. 155r (159r). s. xvi in. C = Ibid. fo. 155v (159v), in copy of inspeximus (1244 × 1258) by P. and C., Ch. Ch. Canterbury.

Omnibus Christi fidelibus ad quos littere presentes pervenerint Ricardus Cantuariensis ecclesie minister humilis salutem in domino. Ad universitatis vestre notitiam volumus pervenire nos concessionem et donationem quam dilectus filius noster Willelmus filius Phillippi et Iuliana uxor eius dilectis filiabus nostris monialibus de Davinton super ecclesia de Newnham*a* pietatis intuitu fecisse noscuntur ratam habere et acceptam. Unde et eam sicut rationabiliter facta est auctoritate qua fungimur confirmamus et tam presentis scripti patrocinio quam nostri*b* appositione sigilli communimus. Hiis testibus: Willelmo archidiacono Glouecestriensi, magistro Roberto de Inglesham*c*, magistro Rogero de Rulveston*d*, magistro Rogero Norwicensi, Rogero decano, Galfrido*e* clerico, et aliis multis*f* clericis et laicis.

> *a* Newnham C; Newham B   *b* nostri C; nostre B   *c* Inglesham C; Inglisham B
> *d*Rulvest' B; Rulvester C   *e* Galfrido C; glalfri B   *f* multis C, *om.* B

> Followed on fo. 155r by the grant of Newnham church by William and Juliana his wife, and by the confirmation by Juliana's son, Robert de Campania, made in the time of archbp Baldwin (see below, no. 267 and note).

122. Dover priory

Grant of an indulgence of five days to all who shall contribute alms to the altar of the Holy Cross in the church of St Martin at Dover.
[28 April 1174 × Sept. 1181]

> B = Lambeth Palace ms. 241 (Dover cartulary) fo. 53v (52v). s. xiv ex.

Ricardus dei gratia Cantuariensis archiepiscopus totius Anglie primas et apostolice sedis legatus universis dei fidelibus ad quos presentes littere pervenerint salutem in Christo. Dignum est et fidei Christiane congruum triumphale signum crucis quo dominus noster Iesus Christus mundum redemit dignis obsequiis et honoribus venerari in terris, per quod nobis omnibus reseratus esse creditur introitus celestis. Unde nos ad eiusdem crucis venerationem singulos attentius invitantes, statuimus ut quicumque fideli devotione altare sancte crucis quod est*a* in ecclesia beati Martini apud Dovorriam ubi monachi commorantur elemosinis et beneficiis sibi a deo collatis honoraverint, de iniuncta sibi penitentia quinque dierum relaxationem obtineant et orationum ac beneficiorum eiusdem ecclesie participes fiant. Valete.

a est: *om.* B

For indulgences granted by archbp Theobald see Saltman, *Theobald* 314–6 nos. 92–4. Besides the present indulgence attached to the altar of the Holy Cross, the cartulary has an indulgence of twenty days granted by the legate Nicholas of Tusculum for those who visit the three altars of the B. V. M., the Holy Cross, and St Katherine, V. and M., on the anniversary of his dedication of these altars on 2 Dec. [1214] (ms. 241 fo. 53v).

123. Dover priory

Mandate to all the priests of Dover to compel their parishioners to pay their tithes fully and without dispute. [28 April 1174 × Sept. 1181]

B = Lambeth Palace ms. 241 (Dover cartulary) fo. 37r (36r). s. xiv ex.

Ricardus dei gratia Cantuariensis archiepiscopus totius Anglie primas et apostolice sedis legatus dilectis in domino filiis universis presbiteris Dovorr' salutem. Pervenit ad audientiam nostram quod parochiani vestri decimas suas integre non persolvant. Eapropter mandamus vobis omnibus et singulis ac districte precipimus quatinus parochianos vestros diligenter moneatis et inducatis ex parte nostra et si opus fuerit ecclesiastica districtione compellatis ut decimas suas integre et sine difficultate persolvant, ita quidem quod si eorum aliqui contumaces inventi fuerint, ipsos ter vocari faciatis, et nisi errorem suum correxerint, ipsos postmodum auctoritate nostra sententia excommunicationis involvatis. Valete.

124. Dover priory

Grant of an indulgence of twenty days to all who out of devotion and for prayer visit the altar of St John the evangelist in the priory church of Dover or contribute alms. Dover, 10 Feb. 1175.

B = Lambeth Palace ms. 241 (Dover cartulary) fo. 55v (54v). s. xiv ex.

Omnibus Christi fidelibus presentes litteras visuris vel audituris Ricardus permissione divina Cantuariensis archiepiscopus salutem in domino sempiternam. De dei misericordia et gloriose virginis Marie genetricis eius omniumque sanctorum meritis confidentes, omnibus parochianis nostris et aliis quorum diocesani hanc nostram indulgentiam ratam habuerint vere contritis et confessis, qui altare sancti Iohannis evangeliste in ecclesia conventuali Dovorr' Cantuariensis diocesis constructum devotionis et orationis causa visitaverint seu de bonis sibi collatis a deo aliquo modo honoraverint, viginti dies de iniuncta sibi penitentia misericorditer relaxamus. Datum Dovorr' iiii^{to} idus Februarii anno domini millesimo C septuagesimo quarto.

125. Dover priory

Confirmation for the monks of St Martin's, Dover, of the charters of archbishops Theobald and Thomas which placed the new church of St Martin and its appurtenances under the protection of the church of Canterbury and the archbishop. The church pertains specially to the archbishops, as was ordained by archbishop Theobald with the assent of king Henry (I) in their charters, and confirmed by popes Eugenius (III), Anastasius (IV), Adrian (IV), and Alexander (III). The Benedictine Rule is to be observed perpetually. The monks' possessions, present and future, are confirmed, especially: by grant of archbishop Theobald and king Henry, the property of the old church of St Martin and its clerks which was on the archbishop's demesne, and the toll due to him; also the tithe of fishing of the burgesses of Dover; the grant of the church of Hougham by Fulbert son of Hugh and archbishop Theobald; the grant of the church of Coldred with the chapel of Popes Hall and all its appurtenances by Walkelin Maminot, of which church the monks had been unjustly deprived and which they recovered in the presence of the archbishop; the grant of the church of 'Bermlinge' by Alfred de Bendevill and Sybil his wife and of the mill which Alfred built there at his own expense; also the old church of St Martin and the rights on land and sea which it possessed; the churches of St Mary, St Peter, St James, founded within the borough of Dover, and the churches of Guston, Appledore, Deal, Buckland, the church in the castle, and the church of St Margaret at Cliffe, with their appurtenances; likewise the land of Harty and 'La Tegh' (B, or 'La Thegei' C) outside the borough of Dover, ten acres of land outside the courtyard gate which the monks got in exchange from Hugh son of Fulbert, and ten acres on the other side of the courtyard which Adelina, wife of Robert de Ver, gave to the church in alms; the prebend of Deal given at the foundation of the monastery of Dover by archbishop William, to be appropriated by the monks to their own uses when Mr Ralph of Sarre, its present holder, dies.   [1177 × Sept. 1181]

B = Canterbury, D. & C. Lit. ms. D 4 fo. 175r. s. xiv in. C = Lambeth Palace ms.
241 (Dover cartulary) fo. 8v (7v). s. xiv ex.

Pd from B in *Literae Cantuarienses* (RS) iii 372–4.

Testibus: magistro Girardo, Willelmo archidiacono Glocestriensi,
magistro Roberto de Inglesham, magistro Rogerio de Rolvestone,[a]
Rogerio Norwycensi, Willelmo de Sotindone,[b] Ricardo et Galfrido
clericis, Thoma de Newesole,[c] et aliis.

[a] Rolvestone C; Roveston B   [b] Sotindone: Schotindone B; Dotintone C
[c] Newesole B; Niewesole C

Charters of Theobald are printed by Saltman, *Theobald* 306–18 nos. 83–97; for
one of archbp Thomas see above, no. 9. Henry I confirmed (1132) archbp
William's proposal to install Austin canons in St Martin's (*Reg. regum anglo-
norm.* ii no. 1736, *Mon. Ang.* iv 538a), but Henry II ratified (Jan. 1156)
Theobald's reconstitution of the house as a Benedictine cell of Christ Church,
Canterbury (*Mon. Ang.* iv 538b). Theobald secured confirmations from popes
Eugenius III, Adrian IV, and Alexander III (1147, 1155–9, 1160–78: *PUE* ii
214, 269, 271, 290, 298, 328, 335, 359 nos. 56, 89, 91, 103, 110, 136, 145, 166).
No bull of Anastasius IV is known. The rehearsal of the possessions in this
charter is taken over almost verbatim in the privilege given by Lucius III, 11
May 1182 (*PUE* ii 414–6 no. 220). It was repeated with specific mention of this
charter and with additions and changes to bring the grant up to date in Celestine
III's privilege of 23 July 1197 (*PUE* ii 483–5 no. 291). If, as seems probable,
'Bermlinge' (C, or 'Bremlyngg' B) = Barming (W. Kent, dioc. Rochester) this
church may have passed out of the hands of St Martin's very soon. Bp Walter of
Rochester — before 26 July 1182 — confirmed for the canons of Leeds the
patronage of Barming (East Barming ?), as granted by the lord of the fee (*Reg.
Roff.* 161). For Mr Ralph of Sarre, prebendary of Deal, one of Bosham's 'eruditi
sancti Thome' who was now dean of Reims (d. *c.*1196) see *Ep. Cant.* pp. xliii–iv,
B. Smalley, *The Becket conflict and the schools* (Oxford 1973) 210–2, and John of
Salisbury, *Letters* i 204, ii pp. xvi, xxxvi.

126. Dover priory

*Confirmation, following grants made by archbishops Theobald and
Thomas, for the monastery of St Martin of Dover of the tithe of all
fishing of the burgesses of Dover.*   [Oct. 1181 × 16 Feb. 1184]

B = Lambeth Palace ms. 241 (Dover cartulary) fo. 37r (36r). s. xiv ex.

Ricardus dei gratia Cantuariensis ecclesie minister humilis venerabili fratri et amico G. Roffensi episcopo et universo clero et populo
totius Cantie salutem et benedictionem. Que deo auctore semel
divinis prestita sunt usibus irrevocabiliter firmare et firmata inviolabiliter conservare debemus. Inde est quod bone memorie Theobaldi
et beati martiris Thome decessorum nostrorum vestigiis inherentes,
decimam totius anni de omni genere piscationis burgensium Dovorr', quam dederunt deo et monasterio beati Martini in usus
monachorum et pauperum perpetualiter, preter illam communem

decimam allecis inter festum sancti Michaelis et Passionem beati
Andree apostoli ab antiquo tempore datam sicut communi assensu
pro salute animarum suarum et omnium successorum incolumitate
eam dederunt, ita eam ad opus monachorum sancti Martini de
Dovorr' confirmamus et ratam huius elemosine donationem et a
monachis orationum promissam burgensibus recompensationem
cum monasterii fraternitate firmam esse volumus. Hanc itaque
elemosinam a nobis confirmatam conservantes, eterne retributionis
gloriam consequantur, diminuere seu aliquatenus inquietare presumentes dei et nostram incurrant maledictionem. Amen. Valete.

In the address G. must be extended to Gualtero or Galeranno. If the bp of
Rochester in question was Walter, the limits of date are Oct. 1181 × 26 July 1182,
if Waleran, the limits are 19 Dec. 1182 × 16 Feb. 1184.

Apart from the reference to the archbp's predecessors, which establishes the
inscription, the charter agrees exactly in wording with that of archbp Thomas,
even to the point of copying the style: 'Cantuariensis ecclesie minister humilis'.
See above, no. 9.

*127.   Dunstable priory

Grants and confirmations for the canons of Dunstable.

[7 April 1174 × 16 Feb. 1184]

Mentioned only in an inventory of the priory's muniments:

B = BL ms. Harl. 1885 (Dunstable cartulary). s. xiii in. fo. 4rb (3rb) *Concessiones
et confirmationes archiepiscoporum.* ... Item Ricardi archiepiscopi confirmatio
generalis. fo. 5ra (4ra) Ricardi archiepiscopi confirmatio de medietate ecclesie
de Cestresham. fo. 5va (4va) *De Asspeleia.* Ricardi archiepiscopi facta inquisi-
tio. Thome archiepiscopi et Ricardi confirmatio.

These items in classified lists may represent different documents, but may
include more than one reference to a single document. For the history of the
moiety of Chesham see *Liber antiquus Hugonis Welles* ed. A. Gibbons (Lincoln
1888) 18, *Ann. mon.* iii 74, and *Dunstable cartulary.* Leicester abbey held the
other moiety: *Liber antiquus* 18 and *CRR* vii 72.

128.   Dunstable priory

*Confirmation of the transaction which has terminated in the arch-
bishop's presence the dispute, brought to him on appeal, between
William son of Fulcher and Alexander the canon. Alexander, for
himself and his brethren, renounced all right in the chapel of Ruxox and
the churches of Flitwick and Husborne (Crawley), surrendered to the
archbishop the charter of Gilbert de Sanderville and all other instruments concerning the chapel and churches, and withdrew his plea on the
condition that the chapel and churches should be transferred to the uses
of the canons of Dunstable. William son of Fulcher and Osmoda his*

wife as patrons granted the chapel and churches with the appurtenant lands to the church of St Peter's, Dunstable, to hold in free and perpetual alms. Alexander son of Gerold, principal lord of the fee and Alice (de Rumilly) his wife confirmed the grant. The archbishop has with their consent received the prior and convent of Dunstable in the chapel and churches and has canonically invested them.

[? Aug. 1174 × Sept. 1175]

B = BL ms. Harl. 1885 (Dunstable cartulary) fo. 21r (20r). s. xiii in.

Pd from B in *EYC* vii 103–4 no. 50, where dated '1174–78'. Calendared from B in *Dunstable cartulary* 43 no. 125.

Hiis testibus: domino Roberto de Novo burgo, Benedicto cancellario etc.

The archbishop is styled legate. For Benedict's tenure of the chancellorship see above, no. 111. The case had probably been referred to the archbishop rather than to Geoffrey, elect of Lincoln, because the latter's appointment was not yet confirmed (1 July 1175: cf. *EEA* i p. xxxviii). The cartulary contains related documents elucidated by C. T. Clay, *EYC* vii 95–107, cf. *Dunstable cartulary* 40–4 nos. 115–28B. A report from Nicholas archdn of Bedford, prior to the archbp's hearing of the case about Ruxox, relates at the request of the parties what he had learnt about the history of the church by enquiry in the rural chapter and from reliable laymen (*Cartulary* 43 no. 126; *EYC* vii 102–3 no. 49). Later letters patent of the archdn announce his induction and investiture of the prior of Dunstable 'ex mandato domini Ricardi Cantuariensis archiepiscopi' (*Cartulary* 42 no. 123). In the cartulary the named witnesses of the archbp's charter appear in the adjoining copy of the grant by William son of Fulcher and his wife to the canons of Dunstable (*EYC* vii 104 no. 51). 'Osmoda' appears elsewhere as 'Osomunda' and, less probably, as 'Sinoda'.

129. Durford abbey

Confirmation for the canons of Durford of the church of St Mary and St John the baptist, Durford, with all its appurtenances, according to the terms of the charter of bishop John of Chichester. Confirmation of the possessions which they may justly acquire in future and of the right which they have by papal privilege to accept persons of the diocese for burial.   [28 April 1174 × 26 April 1180]

B = BL ms. Cotton Vesp. E xxiii (Durford cartulary) fo. 23v (19v, p. 38). s. xiii ex.

Universis sancte matris ecclesie filiis Ricardus dei gratia Cantuariensis archiepiscopus totius Anglie primas et apostolice sedis legatus salutem in domino. Ex iniuncto*a* nobis sollicitudinis officio tenemur omnibus paterna sollicitudine providere, maxime viris religiosis et artioris vie ac vite professionem ingressis, pia diligentia et dili-[fo. 24r]genti providentia prospicere, et ut eorum iura inmutilata serventur vigilanti cura debemus propensius attendere. Inde est quod dilecto filio nostro Roberto abbati de Dureford' et fratribus ibidem deo servientibus omnibusque eorum successoribus canonice substituendis ecclesiam sancte dei genetricis semperque virginis Marie et sancti Iohannis baptiste de Dureford' in qua divino sunt officio mancipati cum omnibus pertinentiis suis, secundum tenorem carte venerabilis fratris nostri Iohannis Cycestrensis episcopi confirmamus et sub nostra protectione suscipimus, in quibus hec propriis duximus exprimenda vocabulis : ex dono Henrici Hosati locum ipsum qui Dereford' dicitur cum adiacentiis suis, sicut terminorum designat positio, et apud Eststanden' terram de Hunria cum omnibus pertinentiis suis et cum incrementis que Henricus Hosatus iunior heres ipsius eis dedit sicut carta ipsius testatur, ex dono Gernagan et uxor eius terram quam Ailwynus Bulluc tenuit, ex dono Walteri Hosati de Stapulford' terram quam Walterus carectarius tenuit. Hec et alia omnia que^b in dyocesi nostra iustis et rationabilibus modis in posterum ipsis obvenerint ipsorum usui perpetuo profutura concedimus et confirmamus. Quod etiam ex privilegio Romane sedis eis indultum est ut quicunque de dyocesi nostra apud eos sepeliri delegerit, nisi excommunicatus vel interdictus fuerit, libere ibi sepeliatur annuimus, salva tamen iustitia illius ecclesie a qua mortui corpus assumitur. Testibus etc.

^{a} iniuncte B ^{b} *om.* que B

The reference to 'our venerable brother' suggests bp John's lifetime.

Apart from the preamble, this uses the wording of bp John's charter (*Chichester acta* 124–5 no. 66: dated 1174 × 1180). At one point only does it refer to another gift by the founder, Henry Hosatus II: 'et apud Eststanden' terram de Hunria cum omnibus pertinentiis suis', and its absence from the charter of bp John may be a copyist's fault. The grant is recorded in later charters of Henry Hosatus III and kg Henry II, with the spellings 'Vure' and 'Hura' (*Mon. Ang.* vii. 937a, 938a), and in a privilege of pope Innocent III, spelt 'Vura' (*Letters of Innocent III* n. 101: 8 April 1199). The place is Standen Manor or Standen Hussey, formerly in Wilts., now part of Hungerford, Berks.

The reference to the papal privilege suggests that Durford relied on a copy of a common privilege for the Premonstratensian Order. The earliest particular privilege preserved with an address to Durford is that of Innocent III (above).

For the foundation and early history of the abbey see Colvin, *White canons* 88–91. Cf. below, nos. 269, 452.

130. East Hanningfield church

Notification of an agreement made in the archbishop's presence between John de Garland, parson, and Gervase, vicar, of the church of East Hanningfield, after a dispute over the vicarage.

Lambeth, 1182 [25 March × 13 Nov. 1182]

B = BL ms. Cotton Appendix xxi (register of Stoke by Clare) fo. 61r (62r, 51r). s. xiii ex.

Pd from B in *Stoke by Clare cartulary* ed. C. Harper-Bill and R. Mortimer, part I (Suffolk Records Soc., Suffolk charters iv 1982) p. 104 no. 130a.

Ricardus dei gratia Cantuariensis archiepiscopus totius Anglie primas universis Christi fidelibus ad quos presentes littere[a] pervenerint eternam in domino salutem. Sciant presentes et futuri quod cum inter Iohannem de Garland et Gervasium clericum controversia super vicaria ecclesie de Esthaningefeld verteretur, tali modo tandem in presentia nostra composuerunt [fo. 61v] pro bono pacis, scilicet quod penes Iohannem residebunt[b] omnes decime curie Agnetis de Munchanesi et domus ecclesie cum universa terra ad ipsam ecclesiam adiacente, preter unam acram terre quam predicta Agnes dedit prefate ecclesie quando adepta est manerium illud contra Ceciliam comitissam Herefordie sororem suam et preter duas acras que sunt de feodo Roberti filii Tecii. Habebit etiam idem Iohannes omnes decimas provenientes de terra quam canonici de Bichenacra modo excolunt in ipsa parochia. Prefatus vero Gervasius habebit omnes decimas, obventiones, omniaque beneficia alia que de ipsa ecclesia pervenient et exhonerabit prefatum Iohannem de omnibus episcopalibus et officialium suorum consuetudinibus. Idem vero Gervasius fidei sue interpositione formavit quod fidem et honorem ac reverentiam portabit Iohanni tamquam persone sepedicte ecclesie et non queret arte vel ingenio[c] modis aliquibus unde possessio ipsius Iohannis turbetur vel ius eius in aliquo diminuatur. Capellanus vero qui in ea ministrabit faciet fidelitatem ipsi Iohanni tamquam persone. Predictus autem Iohannes vice versa hanc transactionem firmiter observandam fide mediante firmavit. Facta est autem hec transactio anno ab incarnatione domini mclxxxii apud Lamhidam, robur perpetuum habitura. Testibus: Ricardo Wintoniensi episcopo, Herberto Cantuariensi archidiacono, magistro Gerardo, magistro Roberto de Inglesham, et aliis.

[a] litterere B   [b] residerunt B   [c] artem vel ingenium B

The transaction occurred before the archbp left England in 1182; he did not return until Aug. 1183. This John de Garland may be the one who appears in the 1190s as royal judge and canon of St Paul's (*Fasti eccl. angl. 1066–1300* i 66). For Agnes, wife of Warin de Muntchenesy, co-heiress with the countess Cicely of Pain FitzJohn, see W. Farrer *Honors and knights' fees* iii (Manchester 1925) 103–6 and *GEC* ix 419, 424–5. For the later history of the manor and church of East Hanningfield see Newcourt, *Repertorium* ii 305–7. The reason for the presence of this record in the Stoke register is not apparent. The compiler assigned it no number, and in the margin is written 'nul ... '.

131. Edinburgh: abbey of Holyrood

Confirmation for the canons of Holyrood, Edinburgh, of the gift of the church of (Great) Paxton and all its appurtenances in free alms by Malcolm (IV) king of Scotland, saving the dignity of the church and bishop of Lincoln. The grant was made in the presence of bishop Robert (II) of Lincoln and confirmed by his charter and by a charter of archbishop Thomas.   [28 April 1174 × autumn 1177]

> B = Lincoln, Lincs. Archives Office, Lincoln D. & C. Mun. A/1/6 ('Registrum') no. 292. s. xiv in.
>
> Pd from B in *Linc. reg. ant.* iii 157–8 no. 811.

Hiis testibus: magistro Gerardo, magistro Petro Blesensi, magistro Ricardo Salopesberiensi, Willelmo de Norhalle, Henrico Baiocensi canonico, Radulfo de Sancto Martino, Rogero Norwicensi, Willelmo de Sotindon'*ᵃ*, Rogerio decano, et pluribus aliis.

> *ᵃ* Dotindon' B

> The archbp is styled legate. Mr Gerard and Mr Peter of Blois left England for Rome in autumn 1177. William of Northolt became archdn of Gloucester May × Dec. 1177.
>   The text uses the words of archbp Thomas's confirmation, above, no. 13; for bp Robert's confirmation cf. *EEA* i no. 111. The arenga and beginning of the text closely resemble a charter for Belvoir (above, no. 56) which includes eight of the same witnesses. 'Dissolvantur' is probably the copyist's misreading of 'divellantur'.

132. Eynsham abbey

Protection and confirmation for the monks of Eynsham of all their present possessions and those which they may justly acquire in future. The following possessions are specified; the churches of Tetbury, Stanton (St John), Northleigh, (South) Newington, Marston, Souldern, Merton, Whitfield, Cornwell, a moiety of the church of (Lower) Heyford, and a mill at Dallington.

[28 April 1174 × autumn 1177]

> B = Oxford, Christ Church, Chapter Libr. ms. 31 (Eynsham cartulary) fo. 20v. s. xii/xiii.
>
> Pd from B in *Eynsham cartulary* i 58 no. 42.

Testibus: magistro Gerardo, Walerano archidiacono Baiocensi, magistro Petro Blesensi, Willelmo de Norhal', Radulfo de Wingham, Radulfo de Sancto Martino, Henrico Baiocensi, Amico clerico, Rogero Norwicensi, Rogero elemosinario, magistro [*sic*] Willelmo de Sottindon et aliis multis.

The archbp is styled legate; William of Northolt became archdn of Gloucester May × Dec. 1177. Mr Gerard and Mr Peter of Blois left England for Rome in autumn 1177.

William of Shottenden nowhere else appears as a master, and the copyist here may have omitted a name or names after 'magistro'. Cf. below, no. 202. The witness-lists are so similar as to suggest the same date for both charters. In that case this one cannot be earlier than Aug. 1176. But in nos. 173 and 174 William's name follows Roger the almoner's immediately.

133. Farleigh priory

Confirmation of an agreement reached in the archbishop's presence between the prior (Hugh III) of Lewes and the noble Margaret de Bohun after dispute about the removal and replacement of the prior of Farleigh and other matters relating to that priory.

[19 Dec. 1182 × 16 Feb. 1184]

B = BL ms. Cotton Vesp. F xv (Lewes cartulary) fo. 165v (194v). s. xv med. Press-mark 'S. xv' in margin.

Pd (calendar) from B in *Cartulary of the priory of St Pancras, Lewes, Wilts., Devon and Dorset portions* (Sussex Rec. Soc. 1948) ed. W. Budgen and L. F. Salzman, 17 no. 28.

Ricardus dei gratia Cantuariensis archiepiscopus totius Anglie primas universis sancte matris ecclesie filiis salutem, gratiam et benedictionem. Cum in presentia nostra contentio*a* fuisset inter priorem de Lewes et nobilem mulierem Margaretam de Boihun super dispositione*b* domus de Ferlegh', concessit eadem Margareta priori de Lewes pro reverentia persone sue ut ipse H. in priore de Farle amovendo et substituendo domui provideat, salva dignitate domini regis et salvo iure nepotis sui Henrici cuius custodiam ipsa habet a*c* domino rege sibi commissam. Promisit etiam eadem domina quod si ipsa vel aliquis de suis de rebus domus quicquam amovit, id ad arbitrium iam dicti prioris restituet, et ipse prior ex parte sua promisit quod si quid ipsa de suo in utilitatem domus expendit id de ipsa domo et reddatur. Hanc pacis formam ratam inter predictas partes manere volentes presenti scripto dignum duximus commendare et sigilli nostri*d* patrocinio communire. Testibus: R. Bathoniensi et P. Meneviensi et Walerano Rofensi episcopis, P. Bathoniensi et W. Gloecestriensi archidiaconis, et multis aliis.

a contessio B   *b* dispositionis B   *c* ad B   *d* sigillo nostro B

Waleran was consecrated bp of Rochester 19 Dec. 1182.

Margaret de Bohun was co-heiress of Miles of Gloucester and now widow of Humphrey (II) de Bohun (d. 1165) who founded the priory of Farleigh. She died in 1197. Her son, Humphrey (III) had died in 1181 and Henry de Bohun, her grandson, was in her wardship. See I. J. Sanders, *English baronies* (Oxford 1960) 91 and D. Walker in *Camden miscellany XXII* (R. Hist. Soc. 1964) 10; and cf. no. 467 below.

134. Godstow abbey

Confirmation for the nuns of Godstow of the church of (High) Wycombe, which they have canonically acquired by the institution of Geoffrey, bishop-elect of Lincoln, on the presentation of king Henry II.

[1177, before autumn]

B = PRO E 164/20 (Godstow cartulary) fo. 153r. s. xv in.

Pd (only from an English abstract s. xv ex.) in the *English register of Godstow nunnery* ed. A. Clark (Early English Text Soc. 1906–11) i 85 no. 88.

Universis sancte matris ecclesie filiis ad quos presentes littere pervenerint Ricardus dei gratia Cantuariensis ecclesie minister humilis, totius Anglie primas et apostolice sedis legatus eternam in domino salutem. Ad universitatis vestre notitiam volumus pervenire nos concessisse et presenti carta nostra confirmasse dilectis in domino filiabus nostris monialibus de Godestowe ecclesiam de Wicumbe cum omnibus eius pertinentiis in perpetuum possidendam, sicut eedem*a* moniales eandem ecclesiam ex institutione venerabilis fratris nostri G. Lincolniensis electi et ad domini regis Anglie presentationem canonice adepte sunt. Volumus ergo et precipimus ut predicte moniales prefatam ecclesiam cum universis ad ecclesiam eandem pertinentibus in terris, decimis, et omnimodis obventionibus libere et integre in perpetuum possideant. Et ut hec nostre confirmationis pagina debita gaudeat stabilitate et posteris temporibus permaneat inconvulsa eam sigilli nostri appositione duximus roborandam. Hiis testibus: Walerano Baiocensi archidiacono, magistro P. Blesensi, Willelmo de Norhall', magistro Roberto de Inglesham, Rogero decano, Iohanne capellano, Willelmo Sotewame, et aliis pluribus.

a eidem B

The royal charter (fo. 152v) has bp John of Norwich as witness: after 14 Dec. 1175. The charter of Geoffrey, elect of Lincoln cannot be earlier than 1177 (*EEA* i no. 288). William of Northolt became archdn of Gloucester May × Dec. 1177. Peter of Blois left England for Rome in autumn 1177.

135. Henry, son of king Henry II

Exhortation to Henry III, king of England, to desist from attacking his father (Henry II), who is devoted to his son's interests. The archbishop quotes biblical texts extolling filial piety and cites numerous examples from classical and biblical history of princes who have refused to take power before their fathers died, as well as a few notorious children whose ambitions led them to disaster. King Henry II guards and strengthens the realm to hand it on to his son; his son should shun false flatterers who, for their own advantage, seduce him into claiming a fixed portion of the royal dominions for himself. He gains more from his father's liberality than he could extort, violently and sinfully, from the kingdom of France. If he abandons his evil ways and his excommunicate associates the archbishop will support him. But if he refuses to listen to the advice of the archbishop and his suffragans, who are writing collectively to him, he must know that the pope has instructed the archbishop to excommunicate him and all who disturb the peace of his lord and father, without appeal. The archbishop, however reluctant, will execute the mandate thoroughly if the prince does not submit within fifteen days. [? May × June 1183]

Petri Blesensis opp. i 141–5 no. 47.

The protocol reads: 'Henrico tertio dei gratia regi Anglie et domini regis filio Ricardus Cantuariensis ecclesie humilis minister spiritum consilii cum salute.' The letter appears in the first and succeeding compilations of Peter of Blois's letters without significant variation. Giles dated it a.d. 1174, connecting it with the rebellion of 1173–74. If this is so, it must have preceded the peace made between Henry II and his sons at Mont-Louis, 30 Sept. 1174, and almost certainly followed the arrival of the new archbp in England in mid-August or later, since the letter implies contact between the archbp and his suffragans. But a more likely date is May or early June 1183. The archbp and Peter of Blois are found at the royal court at Poitiers on 8 March (above, no. 91) and were in France during the next months. There is no record of the papal mandate to which the letter refers, either in 1174 or in 1183; but on Ascension Day (26 May) 1183, at Caen, the archbp of Canterbury and other bps publicly excommunicated disturbers of peace between Henry II and his sons 'excepta regis filii persona', according to the *Gesta Henrici* (i 300). The young king died at Martel on 11 June 1183. His death prompted moral reflections by the dean of St Paul's on the fate of ungrateful sons (Diceto, *Op.* ii 19–20).

136. The church of Hereford

Notification that the dispute between bishop Robert of Hereford and Hugh Parvus, delegated to the archbishop by pope Alexander III, has been terminated in the archbishop's presence. He has found that the churches of Moreton (Valence) and Whaddon, which were claimed by Hugh, were previously granted by his father, Roger Parvus, their patron, to the church of Hereford for a prebend, and confirmed by bishop John of Worcester. The church had enjoyed long and peaceful possession of them. The archbishop adjudges the churches to the bishop and church of Hereford, so that no question of either proprietorship or possession shall again arise. [March 1177]

A = Hereford D. & C. Mun. no. 2770. Endorsed, s. xiii med.: Sententia lata super appropriacione dictarum ecclesiarum per archiepiscopum iudicem delegatum in hac parte. Approx. 220 × 120 + 20 mm. Sealing d.q. 1; seal and counterseal of green wax, damaged. The script is that of nos. 3 and 34, above.

Pd from A in *Hereford charters* 27–28.

Universis Christi fidelibus ad quos presentes littere pervenerint ׃ Ric(ardus) dei gratia Cantuariensis archiepiscopus . totius Anglie primas ׃ et apostolice sedis legatus ׃ salutem in domino. Sicut boni iudicis est semper lites minuere ׃ ita ad ipsius spectat diligentiam ne cum semel decise fuerint rediviva valeant suscitari questione. Eapropter tam ad presentium quam ad futurorum volumus noticiam pervenire ׃ quod causam que inter venerabilem fratrem nostrum .R. Herefordensem episcopum . et Hugonem Parvum super ecclesiis de Mortona et Waddona diutius agitata fuerat ׃ quas idem episcopus ad ius Herefordensis ecclesie pertinere asserebat . a sede apostolica omni appellatione remota cognoscendam et terminandam suscepimus. Partibus itaque sub presentia nostra constitutis cum post diligentem et studiosam examinationem constaret nobis tam per venerabilis fratris nostri .G. Lundonensis episcopi testimonium tunc temporis ecclesie Herefordensi presidentis . quam etiam aliorum multorum integre opinionis virorum . iuratorum attestationibus ׃ pretaxatas ecclesias sepedicte ecclesie Herefordensi a Rogero Parvo patre Hugonis Parvi qui in predictis ecclesiis ius patronatus habebat in perpetuam prebendam concedente et confirmante hoc ׃ bone memorie diocesano episcopo Iohanne canonice fuisse collatas ׃ et ab eadem ecclesia Herefordensi diutius et quiete possessas ׃ predicto episcopo . et ecclesie Herefordensi easdem ecclesias videlicet de Mortona et Waddona . assidentibus nobis viris honestis et discretis adiudicavimus . ita quidem ut tam de proprietate quam de possessione nichil in posterum supersit questionis. Et ne hec decetero in dubium revocentur ׃ et testium subscriptione . et sigilli nostri appositione ea duximus communire. His testibus . magistro Girardo . Waleranno archidiacono Baiocensi . magistro Petro Blesensi . Radulfo de Wingaham . Willelmo de Norhal' . Radulfo de Sancto Martino . magistro Roberto de Inglesham . Willelmo Cadomensi . Nicolao de Leuekenora . magistro Waltero scriptore . Willelmo de Stokes . Amico clerico . et aliis multis.

The original grant by Roger Parvus is Hereford D. & C. Mun. no. 722 (*Hereford charters* 12); this was in the lifetime of earl Roger, i.e. not after 1155. It was confirmed by bp John (of Pagham) of Worcester between 4 March 1151 and 31 March 1157. That the legal proceedings were protracted appears from a decretal of Alexander III, before 1177, which records the appeal by the bp of Hereford, a counter-appeal by Hugh, and action taken by the archbp against Hugh for contumacy (JL 13812: Coll. Lipsiensis 52. 11, Coll. Claustroneoburg. 195, Coll. Wigorn. 7. 4, Coll. Bamberg. 44. 5d, Coll. Sangerm. 5. 4. 6). The settlement can be dated on or before 19 March 1177, when bp Roger of Worcester ratified it in the presence of the archbp and other bps at Westminster. Hugh Parvus was present and submitted to the sentence, kg Henry II gave a confirmatory charter (cf. Eyton, *Itinerary* 211–2). The sentence was confirmed by Alexander III, 5 Feb. 1178 (*PUE* ii 362 no. 179). The relevant documents are printed in *Hereford charters* 27–31, with inaccurate witness-lists and faulty dating.

137. Abbey of St Benet of Holme

Confirmation for Eilward, priest, of the church of North Walsham, with tithes and all appurtenances, as granted and confirmed by Everard and William, bishops of Norwich, and archbishop Theobald.

[1182, before 9 Oct.]

B = BL ms. Cotton Galba E ii (cartulary of St Benet of Holme) fo. 44v (fo. xvv).

Ricardus dei gratia Cantuariensis archiepiscopus totius Anglie primas universis Christi fidelibus ad quos presentes littere pervenerint eternam in domino salutem. Patris et predecessoris nostri felicis memorie Theobaldi Cantuariensis archiepiscopi vestigiis inherentes Eilwardo sacerdoti de Northwalsham ecclesiam de Northwalsham cum decimis et universis pertinentiis suis concedimus et presenti scripti patrocinio canonice confirmamus, sicut memoratus pater et predecessor noster ex concessione et confirmatione Everardi quondam Norwicensis episcopi ac pie memorie Willelmi successoris sui scripti sui testimonio*a* confirmavit. Huius nostre confirmationis testes sunt Waleranus Baiocensis archidiaconus, magister Petrus Blesensis archidiaconus Bathoniensis, etc.

Everard, who received from the abbey of St Benet of Holme the grant of Eilward's lay fee in North Walsham by hereditary tenure (*St Benet's register* i 148 no. 275). Eilward's other title-deeds were not entered in the abbey's cartulary. Pope Lucius III included the church and appurtenances among the possessions of St Benet's in a general privilege of 28 July 1183 (*Mon. Ang.* iii 90; *St Benet's register* i 39 no. 69). By 1186 the abbot had presented, and the bp instituted, Thomas archdn of Norwich to the church of North Walsham, on condition of paying a yearly pension of twenty shillings to the abbey (ibid. i 137 no. 252, i 62 no. 106, i 64 no. 110).

138. Horton priory

Confirmation for the monks of Horton of their possessions, after inspection of the charter of confirmation of king Henry (II).

[1182 × 16 Feb. 1184]

B = Cambridge UL ms. Ee 5 31 (register of prior Henry of Ch. Ch. Canterbury) fo. 99r (100r) in copy of inspeximus (1304) by P. & C. Ch. Ch. s. xiv in. C = BL ms. Stowe 935 (Monks Horton cartulary) fo. 39r (p. 125), in copy of same inspeximus. s. xv med. D = Lambeth Palace, Reg. W. Warham fo. 115v (118v) in copy of same inspeximus. s. xvi in.

Pd (abridged) from B by Kennett, *Parochial antiquities* ii 301.

Omnibus sancte matris ecclesie filiis ad quos presentes littere pervenerint Ricardus dei gratia Cantuariensis archiepiscopus et totius Anglie primas illam que est in domino salutem. Cum ad sollicitudinis nostre pertineat officium subiectorum nostrorum paci et quieti intendere, viros religiosos et eorum possessiones propensiori caritatis affectu debemus protegere et defensare quatinus nostre protectionis beneficio securi in proposito sancte religionis firmius perseverent et nulle malignantium impugnationes eos vel eorum possessiones turbare vel inquietare attemptent. Eapropter ad universitatis vestre notitiam volumus pervenire quod nos inspecto domini H.^{a} illustris Anglorum regis scripto quo dilectis filiis nostris monachis de Horton' concedit et confirmat possessiones a fidelium devotione sibi collatas, easdem possessiones et alias quas iusto possident titulo vel iustis modis poterunt adipisci, eisdem monachis sicut eis rationabiliter collate sunt, concedimus et confirmamus, inter quas quasdam propriis vocabulis duximus exprimendas: ex dono Roberti de Ver et Adeline^b uxoris eius manerium de Horton' cum omnibus pertinentiis suis, scilicet cum terra et hominibus de Haiton'^{c} et de Henxcell' et de marisco et cum operibus que homines faciebant apud Saltwode et cum nemoribus de Redbroc' et de Wytingehangre, decimam etiam de Ecreton'^{d} sicud Robertus capellanus eam habuit, et in Essexia ecclesiam de Purleya cum omnibus decimis et consuetudinibus ad eam pertinentibus, et quinque solidos qui reddebantur de Hayton'^{e} et^f Saltwod', et viginti et quinque denarios qui de eadem terra reddebantur Estbrigg', preterea ex dono eiusdem Roberti et prenominate uxoris sue Adeline^b manerium de Tidinton' cum omnibus pertinentiis et libertatibus eiusdem manerii, et ecclesiam de Stanstede cum omnibus pertinentiis suis, et ecclesiam de Braburne cum omnibus pertinentiis suis, et decimas de Estbregg' et de Hunechild' excepto sale, ex dono Osberti Marescalci et Hermeline uxoris sue terram de Hamton' excepta parte illa quam idem Osbertus dedit^g sorori sue tenendam de predictis monachis, et donationem quam Ermelina fecit eidem ecclesie de mariagio suo in marisco et de dote sua de iugo de Gara, et concessionem quam Walterus filius eiusdem Ermeline inde fecit predictis monachis, ex dono Iohannis comitis de Augo et Adelicie uxoris sue terram quam Goldwynus tenebat de Rysdenn' cum omnibus pertinentiis suis et quindecim solidos de terra que fuit Osberti de Boywik singulis annis, ex dono Symonis de Mallyng' terram de Huleham, ex dono Nicholai et matris sue Avicie in Stutyng' unam virgatam terre, ex dono Stephani Haringod et Wymarc' uxoris sue et Iohannis Haringod et fratrum suorum viginti acras terre apud Stutyngebregg', ex dono Nigelli filii Bertrammi totam terram quam ipse tenebat de feodo Roberti de Ver, et totam aliam terram suam de quibuscumque ipse tenebat, et terram de Heda, ex dono Symonis de Thinegat'[h] unam acram prati que dicitur Langehop', ex dono Normanni de Assactesford, ecclesiam de Assactesford cum terris et decimis et omnibus ad eam pertinentibus et unam virgatam terre quam Fulco presbiter tenuit et terram cuiusdam femine que reddit novem denarios per annum, ex dono Roberti de Aldelos' totam terram illam quam Robertus de Ver tenuit et concessionem quam Hamo filius eiusdem Roberti eis de terra illa fecit, ex dono Hugonis de Sancto Quintino terram de Huleham possidendam per redditum quinque solidorum per annum et per escoctum dimidie virgate terre quod pertinet ad curiam de Sellyng', ex dono Wyberti filii Cole et filiorum suorum terram que dicitur Gare, et ad orientalem eius partem duodecim acras terre ascendentes contra montem, ex dono Rogeri pincerne et uxoris eius terras et virgulta et omnia alia que tenuerunt uno anno et uno die, ex dono Symonis de Thynegate redditum duorum solidorum de terra que vocatur Swanesham, ex dono Walteri filii Roberti de Candos nemus de Fresingheye cum tribus hominibus qui in eodem nemore habitant et terram apud Postling' quam dederat armigero suo Waltero de Malring'[j], ex dono Huberti de Sandherst et concessione Ranulphi et Hadewise neptis predicti Huberti terram que dicitur Weynland[k] in Tydinton', ex dono Godefridi [fo. 99v] de Mallyng' unam virgatam terre in Hunteburne, ex dono Roberti Bretel unam virgatam terre in Strete, ex dono Walteri filii Galfridi Rufi et fratrum suorum terram que dicitur Reginaldi in Strete.[l] Ut autem hec concessionis nostre pagina firma et inconvulsa perseveret, eam et sigilli nostri appositione et testium subscriptione communimus. Hiis testibus: magistro P. Blesensi archidiacono Bathoniensi, Willelmo archidiacono Glowecestriensi, magistro Henrico de Norhamton', Willelmo de Sotindon', Rogero decano, magistro Rogero Norwycensi, Ricardo Lond' et Galfrido clericis, et multis aliis.

[a] H. B; Henrici CD   [b] Adeline CD: Adelue B   [c] Haiton C; Hortone B; Horton D   [d] Ecreton' B; Etreton' C; Etterton D   [e] Hayton' B; Haiton C; Harton' D   [f] om. et B   [g] dedit D; debet BC   [h] Thinegat' B; Thenegate C; Thenegat' D   [j] Malring' B; Marling' CD   [k] Weynland B; Weiland C; Weilond' D   [l] ex dono Walteri ... in Strete CD, om. B

After Peter of Blois became archdn of Bath.

The foundation of the Cluniac priory of Monks Horton by Robert de Vere and his wife was after their marriage c.1130 (PR 31 Hen. I (ed. J. Hunter, Rec. Comm. 1833) 64, and before kg Stephen's confirmation of their gift, 12 July 1140 × Sept. 1143 (Regesta regum iii 155 no. 406). For charters of Robert de Vere and his wife see Mon. Ang. v 34–35. Henry II's charter is pd by J. R. Scott in

Archaeologia Cantiana x (1876) 275. The inspeximus of the archbp's confirmation describes it as 'littere patentes'. Cf. below, no. 497.

139. Order of the Hospital

Confirmation of an amicable composition between the Hospital of St John of Jerusalem and the canons of Dunmow, reached in the presence of the archbishop, acting as papal judge delegate, over the church of Burnham.

[Dec. 1181 × 16 Feb. 1184]

B = BL ms. Cotton Nero E vi (Hospitallers' cartulary) fo. 262r. s. xv med. Probably copied from C, but made the basis of the following text, since C is incomplete. C = Bodl. ms. Rawl. Essex 11 (SC 15998) fos. 3v, 1r. Badly damaged and misplaced leaves of a cartulary of the English Hospitallers. s. xiii/xiv. Cf. Michael Gervers, 'An early cartulary fragment of the Order of St John of Jerusalem in England' *Journal of Soc. of Archivists* v (1974) 8–24.

Pd from BC in M. Gervers, *The Hospitaller cartulary in the British Library* (Toronto 1981) 314; pd (calendar) from B in *Kentish cartulary of the Order of St John of Jerusalem* ed. C. Cotton (Kent Records xi. Kent Archaeol. Soc. 1930) 134.

Universis sancte matris etc. Ricardus Cantuariensis ecclesie minister humilis eternam in Christo salutem. Noverit etc. causam que de mandato domini Lucii pape III coram nobis inter hospitalarios et canonicos de Dunmawe super ecclesia de Burnham[a] diutius ventilata est post varios ipsius excursus tandem de voluntate partium amicabili compositione conquievisse in hunc modum, scilicet quod personatus prescripte ecclesie penes hospitalarios residebit perpetuo et canonici perpetuam vicariam in ea habebunt, solvendo annuatim de eadem ecclesia nomine perpetue vicarie hospitalariis aureum unum quamdiù Walterus filius Walteri vixerit, qui de eisdem canonicis memoratam tenet ecclesiam. Post discessum[b] vero dicti Walteri canonici ecclesiam illam in manum suam omnino recipient et solvent de ea singulis annis ipsis hospitalariis iii marcas argenti ad duos anni terminos, scilicet xx solidos ad Pascha et xx solidos ad festum sancti Michaelis. Et ut presens transactio[c] firma in posterum et inconcussa permaneat, presenti eam scripto duximus commendare et sigilli nostri appositione roborare.[d] Hiis testibus etc.

[a] Burnham B (n *over erasure, orig. rubric* Burgham); Burham C   [b] discessum; dissessum B; diffessum C   [c] transactio B, *om. and interline* + C   [d] roborare: roborari BC

The church of Burnham on Crouch, Essex, was given to Dunmow priory by Walter FitzRobert in 1155 (Newcourt, *Repertorium* ii 113). Newcourt knew of the pension to the Hospitallers but, like *Mon. Ang.* vi 145, treats the rectory as appropriated to Dunmow. The archbp's confirmation is preceded in both mss. by Dunmow's record of the composition, in which the vicar is called 'Walterus clericus filius Walteri filii Roberti', and prior Ralph and the canons undertake to answer 'de omni exactione et consuetudine eiusdem ecclesie episcopo diocesano et archidiacono et officialibus eorum pertinente'. The corresponding record (*mut. mut.*) given by Ralph de Diva, prior of the Hospital in England is printed from the Dunmow cartulary (BL ms. Harl. 662 fo. 69r) by J. Delaville Le Roulx, *Cart. gén. de l'ordre des Hospitaliers* iv (Paris 1906) 320. The case cannot have been heard on a mandate of Lucius III before Dec. 1181.

*140. Kenilworth priory

Notification of an agreement reached between bishop Richard of Coventry and the prior of Kenilworth over the church of Fenny Compton.

[Aug. 1174 × Sept. 1181]

Mentioned only, in a later letter to the bp about the custody of the key of the church (below, no. 141).

141. Kenilworth priory

Notification to bishop Richard of Coventry that in settling the dispute between the bishop and the prior of Kenilworth over the church of Fenny Compton, he made arrangements for the custody of the key of the church. Mandate to institute in the church a fit person when presented by the prior or canons.

[Aug. 1174 × Sept. 1181]

B = BL ms. Harl. 3650 (Kenilworth cartulary) fo. 53r (p. 105). s. xiii in. C = BL ms. Add. 47677 (Kenilworth cartulary) fo. 329r (315r). s. xvi in.

Ricardus dei gratia Cantuariensis archiepiscopus totius Anglie primas et apostolice sedis legatus venerabili fratri R. eadem gratia Coventrensi episcopo salutem in vero salutari. Quoniam in prioribus literis nostris super concordia inter vos et dilectum filium nostrum priorem de Kenill' super ecclesia de Cumton' formatis et emissis nulla de clave ipsius ecclesie tradenda mentio facta est, tandem de ipsius clavis traditione coram nobis questione mota, ipso priore et magistro Ricardo de Gnoueshall' clerico et responsali vestro in presentia nostra constitutis, super hoc quoque pacem inter vos reformare curavimus, scilicet ut omnibus illis que in priori scripto nostro super illa transactione concepto robur omnimodum optinentibus clavis prefate ecclesie in manu vestra per priorem tradatur. Vobis quoque mandamus et in virtute obedientie precipimus ut in clave illa a vobis recipienda vel retinenda seu alii tradenda, sive per vos sive per vestros in preiudicium prefati prioris et ecclesie sue nichil fiat, vel etiam vobis in preiudicium officii episcopalis, addentes etiam in mandatis et firmius iniungentes quatinus cum vel prior seu fratres ecclesie de Kenill' ad prefatam ecclesiam personam idoneam vobis presentabunt, eam sine difficultate et molestia et mora recipiatis et instituatis. Valete.

142.   Kenilworth priory

Confirmation for the canons of Kenilworth of all their possessions (enumerated), following the confirmations of the donors' charters by bishops of Coventry, Worcester, Lincoln, and Bath, and archbishop Theobald.

[Oct. 1181 × 16 Feb. 1184]

B = BL ms. Harl. 3650 (Kenilworth cartulary) fo. 53v (p. 106). s. xiii in. C = BL ms. Add. 47677 (Kenilworth cartulary) fo. 95v (90v). s. xvi in.

Ricardus dei gratia Cantuariensis archiepiscopus totius Anglie primas universis sancte matris ecclesie filiis ad quos presens scriptum pervenerit salutem in domino. Que a venerabilibus fratribus nostris coepiscopis canonice fieri noscuntur ad nostrum spectat officium ea confirmare, et ut futuris maneant temporibus inconcussa perpetuo stabilire. Inde est quod ecclesie beate Marie de Kenill'[a] et religiosis fratribus canonicis regularibus eiusdem loci omnes ecclesias et quascumque possessiones in terris et decimis et aliis quibuslibet redditibus quas bone memorie Rogerus et Walterus Coventrenses et Simon et Alvredus Wigornienses et Alexander et Robertus Lincolnienses et Robertus Bathoniensis episcopi eis cartis suis confirmaverunt, presentis scripti pagina communimus et nostre attestationis auctoritate corroboramus, pie recordationis Teobaldi predecessoris nostri vestigia sequentes, sicut in donatorum cartis continetur. Ex quibus propriis hec duximus exprimenda vocabulis: videlicet ipsam villam de Kenill',[a] manerium de Saltford',[b] manerium de Utilicot' cum duobus pratis, Sexter et Tachesmora, manerium de Neweham, Hichenden' cum omnibus pertinentiis et libertatibus suis, in Lillenton' dimidiam hidam terre, ecclesias de Kinton', de Budiford', de Brailes, de Welesburn', de Cumpton', de Barton', de Stanleg', de Wotton', ecclesiam de Stanes, terram que fuit Bresard' et medietatem totius nemoris, terram que fuit Alani in Waleton' cum essartis, terram Aldewini, terram de Neweton' et de Lodbroc et in Wotton', terras quas habent per Odonem de Turri cum prato et molendino de Kibecliva, ecclesias de Wilmelecton' et de Radeford' et de Hampton' in Arden' et de Stivel' et de Clinton', ecclesiam de Cherleton' in Somersat', sicut in cartis Roberti epis-

copi Bathoniensis et Ricardi de Canvill' continetur, terram que fuit
Cortesi in Tiso, molendinum in Wotton' proximum ecclesie, apud
Stafford' terram Walteri filii Iuete, terram Briani filii Cadio, terram
de Frodeswella, medietatem ecclesie de Stokes, unam hidam terre in
Haleford' ex donatione Willelmi Giffard', ecclesiam sancti Nicholai
in castro de Stafford', ecclesias de Medeleg', de Wolward', et de
Tisso cum virgulto et molendino ecclesie proximo, terram de Broc
cum nemore et essartis, ecclesiam de Eatendon' et ecclesiam de
Smita cum capella Brinkelawe, ecclesias*c* de Cesterton et de Witen-
asse, ecclesias de Laminton' et de Cobinton' ecclesie de Wotton'
pertinentes, ecclesiam de Hugenden', terras et mansuras quas
habent in Warewich', pratum de [fo. 54r] Badechinton*d*, terram que
fuit Milonis in Chinton', ecclesiam de Lokesleg', manerium de
Pachinton', totam Leminton', in Wolvricheston unam hidam terre
et unam virgatam, terram de Stalinton', ecclesiam de Herberbir'.
Hec ergo et omnia alia que iustis modis ac rationabilibus acquirere
poterunt eis similiter confirmamus. Nulli ergo omnino hominum
liceat bona illorum diminuere, pacem temere perturbare, nec aliquo
modo contra iustitiam eorum possessiones inquietare. Pax dei
omnibus eis pacem conservantibus, pacis eorum perturbatores dei
et nostram habeant maledictionem et in districto examine divine
ultionis pene debite subiaceant. Valete.

a Kennel' C   *b* followed by etc. ut supra *and om. rest* C   *c* ecclesiam B
d Radechinton' B

For the charter of archbp Theobald see Saltman, *Theobald* 360–2 no. 139, which
is copied here completely, with trivial changes and the addition of a few
properties, notably the church of Charlton Horethorne. Theobald did not
confirm the charter of bp Robert of Bath concerning this church.

*143. Leeds priory

*Confirmation (?) for the canons of Leeds of the advowson of the church
of Borden.*

[7 April 1174 × May 1183]

Mentioned only, in Lambeth Palace, Carte misc. V/111 (inventory of Leeds
muniments): 'Carta eiusdem [Ricardi] de ecclesia de Bordn' de iure patronatus
et altera de personatu'. s. xiii in. Probably the first charter in this entry, and therefore before May 1183, since the second charter appears to be no. 144 below.

144. Leeds priory

*Confirmation for the canons of Leeds of the church of Borden granted to
them in free and perpetual alms, in the archbishop's presence, by Simon*

son of Peter, and confirmed by the charter of king Henry II. On the
subsequent death of Ralph of St George, parson of the church, the
archbishop has granted it in free and perpetual alms to the canons and
has instituted them canonically as parson.

[Oct. 1181 × ? 25 May 1183]

A = Original lost, probably the second mentioned in Lambeth Palace, Carte misc. V/111 (inventory of Leeds muniments): 'Carta eiusdem [Ricardi] de ecclesia de Bordn' de iure patronatus et altera de personatu et tertia de domino fundi.' s. xiii in.

B = Lambeth Palace, Reg. W. Warham fo. 97r (99r). s. xvi in. C = Ibid. fo. 98r (100r) in copy of inspeximus (1278) by archbp Robert; D = Ibid. fo. 103v (105v) in copy of inspeximus by archbp Hubert; E = Ibid. fo. 104r (106r) in copy of inspeximus (1314) by P. & C. Ch. Ch. Canterbury; F = Cambridge UL ms. Ee 5 31 (register of prior Henry of Ch. Ch.) fo. 152r (154r no. xi) in copy of same inspeximus. s. xiv in.; G = Maidstone, Kent Archives Office ms. U/120 Q/13 (Leeds cartulary) fo. 4v in copy of inspeximus (1278) by archbp Robert. s. xiv med.

Ricardus dei gratia Cantuariensis archiepiscopus totius Anglie primas universis sancte matris ecclesie filiis ad quos littere iste pervenerint eternam in domino salutem. Ad omnium notitiam volumus pervenire dilectum filium nostrum Simonem filium Petri in nostra constitutum presentia, quantum ad laicam spectat personam, sicut scriptum eius auctenticum testatur, concessisse et dedisse in liberam et perpetuam elemosinam dilectis filiis nostris canonicis de Ledes ecclesiam de Bordena. Sed et dominus Anglorum rex illustrissimus eandem donationem ratam habens eam solempniter scripto suo quod vidimus confirmavit. Unde et nos postmodum, cum[a] predictam ecclesiam defuncto Radulfo de Sancto Georgio eiusdem ecclesie persona vacare contigisset, ecclesiam ipsam memoratis canonicis in liberam et perpetuam contulimus elemosinam, ipsosque in eadem ecclesia personam canonice instituimus. Quare volumus et ea qua fungimur auctoritate precipimus ut iidem[b] canonici habeant et teneant libere et pacifice prelibatam ecclesiam quam eis sicut dictum est in liberam et perpetuam elemosinam concessimus et presenti carta confirmavimus, statuentes et sub interminatione anathematis prohibentes ne quis hanc nostre concessionis et confirmationis paginam iniuste infringere vel ei aliquatenus temere contraire presumat. Testibus: magistro Gerardo, Willelmo Glocestriensi archidiacono, magistro Roberto de Inglesham, Willelmo et Moyse capellanis, Henrico Baiocensi, magistro Rogero Norwicensi, Michaele de Burn',[c] Ricardo et[d] Galfrido clericis, Hugone de Brunlegha,[e] Rogero Abbate, Willelmo de Sotindon,[f] Adam de Chering, et aliis.

a om. cum BE *and add* cum *before* vacare E   *b* idem B   *c* Brum B   *d om.* et B
      e Brunlegha BE; Bromlegha CFG; Brumlegh' D   *f* Sotind' BEF; Shotindon' C;
Schotindon' D; Schotyndon' G

Mr Gerard Pucella was elected bp of Coventry ? late May 1183.
    The charter of kg Henry II does not seem to survive, but is cited in kg John's
charter of 31 Oct. 1205 (*Rot. ch.* 159).

145. Leeds priory

Institution of Richard capellanus *to a perpetual vicarage in the church
of Chart (Sutton), at the presentation of the prior and convent of
Leeds, on stated conditions.*   [1177 × Sept. 1181]

A = Original lost, probable mention in Lambeth Palace, Carte misc. V/111
    (inventory of Leeds muniments): 'Carta eiusdem [Ricardi] de ecclesia de
    Chert'.' s. xiii in.

B = Lambeth Palace, Reg. W. Warham fo. 104r (108r) in copy of inspeximus
    (1314) by P. & C. Ch. Ch. Canterbury. s. xvi in. C = Cambridge UL ms. Ee 5
    31 (register of prior Henry of Ch. Ch.) fo. 152r (154r no. xiiii) in copy of same
    inspeximus. s. xiv in.

Ricardus dei gratia Cantuariensis archiepiscopus totius Anglie
primas et apostolice sedis legatus universis ad quos presentes littere
pervenerint eternam in domino salutem. Rerum gestarum memoria
provide scriptis committitur ut futuris temporibus plenior inde
notitia teneatur. Noverit itaque universitas vestra nos ad petitionem
et presentationem dilecti filii nostri Roberti prioris de Ledes et
conventus canonicorum eiusdem loci suscepisse Ricardum capellanum in perpetuam vicariam ecclesie de Chert, que ad predictum
priorem et canonicos suos noscitur pertinere, ipsumque Ricardum
in eadem ecclesia perpetuum vicarium institutum esse, assignatis
sibi certis portionibus, scilicet universis proventibus et obventionibus altaris et decimationibus omnimodis omnium parochianorum
eiusdem ecclesie, excepta terra ad eandem ecclesiam pertinente et
decimationibus de dominio eiusdem ville, quas predictus prior sibi
retinuit ad opus ecclesie sue et ad usus canonicorum suorum. Hanc
igitur institutionem prefati Ricardi vicarii ex presentatione sepedicti
prioris et canonicorum eius factam auctoritate qua fungimur
confirmamus et perpetuum robur decernimus optinere. Testibus:
magistro Gerardo, Walerano archidiacono Baiocensi, Willelmo archidiacono Gloucestriensi, magistro Rogero de Rolveston, magistro
Radulpho de Sancto Martino, Willelmo de Sottindon, Rogero
decano, Rogero Norwycensi, Gaufrido clerico, et aliis.

Cf. no. 146 below. William of Northolt became archdn of Gloucester May × Dec.
1177.

146. Leeds priory

Admission of R. of Leeds capellanus *to the church of St Michael,
Chart (Sutton), at the presentation of the canons of Leeds. The
archbishop has assigned to the canons the tithes of the demesne of Chart
and a yearly pension of twenty shillings to be paid by the rector for the
maintenance of infirm canons.*

[? 1182, before 26 July]

B = Lambeth Palace, Reg. W. Warham fo. 98v (100v) in copy of inspeximus
(1278) by archbp Robert. s. xvi in. C = Maidstone, Kent Archives Office ms.
U/120 Q/13 (Leeds cartulary) fo. 6r in copy of same inspeximus. s. xiv med.

Ricardus dei gratia Cantuariensis archiepiscopus totius Anglie
primas universis sancte matris ecclesie filiis ad quos litere iste
pervenerint eternam in domino salutem. Ad omnium notitiam
volumus pervenire nos admississe dilectum filium R. de Ledes
capellanum ad ecclesiam sancti Michaelis de Chert per presentationem canonicorum de Ledes, assignatis et concessis per nos
eisdem canonicis decimationibus universis provenientibus de dominicis domini eiusdem ville de Chert et viginti solidis*a* annue
pensionis de ipsa ecclesia per manum rectoris qui pro tempore fuerit
imperpetuum solvendis ad sustentationem canonicorum dicte domus de Ledes infirmorum. Testibus his: Henrico Baiocensi et
Waltero Roffensi episcopis, magistro Petro Blesensi archidiacono
Bathoniensi, magistro R. Rolveston,*b* Moyse sacerdote, et aliis.

a solidis C; solidos B   *b* Govelst' B; Rovelst' C

It is possible that the name of bp Walter of Rochester (d. 26 July 1182) is an error
for Waleran, his successor (cons. 19 Dec. 1182); the error is found in some late
copies of archbp Richard's acta. If so, the latest possible date is fixed by the
presence of Moses, elected prior of Coventry *c.*25 May 1183. The archbp's style
and the presence of Peter of Blois as archdn indicate an arrangement superseding
the making of a vicarage in no. 145 above. In the next century Chart Sutton was a
rectory in the patronage of Leeds priory.

147. Leeds priory

*Notification that after dispute between the canons of Leeds and David
de Tymberdene, clerk, and Walter, priest, over the church of Crundale,
through the intervention of friends the parties have made a composition
in the archbishop's presence. Walter is to hold the church as perpetual
vicar for his life-time, paying two loads of wheat yearly to David, who
will pay one load to the canons. After Walter dies or enters religion,
David is to hold the church subject to a yearly pension of twenty-five
shillings to the canons.*   [1182 × 16 Feb. 1184]

A = Original lost, probable mention in Lambeth Palace, Carte misc. V/111 (inventory of Leeds muniments): 'Carta eiusdem [Ricardi] de ecclesia de Crundale.' s. xiii in.

B = Ibid. Reg. W. Warham fo. 99v (193v). s. xvi in. C = Maidstone, Kent Archives Office ms. U/120 Q/13 (Leeds cartulary) fo. 7v, in copy of inspeximus (1278) by archbp Robert. s. xiv in.

Pd from C by C. R. Cheney, *From Becket to Langton* (Manchester 1956) 189–90.

Hiis testibus: magistro P. archidiacono Bathoniensi, Willelmo archidiacono Gloucestriensi, magistro Henrico de Northampton', magistro Roberto de Inglesham, magistro Rogerio de Rolveston', Willelmo de Schotyngdon', Thoma de Newesole, et aliis multis.

The archbp is not styled legate. Peter of Blois became archdn in 1182.

*148. Leeds priory

Confirmation for the canons of Leeds of the church of Goudhurst.
[7 April 1174 × 16 Feb. 1184]

Mentioned only, in Lambeth Palace, Carte misc. V/111 (inventory of Leeds muniments): 'Carta confirmationis Ricardi Cantuariensis archiepiscopi de ecclesia de Gutherst.' s. xiii in.

*149. Leeds priory

Confirmation for the canons of Leeds of possessions in Tetlinesl' *in Goudhurst (?)*   [7 April 1174 × 16 Feb. 1184]

Mentioned only, in Lambeth Palace, Carte misc. V/111 (inventory of Leeds muniments) immediately after no. 148 above: 'Carta eiusdem [Ricardi] de T ... li ... sl' (?) et carta domini fundi'. s. xiii in.

The name is mostly obliterated, but Peter de Otteham granted lands to Leeds in this place in the parish of Goudhurst, ? in the third quarter of the twelfth century (*Cal. ch. rolls* ii 297–8).

*150. Leeds priory

Confirmation (?) for the canons of Leeds of the church of Stockbury.
[7 April 1174 × 16 Feb. 1184]

Mentioned only, in Lambeth Palace, Carte misc. V/111 (inventory of Leeds muniments): 'Carta eiusdem [Ricardi] de ecclesia de Stokingeb', de dono Willelmi filii Heltonis cuius cartam habemus'. s. xiii in.

151. Leeds priory

Confirmation, after enquiry at the instance of R. rector of Mayfield and the canons of Leeds, of the right of the canons' church of Lamberhurst to the tithes of the archbishop's tenants in 'Courthope' and 'Everherst'.

[Oct. 1181 × 16 Feb. 1184]

B = Lambeth Palace, Reg. W. Warham fo. 98r (100r) in copy of inspeximus (1278) by archbp Robert. s. xvi in. C = Maidstone, Kent Archives Office ms. U/120 Q/13 (Leeds cartulary) fo. 5r in copy of same inspeximus. s. xiv med.

Ricardus dei gratia Cantuariensis archiepiscopus totius Anglie primas universis sancte matris ecclesie Cantuariensis et Roffensis diocesum filiis salutem et benedictionem. Noverit universitas vestra nos ad instantiam et de consensu R. rectoris *a* ecclesie*b* de Mage-feud*c* et dilectorum filiorum nostrorum canonicorum de Ledes per viros fidedignos inquisisse cuius ecclesie tenentes nostri de Cour-thope*d* et de Everherst parochiani existant et cui ecclesie eorum decime de iure solvi debeant, qui dicunt per sacramenta sua quod omnes inhabitantes loca de Courthope*d* et de Everherst omnia iura ecclesiastica in ecclesia de Lamberhersta perceperunt et eidem ecclesie omnes decimas suas integre solverunt a tempore cuius non exstat memoria, et ibidem eorum antecessorum ossa quiescunt humata, necnon et huius rei venerabilis fratris nostri W. dei gratia Roffensis episcopi laudabili testimonio veritatem cognovimus. Unde quantum ad nos pertinet omnes decimas predictorum loco-rum memoratis canonicis nostris de Ledes nomine ecclesie sue de Lamberherste concessimus et confirmavimus. In cuius rei testimon-ium huic scripto sigillum nostrum apponi dignum duximus.

a rectoris C; rectores B   *b* add R. C; add S ? B   *c* Magefeud ?: Magester' B; Magefer C   *d* Courthope B; Curthope C

The importance attached to the testimony of the bp of Rochester suggests that this was during the pontificate of bp Walter (d. 26 July 1182) rather than his successor Waleran, who was not in England as bishop with the archbp until Aug. 1183. Courthope and Ewhurst may be places in Wadhurst, like Mayfield in the archbp's great woodland manor of South Malling (Sussex Rec. Soc. lvii (1958) 30). Their tithes are assigned to Lamberhurst in archbp Theobald's charter for Leeds (Saltman, *Theobald* p. 372 no. 148), but when this charter was inspected by archbp Hubert (below, no. 512) the reference to tithes in these places was omitted.

*152. Leicester abbey

Mandate in favour of the canons of St Mary de Pré, Leicester, ordering that their privileges be observed throughout the province of Canterbury.
[7 April 1174 × Sept. 1181]

B = Bodl. ms. Laud misc. 625 (Leicester register) fo. 182r (185r). s. xvi in.

Mentioned only, in an inventory of letters of archbps of Canterbury: 'Mandatum Ricardi Cantuariensis archiepiscopi quod per provinciam suam privilegia nostra faciat observari. Et hoc ad mandatum Alexandri pape'. Perhaps refers to the privilege of Alexander III abridged in the inventory of papal letters, whence printed in *PUE* iii 281 no. 139. Presumably in the lifetime of this pope.

153. Lewes priory

Notification that the archbishop, as judge delegate, has heard and settled in his presence a dispute between the monks of Lewes and Thomas, clerk of Lamport, concerning burial dues of the church of Faxton. Simon de Malesoures and Thomas declared Faxton to be a chapel of Lamport. The prior and convent of Lewes renounced their claim in consideration of a yearly pension of forty shillings. During Thomas's tenure of the church he shall pay only thirty shillings annually.
[Aug. 1174 × Sept. 1181]

A = PRO E 40/15466. Endorsed, s. xii/xiii: Ricardus de Simone de Malesoures et Fakest'; s. xiii: De xl solidis debitis annuatim de Langeport (and in darker ink) Rap de Pavense xii; s. xvi: Fashghton Langport. Approx. 190 × 118 + 18 mm. Sealing d.q. 1; tag remains, seal lost. Scribe I.

B = BL ms. Cotton Vesp. F xv (Lewes cartulary) fo. 71r. s. xv med.

Pd (transl.)from B in *Lewes chartulary* i 126.

.Ric(ardus) . dei gratia Cantuariensis archiepiscopus . totius Anglie primas et apostolice sedis legatus ⁖ universis Christi fidelibus ad quos presentes littere pervenerint ⁖ salutem. Rem gestam in presentia nostra sub scripti nostri testimonio duximus redigendam ⁖ ne ex lapsu memorie litigia semel sopita rediviva questione denuo suscitentur. In communem itaque volumus noticiam devenire ⁖ quod cum inter Osbertum priorem et monachos Sancti Pancratii . et Thomam clericum de Langheport' . super sepultura defunctorum apud Facheston' . quos memorati . prior et fratres ad ecclesiam de Langheport querebantur per violentiam laicalem delatos fuisse . controversia verteretur . et causa nobis a summo pontifice domino Alexandro tertio . fuisset delegata . tandem intervenientibus amicis .

presente et consentiente .S. Malesoures . qui et antedictus Thomas capellam de Fagheston ad ecclesiam suam de Langheport asserebant iure parrochiali ab antiquis retro temporibus pertinere ∴ inter ipsos sub hac pacis forma convenit. Prior et conventus Sancti Pancratii a lite prescripta penitus recedentes ∴ in hoc unanimiter consenserunt ∴ ut persona ecclesie de Langheport ecclesiam de Facheston' cum omnibus eiusdem ville decimationibus . et obventionibus et aliis quibuscumque ad eandem ecclesiam pertinentibus iure perpetuo teneat . reddendo monachis Sancti Pancratii nomine ecclesie de Facheston' ∴ XL solidos . annuos . ita tamen quod prefatus Thomas quoad vixerit . et ecclesiam de Facheston' tenuerit ∴ XXX. tantum solidos monasterio Sancti Pancratii annuatim persolvet . ad Pascha videlicet ∴ XV. solidos . ad festum Sancti Michaelis ∴ XV. solidos. Post cuius decessum ut dictum est prefati monachi annuos .XL. solidos . a persona de Langheport ad terminos prescriptos iure perpetuo percipient. Hec sane transactio hinc inde concessa est . et in nostra presentia fide interposita utrobique firmata. Nos itaque eam inter predictas ecclesias perpetuis temporibus valituram ∴ auctoritate domini pape et nostra duximus confirmandam . et sigilli nostri munimine roborandam ∴

> The archbp is wrongly identified in the PRO List as Richard Weathershed, otherwise le Grant (*List and Index Soc.* vol. 152).

154. The church of Lichfield

Confirmation of the sale of land at 'Cletthull' by Roger Durdent to William, late dean of Lichfield, and of the grant of that land to Henry the dean's chamberlain to be held of the church of Lichfield in fee and heredity.

[May 1177 × Sept. 1181]

> B = Lichfield, D. & C. Mun. Magnum registrum album fo. 246ra. s. xiv in.
>   C = Bodl., ms. Ashmole 1527 (Lichfield cathedral cartulary) fo. 16v. s. xv in.
> Pd (calendar) from B in *Lichfield M. R. A.* 290 no. 605.

Ricardus dei gratia Cantuariensis archiepiscopus totius Anglie primas et apostolice sedis legatus universis Christi fidelibus ad quos presentes littere pervenerint eternam in domino salutem. Ex tenore quorumdam instrumentorum que manibus nostris contrectavimus et diligenter perspeximus, videlicet carte Rogeri Durdent et [fo. 246rb] carte Willelmi quondam decani Lichefeldensis, necnon carte venerabilis fratris nostri Ricardi Coventrensis episcopi et carte capituli Lichefeldensis ecclesie, satis manifeste cognovimus quod predictus Rogerus Durdent de assensu uxoris sue et heredum suorum vendidit prefato Willelmo decano Lichefeldensi terram de Cletthul' cum universis*a* pertinentiis et libertatibus suis quodque idem Willelmus decanus eandem terram cum omnibus pertinentiis et libertatibus suis concessit et dedit Henrico camerario suo in feodo et hereditate tenendam de ecclesia Lich', solvendo singulis annis in festo Inventionis Sancte Crucis pro omni servitio cereos duorum solidorum qui solempniter in processionibus ante crucem faciendis ad honorem et obsequium dominice passionis accendantur et ardeant, quodque venerabilis frater noster Ricardus Coventrensis episcopus ipsam terram concessit et carta sua confirmavit eidem Henrico camerario*b* sicut antedictus Willelmus ei dedit et confirmavit pro servitio suo quod ei per multa tempora in negotiis ecclesie Lichefeldensis noscitur impendisse, quodque etiam capitulum Lichefeldense concessioni et confirmationi prelibati Ricardi episcopi sui gratum prebuit assensum et decani sui factum in prescripta emptione et concessione eiusdem terre facta prelibato Henrico camerario in feodum et hereditatem libere et quiete ab omni servitio seculari vel*c* exactione, solvendo predictos cereos duorum solidorum in prenotato festo Sancte Crucis ratum habuit atque sigillo ecclesie roboravit. Unde quoniam ex officio suscepti regiminis tenemur ea que a subditis nostris rationabiliter facta sunt rata habere et firma, nos tam venditionem supradicti Rogeri quam emptionem prelibati Willelmi decani Lichefeldensis et concessionem eius et donationem factam ipsi Henrico camerario in feodum et hereditatem [fo. 246va] per predictum servitium cereorum duorum solidorum, necnon concessionem memorati episcopi Coventrensis et eius confirmationem, postremo autem concordem assensum capituli Lichefeldensis et confirmationem approbantes, auctoritate qua fungimur confirmamus et presentis scripti testimonio ac sigilli nostri patrocinio communimus, statuentes ut perpetuam obtineant firmitatem sicut auctentica scripta predictorum rationabiliter protestantur. Testibus: magistro Gerardo, Willelmo archidiacono Glouecestriensi, magistro Radulfo de Sancto Martino, magistro Rogero de Rolveston, Gilberto de Pirariis, Thoma de Newesol', Willelmo de Sottindon', Rogero decano, Rogero Wallensi, Rogero Norwicensi, Ricardo Lundoniensi, Gaufrido clerico, et multis aliis clericis et laicis.*d*

---

a universis B; omnibus C   *b* *add* suo C   *c* vel (?): *om.* BC   *d* Thoma de Newesol' ... laicis; etc. B

William of Northolt became archdn of Gloucester May × Dec. 1177. The bp's confirmation of the grant to Henry, the dean's chamberlain was made in or before 1176, in the lifetime of dean William de Lega, and is in Magnum registrum album fo. 246ra (*M. R. A.* 290 no. 604) with related documents (nos. 602–3, 606).

155. The deanery of the church of Lichfield

Confirmation for the deanery of Lichfield of the grants made by bishop Richard of Coventry, on a papal mandate, to re-endow the deanery, which was wasted during time of war.   [May 1177 × Sept. 1181]

B = Lichfield, D. & C. Mun. Magnum registrum album fo. 217ra. s. xiv in.

Pd (calendar) from B in *Lichfield M. R. A.* 239 no. 494.

Ricardus dei gratia Cantuariensis archiepiscopus totius Anglie primas et apostolice sedis legatus universis Christi fidelibus ad quos presens scriptum pervenerit eternam in Christo salutem. Ex inspectione autentici scripti venerabilis fratris nostri Ricardi Coventrensis episcopi ad plenum cognovimus decaniam Lichefeldensis ecclesie, que tempore hostilitatis tota fere in nichilum redacta est, eiusdem episcopi cura et sollicitudine de mandato summi pontificis hoc modo laudabiliter esse reformatam, hiis scilicet honoribus et beneficiis ad reformationem et supplementum eiusdem decanie ab eo assignatis, que quidem omnia propriis duximus exprimenda vocabulis, scilicet decimam cense de Lich' et de parochiis tam infra burgum quam extra, et decimam de firma archidiaconatus Derb' et in Berleswic xx solidos pro decima, sive sit ad firmam sive non, decimam etiam piscin' de vivariis episcopi de Lich' et duas acras et dimidiam de prato eiusdem episcopi et lx acras adiacentes terre de Alreschawe et terram de Torleymor', ipsamque terram de Alreschawe sicut Willelmus quondam decanus eam melius et plenius habuit, et preterea in supplementum decanie prebendam de Brewode cum omnibus suis pertinentiis et libertatibus sicut aliquis canonicus eam melius et plenius unquam tenuit. Quam quidem decaniam eo quo dictum est modo reformatam idem episcopus, sicut ex tenore scripti sui oculata fide didicimus, dilecto filio nostro Ricardo de Dallam cunctisque eius successoribus in eadem decania canonice substituendis libere dedit et concessit possidendam suaque confirmavit auctoritate. Nos ergo honori et dingnitati prescripti Lichefeldensis ecclesie providere volentes, predicti fratris nostri Coventrensis episcopi dispositionem et concessionem canonice factam ratam et firmam decernentes auctoritate qua fungimur sicut rationabiliter facta est confirmamus et sigilli nostri munimine roboramus, statuentes ut prescripta reformatio et ordinatio decanie Lichefeldensis firma et inconvulsa perma-[fo. 217rb]neat inperpetuum. Nullusque memoratum decanum vel eius successores canonice substituendos super eadem decania eiusve possessionibus et libertatibus qualibet temeritate indebite vexare aut molestare presumat. Hiis testibus: Walerano Baiocensi archidiacono, Willelmo Gloecestriensi archidiacono, magistro Roberto de Inglesham*a*, magistro Rogero de Rulveston'*b*, magistro Rogero Norwicensi, Ricardo et Gaufrido clericis, Rogero decano, Philippo canonico Cestrensi, et aliis multis.

a Englesham B   *b* Rulfeston' B

William of Northolt became archdn of Gloucester May × Dec. 1177. Richard de Dalham succeeded William de Lega as dean of Lichfield in 1175 or 1176. The charter of bp Richard, from which the details of the grant are drawn, is in Magnum registrum album fo. 217v (*M. R. A.* 240 no. 497) with related documents (nos. 488–96).

156. The dean and chapter of Lichfield

Mandate to the dean and chapter to send five or six or more of the senior canons to Normandy to meet the archbishop at Caen on 'Viri Galilei' (26 May), empowered by the chapter to elect and receive a new bishop. The archbishop sends his clerk, Peter of Blois, who will give the chapter advice on the procedure to be followed.   [April × May 1183]

B = Lichfield, D. & C. Mun. Magnum registrum album fo. 184ra. s. xiv in.

Pd (calendared imperfectly) from B in *Lichfield M. R. A.* 181 no. 366.

Ricardus dei gratia Cantuariensis archiepiscopus totius Anglie primas dilectis in domino filiis decano et capitulo Lich' salutem, gratiam, et benedictionem. Diu est quod diocesis Coventrensis, cuius desolationem totis compatimur visceribus, suo viduata pastore nonnullam tam in temporalibus quam in spiritualibus sustinuit iacturam. Hoc itaque attendentes ut in predicta*a* et aliis ecclesiis que pastore carent et patre maturius et competentius provideretur, in multa corporis et animi angustia transfretavimus, dominum regem diligenter convenimus, solicite monuimus, et ad hoc tandem per dei [fo. 184rb] misericordiam duximus quod ecclesie Coventrensi per vestram et aliorum quorum interest electionem quam liberam esse volumus et per consilium nostrum divina aspirante gratia providebitur. Desiderio igitur desiderantes in partes Anglicanas sine mora qualibet redire et ecclesie prefate ad honorem dei providere, propter dissencionem filiorum domini regis, quam in proximo per dei misericordiam mitigabimus, et ob hoc ab ipso rege*b* votum nostrum in hac parte non potuimus adimplere. Unde quia dubium est quid parat dies crastina et in hoc negotio moram scimus valde periculosam esse, dilectioni vestre mandamus atque precipimus quatinus vota vestra super episcopo eligendo in quinque aut sex aut plures sicut expedire videritis honestiores et prudentiores ecclesie vestre personas conferatis, que ad Viri Galilei apud Cadomum, omni occasione*c* cessante, cum literis vestris patentibus et ratihabitationem continentibus, se nobis exhibeant patrem et episcopum electure et suscepture. Mittimus itaque propter hoc ad vos dilectum filium et clericum nostrum magistrum P. Blesensem archidiaconum Batthoniensem ut de consilio eius celerius veniant qui venturi sunt et super diutina dilatione festinam et duplicatam recipiant consolationem. Valete in domino.

a predicte B   *b* ? *om.* vocati *or some such word* B   *c* act(i)one B

The archbp was in France with the king in the first half of 1183, and was at Caen on 26 May (Eyton 251). This summons resulted in the choice of Mr Gerard Pucella as bp of Coventry at a date unknown. He appears as 'elect' in no. 167 below and was consecrated by the archbp at Canterbury 25 Sept. 1183. This mandate was produced with other evidence before archbp Stephen Langton 29 Nov. 1223, to substantiate the claim of the dean and chapter of Lichfield to take part in the episcopal election (*M. R. A.* 221 no. 464; *Acta S. Langton* 80 no. 61). The summons for Ascension day, indicated by the introit for the mass, has been misunderstood by the editor, Dean Savage, and some others.

157. Lilleshall abbey

Confirmation for the canons of Lilleshall of the assignment of the church of Atcham to the purposes of hospitality, as confirmed by archbishop Thomas.

[28 April 1174 × Sept. 1181]

B = BL ms. Add. 50121 (Lilleshall cartulary) fo. 25r (p. 49). s. xiii med.

Universis sancte matris ecclesie filiis Ricardus dei gratia Cantuariensis archiepiscopus totius Anglie primas et apostolice sedis legatus salutem in domino. Quoniam ea que laudabilibus et honestis ecclesiarum officiis studio caritatis sunt assignata perpetua stabilitate convenit gaudere, ne in posterum aliqua temeritate divellantur, duximus ea scriptorum auctenticorum patrocinio communire. Ea propter ad omnium Christi fidelium notitiam volumus pervenire nos, vestigia gloriosi martiris Thome predecessoris nostri in quantum possumus sequentes, sicut ipse ratum habuit ita et nos ratum habere et scripti nostri auctoritate [duximus]*a* confirmare quod canonici de Lilleshull' communi assensu super ecclesia de Ettin-

gham canonice statuerunt, videlicet ut ipsa cum omnibus pertinentiis suis de cetero in perpetuos usus hospitalitatis eiusdem domus de
Lilleshull sit deputata. Statuimus quoque et sub interminatione[b]
anathematis prohibemus ne quis hanc 'nostre' confirmationis paginam temere presumat infringere vel ei aliquatenus contraire. Valete.

[a] *om.* duximus ? B (*cf. no. 228 below*)   [b] indeterminatione B

For archbp Thomas's charter see above, no. 21.

158. London: the church of St Paul

*Grant to the chapter of St Paul's, London, of the parsonage of the
church of Barnes, provided that a vicar shall serve the church in the
name of the chapter, to be instituted by the archbishop or his ministri
and to be answerable to them alone for the spirituals.*

[Aug. 1174 × Sept. 1175]

> B = London, St Paul's Cathedral Libr. Liber A (Pilosus) fo. 30v no. 285. s. xiii
> med.
>
> Pd from B in *Early charters of ... St Paul's, London* ed. M. Gibbs (Camden 3s.
> 58, 1939) 228 no. 287.

Testibus: domino Roberto de Novoburgo, Benedicto cancellario, et
aliis nominatis in carta.

> The archbp is styled legate. For Benedict's tenure of the chancellorship see no.
> 111.
>   The appropriation of the parsonage to St Paul's is referred to and confirmed
> by pope Lucius III, 25 July 1185 (*Early charters* 177–8 no. 223, *PUE* i 509–10
> no. 227). For its assignment to the almonry (before 1192) see *Early charters* 247
> no. 308. For dispute in 1225 between the archbp and the chapter over the
> advowson see *CRR* xii 456, 1479, *Early charters* 228–9 no. 288 (*Acta S. Langton*
> 101–2 no. 82).

159. London: the church of St Paul

*Confirmation for Fulcher, priest, of a grant to him by William de
Belmeis, canon of St Paul's, London, of the church of St Pancras as a
perpetual vicarage, subject to a yearly pension of one bezant or two
English shillings to be paid to William and his successors. The grant has
been confirmed by bishop Gilbert of London and the chapter of St
Paul's.*   [May 1177 × Sept. 1181]

> A = Kew (Surrey), B. S. Cron, Esq. 351 Sandycombe Road. Endorsed, s. xiii ex.:
> super ecclesia sancti pancratii. Approx. 178 × 115 + 20 mm. Sealing d.q. 1; seal
> and counterseal (red wax), small part missing at left foot. Scribe II.
>
> Pd (calendar) from A by J. Walton, 'A second calendar of Greenwell deeds',
> *Archaeologia Æliana* 4s. vii (1930) 83 no. 3 [B7]. The seal fully described by W.

Greenwell and C. H. Hunter Blair, *Catalogue of the ecclesiastical seals ... in Durham*, parts vi–viii (Soc. Antiquaries of Newcastle upon Tyne 1917–19) 434 no. 3091A.

Ric(ardus) dei gratia Cantuariensis archiepiscopus totius Anglie primas et apostolice sedis legatus . universis Christi fidelibus ad quos presentes littere pervenerint . eternam in domino salutem. Ex auctentico scripto venerabilis fratris nostri .G. Lundoniensis episcopi . evidenter cognovimus . quod Willelmus de Beaumeis Lundoniensis ecclesie canonicus concessit Fulcherio presbitero ecclesiam sancti Pancratii in perpetuam vicariam sub annua pensione unius bisantii vel duorum solidorum anglicane monete ? quodque idem .G. episcopus prefate concessioni episcopalis robur addidit auctoritatis . et memoratam vicariam ipsi .F. concessit . atque ipsum .F. perpetuum vicarium constituit sub predicta pensione prefato Willelmo vel successoribus suis persolvenda . insuper etiam scripto suo ac sigillo confirmavit. Ex auctentico quoque scripto capituli Lundonensis ecclesie accepimus et intelleximus . quod idem capitulum prescriptam concessionem approbavit et ratam habuit . et scripto suo atque sigillo confirmavit. Unde nos etiam eandem concessionem auctoritate qua fungimur roboramus et sigilli nostri patrocinio et scripti testimonio communimus. Testibus magistro Gerardo . Willelmo archidiacono Glouecestriensi . magistro Rogero de Rolveston . Willelmo de Sottindon' . Rogero decano . Rogero Norwicensi . David' capellano . Ricardo et Gaufrido clericis.

William of Northolt became archdn of Gloucester May × Dec. 1177.
The grant by William de Belmeis, prebendary of St Pancras, is printed in *Facsimiles of royal and other charters in the British Museum* ed. G. F. Warner and H. Ellis (1903) no. 62 and *Early charters of ... St Paul's, London* ed. M. Gibbs (Camden 3s. 58) 124–5 no. 160. For related documents see *Early charters* 123–4 nos. 158–9 and Foliot, *Letters* 442–3, 445 nos. 402–3, 406.

160.   London: the deanery of St Paul's

Confirmation of the grant made to the deanery by the dean, Ralph de Diceto, of his house and chapel in St Paul's churchyard, as confirmed by bishop Gilbert of London.   [1180 × Sept. 1181]

A = London, St Paul's Cathedral Libr. A 78/3016. Endorsed, s. xiv: De domibus decani; s. xv: De mansione domini decani in atrio australi, *and* sub altare iij°. Approx. 190 × 196 + 28 mm. Sealing d.q. 2; seal and counterseal (natural wax, brown varnish), rim totally lost, remains of both obverse and reverse much rubbed. Scribe **IV**.
B = Ibid. Liber A (Pilosus) fo. 57r. s. xiii ex.

.Ric(ardus). dei gratia . Cantuariensis archiepiscopus . tocius Anglie primas et apostolice sedis legatus ? universis sancte matris ecclesie filiis ad quos littere presentes pervenerint ∴ eternam in Christo salutem. Ex inspectione carte venerabilis fratris nostri .G. Lundoniensis . episcopi manifeste cognovimus . quod dilectus filius noster .Radulfus. de Diceto decanus ecclesie beati Pauli . Lundoniensis . ad honorem dei et patroni sui beati Pauli domos suas in atrio iamdicte fundatas ecclesie utensilibus suis et ornamentis munitas . et capellam suam cum libris et ornamentis omnibus concessione et autoritate prefati episcopi decanatui assignando contulit . et donavit . quam donationem idem episcopus ratam habens et acceptam ∴ ut perpetua valeat stabilitate gaudere ∴ autoritate sua confirmavit. Unde et terram in qua iamdicte domus et capella site sunt . decanatui in perpetuum assignavit . statuens ut omnis decanorum ecclesie memorate successio ea*a* sicut scriptum est possideat . ita quod decanus ibidem stacionarius habitet . et domibus sartiendis curam sollicitiorem impendat. Singuli etiam decani decem solidos annuatim in die anniversarii memorati .Radulfi. decani per manum camerarii nomine predicti tenementi solvent ad pitantiam . et hoc se fideliter observaturos coram capitulo in sua institutione cavebunt. Provisum quoque est quod siquis in decanum electus de domibus inhabitandis . et pro tempore sartiendis et utensilibus earum de libris . vasis . et ornamentis spectantibus ad capellam fideliter cum indempnitate custodiendis et de decem solidis annuatim solvendis onus in se suscipere noluerit et cautionem idoneam arbitratu capituli detrectaverit interponere . commodo careat electionis . nec ad decanatum aliquo casu presumat in posterum aspirare. Huic siquidem donationi et constitutioni gratum impertientes assensum . nostre quoque autoritatis robur duximus accommodandum . statuentes et sub interminatione anathematis districtius inhibentes . nequis ei tractu temporis aliquatenus temere contraire presumat. Unde ad maiorem cautelam in posterum ∴ hanc nostre confirmacionis paginam sigilli nostri munimine roboravimus. Hiis testibus . magistro*b* Girardo . Willelmo . Gloecestrensi . archidiacono . Willelmo et Moyse capellanis . magistro Rogerio Norwicensi . magistro Rogerio Walensi . Ricardo . et Gaufrido . clericis . Rogerio decano et aliis multis clericis et laicis.

a ea A; eam B   *b* magistro B; magisto A

Ralph de Diceto became dean Jan. 1180 × Jan. 1181. Bp Gilbert's confirmation of the dean's grant is found in two versions in Liber A (Foliot, *Letters* 445–6 no. 407). The archbp's charter uses much of the wording of the bp's charter (second version), which was also confirmed by bp Richard FitzNeal in 1192 (Cambridge, UL documents 42).

*161.   London: priory of St Mary Clerkenwell

Mandate to the prior and monks of Stanesgate to report to the archbishop by letters patent the terms of their agreements made with the nuns of Clerkenwell and with the canons of St Bartholomew's, respectively, about tithes of the fee of Clerkenwell, notifying him which agreement came first.   [1176 × Sept. 1181]

> Mentioned only, in the report from prior Alexander and the monks of St Mary
> Magdalene, Stanesgate (giving the archbp the style of legate) that they granted
> to the nuns the tithes and twenty pence of rent in the fee for a yearly pension of
> ten shillings, and that this preceded the agreement made with the canons.
> Prior Alexander's grant to the nuns follows this report in the cartulary and is
> dated 1176 (*Clerkenwell cart.* 24–26 no. 32, cf. no. 33).

162.   London: priory of St Mary Clerkenwell

Confirmation for the nuns of Clerkenwell of the church of Sitting-bourne, granted and confirmed to them by king Henry II.

[May 1177 × Sept. 1181]

> B = Lambeth Palace, Reg. W. Warham fo. 118v (121v). s. xvi in. C = Ibid. fo.
> 119v (122v). D = Ibid. fo. 119r (122r), in copy of inspeximus by archbp
> Hubert.

Ricardus dei gratia Cantuariensis archiepiscopus totius Anglie primas et apostolice sedis legatus universis sancte matris ecclesie filiis ad quos presentes littere pervenerint eternam in domino salutem. Ad universitatis vestre notitiam volumus pervenire nos concessisse et hac carta nostra confirmasse in liberam et perpetuam elemosinam ecclesie beate Marie de Fonte clericorum et monialibus ibidem divino [fo. 119r] mancipatis servitio ecclesiam de Sidinge-burna cum omnibus pertinentiis suis, sicut dominus Anglorum rex illustrissimus H. eandem ecclesiam eis concessit et carta sua confirmavit. Unde volumus et ea qua fungimur auctoritate precipimus ut prelibata ecclesia de Fonte clericorum et moniales eiusdem loci habeant et in perpetuum possideant prescriptam ecclesiam de Sidingeburna cum omnibus ad eam pertinentibus, in terris, decimis, et omnimodis obventionibus seu rebus ad ipsam spectantibus. Et ut hec nostre concessionis et confirmationis pagina firma et inconcussa permaneat*a* eam sigilli nostri appositione duximus roborare, statuentes et sub interminatione anathematis prohibentes nequis eandem confirmationis nostre paginam irrationabiliter infringere vel ei aliquatenus temere contraire presumat.*b* Testibus hiis : Walerano*c* Baiocensi, Willelmo Glowecestriensi archidiaconis,[d] magistro Roberto de Inglesham, Henrico Baiocensi, magistro Rogero Norwicensi, Iohanne capellano, Ricardo et Galfrido[e] clericis, Willelmo de Sotindon,[f] et aliis pluribus.

[a] permaneat CD; pertineat B   [b] om. *witness-list* D   [c] Waltero BC
[d] om. archidiaconis, *leaving space* B   [e] om. Ricardo et C, *leaving space* B
[f] Shotund' B; Secundon' C

William of Northolt became archdn of Gloucester May × Dec. 1177.
    The cartulary contains Henry II's charter: *Mon. Ang.* iv 85 and *Clerkenwell cartulary* 9 no. 7. The editor of the latter notes the archiepiscopal charters (nos. 162, 294, 534) but does not print them, p. 276.

163. Abbey of Lonlay

Confirmation for the monks of Lonlay of all the grants of churches, lands, etc. which Nigel of Monville made to them, later confirmed by William of Avranches.   [19 Dec. 1182 × May 1183]

B = Lambeth Palace, Reg. W. Warham fo. 151r (155r). s. xvi in.

Ricardus dei gratia Cantuariensis archiepiscopus totius Anglie primas universis Christi fidelibus ad quos litere nostre pervenerint eternam in domino salutem. Ad omnium notitiam volumus pervenire nos omnes et singulas donationes[a] quas fecit Nigellus de Munevilla et Willelmus de Abrincis[b] postmodum confirmavit dilectis filiis nostris abbati et monachis de Lonleio, sive in [fo. 151v] ecclesiis, sive in terris, sive in decimis, sive in redditibus, sive in aliis quibuscunque rebus sicut rationabiliter facte sunt et confirmate ratas habere et carta presenti confirmare, statuentes et ea qua[c] fungimur auctoritate prohibentes districte ne quis iniuste memoratos abbatem et monachos super donationibus ipsis molestare aut huic nostre confirmationis pagine contraire presumat. Testibus: Walerano Roffensi episcopo, magistro P. Blesensi archidiacono Bathoniensi, Moyse capellano, magistro R. de Rolveston[d], Henrico Baiocensi, Iohanne capellano, Willelmo Sotewame, et aliis.

[a] donationem B   [b] Ambriciis B   [c] om. qua B   [d] Rovestr' B

After the consecration of bp Waleran of Rochester and before the appointment of Moses as prior of Coventry. The gifts of Nigel of Monville, lord of Folkestone, to Lonlay c.1095, constituted the alien priory of Folkestone. William of Avranches, his grandson and successor, died c.1177 (I. J. Sanders, *English baronies* (Oxford 1960) 45). Texts of William's charter (much inflated) are in Reg. W. Warham fo. 149v, and in PRO E 159/179: K. R. Memo. roll Mich. 4 Henr. IV Recorda rot. 10 (whence *Mon. Ang.* iv 673–5).

164. Louis VII, king of the French

The archbishop, prior Alan, and the convent of Christ Church, Canterbury, who have been honoured by the presence of Louis, king of the French, and in consideration of the honour which the king showed to the blessed martyr Thomas in his lifetime, have granted to the king, his queen, his heir, and his children a share in the spiritual benefits of the church of Canterbury. During the king's life a monk shall celebrate the mass of the Holy Spirit daily for him and the queen and his heir and family, and they are to be remembered in the prayers of the other monks. The king's death shall be celebrated with the same service as for an archbishop of Canterbury, and a pauper shall be fed with a monk's portion for a year. There shall be a special office on the anniversary of the king's death. These details are to be recorded in the martyrology and recited annually.

[? 24 × 26 Aug. 1179]

B = BL ms. Cotton Claud. C vi (Ch. Ch. martyrology, etc.) fo. 197r, damaged. s. xii ex. C = BL ms. Arundel 68 (Ch. Ch. martyrology) fo. 41v. s. xv. D = Lambeth Palace, ms. 20 (Ch. Ch. martyrology) fo. 222v. s. xvi in.

Pd from B in *Lettres des rois ... de France et de l'Angleterre* ed. J. J. Champollion-Figeac (Docts inédits sur l'histoire de France i 1839) 13–14 no. viii and Bouquet, etc. *Recueil des historiens* (xvi 1878) 167; from C in *Thomas Becket: Actes du colloque international de Sedières* ed. R. Foreville (Paris 1975) 209.

The address to the kg precedes the archbp's title (which includes the legatine style). Kg Louis visited Canterbury with kg Henry II on 23 Aug. 1179 and embarked again at Dover on 26 Aug. He was received by the archbp and monks and spent the night of the 23rd at the martyr's tomb. Next day he was received in confraternity in the chapterhouse, and assigned by charter a rent of wine to the convent from the castellany of Poissy (Gervas. Cant. i 293, *Lettres des rois* i 12 no. vii, *Actes du colloque* 209). According to Gervase, Louis came 'ob spem recuperandae salutis', but he died 18 Sept. 1180. The rent was confirmed by kg Philip II in 1180 (*Recueil des actes de Philippe Auguste* i (1916) 2–3 no. 2) and by pope Innocent III in 1200 (*Letters of Innocent III* no. 222 p. 216).

165. Hospital of Maiden Bradley

Mandate on behalf of the leper women of Maiden Bradley, addressed to bishop Jocelin of Salisbury, to enforce the decree of pope Alexander concerning the exemption of leper houses from tithe.

[April 1179 × Sept. 1181]

A = PRO E 40/14631, badly dampstained and much of the text obliterated. Occasional isolated letters are visible in the passages noted here as missing. Endorsed, s. xii ex.: De Ricardo archiepiscopo (most of dorse obscured by mount). Approx. 170 × 167 + 13 mm. Sealing d.q. 1; tag and seal lost.

Ricardus dei gratia [Cantuariensis arc]hiepiscopus totius A[ngli]e [prima]s apostol[ice] sedis legatus . venerabili et in Christo dilecto [I]ocelino . eadem gratia . Sareb' ... am ... [s]alutem. S[atis i]nnotuit discretioni vestre [quod ?] dominus noster papa Alexander [constituit] .' ne gens leprosa ..... es eorum ... lab ...... ias. Inde est ... ... essionis per episcopatum vestrum constitutis . immo vice [domin]i pape ..... m[uli?]eres et procuratores earum in pace sancte ecclesie et certior ... . in hospitali de Bradeleia quam funda[verunt Manas]serius B[i]set dapifer re[gis et A]eliz uxor eius ex proprio matrimoni[o] .' quiete et libere [? con-]sistant. Inhibemus vero super christianitate ne de propriis laboribus aut propria pecunia alicui ecclesie dent decimas. Quod siquis contra (?) decretum romanum predictas le[pro]sas et procuratores earum in exigendis decimis vexare presumserit . aut inqui[e]tare .' anathematis spiculo perfodiatur . donec super hoc plenarie satisfecerit. Valete.

The 'decretum romanum' which pope Alexander 'constituit' is presumably 3 Lateran Council c.23, so this letter was written after the death of Manasser Biset (1177). Alexander III had, however, granted to a leprosary exemption from tithe on 'novalia que propriis sumptibus excolunt' and on 'nutrimenta animalium suorum' as early as 1173 × 1174 (JL 12265; PL 200 936-7). In 1202 the leprosary failed to maintain its exemption in the action brought by the canons of Notley to secure payment of these tithes to the parish church of Bradley, which was appropriated to Notley abbey (below, no. 560).

166. Malmesbury abbey

Report to pope Alexander III on an appeal by the abbot of Malmesbury from the archbishop's hearing of a case between the abbot and his diocesan, the bishop of Salisbury. The bishop had appealed against the abbot-elect and persistently forbidden him by papal authority to seek benediction from any but himself; but the elect went secretly to Wales and was clandestinely blessed by the bishop of Llandaff. The archbishop, having carefully investigated the truth of the matter, suspended both the bishop of Llandaff and the abbot pending the production of a justificatory privilege. The parties appeared before the archbishop and privileges of the churches were produced. The only evidence the abbot produced in his favour was a certain letter of exemption ('quasdam exemptionis sue litteras') which appeared to be faulty as to the bulla and thread, and not written in the style of the Roman church, so that the bishop challenged its genuineness. The abbot brought witnesses to prove that his predecessors had been blessed by bishops of their own choosing and had not done obedience. The bishop, on the other hand,

*produced many professions made by abbots of Malmesbury to himself
and his predecessors, by virtue of which he claimed the obedience of the
abbot and the subjection of the abbey. Testimony for the abbot was
heard and put in writing, and the archbishop, at the abbot's earnest
request, appointed a further day for a second production of witnesses.
On that day the archbishop, as was his custom, proposed that the parties
should come to a peaceful settlement. The bishop offered to accept a
settlement or a judgment ('et paci et iudicio humiliter se offerebat');
but the abbot on his counsel's advice resorted to legal chicanery and
would not submit to judgment or come to terms. He declared that he
would only answer to the pope about profession or obedience. Leaving
the session contumaciously, he said: 'abbots are poor mean creatures
who do not totally exclude the power of bishops, when they could get full
freedom from the see of Rome by paying an ounce of gold yearly.' The
archbishop continues with a long diatribe against the lawlessness of
exempt abbots and the disorders of their monasteries, which may lead to
similar insubordination throughout the hierarchy. They acquire forged
privileges. If this disreputable abbot of Malmesbury should come or send
to the pope, let the pope weigh his character. His privileges should not be
admitted until it has been revealed, by comparison of scripts and seals,
at what date and by whom they were granted. Forgery is rife, and will
secure the exemption of all monasteries unless judges are extremely
thorough in their investigations.*

[Sept. × Dec. 1174]

Petri Blesensis opera i 201–5 ep. 68; *PL* cc 1456–9 ep. 95.

The archbp is styled 'ecclesie Cantuariensis humilis minister'; as in some other
letters to the pope from archbishops who were legates, the legatine title is not
used. The date ? 1180, proposed by Giles, is too late. The episode belongs to
autumn 1174, as appears from the papal letter of 22 Dec. (below). The monks of
Malmesbury had presented their abbot-elect, Robert de Veneys', to their
diocesan for benediction. Bp Jocelin would only bless the elect if he professed
obedience. This was refused and the elect went to the bp of Llandaff for
benediction. A letter of bp Nicholas of Llandaff to the bp and dean and chapter
of Salisbury expresses his contrition for having given the blessing illegally, when
the dispute already awaited hearing by the archbp. He admits that he deserved
the suspension from orders and office imposed by the archbp (*Salisbury charters*
41–42). An appeal was lodged by the abbot in time for a mandate to issue on 22
Dec. 1174, appointing the bps of London and Worcester to discharge the abbot
from the claim of the bp of Salisbury if he possessed a suitable papal privilege
(*Reg. Malmesburiense* (RS) i 371–2). No action is recorded by the delegates in
response to this mandate. The suspect papal letter (JE 2140, of Sergius I: pd
Reg. Malmesburiense i 343–5) was accepted by later popes as genuine. Disputes
over the abbey's privileges of exemption produced other papal mandates in 1175
and 1177 (ibid. i 370–1). See M. G. Cheney, *Roger of Worcester* 138–9, 156, and
App. II no. 79.

167. Missenden abbey

Notification that the case delegated to the archbishop by pope Lucius III between the abbot and convent of Missenden and Geoffrey clerk of Turville about the church of Weston (Turville) has been ended in the archbishop's presence by common consent of the parties. Geoffrey and his successors shall, for the sake of peace, pay the canons of Missenden yearly in the church of Taplow a pension of sixty shillings sterling, twenty shillings at Christmas and Easter and Michaelmas; if the first instalment at Christmas is delayed, it shall be taken to the abbey. William de Turville the patron has assented, saving his right of patronage for himself and his heirs. The canons shall claim no right in the church other than the pension of sixty shillings; but on the death of Geoffrey, future parsons presented by the patron shall take oath to make the payment. The canons shall continue to possess the chapel of 'Leie' for a yearly pension of six shillings to the mother church of Weston. All parties have sworn to observe the agreement. The abbot has sworn before the archbishop that the abbot and convent will make no claim on the churches in the patronage of William and his heirs.

[May × 25 Sept. 1183]

B = BL ms. Harl. 3688 (Missenden cartulary) fo. 58v (48v). s. xiv in.

Pd from B in *The cartulary of Missenden abbey* ed. J. G. Jenkins (Bucks. Archaeol. Soc., Records Branch ii 1939) i 218–9 no. 246.

Hiis testibus: magistro G. Coventrensi electo, magistro P. Blesensi archidiacono Batoniensi cancellario nostro, Willelmo Gloecestriensi archidiacono, magistro R. de Inglesham, magistro R. de Rulveston, magistro Aimero de Partimaco,*ᵃ* magistro R. Norwicensi, Ricardo et Gaufrido, Rogerio decano, et aliis.

ᵃ Partinaco B

The archbp is not styled legate. Mr Gerard Pucella was elect of Coventry May — 25 Sept. 1183. Another document recording the settlement (*Cartulary* i 218 no. 245) states that Geoffrey clerk of Turville is brother of William de Turville. If, as is probable, the case was settled in England and recorded without long delay, the date of this notification is after the archbp's return to England in mid August 1183.

168. Monks Kirby priory

Confirmation for the church of Monks Kirby of all its lands, tithes, and obventions and the liberties and free customs which it had in the time of king Henry (I), as confirmed by the charters of bishop Walter of

Coventry and Richard archdeacon of Coventry. Chapels set up since the death of king Henry shall not be used in future.

[? Aug. 1174 × Sept. 1175]

A = PRO E 210/D 119. Endorsed, s. xiii: De ecclesia de Kyrk' et de capellis. Approx. 165 × 118 + 30 mm. Sealing d.q. 1; tag and seal lost. Scribe **II**.

B = PRO E 327/94, incomplete, in inspeximus by archbp Baldwin (below, no. 296).

Pd (calendar) from A in *Calendar of Ancient Deeds* (HMSO) iii 417.

Universis sancte matris ecclesie filiis . Ric(ardus) dei gratia Cantuariensis archiepiscopus totius Anglie primas et apostolice sedis legatus . salutem in domino. Quoniam ea que pro bono utilitatis ecclesiastice facta sunt . perpetua debent stabilitate gaudere ⫶ in communem volumus noticiam devenire . nos presentis carte patrocinio confirmasse ecclesie de Kirkebi omnia tenementa sua . in terris . decimis . et omnimodis obventionibus ad eam pertinentibus ⫶ cum omnibus libertatibus et liberis consuetudinibus quibus tempore Henrici regis melius et liberius tenuit . sicut bone memorie Walterus Coventrensis episcopus et dilectus filius noster Ricardus Coventrensis archidiaconus ea cartis suis rationabiliter confirmaverunt. Precipimus quoque quod omnes capelle illius prefate ecclesie que post mortem regis H. facte sunt ⫶ in perpetuum cessent . sequentes in hoc formam carte predicti episcopi. Si quis igitur aliquo temeritatis ausu hanc nostre confirmationis paginam in irritum revocare temptaverit ⫶ anathematis vinculo se sciat esse innodatum ⫶ donec resipiscat. Testibus . Iohanne Pictavensi episcopo . domino Roberto de Novo burgo . Benedicto cancellario . magistro Gerardo . Willelmo de Norh' . Radulfo de Sancto Martino . magistro Hugone de Sudwell' . Amico clerico . et aliis.

> Bp Walter's charter must be dated before 7 Dec. 1159 and the charter of archdn Richard before he was elected to the bpric in succession to Walter. For Benedict's tenure of the chancellorship see no. 111n.

169. Newhouse abbey

Mandate to the bishops of the province of Canterbury, in accordance with a mandate of pope Alexander III of 23 May 1177 (recited), to maintain a sentence delivered by the pope's judges delegate which awarded the church of East Halton to the abbot and canons of Newhouse, rejecting the claim of the abbess and nuns of Elstow. The nuns are to be punished if they trouble the canons on the matter.

[1177, after June]

A = BL Harl. ch. 43 G 24. Endorsed, s. xii/xiii: R. archiepiscopus Cant'. Approx. 177 × 148 + 10 mm. Sealing s.q.; step torn, seal lost. Scribe **II**.

Pd from A in *Danelaw docts* 215–6 no. 286, and the papal letter only in *PUE* i 418 no. 146; in transl. by S. R. Wigram, *Chronicles of the abbey of Elstow* (1885) 47.

Ric(ardus) dei gratia Cantuariensis archiepiscopus tocius Anglie primas et apostolice sedis legatus . venerabilibus fratribus suis per provinciam Cantuariensem constitutis salutem in vero salutari. Mandatum domini pape suscepimus in hec verba . Alexander episcopus servus servorum dei . venerabili fratri . Cantuariensi archiepiscopo apostolice sedis legato . salutem et apostolicam benedictionem. Ex litteris dilectorum filiorum nostrorum abbatis Rievallensis et prioris de Bridlinton' nobis transmissis evidenter accepimus . quod cum causam que inter abbatem de Neuhus et abbatissam et moniales de Elnest' super ecclesia sancti Petri de 'h'Alton' diutius est agitata . de mandato nostro suscepissent diffiniendam ⸴ post diligentiorem inquisitionem rei veritate cognita scilicet quod canonici eandem ecclesiam ad presentationem dominorum fundi episcopali canonica institutione adepti fuissent ⸴ et quod ita ab antiquioribus et honestioribus viris comprovincialibus iuramento prestito iuratum est set et coram eo qui vices archidiaconatus gerebat in comprovinciali capitulo testificatum est ⸴ quod a quadraginta annis et amplius moniales nunquam eandem ecclesiam possedissent . ordine iudiciario terminarunt. Quia ergo causas concordia vel iudicio terminatas non decet in recidive contentionis scrupulum revocari ⸴ fraternitati tue per apostolica scripta precipiendo mandamus . quatinus prescriptam ecclesiam de Halton' que eisdem canonicis de Neuhus cum omnibus pertinenciis suis est assignata . de cetero inconcusse possidendam decernas . et quiete facias et pacifice possidere. Quod si forte predicte moniales contra sententiam quam predicti iudices quibus causam ipsam commiseramus pro canonicis promulgarunt venire temptaverint ⸴ fraternitati tue firmiter iniungimus . quatinus omni occasione et appellatione cessante ⸴ perpetuum silentium prenominatis monialibus super eadem ecclesia apostolica auctoritate imponas . nullis impedientibus litteris a nobis super hoc impetratis vel impetrandis . ita quidem ut sinceritatem sollicitudinis et obedientie tue ⸴ debeamus non inmerito commendare. Verum quoniam predicti canonici non modicum importunis molestiis predictarum monialium possent gravari . et sui iuris dispendium sustinere ⸴ fraternitati tue per apostolica scripta precipiendo mandamus . quatinus suffraganeis tuis iniungas . ut si forte captata absentia tua memorate moniales aliquando per subreptionem aliquam prelibatos canonicos molestare aut gravare presumpserint ⸴ excessum illum digna studeant severitate punire . ut ceteri timeant similia perpetrare. Dat' Venet' in Rivoalto x .kal. Iunii. Huius auctoritate mandati vestre fraternitati mandamus . atque precipimus . quatinus si quando contigerit sepedictas moniales prelibatis canonicis super prescripta ecclesia molestiam aliquam inferre vel gravamen ⸴ debita sollicitudine eis occurratis . et ab iniustis vexationibus et presumptionibus suis ⸴ apostolica auctoritate et nostra severius eas compescatis.

The mandate to the abbot of Rievaulx and the prior of Bridlington is edited from decretal collections in *Papal decretals relating to the diocese of Lincoln* ed. W. H. Holtzmann and E. W. Kemp (Lincoln Record Soc. 47. 1954) 12–17 No. VI version i. It was issued in response to an appeal by Newhouse against a sentence in favour of Elstow by the dean of Lincoln and archdn of Bedford, judges delegate of the pope. The abbot and prior delivered sentence at Beverley, 10 Jan. 1177 (*Danelaw documents* 214–5 no. 285) and reported to the pope, as his mandate of 23 May shows. Elstow apparently flouted this sentence and Newhouse got a mandate to the archbp of Canterbury and another (*Papal decretals ... Lincoln* 12–17 no. VI version ii, JL 13826, *Extra* 2 8 1). This presumably is the mandate to which the archbp refers in no. 170 below. It gave the new judges authority to end the case 'concordia vel iudicio' if it could not be settled on grounds of prescription. The result was eventually the composition announced by the archbp in no. 170, but intermediate stages of the dispute may be missing.

170. Newhouse abbey

Notification that the dispute between the abbot and canons of Newhouse and the abbess and nuns of Elstow over the church of East Halton has been concluded in the archbishop's presence by a composition which he ratifies.

[1178 × Sept. 1181]

A = BL Harl. ch. 43 G 23. Endorsed, s. xii/xiii: R. archiepiscopus Cant'. Approx. 190 × 176 + 20 mm. Sealing d.q. 2; small remains (brown wax) of seal and counterseal. Top half of chirograph, inverted, divided by straight cut.

Pd from A in *Danelaw docts* 216–7 no. 287; in transl. by S. R. Wigram, *Chronicles of the abbey of Elstow* (1885) 47.

CIRGRPHUM INTER ECCLESIAM DE NIEWEH' ET ECCLESIAM ÆNESTOEN

.Ric(ardus). dei gratia Cantuariensis archiepiscopus . tocius Anglie primas et apostolice sedis legatus ⸴ universis sancte matris ecclesie filiis ad quos presentes littere pervenerint ⸴ illam que est in domino salutem. Ea que in presencia nostra rationabiliter acta sunt ⸴ ne posteris temporibus in dubium revocentur ⸴ aut aliqua malignancium temeritate in redivivam questionem reducantur ⸴ presentis

scripti testimonio duximus commendare. Inde est quod ad communem omnium notitiam volumus pervenire ⁏ quod cum inter dilectos
filios nostros abbatem et canonicos de Niewehus et dilectas filias
nostras abbatissam et moniales de Alnesto super ecclesia de Hauton'
⁏ de sanctitatis apostolice mandato ⁏ in presencia nostra ⁏ controversia diucius fuisset agitata ⁏ tandem sub hac transactionis forma
conquievit. Predicte abbatissa et moniales de Alnesto' ⁏ quicquid
iuris in ecclesia de Halton' sibi vendicaverant ⁏ abbati et canonicis
liberum et quietum in perpetuum concesserunt . et preter hoc ⁏
concesserunt eis ⁏ decimas de dominio de Halton' et totam terram
quam ipse habuerunt in eadem villa unde inter eas et iamdictos
abbatem et canonicos nulla erat querela ⁏ salva tenura eorum qui
terram ipsam de ecclesia de Alnesto' hactenus tenuerunt . et predicti
abbas et canonici pro bono pacis et pro decimis ac terra prenominatis ⁏ sepedictis abbatisse et monialibus .iiii⁰ʳ . marcas argenti
annuatim apud Alnesto' persolvent . duas videlicet marcas ad Natale
domini . et duas in festo sancti Botulfi. Hanc autem transactionem
utrobique fide interposita firmatam ⁏ ut in posterum firma maneat et
inconvulsa presenti scripto et sigilli nostri munimine roboramus.
Testibus hiis . Walerano Baiocensi . et Willelmo Gloecestriensi ⁏
archidiaconis . Willelmo et Moyse capellanis . magistro Roberto de
Inglesham . magistro Rogerio Norwicensi . Iohanne capellano .
Ricardo et Galfrido clericis . Willelmo de Sotindon' et multis aliis.

For the circumstances of this composition see notes to no. 169.

171. Newnham priory

*Notification of an amicable agreement reached in the archbishop's
presence after dispute between Stephen of Ecton and the prior and
canons of St Paul's, Bedford, about tithe in the vill of Holwell of the
demesne of Robert de Bueles and of Simon his son-in-law. Stephen
formerly held the tithe at farm from archdeacon Nicholas of Bedford
who was farmer of Mr Richard de Almaria* ('Amalr' '). *He is to hold it
at farm for life from the canons at a yearly pension of half a silver mark
so long as the canons can warrant the tithe to him. Stephen has
promised* ('in manu nostra fide interposita') *not to deprive the canons
of their title in future on any pretext.*

[Aug. 1174 × Sept. 1181]

B = BL ms. Harl. 3656 (Newnham cartulary) fo. 49v (55v). s. xv.

Pd from B in *Cartulary of Newnham priory* ed. J. Godber (Beds. Hist. Rec. Soc.
43, 1963–4) 56 no. 90.

Testibus: magistro Gerardo, Willelmo, et aliis.

The archbp is styled legate. Nicholas archdn of Bedford may have been a canon of St Paul's, Bedford, the property of which went to the endowment of Newnham priory about 1166. Nicholas is last heard of 1174 × 1178. For Stephen of Ecton cf. *Book of Seals* 143–4, 159–60 nos. 200, 220.

171A.   Newnham priory

Confirmation for prior Auger and the canons of Newnham of their possessions, enumerating (after a missing portion) two thirds of the demesne-tithes of Simon de Beauchamp in Stotfold, Haynes, Keysoe, Linslade, Eversholt and Hunsdon, and of all Simon's fee in Holwell, also one silver mark annually from a mill at Linslade, two-thirds of tithe of a hide and a half once of Richard monachus *in Chicksands, tithe of half a hide of Nigel Malherbe in Houghton (? Conquest), tithe which Jordan* presbiter *had in Haynes, two-thirds of the demesne tithes of Colworth (in Sharnbrook) and Aspley, the mill of Golde and tithes of mills of Bedford castle, of the monks of Bermondsey in Bedford, of Risyngho (in Goldington), Biddenham, Willington, Cardington, and Goldington, half a virgate of land given by Ralph son of Ascelin, ten acres given by Wigan, three acres by Hugh, six virgates which were of the prebends of William, Philip and Gilbert, and three acres in Harrowden which were of the prebends of Richard and Ralph, in Cardington a virgate given by Pain de Beauchamp, half a virgate given by John* pincerna, *a hide in* Fordes *(? Bedford), half a hide in Renhold, demesne-tithe of Puthoe (in Goldington), land in Colworth given by William Druel and land given by Thomas son of Hugh, Pain* campio, *John* pincerna, *Robert* marescallus, *Eylwinus in* Dilewic, *(in Stagsden) and thirty pigs quit of pannage yearly in Cardington wood, all as seen to be confirmed in perpetuity by the sealed charter of Simon de Beauchamp; also all grants by other lords, in the church of All Saints, Bedford, the church of Eynesbury, the church of Wrestlingworth, and five shillings in the church of Holcot.*

[Jan. × May 1177]

B = BL ms. Harl. 3656 (Newnham cartulary) fo. 55r (61r). s. xv. Fos. 53–54 lost; they contained the first part of the charter.

Pd from B in *Cartulary of Newnham priory* ed. Joyce Godber (Beds. Hist. Rec. Soc. 43, 1963–4) i 54–55 no. 87, with ascription to bp Hugh (I) of Lincoln, 1186 × 1200.

Teste magistro Petro Blesensi, Willelmo de Norhal, magistro Hugone de Suell' et aliis.

The remains of the witness-list fixes the date before William of Northolt became archdn of Gloucester, and before the disgrace of Mr Hugh of Southwell (see above, no. 104n.). This charter must have followed the sentence (20 or 25 Jan. 1177) which gave the canons 5s. p. a. from the church of Holcot (*Cartulary* 58–59 no. 94, cf. M. G. Cheney, *Roger of Worcester* 277–8). The surviving fragment is only the tailpiece of a more comprehensive confirmation issued (as shown by the witnesses) by archbp Richard. It lacks the opening clauses and the beginning of the text. Normally the protocol of such a charter would have a general address; but this is a diplomatic freak. The text shows the beneficiary addressed and named in the second person: 'carta dil. fil. Symonis de Bello campo confirmata *vobis*', '*vobis* adiudicata sunt', 'omnes possessiones sicut ecclesie *tue* de Newenham, dilect*e* fil*i* Auger' ... collata *tibi tuis*que successoribus confirmamus'. the reference to the church of Newenham suggests that the address was to the prior and canons of 'Newenham iuxta Bedford' rather than of 'S. Pauli Bedford', as in no. 171 above. The property specified in this remnant (which begins 'has decimas scilicet') mainly comprises land, tithe, and mills. Most of it records gifts by Simon de Beauchamp, founder of the priory on the basis of the collegiate church of Bedford. His two charters (*Cartulary* pp. 9–11 no. 5, pp. 12–13 no. 7), though somewhat irregular in their present form, point to a comprehensive grant *c*.1166 which included twelve churches later in the patronage of Newnham, viz: Ravensden, Renhold, Great Barford, Willington, Cardington, Goldington, Southill, Cockayne Hatley, Wootton, Stagsden, Aspley, Turvey, Gravenhurst, Salford. It may be reasonably assumed that the archbp's charter above recited this list of churches, taken from the Beauchamp charter, before proceeding to rehearse the other possessions in almost precisely the terms in which Simon de Beauchamp had granted them.

172. Thomas of Newsole

Confirmation for Thomas of Newsole of the grant by prior John and the convent of Dover that he may build a chapel for his heirs and household in his curia *on stated conditions and saving the rights of the mother church of Coldred.*

[Oct. 1181 × 9 Oct. 1182]

B = PRO E 164/29 (Langdon cartulary) fo. 19v. s. xiv in. C = Ibid. fo. 19v, much abridged in inspeximus by archbp Hubert (below, no. 501); D = Ibid. 102v, in inspeximus by the abbot of Faversham and others, 25 Dec. 1219. E = Lambeth Palace ms. 241 (Dover cartulary) fo. 185r, in same inspeximus.

Ricardus dei gratia Cantuariensis archiepiscopus totius Anglie primas universis sancte matris ecclesie filiis in Christo salutem. Notum sit omnibus Christi fidelibus ad quos presentes littere pervenerint quod Iohannes prior de Dovor'*a* de communi consensu conventus sui concessit Thome de Newesole quod idem Thomas capellam habeat in curia sua de Newesole fundatam, in qua ipse et heredes sui et familia divina possint officia per capellanum curie sue licenter habere quem ipse et heredes sui sine onere ecclesie de Colrede exibebunt. Thomas autem concessit quod omnes decime de dominio de Newesole ad capellam illam et ad victum capellani pertineant, exceptis terris que permixte sunt cum terris Willelmi de Popeshale. Decime vero de terris que permixte sunt cum terris de Popeshale et preterea decime omnium rusticorum de Newesole integre ad ecclesiam de Colrede pertinebunt, ad quam idem rustici ad divina officia convenient, tam in vita quam in morte, ita tamen quod si aliqui de novo rustici fiant in predicto dominio unde decime sicut dictum est pertinent ad capellam, decime eorumdem rusticorum pertinebunt ad capellam et corpora rusticorum, tam in vita quam in morte, ad ecclesiam de Colrede. Et si terre rusticorum qui tempore huius concessionis tenuerunt ullo umquam casu in dominium memorati Thome vel successorum suorum fuerint devolute, decime tamen de predictorum rusticorum terris ad ecclesiam de Colrede pertinebunt sicut prius pertinebant, set et corpora eorum qui erunt familia Thome vel successorum eius ad ecclesiam eandem de Colrede pertinebunt. Thomas vero pro se et successoribus suis in se et successores suos suscepit omne onus quod de predictis decimis debebit annuatim ad abbatiam Sancti Augustini more debito pertinere. Nos autem predictum negotium ratum habentes illud sigilli nostri munimine duximus roborandum. Hiis testibus: magistro Gerardo, Waleranno, Salomone, et multis aliis.[b]

[a] *for rest of charter read*: etc. sicut in proxima precedenti carta de verbo ad verbum usque ad finem C   [b] magistro Gerardo ... aliis DE; etc. B

The church of Coldred had been confirmed to Dover priory by archbp Richard (above, no. 125). The chapel passed by the gift of Thomas's heirs into the hands of West Langdon abbey after his death, 1193 × 1205 (below, no. 501). The assent of the prior and convent of Dover to the founding of the chapel was granted by charter dated in the year of incarnation 1181 (E 164/29 fo. 20r). The imperfect witness-list in the D text of the archbp's confirmation gives Waleran no title. He was almost certainly archdn of Bayeux at the time. Had he been bp of Rochester his name would come before Mr Gerard's.

173. Newstead-in-Sherwood priory

Confirmation for the canons of Newstead in Sherwood of the church of (Ault) Hucknall with the chapel of Rowthorne and all their appurtenances, as granted and confirmed by bishop Richard of Coventry, who has instituted them at the presentation of king Henry II.

[May 1177 × Sept. 1181]

B = London, College of Arms ms. Arundel 60 (Newstead cartulary) fo. 35r ('confirmationes pontificum .VI.'). s. xiii ex. C = BL ms. Add. 35170 (Newstead cartulary) fo. 148v. s. xiv med.

Universis sancte matris ecclesie filiis[a] ad quos presentes littere pervenerint Ricardus dei gratia Cantuariensis archiepiscopus totius

Anglie primas et apostolice sedis legatus illam que est in domino salutem. Ea que religiosis personis iuste et canonice collata esse noscuntur firma debent stabilitate gaudere et ne aliqua malignantium temeritate divellantur nostra interest attentius providere. Ea propter ad universitatis vestre notitiam deveniat nos concessisse et confirmasse hac carta nostra dilectis filiis nostris canonicis de Novo Loco in Schyrewod' ecclesiam de Hokenhale cum capella de Routhorn' et [fo. 35v] omnibus ad eandem ecclesiam et capellam pertinentibus in perpetuum libere et pacifice possidendam, sicut eis ad presentationem domini regis Anglorum ex institutione venerabilis fratris nostri R. Conventrensis episcopi canonice collata est et confirmata. Volumus ergo et ea qua fungimur auctoritate precipimus ut prelibati canonici pretaxatam ecclesiam cum capella et omnibus aliis ad eam pertinentibus sicut eam rationabiliter adepti sunt in libera et perpetua possideant elemosina, statuentes et sub interminatione anathematis artius inhibentes ne quis huic nostre confirmationis pagine temere et contra iuris ordinem presumat obviare. Testibus hiis: magistro Gerardo[b], Walerano Baiocensi, W. Glocestriensi archidiaconis, magistro Roberto de Inglesham, Henrico Baiocensi, magistro Rogero Norwycensi, Rogero elemosinario, Willelmo de Sotindon', et pluribus aliis.

[a] filiis: *om.* BC   [b] Gerardo C; Berardo B

William of Northolt became archdn of Gloucester May × Dec. 1177.

The charter of bp Richard of Coventry follows, granting the church of Hucknall and the chapel of Rowthorne to the canons of Newstead on the presentation of kg Henry, and revoking a charter which the canons of Croxton had obtained from the bp concerning the church 'falsa suggestione' (ms. Arundel 60 fo. 35v).

174. Northampton: priory of St Andrew

Confirmation for the monks of La Charité dwelling at St Andrew's, Northampton, of all the churches (enumerated) and other ecclesiastical possessions which they have been granted.

[28 April 1174 × autumn 1177]

B = BL ms. Royal 11 B ix (cartulary of St Andrew's) fo. 29r. s. xiii ex. C = ibid. fo. 23v. D = BL ms. Cotton Vesp. E xvii (cartulary of St Andrew's) fo. 292v (275v). s. xv in., probably copied from B. E = ibid. fo. 289r (272r), probably copied from C.

Ricardus dei gratia Cantuariensis archiepiscopus totius Anglie primas et apostolice sedis legatus universis sancte matris ecclesie filiis salutem in domino. Ad solicitudinem et curam nostram pertinere dinoscitur ea que viris ecclesiasticis ac religiosis a fidelibus

dei rationabiliter collata sunt sub protectione dei et sancte Cantuariensis ecclesie clementer suscipere et pastorali provisione et auctoritatis munimine confirmare. Eapropter ad universitatis vestre notitiam volumus[a] pervenire nos presenti scripto confirmasse dilectis
filiis nostris monachis de Caritate apud Norht' in ecclesia sancti
Andree domino[b] famulantibus universa beneficia que eis
rationabiliter collata sunt, queque ipsi in ecclesiis vel ecclesiasticis
possessionibus canonice adepti esse dinoscuntur, specialiter autem,
sicut eis rationabiliter concesse sunt et scriptis auctenticis confirmate, ecclesiam Omnium Sanctorum de Norhampton' et omnes
ecclesias eiusdem ville cum universis pertinentiis suis, et ecclesiam
de Bragefeld'[c] cum terris et decimis suis, et ecclesiam de Hardings-
tor'[d] cum pertinentiis suis, et ecclesiam de Multon' cum pertinentiis
suis, et ecclesiam de Siwelle cum pertinentiis suis, ecclesiam de
Preston' cum pertinentiis suis, et ecclesiam de Billing' cum pertinentiis suis, et ecclesiam de Torp cum pertinentiis suis, ecclesiam
de Exton' cum pertinentiis suis, ecclesiam de Rihal' cum pertinentiis suis, ecclesiam de Hocton'[e] cum pertinentiis suis, ecclesiam de
Sulgrave cum pertinentiis suis, ecclesiam de Quenton' cum pertinentiis suis, ecclesiam [fo. 29v] de Newton'[f] cum pertinentiis suis,
et alias ecclesiasticas possessiones quas canonice adepti sunt, sicut
etiam canonice eis concesse sunt et confirmate, ita eis auctoritate
qua fungimur confirmamus et scripti presentis patrocinio corroboramus et sigilli nostri munimine communimus. Testibus: magistro
Gerardo, Walerano archidiacono Baiocensi, magistro Petro Blesensi, Willelmo de Northal', Radulfo de Wingham, Radulfo de
Sancto Martino, Henrico de Baioc',[g] Rogero elemosinario, Willelmo de Sottindon, Rogero Norwicensi, et aliis.

   [a] volumus DE; volimus BC   [b] domino BD; deo CE   [c] Bragefeld' BC; Brawfelde
D; Braggefeeld' E   [d] Hardingsor B; Hardinstor C; Hardyngysthorn' DE   [e] Hocton' B;
Houton' C; Howton' DE   [f] Newton' BDE; Newenton' C   [g] magistro Petro ... Baioc'
BD, *om*. CE

   Mr Gerard and Mr Peter of Blois left England for Rome in autumn 1177.
   William of Northolt became archdn of Gloucester, May × Dec. 1177. Since the
   witness-list closely resembles that of no. 202 below, the charter is probably not
   earlier than Aug. 1176. Cf. no. 132.

175. Northampton: priory of St Andrew

*Confirmation of the settlement reported to the archbishop by his
delegates, abbot (Adam) of Welford and Mr W. de Estanston, between
the monks of St Andrew's, Northampton and Richard, priest, about the
church of Quinton. Richard has abandoned his claim and received a gift*

of one mark from the priory. Confirmation of the grant of the church made by the priory to John, clerk.

[Oct. 1181 × May 1183]

B = BL ms. Royal 11 B ix (cartulary of St Andrew's) fo. 31r. s. xiii ex. C = BL ms. Cotton Vesp. E xvii (cartulary of St Andrew's) fo. 294v (277v). s. xv in. Probably copied from B.

Ricardus dei gratia Cantuariensis archiepiscopus et totius Anglie primas omnibus Christi fidelibus ad quos presentes littere pervenerint salutem in domino. Cum causam inter dilectos filios nostros monachos*a* sancti Andree de Norhanton et Ricardum presbiterum super ecclesia de Quenton' motam dilectis filiis nostris abbati de*b* Welleford' et magistro W. de Estanston' commisissemus audiendam, partibus in presentia eorum constitutis, cum in mandati nostri executione procedere vellent, prefatus Ricardus sicut littere eorundem iudicum videbantur attestari in medium processit et omni querele et iuri quod in predicta ecclesia sibi vendicabat sponte et sine aliqua coactione renuntiavit. Unde et predicti monachi circa eundem Ricardum pietate moti ad relevandam paupertatem suam unam marcam argenti misericorditer ei contulerunt, sicque omnis controversia hinc inde sopita est. Et quia pacem omnium subiectorum nostrorum procurare et fovere tenemur, nos eandem pacem et litis mote diremptionem*c* ratam habentes et firmam, eam sicut rationabiliter facta est scripti nostri auctoritate et testium subscriptione duximus communire.*d* Concessionem quoque quam sepedicti monachi dilecto filio nostro Iohanni clerico super iamdicta ecclesia fecisse noscuntur, sicut rationabiliter facta est firmam esse decrevimus et auctoritatis nostre munimine communimus. Hiis testibus: magistro Gerardo, Willelmo Glowcestriensi archidia- cono, magistro Roberto de Inglesham, magistro Rogero de Rolveston', Willelmo de Sottindon, Ricardo Londoniarum, Gaufrido clerico, et multis aliis.

a monachos C; monachis B   *b* de: *om.* BC   *c* direptionem BC   *d* communire: precommunire BC, pre- *marked for erasure in* B

Mr Gerard was elected bp of Coventry on or after 26 May 1183. The report of the judges delegate (preceding this in the cartularies, B fo. 30v, C fo. 294r and also fo. 88v) shows that they heard the case in synod. Since the judges delegate address the archbp as legate the synod was probably held in 1181. The monks proved that Thomas, lately deceased, had served the church in their name, and Richard admitted that he held the church as an annual vicar of Thomas. He had now taken the cross to visit the Holy Sepulchre. In later days the church was a rectory in the patronage of St Andrew's priory.

176.   Northampton: abbey of St James

Confirmation for the abbot and canons of St James, Northampton, of their possessions present and future lawfully acquired, including those specified in the confirmation by archbishop Theobald and other churches and possessions here enumerated.   [28 April 1174 × Sept. 1181]

B = BL ms. Cotton Tib. E v (cartulary of St James, Northampton) fo. 87r(85r, 81r). s. xiv in. Badly damaged; doubtful readings in brackets. C = Bodl. ms. Top. Northants. c.5 p. 358 (J. Bridges's transcript of B, abstract). s. xvii.

Ricardus dei gratia Cantuariensis archiepiscopus totius Anglie primas et apostolice sedis legatus universis sancte matris ecclesie filiis ad quos littere presentes pervenerint salutem in vero salutari. Quoniam iuste possidentium quies frequenti temeritate calumpniantium turbatur, consilii prudentioris usus optinuit [ut que] religiosis domibus canonice et rationabiliter sunt collata scriptorum ... -tium auctoritate firmentur. Ea propter in puplicam volumus devenire notitiam nos concessisse et confirmasse abbati Sancti Iacobi de Northampton et fratribus ibi deo*ᵃ* militantibus universa beneficia que a Christi fidelibus ex eorum donatione rationabiliter sunt adepti et que in posterum iustis modis poterunt adipisci. Illis vero possessionibus beneficium confirmationis indulgemus que in confirmatione Teobaldi predecessoris nostri bone memorie eis indulta propriis vocabulis exprimuntur. Insuper eis concedimus et confirmamus ecclesiam de Wicle ex donatione Willelmi ostricarii cum omnibus pertinentiis et appenditiis suis, ecclesiam de Boseg', ecclesiam de Duston, ecclesiam de Horton', ecclesiam de Roda cum omnibus appenditiis et pertinentiis earum, prout carte donatorum testantur, unam carrucatam terre in Lichesbar', et terram que fuit Gocelini in eadem villa, et molendinum de Uptona cum suis holmis et cum alio quodam prato iuxta iacente, et dimidiam marcam redditus, videlicet de quadam scoppa et Alvredo macellario et Gaufrido Peg', et unam virgatam terre in Kysligbir', et redditus xvi denariorum iuxta cimiterium Sancti Petri in Northampton, et quicquid Hugo Gubiun et Ricardus filius eius eis dederunt, et pratum quoddam xiiii acrarum iacens a meridiana parte aque inter molendina de Duston, et quicquid Walterus de Mungumeri eis dedit, et quod Gregorius de Diva eis dedit in Asseby et quod Rogerus de Calz in Duston, et terram quam Robertus*ᵇ* filius Hawise [fo. 87v] eis dedit in Hamtone, et ii virgatas terre in Roda, et exsarta de Horpoll que Robertus de la Sauceia eis confirmavit cum augmento unius acre que*ᶜ* eis Athelardus dedit in eadem et que

Iohannes de Ridun eis dedit, et dimidiam virgatam terre de Hurteligbur' et molendinum de Riston et iii solidatos redditus in alio molendino eiusdem ville, et de Roberto de Sancto Paulo unam[c] virgatam terre in Duston, cum managio quod fuit Iohannis filii Rogeri et quicquid habent[c] ex donatione advocatorum de Prestona et ii solidatos redditus in Hohton, videlicet xii d. de Ricardo filio Rogeri et xii de Iwone de Pavel et vi d. in Touecestr', in Sewella dimidiam virgatam terre. Has possessiones sive in ecclesiis sive in terris eis concedimus et confirmamus cum omnibus appenditiis et pertinentiis et libertatibus earum prout carte donatorum testantur. Preterea quascumque possessiones quecumque bona [donatione] principum largitione fidelium vel aliis rationabilibus modis in futurum[d] poterint adquirere, simili ratione concedimus et confirmamus, salvo iure et dignitate diocesani episcopi. Si qua igitur secularis ecclesiasticave persona ecclesie bona temere invaserit vel minuerit vel quoquo modo iniuste [perturbaverit], secundo tertiove commonita si non satisfecerit canonicis [divine subiaceat ultioni. Cunctis autem] eidem loco sua iura servantibus sit pax domini nostri Iesu Christi. Amen.

[a] deo: de B   [b] ? Robertus B; Radulfus C   [c] *supplied from* C   [d] futurum: futuro B

The confirmation by archbp Theobald is preserved in the cartulary (fo. 228v), even more badly damaged, and ascribed to archbp Thomas; to be edited in *EEA* in the appendix of Theobald's acta.

*177. The church of Norwich

Mandate to the prior and convent to send the prior and five or more 'de discretioribus et sapientioribus domus' *to the king and the archbishop at Oxford on 24 June, armed with letters from the convent, to elect a pastor for their church.* [c. 1 June 1175]

Mentioned only, in *Gesta Henrici II* i 91–92, which notes that letters in the same form went to eleven more vacant religious houses of the province: Abingdon, Grimsby, Crowland, Thorney, St Benet of Holme, Westminster, St Augustine's, Canterbury, Battle, Hyde, Abbotsbury, Muchelney. The letters were sent with similar letters sent by the kg. The kg's messenger was his clerk, Roger of Howden, and the archbp's clerk, Mr Robert of Inglesham, accompanied him with the archbp's mandate, and the list of abbeys presumably shows their itinerary. It is unlikely that the meeting happened at Oxford on 24 June; for the archbp was apparently at Lambeth on 27 June (below, no. 182) and these elections formed part of the business transacted in the great council which met at Woodstock about 1 July (*Gesta* i 92–93). Diceto states that 'priores cum magna parte conventuum sub edicto vocati sunt apud Wdestoc viii[o] idus Iulii' (i 401).

177A.   Nuneaton abbey

Confirmation, following the example of archbishop Theobald, for the
abbey of Eaton, of its possessions and rights, specifying the gifts of earl
Robert of Leicester in Eaton and Kintbury, king Henry's gift of the
church of Chalton, and Gervase Paynel's gift of the mill of Inkpen.

[28 April 1174 × Sept. 1181]

> A = BL Add. ch. 47393. Endorsed, s. xii/xiii(?): Hec carta archiepiscopi de terra
> Etone et de xxv libratis terre in Keneberie et de ecclesia de Chauton' et de
> molendino de Ingepenne; s. xiv in.: Patens. (?) H. de Colecestr' .b. Approx.
> 169 × 190 + 24 mm. Sealing d.q. 2, fine seal and counterseal in brown-
> varnished wax, with faded silk seal-bag.
>
> B = BL Add. ch. 47398 (Nuneaton cartulary roll) no. 3. s. xiv in.

Universis sancte matris ecclesie filiis ad quos presentes littere
pervenerint ⸴ Ricardus . dei gratia Cantuariensis archiepiscopus ⸴
tocius Anglie primas et apostolice sedis legatus ⸴ illam que est in
domino salutem. Ea que religiosis personis divini amoris intuitu
iuste et canonice collata esse noscuntur ⸴ firma debent pace et
tranquillitate gaudere . et ne aliquibus malignantium versutiis
temere perturbentur ⸴ ex iniuncte nobis cure pastoralis officio
tenemur ⸴ sollicite providere. Eapropter vestigiis pie recordationis
.T. predecessoris nostri inherentes ⸴ abbatie*a* que in honorem beate
Marie virginis apud Etton' de ordine monialium de Fonte Ebraudi
fundata est ⸴ universas possessiones et dignitates quas impresentiarum iuste possidet vel in posterum iustis modis poterit adipisci ⸴
concedimus et carta presenti confirmamus. Ex quibus ⸴ hec propriis
duximus exprimenda vocabulis . videlicet ex dono Roberti comitis
Leercestr' ⸴ totam Ettonam ⸴ cum omnibus pertinentiis suis ⸴ in qua
abbatia ipsa fundata est . et in Keneteberga ⸴ xxv libratas terre. Ex
dono regis Henrici ecclesiam de Chauton' cum omnibus pertinentiis
suis. Ex dono Gervasii Paganelli ⸴ molendinum de Ingepenna . cum
omnibus pertinentiis suis. Volumus igitur et precipimus ut in
predicta abbatia*a* de Etton' ordo monialium de Fonte Ebraudi ⸴
perpetuo observetur . et ut eadem abbatia universas possessiones et
dignitates et liberas consuetudines quas ex dono predicti regis vel
memorati comitis seu quorumcumque Christi fidelium largitione
rationabiliter optinet ⸴ aut futuris temporibus iuste et canonice
poterit optinere ⸴ libere et integre possideat in perpetuum. Ea itaque
qua fungimur auctoritate statuimus et sub interminatione anathematis prohibemus ⸴ nequis predictam abbatiam*a* vel eius
possessiones iniuste et contra iuris ordinem perturbare ⸴ vel huic

nostre confirmacionis et constitucionis pagine aliquatenus temere contraire presumat. Quod qui attemptare presumpserit ; dei omnipotentis indignacionem ; et nostre excommunicacionis sententiam ; se noverit incurrisse. Testibus . Walerano Baiocensi archidiacono Willelmo monacho . magistro Roberto de Inglesham . Rogerio elemosinario . Iohanne capellano . Willelmo de Sotindon' et pluribus aliis.

^a abbat- B; abat- A

The only indication of date is the archbp's style.

The charter of earl Robert of Leicester remains in the archives of Fontevrault (*CDF* no. 1062, cf. BL Add. ch. 47384), those of king Henry II and Gervase Paynel are BL Add. ch. 47394 and 47423–4. The sources are ambiguous on the status of Nuneaton. It is described as an abbey in charters of countess Isabel and earl Simon of Northampton, before 1158 (*Danelaw documents* nos. 334–5), in a charter of archbp Theobald, 1154 × 59 (Saltman, *Theobald* no. 187), in a charter of bp Robert II of Lincoln, *c*.1155 × 1166 (*EEA* i no. 207), and in this charter; but most early charters refer simply to the *domus* or the nuns of Eaton. A charter of the abbess and convent of Fontevrault, *c*.1155, refers to a grant made by the prioress and prior and convent of Eaton and another charter, *c*.1160, is attested by William prior and Agnes prioress of Eaton (*Danelaw documents* nos. 331, 336). A succession of prioresses and priors is recorded in the late twelfth century (*HRH* 217), and in 1206 the prioress, Emma, had Simon, prior, as her attorney in the king's court (*CRR* iv 139–40, 172).

178. Osney abbey

Mandate to Philip vice-archdeacon of Oxford to execute a sentence of the bishop of London as papal delegate.

[? summer–autumn 1174]

A = Bodl., deposited deeds Ch. Ch. O 627. Endorsed, s. xiii: Littere Ricardi Cantuariensis archiepiscopi de ecclesia S. Marie Magdalene; s. xvi: S. Marie Magdalene 14 H. Approx. 146 × 45 + 10 (step) mm. Sealing s. q.; tongue, tie, seal and counterseal on tongue (natural wax, brown varnish), wanting about one quarter (bottom right-hand) of seal, and tie. Scribe **II**.

B = BL ms. Cotton Vit. E xv (Osney cartulary) fo. 14r. s. xii/xiii.

Pd from A in *Oseney cartulary* ii 225–6 no. 784.

Ric(ardus) dei gratia Cantuariensis archiepiscopus tocius Anglie primas et apostolice sedis legatus . magistro Philippo vicearchidiacono Oxoniensi^a. salutem. Ex officio nostre legationis . causis que 'de' domini pape precepto vel mandato formam suscipiunt . convenit nos plurimam diligentiam accommodare ; ut finem debitum singule quantum in nobis est sortiantur. Proinde tibi mandantes districte precipimus . quatinus sententiam venerabilis fratris nostri .G. Londoniensis episcopi . quam auctoritate apostolica tibi prescriptam litteris suis a sigillo dependentibus tibi eadem auctoritate

rationabiliter precipit exsecutioni mandare . iuste et sine dilatione
effectui mancipare non differas. Vale.

a Oxoniensi: Oxn' A; Oxenef' B

Bp Gilbert of London's mandate to the vice-archdn ordered him to put the
canons of Osney in possession of the church of St Mary Magdalen, Oxford, from
which they had been forcibly ejected by the canons of St Frideswide's, Oxford.
For this and related documents see *Oseney cartulary* ii 214–26 and Foliot, *Letters*
462–7, where the dating is discussed and this episode placed in its context of a
prolonged lawsuit. Cf. C. R. Cheney, *From Becket to Langton* 114 and M. G.
Cheney, *Roger of Worcester* 138, 163.

*179.   Osney abbey

*Mandate to prohibit the canons of Préaux from building a chapel at
Watcombe in the parish of Watlington, after an appeal from the abbot
and convent of Osney.*   [? *c.*1181]

Mentioned only in two letters of papal judges delegate *c.*1187, who found that
the chapel was built, after appeal and prohibition, and who forbade the
celebration of services in it. *Oseney cartulary* iv 430–1 nos. 401, 401A, cf. iv
428. A manor at Watcombe, in the parish of Watlington, of which the church
belonged to Osney (*Oseney cartulary* iv 405–6), was held by tenants of the
Norman abbey of Préaux, whom Osney repeatedly sued for tithe in
Watcombe. Since the judges state that the case 'iam ultra quinquennium
protracta est', the archbp's mandate may be dated as above, or earlier.

180.   Oxford: priory of St Frideswide

*Confirmation for the canons of St Frideswide, Oxford, of the church of
Churchill in free and perpetual alms, as granted by Henry de Noers,
Juliana his wife, and Jordan their son-in-law.*

[28 April 1174 × June 1181]

B = Oxford, Christ Church, Chapter libr. ms. 224 (Register A of St Frideswide's) p. 228a. s. xv. C = Ibid. p. 232a, in copy of inspeximus by archbp
Hubert.

Pd from B, slightly abridged, in *St Frideswide's cartulary* ii 257–8 no. 1032.

Ricardus dei gratia Cantuariensis archiepiscopus totius Anglie
primas et apostolice sedis legatus universis Christi fidelibus ad quos
presentes litere pervenerint eternam in domino salutem. Ex auctentico scripto Henrici de Noers*a* satis aperte cognovimus quod idem
Henricus assensu et voluntate Iuliane uxoris sue et Iordani generi
sui concessit et dedit deo et Sancte Frideswide de*b* Oxonia et
canonicis ibidem deo servientibus ecclesiam de Chirchehull' cum
omnibus pertinentiis suis in liberam et puram ac perpetuam elemo-

sinam, pro salute animarum eorum et antecessorum suorum liberam et quietam ab omni seculari exactione et servitio. Nichillominus etiam, sicut ex^c eodem scripto cognovimus, idem Henricus et Iuliana uxor eius dederunt corpora sua prefate ecclesie ita quod, si vitam in melius mutare voluerint, in eadem domo ad agendam vitam canonicam reciperentur. Unde quoniam ex officio suscepti regiminis nobis imminet ut caritatis opera que a subditis nostris pietatis et devotionis intuitu facta [p. 228b] esse noscuntur rata habeamus et firma, factum predicti Henrici et Iuliane uxoris sue et Iordani generi sui multipliciter approbantes, prescriptam concessionem et donationem eorum de prelibata ecclesia et pertinentiis suis, necnon de corporibus ipsorum Henrici et Iuliane uxoris sue prelibate ecclesie et domui Sancte Frideswide sub prescripta forma donatis ratam habemus et firmam et auctoritate qua fungimur confirmamus et sigilli nostri patrocinio ac presentis scripti testimonio coroboramus, sicut carta predicti Henrici atque Iuliane uxoris sue et Iordani generi sui sigillis confirmata et consignata quam nos ipsi vidimus rationabiliter testatur.^{d} Hiis testibus etc.

^{a} Noers B; Nuers C ^{b} de C, *om.* B ^{c} ex C; in B ^{d} testatur B; protestatur C

This charter received papal confirmation 25 July 1181 (ibid. ii 258 no. 1033 and *PUE* iii 450 no. 339). The charters of Henry de Noers and his family and lords are in the cartulary (ibid. ii 255–7 nos. 1025–31).

181. Pershore abbey

Confirmation for the monks of Pershore of all their possessions and rights, especially the customs due from the freemen and villeins of St Peter's, Westminster, in the hundred of Pershore, as was granted by abbot Gilbert of Westminster and confirmed by archbishops Theobald and Thomas and by Simon and John bishops of Worcester.

[28 April 1174 × Sept. 1181]

B = PRO E 315/61 (Pershore cartulary) fo. 107v(104v). s. xiv in.

Ricardus dei gratia Cantuariensis archiepiscopus totius Anglie primas et apostolice sedis legatus universis sancte matris ecclesie filiis salutem in domino. Ad sollicitudinem nostram pertinere dinoscitur ea que viris ecclesiasticis et eorum usibus deputata sunt cura propensiore tueri, et ne malignantium versutiis ullatenus turbentur plenissimum eis robur nostris auctoritatibus accommodare. Eapropter ad universitatis vestre notitiam pervenire volumus quod ecclesie sancte Marie de Persora omnes possessiones rationabiliter concessas et collatas omniaque iura que ab antiquis

retro temporibus habere consuevit, sicut ei rationabiliter concessa
sunt et scriptis autenticis confirmata, auctoritate qua fungimur
confirmamus in perpetuum et corroboramus, specialiter autem
omnes rectitudines et consuetudines quas antiquitus habere solebat
et de liberis hominibus et colonis Sancti Petri Westmonasteriensis,
scilicet duas partes decimarum omnium hominum de hundredo de
Persora et alia omnia beneficia que solvi debent matrici ecclesie ubi
corpora defunctorum sepeliuntur, sicut a felicis memorie Gilberto
abbate Westmonasterii et conventu concessa sunt eidem ecclesie de
Persora et scriptis auctenticis que oculis nostris perspeximus
rationabiliter confirmata, et a predecessoribus nostris, Theobaldo
scilicet et gloriosissimo martire Thoma, canonice corroborata, et a
diocesanis episcopis Symone et Iohanne quorum auctentica vidimus
concessa et communita, ita et nos concedimus et confirmamus et
scripti et sigilli nostri patrocinio communimus. Testibus: magistro
Gerardo, domino Roberto de Novoburgo, Walerano archidiacono
Baiocensi, et aliis.

Preceded in the cartulary by 'Confirmatio sancti Thome Cantuariensis archiepiscopi ...' which is actually Theobald's (pd by Saltman, *Theobald* 421 no. 199).
The wording of archbp Richard's charter, from 'omnes rectitudines' to 'oculis
nostris perspeximus' follows Theobald closely. No charter of archbp Thomas
was copied into the cartulary; see above, no. 31.

182. Plympton priory

*Notification of a sentence in favour of Plympton priory by the
archbishop and bishop Roger of Worcester, commissioned by the pope*
sub certa forma, *in a case between the canons of Plympton and Sir Joel
de Vautort, acting as his nephew's guardian and claiming patronage of
the church of Sutton. Sir Joel, who failed to appear on a fourth and
peremptory citation, was accounted contumacious. The judges examined
the original charter of bishop William of Exeter (which adjudged the
church to the canons). Bishop Bartholomew verified its seal by
comparison with others of bishop William. Canon Stephen swore that
he had impetrated the papal commission to the judges on the basis of a
copy of this charter, and he and another canon of Plympton swore that
they had understood from elders of the priory that it was an authentic
instrument of bishop William.*   Lambeth. 27 June 1175.

B = Bodl. ms. James 23 p. 163, among extracts from a lost cartulary of Plympton.
s. xvii in.

Pd from B by M. G. Cheney, *Roger of Worcester* 283–4 no. 53.

Data est autem sententia ista apud Lamhed' anno dominice incarnationis mclxxv v° kal. Iulii, assidentibus nobis venerabili fratre nostro G. Lundon' episcopo, domino Roberto de Novoburgo, Yvone et Amico archidiaconis Rotomagensis ecclesie.

Surviving records of this interesting case include two papal mandates, one of them being the commission *sub certa forma*, calendared in Cheney, *Roger of Worcester* 334–5 App. II no. 37. For the background see ibid. 143–4, 284, 335, 344.

*183. Ramscombe priory

Confirmation for the nuns of 'Ramstede' of lands granted to them by Hugh de Dune, John Grubbe, and Robert the butler.

[7 April 1174 × 16 Feb. 1184]

Mentioned only in inventory of archbpric deeds of 1330, PRO E 36/137 p. 8b, pd in *Canterbury archbpric charters* 8:

Carta Hugonis de Dune de xii acris terre de Estone in la Dune datis religiosis de Ramstede. Donatio et concessio I. Grubbe de viii acris dimidia, dimidia roda religiosis de Ramestede. Duppl'. Carta Roberti pincerne de terra in Ramstede data religiosis ibidem. Carta alia eiusdem Roberti de terra data religiosis in Ramstede. Confirmatio Ricardi archiepiscopi super predictis.

184. Ramscombe priory

Grant to the nuns of 'Ramstede' of all the land on which their house is built, and of the land which Ralph de Dena has released to the archbishop.

[Oct. 1181 × 16 Feb. 1184]

B = Lambeth Palace ms. 1212 (register of the see of Canterbury) fo. 47v (fo. 32v, p. 90), in an inspeximus of archbp Baldwin. s. xiii ex. C = Bodl. ms. Tanner 223 (register of the see) fo. 52v (p. 100), copy of B. s. xvi in.

Omnibus Christi fidelibus ad quos presentes littere pervenerint Ricardus dei gratia Cantuariensis archiepiscopus totius Anglie primas eternam in domino salutem. Ad universitatis vestre notitiam volumus pervenire nos divini amoris intuitu dedisse et concessisse monialibus de Ramstede in perpetuam elemosinam totam terram illam in qua edificia earum constructa sunt, et preterea terram illam quam dilectus filius noster Radulfus de Dena in manu nostra resignavit. Et ut hec concessio nostra firmam obtineat stabilitatem, eam tam scripti nostri patrocinio quam testium subscriptione communimus. Hiis testibus: Willelmo archidiacono de Glowecestrie, magistro Henrico de Northanton, Willelmo de Sotindon',

Rogerio decano, Willelmo persona ecclesie de Fremefeld', Galfrido clerico, et multis aliis.

'Ramstede' has been plausibly located at Ramscombe, near Malling, Sussex (cf. *St Gregory's cartulary* p. xv).

185. Reading abbey

Confirmation of the settlement reached in the lawsuit between the monks of Reading and the canons of St Augustine's, Bristol, over the churches of Berkeley Hernesse. The case was delegated by the pope to bishop Robert of Hereford and abbot Simon of St Albans and terminated in the presence of king Henry II and the archbishop and others.

[18 Oct. 1175 × 24 March 1176]

B = BL ms. Egerton 3031 (Reading cartulary) fo. 50v(37v). s. xii/xiii in. C = BL ms. Cotton Vesp. E xxv (Reading cartulary) fo. 119v, omitting witness-list. s. xiv in.

Ricardus dei gratia Cantuariensis archiepiscopus totius Anglie primas et apostolice sedis legatus universis Christi fidelibus salutem. Causa que inter monachos de Rading' et canonicos de Bristold'*a* ad Sanctum Augustinum apostolica fuit auctoritate venerabili fratri nostro R. Hereford' episcopo et dilecto filio S. abbati Sancti Albani commissa, eisdem fratribus assidentibus sub presentia domini regis Henrici secundi et nostra et aliorum quamplurium religiosorum virorum sub hac transactionis forma conquievit, videlicet quod iamdicti canonici Sancti Augustini de Bristold' ecclesias de Berkelaihernesse cum universis ad eas pertinentibus que ipsis canonici tempore inite transactionis vel aliquis eorum nomine possidebat, nomine monachorum de Rading' perpetuo possidebunt, solvendo monachis pro ipsis ecclesiis annuas xx marcas in perpetuum, x ad Pascha et x ad festum sancti Michaelis. Cum autem de assensu utriusque partis fuerit ut ea que a monachis Gloecestrie vel aliis detinentur*b* sive ecclesie sint sive alia beneficia de Berkelaihernesse mediante iustitia revocentur, ad eorum revocationem sumptus pro equis portionibus debebunt ab utraque partium ministrari et quicquid per sententiam evincere vel pace interveniente potuerint revocare, in usus communes tam monachorum quam canonicorum pro mediis portionibus cedet; ad hec sciendum quod memoratus dominus rex de solutione iamdictarum xx marcarum, quoad Henricus Exoniensis archidiaconus vixerit, ita provisurus est quod et monachi de Rading' singulis annis a prenominatis canonicis singulis annis sine difficultate eas percipient et canonicorum indempnitati providebitur. Hec autem transactio facta fuit anno dominice incarnationis mclxxv. Sicut igitur a predictis fratribus [fo. 51r] nostris Herefordensi episcopo et abbate Sancti Albani apostolica auctoritate qua fungebantur et scripto eorum auctentico quod oculis nostris perspeximus eadem transactio fuit confirmata, sicut etiam in presentia nostra eam fuisse factam recolimus, auctoritate qua fungimur eam communimus et corroboramus, quatinus tantorum testimoniorum vallata presidiis nullis in posterum possit perversionibus perturbari. Testibus: magistro Gerardo, domino Roberto de Novo Burgo, Walerano archidiacono Baiocensi, Amico archidiacono Rothomagensi, et aliis multis.

^a Bristold' B; Bristoll' C   ^b detinentur: *om.* BC

The 'transactio', as recorded by the judges delegate (ms. Egerton 3031 fo. 53v), is dated 18 Oct. 1175. The archbp's confirmation follows its wording closely and it supplies the necessary emendation in note *b* above. Henry archdn of Exeter, who had been kg Henry II's treasurer in 1153, before his accession (*Reg. regum* iii p. xxxvii), was the son of Robert FitzHarding, lord of Berkeley. For the circumstances of this settlement see B. R. Kemp, 'The churches of Berkeley Hernesse' *Trans. Bristol and Gloucs. Archaeol. Soc.* 87 (1968) 96–110, esp. 107.

186. Repton priory

Grant of an indulgence of fifteen days for visitors to Repton priory on the day when divine office shall first be celebrated in the church of Holy Trinity, or within the octave of that ceremony. Visitors shall also participate in the spiritual benefits of the church of Canterbury.

[28 April 1174 × Sept. 1181]

A = PRO C 109/86/39 (Chancery Masters' exhibits, Mr Humphrey). Endorsed, s. xii ex.: Indulgentia Ricardi Cantuariensis archiepiscopi s. xiii ex.: Per dominum Ricardum Cantuariensem archiepiscopum quindecim dies et quod sint participes omnium bonorum in ecclesia Cantuariensi. Approx. 180 × 58 + 20 mm. step. Sealing s. q.; tongue and tie remain, seal lost. On tie: De relaxatione domini Cantuariensis. Scribe V.

Pd (calendar) from A by F. Williamson, 'Repton charters', *Journal of Derbyshire Archaeol. and Nat. Hist. Soc.* 53 no. 6 (1933) 74–5 no. 31.

Ric(ardus) dei gratia Cantuariensis archiepiscopus totius Anglie primas et apostolice sedis legatus ⫶ omnibus Christi fidelibus ad quos presentes littere pervenerint . eternam in domino salutem. Ad universitatis vestre noticiam volumus pervenire . quod nos devocionem dilecte filie nostre .M. illustris comitisse . Cestr' . et fervorem religionis dilectorum filiorum nostrorum canonicorum de Rapindon' . ex eorumdem celebri opinione plenius attendentes .

omnibus quicumque devotionis causa . aut pietatis studio . ecclesiam de Rapindon' in honore sancte Trinitatis fundatam . ea die sollempnitatis qua primo in eadem ecclesia divina officia celebrabuntur *.*' visitaverint . aut infra octavum eiusdem sollempnitatis diem pro statu eiusdem ecclesie et benefactorum eius domino supplicaverint *.*' vere penitentibus et confessis *.*' de iniuncta sibi penitencia . quindecim dies relaxamus . omniumque bonorum que in Cantuariensi ecclesia fiunt *.*' participes esse concedimus.[a] Valete.

[a] "concedimus"esse *marked thus for transposition* A

The Augustinian priory of Repton was set up and settled with canons from Calke by countess Matilda of Chester, widow of earl Ranulf II 'aux Grenons' (or 'de Gernons', d. 1153). The date of the canons' removal from Calke is uncertain (? c.1153 × 1160) and the main transfer is said to have only been accomplished in 1172. This indulgence shows that a new priory church of Holy Trinity was under construction. The parish church of St Wistan, given by earl Ranulf to the canons, was probably used meanwhile. Cf. *Mon. Ang.* vi 430a and I. H. Jeayes, *Derbyshire charters* (1906) 243.

187.   Robertsbridge abbey

Confirmation for the abbot and monks of Robertsbridge of the fee of Robertsbridge given them by their founder, Alfred de Sancto Martino, and of his other gifts and of the liberties granted to them by king Henry II by his charter.   [29 March 1176 × Sept. 1181]

A = Maidstone, Kent Archives Office, T 264/12. Endorsed, s. xii/xiii: Ric' archiepiscopus. + XXV. Approx. 146 × 178 + 20 mm. (double fold). Sealed d.q. 1; seal and counterseal, (natural wax, brown varnish), in fair condition. Scribe **II**.

Pd from A in *Report on mss. of Lord de L'Isle and Dudley preserved at Penshurst Place* (HMCR 77, 1925) i 37–38 no. 406.

Ricardus dei gratia Cantuariensis archiepiscopus totius Anglie primas et apostolice sedis legatus . universis sancte matris ecclesie filiis . eternam in domino salutem. Viros religiosos pastorali tenemur sollicitudine promovere . et paci eorum ac quieti quantum nobis possibile est attentius providere. Inde est quod nos dilectos filios nostros abbatem de Ponte Roberti et fratres suos monachos regulam beati Benedicti atque institutionem Cisterciensium fratrum profitentes . sub protectione dei et ecclesie Cantuariensis ac nostre suscipientes *.*' quascunque possessiones quecunque bona inpresenciarum iuste et canonice possident . aut in futurum quibuscunque iustis modis prestante domino poterunt adipisci . ea qua fungimur auctoritate eis in perpetuum confirmamus . specialiter vero totum feodum Pontis Roberti ubi ecclesia eorundem fratrum sita est . quod dilectus filius noster Alvredus de Sancto Martino fundator illius domus eis dedit in perpetuam elemosinam . cum parco et domibus et universis pertinentiis suis . cum terris cultis . et bosco et plano . cum pascuis et pratis . cum molendinis . vivariis et stagnis . viis et semitis . et omnibus aliis rebus . sicut carta eiusdem Aufredi testatur . totam quoque terram quam idem Aufredus tenuerat in feodofirma de canonicis Sancte Marie de Hasting' . reddendo annuatim sex solidos pro omni servitio . terram quoque quam idem Aufredus habuerat inter Winchelse . et Clivesende . cum domibus suis . sicut ipse Aufredus eam eis concessit et dedit . terram quoque de Farleia . et terram Gencelini . et terram de Pochelesesse quas memoratus Aufredus propriis sumptibus comparatas eis dedit et confirmavit . libertates etiam et inmunitates quarunlibet consuetudinum quas illustris rex Anglie Henricus .ii. regia largitate eis concessit et carta sua confirmavit. Statuimus igitur et ea qua fungimur auctoritate prohibemus ∴ ne quis eosdem fratres super prescriptis possessionibus suis temere turbare vel inquietare presumat . aut quibuscunque vexationibus vel molestiis ullatenus infestare . aut libertatibus et inmunitatibus ab apostolica celsitudine sibi indultis . audeat contraire. Quod si quis facere presumpserit ∴ nisi commonitus congrue satisfecerit et emendaverit ∴ divine ultioni et ecclesie Cantuariensis indignationi se noverit subiacere.

188. The church of Rochester

Confirmation for the church of St Andrew and the monks of Rochester of the church of Norton with all its appurtenances, as granted by Fulk of Newnham, lord of the fee, and witnessed by his charter.

[7 April 1174 × 29 Sept. 1175]

B = BL ms. Cotton Domit. A x (Rochester register) fo. 132r(133r). s. xiii in.

Pd from B in *Reg. Roff.* 508.

Hiis testibus: Benedicto cancellario etc.

The archbp's style is like that used by Thomas: 'ecclesie Christi Cantuariensis humilis minister', without mention of primacy or legation. Cf. no. 126. It follows a general address. For Benedict's tenure of the chancellorship see no. 111 note.

The register includes the confirmation by archbp Ralph of the original grant by Hugh of Newnham, father of Fulk, also Fulk's charter, archbp Theobald's confirmation, confirmation by Robert de Campania, Fulk's grandson, and his mother Juliana, and a final concord between the monks of Rochester and Juliana to the same purpose, made in the kg's court, 30 Oct. 1183 (*Reg. Roff.* 507–8).

189. The church of Rochester

Confirmation for the monks of Rochester of the church of Northfleet.
Abstract only..   [28 April 1174 × Sept. 1181]

B = BL ms. Cotton Domit. A x (Rochester register) fo. 118v(119v). s. xiii in.

Ricardus Cantuariensis archiepiscopus totius Anglie primas et
apostolice sedis legatus confirmat eandem ecclesiam de Norfliete
autentico suo predictis monachis.

> This abstract, assigned no number and marked 'vacat' in the register is appended
> to the document there numbered xxxiii: Testimonium de ecclesia de Norfliete.
> *inc.* Hardingus sacerdotum humillimus ... (not printed in *Reg. Roff.*). It may be
> the charter of archbp Richard referred to in no. †593, ascribed to Hubert, which
> may preserve parts of the original of no. 189 containing details not found in the
> general confirmations of possessions, nos. †194, †195.

190. The church of Rochester

*Notification of the sentence delivered by the archbishop after hearing an
action of the monks of Rochester against John parson of Hayes for
failing to pay an agreed pension to the monks in lieu of tithes of Alan de
Geddinges. The church of Rochester is absolved from any claim by John
to the tithes of 'Geddinges'.*   [Aug. 1174 × Sept. 1181]

B = BL ms. Cotton Domit. A x (Rochester register) fo. 181r(182r). s. xiii in.

Ricardus dei gratia Cantuariensis archiepiscopus totius Anglie
primas et apostolice sedis legatus universis sancte matris ecclesie
filiis ad quos littere presentes pervenerint eternam in domino
salutem. Cum essent in presentia nostra constituti Aufredus prior
de Waletune et Osbertus camerarius, monachi Roffensis ecclesie et
ad agendam ecclesie sue causam destinati, proponerentque adversus
Iohannem clericum personam ecclesie de Hesa, quod idem
Iohannes per duos annos detinuerat ecclesie Roffensis decem solidos annuos quos pro decimis Alani de Geddinges ei solvere tenebatur, secundum conventionem inter ecclesiam Roffensem et ipsum
Iohannem factam in pleno capitulo Roffensi et promisso ipsius
Iohannis in verbo veritatis facto firmatam atque etiam cyrographo
confirmatam, sepedictus Iohannes prelibato Aufredo priori detulit
iusiurandum ut si ipse ita esse iuraret sicut proposuerat de prescripta querela, cederet in universum et decimas dimitteret ecclesie
Roffensi pacifice possidendas. Cumque memoratus Aufredus iusiurandum susciperet et sub prescripta forma iuraret sacrosanctis
ewangeliis in medio propositis et tactis, nos auctoritate qua fungi-

mur [fo. 181v] adiudicavimus easdem decimas de Geddinges ecclesie Roffensi ab omni reclamatione prefati Iohannis in perpetuum
liberas et absolutas. Testibus: Waleranno Baiocensi archidiacono,
etc.

Used in the composition of no. †194. Anfredus, prior of the Rochester cell of
Walton, or Felixstowe, may have been later prior of Rochester and abbot of
Abingdon.

191. The church of Rochester

Confirmation of a settlement, made in the presence of the archbishop,
acting as papal delegate, of the dispute between the monks of the church
of Rochester and Roger the priest about the chapel of Kingsey. Roger
has eventually admitted that the chapel pertains to the mother church of
Haddenham and to the monks, and has resigned the chapel into the
archbishop's hand and has renounced all claim in it. The monks have
granted the chapel to him as a perpetual vicarage for his lifetime,
subject to a yearly pension of twenty marks to be paid to them at
Michaelmas and Easter. When Roger dies or enters religion, that
chapel shall revert freely and without dispute to the mother church of
Haddenham. [? Aug. 1174 × 25 March 1175]

B = BL ms. Cotton Domit. A x (Rochester register) fo. 173r(172r). s. xiii in.
C = Lincoln, D. & C. Archives Dij/73/1/31, a damaged sheet with transcript of
this and another act concerning the church of Haddenham. s. xiii in.

Pd from B in *Reg. Roff.* p. 384; from C in *Lincoln reg. ant.* iii 224 no. 659.

Hiis testibus: Roberto Call' etc.[a]

[a] Rob' Call' etc. (*sic*) B, *om.* C

The archbp is styled legate.
C is followed by the note: 'Facta est hec carta a. d. m^o c^o lxx ^{o} iiii^o. Postea
fluxerunt anni lvi$^{o'}$', the last four words being added later. '1174' may be only a
guess based on the date of archbp Richard's accession. The accompanying
charter of bp Hugh II of Lincoln is dated (as also in Domit. A x) : Eynsham 18
Aug. 1218.
Related records, some in *Reg. Roff.* 384–7, some in *Lincoln reg. ant.* iii 21–32,
show that the terms of the vicarage were changed, probably after Roger's
departure, early in the thirteenth century.

192. The church of Rochester

Notification of the judgment given by the archbishop as delegate of pope
Alexander III in a case between the churches of Chislehurst and
Eltham and their parsons concerning the tithes of Mottingham. Pichard
parson of Eltham appeared and appointed R. his vicar as proctor. In

*order to spare the parties trouble and expense the archbishop, having
heard witnesses, referred the case to Paris archdeacon of Rochester, Mr
Walter Tonitruus, and Mr Ralph of Frindsbury, to take evidence and
send it under seal with the parties to the archbishop. The parties
appeared and renounced further production of witnesses; the testimony
was published and discussed. Finally the archbishop adjudged the
possession of the tithes of Mottingham to the church of Chislehurst,
saving the question of right of the church and parson of Eltham.
According to the papal mandate he ordered that the parson of Eltham
should pay to the church of Chislehurst the tithes which had been
withheld in accordance with the assessment of a reliable man, and
should not cause unreasonable trouble in future. At the parson's
instance the archbishop appointed a day in his presence for hearing the
proprietary question and for assessing the detained tithes, but Pichard
and his proctor failed to appear personally or send a representative.
The archbishop declares that the church of Chislehurst shall enjoy the
tithes of Mottingham freely and peaceably without obligation to answer
to the church of Eltham and its parson on the proprietary question until
proper recompense has been made for tithes withheld.*

[Aug. 1174 × Sept. 1181]

B = BL ms. Cotton Domit. A x (Rochester register) fo. 133v(134v). s. xiii in.
Pd from B in *Reg. Roff.* 347–8.

Testibus hiis: magistro Gerardo etc.

The full list of witnesses may be preserved in the document next following (no.
†193), a forgery which uses much of the language of this document. The dating
clause may also be derived from the same source; if so, this should be dated 25
March 1176 × 24 March 1177. The original was probably destroyed when no.
†193 was composed to replace it. The title follows a general address.

†193.   The church of Rochester *(spurious)*

*Notification that in the archbishop's visitation of the diocese of
Rochester he heard the case between the monks of Rochester, rectors of
the church of Chislehurst and Pichard rector of the church of Eltham,
about tithes of Mottingham. In order to spare the parties trouble and
expense, he referred the case to 'N.' archdeacon of Rochester, Mr
Walter Tonitruus, and Mr Ralph of Frindsbury. The archbishop
finally gives sentence, awarding all the tithes of Mottingham in both the
parishes of Chislehurst and of Eltham to the monks and church of
Rochester.*   1176 [25 March 1176 × 24 March 1177]

A = Maidstone, Kent Archives Office DRc/L 16/1 (Rochester D. & C. Mun. B
1303(N 59)). Endorsed, s. xiii: Adiudicacio archiepiscopi Ricardi de decimis

de Modingeham; s. xiv: Russel (? *notarial sign-manual*) *and* .v. *and* exh'.
Approx. 164 × 198 + 25 mm. Sealing d.q. 2; seal in canvas bag.

B = Ibid. DRc/R3 (Rochester Registrum temporalium) fo. 22r. s. xiv med.
C = Rochester mun., original of notarial copy of this and other documents by
William Dene, 30 Sept. 1316; now lost. D = Ibid. DRc/R9 fo. 22r. s. xvi ex.
E = Ibid. fo. 23v. s. xvi ex. from C.

Pd from A in *Reg. Roff.* 347 and from C, ibid. 350.

Universis sancte matris ecclesie filiis ad quos presentes littere
pervenerint . Ric(ardus) dei gracia Cantuariensis archiepiscopus
tocius Anglie primas et apostolice sedis legatus eternam in domino
salutem. Cum causa inter monachos Roffenses rectores ecclesie de
Chiselherst . et Pichardum rectorem ecclesie de Altham super
decimis de Modingham in nostra visitacione in diocesi Roffensi
coram nobis mota fuisset partibus ante nos vocatis et per procuratores legittime constitutos litteras suas de ratihabicione tocius cause
nobis porrectas comparentibus ut earum parceremus laboribus et
expensis . dilectis filiis nostris .N. archidiacono Roffensi magistro
Waltero Tonitruo et magistro Radulfo de Frendesberi . viris
equidem probate opinionis dedimus in mandatis . ut testes quos
utrobique erant producturi super iure et percepcione predictarum
decimarum audirent diligenter et attestaciones eorum conscriptas
sub sigillis suis ad diem certum cum ipsis partibus ad nostram
transmitterent audienciam . qui quidem diligenter et devote mandatum nostrum executi sunt. Die ergo constituta cum partes copiam
sui nobis facerent et testium fuisset renunciatum productioni .
publicatis tandem attestacionibus cum hinc inde in testes et dicta
testium adinvicem multa fuissent proposita et de consensu parcium
in causa conclusum demum de iure monachorum Roffensium et
possessione antiqua dictas decimas percipiendi plenius instructi et
certificati quia tam per dicta testium quam per autenticas litteras
Radulfi . Willelmi . Theobaldi . predecessorum nostrorum Cantuariensium archiepiscoporum . necnon Gundulfi et . Iohannis Roffensium episcoporum quas diligenter inspeximus et manibus tractavi-
mus ac aliis legittimis documentis nobis constat fide plena predictos
monachos et eorum ecclesiam Roffensem quaterviginti quatuorde-
cim annis post donacionem ecclesie de Chiselherste quam Gundulfus episcopus eis fecit et ante predictam donacionem . tempore
prescripto de benivolencia Ansgoti decimas prescriptas ecclesie sue
Roffensis nomine pacifice et inconcusse possedisse . et postea ex
certa sciencia cognoscentes eosdem monachos et eorum ecclesiam
Roffensem in omnibus decimis de Modingham in utraque parochia
de Chiselherst et Altham existentes . antequam ecclesie de Chisel-

herst fuerant rectores ius sufficiens optinere tanquam ius ecclesie Roffensi appropriatum sine dependencia aliquali ad ecclesias de Chiselherst vel Altham pertinente ipsis monachis et ecclesie Roffensi omnes decimas de Modingham provenientes invocato nomine domini sentencialiter et diffinitive adiudicamus . inhibentes sub pena excommunicacionis ne quis eos de eisdem decimis de cetero inquietet. Act'. anno . incarnacionis dominice . m^{mo}. c^o . lxx^o . vi^o . Testibus . hiis . magistro Gerardo . Walerano . Baiocensi^a . archidiacono . magistro .P^b. Blesensi . magistro Roberto de Inglesham . magistro Rogerio Norwicensi . Henrico Baiocensi^a . Rogerio elemosinario . Willelmo^c de Sotindon' . et aliorum . multorum testimonio.

^{a} Baiōe A ^{b} .N. A ^{c} Willelmio A

Probably spurious. On parchment of poor quality, in format and writing unlike other originals of archbp Richard, probably written s. xiii ex. with studied archaism. The top of the seal (white wax) is lost, and much besides; the counterseal may be archbp Richard's; but it may have been re-attached to the tag. Cf. no. 192 above, which is perhaps an authentic record of the proceedings over the tithes of Mottingham, out of which this was made. Another spurious charter on the subject is ascribed to archbp William, 1131 (*Reg. Roff.* 346). The first half of no. †193 follows the wording of no. 192 with significant changes. Unlike no. 192 this does not refer to a papal mandate. Whereas no. 192 speaks of an action between the churches of Chislehurst and Eltham, here the plaintiffs are the monks of Rochester, rectors of Chislehurst, although in the thirteenth century and after the rector of Chislehurst was a secular clerk. (The word *rector* is used throughout this document in place of the *persona* of no. 192). The judgment determines the question, not of possession, but of right; no. 192 specially reserves the matter of right. Here the archdn of Rochester has the initial 'N', although in no. 192 he is correctly called Paris, archdn c.1145–90. (Another charter, supposedly of bp Walter of Rochester (1148–82) names the archdn 'Walter': *Reg. Roff.* 528). The witness-list contains blunders which result from careless copying, possibly of the original of no. 192: Baiōe for Baiocensi, N. Blesensi for P. Blesensi. The ending 'et aliorum multorum testimonio' corresponds to that of the forged charter of archbp William on Mottingham. The notarial endorsement may be the sign of William filius Roberti Russel de Estbriggeford, who acted in the Court of Arches in 1312–13. Cf. no. †594 below.

†194.   The church of Rochester (*spurious*)

Notification of the archbishop's sentence in the case between the monks of Rochester and the parson of Hayes (as in no. 190); with confirmation for the monks of their tithes and churches (enumerated) in the diocese of Canterbury and general confirmation of all their possessions and liberties.   15 May 1177

A = Maidstone, Kent Archives Office DRc/L 17 (Rochester D. & C. Mun. B 794 (N 59)). Endorsed, s. xiii in.: Ricardus archiepiscopus de Gedding' . et de omnibus aliis rebus; s. xiv: De decimis de Gillingham et diversis aliis locis, *and two notarial marks*. Approx. 230 × 288 + 30mm. Sealing d.q. 2; tag remains, seal lost.

B = BL ms. Cotton Domit. A x (Rochester register) fo. 204r(205r). s. xiii in. C = BL ms. Royal 5 A iv (Rochester register) fo. 197r. s. xiii ex. D = Maidstone, Kent Archives Office DRc/T 56 (Rochester D. & C. Mun. B 861), fragment (approx. 142 × 93 mm.) from bottom right-hand corner of a single-sheet copy, cut up to make a seal-bag. s. xiii ex., in the same hand as the fragment of an act attributed to archbp Hubert, *EEA* iii no. †593 text D.

Pd from B in *Reg. Roff.* 410–1.

Ricardus dei gratia Cantuariensis archiepiscopus totius Anglie primas et apostolice sedis legatus . universis sancte matris ecclesie filiis ad quos presens scriptum pervenerit eternam in domino salutem. Cum essent in presentia nostra constituti Aufredus prior de Waleton' et Osbertus camerarius monachi Roffensis ecclesie et ad agendam ecclesie sue causam destinati . proponerentque adversus Iohannem clericum personam ecclesie de Hesa quod idem Iohannes per duos annos detinuerat ecclesie Roffensis decem solidos annuos quos pro decimis Alani de Geddingis ei solvere tenebatur secundum conventionem inter ecclesiam Roffensem et ipsum Iohannem factam in pleno capitulo Roffensi et promisso ipsius Iohannis in verbo veritatis facto firmatam atque etiam cyrographo confirmatam : sepedictus Iohannes prelibato Aufredo priori detulit iusiurandum ut si ipse ita esse iuraret sicut proposuerat de prescripta querela cederet in universum et decimas dimitteret ecclesie Roffensi pacifice possidendas. Cumque memoratus Aufredus iusiurandum susciperet et sub prescripta forma iuraret sacrosanctis ewangeliis in medio propositis et tactis . nos auctoritate qua fungimur adiudicavimus easdem decimas de Gedding' ecclesie Roffensi ab omni reclamatione prefati Iohannis et omnium successorum suorum in perpetuum liberas et absolutas. Et quoniam artioris affectu dilectionis ecclesiam Roffensem et fratres in ea domino famulantes diligimus necessarium duximus illorum utilitati honori et quieti perpetue prospicere . et ne a quoquam valeant indebite molestari in posterum super possessionibus suis et libertatibus providere . prehabito igitur consilio et diligenti tractatu cum conventu nostro et aliis viris prudentibus et discretis . cognito iure predictorum monachorum per inspectionem instrumentorum suorum . considerata etiam diutius illorum possessione per diligentem inquisitionem : ad instantiam et petitionem .S. prioris Roffensis et fratrum eiusdem ecclesie . auctoritate Cantuariensis ecclesie de assensu et voluntate conventus nostri concedimus et confirmamus prenominatis monachis decimas predictas . similiter et omnes decimas quas percipiunt in diocesi

nostra . decimam scilicet quam percipiunt in parrochia de Gillinge-
ham . decimam etiam de Sreambroke[a] in parrochia de Clive .
decimam de Ealdeham in parrochia de Wroteham ? decimam de
Hamwolde in parrochia de Wednesberge . decimam de Merile in
parrochia de Herietesham . decimam de Buggele in parrochia de
Boctune . decimam de Benchesham in parrochia de Croindenne .
decimas etiam quas percipiunt in Dudindale . in Stalesfeld . in
Bilsintune. Concedimus etiam et confirmamus eisdem monachis
ecclesias quas habent in diocesi nostra . ecclesiam scilicet de Boxle
cum omnibus pertinentiis suis quam habent ex dono Henrici regis
primi . et ecclesiam de Nortune cum pertinentiis suis ex dono
Fulconis de Newenham . et ecclesiam de Sturmuth' cum pertinentiis suis ex dono Willelmi filii Hamonis . et ecclesiam de Norefl'[b]
cum decimis de Yfeld et de la Dune et cum omnibus aliis pertinentiis suis ex dono venerabilis patris Anselmi predecessoris nostri . et
in predictis ecclesiis vicariorum presentationem . quam quidem
predictos monachos ante tempora nostra libere obtinuisse per
evidentes probationes nobis innotuit. Concedimus etiam et confirmamus eisdem monachis omnes redditus et omnes terras et omnes
possessiones et omnes libertates quas ex collatione regum Anglie
sive archiepiscoporum Cantuariensium . seu episcoporum . vel
comitum aut baronum . sive aliorum Christi fidelium ante tempora
nostra obtinuerunt. Quantum etiam in nobis est concedimus et
confirmamus eisdem monachis omnia maneria . omnes redditus .
omnes ecclesias . omnes decimas . et omnes possessiones a bone
memorie Gundulfo ipsius ecclesie episcopo sive a successoribus suis
. ipsis ad victum suum assignatas et ordinatas . ut ea omnia libere
pacifice et hereditarie habeant in perpetuum et possideant. Hanc
autem concessionem et confirmationem nostram ab omnibus volumus inviolabiliter observari . ut si quis eam infirmare temptaverit ?
iram et indignationem dei omnipotentis incurrat . et nisi ad congruam satisfactionem venerit . cum Iuda proditore eternam accipiat
condempnationem. Ut igitur hec rata et inconcussa permaneant ?
presens scriptum sigilli nostri testimonio roboravimus. Huius
confirmationis testes sunt . Guerricus abbas de Favresham . Benedictus cancellarius . magister Galerannus . Baiocensis archidiaconus
. magister Gerardus Pulcellus . Guillelmus de Norhale[c] . magister
Robertus de Inglesham[d] . magister Hugo de Suthwell' . Radulfus
pincerna . et alii multi. Facta est autem hec carta anno ab incarnatione domini MCLXXVII idus Maii.

[a] Sreambrok' AB; Screhambroc' C   [b] Norefl' A; Nortflete B; Noreflet C   [c] Norhale
A; Northal' B   [d] Inglesham: Ignesham A; Hignesham B

The arrangement of this document, combining a sentence in a particular case with a general confirmation, is unusual, and it is to be noted that the sentence exists separately (no. 190). The witnesses include incompatibles: abbot Guerricus of Faversham, elected early in 1178, and Benedict the archbp's chancellor, who became prior of Canterbury in Sept. 1175 and is unlikely to be recorded as witness without that title in May 1177. Cf. no. †193n. The script is neat and accomplished charter-hand, but is not identifiable with that of other originals of archbp Richard. The spellings 'Pulcellus' and 'Guillelmus', the mistake in the name of Robert of Inglesham, and the putting of the witnesses in the nominative, are noteworthy.

This may be one of two attempts made at Rochester to produce a general title-deed in the name of archbp Richard. It should be compared with no. †195, of which the abridged witness-list presents the same anomaly. Perhaps no. †195 was an earlier essay, drawing heavily on the charter attributed to archbp Theobald and retaining the use of the first person singular, whereas this charter uses the first person plural throughout.

†195. **The church of Rochester** *(spurious)*

Confirmation for the monks of all grants of lands, churches, and tithes granted to the church of St Andrew of Rochester by kings, archbishops, and others, in particular the lands (enumerated) assigned by bishop Gundulf for the use of the monks; with confirmation of their churches and tithes (enumerated) in the diocese of Canterbury.

[28 April 1174 × Sept. 1181]

B = BL ms. Cotton Domit. A x (Rochester register) fo. 113r (114r). s. xiii in.

Pd from B in *Reg. Roff.* 44–45, and in A. C. Ducarel, *Hist. and antiquities of Lambeth parish* (1786) Appendix p. 18 (in Nichols, *Bibliotheca* vol. ii no. XXXIX).

Ricardus dei gratia Cantuariensis archiepiscopus totius Anglie primas et apostolice sedis legatus omnibus sancte matris ecclesie filiis salutem, gratiam, et benedictionem. Quanto artioris affectu dilectionis ecclesiam Roffensem et fratres in ea deo servientes diligimus eo propensius eorum utilitati, honori, et quieti prospicere dignum duximus. Inde est quod universitati vestre notum esse volumus quod omnes donationes et concessiones omnium maneriorum et omnium terrarum et omnium ecclesiarum cum omnibus redditibus et rectitudinibus suis et omnium decimarum que hactenus concesse et donate sunt ecclesie sancti Andree apostoli que sita est in civitate Rouecestrie a quibuscumque sive regibus sive archiepiscopis vel episcopis seu comitibus seu aliis quibuslibet huius regni nobilibus concesse sunt aut donate, ego Ricardus dei gratia*a* Cantuariensis archiepiscopus totius Anglie primas et apostolice sedis legatus auctoritate michi a deo collata omnimodo ratas et in perpetuum stabiles esse confirmo et eas nominatim quas Gundulfus ecclesie illius episcopus, ut ad usum mo-[fo. 113v]nachorum illorum domino Christo et predicto apostolo devote famulantium permaneant, ordinavit, ego eidem ecclesie et eisdem monachis iure eterne hereditatis habendas et libere atque quiete confirmo possidendas, et sicut prenominatus episcopus qui monachos illos in Roffensi ecclesia congregavit, et ipsa maneria et terras quas in suo dominico habebat ipsis monachis a suo proprio victu discrevit discretas dedit, videlicet Wldeham cum omnibus appenditiis suis, Frendesberiam cum omnibus pertinentiis suis, Stoches cum omnibus appenditiis suis, Danintunam cum omnibus pertinentiis suis, Sufflietham cum omnibus appenditiis suis, Lamhetha cum omnibus pertinentiis suis, Hedenham cum manerio Cudintuna nomine et cum omnibus XL hidis terre que appendent et omnes alias minutas terras et omnes redditus omnium terrarum quas suo tempore adquisivit et illis dedit, ita firmiter et stabiliter in omnibus, omnia ista monachis illis confirmo et corroboro. Confirmo etiam eis ecclesias quas habent in Cantuariensi diocesi, seu regum Anglorum sive antecessorum nostrorum vel aliorum fidelium liberalitate eis collatas, similiter et decimas in diocesi nostra a dei fidelibus sibi [fo. 114r] concessas, ecclesiam de Norfliete cum pertinentiis suis cum decimis de Ifeld et de la Dune, ecclesiam de Boxle cum pertinentiis suis, ecclesiam de Sturemutha cum omnibus ad eam pertinentibus, ecclesiam de Nortune cum omnibus adiacentiis, decimas de Hamwolde, de Dudindale, de Bilsintune, decimam de Bugel, de Stalesfeld, de Gillingham, decimam de Geddinges et de Benchesham, et alias ecclesias vel decimas quas adquisierunt vel inposterum rationabiliter adquirere poterunt, et sicut beate memorie Anselmus et Theobaldus Cantuarienses archiepiscopi et Gundulfus et Ascelinus Roffenses episcopi possessiones et maneria omnia a rege Henrico confirmata confirmaverunt et eidem ecclesie et monachis predictis atque post illos in perpetuum victuris firmiter stabilia et stabiliter firma et illibata permanere sanxerunt et auctoritate dei omnipotentis patris, filii, et spiritus sancti, et omnium sanctorum omnes illos qui aliquid de regia concessione et illorum institutione vel confirmatione infringerent excommunicaverunt, ita et ego tantorum virorum exempla secutus institutiones, concessiones, confirmationes, et omnia [fo. 114v] predicta ipsis monachis in perpetuum habenda firmiter stabilia et stabiliter firma et illibata permanere sanctio, et sub eadem interminatione omnes qui vel eorum vel nostram confirmationem infirmare, vel absque communi fratrum ecclesie illius consilio et consensu immutare presumpserint, a liminibus sancte matris ecclesie ex auctoritate dei omnipotentis patris, filii, et spiritus sancti, omniumque sanctorum sequestro et nisi ad congruam satisfactionem venerint eterni iudicis iram, indignationem, et maledictionem incurrant. Huius confirmationis testes sunt Guerricus abbas de Faversham, Benedictus cancellarius, magister Galerannus Baiocensis archidiaconus etc.

a dei gratia: gratia diei B

The text is printed in full to permit comparison with nos. 190, 194 and with the later confirmation in the name of archbp Baldwin (nos. †304–5). There are two difficulties in the way of accepting this as genuine: i. the witness-list, curtailed though it is, has the anomaly seen in no. †194; ii. the first person singular is used for most of the charter. The latter peculiarity is explained by the fact that the whole text after the arenga (which uses the plural) copies the wording of a charter of archbp Theobald (? 1145 × 1148: Saltman, *Theobald* 444–5 no. 220) found in the Textus Roffensis. Note that archbp Hubert's surviving acta include an inspeximus (no. 590) of archbp Theobald's charter, but no inspeximus of the charters of Richard and Baldwin.

196. The church of Rochester

Confirmation of a conventio *between the monks of Boxley and the monks of Rochester. The latter have granted to the monks of Boxley a field on the hills, belonging to the parish church, retaining half an acre of wood in the field for fencing. The monks of Rochester have also granted to the monks of Boxley all tithes of lands on the hills which they hold by the king's gift or which they have acquired or shall acquire by agreement with the villeinage for their own cultivation. They have also granted to the monks of Boxley land of the parish church below the hills with a meadow lying between the abbey and the vill. The monks of Boxley have granted to the monks of Rochester all their tithes below the hills outside the bounds of the abbey and the grange. The monks of Rochester shall also have the tithes of all lands on the slopes of the hills formerly cultivated, except for the field which the monks of Boxley bought from John de Horepole.*

[25 March 1180 × Sept. 1181]

B = BL ms. Cotton Domit. A x (Rochester register) fo. 135v(136v). s. xiii in.

Pd from B in *Reg. Roff.* 179–80.

Hiis testibus: magistro Girardo, etc.

The archbp is styled legate. His confirmation reproduces verbatim the substance of a composition dated 'anno ab incarnatione domini 1180' (*Reg. Roff.* 178). Many years earlier the pope (Adrian IV or Alexander III) had heard a complaint that Boxley abbey withheld tithe due to the parish church and ordered the archbp (Theobald or Thomas) to enforce payment by the monks on all land which had paid tithe before it came into their hands (JL 11660. *MTB* v 129 no.

66. In English decretal collections and finally in *Extra* 3 30 4). This incident may be connected with the general complaint about Cistercian retention of tithes which archbp Richard addressed to Cîteaux (above, no. 106).

197. The church of Rochester

Confirmation of the grant by the prior and convent of Rochester to Gilbert de Perieres of their tithe of Bilsington to be held of them for nine years from Michaelmas next after the death of archbishop Roger of York, for a yearly payment of half a mark at Easter.

[26 Nov. 1181 × Feb. 1184]

B = BL ms. Cotton Domit. A x (Rochester register) fo. 130r(131r). s. xiii in.

Pd from B in *Reg. Roff.* 168.

Archbp Richard is not styled legate. Archbp Roger died 26 Nov. 1181. The lease here confirmed was presumably made before the next Michaelmas.

198. Abbey of St Albans

Confirmation of a compromise formerly reached between bishop Robert (II) of Lincoln and abbot Robert of St Albans and confirmed by archbishop Thomas and king Henry (II).

[28 April 1174 × Sept. 1175]

B = BL ms. Cotton Otho D iii (St Albans cartulary) fo. 109r, damaged in the Cottonian fire. s. xiv/xv.

Ricardus dei gratia Cantuariensis archiepiscopus totius Anglie primas et apostolice sedis legatus omnibus sancte matris ecclesie fidelibus ad quos litere iste pervenerint salutem. Ne semel sopite lites iterum suscitentur et bonum pacis contentio rediviva perturbet, cause legitimo fine decise dispositione provida literis commendantur. Inde est quod nos decessoris nostri gloriosi martiris Thome vestigiis inherentes, transactionem factam inter ecclesiam Lincolniensem et monasterium Sancti Albani per bone memorie Robertum quondam Lincolniensem episcopum et Robertum quondam abbatem Sancti Albani super controversia subiectionis quam episcopus et ecclesia Lincolniensis ab abbate Sancti Albani et eius monasterio petebant, utriusque ... ... consentiente capitulo et ... ... eam ad invicem literis legitime corroborante, ratam habemus, et sicut dominus noster illustris Anglorum rex Henricus carta sua confirmavit auctoritate qua fungimur confirmamus, modis omnibus inhibentes ne quis de cetero pacem ecclesiarum salubriter et legitime reformatam et firmatam perturbare presumat. Hiis testibus: Gualeranno archidiacono Baiocensi, dompno Benedicto cancellario nostro, Herelewino et Radulfo capellanis, magistro Ricardo de Suduuel, magistro Petro Blesensi, Willelmo de Norhal', Radulfo de Wengham, Thurstano de Hachest', Willelmo medico de Wauton', Iohanne de Cantuaria, Henrico Baiocensi, Henrico ... .

For Benedict's tenure of the chancellorship see no. 111n.
For the settlement made in the king's court at Westminster in March 1163 see above, no. 37.

199. Abbey of St Albans

Confirmation for the monks of St Albans of the churches of Luton and Houghton with their lands, tithes, and all appurtenances as given by earl William of Gloucester, and also of the land held by William the chamberlain of the earl's fee in the soke of Luton and in Hartwell and Battlesden and Potsgrove, as granted and confirmed by the earl's charter. [28 April 1174 × autumn 1177]

B = BL ms. Cotton Otho D iii (St Albans cartulary) fo. 117r, damaged in the Cottonian fire. s. xiv/xv.

Ricardus dei gratia Cantuariensis archiepiscopus totius Anglie primas et apostolice sedis legatus universis sancte matris ecclesie filiis ad quos littere iste pervenerint salutem. Ea que locis venerabilibus et viris religiosis et pietatis intuitu fidelium sunt devotione collata, pontificalis est officii*a* stabilire et valituris in perpetuum munimentis*b* roborare. Unde ad communem universorum volumus pervenire notitiam nos in perpetuam elemosinam confirmasse ecclesie Sancti Albani et monachis eiusdem loci ecclesiam de Luytona et ecclesiam de Houghinton cum terris et decimis et omnibus pertinentiis suis sicut comes Gloucestrie Willelmus eis illas dedit et carta sua rationabiliter et iuste confirmavit. Terram etiam quam Willelmus camerarius tenuit de feodo eiusdem comitis, videlicet quicquid tenuit in soca de Luitona et in Hertewella et in Badelesdona et in Potesgrava eisdem confirmamus sicut idem comes eis ration-[fo. 117v]abiliter concessit et carta sua confirmavit. Ut hec autem*c* nostra confirmatio stabilis et inconcussa perseveret, eandem sigilli nostri appensione roboramus et testium subscriptione communimus. Testes: magister Gerardus, Waleranus archidiaconus Baiocensis, magister Petrus Blesensis, Willelmus de Norhall', Radulfus*d* de Wengham, Henricus Baiocensis canonicus, Radulfus*d* de Sancto Martino, et alii.

a est officii *doubtful* B   *b* munimentis *doubtful* B   *c* hec *repeated* B   *d* Radulfo B

Mr Gerard and Mr Peter of Blois left England for Rome in autumn 1177. William of Northolt became archdn of Gloucester May × Dec. 1177.

For the background of this charter see charters of earl William (*Earldom of Gloucester charters* ed. R. B. Patterson (Oxford 1973) 153 no. 168 and note, 177 no. 282), a confirmation of the earl's original grant by archbp Theobald which burdened the abbey with the service of half a knight's fee which William the chamberlain had owed (Saltman, *Theobald* 456–7 no. 229), and the St Albans story of Luton church in *Gesta abbatum S. Albani* (RS) i 113–24. The earl's charter was confirmed by pope Anastasius IV, 2 June 1154 (*PUE* iii 227 no. 93, cf. 235, 243, 275 nos. 100, 106, 133). Cf. L. F. Rushbrook Williams, 'William the chamberlain and Luton church' *EHR* xxviii (1913) 719–30. A settlement before judges delegate relating to Luton church was made in London on 22 Nov. 1174 (ms. Cotton Otho D iii fo. 115v; M. G. Cheney, *Roger of Worcester*, app. I no. 54).

200.   Abbey of St Albans

Mandate addressed to archdeacons, deans, and ecclesiastical officials of Hertfordshire to enforce payment to the church of St Albans of three half-pence yearly from every ploughland in Hertfordshire, as granted and confirmed in the past by kings of England.

[28 April 1174 × Sept. 1181]

B = Cambridge UL ms. Ee 4 20 (St Albans formulary) fo. 80v (51v). s. xiv ex.

Ricardus dei gratia Cantuariensis archiepiscopus totius Anglie primas et apostolice sedis legatus dilectis filiis archidiaconis, decanis, ministris ecclesiasticis de Herfordsira[a] salutem, gratiam, et benedictionem. Cum satis manifestum sit de singulis carugiis de Herfordsira de donationibus regum Anglie unum denarium et obolum in perpetuam elemosinam ecclesie Sancti Albani annuatim esse concessum et collatum, solicitudini vestre mandamus et districte precipimus quatinus universos per officia vestra constitutos moneatis attentius et instantius inducatis atque ad salutem animarum vestrarum eis iniungatis ut prescriptam elemosinam sicut ab antiquo concessa est et scriptis regiis confirmata, ita eam annuatim sine difficultate et contradictione cessante reddant et cum omni integritate et absque diminutione persolvant, ut ab omnipotenti[b] deo premium recipiant et retributionem. Alioquin precipimus ut detentores eiusdem beneficii ecclesiastica mediante iustitia non differatis acrius cohercere, ne dilecti filii nostri monachi Sancti Albani pro defectu iustitie iustam debeant ad nos querimoniam reportare. Valete.

[a] Herfordsira B   [b] omnipotente B

The fact that the mandate does not name the bp of Lincoln may indicate that it was impetrated before Geoffrey's election was confirmed, 9 July 1175 (Diceto i 401).

The custom is confirmed by a mandate of kg Stephen (*Regesta regum* iii 273 no.

742). A papal mandate of 2 Aug. 1147 to enforce payment describes it as a halfpenny due on Friday after Ascension and a penny due on the second feast of St Alban (2 Aug.) from every plough (*PUE* iii 200–1 no. 69).

*201. Abbey of St-Bertin

Notification to the abbots of Faversham and Boxley, judges delegate of pope Alexander III in a suit between the monks of St-Bertin and Nathaniel, a knight, over the chapel of Leaveland. The archbishop claims a right in the chapel, and appeals against the granting of possession to the monks. [Aug. 1174 × June 1176]

> Mentioned only, in a later mandate from Alexander III to the bps of Exeter and Worcester to hear the case (JL 12676[G[a]G], *Chartes de St-Bertin* i 125 no. 275, *CDF* 486 no. 1339, M. G. Cheney, *Roger of Worcester* 319–20). The later mandate, dated at Anagni 27 July, cannot have been issued before the archbp's arrival in England c.Aug. 1174, and therefore can be assigned to 1176. The consequential action by the bps is implied by nos. 202–3.

202. Abbey of St-Bertin

Confirmation for the monastery of St-Bertin of the church of Throwley with its chapels, in particular the chapel of Leaveland, and all its appurtenances, as confirmed by the charters of archbishops Theobald and Thomas, which have been inspected. [Aug. 1176 × autumn 1177]

> A = Original lost, from abbey of St-Bertin, St-Omer.
>
> B = St-Omer, Bibliothèque municipale, ms. 803 (Grand cartulaire de St-Bertin) vol. i p. 364 no. 248.189. 1°, with description: 'Ex originali in Theca Angleterre no. 4. 4° loco. Cet original a 5 pouces d'hauteur sur 5 pouces et 3-quarts de largeur', and with sketch of archbishop's seal (diapered background) and counterseal. Transcript of A by Dom C. J. Dewitte. s. xviii ex. C = Ibid. ms. 746 (fragment of a cartulary fo. 206v. s. xv in. D = PRO, P. R. O. 31/8/144 (part 6) fo. 73r no. 10: transcript of B. s. xix med.
>
> Pd (abridged) from B in *Chartes de St-Bertin* i 123 no. 269, and in *Archaeologia Cantiana* iv (1861) 211 no. xii. Calendared from D in *CDF* 488 no. 1343, where dated 1179–82.

Ricardus dei gratia Cantuariensis archiepiscopus totius Anglię primas et apostolicę sedis legatus universis sanctę matris ecclesię filiis ad quos presentes litterę pervenerint eternam in domino salutem. Ex ininunctę nobis administrationis officio tenemur iura ecclesiarum in quantum possumus integre et illesa conservare, et ut ea quę deo et ecclesię semel iuste collata sunt debita gaudeant tranquillitate sollicite providere. Inde est quod in communem omnium notitiam volumus devenire nos inherentes vestigiis pię recordationis Theobaldi et beatissimi martiris Thomę predecessorum nostrorum, quorum cartas conspeximus et propriis manibus nostris contrectavimus , concessisse et presenti carta confirmasse dilectis in domino filiis monachis de Sancto Bertino et monasterio eorumdem ecclesiam de Trulegha*a* cum capellis ad eam pertinentibus, quarum unam,*b* scilicet de Levelanda nominatim duximus exprimendam. Volumus itaque et precipimus ut idem monachi prelibatam ecclesiam cum universis eiusdem pertinentiis in capellis, in terris, decimis, et omnimodis obventionibus libere et pacifice possideant sicut eis iuste et canonice concessa est et a predictis decessoribus nostris rationabiliter confirmata. Et ut hęc nostrę confirmationis pagina in posterum inconvulsa permaneat, eam sigilli nostri munimine duximus roborare. Hiis testibus: magistro Gerardo, Walerano Baiocensi archidiacono, magistro Petro Blesensi, Willelmo de Norhall*c*, Radulfo de Wingham, Henrico Baiocensi canonico, Radulfo de Sancto Martino, Amico clerico, Rogerio elemosinario, Roberto de Bavento, magistro Iohanne Dovr', Willelmo Beivino, Willelmo de Sotindona, et pluribus aliis.

a Trulegha B; Trullega C   *b* unam C; una B   *c* Norhall C; Norhast B (*emended in* CDF *to* Norhantona)

The reference to Leaveland shows that this charter followed settlement of the dispute over this chapel (above, no. 201) which is not likely to have been earlier than receipt of the papal mandate of 27 July 1176. Mr Gerard and Mr Peter of Blois left England for Rome in autumn 1177. William of Northolt became archdn of Gloucester, May × Dec. 1177.

For the charters of archbps Theobald and Thomas see Saltman, *Theobald* 464 no. 239 and above, no. 39.

The narrative 'chartularium Bertinianum' (ed. B. Guérard, *Cartulaire de l'abbaye de St Bertin* (Coll. des docts. inédits sur l'hist. de France. Paris 1841) 370–1, cf. 326) tells how Henry de Insula, after trying to avoid the parochial jurisdiction of Throwley, acknowledged its rights 'Cantuarie, in capitulo presbiterorum, assistente Huberto [*recte* Herberto] archidiacono Cantuariensi ac magistro Willelmo de Sancta Fide' in the year 1176.

Cf. the witness-list with those of nos. 132, 174 above.

203. Abbey of St-Bertin

Notification that the monks of St-Bertin have granted to William Beivin the chapel of Leaveland in perpetual alms for a yearly pension of one gold piece. After William's death the monks may make arrangements for the chapel to their own advantage.

[Aug. 1176 × Sept. 1181]

B = St-Omer, Bibliothèque municipale ms. 803 (Grand cartulaire de St-Bertin) vol. ii pp. 76–7 no. 331.64: transcript by Dom C. J. Dewitte of an original inspeximus by bp John of Thérouanne, c.1208. s. xviii ex. C = Ibid. ms. 746

(fragment of a cartulary) fo. 217v, in copy of the same inspeximus. D = PRO, P. R. O. 31/8/144 (part 6) fo. 86 no. 27: transcript of B. s. xix med.

Pd from B in *Chartes de St-Bertin* i 148 no. 336; calendared from D in *CDF* 487 no. 1341.

Ricardus dei gratia Cantuariensis archiepiscopus totius Anglie primas et apostolice sedis legatus omnibus Christi fidelibus ad quos presens scriptum pervenerit salutem [p. 77] in domino. Ad universitatis vestre notitiam volumus pervenire dilectos filios nostros monachos Sancti Bertini concessisse dilecto filio nostro Willelmo Baivin capellam de Livelande in perpetuam elemosinam, sub annua pensione videlicet unius aurei eisdem monachis persolvenda nomine matricis ecclesie de Trulega ad quam eadem capella dinoscitur pertinere. Predictus autem Willelmus faciet celebrari divina in eadem capella per tres dies in septimana secundum antiquam consuetudinem, in quatuor autem festis anni videlicet in Natali domini, in Purificatione beate Marie Virginis et in die Resurrectionis domini , et in festo sancti Michaelis visitabunt parochiani predicte capelle matricem ecclesiam*a* de Trulega et ibi sicut viri catholici audient missas ceterorumque divinorum sollemnia. Post decessum vero predicti Willelmi licebit iamdictis monachis de predicta capella ordinare et ad utilitatem suam disponere. Ut autem hec concessio firma et inconvulsa perseveret eam presentis scripti testimonio confirmamus. Hiis testibus: magistro Girardo, Walerano*b* Baiocensi, et aliis multis.

a add suam C   *b* Walerano C; Waltero B

This grant was probably part of the settlement after the archbp appealed against the granting of possession of the chapel to the monks (no. 201 above), and was contemporary with his confirmation to them of the church and the chapel.
For William Baivin or Beivin cf. no. 4 above.

204. Abbey of St-Bertin

Confirmation for the monastery of St-Bertin of the church of Chilham with all its appurtenances. The archbishop has inspected and handled the charter of archbishop Thomas, who confirmed the church as archbishop Theobald had done. [29 May 1177 × Sept. 1181]

A = Original lost, from abbey of St-Bertin.

B = St-Omer, Bibliothèque municipale ms. 803 (Grand cartulaire de St-Bertin) vol. i p. 365 no. 249.189. 2⁰, with description: 'Ex originali in Theca Angletere no. 4. 3⁰ loco. Cet original a 3 pouces et demi d'hauteur sur sept pouces et 3-quarts de largeur', and note that seal and counterseal correspond to those on the preceding page (no. 202 here): transcript of A by Dom C. J. Dewitte. s.

xviii ex. C = Ibid. ms. 746 (fragment of a cartulary) fo. 205r. s. xv in. D = Ibid. ms. 746 fo. 207v. E = PRO, P. R. O. 31/8/144 (part 6) fo. 73*bis* unnumbered, no. 11: transcript of B. s. xix med.

Pd (calendar) from B in *Chartes de St-Bertin* i 123–4 no. 270 and in *Archaeologia Cantiana* iv (1861) 212 no. xiii; from E in *CDF* 487 no. 1340.

Ricardus dei gratia Cantuariensis archiepiscopus totius Anglie primas et apostolice sedis legatus, universis Christi fidelibus ad quos presentes littere pervenerint eternam in domino salutem. Ex scripto gloriosissimi martiris Thomę predecessoris nostri, quod manibus nostris contrectavimus et oculis nostris perspeximus, evidenter cognovimus quod idem gloriosus predecessor noster Thomas monasterio Sancti Bertini concessit ecclesiam de Chileham*a* cum universis pertinentiis suis iuste et canonice possidendam, et carta sua confirmavit sicut eam bonę memorię Theodbaldus Cantuariensis archiepiscopus eidem monasterio Sancti Bertini concessit et carta sua confirmavit. Nos igitur 'predictorum' predecessorum nostrorum vestigiis inherentes, prescriptam ecclesiam de Chileham*b* cum universis pertinentiis 'suis' prelibato monasterio Sancti Bertini in perpetuum confirmamus et sigilli nostri patrocinio communimus. Testibus: Benedicto abbate de Burgo, Walerano*c* archidiacono Baiocensi, magistro Roberto de Inglessham*d*, Henrico Baiocensi, Wilelmo de Vallibus, Rogero Norwicensi, et aliis multis.

a Chileham B; Chilleham C   *b* Chileham B; Chilleham C   *c* Walerano C; Waltero (t *del.*) B   *d* Inglessham B; Inglesham C

Prior Benedict of Canterbury was elected abbot of Peterborough 29 May 1177. For the charters of archbps Theobald and Thomas see Saltman, *Theobald* 465 no. 240 and above, no. 40.

*204A.   St David's: tithe-payers of the diocese

Mandate to the people of the diocese to pay tithe on wool and cheese, which because of the slackness of the clergy has not been collected. To those who pay the archbishop remits a third of the penance enjoined on them for non-payment, and orders that those who obstinately resist shall be coerced with ecclesiastical censures.   [Aug. 1174 × 1175]

Mentioned only, by Gerald of Wales (*Opp.* i 24 (De rebus a se gestis), and cf. *Welsh ep. acts* i 276–7). Gerald claims that he went himself to the archbp to get this mandate, and was despatched as the archbp's legate to enforce it in the diocese, accompanied by Mr Michael (i 26). The archbp had almost certainly arrived in England, and this occurred before Gerald became archdn of Brecon some time in 1175. The mandate was perhaps a measure intended to implement canon 13 of the provincial council of Westminster, May 1175, but it may have anticipated it.

*204B. St David's: tithe-payers of the diocese

Mandate to bishop David of St David's to renew recent censures on withholders of tithe, except for the Flemings dwelling in the cantref of Rhos, who had been granted some remission by the archbishop at the king's request.   [1175 × 8 May 1176]

Mentioned only, by Gerald of Wales (*Opp.* i 28 (De rebus a se gestis) and cf. *Welsh ep. acts* i 279). This followed no. 204A, after Gerald was made archdn of Brecon and before the death of his uncle, bp David, on 8 May 1176.

*205. Priory of St Neots

Mandate to the priors of Huntingdon and Newnham to hear and decide a case about a fishery lying between the mill of Eynesbury and the land of William de Sudbir' between the prior and monks of St Neots, who possess it, and Nicholas de Bello Campo, parson of Eaton Socon, who claims it.   [? June 1182 × 16 Feb. 1184]

Mentioned only, in notification by prior W(illiam) of Huntingdon and prior R(alph) of Newnham (not in office before May 1182) of an amicable composition, by which Nicholas withdrew his claim and received a messuage and croft, granted by Hugh de Beauchamp, patron of the church (BL ms. Cotton Faust. A iv (St Neots cartulary) fo. 82r no. xiiii). The judges do not name the archbp who commissioned them; he was almost certainly Richard or Baldwin. Hugh was probably the Beauchamp of that name who flourished 1157–87, went on pilgrimage early in 1186, and fell at Hattin in 1187 (W. Farrer, *Honors and knights' fees* iii (Manchester 1925) 249–50). His grandson of the same name, who appears from 1194 onwards, can probably be excluded, since he is described in charters of St Neots as Hugh son of Oliver. Cf. no. 309 below.

206. Priory of St Neots

Confirmation for the prior and monks of St Neots of the churches of Brampton, Hemington, and Clopton. The archbishop has inspected charters by Geoffrey elect of Lincoln which state that he has instituted the prior and convent as parson of the first two churches and a charter of Savaric archdeacon of Northampton which states that he has conferred on the prior and convent the parsonage of Clopton. The archbishop has also inspected charters by the former patrons.
                                           [6 Jan. × 9 Oct. 1182]

A = Northampton, Northants Record Office, Montagu (Buccleuch) mss. 'Old' box 25 no. 6. Endorsed, s. xiii: Carta Ricardi Cantuariensis archiepiscopi de ecclesiis Bramton. Hemmigt'. Clopton'.; s. xiv: Titulus Cant' pont' VI*a*. Approx. 156 × 76 + 13 (tongue) + 2 (tie) mm. Sealing s. q.; tongue and tie remain; seal lost (stain left on tongue).

B = BL ms. Cotton Faust. A iv (St Neots cartulary) fo. 40v(39v) no. xxv, omitting witnesses. s. xiii med.

Pd from A in *Northants charters* 68–69 no. xxiv(a), with facsimile.

.Ric(ardus) dei gratia Cantuariensis archiepiscopus . totius Anglie primas . universis sancte matris ecclesie filiis : salutem in domino. Inspectis auctenticis scriptis .G. quondam electi Lincolniensis nobis manifestius innotuit . ipsum ad presentationem Radulfi filii Radulfi ecclesiam sancte Marie de Bramton' et ad presentationem Ivonis de Gunnetorp' et Turstani presbiteri ecclesiam de Haminton' dilectis filiis nostris .H. priori et conventui Sancti Neoti dedisse ac concessisse et ipsos in easdem ecclesias canonice instituisse personam. Inspeximus quoque cartam dilecti filii nostri Savarici archidiaconi Noramtonensis ex qua intelleximus quod ipse ad presentationem Willelmi de Clotton' ecclesiam de Clotton eisdem priori et conventui concessit . et quod eis eiusdem ecclesie canonice contulit personatum. Cartas etiam predictorum advocatorum vidimus que liquide protestantur prefatum priorem et conventum ipsorum presentatione et assensu iamdictas ecclesias fuisse adeptos. Nos autem tam predicti electi quam archidiaconi concessionem ac institutionem ratam habentes : eam sicut rationabiliter facta est . confirmamus et presenti scripto ac sigillo nostro communimus. Testibus magistro Girardo . Waleranno Baiocensi . magistro Petro Baptoniensi . Willelmo Glocestriensi archidiaconis . magistro Rogero de Rolvest' . Willelmo de Sottend' . magistro Rogero Norwicensi . Galfrido clerico . magistro Rogero Walensi . Ricardo de Lond' et multis aliis.

After the resignation of Geoffrey elect of Lincoln and before the election of Waleran to Rochester.

Other original documents concerned with the transaction, mostly concerning the church of Hemington, survive and are edited by Stenton, *Northants charters* 62–77. For the charter of Geoffrey, elect, about Hemington see also *EEA* i no. 292, and for his charter concerning Brampton ibid. no. 293.

*207.   Abbey of St Osyth

Confirmation for the canons of St Osyth of Chich of the church of Petham, granted and confirmed to them by charters of archbishops Ralph and William.   [7 April 1174 × 16 Feb. 1184]

Mentioned only, in a confirmation charter by archbp Hubert, below, no. 600.

*208. Abbey of St Victor-en-Caux

Confirmation of the possessions of the monastery of St Victor-en-Caux in England. [7 April 1174 × 16 Feb. 1184]

Mentioned only, in the confirmation by archbp Hubert, below, no. 601.

209. Salisbury: lands of the see

Confirmation for Walter son of Sweyn de Legha and his heirs of all the land of Wootton and Whitechurch and land and buildings in Sherborne, held by Nicholas, as granted by bishop Jocelin of Salisbury, and confirmed by his seal, to be held for a quarter of one knight's service. [Aug. 1174 × Sept. 1175]

B = Salisbury, D. & C. Mun., Liber evid. C p. 163 (fo. 64r) no. 213. s. xiii ex. C = London, Inner Temple Libr. ms. Petyt 511.18 (Salisbury D. & C. cartulary) fo. 39r (p. 67). s. xiii ex. D = Trowbridge, Dioc. Record Office, Liber evid. B fo. 92v(56v) no. 176. s. xiii/xiv. E = Ibid. Reg. rubrum fo. 48r no. 176, copied from B. s. xiii/xiv.

Pd from BDE in *Salisbury charters* 43 no. 51.

Testibus: Benedicto cancellario, Radulfo et Herlewer*ª* monachis, magistro Gerardo, Radulfo de Wingeham et aliis.

ª et Herlewer DE; de Herewer B; *om. witnesses* C

The archbp is styled legate and was evidently in England. Benedict probably ceased to use the title of chancellor on becoming prior of Canterbury, Sept. 1175.
  Whitechurch is spelt Wyteahe (B), Whytehach' (C), de la Witehache (D), de la Whitecherche (E).

*210. Abbey of Savigny

Confirmation for the monks of Savigny of the church of Long Bennington. [7 April 1174 × 16 Feb. 1184]

Mentioned only, in the confirmation by archbp Baldwin, below, no. 311. The gift of the church to Savigny by Ralph of Fougères was confirmed by Conan, duke of Brittany, in 1166 (*CDF* 305 nos. 846–8), and later by kg Henry II (*Recueil des actes* ii 138–9 no. DLVIII) and pope Alexander III (*PU Normandie*, ed. J. Ramackers, 250 no. 158).

211. Sele priory

Notification that a dispute between the prior and monks of Sele and the church of Tarring over certain tithes of Durrington has been settled in the archbishop's presence. [Aug. 1174 × Sept. 1181]

A = Oxford, Magdalen Coll. Deeds, Durrington 3. Endorsed, s. xiii: Confirmacio Ricardi Cantuariensis archiepiscopi de decimis de Durinton'. Approx. 174 × 137 + 25 mm. Sealing d. q. 2; tag remains, seal lost. Scribe **IV**. Bottom half of chirograph, divided by a straight cut.

B = Ibid. Durrington 4, in inspeximus by bp John of Chichester, 15 Aug. 1257. C = Ibid. ms. 274 (Sele cartulary) fo. 8v. s. xiii.

Pd (English abstract) from C by L. F. Salzman, *The chartulary of the priory of St Peter at Sele* (Cambridge 1923) 14, 15 nos. 21, 23.

CIROGRAPHUM

.Ric(ardus) dei gracia . Cantuariensis . archiepiscopus . tocius Anglie primas et apostolice sedis legatus .' universis Christi fidelibus ad quos presentes littere pervenerint .' salutem in eo qui est salus universorum. In communem volumus devenire noticiam quod cum inter dilectos filios nostros priorem et monacos de Sele et ecclesiam de Terring' super decimis quibusdam de Derinton' controversia diutius ageretur .' tandem in presentia nostra hoc fine conquievit . scilicet quod prefati monaci de Sele . et ecclesia de Terring' prescriptas decimas de Derinton' communibus expensis colligent .' singulis annis . et eas in domo quadam que in cimiterio de Derinton' fieri debet .' communibus expensis reponent . et easdem decimas inter se penitus ex equo divident . ita scilicet quod sicut circa decimas colligendas . labores et expensas prorsus communicant .' ita etiam divisa ex equo inter se decimarum emolumenta percipient. Curam quoque prefati horrei communiter inter se gerent . ita quod utraque pars suam adhibebit seram .' et sere custodem. Et ut hec compositio firma et stabilis perseveret .' eam scripti et sigilli nostri munimine roboramus. Hiis testibus . Guarino priore de Sele . Roberto monaco . Bovone presbitero de Guassinghet' . Roberto capellano de Sele . Rogero clerico . Roberto presbitero de Suntingh' . Heimerico de Cnelle . Cusino de Selvinton' . Willelmo capellano de Terring' . Avico de Lacote . Radulfo Scotto . et multis aliis.

212.   Tavistock abbey

Confirmation for the monks of St Mary and St Rumon of Tavistock of the churches of Sheviock, Antony, and St John, with all their appurtenances. The archbishop has inspected and handled the charters with which these churches were confirmed by former bishops of Exeter, William, Robert I, and Robert II. He also confirms for them the church of Lamerton with its appurtenances, according to a charter of bishop Bartholomew.   [28 April 1174 × Sept. 1181]

B = Woburn Abbey, Duke of Bedford, Muniments 3 A 3 (Tavistock cartulary) fo. 14r. s. xiii. Witness-list omitted.

Pd from B by H. P. R. Finberg in 'Some early Tavistock charters' *EHR* lxii (1947) 364.

The archbp is styled legate.

Charters of the four bps named are also in the cartulary: *EHR* lxii 355, 356, 358, 361. The church of St John is probably that of St John the baptist, Hatherleigh (see below, no. 316).

213. Order of the Temple: Sompting

Notification that Elias son of Bernard admits that his chapel of Sompting is an appurtenance of the parish church and has granted the chapel with lands at Sompting and Broadwater to the brethren of the Order of the Knights of the Temple of Solomon.

[May 1177 × Sept. 1181]

B = BL ms. Cotton Nero E vi (Hospitallers' cartulary) fo. 156r. s. xv med.

Ricardus dei gratia Cantuariensis archiepiscopus totius Anglie primas et apostolice sedis legatus universis sancte matris ecclesie filiis salutem in domino. Cartam dilecti filii nostri Helie filii Bernardi inspeximus, ex qua nobis innotuit ipsum reddidisse ecclesie de Suntynges capellaniam domus sue de eadem villa, scilicet dimidiam hydam terre quam Geroboldus presbiter tenuit in eadem villa et duas garbas decime de dominico suo et totam decimam rerum decimabilium de curia ipsius H. et decimam hydarum duarum de Bradewatere et quatuor bovibus et uni equo pasturam in dominica pastura sua, preter alios quatuor boves et unum equum quos ecclesia ville habet in eadem pastura, que omnia sicut in prescripta carta perpendi potest. Ipse H. intellexerat capellaniam domus sue separatim ab ecclesia debere habere, set postea intellecta veritate quod predicta capellania cum predictis pertinentiis suis ad predictam ecclesiam pertinebant et pertinere debent, illam ei et fratribus militie Templi Salomonis reddidit et cartam quam inspeximus confirmavit. Ut eam cum omnibus pertinentiis suis libere et quiete, integre et honorifice imperpetuum habeant et teneant, preterea concessit eis decimam dominici feni sui de eadem villa quam Willelmus de Harecourt dedit predicte ecclesie ad lumen inveniendum in ea in omnibus noctibus dominicis. Predicti autem fratres Templi debent invenire prescripto H. , uxori [fo. 156v], et familie sue in predicta ecclesia cum fuerint in eadem villa plenarium servitium divinum. Nos autem hanc conventionem et donationem ratam habentes, eam sicut rationabiliter facta est confirmamus et tam sigilli quam scripti nostri robore*a* communimus. Testibus: magistro Gerardo, Walerano*b* archidiacono Baiocensi*c*, Willelmo archidiacono Gloucestriensi, magistro Rogero de Roveleston', Rogero decano de Cranebroc*d*, Henrico Baiocensi,*e* Galfrido et Ricardo clericis et multis aliis.

a roborare B   *b* Walerer' B   *c* Baioren' B   *d* Cranewer' B   *e* Baiocenenc' B

After William of Northolt became archdn, May × Dec. 1177.

The charter of Elias (on fo. 155v) has for its first witnesses 'G. Eliensi episcopo, magistro Andrea Wynton', magistro Helia, magistro Andrea de Beddingham, magistro Amando, magistro G. de Insula', and Robert, Thomas, and William, sons of Bernard.

A notification in the same terms by bp Seffrid II of Chichester (consec. 16 Nov. 1180) may well have been issued on the same occasion, therefore 16 Nov. 1180 × Sept. 1181 (*Chichester acta* 189–90 no. 138). Roger dean of 'Cranewer' is probably the dean of 'Cranebroc' in nos. 54, 114 and *St Gregory's cartulary* 57 no. 73 (on the supposition that he was rector of Cranbrook, Kent, a hundredal centre), and the 'Roger dean' of many other acta of this archbp.

214.   Tewkesbury abbey

Recommendation to the abbot of Tewkesbury on behalf of P., bearer of the archbishop's letter. The man admits to being a professed monk of Tewkesbury who has forsaken the cloister for the world. The archbishop pleads with a wealth of scriptural citations for a welcome to the prodigal. If the abbot is unforgiving, the archbishop will proceed to judgment and oblige him to be merciful.

[? Aug. 1174 × autumn 1177]

Petri Blesensis opera i 272–4 ep. 88.

The archbp is styled 'dei gratia Cantuariensis archiepiscopus totius Anglie primas et apostolice sedis legatus'. The initial 'P', missing in Giles's text, is in Cambridge, Corpus Christi Coll. ms. 214 fo. 127r. Apparently Tewkesbury lacked an abbot between the death of Fromundus, May 1178, and the accession of Robert, 1182. If so, Mr Peter of Blois wrote this letter before he left England for Rome, autumn 1177.

215.   Thoby priory

Confirmation for the brethren of the church of St Mary and St Leonard in the wood of Ginges of the gift by Michael Capra, as confirmed by bishop Richard (II) of London and archbishop Theobald.

Canterbury [July 1175 × 24 March 1176]

A = Chelmsford, Essex Record Office D/DP T 1/274. Endorsed, s. xiii ex.: Cart' archiepiscoporum Cantuar'. Approx. 206 × 166 + 21 mm. Sealing d. q. 2; with seal and counterseal (green wax). Scribe I.

Pd (calendar) from A by J. L. Fisher 'The Petre muniments' *Essex Archaeol. Soc. Transactions* n. s. 23 (1942–5) 79.

.R. dei gratia Cantuariensis archiepiscopus totius Anglie primas et apostolice sedis legatus . universis sancte matris ecclesie filiis ad quos presentes littere pervenerint . salutem in vero salutari. Quoniam diebus nostris ita invaluit et exarsit exsecrabilis fames avaricie . ut exquisitis calumpniantium versutiis veritas multipliciter impugnetur . et quies iuste possidentium assidue molestetur ./ necesse est ea que deo et ecclesiis . vel ecclesiasticis personis in liberam et perpetuam elemosinam iuste collata noscuntur . scriptorum autenticorum et testium patrocinio communiri. Inde est quod ad universitatis vestre noticiam volumus pervenire . quod donationem Michaelis Capre deo et ecclesie beate Marie et sancti Leonardi de bosco de Ginges et fratribus ibidem divino obsequio mancipatis ./ factam . et tam a bone memorie Ricardo . Londoniensi episcopo . quam a sancte recordationis Theobaldo . Cantuariensi archiepiscopo confirmatam ./ de una hida terre que est circa predictam ecclesiam . et de pasnagio . et de decima de proprio feno ipsius Michaelis . et de molendino suo . et de ligno ad ignem suum . ut hec omnia habeant libere et quiete et absque omni servicio seculari . sicut prefati Michaelis et predicti Londoniensis episcopi Ricardi carte testantur illis esse concessam et donatam ./ nos quoque concedimus et confirmamus et presentis scripti patrocinio communimus. Facta est autem hec nostra confirmatio anno ab incarnatione domini millesimo centesimo septuagesimo quinto ordinationis autem nostre secundo. Aput Cantuariam . Hiis testibus . Benedicto priore Cantuariensi . magistro Gerardo . magistro Petro Blesensi . Rogerio et Willelmo clericis . et aliis.

After Benedict became prior of Christ Church, July × Sept. 1175 and before the end of the year 1175/6.

For the original grant and archbp Theobald's confirmation see Fisher, *loc. cit.* and for kg Stephen's charter *Essex Review* xlviii (1939) 67 (with facsimile) and *Regesta regum* iii 321 no. 877. Michael Capra was also a benefactor of the nuns of Clerkenwell.

*216. Trentham priory

Mandate to the bishop of Coventry to hear the complaint of Vivian de Stoch, as proctor of Robert de Costentin, who had brought his complaint personally to the archbishop against the prior and canons of Trentham, concerning the rights of the parties in the chapels of Newcastle-under-Lyme and Whitmore.

[Aug. 1174 × summer 1182 ?]

Mentioned only, in a chirograph recording a *transactio* reached before the bp of Coventry 'in plena sinodo' (Madox, *Formulare* 22 no. XXXIX, from PRO E 327/39, whence *Collections for the history of Staffordshire* (William Salt Archaeol. Soc.) xi (1891) 322–3, where dated *c.*1175 × 1180); cf. *VCH Staffs.* viii (1963) 16, 186, where this document is dated 1175 × 1182. Both datings assume that the bp who held the synod was Richard Peche, who died after resigning his see, on 6 Oct. 1182, and therefore that the mandate came from archbp Richard. It is unlikely that the bp was Gerard Pucella (consec. 25 Sept. 1183, d. 13 Jan. 1184). The proceedings could have been in a synod of bp Hugh Nonant, if he held one between his consecration (31 Jan. 1188) and his departure for Normandy in March 1190; in this case the mandate emanated from archbp Baldwin (below, no. 321). A later date is precluded by the presence in the synod of archdn Alan of Stafford (before April 1192).

217. Tutbury priory

Confirmation for the monks of Tutbury of all their possessions and other benefices, after inspection of their charter from the late earl Robert the younger, of Nottingham, which confirmed all things given by his grandfather Henry, his uncle Engenulfus, and his father Robert, and their wives, barons, knights, and men.

[28 April 1174 × Sept. 1181]

B = London, College of Arms ms. Arundel 59 (Tutbury cartulary) fo. 20r. s. xv med.

Pd from B in *Tutbury cartulary* 28–29 no. 8, where dated 1174–83.

His testibus: magistro Girardo et ceteris quam pluribus.

The archbp is styled legate.
   For the charter (1140 × 1150) of Robert de Ferrers II see *Cartulary* 74–75 no. 70 and, with witnesses, *CDF* 203 no. 581. Various charters of his forebears are in the cartulary and in *CDF* 203–6.

218. Tutbury priory

Confirmation for the monks of Tutbury, after inspection of their charter from earl William de Ferrers, of the grant by the earl and his forebears of two thirds of the tithes of his demesne in Stanford(-in-the-Vale).

[28 April 1174 × Sept. 1181]

B = London, College of Arms ms. Arundel 59 (Tutbury cartulary) fo. 29v. s. xv med.

Pd in *Tutbury cartulary* 41–42 no. 28, where dated 1174–1184.

Hiis testibus etc.

The archbp is styled legate.
   For charters of earl William de Ferrers I, granting these tithes (1161 × 1181) see *Cartulary* 67–68 nos. 54–55.

219. Tutbury priory

Mandate addressed to all bishops and archdeacons and their officials in the province of Canterbury in whose jurisdiction the monks of Tutbury have possessions. The archbishop has inspected and confirms a mandate of archbishop Theobald which ordered the addressees and their predecessors in office to protect the monks' possession of tithes to which they justly laid claim in the demesne of the earl of Tutbury and in the lands of the earl's barons and to compel defaulters.

[28 April 1174 × Sept. 1181]

B = London, College of Arms ms. Arundel 59 (Tutbury cartulary) fo. 19v. s. xv med.

Pd from B in *Tutbury cartulary* 27–28 no. 7, where dated 1174–84.

The archbp is styled legate.
Theobald's mandate is printed by Saltman, *Theobald* 497–8 no. 265 and *Cartulary* 27 no. 6, dated 1151–7. Archbp Richard significantly fails to mention a similar mandate attributed in the cartulary to archbp Thomas (styled primate and legate). This was probably issued by Theobald (*Cartulary* 29–30 no. 9). Perhaps the words 'dominii comitis de Tuttesbiri' should be rendered 'of the earl's demesne of Tutbury'.

220. Walden priory

Confirmation for the church of Walden of its possessions (enumerated) as granted and confirmed by the earls of Essex, bishop Gilbert of London, king Henry II, and pope Eugenius (III).

[28 April 1174 × 1176]

B = BL ms. Harl. 3697 (Walden cartulary) fo. 42v (26v). s. xiv ex. No. V in the 'privilegia archiepiscoporum Cantuariensium'.

Ricardus dei gratia Cantuariensis archiepiscopus totius Anglie primas et apostolice sedis legatus universis sancte matris ecclesie filiis ad quos presentes littere pervenerint salutem in vero salutari. Quia iuste possidentium quies exquisitis calumpniantium versutiis hodie multipliciter inpugnatur, publice interest ea que viri religiosi de magnatum munificentia susceperunt*a* autoritate multiplici confirmari. Nos itaque, inspectis confirmationibus Galfridi comitis de Essexia et Galfridi comitis filii eius, Gilberti etiam Londoniensis episcopi, illustrissimi etiam regis Anglorum Henrici secundi, et preterea felicis memorie patris nostri Eugenii pape super donationibus et concessionibus quas fecit senior Galfridus comes ecclesie de Waleden' fundate in honore beate Marie et beati Iacobi, volentes prefatas donationes robur habere perpetuum, easdem nostre autoritatis munimine duximus roborare propriisque vocabulis designare, scilicet ecclesiam de Waleden', ecclesiam de Edelmeton', ecclesiam de Enefeld, ecclesiam de Mymmes, ecclesiam de Senleia, ecclesiam de Norhale, ecclesiam de Kaingham, ecclesiam de Ainho, ecclesiam de Cumton', ecclesiam de Almodesham, ecclesiam de Strateleia, ecclesiam de Sabricthtesword', ecclesiam de Gedelstona, ecclesiam de Torleia, ecclesiam de Chipenham, ecclesiam de Estra, ecclesiam de Waltham, ecclesiam de Chishelle, cum omnibus beneficiis et libertatibus eisdem ecclesiis pertinentibus, molendinum insuper unum apud Parcum et dimidiam virgatam terre ad idem molendinum pertinentem, apud Waldenam molendinum unum et centum et viginti acras terre arabilis in essarto de Waleden' et centum acras de bosco et unum pratum in Waleden quod vocatur Fulefen et pannagium quietum de porcis prefate ecclesie in bosco de Waleden' et in foresta de Parco. Has igitur possessiones sicut predicte ecclesie iuste et canonice concesse sunt nos quoque concedimus et confirmamus et presentis scripti patrocinio communimus. Hiis testibus: magistro Gerardo, magistro Petro Blesensi, Radulpho et Alexandro monachis, Henrico de Norhanton',[b] Henrico Baiocensi canonico, Radulfo de Sancto Martino, Rogero decano, Willelmo de Sotindon', et pluribus aliis tam clericis quam laicis.[c]

[a] susciperent B   [b] Norhanton'? : Norhale B   [c] add Exhibitum archiepiscopo vii B

The suggested terminal date, 1176, depends on the dating of Alexander III's letter for Walden: Benevento, 30 Dec. (*PUE* i 375 no. 110, from the cartulary). The year 1176, when the pope was at Benevento, seems more probable than the years 1167–9 to which Holtzmann assigned the letter. Churches recited in the bull include Elsenham and the chapel of 'Einswrda', which do not appear here (see below, no. 222 and cf. Foliot, *Letters* 476–7 nos. 442–4), and the bull is not mentioned.

   Charters of the founder and his family are in *Mon. Ang.* iv 148b--151. The confirmation by bp Gilbert is in *Letters* 474–5 no. 439 dated 1163–1172, ? 1169–1172. Henry II's charter is in *Cartae Antiquae Rolls 1–10* (PRS n. s. 17 1939) 58 no. 97 and *Mon. Ang.* iv 152. For the bull of Eugenius III, 25 April 1148, see *PUE* i 279 no. 43. All these records are drawn from the cartulary except for the royal charter.

221. Walden priory

Confirmation for the prior and monks of Walden of the grant of the patronage of the church of Arkesden by Eudo of Arkesden and William son of Ernulf, and of the institution of the monks in the church by bishop Gilbert of London, whose charter the archbishop has inspected.

[1180 × Sept. 1181]

B = BL ms. Harl. 3697 (Walden cartulary) fo. 42r (26r). s. xiv ex. No. III in the 'privilegia archiepiscoporum Cantuariensium'. C = Ibid. fo. 42r (26r). No. IV, the first six lines of the same, noted 'Ista scribitur ante'.

Ricardus dei gratia Cantuariensis archiepiscopus totius Anglie primas et apostolice sedis legatus universis sancte matris ecclesie filiis ad quos presentes littere pervenerint eternam in Christo salutem. Quoniam exquisitis calumpniantium versutiis ecclesiastica libertas hodie multipliciter impugnatur, necesse est ea que religiosis domibus caritatis intuitu sunt collata autenticorum scriptorum munimine roborari ut ad sustentationem eorum qui divinis assidue famulantibus*a* perpetua stabilitate firmentur. Eapropter universitati vestre volumus innotescere Eudonem de Arkesdena et Willelmum filium Ernulfi ius patronatus quod in ecclesia de Arkesdena habebant dilectis filiis nostris priori et monachis de Waledena in perpetuam elemosinam concessisse et carta sua confirmasse et prefatos priorem et monachos de Waleden' autoritate*b* venerabilis fratris nostri Gilberti Londoniensis episcopi in ecclesia eadem canonice esse institutos, sicut autenticum scriptum eiusdem episcopi super hoc eis indultum evidenter ostendit. Hanc itaque predictorum militum donationem et prefati episcopi institutionem sicut rationabiliter facte sunt ratas habentes et firmas, ad habundantiorem*c* cautelam in posterum prescriptam ecclesiam memoratis monachis autoritate qua fungimur confirmamus, hanc nostre confirmationis paginam sigilli nostri munimine roborantes, statuentes ut nemo ausu sacrilego eam presumat infringere vel ei quacunque temeritate in detrimentum eorumdem monachorum contraire. Hiis testibus : magistro Girardo Pulcell', Walerano Baiocensi archidiacono, Willelmo et Moyse capellanis, Henrico Baiocensi, magistro Rogero Walensi, Iohanne capellano, Michaele de Burn', Gaufrido clerico, Rogero decano, et aliis multis.

a familatibus *corr. (s. xv) to* famulantibus B   *b* autoritate *repeated* B   *c* habuntiorem B

The bp's letter of institution (Foliot, *Letters* 478–9 no. 446) cannot be before 1180 since Ralph de Diceto witnesses as dean of St Paul's; the final date is fixed by the archbp's legatine title.

Eudo's charter is in the cartulary, fo. 42r.

222. Walden priory

Confirmation for the monastery of Walden of its possessions (enumerated) as granted and confirmed by the earls of Essex, bishop Gilbert of London, king Henry II, and popes Eugenius (III) and Alexander (III), with the addition of gifts by other donors.

[Oct. 1181 × May 1183]

B = BL ms. Harl. 3697 (Walden cartulary) fo. 42v (26v). s. xiv ex. No. VI in the
'privilegia archiepiscoporum Cantuariensium'.

Universis sancte matris ecclesie filiis ad quos presens scriptum
pervenerit Ricardus Cantuariensis ecclesie minister humilis salutem
in domino. Quia iuste possidentium quies exquisitis calumpniantium versutiis hodie multipliciter impugnatur, publice interest ea
que viri religiosi ex magnatum munificentia susceperunt autoritate
multiplici confirmari. Nos itaque inspectis confirmationibus Gaufridi comitis[a] de Essexia et Gaufridi comitis filii eius, Gilberti
quoque Lundoniensis episcopi, illustrissimi etiam regis Anglorum
Henrici secundi, et preterea felicis memorie patrum nostrorum
Eugenii et Alexandri Romanorum pontificum super donationibus et
concessionbius quas fecit senior Gaufredus comes monasterio de
Waleden' fundato in honore beate Marie et beati Iacobi apostoli,
volentes prefatas donationes robur habere perpetuum easdem nostre
autoritatis munimine duximus roborare propriisque vocabulis designare, scilicet ecclesiam parochialem de Waledena, ecclesiam de
Edelmetona, ecclesiam de Enefeld, ecclesiam de Mimmes, ecclesiam de Senlee, ecclesiam de Norhale, ecclesiam de Kaingham,
ecclesiam de Cumton', ecclesiam de Ainho, ecclesiam de Stradlee,
ecclesiam de Amodesham, ecclesiam de Sabrichtesword, ecclesiam
de Gedelston', ecclesiam de Digheneswell', ecclesiam de Torleia,
ecclesiam de Chippenham, ecclesiam de Chishell', ecclesiam de
Estra, ecclesiam de Waltham, ecclesiam de Elsenham, cum omnibus
beneficiis et libertatibus ad easdem ecclesias pertinentibus, molendinum insuper unum apud Parcum et dimidiam virgatam terre ad
idem molendinum pertinentem, apud Waledene molendinum unum
et centum et viginti acras terre arabilis in assarto[b] de Waledena et
centum acras de bosco et unum pratum in Waleden' quod vocatur
Fulefen, terram que iacet inter portam monachorum et vadum
versus Neuport, et pannagium quietum de porcis prefati monasterii
in bosco de Waledena et in foresta de Parco. Preterea de dono
Radulfi Pirot ecclesiam de Lindesele cum capella de Lachell', de
dono Willelmi Guhet capellam de Einesword, de abbate et conventu
sancti Salvii de Musteriolo capellam sancti Wingaloec de Coken-
hach, de terris et redditibus de feodo comitis Willelmi et Roberti de
Burun, et aliis omnibus ad eundem locum pertinentibus. Preterea
ecclesiam de Haiden. Has ergo possessiones sicut predicto monasterio iuste et canonice concesse sunt nos quoque concedimus et
confirmamus ac presentis scripti patrocinio communimus. Hiis
testibus: magistro Girardo, Willelmo Gloecestriensi archidiacono,
Willelmo et Moyse capellanis, Henrico Baiocensi, Ricardo de

Lundonia, magistro Rogero Walensi, Gaufrido clerico, Michaele de Burnis, Rogero decano, et aliis multis clericis et laicis.*c*

a comes: *om.* B   *b* asserto B   *c* *add* Exhibitum apud Stort' .I. Hasselerton' B

After the death of Alexander III and before the election of Mr Gerard Pucella to the bpric of Coventry.

The charter is based on no. 220 above; it is substantially the same as far as the words 'quod vocatur Fulefen', apart from the added reference to Alexander III and the inclusion of the churches of Digswell (after Gedelston) and Elsenham (after Waltham). For the grants of Lindsell church with Lashley and 'Einesword' chapel (in Arkesden) see Foliot *Letters* 475–9 nos. 440–5 and *PUE* i 448–9 no. 179. For the chapel of St Wingaloec, or Winwaloc (in Nuthampstead), given by the abbey of St Saulve de Montreuil see *VCH Herts* iv (1914) 32b: the grant was confirmed to Walden by Lucius III, 7 April 1184 (*PUE* i 493 no. 218).

223. Walden priory

Letters of protection for the monks of Walden, and grant of an indulgence of fifteen days for visitors to the monastery who give alms and those who are received into confraternity with the monks. The grant includes participation in the spiritual benefits of the church of Canterbury.   [? Oct. 1181 × 16 Feb. 1184]

B = BL ms. Harl. 3697 (Walden cartulary) fo. 42r (25r). s. xiv ex.

Universis sancte matris ecclesie filiis ad quos presentes littere pervenerint Ricardus Cantuariensis ecclesie minister humilis eternam in Christo salutem. Cum ex iniuncto nobis cure pastoralis officio omnium subditorum nostrorum profectibus intendere debeamus, viris tamen religiosis tanto propensiori cura providere tenemur quanto minus suo inhibente proposito circa exteriora possunt occupari. Attendentes siquidem dilectorum filiorum nostrorum devotionem monachorum de Waleden' pariterque sui monasterii novitatem, quod licet paucis ad modum dotatum redditibus mirifica tamen structura in honorem gloriose dei genetricis et virginis Marie et beati Iacobi apostoli ex elemosinis et impendiis fidelium videtur consurgere, ipsos et prefatum locum cum omnibus pertinentiis et possessionibus quas vel in presenti habent vel futuris temporibus iustis modis poterunt adipisci sub protectione sancte Cantuariensis ecclesie et nostra recipimus, districtius ea qua fungimur autoritate prohibentes ne quis eorum bona aut iura turbare, diminuere, vel auferre presumat. Rogamus caritatem vestram et attentius exhortamur in domino quatinus intuitu divine pietatis et beate matris domini sanctique Iacobi memoratos fratres et locum suum ametis, honoretis, et de facultatibus vobis a deo collatis misericorditer prospicere ac promovere curetis ut ad ipso autore ac retributore omnium bonorum eterne felicitatis premia in celo capiatis. Omnibus autem Christi fidelibus qui memoratum locum cum devotis orationibus et elemosinis visitaverint vel in eorum fraternitate ascribi ac recipi meruerint vel in diversis sanctorum festivitatibus processiones que ad monasterium illud fieri solent devote secuti fuerint, vere scilicet penitentibus et confessis, de misericordia Christi et genetricis sue meritisque sancti Iacobi apostoli confidentes, de iniuncta sibi penitentia quindecim dies relaxamus et orationum ac beneficiorum Cantuariensis ecclesie tam in morte quam in vita participes esse concedimus. Valete.

> The archbp is not styled legate, but the form of the *intitulatio* is unusual (cf. above, p. lv).
> Building activity at Walden is referred to in an indulgence granted by bp Gilbert of London, 1163–87 (Foliot, *Letters* 479 no. 447).

224. Waltham abbey

Grant to Waltham abbey of the protection of the church of Canterbury, and exhortation to the faithful to honour the abbey. Grant of fifteen days' indulgence for all who visit the new abbey of Austin canons and give alms, on the feasts of the Invention and Elevation of the Holy Cross or within the octaves of these festivals. The grant includes participation in the spiritual benefits of the church of Canterbury.

[11 June 1177 (? Oct. 1181) × 16 Feb. 1184]

B = BL ms. Harl. 391 (Waltham cartulary) fo. 100v. s. xiii in.

Universis Christi fidelibus ad quos presentes littere pervenerint Ricardus Cantuariensis ecclesie minister humilis eternam in Christo salutem. Cum omnium sanctorum merita devotis obsequiis cristianam religionem deceat venerari, ipsum tamen sanctum sanctorum qui per crucem suam cunctos redemit sanctos precipua oportet devotione colere et adorare, et in eius nomine crucis sue signaculum glorificare, de quo dicit apostolus: Michi autem absit gloriari nisi in cruce domini nostri Iesu Christi. Cum ergo apud Waltham in honore eiusdem salutifere crucis ex antiqua devotione fidelium populique frequentia venerabile templum existat, illud tamen maiori veneratione censemus dignum quod et nove religionis cultus sanctificat et mirabilis structure de novo surgentis decor exornat. Attendentes siquidem memorati loci reverentiam pariterque devotionem dilectorum filiorum nostrorum canonicorum sub regula beati doctoris Augustini ibidem deo militantium, prefatum locum et canonicos cum omnibus pertinentiis suis sub protectione sancte

Cantuariensis ecclesie et nostra recipimus, fraternitatem vestram rogantes, monentes, et attentius exhortantes in domino quatinus eundem locum et canonicos ob reverentiam et honorem sancte crucis ametis, honoretis, et in quibus secundum deum poteritis promovere curetis ut ab ipso salvatore et crucis sanctificatore eterne salutis premia [fo. 101r] in celo recipiatis. Omnibus autem Christi fidelibus qui prefatam ecclesiam sive in festis Inventionis sive Exaltationis sacrosancte crucis vel in octavis earundem festivitatum cum devotis orationibus seu elemosinis visitaverint, vere scilicet penitentibus et confessis de misericordia salvatoris confidentes, quindecim dies de iniuncta sibi penitentia relaxamus et orationum ac beneficiorum sancte Cantuariensis ecclesie inperpetuum participes esse concedimus. Bene valeat fraternitas vestra in Christo.

Archbp Richard was not himself present at the induction of canons regular to replace the secular canons at Waltham on 11 June 1177 (Eyton 212). This indulgence may have been granted soon afterwards, but note the absence of the legatine title and compare other occasions when the archbp is styled 'minister humilis'.

225. The church of Wells

Notification that Richard de Camville has resigned his right in the church of Henstridge in the hand of bishop Reginald of Bath, to make it a perpetual prebend of the church of Wells, saving the right of John son of Luke, the present parson of the church.

[? March 1176]

B = Wells, D. & C. Libr. Liber albus I (Reg. I) fo. 22r. no. lx. s. xiii med.
  C = Ibid. Liber albus II (Reg. III) fo. 160v. s. xv/xvi.

Pd (calendar) from B and C in *HMCR Wells* i (1907) 22.

Universis sancte matris ecclesie filiis ad quos presentes littere pervenerint Ricardus dei gratia Cantuariensis archiepiscopus totius Anglie primas et apostolice sedis legatus salutem in vero salutari. Quia publice interest perhibere testimonium veritati, volumus in publicam devenire notitiam quod Ricardus de Camvill'ᵃ in presentia nostra et venerabilium fratrum nostrorum G. Londoniensis, R. Wintoniensis, G. Eliensis, B. Exoniensis, R. Wigorniensis, R. Cestrensis, I. Cicestrensis, et A. Sancti Asaphi episcoporum donavit et concessit in prebendam perpetuam Wellensi ecclesie in manu venerabilis fratris nostri R. Bathonie episcopi ecclesie de Hengestr'ᵇ liberam ab omni servitute et quietam cum omnibus pertinentiis suis, resignans in manu eiusdem quicquid in ea cognoscebatur antiquitus habuisse, salvo iure Iohannis filii Luce qui eo tempore eiusdem ecclesie persona extabat. Ut ergo hec resignatio*c* prescripte ecclesie et prebende institutio firma inperpetuum et stabilis perseveret, eam cum predictis fratribus nostris testamur et scripti ac sigilli nostri munimine roboramus. Sunt hiis*d* testes:*e* magister Walterus de Constantiis archidiaconus Oxeneford', Waleranus archidiaconus Baiocensis, magister Petrus Blesensis.

a Camvill' B; Canvill' C   *b* Hengestr' B; Hengestrig' C   *c* ressignatio B   *d* hii B; et alii C   *e* names of witnesses, om. in B, supplied from C.

The presence of bp Adam of St Asaph dates the gathering after his consecration, 12 Oct. 1175, and no time seems more probable than March 1176, when bps assembled at Westminster for the council of the legate Hugh (14 March). Cardinal Hugh had landed in England late in Oct. 1175.

Charter liiii in Reg. I is Richard de Camville's grant, witnessed in Reg. III by the archbp and bps and others named as witnesses above (the archdn of Oxford being also styled keeper of the kg's seal), and with the names of Walter precentor of Salisbury, Geoffrey archdn of Berkshire, and William de Sancta Fide. Other documents relating to Henstridge follow (cf. no. 227 below), including a notification by bp Roger of Worcester attested by the archbp and most of the bps named above (M. G. Cheney, *Roger of Worcester* 302–3 App. I no. 71), and a confirmation by the cardinal legate Hugh, which cites the acta of the archbp and the bp of Worcester (*PUE* ii 344–5 no. 155).

226. The church of Wells

Confirmation for the church of Wells of all grants of churches and prebends recorded in the donors' charters and in the confirmation by bishop Reginald of Bath which the archbishop has seen.

[Aug. 1174 × Sept. 1181]

B = Wells, D. & C. Libr. Liber albus I (Reg. I) fo. 21v no. lvii. s. xiii med. C = Ibid. Liber fuscus (Reg. IV) fo. 6v. s. xiv med. D = Ibid. Liber albus II (Reg. III) fo. 9r, copied from C. s. xv/xvi.

Pd (calendar) from B and D in *HMCR Wells* i 22.

Ricardus dei gratia Cantuariensis archiepiscopus totius Anglie primas et apostolice sedis legatus universis ad quos presentes littere pervenerint salutem in Christo. Ea que sacrosanctis ecclesiis in perpetuum*a* patrimonium Christi pia quorumlibet fidelium devotione collata sunt rata convenit et inconvulsa permanere,*b* et nobis qui ecclesie dei preesse videmur studiosius est providendum ne aliquorum temeritas contra rationem audeat ea in posterum avellere aut irrationabiliter perturbare. Ad omnium itaque volumus notitiam pervenire quod universas donationes quecumque Wellensi ecclesie rationabiliter facte sunt sive in ecclesiis sive prebendis, sicut venerabilis frater noster Reginaldus Bathonie episcopus eidem ecclesie Wellensi scripto suo quod*c* nos ipsi vidimus confirmavit et sicut donatorum carte et instrumenta testantur nostra quoque auctoritate confirmamus et sigilli munimine imperpetuum roboramus, statuentes ne quis eas ausu temerario revocare, diminuere, aut perturbare presumat, set eidem ecclesie ad perpetuam dei laudem et gloriam perhenniter maneant instituta. Testibus:^c Walerano archidiacono Baiocensi, Henrico Baiocensi, Willelmo de Sottindon', Rogero Norwicensi, Gaufrido clerico, et aliis multis.

^a in perp. CD; imperp. B   ^b permanere B; manere CD   ^c Names of witnesses, om. in B, supplied from CD

Although the bp could have issued his charter and the archbp given this confirmation immediately after Reginald's consecration at St Jean de Maurienne, 23 June 1174, such action was unlikely until their return to England, and was probably much later.

227. The church of Wells

Notification by archbishop Richard and bishops John of Norwich, Baldwin of Worcester, and Seffrid of Chichester that Gerard de Camville, son and heir of Richard de Camville, has confirmed in their presence and that of the king's justiciar, Ranulf de Glanvill, and of Roger FitzReinfrid and many others of the Exchequer the grant which his father had made and confirmed by charter of the church of Henstridge, to be a perpetual prebend of the church of Wells. Gerard placed the church in the hand of bishop Reginald of Bath to be collated by him to whomsoever he wished, like other prebends of Wells. The bishops were present and have recorded this grant in this charter with their seals. [Westminster. Early 1182]

B = Wells, D. & C. Libr. Liber albus I (Reg. I) fo. 21v, unnumbered item after no. lvi. s. xiii med. C = Ibid. Liber albus II (Reg. III) fo. 160r. s. xv/xvi.

Pd from B and C in *Chichester acta* 192–3 no. 141; and (calendar) from B and C in *HMCR Wells* i (1907) 21–2.

Interfuerunt etiam Herebertus Cantuariensis,^a Ricardus Elyensis, Petrus Bathoniensis, Willelmus Gloecestriensis, Iocelinus Cicestrensis, et Radulfus Herefordensis archidiaconi, Osbertus de Camera, Hubertus Walteri, Willelmus de Glanvill' clericus, Baldwinus cancellarius Saresberiensis, Hugo de Gaherst, Elyas de Chivelai, Stephanus de Clai, Thomas Brito, Willelmus et Iocelinus capellani, Thomas filius Bernardi, Michael Belet, Willelmus Basset, Gillebertus Malet, Radulfus filius Stephani, Willelmus filius Stephani, Willelmus Rufus, Willelmus de Bendeng', Robertus Witefeld', Robertus Poher, Iohannes de Sandford', Henricus de Novomercato, Eustachius de Bailluel, Willelmus Torel, Gillebertus de Colevill constabularius Londonie, Hugo de Canvill, Willelmus de Canvill.

a Names of following witnesses, om. in B, supplied from C.

The archbp is not styled legate; Peter of Blois became archdn of Bath early in 1182. The text of Gerard de Camville's confirmation in Reg. III fo. 161r is witnessed by the archbp and three of the bps and all but two of the other witnesses in the list given here, and it is dated at Westminster in the kg's chamber, 1182 (*HMCR Wells* i 21). Since Peter of Blois is a witness this must precede his departure abroad in June (J. Armitage Robinson, *Somerset hist. essays* (Brit. Acad. 1921) 114).

228. Westwood priory

Confirmation for the nuns of Westwood of all their possessions, enumerated. [23 June 1174 × Sept. 1175]

A = Birmingham, Reference Libr. ms. 473629. Endorsed, s. xv ex. (twice): Strowes (?); s. xvi: A confirmation of the bishop of Canterbury to Westwode (?). Approx. 245 × 247 + 57 mm. Sealing d. q. 1, with double fold and slit through three thicknesses; tag and seal lost. Stained. Scribe I.

. Ric(ardus) dei gratia Cantuariensis archiepiscopus . totius Anglie primas . et apostolice sedis legatus ∴ universis sancte matris ecclesie filiis ad quos littere presentes pervenerint ∴ salutem que est in Christo Iesu. Quoniam ea que domibus religiosis pietatis intuitu sunt concessa perpetua debent stabilitate gaudere ∴ ut pie humanitatis beneficia nulla in posterum calumpniantium temeritate divellantur ∴ nos dilectis in Christo filiabus monialibus de Westwude divino ibidem servicio mancipatis ∴ omnes possessiones quas ex donatione virorum aut mulierum nobilium . vel aliis iustis titulis rationabiliter sunt adepte ∴ nostri scripti auctoritate duximus confirmare. Specialiter autem possessiones subscriptis nominibus designatas . super quibus cartas et instrumenta donatorum contrectavimus . et oculis propriis inspeximus . ecclesiam sancti Augustini de Duderhull' cum pertinentiis suis . terram de Westwude cum essartis . in bosco . et plano . et in omnibus consuetudinibus . terram de Cruche cum omnibus pertinentiis . in bosco . et plano . cum salina apud Wicham ∴ cum hominibus . ecclesiam de Codderegghe cum suis pertinentiis . redditum molendini de Westwude cum omnibus pertinentiis . terris . pratis . pascuis . cum multura hominum terre illius . salvo iure ecclesie sancti Augustini de Dudderhull' . et multura Hugonis de Ardena quoad vixerit . pasturam quoque .lx. porcorum ∴ sine pasnagio a festo sancti Michaelis ∴ usque ad festum sancti Martini . virgatam terre . et dimidiam apud Brumfeld' . ex donatione comitis Rannulfi Cestrie ∴ singulis annis .xl. solidos in elemosinam . de

nundinis de Warewich' unam marcam argenti ad Vincula beati Petri
. virgatam unam terre ꞏ quam tenet Radulfus Vilain . per quatuor
solidos . et dimidiam virgatam terre quam tenet Alfricus pro tribus
solidis . et unam mansuram quam tenet Walchelinus faber in
Oureleya . pro .ix. denariis . terram de parva Estona ꞏ cum omnibus
pertinentiis . in terris . pratis . pascuis . capellam de Piritona ꞏ post
decessum Walteri persone eiusdem capelle . terciam partem omnium decimarum de Guttingh' . apud Wich' unum molendinum ꞏ et
dimidiam virgatam terre prope molendinum. Generaliter ergo sub
interminatione anathematis inhibemus . ne quis beneficia
rationabiliter eis collata iniuste diminuat . aut temere perturbare
presumat. Hiis testibus . Reginaldo Baton(iensi) episcopo . Benedicto cancellario . magistro Gerardo . Waleramo (sic) Baiocensi
archidiacono . magistro Petro Blesensi . Willelmo de Norhal .
Radulfo de Wingham . magistro Andrea . magistro Hugone de
Suwell' . Radulfo clerico . Henrico Baiocensi . magistro Willelmo
Cadomensi . magistro Willelmo de Wintonia . Ricardo Pictav(ensi) .
Petro clerico . Rogero . Amicio scriptoribus . et aliis.

The first two witnesses give the limits of dating.

The first item in this confirmation, the church of St Augustine of Dodderhill
in Droitwich, had been granted to the monks of Worcester by Osbert before
1100, and confirmed to them by bp Samson (*Worcester cartulary* (PRS n. s. 38)
82–83 nos. 147–148); but it was given to the nuns of Westwood by the donor's
grandson, Osbert FitzHugh, when his mother Eustachia de Say and he established nuns of Fontevrault at Westwood by 1158. The grant was allegedly
confirmed by bp Alfred, 1158 × 1160, and by kg Henry II. At about the time of
this confirmation by the archbp, the abbess of Fontevrault complained that the
monks of Worcester were claiming the church. To avoid litigation ('quia servum
dei non oportet litigare, ut ait apostolus') she submitted the matter to the
decision of bp Roger of Worcester and others. A compromise was reached in the
bp's presence, 4 Nov. 1178, and later confirmed by bp Baldwin (according to
pope Clement III's bull). As a result Westwood was to hold the land of Clethale
in Westwood Park and enjoy certain tithes, burial rights, and offerings;
Worcester recovered the church of St Augustine, Dodderhill, subject to the
interest of Osbert FitzHugh and his next heir. For documents bearing on this
case see *Worcester cartulary* 88–96 nos. 162–178, and p. xxxv; see also M. G.
Cheney, *Roger of Worcester* 93, 95. Other gifts to Westwood are recorded in *Mon.
Ang.* vii 1004–10. Fontevrault obtained a privilege in favour of the nuns of
Westwood from Clement III, 12 Nov. 1188, which confirms and enumerates
their possessions (Facs. of a *copie figurée* in Angers, Archives de Maine-et-Loire,
fonds Fontevrault, prieurés de l'Angleterre 15. 1, in A. de Boüard, *Manuel de
diplomatique* i (album) pl. XIX–XIX*bis*). Some possessions are there specified
more precisely than in the confirmation above, and their donors named.

229. The bishops of Winchester, Ely, and Norwich

Exhortation to bishops Richard of Winchester, Geoffrey of Ely, and John of Norwich to work for the abolition of an evil custom which has grown up in the English church, which will increase unless they check it. Whereas laymen are hanged for murdering laymen, the church does not invoke the secular arm to punish the murderers of clerks. Instead, it only uses the ineffective penalty of excommunication, proudly and ambitiously claiming jurisdiction in matters which lay judges ought to punish. Recently a worthy priest of Winchester was murdered. William Freschet and his wife admitted to the crime. They are ready to go to the Roman curia, because the man is confident of getting absolution there and, into the bargain, will make money on the journey by trading on his wife's good looks. The addressees should counter this evil with a more timely policy. Let the church first exercise her jurisdiction; and if this is not enough, let the secular sword meet the deficiency. The archbishop cites canons (C. 12 q. 2 c. 46, etc.) to justify this. Let no one say that a man is punished twice for the same thing when what is begun by one authority is finished by the other. There are two swords which require mutual help, the priestly power to aid the kings, the royal power the priesthood. According to the council of Mainz (C. 13 q. 2 c. 30) criminals condemned to death are first punished spiritually by penitence, contrition, and satisfaction. Let us therefore render to God the things that are God's, to Caesar the things that are Caesar's. As the king requests, leave to him the avenging of such crimes, and give such criminals absolution in mortis articulo *for the excommunication which they have incurred by the* sententia lati canonis *(C. 17 q. 4 c. 29).*

[? 14 Dec. 1175 × 3 July 1176]

Petri Blesensis opera i 217–9 ep. 73 (n. d.). Whence *MTB* vii 560 ep. 794 (s. a. 1176), and transl. by W. F. Hook, *Lives of the archbishops of Canterbury* ii (2nd ed. 1862) 516–9.

The archbp is styled legate. Bp John of Norwich was consecrated 14 Dec. 1175. The dating is based on the observation of Foreville, *L'Église et la royauté* 427–8, 436–7, that it is connected with the negotations between kg Henry II and the legate Hugh Pierleone. This resulted in a letter from the kg to the pope (probably before the legate left, 3 July 1176) which records a promise by the kg relating to prosecution of clerks before secular judges and his undertaking that convicted or confessed murderers of clerks should be penalized like murderers of laymen and also suffer disinheritance of heirs (Diceto i 410).

The archbp's letter was a brief for the three bps who were then the most influential prelates at the royal court, concerned especially with judicial business. Cf. below, no. 230.

230. The bishops of Winchester, Ely, and Norwich

Testimonial for bishops Richard of Winchester, Geoffrey of Ely, and John of Norwich, addressed to pope Alexander III, contradicting reports that they are grasping, preoccupied with secular business, and neglectful of their pastoral duties. They are said to engage in trials which entail the shedding of blood. The pope has ordered the archbishop to punish their excesses canonically; but the reports are untrue. The archbishop praises the bishop of Winchester specially for his almsgiving. The bishop of Ely has purged his ill-fame as the pope required and has confounded his accusers by a holy and upright life. The virtue and prudence of the bishop of Norwich have been seen by the pope on his frequent missions from the king. The bishops have greatly improved the material state of their dioceses. The archbishop enlarges on the importance of employing wise and compassionate men in the adminis-tration of the state (rei publice): *it is no new thing for bishops to be counsellors of kings. With these bishops as the king's confidants, the clergy are less exposed to the presumption of laymen. Any attack on the church is now corrected by episcopal authority or, if ecclesiastical censure is not enough, the civil authority makes up for the deficiency of the spiritual sword. Other advantages accrue to the clergy and to other classes of society. The decrees of Rome are enforced and ecclesiastical possessions are enlarged. Unlike the bishops of Sicily, these bishops attend their churches on the major festivals and redeem with good works the days passed at court. The archbishop begs the pope to weigh these great benefits to the English church against the inconvenience of the bishops' residence at court. He will execute the pope's command when he receives it.*   [July 1176 × Sept. 1181]

Petri Blesensis opera i 252–5 ep. 84; *PL* cc 1459–61 ep. 96.

The archbp is styled 'Cantuariensis ecclesie humilis minister' (cf. above, no. 166n.).

The reference to secular penalties for those who attack the church suggests a date after the settlement of 1176 (above, no. 229n.). The particular notoriety of these three bps probably increased with their commission as *archiiusticiarii regni* at Easter 1179 which prompted an apologia from Ralph de Diceto (Diceto i 434–5), so that a date in or after 1179 is likely.

231. Wix priory

Confirmation for the nuns of Wix of the grant by Walter of Windsor and Christine, his mother, of the churches of Wormingford and Swilland, confirmed by the bishops of London and Norwich.

[1177 × Sept. 1181]

B = Cambridge, Christ's College muniments, Manorbier box no. A (6), in an inspeximus by D. & C. St Paul's, London, 3 Oct. 1310.

Ricardus dei gratia Cantuariensis archiepiscopus totius Anglie primas et apostolice sedis legatus omnibus Christi fidelibus ad quos presens scriptum pervenerit eternam in Christo salutem. Ut ea que religiosis locis caritatis intuitu ex fidelium munificentia et devotione sunt collata perpetua valeant in posterum stabilitate gaudere, necesse est ea virorum autenticorum scriptis et patrocinio confirmari, ne temeraria calumpniantium presumptione in posterum convellantur. Eapropter universitati vestre volumus innotescere ecclesias de Wythermundeford' et de Swineland' sustentationi dilectarum filiarum nostrarum in Christo apud Wykes et ecclesie sue ex donationibus nobilium personarum Walteri de Wyndelesor' et Cristine matris sue in perpetuam elemosinam collatas, et auctoritate venerabilium fratrum nostrorum Londoniensis et Norwycensis episcoporum eis esse confirmatas. Unde eisdem monialibus in posterum[a] providere volentes, memoratas ecclesias cum omnibus pertinentiis suis sicut eas canonice possedisse vel possidere noscuntur seu ex donatione dominorum fundi seu ex confirmatione diocesanorum[b] episcoporum auctoritate qua fungimur confirmamus et presentis scripti munimine roboramus, districtius inhibentes ne quis eas super prescriptis ecclesiis vel earum pertinentiis indebite vexare vel molestare presumat. Hiis testibus: magistro Girardo, Walerano Baiocensi et Willelmo Gloecestriensi archidiaconis, magistro Roberto de Inglesham, Willelmo de Sotind', Ricardo dec' et aliis.

[a] postterum B   [b] diocesanarum B

After William of Northolt became archdn of Gloucester, and probably of the same date as no. 232 (if that is genuine).

'Ricardo dec' ' may be a contraction of 'Ricardo clerico de Lundonia, Rogerio decano', the last two witnesses of no. 232. The confirmation by bp Gilbert of London of the grant of Wormingford church here cited is no. 4 in the same inspeximus.

232. Wix priory

Confirmation for the nuns of Wix of all the grants of their benefactors, confirmed by charters of king Henry I and king Henry II, archbishop Theobald, and bishops Robert, Richard (II), and Gilbert of London, which archbishop Richard has inspected.   [1177 × Sept. 1181]

A = PRO E 40/5269. Endorsed, s. xiii in.: Confirmacio Ric' archiepiscopi de ecclesia de Wykes et omnibus donacionibus eis collatis; s. xv: Kenyngton' (with notarial flourishes). Approx. 183 × 123 + 24 mm. Sealing d. q. 2; tag remains, seal lost. Scribe **IV**.

B = Cambridge, Christ's College muniments, Manorbier box no. A (7), in
inspeximus by D. & C. St Paul's, London, 3 Oct. 1310 (a very faithful
transcript, reading 'Wykes' for 'Wiches').

Pd from A by C. N. L. Brooke, 'Episcopal charters' 59–60 no. 2, cf. p. 51;
partially, by V. H. Galbraith in *EHR* lii (1937) 72; calendared in *Cat. of
ancient deeds* iii (HMSO 1900) 157–8 no. A 5269.

.Ric(ardus) . dei gracia . Cantuariensis . archiepiscopus . tocius
Anglie primas et apostolice sedis legatus ; omnibus sancte matris
ecclesie filiis ad quos presens scriptum pervenerit ; eternam in
Christo salutem. Cum omnia religiosa loca nostra iurisdictioni
subiecta ex officii nostri debito tueri ac promovere debeamus ; illis
tamen propensius intendere ac providere tenemur ; in quibus fragilis
mulierum sexus sub habitu regulari deo assidue noscitur deservire .
et earum paci et tranquillitati tanto diligentius invigilare ; quanto
minus suscepte religionis inhibente proposito et sexus sui fragilitate ;
curis secularibus operam possunt adhibere. In communem siquidem
volumus devenire noticiam . quod cum autentica scripta ecclesie
sanctimonialium de Wiches nobis essent oblata ; cartas regum
illustrium domini Henrici senioris . et domini nostri Henrici iunioris
filii scilicet Mathildis imperatricis . cartam etiam Teobaldi . predecessoris nostri . et cartas . Lundoniensium . episcoporum . Roberti .
Ricardi . Gilleberti ; inspeximus . quibus memoratis monialibus de .
Wich' . ecclesia beate Marie ibi fundata et omnia eidem ecclesie
donatione fidelium collata ; in perpetuam elemosinam habenda tam
regali quam episcopali autoritate confirmantur. Nos quoque eisdem
monialibus nostre autoritatis robur impertiri volentes ; easdem et
locum earum . et omnes earundem possessiones quascunque inpresentiarum iustis titulis possident vel deo autore in futuro poterunt
adipisci ; sub nostram protectionem . necnon et sancti martyris Tome
et omnium sanctorum quorum patrocinio specialiter sancta Cantuariensis ecclesia nititur ; suscipimus . et omnia earum bona sicut eis
canonice sunt collata et confirmata ; autoritate qua fungimur
confirmamus . et presentis scripti patrocinio et sigilli nostri appositione communimus . statuentes . et ex parte omnipotentis dei et
gloriosi martyris Tome et nostra districtius inhibentes . nequis hanc
nostre confirmationis paginam ausu sacrilego presumat infringere .
vel ei temerarie contraire. Hiis testibus . magistro . Girardo .
Walerano Baiocensi . et Willelmo Gloecestriensi . archidiaconis .
magistro Roberto de Inglesham . Henrico Baiocensi . Willelmo
clerico de Wedecherche . magistro Rog' . Norwicensi . Gilleberto . de
Pirariis . Ricardo clerico de Lundonia . Rogerio decano . et aliis
multis tam clericis quam laicis.

After William of Northolt became archdn of Gloucester.

Brooke (loc. cit. 51) argues that this charter is genuine but, in discussing the many forgeries of the nuns of Wix, observes that we cannot answer for any of the charters which archbp Richard cites. In no other archiepiscopal actum is the protection of St Thomas invoked in this way. In no other original actum of archbp Richard does the address read 'presens scriptum' (but cf. no. †194). None the less, in favour of its authenticity is the script, which is that of a scribe identified by Mr Bishop in acta for Christ Church (84), Combwell (114), London deanery (160) and Sele (211), and by Prof. Brooke in nos. 77, 80, 84–5, for Christ Church.

BALDWIN OF FORDE, 1184–1190

233. Battle abbey

Inspeximus and confirmation for the abbot and monks of Battle of a charter of archbishop Richard confirming to them the church of Wye.
[Jan. 1186 × Dec. 1187]

> B = San Marino (Calif.) Huntington Libr. ms. B. A. 29 (Battle cartulary) fo. 6ov (49v). Described as of archbp Boniface in title at head of page. s. xiii ex. C = London, Lincoln's Inn ms. Hale 87 (Battle cartulary) fo. 25r. s. xiii med. Protocol and witness list abridged and the text of archbp Richard breaks off at 'Quonian exquisitis etc.'

B.*a* dei gratia Cantuariensis archiepiscopus totius Anglie primas et apostolice sedis legatus omnibus fidelibus ad quos presens scriptura pervenerit salutem in domino. Ad universitatis vestre notitiam volumus pervenire litteras bone memorie R. Cantuariensis archiepiscopi decessoris*b* nostri nobis presentatas fuisse in hec verba: Ricardus dei gratia Cantuariensis archiepiscopus [*above, no. 54 ... fo. 61r ...*] et aliis. Nos autem predicti decessoris nostri confirmationem sicut rationabiliter facta est ratam habentes, eam presenti scripto et sigilli nostri appositione communimus. Hiis testibus: magistro Silvestro,*c* magistro R. de Sancto Martino, Rogero de Cheriton, Iohanne de Exonia, Galfrido Forti, Henrico et Eustachio clericis, Willelmo Prudhum*d* et aliis.

a B. B; Baldewynus C   *b* decessoris B; predecessoris C   *c* Silv' B; Silvano C
d Rogero ... Prudhum B, *om.* C

234. Belvoir priory

Notification that Alexander brother of Alfred of Haddington has in the archbishop's presence renounced all rights which he claimed in the church of Aubourn.
[Sept. 1185 × Jan. 1186]

> B = Belvoir Castle ms. Add. 105 (Belvoir cartulary) fo. 27r. s. xv in.
>
> Pd (calendar) from B in *HMCR Rutland* iv (1905) 113.

Omnibus Christi fidelibus ad quos presentes littere pervenerint B. dei gratia Cantuariensis archiepiscopus totius Anglie primas eternam in domino salutem. Ad universitatis vestre notitiam volumus pervenire quod Alexander frater Alveredi de Hadinton' in nostra constitutus presentia sponte et sine aliqua coactione quicquid iuris in ecclesia de Alburna se dicebat habere*a* in manu dilecti filii nostri R. vicearchidiaconi Lincolniensis resignavit. Quod ne processu temporis in dubium revocetur id ipsum presenti scripto duximus commendare.

a haberi B

Cf. no. 57, above. The incumbent's resignation made effective the earlier grant by Ralph d'Aubigny, which he now renewed in a letter addressed to archbp Baldwin (fo. 26v). In renewing his grant Ralph states that the monks may appoint 'quamcunque voluerint honestam personam' to celebrate divine office in the church. An accompanying letter by Robert of Hardres ('Haydr' '), canon of Lincoln and vice-archdn, records that with the assent of the archbp and on the presentation of Ralph d'Aubigny, patron of the church, he has canonically instituted the prior and convent of Belvoir 'vacante personatu'. He states that Alexander's renunciation was made in the presence of the archbp, bp Gilbert of Rochester, Godfrey de Lucy, William of Northolt, Mr Henry of Northampton, Peter of Blois, and many others. Mention of bp Gilbert fixes the earliest date as 29 Sept. 1185. The see of Lincoln is vacant, and the archbp is not styled legate. The corporal institution, or induction, of the prior and convent 'sicut personam' was performed by the rural dean of Swinderby, instructed by the vice-archdn. Alexander the clerk was again called upon to renounce his rights in the church on 22 March 1194.

235. Bordesley abbey

Confirmation for the monks of Bordesley of the grant of Tardebigg and the advowson of the church there by king Henry II, according to the charter which the archbishop inspected and confirmed when he was bishop of Worcester.

[April 1185 × Jan. 1186 or Dec. 1187 × July 1189]

A = PRO E 326/10443. No medieval endorsement. Approx. 157 × 89 + 24 mm. Sealing d. q. 2; small remains of middle of seal and counterseal (brown varnish).

Universis sancte matris ecclesie filiis ad quos presentes littere pervenerint ∴ B. divina miseratione sancte Cantuariensis ecclesie minister . eternam in 'domino' salutem. Ad universitatis vestre noticiam volumus pervenire . quod cum domino permittente administrationem . Wigorn' ecclesie gereremus . cartam domini nostri Henrici illustris Anglorum regis secundi . qua idem dominus rex dilectis filiis nostris monachis de Bordesleya . concedit et confirmat Tardebigam cum omnibus pertinentiis suis . et ius advocationis et donationis ecclesie eiusdem ville in perpetuam elemosinam . oculis nostris inspeximus et propriis manibus contrectavimus unde et nos concessionem illam sicut eam tunc scripto auctentico fecimus roborari*a* . ita et ea qua nunc fungimur auctoritate ad abundantioris cautele securitatem duximus communire.

a corr. from roborare A

With neither witness-list nor final greeting.

The archbp is not styled legate; Henry II is almost certainly alive.

Henry II's charter, confirming to Bordesley among other things 'ius advocationis et dominationis (*sic*) ecclesie eiusdem ville de Terdebigga', is pd in *Recueil des actes* i 221–2 no. 117 (dated 1156 × 1159) from an original in BL ms. Cotton Nero C iii fo. 176 (reading 'dñationis'). *Cal. Ch. Rolls* ii 64–65 has an inspeximus of this charter of Henry II (reading 'donationis') with a charter of the empress Matilda given at the same time. For earlier charters of the empress (1141 × 1142), see *Regesta regum* iii nos. 115–6; no. 115 reads 'dominationis', no. 116 'dñationis'.

236. Boxgrove priory

Confirmation for the monks of Boxgrove of all their possessions as confirmed by archbishop Richard and bishop Seffrid of Chichester, in the charters which archbishop Baldwin has inspected.

[April 1185 × Jan. 1186]

B = BL ms. Cotton Claud. A vi (Boxgrove cartulary) fo. 63r (60r). s. xiii med.
 C = Ibid. fo. 64r (61r) in inspeximus by archbp Hubert (*EEA* iii no. 342).

Pd (transl.) from B in *Boxgrove chartulary* 58 no. 68.

Universis sancte matris ecclesie filiis ad quos presentes littere pervenerint B.*a* dei gratia Cantuariensis archiepiscopus totius Anglie primas eternam in domino salutem. Ad universitatis vestre notitiam [fo. 63v] volumus pervenire nos tam bone memorie patris et predecessoris nostri Ricardi Cantuariensis archiepiscopi quam venerabilis fratris nostri S.*b* Cicestrensis episcopi autentica scripta inspexisse, quibus dilecti filii nostri monachi de Boxgrava possessiones sibi et ecclesie sue fidelium devotione collatas impetraverunt confirmari. Nos igitur que a predicto predecessore nostro et memorato episcopo rationabiliter ordinata sunt debito firmitate gaudere volentes, predictorum monachorum possessiones, sicut eas canonice ac rationabiliter adepti sunt et in memoratis scriptis continetur expressum, auctoritate qua fungimur confirmamus et sigilli nostri appositione communimus, inhibentes nequis memoratos monachos super possessionibus predictis iniuste vel citra iuris ordinem molestare aut gravare presumat.

a add -alduinus B *corrector*   *b add* -effridus B *corrector*

This or the next charter is no. 11 in the list of confirmations on fo. 4r (1r) of the cartulary, no. 12 in the list on fo. 15r (12r): 'Confirmatio generalis'. The number *xii* is beside the text. Since the agreement with the abbot of Lessay is not mentioned (see below, no. 237) the order of documents in the cartulary is probably correct. This charter therefore antedates Baldwin's legation.

237. Boxgrove priory

Confirmation for the monks of Boxgrove of their possessions granted by William of St John and his ancestors and his knights, as confirmed by bishops Hilary, John, and Seffrid of Chichester. Confirmation also of the written agreement about the ordering of the convent of Boxgrove made by abbot Thomas of Lessay.   [Jan. 1186 × Feb. 1187]

B = BL ms. Cotton Claud. A vi (Boxgrove cartulary) fo. 63v (60v). s. xiii med.
Pd (transl.) from B in *Boxgrove chartulary* 58–59 no. 69.

Balduinus dei gratia Cantuariensis archiepiscopus totius Anglie primas et apostolice sedis legatus omnibus Christi fidelibus ad quos presentes littere pervenerint illam que est in domino salutem. Quoniam ad officii nostri pertinet debitum paci et tranquillitati*a* subiectorum nostrorum et maxime virorum religiosorum attentius providere, possessiones ecclesie sancte Marie de Boxgrava a nobili viro Willelmo de Sancto Iohanne et antecessoribus suis eiusdemque Willelmi militibus in sustentationem fratrum ibidem deo servientibus pia consideratione ad assensu Hylarii, Iohannis, et Seffridi Cicestrensis ecclesie episcoporum collatas, in nostra suscipimus protectione et omnes donationes tam veteres [fo. 64r] quam novas ipsius Willelmi et antecessorum suorum necnon et militum eiusdem Willelmi, sicut predicte ecclesie de Boxgrava karitatis affectu et rationabiliter facte sunt et episcopali auctoritate confirmate, stabilem et firmam esse concedimus et auctoritate qua fungimur confirmamus. Concessionem quoque venerabilis viri Thome abbatis de Exaquio quam dilectis filiis nostris conventui de Boxgrava super cuiusdam dispositionis conventione domus de Boxgrava scripto autentico se fecisse protestatur, sicut iuste et rationabiliter facta est, stabilem et perpetuam esse concedimus et auctoritatis nostre robore et sigilli nostri appositione communimus. Hiis testibus: P. Blesensi archidiacono Bathoniensi, magistro Henrico de Norhanton, magistro Silvestro, Iohanne de Exonia, Willelmo Prudum, Gileberto filio Willelmi, Galfrido Forti, et aliis.

a transquillitati B

This charter is no. 13 in the list of confirmations on fo. 15r (12r) of the cartulary: 'Eiusdem ... confirmatio secunda'. The no. *xiii* is beside the text.

The 'conventio' (after 1178) of abbot Thomas of Lessay and the prior of Boxgrove is pd (*Mon. Ang.* iv 647) along with various benefactors' charters, all taken from the cartulary. For the episcopal charters see *Chichester acta* 87, 116–21, 134–41 nos. 20, 58–60, 76–78.

Peter of Blois was sent to the Curia by the archbp late in Feb. 1187 and did not rejoin him until Dec. 1187.

238. Bradenstoke priory

Confirmation for the canons of Bradenstoke of its churches and other possessions (enumerated) as confirmed by a charter of king Henry II.
[Jan. 1186 × Dec. 1187]

B = BL ms. Cotton Vitell. A xi (Bradenstoke cartulary) fo. 144r. s. xiv med.
C = BL ms. Stowe 925 (Bradenstoke cartulary) fo. 27v. s. xiv ex.

Pd (calendar) from B and C in *Bradenstoke cartulary* 29 no. 6.

B.[a] dei gratia Cantuariensis archiepiscopus totius Anglie primas et apostolice sedis legatus omnibus Christi fidelibus ad quos presens scriptum pervenerit eternam in domino salutem. Ea que in subsidium religionis a Christi fidelibus in nostra provincia pia consideratione collata sunt et auctentico scripto confirmata, ad perpetue[b] [fo. 144v] firmitatis securitatem nostra qua fungimur auctoritate duximus communire. Quapropter ad universitatis vestre notitiam volumus pervenire quod nos domini nostri illustris Anglorum regis Henrici secundi viso confirmationis scripto dilectis filiis nostris canonicis de Bradenestok' super possessionibus in perpetuam elemosinam sibi collatis indulto, id quod a regia magestate confirmatum est nostro quoque scripto duximus communire, eas possessiones que in carta domini regis continentur expresse[c] in nostris litteris certis vocabulis exprimentes: ex dono videlicet Walteri de Saresburia totam villam de Bradenstok' et quicquid ad eam pertinet cum ecclesia eiusdem ville et unam hydam terre in Echesigneton'[d] et quicquid ad eam pertinet et capellam de Lacha cum omnibus pertinentiis suis; ex dono comitis Patricii totam villam de Wylcote et quicquid ad eam pertinet et ecclesiam eiusdem ville cum omnibus pertinentiis suis et salinam quandam de Canefort que est apud Waldefletam cum omnibus pertinentiis suis; ex dono comitis Willelmi de Saresburia ecclesiam de Canefort cum omnibus pertinentiis suis et capellam sancti Andree de Cettra; ex dono Willelmi de Littelcote terram illam que adiacet vicinius et competentius terre de Bradenestok'; terram etiam illam quam Willelmus Malcuvenant prefate ecclesie rationabiliter dedit; ex dono Ricardi Cotel unam virgatam terre in villa de Laka, et apud Eston' ecclesiam eiusdem ville cum omnibus pertinentiis suis; et ex dono Willelmi de Eston' quinquaginta acras de inlanda sua concessione Osberti filii sui cum tribus mansuris, et unam virgatam terre in eadem villa quam predicti canonici rationabiliter emerunt de Reginaldo de Sancto Paulo. Ut igitur quod a regia magestate predictis fratribus super iamdictis possessionibus concessum est et confirmatum·perpetuam habeat stabilitatem, ipsius domini regis concessionem*e* sicut rationabiliter factum est firmam esse concedimus et scripti nostri munimine roboramus. Hiis testibus: magistro Henrico de Northamton', magistro Silvestro, magistro Radulfo de Sancto Martino, et multis aliis.*f*

a H. C   *b* ad perpetue C, *oblit. in* B   *c* expressa BC   *d* Echesingetingeton B *and in* C *by second hand over erasure*   *e* confessionem B   *f* add etc. B

The royal charter is calendared in *Bradenstoke cartulary* 161–2 no. 549, dated by the editor 6 Oct. 1174 × April 1179. In confirming the properties named there, the archbp does not include others named in privileges of pope Lucius III in 1182 and 1184 (*PUE* i 483–5, 496–500 nos. 209, 220; *Cartulary* 32–3 nos. 18–9). Cf. *EEA* iii no. 346.

239. Brecon priory

Confirmation for the monks of Brecon of the charter of bishop Peter of St David's which the archbishop has seen. The bishop has confirmed the gifts of the patrons of the priory, Bernard of Neufmarché, Roger earl of Hereford and his brothers, Walter, Henry, and Mahel, and William de Braose, lord of Brecon, and other benefactors.   [March 1188]

B = Bodl. ms. Carte 108 (SC 10553: collections for Wales) fo. 276v. (272v, 136v). s. xviii in. C = BL ms. Harl 6976 (M. Hutton's collections) fo. 11r, abstract with witness-list. s. xvii ex.

Pd from B in *Archaeologia Cambrensis* 4s. xiv (1883) 42, attributed to archbp Boniface; (calendar) in *Welsh. ep. acts* i 292 (D 243) identified as of archbp Baldwin.

Hiis testibus: G. archidiacono Menevensi, magistro Alexandro Walensi, magistro Silvestro, Gilberto filio Willelmi, Reginaldo de Oilli, Ricardo de Umframvill, Galfrido Forti, Eustachio de Wilton, et aliis.

The archbp is not styled legate. The attestation of archdn Gerald indicates a date during the archbp's Welsh visitation in March 1188, when he was accompanied by Giraldus Cambrensis, archdn of Brecon (here styled 'Menevensis'), and when he met bp Peter of St David's (*Welsh ep. acts* i 292 (D 242)).

Bp Peter's charter is printed from B (fo. 279v) in *Archaeol. Cambr.* 4s. xiv 137–8; and various charters of the patrons ibid. 143–54, *Mon. Ang.* iii 251–3, 264–6, *Cal. Ch. Rolls* iii 444–5. See also 'Charters of the earldom of Hereford 1095–1201' ed. D. Walker, *Camden miscellany XXII* (R. Hist. Soc. 1964).

240. Burton abbey

Inspeximus and confirmation for the abbot and monks of Burton of the charter granted by archbishop Richard, confirming their liberties and possessions.   [Jan. 1186 × Dec. 1187]

B = BL ms. Loan 30 (Burton cartulary) fo. 23va (12va). s. xiii in. C = Burton-upon-Trent Library, D 27/164 in inspeximus with other charters inspected in Benedictine Gen. Chapter, Gloucester, 26 March 1260.

Pd (brief calendar) from B in *Burton chartulary* 18.

Baldwinus dei gratia Cantuariensis archiepiscopus totius Anglie primas et apostolice sedis legatus universis Christi fidelibus ad quos presentes littere pervenerint illam que est in domino salutem. Ad universitatis vestre notitiam volumus pervenire dilectos filios nostros abbatem et monachos de Burthon' scriptum auctenticum bone memorie Ricardi predecessoris nostri Cantuariensis archiepiscopi nobis in hec verba exhibuisse. Ricardus dei gratia Cantuariensis archiepiscopus*a* ... [*above, no. 63*] ... [fo. 23vb] et pluribus aliis. Ut igitur concessio et confirmatio memorati predecessoris nostri firmam et perpetuam habeat stabilitatem, auctoritati ipsius nostre auctoritatis robur dignum duximus accommodare et ipsius concessionis ac protectionis scriptum sicut iuste et rationabiliter memoratis fratribus de Burton' indultum est firmum esse concedimus et auctoritatis nostre patrocinio idem communimus. Hiis testibus: magistro Henrico de Norh', magistro Silvestro, Willelmo de Sotindon',*b* Reginaldo de Oyli, Willelmo Prudume, Ricardo de Humframvile, Eustachio de Wilton, Galfrido Forti, et aliis.

a add etc. de verbo ad verbum sicut precedens usque ad hanc clausulam *and om. rest of Richard's charter* C   *b* Sotindon': Sodinton BC

241. See of Canterbury

Institution of a fraternity throughout the province of Canterbury to last for seven years from the present year of the Lord's incarnation 1186. The blessed archbishop Anselm and St Thomas the martyr intended to found a collegiate church near Canterbury in honour of St Stephen, but left the project to be carried out by their successors. St Thomas has churches dedicated to him abroad, but none in England. Archbishop Baldwin has decided to carry out the project, with the approval of the pope, the king, the suffragans of Canterbury, and the magnates of the land. For those who join the fraternity and send a donation annually for the fabric or bequeath it at death he remits a third of the penance for those sins truly confessed for which they are doing seven years or more of penance; if their penance is less, sixty days are remitted. Slight sins and those forgotten, and offences against parents which fall short of violence, are covered by the penance imposed for other sins. Members of the fraternity are in some circumstances pardoned certain penalties concerning access to churches and christian burial. They share, more-

over, in all the masses, prayers, and observances for the departed in all
the churches of the province. Their children below the age of fifteen
enjoy the benefit of the fraternity.   [Nov. 1186 × 24 March 1187]

B = Lambeth Palace ms. 415 (Ch. Ch. letter-collection) fo. 2v. s. xiii in.

Pd from B in *Ep. Cant.* 8–9 no. 8.

The archbp is styled legate (but the primatial title is omitted). The year of
incarnation probably begins with the Annunciation. The reference to papal
approval (see below) determines the earlier limit of date. The address is
'omnibus Christi fidelibus ad quos presens scriptum pervenerit'.
      For the project to found a collegiate church at Hackington, outside Canter-
bury, which aroused violent opposition from the monks of Christ Church, see
Gervas. Cant. *Opp.* i 29–68, 337–484, and many letters in *Ep. Cant.* See also
Stubbs in *Ep. Cant.* pp. xl--xci. For the comment by Gervase on this letter see
Opp i 361. On 1 Oct. 1186 pope Urban III authorized the archbp to found a
collegiate church in honour of St Stephen and St Thomas, but on 9 May 1187
ordered the archbp to cease work on the building, not to appoint canons, and to
suppress the fraternity (*Ep. Cant.* 7, 34–35 nos. 6, 40–41; Gervase, *Opp.* i 58–59,
363–5). An undated royal confirmation is preserved (*Ep. Cant.* 16–17 no. 21, cf.
a later letter from Henry II (? Aug. 1187) which confirms the pope's original
indult. Ibid. 7–8 no. 7).
      For comparable fraternities in English churches see Cheney, *Med. texts and*
studies 359–61.

242.   See of Canterbury

Notification to the suffragans of Canterbury that the archbishop's
predecessors, Anselm and the blessed martyr Thomas, and others,
intended to found a collegiate church with prebends formed out of parish
churches in the archbishops' gift, where clerks should live in common
and worship God in the service of the church of Canterbury. This was
intended not only for the advantage of the church of Canterbury but for
the strengthening of the whole realm and church of England. The
archbishop, having obtained approval from pope Urban III and king
Henry and those of his fellow bishops he was able to consult, has begun
to found a church in honour of God and the martyr Thomas near to
Canterbury. Because the monks of Holy Trinity, Canterbury, try to
obstruct the plan, the archbishop asks that the suffragans shall address
letters to the pope in support, using if they wish the form of letter which
the king has sent. Will they please send their sealed letters, when
written, with copies of them, to the archbishop. They should be moved
by the consideration that the martyr, although honoured in other lands
by many churches dedicated to him, is as it were a stranger in his own
country and province, where altars have been raised to him but no
church dedicated in his honour.   [Nov. 1186 × 24 March 1187]

B = Lambeth Palace ms. 415 (Ch. Ch. letter-collection) fo. 4v. s. xiii in.

Pd from B in *Ep. Cant.* 17–18 no. 22.

The archbp is styled legate (but the primatial title is omitted). Probably written at about the same time as the institution of the fraternity of the fabric (above, no. 241). The wording corresponds at several points, but the dedication to St Stephen proposed by Baldwin's predecessors is not mentioned here. The parish church of Hackington was, it seems, already dedicated to St Stephen (Gervase, *Opp.* i 337).

The letter-collection includes the letters addressed to the pope in support of the project by the bps of Ely and Exeter, and records others. The former (Geoffrey Ridel) states that saint Thomas ('cui tunc temporis eius archidiaconus adhesi') often expressed to him in conversation his desire to carry out the project (*Ep. Cant.* 18–21 nos. 23, 24). These were probably written after the appeal of the monks to Rome, which appointed 8 March 1187 as the term, and which was announced to the archbp 8 × 14 Dec. 1186 (ibid. 8 no. 9 and Gervase, *Opp.* i 38, 343–4, 352).

243. See of Canterbury

Exhortation to Robert de Bechetun, Master Samson, and other canons of Hackington, who serve God in the church of the blessed martyrs Stephen and Thomas, to rejoice and praise the blessed Virgin Mary and the two martyrs, extolling God because of his works on their behalf. The counsel of Achitophel is turned into foolishness and mandates which their enemies had obtained from the apostolic see are quashed and annulled. Let them trust in God, who exalts those who mourn to safety, and no longer fear threats nor let their hearts be troubled by rumours.

[Nov. 1187]

B = Lambeth Palace ms. 415 (Ch. Ch. letter-collection) fo. 29ra. s. xiii in.

Pd from B in *Ep. Cant.* 112 no. 140.

Protocol omitted. The letter refers by implication to the death (20 Oct.) of pope Urban III, who had supported the monks of Christ Church in their opposition to the archbp over the collegiate church of Hackington (cf. Gervase, *Opp.* i 389, 391), and follows receipt of the letter of Gregory VIII (Ferrara, 29 Oct. 1187: *Ep. Cant.* 112 no. 139) which annulled letters obtained from pope Urban against the archbp and his clerks (Ferrara, 3 Oct. 1187: *Ep. Cant.* 100–4 nos. 128–30). The archbp's letter is referred to by Gervase (*Opp.* i 422).

244. See of Canterbury

Notification that, at the request of king Richard and the archbishop and his suffragans, the bishop of Rochester with prior Osbern and the monks of Rochester have granted part of their curia at Lambeth, on the Thames, to the archbishop and his successors for them to build a church in honour of the blessed martyr Thomas, with dwellings for the canons who will minister there. The bishop and monks of Rochester have also granted twenty-four acres and one perch outside the curia *and the service from the four acres of Hawise. They reserve their rights over the parish church of Lambeth and its parishioners and tithes and offerings except from the parts granted to the archbishop. Neither the archbishop and his household nor the canons and their households shall acquire any of the land retained and occupied by the monks and their men without leave of the bishop and convent. In exchange for this the archbishop has granted to the bishop and convent of Rochester a sheep-walk* (bercaria) *in the Isle of Grain which is held by John son of Eilgar at an annual rent of sixty shillings and certain services, to be free of all service to the archbishop. He has also granted that the service due from three other sheep-walks in the Isle of Grain, which the bishop and monks of Rochester used to hold of the archbishop, shall be paid to the archbishop by the monks, and the tenant shall be answerable to them. The agreement is corroborated by the seals of the archbishop and his fellow bishops and enrolled before the king's justices in the exchequer. The first year of king Richard.* [? Normandy. March 1190]

B = BL ms. Cotton Domit. A x (Rochester register) fo. 164r (165r). s. xiii in.

Pd from B (curtailed) in *Reg. Roff.* 434, *Ep. Cant.* 547 no. 565, and A. C. Ducarel, *Hist. and antiquities of Lambeth parish* (1786) App. 24–5 (in Nichols, *Bibliotheca* vol. ii no. XXXIX). The ms. appears to record two versions of the ending, of which the second is omitted in the editions cited. In B the words 'hanc concessionem nostram et mutuam conventionem' continue with I below, followed without break by II.

I

ut inposterum firmiori gaudeat stabilitate tam nostri quam coepiscoporum nostrorum sigilli appositione fecimus roborari et coram iustitiis domini regis apud scaccarium inrollari. Facta est autem hec conventio anno primo coronationis Ricardi illustris regis Anglie. Huic carte apposita sunt vii sigilla.

II

presenti scripto et sigilli nostri appositione roboravimus. Facta est autem hec conventio anno primo coronationis regis illustris Anglie Ricardi.

The archbp is not styled legate in the title, which follows a general address. The agreement is said to be in the year after Richard's coronation (3 Sept. 1189) but can be dated more closely. It came after archbp Baldwin's abandonment of his plan for a collegiate church at Hackington (early Dec. 1189: *Ep. Cant.* 323 no.

335) and before he left France on crusade, probably when the king was at hand and at least some of Canterbury's suffragans were present. The king confirmed the transaction at Rouen, 20 March 1190 (*Ep. Cant.* 324 no. 337 and *Cartae antiquae 11–20* (PRS n. s. 33 1960) 96–97 no. 460). The archbp and the bp of Rochester were both at court on this day, as well as many other bps (*Itinerary of Richard I* 28). Probably the archbp's notification was drafted by then. The absence of witnesses and of precise date in this only copy does not permit certainty about the time or times at which original engrossments were prepared.

After Baldwin's departure to the East and his death at Acre the plans for setting up a collegiate church at Lambeth lapsed. That this transaction, or part of it, was carried through emerges from a consequential grant to Rochester by John son of Eilgar (*Reg. Roff.* 435, here called John de Grean) and from archbp Hubert's reference to the marsh in 'Gren' which archbp Baldwin had given to the monks of Rochester. Baldwin's agreement was eventually superseded by archbp Hubert's more comprehensive exchange with Rochester (*EEA* iii no. 370).

245. See of Canterbury

Notification that the archbishop has, for the period of his pilgrimage, committed to the bishop of Rochester the care and administration of the spiritualities and temporalities in Kent and elsewhere of the dioceses of Canterbury and Rochester and of the peculiars in the immediate jurisdiction of the archbishop 'ut ipse ... vices nostras ... exequatur'. *He ratifies whatever the bishop shall do on his behalf in spiritual matters with the advice of Master Samson, Master Ralph de Sancto Martino, Master William de Sancta Fide, or any two or one of them; likewise in temporal matters, where the bishop shall use the advice of Robert de Bekynton, Roger de Cheryton, and Roger de Gruscy the archbishop's steward.* [? Feb. × 6 March 1190]

B = Maidstone, Kent Archives Office DRc/R 3 (Rochester registrum temporalium) fo. 138r. s. xiv med.

Pd from B in *Reg. Roff.* 50 (reading 'H' for 'B' in title); Churchill, *Canterbury administration* ii 1.

The title, following a general address, does not style the archbp legate. Presumably issued very shortly before he left England on 6 March 1190. He took the pilgrim's staff and scrip from the altar in Christ Church on 24 Feb. (Gervas. Cant. *Opp.* i 484–5).

Ralph de Diceto (ii 75) naturally refers to the rights of the bp of London as dean of the province: Baldwin 'de communi consilio suffraganeorum suorum vices suas episcopo Lundoniensi Ricardo commisit. Rofensis episcopus, ab antiquo vicarius archiepiscopi, tam in territorio Cantiae quam in ecclesiis maneriorum archiepiscopi, curam pastoralem suscepit'. It was later reported to archbp Stephen by James Salvagius that in the time of archbps Baldwin and Hubert the custodians of temporalities paid the bp for expenses incurred in performing his duties at Canterbury in the absence of the archbps, and Robert de Grusci is named as Baldwin's steward when the archbp was in Syria (*Reg. Roff.* 98).

246. See of Canterbury

Mandate to bishop Gilbert of Rochester about filling the vacant see of Worcester. Since it is an old right of the church of Canterbury that elections of suffragans are invalid if made without the advice and consent of the metropolitan, the bishop is to act for the archbishop in this occasion with bishop Richard of London. When an election has been confirmed by the archbishop's authority, the suffragans are to be summoned by the bishop of London in the usual way to attend the consecration of the elect in the church of Canterbury as custom requires lest, if it were performed elsewhere in the archbishop's absence, disturbance or obstruction should arise or the church of Canterbury be prejudiced.   [May × June 1190]

B = Lambeth Palace ms. 415 (Ch. Ch. letter-collection) fo. 85r. s. xiii in.

Pd from B in *Ep. Cant.* 324–5 no. cccxxxviii.

Bp William of Worcester died 2/3 May 1190, when the archbp was in France. Robert FitzRalph was elected 1 July, and consecrated at Canterbury 5 May 1191. The emphasis in this letter on consecration at Canterbury shows a rare coincidence of views between the archbp and his cathedral convent (cf. Cheney, *Med. texts and studies* 88–89). The archbp is not styled legate.

247. Canterbury: suffragans of the province

Instructions to the suffragans of the church of Canterbury about the levy of a tax (collecta) *for the relief of the Holy Land. Heraclius, patriarch of Jerusalem, and other great men of the Holy Land, being driven by necessity, have come to England to seek help from the king against the invaders of the Latin kingdom of Jerusalem. King Henry has made a lavish grant from his treasure and has ordained by the common advice of bishops, earls, and barons a levy which the bishops are to organize in every parish of their dioceses, according to the method described below, for the relief of Jerusalem.*
                                      [March 1185 × Jan. 1186]

Petri Blesensis opera i 307–9 no. 98.

The archbp is not styled legate. The patriarch Heraclius arrived in England late in January 1185. On the circumstances of his mission see H.E. Mayer, *EHR* xcvii (1982) 731–4. The decision on the tax was probably made at a great council at London on 18 March, after a meeting between Heraclius and the king at Reading. On 16 April the patriarch left England with the king.

   The surviving texts of the letter do not include the detailed instructions said to be appended; nor are they known from any other source. The patriarch had brought a letter from Lucius III, urging the king to give all the support he had previously promised for the Holy Land (JL 15151, *Gesta Henrici* i 332–3, etc.).

See W. E. Lunt, *Financial relations of the papacy with England to 1327* (Mediaeval Academy of America, 1939) 177, 419, who observes that the tax probably fell upon both clergy and laymen; but nothing is recorded of the result.

248. Canterbury: Christ Church

Notification that on the presentation of the prior and convent of Christ Church, Canterbury, the archbishop has granted to John of London, nephew of the blessed martyr Thomas, the church of Halstow in perpetual alms, saving a yearly pension of a mark to the monks.

[Jan. × May 1186]

A = Canterbury, D. & C. C.A. H 90 (N 69, H 183). Endorsed, s. xiii ex.: Baldwinus archiepiscopus instituit .I. de Lond' nepotem sancti Thome martiris in ecclesia sancte Margarete de Halestowe . ad presentacionem nostram . sub annua pensione unius marce, *and* .VIII. *del.* Approx. 180 × 106 + 27 mm. Sealing d. q. 2; tag and seal lost.

B = Ibid. Reg. E fo. 61r (31r). s. xiii ex. C = Ibid. Reg. A fo. 164v (186v). s. xiii/xiv.

Universis sancte matris ecclesie filiis ad quos presentes littere pervenerint .B. dei gratia Cantuariensis archiepiscopus . totius Anglie primas et apostolice sedis legatus ⁒ eternam in domino salutem. Ad universitatis vestre noticiam volumus pervenire . nos ad presentationem dilectorum filiorum nostrorum prioris et conventus ecclesie Christi Cantuariensis dedisse et concessisse dilecto filio nostro Iohanni de Londonia nepoti beati martiris Thome ecclesiam sancte Margarite de Halgestowa in perpetuam elemosinam salva pensione unius marce quam idem . Iohannes ⁒ memoratis monachis in duobus terminis singulis annis tenetur persolvere . imfra videlicet .xv. dies post Pasca ⁒ dimidiam marcam . et imfra .xv. dies post festum sancti Michaelis ⁒ dimidiam marcam. Quare volumus et precipimus ut prefatus .I. quem in predicta ecclesia canonice instituimus ⁒ eandem ecclesiam quiete in perpetuum et pacifice sub prenotata teneat et possideat pensione. Et ut hec nostra donatio firma et stabilis perseveret ⁒ eam presentis scripti munimine duximus robborandam. Hiis testibus Willelmo Gloecestriensi et magistro Petro Blesensi ⁒ Bathoniensi archidiaconis . magistro Silvestro . magistro Henrico . Iohanne de Exonia . Galfrido Forti . Eustachio . et aliis.,

William of Northolt, archdn of Gloucester, was elected to the see of Worcester *c.*25 May 1186 (cf. no. 273). The witnesses Mr Henry and Eustace are almost certainly Mr Henry of Northampton and Eustace de Wilton who witness the archbp's grant to another nephew of the martyr named John (below, no. 249). The similarity of witness-lists in nos. 248 and 249 suggests that the institutions occurred on the same occasion, but the documents are not in the same hand. The grant of a vicarage in the church of Halstow by prior Alan and the convent is D. & C. C.A. H 89, from which it appears that John of London was son of St Thomas's sister Agnes.

This church of Lower Halstow (east of Rochester, dioc. Canterbury) must not be confused with the church of High Halstow (across the R. Medway, to the north, dioc. Rochester). Both are dedicated to St Margaret.

249. Canterbury: Christ Church

Notification that on the presentation of the prior and convent of Christ Church, Canterbury, the archbishop has granted to John, nephew of the blessed martyr Thomas, the church of St Mary Bothaw in London in perpetual alms, saving a yearly pension of five shillings to the monks.

[Jan. × May 1186]

A = Canterbury, D. & C. C.A. L 39 (L 398), badly holed. Endorsed (on three lines on the top half of the dorse) s. xii/xiii: Magistro Ricardo [cancellario Ranulfo t]h' Sar' . magistris G. de Bocland' . S. de Siwell' . G. de Insula . W. de ... et W. de Calna . W. de Melan' . Gervasio . I. de Sancto Laurentio . Simone de Camera . Adam de Wasingeham . Iohanne de Brancestr' . Ric' Aaron; s. xiii ex.: Baldewinus archiepiscopus contulit ecclesiam ' sancte Marie ' de Bothag' in Lond' ad nostram presentationem . Iohanni nepoti sancti Thome martiris . sub annua pensione .v. solidorum. Approx. 174 × 76 + 22 mm. Sealing d. q. 2; tag and seal and part of fold lost. The upper endorsement is perhaps the draft of a witness-list prepared for a charter of archbp Hubert.

B = Ibid. Reg. B fo. 244v (249v). s. xiv/xv. Missing parts of A are replaced below from B, in square brackets.

Universis sancte matris ecclesie filiis ad quos presentes littere pervenerint .B. dei [gratia Cantuariensis archiepiscopus totius An-]glie primas et apostolice sedis legatus : eternam in domino salutem. Ad universitatis vestre noticiam volumus pervenire . [nos ad presentationem dilect-]orum filiorum nostrorum prioris et conventus ecclesie Christi Cantuariensis dedisse et concessisse dilecto filio nostro .Iohanni. nepoti beati martiris Thome ecclesiam sancte Marie de Bothag' in Londonia . in perpetuam elemosinam . salva pensione .v. solidorum quam idem Iohannes memoratis monachis in festo beati Andree apostoli singulis annis : tenetur persolvere. Quare volumus et precipimus ut prefatus Iohannes memoratam ecclesiam ita quiete et pacifice possideat : sicut unquam aliquis predecessorum suorum sub prenotata pensione quietius et melius noscitur possedisse. Ut autem hec nostra donatio firma et inconvulsa perseveret . eam presentis scripti patrocinio duximus roborandam. Hiis testibus . Willelmo Glowecestriensi . et magistro .P. Blesensi . Bathoniensi archidiaconis . magistro Henrico [de] Norhamton' . magistro Silvestro . Iohanne de Exonia . Eustachio de Wilton' . Galfrido Forti et aliis.

Cf. no. 248 above for date.

The grant of a perpetual vicarage in the church by prior Alan and the convent, in chirograph form, is D. & C. C.A. L 4. It describes the recipient as nephew of St Thomas 'ex sorore sua Rohesia'. The church had been granted (1145 × 1161) to Christ Church 'et nominatim priori eiusdem ecclesie' by Peter 'sacerdos de Bothahe', whose patrimony it was. The prior was to receive a pension of five shillings yearly (*Literae cantuarienses* (RS) iii 357 and Saltman, *Theobald* 268 no. 41, where dated 1141 × 1161).

250. Canterbury: Christ Church

Mandate to the convent of Canterbury to enforce thorough observance of the ordinance he has made for the management of their house on account of the absence of the prior, as their brethren who bring this letter will expound.   [Jan. 1187]

B = Lambeth Palace ms. 415 fo. 18rb. s. xiii in.

Pd from B in *Ep. Cant.* 71 no. 84.

Protocol omitted. For the date and circumstances see Gervas. Cant. *Opp.* i 347–8. Prior Honorius had left England 19 Dec. 1186, to appeal in the Curia against the archbp's foundation at Hackington (cf. above, nos. 241–3). The convent refused to receive the three monks to whom the archbp, acting on his own authority, had entrusted the custody of the house (*Ep. Cant.* 71–72 no. 85).

251. Canterbury: Christ Church

Mandate to Geoffrey, subprior of Christ Church, Canterbury, to forbid Ralph of Orpington and John of Bocking, by the archbishop's author- ity, to leave the cloister or to take part in the management of the church.
[? April 1187]

B = Lambeth Palace ms. 415 fo. 7v. s. xiii in.

Pd from B in *Ep. Cant.* 28 no. 32.

The archbp is styled legate. His mandate is reported in a letter of the convent to pope Urban III after 11 April 1187 (*Ep. Cant.* 28–29 no. 33). The two monks named, described by Stubbs as stewards of the manors (ibid. pp. 29, 70), defied the order and were excommunicated by the archbp (below, no. 252). One Ralph of Orpington, with another monk named John of Dover, appeared as proctors of Christ Church in the king's court in a suit over land in Southchurch, 4 May 1198 (Canterbury, D. & C. C. A. S 231). A Ralph of Orpington was involved long afterwards in the manufacture of the Magna Carta of St Thomas (cf. above, no. 6).

252. Canterbury: Christ Church

Notification to Geoffrey, subprior of Christ Church, Canterbury, that the archbishop has excommunicated John of Bocking and Ralph of Orpington, monks, on account of their manifest disobedience and insufferable contempt for the archbishop's order. Mandate to treat them

as incorrigible excommunicates and to order his brethren to shun them
until they have made proper satisfaction. [23 June × 25 July 1187]

B = Lambeth Palace ms. 415 fo. 15rb. s. xiii in.

Pd from B in *Ep. Cant.* 60 no. 73.

Protocol omitted. For the date see Stubbs, 60 n. 3. The two monks, excommunicated because they resisted the archbp's attempt to take over the conventual
estates (ibid. 70 no. 83, cf. 64–65 no. 77) were absolved immediately on arrival at
the Curia, whither they took the convent's appeal (ibid. 75 no. 90).

253. Canterbury: Christ Church

Notification to bishop Gilbert of Rochester that at the king's court at
Alençon Roger Noreis, monk of Christ Church, accepted the office of
cellarer at the archbishop's hand and Robert the sacrist the office of
sacrist. Mandate to the bishop to commit to Roger and Robert all the
possessions of their offices on the archbishop's behalf (vice nostra), *to*
administer their offices by authority of the archbishop; also to commit to
Simon, monk and formerly chamberlain, on the archbishop's authority
(ex parte nostra), *the custody and ordering of all things which pertain*
to the chamber.   [28 Aug. × Sept. 1187]

B = Lambeth Palace ms. 415 fo. 22vb. s. xiii in.

Pd from B in *Ep. Cant.* 89 no. 111.

Protocol omitted. For the date and circumstances see Stubbs, *Ep. Cant.* pp. lii–
liii, cxxx, and above, nos. 250–1.
        The letter was sent as a letter close (see above, pp. xlvii–viii).

254. Canterbury: Christ Church

A letter to pope Clement III, refuting the slanders of the monks of
Canterbury. The pope knows how pertinaciously and at what expense
and by what various devices the monks have tried to prove that the
archbishop is disobedient to the Roman church. He vigorously defends
himself from the charge of rebelliousness in thought or deed.

[*c.*Feb. 1188]

B = Lambeth Palace ms. 415 fo. 46r. s. xiii in.

Pd from B in *Ep. Cant.* 173–4 no. 191.

Protocol omitted. Clement III was elected 19 Dec. 1187 after the death of pope
Gregory VIII. This was probably written before the receipt of Clement's
mandate of 26 Jan. 1188 which ordered the destruction of the 'chapel' of
Hackington and forbade the establishment of canons there, and which was served
on the archbp by the monks on 22 March (*Ep. Cant.* 174–5, 204–5, nos. 193,
223).

The report to the convent from br. John de Bremble in the Curia (*c*.17 March) shows that the archbp had either written earlier with more specific complaints or else left it to the bearers of this letter to enlarge on the monks' offences by word of mouth (ibid. 193–4 no. 209).

255. Canterbury: Christ Church

Notification to (Seffrid) bishop of Chichester, (William) bishop of Worcester, (William) bishop of Hereford, (Walter) abbot of Wal-tham, and Mr Osbern de Camera that he warrants the safe-conduct they have promised to the monks of Canterbury in going, in the king's peace, to the king's court and in returning.   [Feb. 1188]

B = Lambeth Palace ms. 415 fo. 44v. s. xiii in.

Pd from B in *Ep. Cant.* 168 no. 186.

Contained, with a copy of the letters patent of safe-conduct given by the commissioners, in the convent's report to prior Honorius in Rome on the events leading up to their sending of four monks to court on 24 Feb. Mr Osbern has been identified with Mr Osbert, incumbent of Faversham (*EEA* iii no. 394n.).

*256. Canterbury: Christ Church

Mandate to Mr R. and Laurence the archbishop's clerk, expressing surprise that chrism has not been distributed according to custom in his diocese (parochia). *He sends it to them to be distributed by those who usually do so. If the monks of Canterbury will not do so, the addressees are to make careful arrangement for its distribution.*   [April 1188]

Mentioned only, in a report from the convent to prior Honorius in Rome (*Ep. Cant.* 203–4 no. 222); nos. 220–3 explain the circumstances.

The archbishop was in Wales at the time.

257. Canterbury: Christ Church

Report to prior Osbert and the convent of Christ Church on the archbishop's arrival in the Holy Land. He and his companions reached Tyre safe and sound on 16 September, and stayed there for nearly a month, because most of their company fell sick there. After they had recovered they went on, on 12 October, to the crusaders' camp at Acre, where the kings of England and France are expected to arrive shortly. At the time of sending this messenger they are all well, and ask that the monks will, for the love of God, remember them in their prayers.

[Acre. ? 21 Oct. 1190]

B = Lambeth Palace ms. 415 f. 86ra. s. xiii in.

Pd from B in *Ep. Cant.* 328 no. 345.

The archbp is not styled legate.

A letter from the archbp's chaplain to the convent, in very gloomy terms, was probably sent by the same messenger and is said to be despatched on 21 Oct. (*Ep. Cant.* 328 no. 345). The rumour of the kings' coming was unfounded: they wintered in Sicily.

258. Canterbury, priory of St Gregory

Confirmation for the prior and canons of St Gregory, Canterbury, of their possessions present and future.
                [April 1185 × Jan. 1186 or Dec. 1187 × March 1190]

B = Cambridge UL ms. Ll 2 15 (cartulary of St Gregory's) fo. 9vb. s. xiii med.

Pd from B in *St Gregory's cartulary* 12–13 no. 16.

Hiis testibus: magistro Silvestro, magistro Samsone, Willelmo de Sotindon', Adam de Cherringe, Galfrido[a] le Fort', et multis aliis.

[a] Galfridus B

The archbp is not styled legate.

In precisely the same terms as those of archbp Richard's confirmation (above, no. 92), without mention of it. It contains none of the numerous other properties named in the privilege of pope Lucius III, 13 July 1185 (*Cart.* 22–24 no. 27; *PUE* iii 473–4 no. 373). Mr Samson did not go on crusade in 1190.

259. Carisbrooke priory

Confirmation for the monks of Lire of churches, tithes, lands, and other possessions confirmed to them by suffragans of the province of Canterbury.   [April 1185 × Jan. 1186 or Dec. 1187 × March 1190]

B = Évreux, Archives dép. de l'Eure, 1 M 2. Microfilm of transcripts of Dom J. L. Lenoir (s. xviii) vol. XXIII (p. 493 no. 103), now the property of le Marquis de Mathan, S. Pierre-de-Semilly, Manche, taken from a lost cartulary of Lire, s. xiii. C = BL ms. Cotton Otho B xiv (inventory of Sheen charterhouse) fo. 47v (45v, 46v). s. xv ex. Abstract only, in section of Carisbrooke deeds.

Universis Christi fidelibus ad quos presens scriptum pervenerit .B.[a] divina misericordia Cantuariensis archiepiscopus totius Anglie primas perpetuam in domino salutem. Ut ea que viris religiosis pia fidelium largitione et suffraganeorum concessione conferuntur firmiori gaudeant stabilitate, dignum est ut auctoritate nostra muniantur.[b] Nos itaque religionem et honestatem fratrum Lirensis monasterii intuitu benigno considerantes, eis que per scripta autentica tam in ecclesiis, decimis, terris et aliis possessionibus a venerabilibus fratribus provincie nostre episcopis confirmata sunt plenum auctoritatis nostre robur accomodamus et eorum concessiones que rationabiliter facte sunt confirmamus et presentis scripti patrocinio communimus. Testibus: magistro Petro archidiacono Bathoniensi, magistro Silvestro, Willelmo de Sancta Fide, magistro Radulfo de Sancto Martino.

a .B. C; .G. B   *b* muniatur B

The archbp is not styled legate; and the witnesses show that the date is earlier than his departure for the East (cf. no. 245). All four witnesses occur together in other acta (nos. 295, 298).

The abstract in C shows that Carisbrooke, a cell of Lire, kept a text of this charter; but it was not copied in the priory's cartulary (BL ms. Egerton 3667) which contains charters of bps Henry of Winchester and Jocelin of Salisbury.

260. Chester abbey

Grant to St Werburgh's abbey, Chester, of the protection of the church of Canterbury for all its possessions, confirming especially half of the church of Wallasey given by William de Waleya, an annual rent of eight shillings from the church of Handley given by Helto de Boydel, the church of Astbury given by William de Venables, and the church of Prestbury with all its appurtenances which earl Hugh of Chester gave with his body, as his charter witnesses. Abstract only.

[? 24 × 27 June 1187 or 14 × 18 April 1188]

B = BL ms. Harl. 1965 (Chester cartulary) fo. 29v. s. xiv in.

Pd from B in *Chester cartulary* i 335–6 no. 594.

Archbp Baldwin visited Chester abbey 24–27 June 1187 (*Annales cestrienses* ed. R. C. Christie (Record Soc. Lancs. and Cheshire. xiv 1886) 36). He stayed again at Chester for Easter 1188 after preaching the crusade in Wales (Gir. Cambr. *Opp.* vi 139, 142).

261. Order of Cîteaux

Request to the abbots assembled in the general chapter of Cîteaux for their prayers. The archbishop had hoped to be present, but the cares of his new position prevent him.   [early 1185]

Petri Blesensis opera i 302–4 ep. 96; *PL* ccvii 302–4 ep. 96.

The archbp's style is 'dei permissione Cantuariensis ecclesie minister'. The initial is *R*, but the writer is revealed as a Cistercian by some references in the body of the letter (e. g., Memor communionis vestre ... ; Vos enim estis gloria mea et gaudium; Vinculum fraternitatis, professionis communio), so that the archbp must be Baldwin, not Richard, as noted by E. S. Cohn, *EHR* xli (1926) 58. The archbp refers to his office as new. This letter is not in the first collection of Peter of Blois's letters, dated by Southern 1184, and appears in the second collection *c.*1189 (*Medieval humanism* (1970) 130–2). Pd and commented upon by A. Manrique *Annales cistercienses* ii (Lyon 1642) p. 540*b*, anno 1173 cap. II, on the assumption that the author is Richard of Dover; whence J. M. Canivez *Statuta generalium capitulorum ord. Cist.* i (Louvain 1933) 79–81.

262. Combe abbey

Record, in impersonal form, of an agreement between the monks of Combe and the canons of Kenilworth over the churches of Smite and Charlton Horethorne and the chapel of Brinklow, after a dispute in which the monks obtained a mandate from pope Urban III delegating the case to the archbishop.

1187 [25 March 1187 × 24 March 1188]

A = Stratford-upon-Avon, Shakespeare Birthplace Trust, Gregory-Hood collection DR 10/195, from Combe abbey; almost whole right-hand half eaten by rodents. Endorsed, much faded, s. xiv/xv: Composicio inter nos et domum de Kenlwrth super ecclesiam de Smyta; and by Arthur Gregory, s. xvi ex.: capella de Brinkelawe. Approx. 160 × 195 + 24 mm. Sealing d. q. 2; fold torn, originally place for two seals; lefthand tag remains, righthand tag and both seals lost. Top half of chirograph, inverted, divided by a straight cut.

B = BL ms. Cotton Vit. A i (Combe cartulary) fo. 45v (41v). s. xiii med. C = BL ms. Cotton Vit. D xviii fo. 65r. s. xiii. Seen by W. Dugdale, 1637, but no longer among surviving fragments. D = BL ms. Add. 47677 (Kenilworth cartulary) fo. 96r (91r). s. xvi in. E = Bodl. ms. Dugdale 12 (SC 6502) p. 120. Transcript by Dugdale from C.

Pd (calendar) from B by Dugdale, *Hist. of Warwickshire* (1656) 147, whence *Mon. Ang.* v 583.

Pd here from A, collated with BDE, completed so far as possible from B.

[CIROGR]APH[UM]

Anno incarnationis domini m° c ° lxxxvii [cum cognitio cause que vertebatur inter monachos] de Cumba et canonicos de Kynillewrd'. [super ecclesia de Smita et eius pertinentiis et octo marcarum] pensione canonicis a monachis annuatim [prestanda domino archiepiscopo B. totius Anglie] primati et apostolice sedis legato a domino papa Urb[ano III ad conquestionem monachorum delegata] fuisset ∴ controversia exinde suborta huiusmodi [transactione mediante sopita est quod mona]chi in ecclesia de Smita divina facient hon[este celebrari et pro ea de episcopalibus et archidiaco]nalibus satisfacient . nisi per indulgenciam apostolic[e sedis exinde sint immunes. Super octo marcarum] pensione solvenda canonicis expressum [est quod canonicis satisfactum est de sex marcis] annuis in ecclesia de Cherletona. De du[abus marcis annuis satisfactum est eis in capel]la*ᵃ* de Brinkelawa . quam monachi sub an[nua duorum solidorum pensione ad luminare mo]nasterii de C[umba] pro bono pacis ad festum s[ancti Michaelis a canonicis solvenda] concesserunt . ita etiam quod si monachi terras ali[quas de quibus capella de Brinkelawa decimas] ante tempus conventionis huius percipere consuev[it excoluerint decimationes exinde provenientes] capelle persolvent . exceptis novalibus monac[horum si qua forte de nemore ad frugum fer]tilitatem perduxerint et excoluerint . et ex[ceptis ortis] et virgultis intra [sep]ta grangie monachorum . et his que provenerint de nutrimentis animalium suorum. Testibus his . Gilleberto episcopo Roffensi . Radulfo decano London'[b] . m[agistro] ... d' magistro Hugone de Lond' . magistro Radulfo de Sancto Ma[rtino] ... Ricardo de Umframvill' . Iohanne de Exonia cancellario domini arch[iepiscopi] ... Iordano canonico de Warewic' . Gaufrido Forti . magistro Roberti d ... aliis.

^{a} ...la A; capella D; ecclesia BE $\qquad^b$ add et aliis and omit following names BE; om. all witnesses D

Since Urban III (d. 20 Oct. 1187) is not described as dead and the archbp is styled legate, this *transactio* was probably made before the end of Dec. 1187.

An earlier composition is recorded in an undated letter of pope Alexander III (*PUE* iii 413 no. 290 from BL ms. Add. 47677 fo. 95r). For the early history of Smite church see *Charters of the honour of Mowbray*, ed. D. E. Greenway (Brit. Acad. Records of Social and Econ. Hist. n. s. I (1972)) 126–9, 210. Charlton Horethorne also appears in records as Charlton Camvill or Campfield. 'Jordan, canon of Warwick' is probably 'Jordan, *dean* of Warwick' who witnesses two acta of Baldwin as bp of Worcester for Kenilworth (BL ms. Harl. 3650 fos. 45v, 46r), and 'Jordan, dean' in an abridged act of bp William of Hereford for Haughmond (no. 278 below).

263. Combermere abbey

Confirmation for the monks of Combermere of the churches of Acton, Nantwich, Sandon, and Alstonfield, and their chapels, granted to the abbey by William Malbanc and confirmed by bishop Richard of Coventry. [April 1185 × Jan. 1186 or Dec. 1187 × Nov. 1190]

B = copy in inspeximus by archbp Hubert, now lost, which belonged to the family of Cotton of Combermere s. xvii (and probably s. xix in.).

Pd from B in *Mon. Ang.* ii (1661) 914; reprinted *Mon. Ang.* (1846) v 326–7.

The archbp is not styled legate in the title, which follows a general address. William Malbanc, son of the founder of Combermere, died in 1176 (W. Farrer, *Honors and knights' fees* ii (1924) 261), and bp Richard in 1182.

264. Combwell abbey

Confirmation for the canons of Combwell of all their possessions and benefices, as set out in a charter of king Henry II and a confirmation by archbishop Richard. [Jan. 1186 × Dec. 1187]

A = London, College of Arms, Combwell charters XL/2. Endorsed, s. xiii: Confirmacio B. Cant' arch'; s. xvii/xviii: description by Peter Le Neve. Approx. 167 × 158 + 24 mm. Sealing d. q. 2; seal and counterseal (natural wax, brown varnish) badly damaged.

Pd from A in *Archaeologia Cantiana* vi (1864) 206–7 no. XL.

.B. dei gratia Cantuariensis archiepiscopus totius Anglie primas et apostolice sedis legatus . universis Christi fidelibus ad quos presentes littere pervenerint ; illam que est in domino salutem. Ad nostre sollicitudinis pertinet officium subiectos nostros et maxime viros religiosos protegere . et paci et securitati eorum studiosius providere. Eapropter nos devotionem et laudabilem conversationem dilectorum filiorum nostrorum canonicorum de Cumbwell' ex multorum relatione attendentes ; eosdem canonicos et ecclesiam ac possessiones eorum universas in protectione dei et nostra recepimus . et omnes possessiones et beneficia . que ipsis canonicis in subsidium religionis pia devotione collata sunt et tam regia quam episcopali auctoritate confirmata ; eis concedimus ; et sicut in auctentico scripto domini illustris Anglorum regis . Henrici . secundi . et in litteris confirmationis . Ricardi . bone memorie predecessoris nostri . Cantuariensis archiepiscopi continentur expressa ; auctoritate qua fungimur ; confirmamus . et sigilli nostri appositione communimus . sub interminatione anathematis distinctius inhibentes . nequis predictos canonicos super possessionibus suis iniuste aut contra iuris ordinem turbare vel molestare presumat. Et ut hec confirmatio nostra firma et inconvulsa perseveret . eandem presenti pagina et testium subscriptione duximus roborandam. Hiis testibus . magistro Henrico de Norhamton . magistro Silvestro . Gileberto filio Willelmi Reginaldo de Oylli magistro Nicolao de Lideford' . Ricardo de Hunfranvill' Eustachio de Wilton' . Galfrido Forti et aliis.

Cf. above, no. 111; the royal charter is not known.

265. See of Coventry

Inspeximus and confirmation for Hugh bishop-elect of Coventry of king Henry II's charter which grants to him the priory of Coventry, with power to institute the prior and regulate all the affairs of the church both within and without.   [? late August 1187]

B = Lichfield, D. & C. Mun. Magnum registrum album fo. 241va. s. xiv in.

Pd (calendar) from B in *Lichfield M. R. A.* 284 no. 590.

B. dei gratia Cantuariensis archiepiscopus totius Anglie primas et apostolice 'sedis' legatus omnibus ad quos littere presentes pervenerint salutem in vero salutari. Universitati vestre notum facimus quod dominus rex Angl' H. prioratum Coventrensem concessit et donavit dilecto et familiari suo H. eiusdem ecclesie electo, integre et plenarie tenendum sicut carta ipsius regis testatur quam ad notitiam posterorum duximus annotandam. H. dei gratia rex Angl' et dux Normann' et Aquitann' et comes And' archiepiscopis, episcopis, abbatibus, comitibus, baronibus, iustitiis, vicecomitibus, et omnibus ballivis et fidelibus suis salutem. Sciatis me concessisse et donasse Hugoni de Nonant Coventrensi electo dilecto et familiari nostro prioratum ecclesie Coventrensis et quicquid ad ipsum prioratum pertinet in ea libertate et possessionum integritate et omnimoda dignitate in qua Rogerus episcopus Coventrensis aut aliquis [fo. 241vb] predecessorum ipsius electi prioratum illum unquam melius aut liberius habuit, ut ad eius pertineat paternitatem tam institutio prioris quam ordinatio interiorum et exteriorum ad ecclesiam illam pertinentium. Quare volo et firmiter precipio ut predictus electus habeat et teneat bene et in pace, libere et quiete, integre et plenarie, honorifice et inconcusse prioratum illum et omnia ad ipsum pertinentia cum omnibus possessionibus et libertatibus et liberis consuetudinibus suis omnibus diebus vite sue quibus episcopatum habuerit Coventrensem. Ne igitur quod in presentia nostra et domini Bobonis Sancti Angeli diaconi cardinalis tunc apostolice sedis legati solempniter factum est et a domino rege carta precedente firmatum ad lesionem prefati electi aliqua posset in posterum malignitate converti, donationem illam et concessionem regiam quam vidimus sigilli nostri testimonio communimus et auctoritatis nostre munimine confirmamus.

Hugh Nonant was elected to the bpric in Jan. 1185 but not consecrated until 31 Jan. 1188. The copy of Henry II's charter which follows this inspeximus of it in the Magnum registrum names the witnesses: B. cardinal deacon of St Angelo, B. archbp of Canterbury and legate, Ralph archdn of Hereford, William of Ste-Mère-Église, clerk of the chamber. This points to late summer as the date of both charters. Cardinals Bobo and Soffredus had negotiated a truce between Philip Augustus of France and Henry II of England at Châteauroux on 23 June, and may have attended a meeting of the kings at Alençon, 28 Aug., at which archbp Baldwin was present, having recently come from England (Gervas. Cant. i 379, 380). The date proposed by Eyton (*Itinerary* 284), *c*.25 Jan. 1188, which is followed by Savage in *Lichfield M. R. A.* 284 and by W. Janssen *Die päpstlichen Legaten in Frankreich 1130–1198* (Kölner hist. Abh. vi 1961) 129, is less probable. It is unlikely that Baldwin would use the legatine title in France as late as 25 Jan. 1188. Hugh Nonant had armed himself with a papal indult from Urban III to appoint the prior of Coventry according to English custom (18 June 1186 or 1187: *PUE* ii 435–6 no. 243). On 12 Feb. 1189 Clement III confirmed for bp Hugh the grant which had been made by authority of the king, the legate, and the archbp (*PUE* ii 449–50 no. 253). This was preliminary to the emergence of bp Hugh's plan to replace the monks by secular canons, a plan finally completed in 1191.

266. Coventry: bishop Hugh Nonant

Mandate to Richard bishop of London. When the archbishop was at Rouen, he suspended Hugh bishop of Coventry from the use of his episcopal orders for exercising the incompatible office of sheriff and for other reasonable causes. The bishop later obtained release from suspension and has promised in letters patent addressed to the king that he will resign his shrievalty into the king's hands within a fortnight of Easter and will not concern himself with such business in future. Respecting the other charges, he has given letters patent to the archbishop renouncing appeal, which the archbishop sends to the bishop of London. The bishop of London is to bring together the bishop of Rochester, the archbishop's clerks, and others of his own choice, to meet the bishop of Coventry and do what is needful about the charges against him. They are to cause the bishop of Coventry to fulfil the promises which he has made in writing.

[24 March × 15 April 1190]

B = Lambeth Palace ms. 8 (Diceto, Ymagines) fo. 117v (s. a. 1190). s. xii/xiii.
    C = BL ms. Royal 13 E vi fo. 114r, copied from B. s. xii/xiii.

Pd from B in Diceto, *Op. Hist.* ii 77–8, from C in Roger Wendover *Flores historiarum* (RS) i 175 and Paris *Chron. Maj.* ii 358.

Like other documents preserved by Diceto this may be an abridged or garbled version. The last sentence comes as an afterthought, following 'Valete': it is omitted by Wendover and Paris. In the *Ymagines* the letter is followed by a letter of the bp of Coventry to the bp of London, undertaking to abide by his judgment 'super querela monachorum de Coventria et capelle sancti Michaelis de Coventria' and all other charges against him, if he will appoint suitable time and place for a hearing. The archbp's letter was apparently written before the quindene of Easter (15 April) and after he left Rouen, where he is last recorded on 24 March, in the company of the kg and the bp of Coventry. It had no effect. Late in June 1190 bp Hugh was at court at Montrichard and struck bargains with the kg 'pro prioratu de Coventre habendo' and 'pro habendis vicecomitatibus de Warewichsira et Legecestresira et Staffordsira' (*PR 3 & 4 Richard I* (PRS n. s. 2) 248 and *Itinerary of Richard I* 35).

267. Davington priory

Confirmation for the nuns of Davington of the church of Newnham, granted to them by William son of Philip and Juliana, William's wife, and confirmed by Juliana's son Robert de Campania.

[Jan. 1186 × Dec. 1187]

B = Lambeth Palace, Reg. W. Warham fo. 155v (159v), in copy of inspeximus (1244 × 1258) by P. & C. Ch. Ch. s. xvi in.

B. dei gratia Cantuariensis archiepiscopus totius Anglie primas et apostolice sedis legatus omnibus Christi fidelibus ad quos presentes littere pervenerint eternam in domino salutem. Ad omnium[a] notitiam volumus pervenire nobis[b] innotuisse dilectum filium nostrum Willelmum filium Phillippi et Iulianam uxorem suam dedisse et concessisse, quantum ad laicam pertinet donationem, ecclesiam de Newnham monialibus in ecclesia beate Marie Magdalene de Davinton deo servientibus, quorum concessionem Ricardus bone memorie Cantuariensis archiepiscopus predecessor noster sicut in autentico scripto ipsius continetur confirmavit, sed et dilectus filius noster Robertus de Campania donationem a memorato Willelmo et Iuliana matre sua predictis monialibus super ecclesia de Newnham factam coram nobis se ratam[c] habere proposuit et scripto suo confirmari fecit. Ut igitur quod a predictis viris Willelmo videlicet filio Phillippi et Iuliana uxore sua et Roberto de Campania filio eiusdem Iuliane memoratis monialibus pia consideratione concessum est firmam et perpetuam habeat stabilitatem, eandem concessionem sicut rationabiliter facta est ratam habemus et auctoritate qua fungimur confirmamus et sigilli nostri appositione communimus. Hiis testibus: magistro Henrico de Northamton', magistro [fo. 156r] Silvestro, magistro Radulpho de Sancto Martino, Iohanne de Exonia, Galfrido filio Terrici, Willelmo Prudumma, Ricardo de Humframvill',[d] Eustachio de Wilton', Galfrido Forti et aliis, scilicet Willelmo filio Phillippi, Hugone de Dudinton', Iohanne de Borg', Waltero et Osberto capellanis.

[a] Ad omnium: et dominium B   [b] vobis: nobis B   [c] seratam B   [d] Humframill' B

On fo. 155r are the grants of William and Juliana and the confirmation of Robert de Campania. The latter is attested by the first four and last five witnesses of Baldwin's charter (reading 'J. de Berg' ' for 'J. de Borg' '). For archbp Richard's confirmation see above, no. 121.

*267A. Dover priory

Institution of Robert of Rouen in the church of Hougham.

[April 1185 × March 1190]

Mentioned only, as a charter which Robert of Rouen received from the archbp, in a sentence of judges delegate, in Lambeth Palace ms. 241 (Dover cartulary) fo. 191r. The charter was probably in the form of no. 268, below (and cf. nos. 248, 249, 326).

The papal mandate to the judges, 29 May 1192, concerns the churches of Hougham and Coldred, and states that Dover priory has been deprived of their peaceful possession by archbp Baldwin, who had given the churches to his clerks. Cited before the judges, Robert of Rouen and Peter of Hougham, clerk, renounced claims to any right in the church of Hougham. Robert promised on oath to surrender the archbp's charter which he had concerning the church.

Archbp Hubert gave his approval to the restoration of the church and its appurtenances to the prior and monks of Dover; they agreed to pay Robert six marks yearly from their chamber until they found him a benefice (cf. *EEA* iii no. 437). Robert of Rouen was acting for Baldwin in the Curia in 1189 (*Ep. Cant.* 277, 288 epp. 292, 305).

268. Dover priory

Notification that at the request and presentation of prior Osbern of Dover the archbishop has instituted his clerk, Mr Joseph, in the church of Appledore on condition of his paying to the monks of Dover the customary yearly pension.   [1189 × March 1190]

B = Lambeth Palace ms. 241 (Dover cartulary) fo. 225v (227v). s. xiv ex.

Universis sancte matris ecclesie filiis ad quos presentes littere pervenerint B. dei gratia Cantuariensis archiepiscopus totius Anglie primas eternam in domino salutem. Ad universitatis vestre notitiam volumus pervenire quod nos ad petitionem et presentationem dilecti filii nostri O. prioris Dovorr' dedimus et concessimus dilecto filio et clerico nostro magistro Iosepho in perpetuam elemosinam ecclesiam de Apoldre cum universis pertinentiis suis sub debita et consueta pensione quam dilectis filiis nostris priori et monachis Dovorr' singulis annis persolvet perpetuo tenendam. Quare volumus et precipimus ut idem Iosephus eandem ecclesiam de Apoldre cum universis pertinentiis suis sub predicta pensione perpetuo teneat et possideat. Et ut hec nostra concessio firmam et perpetuam optineat stabilitatem, eam presenti scripto et sigilli nostri appositione communimus. Hiis testibus: magistro Silvestro, magistro R. de Sancto Martino, magistro Willelmo de Sancta Fide, Willelmo de Sotindon', magistro Godefrido de Sildon', Iohanne de Exonia, Galfrido filio Terrici, Willelmo Prudum', Galfrido Forti, Eustachio de Wilton', Roberto clerico.

Osbern or Osbert is thought to have become prior of Dover in 1189. Mr Ralph de Sancto Martino and Mr William de Sancta Fide were left at home by archbp Baldwin when he went on crusade, which means that this charter was issued in England before the archbp's departure.

Mr Joseph is probably the author known as Joseph of Exeter, or 'Iscanus', said by Giraldus Cambrensis (*Opp.* i 79) to have been a nephew of archbp Baldwin. For his writings see M. Manitius, *Gesch. der lateinischen Literatur des Mittelalters* iii (1931) 649–53, F. J. E. Raby, *A hist. of secular Latin poetry in the Middle Ages* ii (Oxford 1934) 132–37, and Josephus Iscanus, *Werke u. Briefe* ed. L. Gompf (Mittellat. Studien u. Texte, 1970). Mr Joseph had vacated the rectory of Appledore by death or resignation before 1204, when John of Kent was rector (*EEA* iii nos. 445, 447).

269. Durford abbey

Inspeximus and confirmation for the canons of Durford of a charter of archbishop Richard. [Jan. 1186 × Dec. 1187]

B = BL ms. Cotton Vesp. E xxiii (Durford cartulary) fo. 24r (20r, p. 39). s. xiii ex.

B.*ᵃ* dei gratia Cantuariensis archiepiscopus totius Anglie primas et apostolice sedis legatus omnibus Christi fidelibus ad quos presentes littere pervenerint eternam in domino salutem. Ad universitatis vestre notitiam volumus pervenire dilectos filios nostros canonicos de Dureford' scriptum bone memorie Ricardi Cantuariensis archiepiscopi predecessoris nostri in hec verba presentasse. sicut superius dictum est. [above, no. 129]. Ut igitur quod a memorato predecessore nostro iamdictis canonicis concessum est et autentico ipsius scripto roboratum firmam et perpetuam optineat stabilitatem eandem concessionem sicut iuste et canonice facta est stabilem esse concedimus et auctoritate qua fungimur confirmamus ac sigilli nostri appositione communimus. Testibus etc.

ᵃ B.: R. B

The reference to Richard our predecessor shows that the title is wrong. The formula introducing the inspected charter resembles those of Baldwin's time rather than the more standardized pattern of later inspeximus charters. Cf. the use of 'presentasse' here and in no. 300, issued in the same period.

270. Exeter: priory of St James

Inspeximus and confirmation for prior Angerus and the monks of St James, Exeter, of a charter by bishop Bartholomew of Exeter confirming the award of bishop Robert (II) about the monks' rights in the church of Tiverton. [April × May 1185]

A = Cambridge, King's Coll. Mun. 2 W 10. Endorsed, s. xiii ex.: Confirmacio archiepiscopi super ecclesia de Twivert'. Approx. 305 × 342 + 28 mm. Sealing d. q. 2; seal and counterseal (natural wax, brown varnish).

B = Ibid. 2 W 9 (original charter of bp Bartholomew).

Pd (B only) by Morey, *Bartholomew of Exeter* 148–9.

Bald(ewinus) dei gratia Cantuariensis archiepiscopus tocius Anglie primas ː universis sancte matris ecclesię filiis ad quos presens scriptura pervenerit salutem in domino. Notum facimus universitati vestrę quod dilectus filius noster Angerus prior Sancti Iacobi prope Exoniam presentavit nobis cartam bonę memorię Bartholomei quondam Exoniensis episcopi in hec verba. Omnibus fidelibus ad quos presens scriptura pervenerit ⸵ Bartholomeus divina miseratione dictus episcopus Exoniensis ⸵ salutem in domino. Noverit universitas vestra quod cum bonę memorię venerabilis Ricardus comes Devonię ⸵ et monachi Sancti Iacobi super ecclesia de Twivertona aliquandiu contendissent . monachis ex donatione Baldewini patris ipsius Ricardi totam ecclesiam sibi vendicantibus ⸵ tandem auctoritate pie recordationis Roberti predecessoris mei . me tunc archidiacono[a] suo ei assistente consensu partium controversia super hoc amicabiliter in perpetuum sopita est in hunc modum. Medietas ecclesię Twivertonę per divisum[b] ut in sequentibus patentius exprimetur cum omnibus pertinentiis suis terris . decimis . oblationibus . sepulturis . capellis . et omnimodis fructibus et obventionibus ⸵ monasterio Sancti Iacobi Ricardo comite concedente et plenarium assensum prebente . ac priorem predicti monasterii Alveredum vice monasterii prefato predecessori meo presentante ⸵ ipsius auctoritate et per manus eius investituram in perpetuum concessa atque donata est. Altera vero medietas cum omnibus pertinentiis suis terris . decimis . oblationibus . sepulturis . capellis et omnimodis fructibus et obventionibus eiusdem ęcclesię ministerio in perpetuum reservata est . ita ut in ea per episcopi vel archidiaconi Exon' donationem et investituram Ricardo comite vel aliquo eius successore eligente ac presentante . duo clerici ordinentur et constituantur . qui perpetuo ecclesie ministerio et parrochianorum spiritualibus necessitatibus assidue deputati ⸵ omnium episcopalium consuetudinum onera in se suscipiant atque perficiant . ita tamen ut Willelmus frater Alexandri quondam decani et Willelmus de Manelega[c] et Sewacar frater eius qui tunc illam medietatem possidebant hac compositione non gravarentur. Monachi quoque prefati medietatis integra perceptione contenti . omnium episcopalium consuetudinum immunitate gaudentes orationi vacent et quieti . ministrandi vel non ministrandi in ęcclesia liberam habentes potestatem. Medietas que in monachorum ius et possessionem cessit ⸵ integre continet .iiii.[or] illas portiones . quarum .ii[as]. a multis temporibus possedit Alexander quondam decanus . quas et Walterio filio Alexandri ⸵ monachi concesserunt tenendas quoad vixerit pro marca argenti annuatim solvenda monasterio Sancti Iacobi in[d] .ii[obus]. terminis . in natali et in festo sancti Iohannis ⸵ iurisiurandi religione monachis ab eodem Walterio prestita super fidelitate . de predicta possessione et pensione monachis servanda et exhibenda. Reliquas vero duas ⸵ Pagano capellano concessit[e] tota vita sua tenendas pro dimidia marca annuatim monachis solvenda . eadem fidelitatis iuratoria cautione ab ipso prestita. Preterea concessit

memoratus Ricardus comes atque per manum prenominati decessoris mei donavit *:* sepedictis monachis Sancti Iacobi totam terram
et totum boscum de Cottalega . et forestarium nomine Robertum
cum omni possessione sua mobili et immobili . sola sibi usuaria
necessitate in bosco retenta *:* ad exclusam piscinę suę et caulas
proprias reficiendas . ita ut nec ipsi nec alicui successorum eius *:*
aliquid inde vendere liceat aut donare. Monachis vero plenarium
dominium et possessio atque omnis usus concessus et donatus est
excepto quod boscum eradicare et in novalia convertere non licebit.
Hoc autem totum per predictos decessorem meum bonę memorię
Robertum et Ricardum comitem Devonie *:* ego tunc archidiaconus
Exoniensis oculata fide sic factum esse . inspexi et cognovi. Quod ne
tractu[f] temporis vel malignantium versutiis in dubium revocetur *:*
ego postea divina permissione Exoniensis episcopus . petitione
prioris et monachorum predicti monasterii Sancti Iacobi presenti
scripto et sigilli mei appositione confirmavi. His testibus . magistro
Roberto archidiacono Toton' . magistro Rogero Barnast' . magistro
Gualterio archidiacono Cornubie . magistro Baldewino filio Albreę .
magistro Roberto de Auc . Pagano capellano . Petro de Mandevill' .
Petro Pichot . Petro filio Ricardi . Helia de Cridiat' . Martino de
Dovlis . Turstano canonico . Willelmo Lumbardo . Willelmo filio
comitis Reginaldi . Gaufrido Cornuto . Osberto de Camera . Thoma
filio Ricardi . Iohanne cantore . Serlone canonico . et Osberto
cognato suo canonico . Alano de Furnellis iuvene . Arnulfo canonico
. Willelmo de Burdevile . Stephano serviente domini episcopi .
Eadmundo . Henrico Coco . Walterio de Camera . Radulfo Saxone .
Ricardo de Toteneis . Roberto de Mortuna. Nos autem predicti
episcopi confirmationem ratam habentes *:* eam quantum in nobis est
presenti scripto et sigillo nostro confirmamus. His testibus . Willelmo archidiacono Gloucestriensi . Gileberto archidiacono Lexoviensi . magistro Petro archidiacono Bathoniensi . magistro Henrico
de Londonia . magistro Godefrido . Willelmo filio Roberti . Iohanne
de Exonia . Willelmo Prudum . Ricardo novo capellano ;

a archidiacono B; archidiano A   *b* per divisum B; pro diviso A   *c* Manelega B;
Manalega A   *d* in A, *om.* B   *e* concessit B; concesserunt A   *f* tractu A; lapsu B

This must be dated after the archbp's postulation was confirmed by Urban III
(15 March 1185) and before Gilbert Glanvill, archdn of Lisieux, was elected to
the see of Rochester.
   The formulas of this inspeximus correspond exactly with those of no. 271
below, and the witness-lists are identical. They were probably written on one
occasion. The scripts of both suggest external writing by two hands; that of no.
270 is the more elegant.

271.   Exeter: priory of St James

Inspeximus and confirmation for prior Angerius and the monks of St James, Exeter, of a charter by bishop Robert (I) of Exeter confirming to them the grants which Baldwin de Redvers, earl of Exeter, and his family made to the monasteries of Cluny and St-Martin-des-Champs for the maintenance of monks of Cluny at Exeter.

[April × May 1185]

A = Cambridge, King's Coll. Mun. 2 W 3. Endorsed, s. xiii ex.: Confirmacio archiepiscopi omnium instrumentorum. Approx. 252 × 367 + 42 mm. Sealing d. q. 2; seal lost.

B = Ibid. 2 W 2 (original charter of bishop Robert I).

Pd (B only) in *Mon. Exon.* 194–5 no. VII.

archiepiscopus.

Baldewin(us) dei gratia Cantuariensis . totius Anglie primas . universis sancte matris ecclesie filiis . ad quos presens scriptura pervenerit : salutem : in domino. Notum facimus universitati vestre quod dilectus filius noster Angerius prior Sancti Iacobi prope Exoniam . presentavit nobis cartam bone memorie Roberti . quondam Exoniensis episcopi . in hec verba. Omnibus ad quos presens scriptum pervenerit : Robertus dei gratia Exoniensis episcopus : salutem in domino. Noverit universitas vestra . quod venerabilis Baldewinus de Riveriis*a* Exoniensis comes . filio suo Ricardo concedente . et plenarium assensum prebente . pro remedio anime sue . et precipue pro anima uxoris sue Adeliz . et patris sui . Ricardi . et matris sue .A.*b* et pro omnium predecessorum successorumque suorum animabus . totam terram . cum capella sancti Iacobi extra Exoniam . et cum decima . et omnibus pertinenciis suis . quas . Walterius filius Wlwardi ex eo libere . et quiete tenuit . ipso Walterio rogante . et concedente . quicquid iuris . et dominii in eis habebat . herede*c* Edith assentiente . deo . et monasterio . sancti Petri de Cluniaco . et Sancti Martini de campis . ad sustentationem monachorum Cluniacensium . ibidem deo . et sancto Iacobo servientium . per manuum mearum investituram donavit . et irrevocabiliter confirmavit . cum eadem libertate . et liberis consuetudinibus . quibus terram suam de Toppesham*d* tenuit et habuit. Insuper concessit iamdictis monachis . ut omnes terras suas . et homines . et*e* possessiones . et elemosinas . quas habent . vel in posterum iure . ac legaliter adquirere poterunt . infra fines totius terre sue . et feodi sui . habeant . et teneant . solutas . liberas . et quietas . ab omnibus exactionibus subiectionibus . hundredis . placitis . querelis . et omni servitio . et opere servili . et theloneo . et omnibus consuetudinibus :

que excogitari poterunt. Preterea vero pia devotione . concessit . ut prefati monachi et homines eorum . habeant quamlibet mensuram . et libertatem . vendendi . et emendi . et res suas modis omnibus iuste multiplicandi. In terra etiam sua concessit ut habeant absque omni impeditione liberum introitum[f] . et reditum . cum rebus suis . et communes pascuas animalibus suis . et iuncos in marisco : absque emptione[g] . et omnem communitatem . profectum . et refugium in omni loco . qui ad se spectare dinoscitur. Siquid vero foresfacti vel querele . inter homines eius . et homines monachorum . quacunque occasione inciderit : monachi plenarie de qualibet causa . curiam . et[h] iusticiam suam habeant propriam : et emendacionem. Hec itaque omnia sepedictis monachis donavit . et iure proprietatis : transactavit . ita . quod in eos . nec . sibi . nec . alicui ex heredibus suis . aliquid violente potestatis exercere licebit . nisi tantummodo contra adversantium molestias : defensionis auxilium. Et quia[j] predicta . predictorum fratrum sustentationi minime sufficere estimavit : divini amoris instinctu totam ecclesiam de Tuiverton' . cum capellis . et omnibus pertinentiis suis . permissione et assensu meo donavit . et scripto auctentico : confirmavit . volens ut monachi ab omni vexatione . liberi . et immunes : orationi vacent . et deum . pro se et suis : indesinenter exorent. Preterea prefatus .B. illustris comes Exoniensis ecclesie sancti Iacobi . tantum beneficii ex voto conferre tenetur : unde sacer monachorum conventus constitui . et sustentari poterit. Quod ne tractu temporis vel malignantium versutiis in dubium revocetur : ego sicut diocesanus episcopus . ad petitionem tam .B.[k] comitis . quam Ricardi . eiusdem monasterii prioris . presenti scripto . et sigilli mei appositione : confirmavi . salva semper auctoritate nostra : et successorum nostrorum episcoporum. Actum . ab incarnatione domini . anno . millesimo . centesimo . quadragesimo . sexto : apud Exoniam. Hiis testibus . Walterio de Piriton' . Hugone de Auco . Radulfo filio Iocelini . archidiaconis[l] . magistro Willelmo de[m] Cucufel . Philippo de Furnell'[n] . Iohanne Paz . Stephano de Mandevilla . Huberto de .Vaus. Radulfo Patrich[o] . Roberto de Scocis . Rogero abbate . Willelmo filio Radulfi . et fratre suo Roberto . Hugone clerico de Coleford' . Roberto de Gernun[p] . Guidone de Britevill' . Willelmo de Musters . domino Roberto[q] abbate de Tavistoke . Ricardo filio Radulfi . Willelmo de Morevill' . et filiis . sepedicti .B.[k] comitis . Ricardo . Willelmo . et[r] Henrico . Iocelino filio Nigelli . Gaufredo de Lega militibus . Ricardo et Edwardo . monachis. Nos autem predicti episcopi confirmationem ratam habentes : eam quantum in nobis est . presenti scripto . et sigillo nostro confirmamus. Hiis testibus .

Willelmo archidiacono Gloucestrensi . Gilleberto archidiacono Lexoviensi . magistro Petro archidiacono Bath*oniensi* . magistro Henrico de Londonia . magistro Godefrido . Willelmo filio Roberti . Iohanne de Exonia . Willelmo Prudum . Ricardo novo capellano.

a Riveriis A; Reveriis B *b* A. A; Adelize B *c* add sua B *d* Toppesham A; Topesham B *e* et A, *om.* B *f* introitum B; itum A *g* emptione A; impetitione B *h* et A; ad B *j* add hec B *k* B. A; Baldwini B *l* archidiaconis: archidiaconi A; archidiacono B *m* de A, *om.* B *n* Furnell' B; Funell' A *o* Patrich A; Partirch B *p* Gernun A; Giver B *q* Roberto A; Rogero B *r* et A, *om.* B

For the date, see no. 270 above, which has the same witnesses.
The script is irregular, and badly spaced.

272.   Exeter: priory of St James

Confirmation for the monastery of St James outside the south gate of Exeter of the grant by Richard de Redvers of three marks' worth of land at Topsham to maintain a monk priest who will minister for the souls of Richard's brother, earl Baldwin, and others.

[10 May 1188 × 6 July 1189]

A = Cambridge, King's Coll. Mun. 2 W 13. No lengthy or legible endorsement. Approx. 163 × 177 + 42 mm. Sealing d. q. 2; traces of seal (red wax).

Bald(ewinus) dei gratia Cantuariensis archiepiscopus totius Anglie primas ∴ universis sancte matris ecclesie filiis ad quos presens scriptura pervenerit ∴ salutem in domino. Notum facimus universitati vestre quod venerabilis et dilectus filius noster Ricardus de Riveriis . pro remedio anime fratris sui Baldewini comitis . et pro animabus predecessorum successorumque parentum suorum . et pro salute sua . permissione et assensu domini Henrici regis in presentia nostra donavit monasterio sancti Iacobi extra portam australem civitatis Exoniensis fundato . et monachis ibidem deo servientibus ∴ tres marcatas terre in manerio de Toppesham . quod est contiguum terre ipsorum monachorum. Has itaque tres marcatas terre ad sustentationem unius monachi sacerdotis . qui pro animabus predictorum parentum suorum ministrabit ∴ in perpetuam elemosinam donavit . et carta sua confirmavit . ab omni servitio et ab omnibus consuetudinibus et occasionibus que excogitari possunt ∴ liberas . et quietas . in viis . in semitis . in marisco . in pascuis . in pasturis . in mari . in portu . in aquis . et in omnibus aliis locis. Nos autem predicti Ricardi donationem gratam habentes ∴ eam presenti scripto et sigillo nostro confirmavimus. Hiis testibus . Gaultero Rotomagensi archiepiscopo . Gileberto Pipard . Radulfo filio Stephani . Reginaldo filio Hereberti . Gaultero Mautravers . Guillelmo Maskerel . Iuelo de Bukintone*a* . militibus ipsius Ricardi de Riveriis;

a -e *changed from* -a A

Well written, but in an unusual hand. Wide-ruled parchment, with a margin 7 mm. wide on left.

After the death of earl Baldwin II, 10 or 18 May 1188, but probably in the lifetime of Henry II. The kg left England for the last time on 10 July 1188, and this confirmation may belong to a time when the archbps of Canterbury and Rouen were with the court in Normandy or Maine in spring 1189.

273. Eynsham abbey

Inspeximus and confirmation for the monks of Eynsham of the charter of protection and confirmation given to them by archbishop Richard.

[Jan. × May 1186]

B = Oxford, Christ Church, Chapter Libr. ms. 31 (Eynsham cartulary) fo. 21r. s. xii/xiii.

Pd from B in *Eynsham cartulary* i 59 no. 43.

Hiis testibus: Willelmo Gloecestriensi, magistro Petro Blesensi Bathoniensi archidiaconis, magistro Silvestro, magistro Henrico de Norhamton'.

The archbp is styled legate. Baldwin visited Eynsham late in May 1186 when William archdn of Gloucester was apparently elected to the see of Worcester, along with other episcopal appointments (Gervas. Cant. i 335).

*274. Forde abbey

Confirmation for Forde abbey of the grant by bishop John of Exeter of the church of Thorncombe with the chapel of Holditch, safeguarding the incumbency of Mr Milo, and providing that after his death a vicar shall be appointed. [Oct 1186 (? Sept. 1189) × Nov. 1190]

Mentioned only, when the charter was produced, with a confirmation by archbp Hubert, in the king's court in Michaelmas term 1214 (*CRR* vii 301–2; *Mon. Exon.* 347–8). Possibly after the royal charter confirming the church and manor to Forde, 16 Sept. 1189 (*Cartae antiquae rolls 11–20* (PRS n. s. 33, 1960) 162–4 and from this source in *Mon. Ang.* v 382 and *Mon. Exon.* 346).

*275. Gent: abbey of St Peter

Notification of a settlement in the archbishop's presence, on a mandate from pope Clement III, of a dispute between St Peter's abbey, Gent, and bishop Gilbert of Rochester, concerning the churches of East Greenwich and Lewisham. The abbey's proctor submitted to an ordination of vicarages in the two churches to be made by the bishop of Rochester. [1188 × March 1190]

Mentioned only, in an ordination of vicarages by bp Benedict of Rochester (1218) who stated that no ordination had hitherto been made (Gent, Rijksarchief, cartulary of Lewisham priory fo. 17v. s. xiii med. Also in register of bp Hamo de Hethe, whence pd in *Reg. H. Hethe* i 39–40).

276. Gloucester abbey

Inspeximus and confirmation of the award made by bishop William of Worcester after a dispute between the abbot and convent of St Peter's, Gloucester, and the prior and monks of (Leonard) Stanley, of the one part, and William of Berkeley, of the other part, over the advowson of the church of Coberley.   [Feb. × May 1188]

A = Bodl. ms. Gloucester ch. 22. No endorsement visible, the charter being mounted on parchment. Approx. 163 × 178 + 20 mm. Sealing d. q. 2; tag remains, seal lost. Badly damaged, with several holes.

Pd from A by C. Swynnerton in *Trans. Bristol and Gloucs. Archaeological Soc.* xliv (1922) 267–8, with facsimile.

B(aldwinus) dei gratia Cantuariensis archiepiscopus totius Anglie primas . omnibus Christi fidelibus ad quos presens scriptum pervenerit ꞉ salutem in domino. Notum sit universitati vestre . literas venerabilis fratris nostri Willelmi Wigorniensis episcopi nobis exhibitas fuisse in hec verba ꞉ Universis sancte matris ecclesie filiis . Willelmus divina miseratione Wigorniensis ecclesie minister ꞉ salutem in domino. Ad universitatis vestre volumus pervenire noticiam . quod controversia que vertebatur inter abbatem et conventum ecclesie sancti Petri Gloecestrensis . et priorem et monachos de Stanleis ꞉ et Willelmum de Berchelai super iure advocacionis ecclesie de Cutberleia ex utraque parte in nos compromissione facta ꞉ nostra dispositione de consilio prudentum virorum qui nobis assistebant[a] consentiente magistro Petro de Lech' tunc temporis persona ipsius ecclesie . hoc modo finem sortita est. Prefati siquidem abbas et conventus Gloecestrie et prior de Stanleia quicquid iuris in advocatione predicte ecclesie de Cutberleia se habere proposuerant . [prenominato] Willelmo de Berkelai qui eam clamabat et heredibus suis in perpetuum remiserunt. Quia vero ecclesia sancti [Leon]ardi de Stanleia ad virorum religiosorum ibi existentium sustentationem de prelibata [ecclesia de Cutberleia quinque] solidos quos ulterius non est perceptura nomine [pensionis accipiebat (?) ne suo penitus commodo] frustraretur [nos statui]mus ut ipsa medietatem decimarum [frugum totius dominii eiusdem Willelmi de] Berkeleia [et omnium cotariorum suorum in Cutberleia quicumque] terras excoluerit . per m[anus] propriorum servientium in] perpetuam elemosinam percipiat. [Ut hoc statutum sicut coram]^b nobis compositio facta est perpetuum et incon[vul-sum perm]^{b}aneat eum presenti scripto commendare et testium subscriptione sigillique nostri appositione confirmare dignum duximus. Hiis testibus . magistro Petro de [Lech'.] magistro Godefrido de Lanton' . magistro Willelmo de Tunebrig' . Roberto de Bellocampo . Roberto de Lech' . [Willelmo] filio Godefridi . Iohanne de Draiton . Hugone pincerna . Walterio nepote magistri Petri . Galfrido filio Restwoldi . ... Mainard'. Nos igitur quod a prefat[o episcopo] in hac parte statutum est ratum habentes et gratum $\cdot$ illud [quod iuste] et canonice factum est presentis scripti attestatione^c et sigilli nostri appositione communivimus. Hiis testibus . Giraldo archidiacono Menevensi, magistro Petro Blesensi Bathoniensi archidiacono . magistro Silvestro . magistro Alexandro Walensi . Ricardo de Umfranvilla . Reginaldo de Oilli . Nicholao de Lideford' . magistro Michaele de Buk... . magistro Reginaldo de Hamma . Willelmo de Botinton' . Eustachio de Wilton' . et multis aliis . ,

^{a} asistebant A ^{b} *conjectural* ^{c} attestione A

The attestation of Gerald 'archid. Menev.' points to a time during the archbp's journey to Wales, between Feb. and June 1188. Cf. above, no. 239n.

Three witnesses' names suggest local men. Mr Michael de Buk... may take his name from Buckland and Mr Reginald of Hamme from Churcham, Gloucs., churches in the abbey's gift. William de Botinton occurs as witness to a charter of abbot Hamelin before 1179 (*Trans.* xliv 240). Bp William's charter only exists in this inspeximus, but Bodl. ms. Glouc. ch. 21 (pd in *Trans.* xliv 266) is a chirograph recording the settlement, which permits the filling of some gaps in the inspeximus (noted above by square brackets). The witness Nicholas de Lideford' appears in an earlier list (no. 264 above), with the title of 'master'.

*277. Gloucester abbey

Mandate to bishop William of Llandaff, following a complaint from the monks of St Peter's abbey, Gloucester, about the ministry of the chapel in the castle of Newport. [1187 × March 1190]

Mentioned only, in the bp's record (*Gloucester cartulary* ii 48–49 and 56) that William de Bendingis, castellan of Newport, after legal proceedings in the chapter at Striguil (Chepstow) had admitted that the chapel should be served from the parish church of Newport. Before the monks brought this mandate to the bp, he had already heard frequent complaints from the monks and from the incumbent, Elias the dean.

Bp William was consecrated 10 Aug. 1186 and the archbp left England finally in March 1190; but the complaints and the settlement probably occurred on the archbp's visit to Wales in March 1188, when the two prelates spent a night together at Newport (Gir. Cambrensis *Opp.* vi 55).

278. Haughmond abbey

*Confirmation for the canons of Haughmond of the church of Stokesay,
with inspection of the charter by which bishop William of Hereford
granted them the church and invested abbot Richard with it.*

[Aug. 1186 × Aug. 1187, probably June 1187]

B = Shrewsbury Public Libr. ms. 1 (Haughmond cartulary) fo. 206r. s. xv ex.

B. dei gratia Cantuariensis archiepiscopus totius Anglie primas et
apostolice sedis legatus omnibus sancte matris ecclesie filiis ad quos
presens scriptura pervenerit eternam in domino salutem. Universitatem vestram scire volumus dilectos filios nostros Ricardum abbatem et canonicos de Haghmon' litteras venerabilis fratris nostri
Willelmi Herefordensis episcopi nobis exhibuisse in hec verba:
Willelmus dei gratia Herefordensis episcopus *ᵃ*-omnibus matris
ecclesie filiis ad quos presens carta pervenerit salutem. Notum sit
universitati vestre quod nos ecclesie Hamonensi concessimus ecclesiam de Suthstoke perpetuo iure possidendam cum omnibus pertinentiis suis ipsumque abbatem fratrem Ricardum vice sue ecclesie
predicta ecclesia de Stok' investimus, et ei investituram et donationem eiusque successoribus canonice instituendis presentis scripti
auctoritate confirmamus. Testibus: Ada abbate de Dore et Iordano
decano etc.-*ᵃ* Et nos prefati episcopi concessionem grato acceptantes
assensu eam sicut rationabiliter facta est auctoritate qua fungimur
presentis scripti testimonio et sigilli nostri patrocinio confirmamus.
Hiis testibus: venerabili fratre nostro Reinero episcopo Sancti
Assaph, Radulpho abbate Salopesbur', Radulpho abbate de Bil-
dewas, Waltero abbate de Lilleshull' etc.

ᵃ⁻ᵃ omnibus ... decano etc. (*supplied from next text in cartulary*); etc. ut inferius B

Limits of date are the consecration of bp William de Vere at Lambeth, 10 Aug.
1186, and the death of abbot Ranulf of Buildwas a year later. The archbp's
inspeximus (in an unusual form) probably belongs to June 1187, when he visited
Shropshire: note the local prelates as witnesses.

279. Order of the Hospital: Buckland

*Inspeximus and confirmation for the brethren of the Hospital of St John
of Jerusalem of a charter of king Henry II granting them Buckland
with the church of St Mary and St Nicholas, on condition that they
will maintain sisters of their Order in no other house in England.*

[7 July 1189 × March 1190]

B = Taunton, Somerset Records Office, DD/SAS SX 133 (Buckland cartulary) fo. 2v. s. xv med.

Pd (calendar) in *Buckland cartulary* 6 no. 8.

Universis sancte matris ecclesie filiis ad quos presens scriptum pervenerit, B. dei gratia Cantuariensis archiepiscopus totius Anglie primas eternam salutem in domino. Nostre solicitudinis incumbit officio studiosius providere ut que in subsidium religionis collata sunt[a] sub nostra confirmante auctoritate in perpetua perseverent tranquillitate. Nos enim paci et tranquillitati fratrum hospitalis Ierusalem attentius providere volentes, vestre notitie duximus significandum priorem et fratres dicti hospitalis cartam H. secundi quondam illustris Anglie regis sub hoc tenore nobis exhibuisse. H. dei gratia rex Anglorum[b] et dux Normannorum et Aquitanorum et comes Andegavorum archiepiscopis, episcopis, abbatibus, prioribus, comitibus, baronibus, iustitiariis, vicecomitibus, et omnibus ballivis et fidelibus suis salutem. Sciatis me pro salute anime mee et patris mei et matris mee et antecessorum et successorum meorum et omnium fidelium defunctorum dedisse et concessisse in liberam et perpetuam elemosinam et presenti carta mea confirmasse deo et beate Marie et sancto Iohanni baptiste et beatis pauperibus sancte domus hospitalis Ierusalem et fratribus in eadem domo deo servientibus ad collocandas et sustentandas ibidem[c] sorores ordinis sui locum de Bochland' in quo ecclesia[d] beate Marie et sancti Nicholai sita est cum omnibus pertinentiis suis, ita quod prior hospitalis Ierusalem[e] conventionavit michi quod in nulla alia domo sua in Anglia retinebit sorores ordinis sui nisi in predicta domo de Bochland'. Quare volo et firmiter precipio quod domus hospitalis Ierusalem et fratres in ea domo deo servientes omnia predicta habeant et teneant in libera et perpetua elemosina ad collocandas et sustentandas memoratas sorores ordinis sui, sicut predeterminatum est, bene et in pace, libere et quiete, integre et plenarie et honorifice in ecclesiis et capellis, in terris, in bosco et in plano, in pratis et pasturis, in communitate nemoris, in moris et mariscis, in vivariis et stagnis et piscariis, in aquis et molendinis, in viis et semitis, et in omnibus aliis locis et aliis rebus ad ea pertinentibus cum omnibus libertatibus et liberis consuetudinibus suis. Testibus: B. archiepiscopo Cantuariensi, G. Eliensi et G. Roffensi episcopis, H. decano Eboracensi, Godefrido de Lucy archidiacono Richemondie, Hamelino comite Warenn', Willelmo comite Arundell', Ranulfo de Glanvyll', Hugone de Cressy,[f] Rogero filio Rainfridi, Hugone de[g] Morewich', et Hugone Bardulf' dapiferis, Michaele Belet, Willelmo de Bendeng', apud Westmonasterium. Nos igitur concessioni et donationi predicti regis gratum prebentes assensum, ea que in carta ipsius comprehensa sunt et iuste et rationabiliter memoratis fratribus hospitalis Ierusalem ab ipso rege collata auctoritate qua fungimur confirmamus et sigilli nostri appositione communimus. Hiis testibus: magistro Silvestro, magistro Sampsone, Roberto de Bekynton', Willelmo de Sotyndon',ʰ Iohanne de Exonia, Willelmo Produm', Galfrido Forti, Galfrido filio Terrici, Eustachio de Wilton', Iosepho.

ᵃ om. sunt B   ᵇ Anglie B, *endings of other titles suspended*   ᶜ ibidem B, *omitted in preceding text of royal charter, but included in confirmation by bp Reginald of Bath, fo. 6v*   ᵈ ecclesia B *and bp Reginald's charter*; capella *royal charter*   ᵉ Ierusalem B, *om. royal charter*   ᶠ Cressy B; Crassy *royal charter*   ᵍ de *royal charter, om.* B   ʰ Satyndon' B

The inspected charter of Henry II (who was dead when the inspeximus was given) was after Hubert Walter became dean of York, July 1186, and before 8 Nov. 1186, when bp Reginald of Bath confirmed it and enlarged upon it in synod at Taunton (Cartulary fos. 6v-7r). The royal charter is mentioned in confirmations by pope Urban III, 6 June (1187), ibid. fo. 6v.

*280. John, count of Mortain

Remonstrance about the prince's marriage with Isabella daughter of the earl of Gloucester, related to him in the third degree of consanguinity. Mandate to abstain from relations with her under pain of anathema and to appear before the archbishop to answer for his offence.

[Aug. × Sept. 1189]

Mentioned only, by Gervase of Canterbury, *Opp.* i 458: 'comminatoriam misit epistolam ... '. The marriage took place at Marlborough, 29 Aug. 1189, 'contra prohibitionem Baldewini Cantuariensis archiepiscopi' (*Gesta regis Henrici II* (RS) ii 78).

For a commentary on the circumstances and outcome see H. G. Richardson in *EHR* lxi (1946) 289–91, lxv (1950) 361–2, cf. ibid. lxiii (1948) 89.

281. Langdon abbey

Inspeximus and confirmation for the canons of Langdon of the grants made by William de Auberville for the endowment of a Premonstratensian abbey at (West) Langdon.   [15 Sept. 1189 × March 1190]

B = Lambeth Palace, Reg. W. Warham fo. 133r (137r). s. xvi in. C = PRO E 164/29 (Langdon cartulary) fo. 2v, omitting the inspected charter. s. xiv in.

Baldewinus dei gratiaᵃ Cantuariensis archiepiscopus totius Anglie primas universis Christi fidelibus ad quos presens carta pervenerit salutem in domino. Noverit universitas vestra nosᵇ inspexisse et manibus propriis contrectasseᶜ cartam venerabilis filii nostri Willelmi de Aubervill' sub hac forma.[d] Universis sancte matris ecclesie filiis presentibus et futuris Willelmus de Aubervilla salutem. Noverit universitas vestra me dedisse et concessisse deo et beato martiri Thome et canonicis ordinis Premonstratensis concensu et assensu Matildis uxoris mee et heredum meorum totam villam meam de Langdon' ad faciendam in ea abbatiam ordinis Premonstratensis per manum Roberti abbatis de Leistun. Hanc autem villam dedi et concessi eis totam cum omnibus pertinentiis suis in boscis et plano et pastura et cum omnibus aliis eeisiamentis suis ad eandem villam pertinentibus et cum omnibus servitiis omnium hominum meorum in eadem villa manentium. Preterea eis dedi et concessi ecclesiam beate Marie de eadem villa et ecclesiam beate Marie de Walemere et ecclesiam sancti Nicolai de Oxeneia et ecclesiam beate Marie de Liden'. Hec autem omnia eis concessi pro anima cari domini mei regis[e] Henrici secundi et pro anima Willelmi filii mei et Emme filie mee et pro anima Hugonis patris mei et Wimarc matris mee et Ranulphi de Glanvill' et Berte uxoris sue et pro salute anime mee et Matildis uxoris mee et heredum nostrorum et pro animabus predecessorum et successorum nostrorum. Quare volo et firmiter precipio quod prefati canonici habeant et teneant omnia prenominata que eis dedi et concessi libere et quiete, integre et plenarie et honorifice in puram[f] et perpetuam elimosinam, libera et quieta ab omni seculari servitio et exactione, ita quod si aliquod servitium de predicta villa exigatur, ego et heredes mei dominium canonicorum quod meum fuit in omnibus erga omnes homines et feminas acquietabimus, warantizabimus, et defendemus imperpetuum. Hiis testibus: Iohanne Norwicensi episcopo, Huberto Saresberiensi[g] electo, Henrico abbate de Meldune, G. priore de Butteley, Ranulpho de Glanvill', Willelmo de Glanvill' clerico, Ranulpho capellano, Alano de Valeines, Iosepho clerico, Philippo capellano. Nos igitur, petitione iam dicti Willelmi et interveniente, predicte ecclesie et canonicorum in ea ministrantium securitati et tranquillitati imposterum providere volentes, que iam dicta et scripta[h] sunt auctoritate nostra confirmamus et sigilli nostri appositione communimus. Testibus hiis:[j] G. Roffensi episcopo, H. Cantuariensi archidiacono,[k] magistro Silvestro, magistro Radulpho de Sancto Martino, magistro Willelmo de Sancta Fide, magistro H. de Norh', magistro Galfrido Forti, magistro Iohanne.

---

[a] dei gratia C, *om.* B   [b] nos C, *om.* B   [c] contractasse B   [d] *add* etc. *and omit* William's charter C   [e] *add* Anglie *text of William's charter in cartulary*   [f] puram *text of William's charter in cartulary*; piam B   [g] Sarab' B   [h] scripta C; subscripta B   [j] Testibus hiis: T' hiis etc. *and omit witnesses* C; Testant' B   [k] archiepiscopo B

The formal foundation of the abbey may be dated by the witness of Hubert Walter, elect of Salisbury, between 15 Sept. and 22 Oct. 1189. See Colvin, *White canons* 135–6; the founder's charter is printed ibid. 349–50 and *Mon. Ang.* vii 898 from the cartulary, fo. 2r.

Geoffrey Fortis, or Le Fort, is not elsewhere described as a master.

282. Leeds priory

Grant to the canons of Leeds of forty shillings yearly from the church of Acrise, nomine pensionis *or* nomine personatus.

Otford. 21 April 1185

B = Lambeth Palace, Reg. W. Warham fo. 98v (100v) in copy of inspeximus (1278) by archbp Robert. s. xvi in. C = Cambridge UL ms. Ee 5 31 (register of prior Henry of Ch. Ch. Canterbury) fo. 24r no. v in copy of inspeximus (1286) by P. & C. Ch. Ch. s. xiii/xiv. D = Maidstone, Kent Archives Office ms. U/120 Q/13 (Leeds cartulary) fo. 6v in copy of inspeximus (1278) by archbp Robert. s. xiv med. E = PRO C 53/150 m. 9 in copy of royal inspeximus of March 1367.

Pd (calendar only) from E in *Cal. Ch. Rolls* v 201.

Omnibus sancte matris ecclesie filiis presentes literas inspecturis Baldwinus dei gratia Cantuariensis archiepiscopus totius Anglie primas salutem in domino. Ad universitatis vestre notitiam volumus pervenire nos intuitu dei contulisse dilectis nobis*a* in Christo filiis canonicis nostris de Ledes nomine pensionis*b* annuos quadraginta solidos de ecclesia de Acryse annuatim imperpetuum percipiendos et in*c* usus proprios convertendos. In cuius rei testimonium presentibus literis sigillum nostrum apponi fecimus. Dat' apud Otteford' xi kal. mensis Maii anno ab incarnatione domini millesimo c l xxx quinto.*d*

a nobis D, *om.* BCE   *b* pensionis BE; personatus CD   *c* in CDE, *om.* B   *d* *add* consecrationis nostre anno secundo CDE

The additional date in CDE (note *d*) cannot be correct: archbp Baldwin had been consecrated to Worcester 10 Aug. 1180 and was enthroned at Canterbury 19 May 1185. The variant (and that in note *b*) raises a difficult textual problem.

283. Leeds priory

Inspeximus and confirmation for the canons of Leeds of the grant of the church of Acrise by William de Cosynton to the canons in free and perpetual alms.   [Jan. 1186 × Dec. 1187]

A = Original lost, probable mention in Lambeth Palace, Carte misc. V/111 (inventory of Leeds muniments): 'Carta Baldewini de ecclesia de Acrise et alia de iure personatus in eadem.' s. xiii in.

B = Ibid. Reg. W. Warham fo. 98v (100v) in copy of inspeximus (1278) of archbp Robert. s. xvi in. C = Maidstone, Kent Archives Office ms. U/120 Q/13 (Leeds cartulary) fo. 6v, in copy of same inspeximus. s. xiv med.

B. dei gratia Cantuariensis archiepiscopus totius Anglie primas et apostolice sedis legatus omnibus Christi fidelibus ad quos presentes littere pervenerint illam que est in domino salutem. Ad universitatis vestre notitiam volumus pervenire dilectos filios nostros canonicos de Ledes scriptum Willelmi de Cosynton' in hec verba nobis exhibuisse. Omnibus sancte matris ecclesie filiis ad quos presentes littere pervenerint Willelmus de Cosynton' salutem. Ad universitatis vestre notitiam pervenire semper desidero me divini amoris intuitu et pro salute anime mee et pro salute anime patris mei Wymundi et pro animabus omnium propinquorum meorum concessisse et dedisse et hac mea carta confirmasse in liberam et perpetuam elemosinam ecclesiam de Acrise cum omnibus pertinentiis suis, quantum ad me spectare dinoscitur, ecclesie sancte Marie et sancti Nicholai de Ledes et fratribus meis eiusdem loci canonicis. Corpus etiam meum cum anima deo iubente a carne migraverit eidem ecclesie dedi. Hiis testibus: Thoma capellano de Ledes, Radulfo capellano domini Roberti de Crevequer, Radulfo capellano de Chert, magistro Roberto de Cantuaria, et aliis. Nos igitur quod a prefato milite laudabili consideratione et pio caritatis affectu memoratis canonicis concessum est ratum habentes et acceptum, eandem concessionem sicut iuste et rationabiliter facta est auctoritate qua fungimur confirmamus. Hiis testibus: magistro Henrico de Northampton', magistro Silvestro, Iohanne de Exonia, Gilberto filio Willelmi, Eustachio de Wilton', Galfrido Forti, et aliis.

*284. Leeds priory

Institution (?) of the canons of Leeds in the parsonage of Acrise.
[Jan. 1186 × March 1190]

Mentioned only, in Lambeth Palace, Carte misc. V/111 (inventory of Leeds muniments): 'Carta Baldewini de ecclesia de Acrise et alia de iure personatus in eadem'. s. xiii in. Probably the second charter in this entry, the first being either no. 282 or no. 283 above.

285. Leeds priory

Grant to the canons of Leeds in proprios usus *of the church of Holy Cross, Bearsted, for the provision of lights and ornaments in their church.*   [April 1185 × Jan. 1186 or Dec. 1187 × March 1190]

B = Lambeth Palace, Reg. W. Warham fo. 98r (100r) in copy of inspeximus (1278) by archbp Robert. s. xvi in. C = Ibid. fo. 104v (106v) in copy of inspeximus (1314) by P. & C. Ch. Ch. Canterbury. D = Cambridge UL ms. Ee 5 31 (register of prior Henry of Ch. Ch.) fo. 152r (154r. no. xiii) in copy of same inspeximus. s. xiv in. E = Maidstone, Kent Archives Office U/120 Q/13 (Leeds cartulary) fo. 4v, in copy of inspeximus (1278) by archbp Robert. s. xiv med.

Universis Christi fidelibus ad quos presens scriptum pervenerit Baldewynus dei gratia Cantuariensis archiepiscopus totius Anglie primas eternam in domino salutem. Ad universitatis vestre notitiam volumus pervenire nos concessisse et in proprios usus dedisse ecclesiam Sancte Crucis de*a* Berghsted canonicis de Ledes ibi deo servientibus et imperpetuum servituris, ad luminaria et alia ornamenta in eadem ecclesia de Ledes invenienda. Et ut hec nostra donatio et concessio perpetuitatis robur obtineat, presens scriptum sigilli nostri munimine roboravimus. Hiis testibus: magistro Waltero de Frehan,*b* magistro Silvestro, domino Iohanne senescallo, magistro Willelmo de Sancta Fide, Iohanne de Exonia, Eustachio de Wilton,*c* Roberto de Seven',*d* et multis aliis.

a om. Sancte Crucis de B *b* Frehan' BE; Frean' CD *c* Wilton: Wyltes' B; Wilt' C; Wylt' D; Wiltesir' E *d* Seven' CDE; Meneu (?) B

*286. Leeds priory

Institution (?) of the canons of Leeds in the parsonage of Boughton (Monchelsea). [April 1185 × March 1190]

Mentioned only, in Lambeth Palace, Carte misc. V/111 (inventory of Leeds muniments): 'Carta eiusdem [Baldewini] de personatu de Botun'.' Followed by a line deleted: 'Item alia de resignatione magistri R.'. s. xiii in. Cf. *EEA* iii no. 513.

287. Leeds priory

Confirmation for the canons of Leeds of the church of Chillenden, granted to them in perpetual alms by William de Norfuco.
[April 1185 × Jan. 1186 or Dec. 1187 × March 1190]

A = Original lost, probable mention in Lambeth Palace, Carte misc. V/111 (inventory of Leeds muniments): 'Carta eiusdem [Baldewini] ecclesie de Chilindun'.' s. xiii in.

B = Ibid. Reg. W. Warham fo. 99r (101r) in copy of inspeximus (1278) by archbp Robert. s. xvi in. C = Maidstone, Kent Archives Office ms. U/120 Q/13 (Leeds cartulary) fo. 7v in copy of same inspeximus. s. xiv med.

Omnibus Christi fidelibus ad quos presens scriptum pervenerit Baldewynus dei gratia Cantuariensis archiepiscopus totius Anglie primas eternam in domino salutem. Ad notitiam omnium volumus pervenire quod Willelmus de Norfuco*a* in presentia nostra constitutus quicquid iuris in ecclesia de Chillendenn' habebat dilectis filiis nostris priori et canonicis de Ledes in perpetuam contulit elemosinam. Nos igitur eiusdem Willelmi concessionem ratam habentes eam presenti scripto et sigilli nostri appositione communimus. Hiis testibus: magistro Silvestro, magistro Radulfo de Sancto Martino, magistro W. de Sancta Fide, Roberto de Bukinton',*b* Iohanne de Exonia, et aliis.

a Norfuco B; Northwico C   *b* Bukinton' B; Bykinton' C

*288. Leeds priory

Confirmation (?) for the canons of Leeds of the church of Crundale.
[April 1185 × March 1190]

Mentioned only, in Lambeth Palace, Carte misc. V/111 (inventory of Leeds muniments): 'Carta eiusdem [Baldewini] de ecclesia de Crundale.' s. xiii in.

289. Leeds priory

Notification that Stephen of Leybourne, clerk, has resigned into the archbishop's hand the parsonage of Ham (near Sandwich) and that at the request of William de Norfuco, lord of the fee, the archbishop has granted the church to the canons of Leeds in perpetual alms and has constituted them parsons of the same.
[April 1185 × Jan. 1186 or Dec. 1187 × March 1190]

A = Original lost, probable mention in Lambeth Palace, Carte misc. V/111 (inventory of Leeds muniments): 'Carta eiusdem [Baldewini] de ecclesia de Hammes.' s. xiii in.

B = Ibid. Reg. W. Warham fo. 99r (101r) in copy of inspeximus (1278) by archbp Robert. s. xvi in. C = Ibid. fo. 104v (106v) in copy of inspeximus (1314) by P. & C. Ch. Ch. Canterbury. D = Cambridge UL ms. Ee 5 31 (register of prior Henry of Ch. Ch.) fo. 152v (154v no. xviii) in copy of same inspeximus. s. xiv in. E = Maidstone, Kent Archives Office ms. U/120 Q/13 (Leeds cartulary) fo. 7v in copy of inspeximus (1278) by archbp Robert. s. xiv med.

Omnibus Christi fidelibus ad quos presens scriptum pervenerit Baldewynus dei gratia Cantuariensis archiepiscopus totius Anglie primas eternam in domino salutem. Ad notitiam vestram volumus pervenire quod cum Stephanus de Leybourn' clericus ecclesiam de Hamme cuius aliquando gerebat personatum in manum nostram resignasset, ad petitionem et presentationem Willelmi de Norfuco militis domini fundi eandem ecclesiam dilectis filiis priori et canonicis de Ledes in perpetuam elemosinam contulimus ipsosque in eadem ecclesia personas canonice instituimus. Unde ut hec nostra donatio firmam et perpetuam habeat stabilitatem, eam auctoritate qua fungimur confirmamus et sigilli nostri appositione communimus. Hiis testibus: magistro Silvestro, magistro Godefrido de Sildon', Roberto de Bekinton', Iohanne de Exonia, Galfrido Forti, magistro Ioseph, Eustachio de Wiltone clerico, Roberto clerico.[a]

    [a] magistro Ioseph (Isope D) ... clerico CD; et aliis BE

290. Leiston abbey

Inspeximus and confirmation for the canons of Leiston of a charter of king Richard. The king, at the petition of Ranulf de Glanvill, confirms Ranulf's gift to the Premonstratensian canons of the manor of Leiston and of the churches of St Margaret of Leiston and St Andrew of Aldringham, which Ranulf formerly gave to the canons of Butley, and which they have resigned to the canons of Leiston. He confirms all their possessions, with the usual liberties and free customs, subject to the restrictions laid down by the founder. The royal charter is dated at Arundel by the hand of William Longchamp, the king's chancellor and elect of Ely, 14 October, the first year of king Richard. The archbishop confirms the grant with his authority and his seal.

[14 Oct. 1189 × March 1190]

    B = BL ms. Cotton Vesp. E xiv (Leiston cartulary) fo. 11r, reading 'R' for 'B' in the title and 'Ric'' in the rubric. s. xiii in. C = Ibid. fo. 17r, included in inspeximus by archbp Hubert (*EEA* iii no. 523), which omits most of the royal charter.

    Pd from B in *Mon. Ang.* vii 881 no. 5, and by A. Suckling, *Hist. and antiquities of the county of Suffolk* (1846–8) ii 447–8, reading 'Ricardus' in title; and in *Leiston cart.* p. 61 no. 8 and pp. 71–73 no. 23.

[a]Testibus: G. Rofensi episcopo, Herberto Canthuariensi archidiacono, magistro Silvestro, magistro Radulfo[b] de Sancto Martino.

    [a] Testibus inscriptis (*om. names*) C   [b] Radulfo: Ricardo B

The archbp is not styled legate. The witnesses are those to whom the archbp entrusted the see of Canterbury on his departure for the Third Crusade. Ranulf also went, and died, on the crusade. Cf. the witnesses here with the list in no. 281.

    For the foundation and early history of Leiston abbey see Colvin, *White canons* 118–24 and R. Mortimer, *Leiston cart.* 2–3.

291. Lilleshall abbey

Confirmation for the canons of Lilleshall of the grants by king Henry II and the empress (Matilda). Abbot Walter has exhibited the king's charter to the archbishop.   [Jan. 1186 × Dec. 1187]

B = BL ms. Harl. 3868 (Lichfield register) fo. 23rb (197rb). s. xiv in. C = Ibid. ms. Add. 50121 (Lilleshall cartulary) fo. 24r (p. 46). s. xiii med.

B. dei gratia Cantuariensis archiepiscopus totius Anglie primas et apostolice sedis legatus omnibus Christi fidelibus ad quos presentes littere pervenerint illam que est in domino salutem. Dilectus filius noster W. abbas ecclesie sancte Marie de Lilleshull' cartam domini regis Anglorum Henrici secundi nobis exhibuit, ex cuius tenore intelleximus ipsum dominum regem in perpetuam elemosinam concessisse dilectis filiis nostris canonicis de Lilleshull' ecclesiam sancte Marie de Lilleshull' et locum in quo ecclesia eorundem canonicorum sita est, et ecclesiam sancti Alcmundi de Salop' cum omnibus pertinentiis suis, in terris et ecclesiis et capellis et decimis et libertatibus et consuetudinibus et quietantiis suis cum soca et saca et toll' et theam et infangethef, sicut domina imperatrix eisdem canonicis concessit et carta sua confirmavit. Nos igitur quod a regis maiestate memoratis canonicis intuitu caritatis collatum est et scripto ipsius confirmatum ratum habentes et acceptum, eiusdem domini regis concessionem sicut rationabiliter facta est iuxta officii nostri debitum auctoritate qua fungimur confirmamus et sigilli nostri appositione communimus. Hiis testibus: magistro Henrico de Northamton, magistro Silvestro, Willelmo de Sotindon', Reginaldo^a de Oylli, Willelmo de Prudumma, Ricardo de Hunfranvill', Eustachio de Wilton', Salomone de Dovera, Galfrido Forti, et aliis.

^a Reginaldo: Rag' BC

See *Regesta regum* iii 173–4 nos. 460–2 for the charter of the empress (1148 × 1151) and that of her son as duke of Normandy (1150 × 1151), with the charter of king Stephen (1145) which had confirmed the gift of the prebends of St Alcmund's, Shrewsbury, to the Arrouaisian canons at Donnington, before they were established at Lilleshall. Henry II's confirmation as king, which refers to his mother's charter, is dated 'apud Alrewas in exercitu' (c.Feb. 1155). It is in BL ms. Add. 50121 fo. 23r (p. 44) and ms. Harl. 3868 fo. 21rb; the former also has (fo. 23v) a writ-charter granting the canons freedom from tolls, issued at the same time.

292. See of London

Mandate to the custodians of the temporalities of the bishopric of London sede vacante. The late bishop Gilbert sequestrated the church of Hormead pending settlement of a dispute between Philip clerk of Hormead and Adam de Samford. The custodians have required Philip to surrender the key of the church to them. They have no authority to interfere with spiritual matters and are to allow Gilbert, archdeacon of Middlesex, to have custody of the church. [1187, after 18 Feb.]

The substance of the mandate is reported (probably verbatim) by Ralph de
Diceto s. a. 1187: Idem archiepiscopus custodibus episcopatus Lundoniensis
scripsit in hec verba (Diceto ii 48). As dean of St Paul's, Diceto was concerned
with the administration of the spirituals *sede vacante*. The crown's custodians
of the temporalities were Ralph archdn of Colchester and Richard archdn of
Coventry (*PR 33 Henry II* (PRS 37. 1915) 29). Philip was named as former
chaplain of the church when bp William ordained a vicarage later (Newcourt,
Repertorium i 834). The Sampford family had the patronage.

293.   London: church of St Paul

*Mandate to Ralph the dean and the chapter of London. The archbishop
is detained abroad by the need to restore peace between the kings of
England and France and to work for the recovery of the cross of Christ
which is in enemy hands. To avoid delay in the appointment of a bishop
of London he orders them to send eight of their wiser canons* ('sanioris et
melioris consilii') *to come to his presence in Normandy on the Sunday*
Isti sunt dies *(26 March 1189) with ratificatory letters* ('de ratihabi-
tione') *of the chapter, to elect a fit pastor.*   [March 1189]

B = Lambeth Palace ms. 145 (Ralph de Diceto, *Ymagines historiarum*) fo. 114rb.
s. xii/xiii.

Pd from B in Diceto ii 62.

The archbp's style is probably abridged: Baldewinus Cantuariensis archiepiscopus.
    Dean Ralph couples with this mandate the kg's writ which orders the dean and
chapter to send eight canons ('quos ad hoc magis idoneos esse videritis') to him,
wherever he should be on the Sunday *Isti sunt dies* to make an election.
According to Ralph de Diceto, the chapter sent a large contingent to Normandy
with him who spent fourteen fruitless weeks there. Richard FitzNeal, dean of
Lincoln, archdn of Ely, and canon of London, was elected bp at kg Richard's
great council at Pipewell, 15 Sept. 1189, and consecrated 31 Dec. Bp Gilbert
Foliot had died 18 Feb. 1187.

294.   London: priory of St Mary, Clerkenwell

*Confirmation for the nuns of Clerkenwell of the church of Sitting-
bourne, granted and confirmed to them by king Henry II.*
                                      [Jan. 1186 × Dec. 1187]

B = Lambeth Palace, Reg. W. Warham fo. 119r (122r). s. xvi in.

Baldewinus dei gratia Cantuariensis archiepiscopus totius Anglie
primas et apostolice sedis legatus omnibus Christi fidelibus ad quos
presentes littere pervenerint eternam in domino salutem. Ad universitatis vestre notitiam volumus pervenire dilectas filias nostras
priorissam et moniales de Clerkenwell' cartam illustris Anglorum
regis Henrici secundi nobis exhibuisse, ex cuius tenore intelleximus

dominum regem ecclesiam de Sidingeburn' in Cantia ecclesie sancte Marie de Clerkenwell et iamdictis monialibus ibidem deo famulantibus in liberam et perpetuam elemosinam concessisse et dedisse cum omnibus pertinentiis suis. Nos vero concessionem et donationem a domino rege factam grato acceptantes assensu eam auctoritate qua fungimur presentis scripti serie confirmamus et ipsam sicut rationabiliter facta est sigilli nostri patrocinio communimus. Hiis testibus : magistro Henrico de Norham', magistro Silvestro, magistro Radulpho de Sancto Martino, Iohanne de Exonia, Willelmo de Sotindon, Gileberto filio Willelmi, Henrico de Exonia, Ricardo de Umframvill', Willelmo Prudum', Galfrido Forti, Vincentio, Salomone, Eustachio de Wilton, et aliis.

The cartulary of Clerkenwell contains Henry II's charter: *Mon. Ang.* iv 85 and *Clerkenwell cartulary* 9 no. 7. The editor of the latter notes the archiepiscopal charters in Reg. W. Warham but does not print them. Cf. above, no. 162.

295. South Malling: collegiate church of St Michael

Inspeximus and confirmation for the canons of the church of St Michael of Malling of the charter of archbishop Theobald.

[April 1185 × Jan. 1186 or Dec. 1187 × Nov. 1190]

B = Lambeth Palace ms. 1212 (register of the see of Canterbury) fo. 56r (fo. 41r, p. 107). s. xiii ex. C = Bodl. ms. Tanner 223 (register of the see) fo. 63r (p. 121). s. xvi in. Copied from B. D = BL ms. Add. 33182 (court book of South Malling) fo. 8r (p. 12). s. xvi med. Probably copied from B (see *BIHR* xxxii (1959) 58–62).

Universis sancte matris ecclesie filiis ad quos presens scriptum pervenerit B. dei gratia Cantuariensis archiepiscopus totius Anglie primas illam que est in domino salutem. Ad universitatis vestre notitiam volumus pervenire nos cartam bone memorie Theobaldi predecessoris nostri quondam Cantuariensis archiepiscopi sub hiis verbis comprehensam inspexisse. T. dei gratia etc. de verbo ad verbum ut supra proximo. Nos igitur quod a prefato predecessore nostro rationabiliter in hac parte factum est ratum et gratum habemus illudque presentis scripti serie et sigilli nostri appositione communimus et confirmamus. Hiis testibus: magistro Petro Blesensi Bathoniensi archidiacono, Hereberto Cantuariensi archidiacono, magistro Silvestro, magistro Radulfo de Sancto Martino, magistro Willelmo de Sancta Fide precentore Wellensi, Roberto de Buckenton', Iohanne de Exonia, Galfrido Forti, Galfrido filio Terrici, Willelmo Prudome, Eustachio de Wilton, et multis aliis.

Theobald's charter (B fo. 56r, printed by Saltman, *Theobald* 403–4 no. 180) granted the canons the tithe of pannage 'tam in denariis quam in porcis' and the right to keep twenty-four pigs of their demesne in the archbp's forest free of pannage.

296. Monks Kirby priory

Inspeximus (incomplete) and confirmation for the monks of (Monks) Kirby of a charter of archbishop Richard. [Jan. 1186 × Dec. 1187]

A = PRO E 327/94. Endorsed, s. xiii ex.: Confirmacio Cant' archiepiscopi. Approx. 149 × 152 + 18 mm. Sealing d. q. 2; tag remains, seal lost. Badly damaged, with several holes.

Pd from A in *Formulare anglicanum* 51 no. xciv (omitting 7 witnesses).

Omnibus fidelibus ad quos presens scriptura pervenerit . Bald(ewinus) dei gratia Cantuariensis archiepiscopus . totius Anglie primas . et apostolice sedis legatus . salutem in domino. Noverit universitas vestra . dilectum filium nostrum .B. priorem de Kirkebi . cartam bone memorie Ricardi Cantuariensis archiepiscopi decessoris nostri nobis exhibuisse in hec verba. Universis sancte matris ecclesie filiis Ricardus dei gratia Cantuariensis archiepiscopus totius Anglie primas . et apostolice sedis legatus . salutem in domino. Quoniam ea que pro bono utilitatis ecclesiastice facta sunt . perpetua debent stabilitate gaudere . in communem volumus noticiam devenire . nos presentis carte patrocinio confirmasse ecclesie de Kirkebi omnia tenementa sua . in terris decimis . et omnimodis obventionibus ad eam pertinentibus . cum omnibus libertatibus et liberis consuetudinibus quibus tempore Henrici regis melius et liberius tenuit . sicut bone memorie Walterus Coventrensis episcopus et dilectus filius noster Ricardus Coventrensis archidiaconus ea cartis suis rationabiliter confirmaverunt.[a] Testibus Iohanne Pictavensi episcopo .[b]Roberto de Novoburgo . Benedicto cancellario . magistro Gerardo . Willelmo . de Norhal'.[c] et aliis. Nos autem hanc decessoris nostri confirmationem sicut rationabiliter facta est ratam habentes.' eam presenti scripto et sigilli nostri appositione confirmamus. Testibus magistro Henrico de Norhamt' . magistro Silvestro . magistro Godefrido . Galfrido filio Therrici . Iohanne de Exonia . Galfrido Forti . Henrico de Cruce . Willelmo Prudhum';

[a] *om. two clauses of archbp Richard's charter (see above, no. 168):* Precipimus quoque quod ... , Si quis igitur ... A   [b] *om.* domino A   [c] *three witnesses omitted* A

The inspeximus formula is quoted and commented upon by V. H. Galbraith in *EHR* lii (1937) 72. The script resembles that of no. 311. Cf. the witness-lists. Prior B(aldwin) was a relative of the archbp.

297. Newton Longville priory

Notification of a composition made in the archbishop's presence after dispute between William, monk and proctor of the monks of Longueville, and Roger son of William, canon of Lincoln, over tithes of demesne of Moulsoe. Canon Roger resigned the tithes into the hand of the archbishop, who restored them to the monk; the latter then granted them to Roger to be held saving a yearly pension of five shillings to the monks of Longueville. After Roger's death the tithes shall be at the free disposal of the monks. [April 1185 × Jan. 1186]

B = Oxford, New Coll. Mun. 'Liber niger' fo. 66r. s. xvi in.

Pd from B in *Newington Longeville charters* 50–51 no. 55.

The archbp is not styled legate. Roger, canon of an unidentified prebend from *c.*1150×1154, is not in the second list of canons *c.*1187 (*Fasti eccl. angl. 1066–1300* iii 142). While the archbp's name is omitted in this copy of his charter, he is named in canon Roger's record of the agreement (ibid. 51 no. 56). Undated letters of canon Roger and of Robert of Burnham, archdn of Buckingham, show that Roger later resigned all right to these tithes (ibid. 51–52 nos. 57–58).
The case was heard by the archbp during the vacancy of the see of Lincoln.

297A. Nuneaton priory

Confirmation for the nuns of Eaton of the churches (enumerated) granted to them by various named donors and confirmed by the diocesan bishops. [Jan. × May 1186]

B = BL Add. ch. 47398 (Nuneaton cartulary roll) no. 7. s. xiv in.

B. dei gratia Cantuariensis archiepiscopus totius Anglie primas et apostolice sedis legatus universis Christi fidelibus ad quos presentes littere pervenerint eternam in domino salutem. Cum ad officii nostri pertineat sollicitudinem circa pacem subditis nostris conservandam operam et diligentiam exibere, eos et eorum possessiones propensiori benignitatis studio debemus protegere qui se artioris religionis voto noscuntur obligasse. Nos igitur dilectas filias nostras moniales de Etton' ordinem Fontis Ebraldi professas sub nostra protectione in securo statu et tranquilla pace permanere volentes, possessiones quas fidelium in subsidium religionis pia eis devotio rationabiliter contulit et episcopalis auctoritas canonice confirmavit auctoritatis nostre patrocinio dignum duximus communire. De quibus quasdam propriis nominibus censuimus exprimendas; ex dono illustris 'Anglorum' regis Henrici secundi ecclesiam de Chalton' cum omnibus pertinentiis suis, ex dono et concessione Roberti prioris et conven-

tus de Kinilewurde ecclesiam de Hodnilla, ex dono Ricardi Wintoniensis episcopi et concessione David de Armentariis ecclesiam de
Burgeleya, ex dono Radulfi de Turri ecclesiam de Burgton' cum
omnibus pertinentiis suis, ex dono Willelmi comitis Gloec' ecclesiam sancti Gregorii de Sudbiria cum omnibus ad eam pertinentibus, ex dono Gervasii Painelli ecclesiam de Waltham, ex dono
Ricardi filii Nigelli ecclesiam de Mureslay cum omnibus pertinentiis suis, ex dono Arnoldi de Bosco ecclesiam de Claybrok' cum
omnibus pertinentiis suis, 'ex dono Roberti de Craft' (?) ecclesiam
de Merton' cum omnibus pertinentiis suis.' Ut autem donationes et
concessiones memoratis monialibus a predictis viris facte firmam et
perpetuam habeant stabilitatem, easdem sicut rationabiliter et
canonice facte sunt auctoritate qua fungimur confirmamus et sigilli
nostri appositione communimus. Hiis testibus: Willelmo Glowec',
magistro P. Blesensi Bathon' archidiaconis, magistro Radulfo de
Sancto Martino, Iohanne de Exonia, Gileberto filio Willelmi,
Galfrido Forti et aliis.

> The archbp is styled legate and the archdn of Gloucester is not yet elected to the
> see of Worcester (c.25 May 1186).
>   Records of the separate grants are mostly – in original or in copy – among the
> charters of the Astons of Aston Hall, Runcorn, now BL Add. ch. 47423–4,
> 47556–8, 47573, 48299–48301.
>   On the status of Nuneaton – abbey or priory – see above, no. 179.

297B.   Nuneaton priory

*Mandate to T(homas) prior of Warwick and John vice-archdeacon of
Coventry, on the complaint of the nuns of Nuneaton that certain
knights dwelling in the archdeaconry withhold rents due to the nuns.
The addressees are to summon the parties before them, investigate the
charge, and do full justice to the nuns.*   [Jan. 1186 × Dec. 1187]

> A = BL Add. ch. 48306. Endorsed, s. xiii/xiv: Commissio episcopi Cantuar' ad
> inquirendum de iniuriis factis ecclesie de Mertun' (and added): Non irrotula-
> tur nec mensio sit. Approx. 145 × 47 + 9 mm. tongue. Sealed s. q., tongue but
> no tie, fragments of seal sewn in silk bag, pattern as no. 177A.

.B. dei gratia Cantuariensis archiepiscopus tocius Anglie primas et
apostolice sedis legatus ⫶ dilectis filiis .T. priori de Warewico et
Iohanni vicearchidiacono Coventr' salutem et benedictionem.
Querelam monialium de Ettona ad nos transmissam ⫶ recepimus
quod quidam milites in archidiaconatu Coventr' commorantes
redditus quosdam quos ecclesie de Merton' ad ipsas moniales sicut
accepimus pertinenti^a . solvere tenentur . iniuste detinere presumunt. Unde quoniam iuri predictarum monialium volumus sicut et

debemus providere ; vobis de quorum confidimus discrecione huius rei cognicionem duximus committendam mandantes quatinus partibus ante presentiam vestram convocatis veritatem inquiratis et prefatis monialibus plenam super proposita querela iusticiam faciatis exhibere ne pro iusticie defectu iustam habeant iterande querele occasionem. Valete.

a pertinentis A

298. Plympton priory

Inspeximus and confirmation for prior Johel and the canons of Plympton of the charter of bishop Bartholomew of Exeter which confirmed to them the grants of his predecessors, bishops William, Robert, and Robert II. [6 Oct. × 30 Nov. 1189]

> A = Exeter, Devon Record Office, Exeter City Archives misc. deeds 226. Endorsed, s. xiii: Carta B. archiepiscopi de prebenda Exon'. Approx. 170 × 240 + 25 mm. Sealing d. q. 2; seal and counterseal (natural wax).
>
> Pd from A in *Mon. Exon.* 137–8 no. XI.

.B. dei gratia Cantuariensis archiepiscopus totius Anglie primas omnibus Christi fidelibus ad quos presens scriptum pervenerit ; eternam in domino salutem. Ad universitatis vestre noticiam volumus pervenire ; dilectos filios nostros Iohellum 'priorem' et canonicos de Plimton' . cartam bone memorie .B. quondam Exoniensis episcopus nobis exhibuisse in hec verba .B. dei gratia episcopus Exoniensis . omnibus ad quos presens carta pervenerit ; in Christo salutem. Noverit universitas vestra quod Willelmus episcopus tercius predecessor noster sicut ex carta ipsius et ex testimonio multorum cognovimus ; dedit et concessit ecclesie beati Petri Plimton'*a* sexaginta solidos de prebenda cuiuscumque canonici Exoniensis ecclesie sive defuncti sive ad ordinem religionis conversi. Hanc vero donationem successor eius bone memorie Robertus episcopus ratam habuit et carta sua confirmavit. Insuper de dono liberalitatis sue intuitu pietatis viginti solidos superaddidit . ut deinceps Plimton' ecclesia in obitu cuiuscumque canonici Exoniensis ecclesie sive in conversione eius ad religionem ; quatuor libras de prebenda ipsius canonici quatuor terminis quibus prebende reddi solent ; percipere debeat. Robertus vero secundus pie recordationis episcopus ; predictam donationem quatuor librarum ratam habuit . et carta sua confirmavit. Nos vero que a predecessoribus nostris venerabilibus episcopis rite facta sunt perpetua stabilitate permanere volentes ; memoratam donationem .iiii^{or} . librarum Plimton' ecclesie assensu capituli nostri presenti carta et impressione sigilli nostri ut inconcussa permaneat *a* confirmamus. Teste capitulo. Nos igitur quod a prenominatis episcopis pia et rationabili consideratione factum esse in hac parte dinoscitur gratum habentes et ratum *a* illud sicut rationabiliter factum est confirmamus et sigilli nostri appositione communimus. Hiis testibus . Willelmo abbate Sireburn' . Rogero priore Cantuariensi . Petro archidiacono Bathoniensi . Willelmo precentore Wellensi . magistro Silvestro . magistro Radulfo de Sancto Martino . Iohanne de Exonia . Galfrido filio Terrici . Willelmo Prudum' . Galfrido Forti . Henrico de Cruce . Eustachio de Wilton' . et multis aliis.

a Plūton' A

Roger Norreis was appointed prior of Christ Church by the archbp 6 Oct. and removed 30 Nov. 1189.

The charter of bp William, dated 2 July 1133, is printed from Exeter City Archives in *Mon. Exon.* 136 no. VII.

299.   Pont-Audemer: hospital of St Gilles

Confirmation for the leper brethren of the hospital of St Gilles, Pont-Audemer, of the grant by count Waleran of Meulan of the church of St Peter, Sturminster Marshal, and of a composition between the brethren and Walter the clerk recorded by archbishop Thomas.

[Jan. 1186 × Dec. 1187]

B = Rouen, Bibl. municipale ms. Y 200 (cartulary of hospital of St Gilles) fo. 28v. s. xiii in.

Pd (calendar) from B in *CDF* 86 no. 255.

B. dei gratia Cantuariensis archiepiscopus totius Anglie primas et apostolice sedis legatus omnibus Christi fidelibus ad quos presentes litere pervenerint illam que est in domino salutem. Ad universitatis vestre notitiam volumus pervenire nos ex carta .G. quondam comitis de Mellent intellexisse eundem comitem ecclesiam sancti Petri Sturministre, quantum ad laicam pertinet donationem, fratribus leprosis in hospitali sancti Egidii de Ponteaud' commorantibus in perpetuam elemosinam contulisse, quam donationem dominus illustris rex Anglorum Henricus secundus et bone memorie Iocelinus quondam episcopus Saresburiensis ecclesie, sicut scripta eorum auctentica protestantur, confirmaverunt. Ex scriptis quoque gloriosi martiris Thome et memorati episcopi nobis innotuit quandam compositionem inter Galterum clericum et procuratores predictorum infirmorum super eadem ecclesia factam et utriusque auctoritate roboratam esse. Ut igitur quod a predicto comite memoratis leprosis pia devotione collatum est et tam regia quam episcopali auctoritate firmatum perpetua gaudeat stabilitate, utrique concessioni iuxta quod in scriptis auctenticis continetur expressum nostrum accommodantes assensum, ipsam et prefatam compositionem sicut iuste et rationabiliter facte sunt firma esse concedimus et auctoritate qua fungimur communimus.

> Count Waleran of Meulan (1104–66) founded the hospital of St Gilles in 1135. The grant of Sturminster church, recorded in the cartulary (*CDF* 84 nos. 243–4) was confirmed by kg Henry II (*Recueil des actes de Henri II* i 326–8 no. 195: 1155 × 1161). For archbp Thomas's confirmation of the agreement with Walter the clerk, see no. 32 above. A witness-list may have been omitted by the copyist, for the other charters in the cartulary are devoid of lists; but cf. no. 235 above.

300.   Ramscombe priory

Inspeximus and confirmation for the nuns of 'Ramstede' of the charter by which archbishop Richard granted them all the land on which their house is built, and the land which Ralph de Dena released to the archbishop.   [Jan. 1186 × Dec. 1187]

> A = lost original listed (in 'Vas xiiii') in inventory of archbpric deeds of 1330, PRO E 36/137 p. 9a, whence pd in 'Canterbury archbpric charters' 13.
>
> B = Lambeth Palace ms. 1212 (register of the see of Canterbury) fo. 47v (32v, p. 90) no. xxix. s. xiii ex. C = Bodl. ms. Tanner 223 (register of the see) fo. 52v (p. 100). Copy of B. s. xvi in.

B. dei gratia Cantuariensis archiepiscopus totius Anglie primas et apostolice sedis legatus omnibus Christi fidelibus ad quos presentes littere pervenerint salutem in domino. Ad universitatis vestre notitiam volumus pervenire moniales de Ramstede scriptum bone memorie Ricardi predecessoris nostri Cantuariensis archiepiscopi nobis in hec verba presentasse. Omnibus Christi fidelibus ad quos presentes littere pervenerint Ricardus dei gratia ... [above, no. 184] ... Galfrido clerico, et multis aliis. Volentes igitur quod a predicto predecessore nostro memoratis monialibus concessum est firmum et stabile permanere, ipsius concessionem sicut iuste et rationabiliter facta est firmam [fo. 48r] et perpetuam manere concedimus et ipsam auctoritate qua fungimur communimus. Hiis testibus: magistro Silvestro, magistro Radulfo de Sancto Martino, Iohanne de Exonia, Galfrido filio Terrici, Henrico canonico Malling', Eustagio de Wilton', Galfrido Forti, et aliis.

301. Ranton priory

Confirmation for the canons of Ranton of the grant made by the late Robert Noel 'de loco qui dicitur ad S. Mariam de Essarz' to God and St Mary and the canons serving God under the rule of the church of Haughmond. [April 1185 × Nov. 1190]

A = 'Penes Walterum Harcourt de Ellenhall in comitatu Staff.' c.1640, original now lost.

Pd from A, abridged, in *Mon. Ang.* vi 257 no. III.

The archbp's abridged title ('B. dei gratia Cantuariensis archiepiscopus') gives no clue to date. Ranton (or Ronton) priory was founded mid-twelfth century: the charters of Robert Noel and his son Thomas are in *Mon. Ang.* vi 257–8. They use the term 'sub regula et obedientia Hagemanensis ecclesie', but archbp Baldwin's confirmation omits the words 'et obedientia'. Subordination to Haughmond abbey was a matter of dispute in the next century: see *Mon. Ang.* vii 750 and *EEA* iii no. 583.

302. Reading abbey

Inspeximus and confirmation for the monks of Reading of a charter of archbishop Theobald which confirmed the charter of king Henry I their founder and the confirmation of his gifts by archbishop William. Theobald's charter specifies the grant of Reading and its churches and chapels, the churches of Thatcham, Cholsey, Wargrave, Stanton (Harcourt), (Long) Handborough, and Aston, and property in Wigston (Parva) which bishop Robert (II) of Lincoln confirmed by charter, with all else which the monks canonically possess or may acquire in future. [April 1185 × Jan. 1186 or Dec. 1187 × March 1190]

B = BL ms. Egerton 3031 (Reading cartulary) fo. 51r (38r). s. xiii in. C = BL ms. Harl. 1708 (Reading cartulary) fo. 188v, abridged by reference to preceding text (fo. 188r) of Theobald's charter, and omitting witness-list. s. xiii med. D = BL ms. Cotton Vesp. E xxv (Reading cartulary) fo. 109r, abridged as C. s. xiv in. Probably copied from C.

Pd (Theobald's charter only) from ms. Egerton 3031 fo. 50r collated with C, by Saltman, *Theobald* 437–9 no. 215.

Universis sancte matris ecclesie filiis ad quos presens scriptum pervenerit B. dei gratia Cantuariensis archiepiscopus totius Anglie primas eternam in domino salutem. Ad notitiam vestram volumus pervenire nos scriptum bone memorie Theodbaldi predecessoris nostri in hec verba inspexisse. T. dei gratia Cantuariensis archiepiscopus ... [Saltman, *Theobald* no. 215] ... subiaceat. Amen. Valete. Nos igitur ut quod a memorato predecessore nostro iuste et rationabiliter ordinatum est et confirmatum firmam et perpetuam habeat stabilitatem, eandem confirmationem auctoritate qua fungimur communimus et sigilli nostri appositione roboramus. Hiis testibus: magistro Silvestro, magistro R. de Sancto Martino, magistro Edmundo, et multis aliis.

For the charter of bp Robert II of Lincoln see *EEA* i 144–5 no. 230.

303. The church of Rochester

Confirmation for the monks of Rochester of the grant of a messuage within the city walls by Albreda daughter of Robert the moneyer, saving the customary service to the archbishop's court of Darenth.

[29 Sept. 1185 × Jan. 1186 or Dec. 1187 × March 1190]

A = Maidstone, Kent Archives Office DRc/T 293 (Rochester D. & C. Mun. B 816 (N 2)). Endorsed. s. xii/xiii: Confirmatio Bald' archiepiscopi de terra Ric' palmarii in Roffa; s. xiii : De terris Albrede filie Rodberti monetarii ... domus quam tenent heredes Potyn de qua debentur xxvi d. ad manerium de Derente; s. xvi : De quodam messuagio infra muros civitatis Roffensis. Approx. 194 × 108 + 26 mm. Sealing d. q. 2, but with no slit on crease; tag remains, seal lost.

B = BL ms. Cotton Domit. A x (Rochester register) fo. 165r (166r). s. xiii in. Witnesses omitted.

Pd from B in *Reg. Roff.* 527.

.B. dei gracia Cantuariensis archiepiscopus . tocius Anglie primas . omnibus Christi fidelibus eternam in domino salutem. Noverit universitas vestra nos divina pietatis intuitu concessisse et presenti carta nostra confirmasse ecclesie beati Andree Rouec' . et monachis ibidem deo servientibus donationem quam Albreda filia Rodberti monetarii fecit predicte ecclesie de quodam masagio suo quod habuit et tenuit iure hereditario infra muros civitatis Roffensis . ita ut prefata ecclesia et predicti monachi habeant et teneant prenominatum masagium . libere . integre . plenarie . sicut predicta Albreda vel aliquis antecessorum eius melius et liberius illud tenuit . salvo debito et consueto servitio quod prefatum masagium debet annuatim curie nostre de Derente. His testibus . domno Gileberto Roffensi episcopo . magistro Silvestro . magistro Willelmo de Sancta Fide . magistro Radulfo de Sancto Martino . Gaufrido notario . Michaele clerico de Ospring' . Osberto de Wrinedel . Radulfo le Bor . Rogero de Pundherste et multis aliis.

After the consecration of Gilbert Glanvill as bp of Rochester.

†304.   The church of Rochester *(? spurious)*

Confirmation for the monks of Rochester of their churches and tithes (enumerated) in the diocese of Canterbury and of all possessions and privileges granted by kings, archbishops, and others, whose charters the archbishop has inspected.

Canterbury, in synod, in the first year of
king Richard [Sept. 1189 × March 1190]

B = BL ms. Cotton Domit. A x (Rochester register) fo. 205r (206r). s. xiii in.
C = BL ms. Royal 5 A iv (Rochester register) fo. 198v. s. xiii ex.

Pd from B in *Reg. Roff.* 48–49.

Universis sancte matris ecclesie filiis ad quos presens scriptum pervenerit Baldewinus dei gratia Cantuariensis archiepiscopus totius Anglie primas eternam in domino salutem. Quanto magis ecclesiam Roffensem et fratres in ea domino famulantes ratione multiplici*ᵃ* paterno affectu diligere ac fovere tenemur, eo attentius illorum utilitati, honori,*ᵇ* et tranquillitati perpetue intendere ac providere dignum duximus. Ad omnium igitur notitiam volumus pervenire nos auctoritate Cantuariensis ecclesie cui divina miseratione presidemus, habito consilio cum viris*ᶜ* prudentibus et discretis, de assensu etiam et voluntate capituli nostri, concessisse et confirmasse monachis Roffensibus ecclesias quas habent in dyocesi nostra ex collatione regum vel archiepiscoporum seu aliorum Christi fidelium: ecclesiam scilicet de Boxle cum omnibus pertinentiis suis, ecclesiam de Sturmue cum omnibus pertinentiis suis, ecclesiam de Northune cum omnibus pertinentiis suis, ecclesiam de Nortflete cum decimis de Hyfeld et de la Dune et cum omnibus aliis pertinentiis suis, et in predictis ecclesiis vicariorum presentationem inperpetuum, qua quidem ante tempora nostra se gavisos fuisse in presentia nostra efficaciter docuerunt, similiterque omnes redditus et omnes decimas a quibuscumque dei fidelibus hactenus eisdem monachis in dyocesi nostra collatas: decimam scilicet quam percipiunt in parochia de Gilling' et decimam de Screhambroch*ᵈ* in parochia de Clive, decimam etiam de Ealdeham in parochia de Wroteham, decimam de Gedding' in parochia de Hese, decimam de Hamwold in parochia de Wednesberg', decimam de Merile in parochia de Herietesham, decimam de Buggele in parochia de Boctune, decimam de Bengesham in parochia de Croindene, decimas etiam quas percipiunt in Dudendale, in Stalesfeld,*ᵉ* in Bilsintune, quas quidem decimas universas a quadraginta annis et amplius ante tempora nostra predictos monachos pacifice et [fo. 205v] inconcusse possedisse et libere percepisse ex donatione Christi fidelium testimonio virorum fide dignorum et aliis documentis evidentissimis cognovimus facta super hiis diligenti inquisitione, quantum etiam ad nos pertinet concedimus et confirmamus eisdem monachis omnes terras et omnes redditus et omnes libertates et omnia beneficia, sive a regibus Anglie, Willelmo, scilicet, Henrico primo, Henrico secundo et aliis omnibus sive ab archiepiscopis Cantuariensibus, Lanfranco scilicet, et Anselmo, Radulfo, Willelmo, et Ricardo, quorum cartas inspeximus, sive ab aliis predecessoribus nostris seu etiam ab episcopis eiusdem ecclesie vel ab aliis Christi fidelibus ipsis monachis concessa et ab eisdem optenta, ut ea omnia ita libere et pacifice, integre et plenarie habeant inperpetuum et possideant, ut nulli omnino hominum neque clerico neque laico super eisdem liceat predictis monachis gravamen inferre vel molestiam. Observatores autem huius nostre concessionis et confirmationis dextera dei omnipotentis protegat et benedicat, et qui ea infirmare temptaverint iram eterni iudicis et indignationem nisi ad congruam satisfactionem venerint incurrant. Ut igitur hec nostra concessio et confirmatio perpetue firmitatis robur obtineat, eam presenti scripto et sigilli nostri testimonio duximus roborandam. Hiis testibus: magistro Petro Blesensi, domino Roberto de Bekintune,[f] magistro Silvestro, Radulfo de Sancto Martino, domino Rogero de Cirintun', Willelmo de Sancta Fide, Willelmo Prudumme, domino Iohanne cancellario, Martino camerario,[g] domino Roberto de Cruci,[h] Radulfo de Vaus, Petro pincerna, Roberto de Bristo, et multis aliis clericis et laicis. Facta est autem[j] hec confirmatio apud Cantuariam in synodo anno primo coronationis Ricardi illustris regis Anglorum.

[a] multipli B   [b] et C; -que B   [c] viris *follows* discretis B   [d] Schrehambroch C; Srestinbroke B   [e] Stalesfeld C; Stanesfeld B   [f] Bekintune C, *omitting rest of names*; Belrint' B   [g] Camberar' B   [h] ? *for* Rogero de Grusci B   [j] autem C, *om.* B

The latest time at which archbp Baldwin can have attended a synod at Canterbury was the first days of March 1190; he crossed to France 6 March (Gervas. i. 485).

There is no other record of a diocesan synod at Canterbury 1189–1190.

This charter is suspect because of its close similarities to no. 194 above, thus forming one of a highly suspect group with nos. 194, 195, 305, and 594 (*EEA* iii). The witness-list may be taken from a genuine text, but note that Peter of Blois is not given his title of archdn of Bath.

†305.   The church of Rochester *(? spurious)*

Confirmation for the monks of Rochester of all grants of lands, churches, rents, and tithes granted to their church by kings, archbishops, and others, (in particular the lands enumerated) assigned by bishop Gundulf to the use of the monks; with confirmation of their churches and tithes (enumerated) in the diocese of Canterbury.

[? Dec. 1189 × March 1190]

B = BL ms. Cotton Domit. A x (Rochester register) fo. 182v (183v). s. xiii in.
Pd in *Reg. Roff.* 46–47, and in A. C. Ducarel, *Hist. and antiquities of Lambeth parish* (1785) Appendix p. 19 (in J. Nichols, *Bibliotheca* (1780–90) no. V).

Universis sancte matris ecclesie filiis ad quos presens scriptum pervenerit B. dei gratia Cantuariensis archiepiscopus totius Anglie primas eternam in domino salutem. Quoniam Rofensem ecclesiam et fratres in ea domino famulantes ratione [fo. 183r] multiplici diligere tenemur, eo attentius eorum utilitati, honori et quieti intendere dignum duximus. Hinc est quod ad communem omnium vestrum volumus devenire notitiam quod omnes donationes et concessiones omnium maneriorum et omnium terrarum et omnium ecclesiarum cum omnibus redditibus suis et omnium decimarum que hactenus concesse sunt et donate ecclesie beati Andree apostoli que sita est in civitate Rouecestrie a quibuscumque sive regibus sive archiepiscopis vel episcopis sive comitibus sive*a* aliis quibuslibet huius regni nobilibus concesse sunt aut donate, ego B. dei gratia Cantuariensis archiepiscopus totius Anglie primas auctoritate a deo michi collata omnimodo ratas et in perpetuum stabiles esse confirmo et eas nominatim quas Gundulfus ecclesie illius episcopus ut ad usum monachorum illorum domino Christo et predicto apostolo devote famulantium permaneant*b* ordinavit, ego eidem ecclesie et eisdem monachis iure eterne hereditatis habendas libere atque quiete confirmo possidendas, et sicut prenominatus episcopus qui monachos illos in Rofensi ecclesia congregavit et ipsa maneria et terras quas in suo dominico habebat ipsis monachis a suo proprio victu discrevit discretas dedit, videlicet Wldeham cum omnibus appenditiis suis, Frendesberiam cum omnibus appenditiis suis, Stoches cum omnibus appenditiis suis, Denintune cum omnibus pertinentiis suis, Sufflet' cum omnibus appenditiis suis, Lamhetham cum omnibus appenditiis suis, excepta*c* illa parte curie sue super Thamisiam prout certis limitibus distincta est et viginti et quattuor acris et una perticata terre de dominico suo et servitio quod habuerunt [fo. 183v] de quattuor acris Hawise super Thamisiam, sicut continetur in autentico scripto inter nos et ecclesiam et

prefatos monachos inde confecto, Hedenham cum manerio Cuden-
tune nomine et cum omnibus XL hidis terre que appendent et omnes
alias minutas terras et omnes redditus omnium terrarum quas suo
tempore adquisivit et illis dedit, ita firmiter et stabiliter in^d omnibus,
omnia ista monachis illis confirmo et corroboro. Confirmo etiam eis
ecclesias quas habent in Cantuariensi diocesi seu regum Anglie sive
antecessorum nostrorum vel aliorum fidelium liberalitate eis collatas:
ecclesiam de Norfliet' cum omnibus ad eam pertinentibus, ecclesiam
de Boxle cum omnibus pertinentiis suis, ecclesiam de Sturemuthe
cum omnibus ad eam pertinentibus, ecclesiam de Nortune cum
omnibus pertinentiis suis, similiter decimas^e quas habent in diocesi
nostra a dei fidelibus sibi concessas: videlicet decimam de Hamwolde, decimam de Dudindale, decimam de Bilsintune, decimam de
Merile, decimam de Bugele, decimam de Stalesfeld,^{f} decimam de
Gilingeham, decimam de Srembroc, decimam de Aldeham, decimam de Bengesham, decimam de Geddinges, et alias ecclesias vel
decimas quas adquisierunt vel in posterum rationabiliter adquirere
poterunt, et sicut beate memorie Anselmus et Theobaldus et
Ricardus Cantuarienses archiepiscopi et Gundulfus et Ascelinus^g et
Walterus Rofenses episcopi possessiones et maneria omnia a rege
Henrico primo et Henrico secundo confirmata confirmaverunt, et
eidem ecclesie et monachis predictis aut post illos inperpetuum
victuris firmiter stabilia et stabiliter firma et illibata perma-[fo.
184r]nere xanctierunt, et auctoritate dei omnipotentis patris et filii et
spiritus sancti et omnium sanctorum omnes illos qui aliquid de regis
concessione 'et' illorum institutione vel confirmatione infringerent
excommunicaverunt, ita et nos tantorum virorum exempla secuti,
institutiones, confirmationes, et omnia predicta ipsis monachis in
perpetuum habenda firmiter stabilia et stabiliter firma et illibata
permanere xanctio, et sub eadem interminatione omnes qui vel
eorum vel nostram confirmationem infirmare vel absque communi
fratrum ecclesie illius consilio et consensu immutare presumpserint^h
a liminibus sancte matris ecclesie ex auctoritate dei patris omnipotentis et filii et spiritus sancti omniumque sanctorum sequestro, et nisi
ad congruam satisfactionem venerint eterni iudicis iram, indignationem et maledictionem incurrant. Ut igitur hec nostra confirmatio
perpetue firmitatis robur optineat eam presenti scripto et sigilli nostri
testimonio duximus roborandam. Hiis testibus: domino Roberto de
Bechinton, magistro P. Blesensi etc.

---

^{a} sive: se B ^{b} fam. perm.: famulantur permaneat B ^{c} excepcepta B
^{d} in: 'cum' B ^{e} decimas *added in margin* B ^{f} Stanesfeld B ^{g} A *followed by erasure* B
^{h} presumpserit B

The reference to the transaction between the archbp and the church of Rochester 'sicut continetur in autentico scripto' must relate to no. 244, not earlier than Dec. 1189 and probably of March 1190. The relative positions of Robert de Bechinton and Peter of Blois in the fragmentary witness-list is surprising (cf. no. 304), even though Robert was one of those appointed to manage the temporal affairs of the see during Baldwin's absence on crusade (no. 244). The charter is suspect because it belongs to a highly suspect group, including nos. 194, 195, 304. The use in some places of the first person singular (taken over from no. 195) is inconsistent and confused.

306. Romney: hospital of St Thomas

Inspeximus and confirmation of a charter of Adam of Charing, which grants property to the lepers in the hospital of St Thomas the martyr at Romney, with confirmation of further grants by Adam.

[Sept. 1185 × Jan. 1186 or Dec. 1187 × March 1190]

A = Oxford, Magdalen Coll. Deeds, Romney 59. Endorsed, s. xiii: Confirmatio domini Baldewini archiepiscopi Cantuariensis. Approx. 183 × 225 + 21 mm. Sealing d. q. 2; tag remains, with broken bits of seal in canvas bag.

.B. dei gracia Cantuariensis archiepiscopus . tocius Anglie primas universis Christi fidelibus ad quos presens carta pervenerit ∙ eternam in domino salutem. Cartam dilecti filii nostri Ade de Charringes recepimus et vidimus . in hec verba .A. de Cherringes universis Christi fidelibus ad quos presens scriptum pervenerit salutem. Sciatis quod pro amore dei . et pro honore . et reverentia gloriosi martyris Tome . et pro salute anime mee . et antecessorum meorum concessi et dedi . et hac carta mea confirmavi in perpetuam elemosinam leprosis apud Rumenellum in hospitali sancti Tome . commorantibus . et in posterum commoraturis terram que fuit Galfridi Turcople . et quam gloriosus martyr Tomas . eidem .G. donavit . quam etiam terram idem G. Iohanni nepoti Waleranni Roffensis episcopi . et idem Iohannes venerabili domino . et patri nostro .B. Cantuariensi archiepiscopo . et idem archiepiscopus michi pro quindecim marcis argenti vendidit. Et ideo volo quod predicti leprosi habeant in perpetuum predictam terram sicut memoratus dominus archiepiscopus eam michi concessit . solvendo inde annuatim curie de Aldinton' . ad festum sancti Michaelis . duos solidos pro omni servitio . et per defensionem Walle que ad predictam terram pertinet. Predictam igitur concessionem et donationem pretaxatis leprosis a prenominato A. factam ∙ ratam habentes et acceptam . eam presentis scripti patrocinio . et sigilli nostri appositione roboramus. Preterea quadraginta acras terre apud Snergath' . quas supradictus .A. memoratis leprosis dedit et confirmavit liberas et quietas ab omni servitio . excepta defensione Walle que ad eas pertinet . cum viginti solidis annui redditus de tenemento suo de Langeporth' . quos eisdem leprosis dedit et confirmavit *.* nos quoque concedimus et in perpetuam elemosinam confirmamus *.* sicut in carta ipsius A. rationabiliter distinguitur et iuste continetur. Testibus his .G. Roffensi episcopo . magistro Silvestro . magistro Radulfo de Sancto Martino . magistro Willelmo de Sancta Fide . Roberto de Becheton' . Willelmo de Sotindon' . Iohanne Exoniensi . Galfrido filio Terrici . Willelmo Prudum . Rogero de Tanton' . Galfrido Forti . Godefrido de Sildon' . Radulfo clerico . Rogero de Grusci senescallo . Adam de Saxinherst'. et aliis.

For Adam of Charing, excommunicated by archbp Thomas in 1169, and his foundation of the leprosary at Romney, see above, no. 67n. and *Mon. Ang.* vii 640–1. Baldwin's confirmation of the foundation is mentioned when the hospital was reconstituted in 1363 (ibid. vii 641). In 1188 Adam of Charing was the archbp's steward (*PR 34 Henry II* 202).

The witnesses of the charter include six of those, headed by the bp of Rochester, whom the archbp left in charge when he went on crusade in March 1190. Cf. no. 281 above, which also has the phrase in the address: 'ad quos presens carta perv.', unusual in Baldwin's charters. A. F. Butcher, 'The hospital of St Stephen and St Thomas New Romney: the documentary evidence', *Archaeologia Cantiana* xcvi (1981) 17–26, gives other details of the endowment and early history of the hospital from Magdalen College deeds.

307. Abbey of St-Bertin

Inspeximus and confirmation for the monks of St-Bertin of the charter of archbishop Richard, by which he confirmed to them the church of Throwley with its chapels and appurtenances.

[April 1185 × Jan. 1186 or Dec. 1187 × March 1190]

A = Original lost, from abbey of St-Bertin, St-Omer.

B = St-Omer, Bibliothèque municipale ms. 803 (Grand cartulaire de St-Bertin) vol. i p. 462 no. 333, with description: 'Ex originali in Theca Angletterre no. 4 8° loco. Cet original a 6 pouces et demi d'hauteur et 7 pouces de largeur. Registrata tomo 36 pagina 263', without mention of any seal. Transcript of A by Dom C. J. Dewitte. s. xviii ex. C = PRO, P. R. O. 31/8/144 (part 6) fo. 78 no. 17.

Pd (abridged) from B in *Chartes de St-Bertin* i 166 no. 378. Calendared from B in *Archaeologia Cantiana* iv (1861) 216 no. xix and from C in *CDF* 489 no. 1345.

Balduinus dei gratia Cantuariensis archiepiscopus totius Anglię primas universis Christi fidelibus ad quos presentes litterę pervenerint perpetuam in domino salutem. Ad universitatis vestrę notitiam volumus pervenire dilectos nobis in Christo monachos Sancti Bertini scriptum bonę memorię Ricardi predecessoris nostri Cantuariensis archiepiscopi nobis in hec verba presentasse. Ricardus dei gratia Cantuariensis archiepiscopus totius Anglię primas etc., etc.

Voyez ci devant à la page 364 à l'année 1175 au 248ème titre [*above, no. 202*]. Nos quoque ad securitatem predictorum fratrum memorati predecessoris nostri confirmationi nostrum prebentes assensum, quod ab ipso predictis fratribus iuste concessum est et rationabiliter super predicta ecclesia confirmatum ratum habemus, et ea qua fungimur auctoritate confirmamus. Hiis testibus: magistro Henrico de Norhanton, magistro Silvestro, Reginaldo de Oilly,*ᵃ* magistro Nicolao de Exonia,*ᵇ* Ricardo de Hunfranvill', Galfrido Forti,*ᶜ* et multis aliis.

ᵃ Oilly: Olly B   *ᵇ* Exonia: Exoniensi B   *ᶜ* Forti: Fotti B

*308. Priory of St Germans

Confirmation for the church of St Germans of a grant establishing regular canons in place of secular clergy, made by bishop Bartholomew of Exeter.   [Jan. 1185 × Nov. 1190]

> Mentioned only, in a note made by John Leland, which follows his abstract of a charter of bp Bartholomew: 'Balduinus archiepiscopus Cantuariensis factum approbavit' (J. Leland, *Collectanea*, ed. 1771, i 75, whence *Mon. Ang.* ii 468*b*). The note implies that Leland saw a written confirmation.

*309. Priory of St Neots

Mandate to delegates to hear and decide a case between the prior and monks of St Neots and Nicholas de Bello campo, parson of Eaton Socon.   [? Dec. 1184 × Jan. 1186]

> Mentioned only; possibly issued by archbp Richard. See above, no. 205.

*310. Abbey of St Osyth

Confirmation for the canons of ˙St Osyth of Chich of the church of Petham, granted and confirmed to them by charters of archbishops Ralph and William and Richard. Provision is made for a perpetual vicar.   [May 1185 × Nov. 1190]

> Mentioned only, in the confirmation of the grant and the notification of the regularizing of the perpetual vicar's position by archbp Hubert (*EEA* iii no. 600).

311. Abbey of Savigny

Confirmation for the monks of Savigny of their right in the church of [Long] Bennington, according to the charter by which archbishop Richard of Canterbury confirmed to them the church and its appurtenances.   [April 1185 × Jan. 1186]

A = Paris, Archives nationales L 968 (L 1146) no. 225. Endorsed, s. xii/xiii : Carta domni Balduini archiepiscopi Cantuarie de ecclesia de Belintonia. .T. ii. Approx. 150 × 84 + 17 mm. Holes in fold: on left, leather thong drawn through two holes (badly fitting in upper hole); on right, yellow silk cord drawn through one hole. Seals lost. Perhaps neither thong nor cord is an original attachment.

Pd (calendar) from A in *CDF* 307 no. 854.

Omnibus fidelibus ad quos presentes littere pervenerint . Bald(uinus) divina miseratione Cantuariensis ecclesie minister eternam in domino salutem. Ad universitatis vestre notitiam volumus pervenire . nos inspexisse litteras bone memorie R. Cantuariensis archiepiscopi predecessoris nostri . in quibus continebatur ipsum ecclesiam de Belinton' . cum omnibus ad eam pertinentibus . dilectis fratribus nostris monachis Savigniensibus ∴ confirmasse. Nos autem predicti predecessoris nostri vestigiis inherentes ∴ memoratis monachis quicquid iuris in prefata ecclesia habere noscuntur . sicut eis rationabiliter collatum est ∴ ea qua fungimur auctoritate confirmamus . et presentis scripti et sigilli nostri patrocinio communimus. Hiis testibus Willelmo archidiacono Gloucestriensi . magistro .P. archidiacono Bathoniensi . magistro Henrico de Norhanthon' . magistro Silvestro . Iohanne de Exonia . Galfrido filio Therrici . Willelmo Prudhum' . Henrico clerico.

The latest possible date is before archdn William was elected to the see of Worcester (late May 1186). The absence from the archbp's style of the legatine title points to a date before Feb. 1186, but the style 'ecclesie minister' is unusual. For early charters concerned with Long Bennington see *CDF* 296–7, 305–8 nos. 817–8, 846–58. Cf. *EEA* iv no. 172, *Mon. Ang.* vii 1024, and *Book of seals* 171–3 no. 236. The script resembles that of no. 296 above. Cf. the witness-lists.

312. Stafford: priory of St Thomas

Confirmation and protection for the canons of St Thomas the martyr near Stafford of their possessions,including those granted by Richard late bishop of Coventry and Gerard of Stafford and by other donors, as witnessed by their charters and the charter of king Henry II.

[Jan. 1186 × Dec. 1187]

A = Stafford, County Record Office, Acc. 938/5 (7967). Endorsed, s. xii ex.: Balduini archiepiscopi. Approx. 222 × 118 + 26 mm. Two holes in fold for plaited cord, fragment of seal (green wax), repaired.

B. dei gracia Cantuariensis archiepiscopus tocius Anglie primas et apostolice sedis legatus ∴ omnibus Christi fidelibus ad quos presentes litere pervenerint ∴ eternam in domino salutem. Ad dignitatis qua preminemus pertinet sollicitudinem . viros religiosos in provintia nostra constitutos ./ fovere . manutenere et eis protectionis nostre munimen inquantum ad nos pertinet impendere . eorumque possessiones protegere. Inde est quod ad vestram volumus noticiam pervenire . quod nos dilectos filios nostros canonicos gloriosi martiris nostri Thome iuxta Stafford' . et locum eorum in quo ipsi divinis mancipati officiis commorantur . eorumque res et possessiones quas iuste et canonice adepti sunt sive ex dono pie recordationis . Ricardi quondam Coventrensis episcopi et dilecti filii nostri Gerardi de Stafford' . sive ex beneficiis aliorum quorumlibet Christi fidelium sicut ipsorum donatorum et eciam domini regis Henrici secundi carte testantur . et iuste adepti esse dinoscuntur vel quolibet iusto modo in posterum poterunt adipisci ./ sub nostra volumus esse protectione ./ ipsasque donationes sicut rationabiliter facte sunt presentis*a* scripti testimonio et sigilli nostri patrocinio confirmamus. Hiis testibus . Alano de Stafford' et Ricardo de Salopesbir' archidiaconis . magistro Roberto de Salopesbir' . magistro Henri de Norhamt' . magistro Silvestro . magistro Radulfo de hospitali decano ecclesie de Stafford' . Willelmo Prudum' . Henri de Exon' . Adam decano de Chebbeseya . magistro Rogero et magistro Gileberto . clericis Staffordie . Galfrido forti . Salomone . Eustachio de Wilton' . et aliis.

a i *inserted over* e, *expunged* A

The charter of bp Richard of Coventry is in the same collection, Acc. 938/1 (7972), pd in *Staffs. Hist. Coll.* (Wm Salt Soc.) VIII i (1887) 133–4. Two other grants by bp Richard are Acc. 938/1 and 2 (7973 and 7974). A facsimile of Gerard of Stafford's charter is in *Staffs. Hist. Coll.* VIII i facing 155. Cf. *VCH Staffs.* iii (1970) 260–2.

The hand, not found in other acta of the archbp, differs from the neat, small charter-hands of most of the originals. Note the use of 'Henri' for 'Henrico' in the witness-list.

313. Stanlow abbey

Inspeximus and confirmation for the monks of Stanlow (Stanlawe) *of a charter given by the late bishop Richard of Coventry, granting to them Stanlow, otherwise known as* Benedictus locus, *and the vill called* Maurich' Eston *(? Aston Grange) and other rights. Also confirmation of other liberties and gifts* (beneficia) *conferred by the earl of Chester and John constable of Chester as appear from their charters: by the earl, quittance of toll in the town of Chester on purchases by the monks for their own use; by John the constable the tithe of his salt in Northwich* (Norwyco), *in money or salt. If the monks prefer salt they shall have a 'summa salis' for 2½d.*

[Jan. 1186 × Dec. 1187, probably late June 1187]

B = BL ms. Egerton 3126 (Whalley cartulary) fo. 35r no. 15. s. xiv med.

Pd from B in *The coucher book or chartulary of Whalley abbey* ed. W. A. Hulton (Chetham Soc. x 1847) i 15–16 no. xv.

Hiis testibus: magistro Henrico de Northhampton', magistro Silvestro, Willelmo de Sotyndon', Raginaldo de Oilly, Willelmo Prudhome, Ricardo de Humfraville, Eustachio de Wilton', Salomone clerico, Galfrido Forti, et aliis.

> The archbp is styled legate. He almost certainly issued this and the next charter when he held his legatine visitation in these parts. He is said to have stayed at St Werburgh's abbey. Chester, 24–27 June 1187. The inspected charter of bp Richard precedes this confirmation in the coucher book, fo. 34v no. xiv.
>
> For the identification of Maurich' Eston as Aston Grange, Cheshire, see *VCH Lancs* ii 131 note 256.

314. Stanlow abbey

Confirmation for the monks of Stanlow of chirographs which the archbishop has inspected, one recording the settlement of their dispute with the monks of St Werburgh's abbey, Chester, concerning tithes of Stanney, the other recording the settlement of their dispute with the canons of Norton concerning two bovates of land in Stanney and the tithes of the demesne of the vill and of the tithes of Maurich' Eston (? Aston Grange).

[Jan. 1186 × Dec. 1187, probably late June 1187]

B = BL ms. Egerton 3126 (Whalley cartulary) fo. 213r (208r) no. 3. s. xiv med.

Pd from B in *The coucher book or chartulary of Whalley abbey* ed. W. A. Hulton (Chetham Soc. xi 1847) ii 534 no. iii.

Hiis testibus: magistro Henrico de Northampton', magistro Silvestro, Raginaldo de Oylly, Willelmo Prudhom', Ricardo de Humfrayville, Salomone clerico, Galfrido Forti, et aliis.

> The archbp is styled legate. The charter was almost certainly given late June 1187 on the archbp's visit to Cheshire: see nos. 260, 313, above and cf. witness-lists. The agreement between Stanlow and Chester is attested by abbot Ranulf of Buildwas, died c.Aug. 1187.
>
> The caption, by the scribe of the cartulary, reads 'Confirmacio B. archiepiscopi ... '. The red illuminated initial at the beginning of the text reads 'R.'.

315. Abbey of Stratford Langthorne

Confirmation for the monks of Stratford of the grant of the church of West Ham and its appropriation to them by bishop Gilbert of London, with the assent of Gilbert de Muntfichet, lord of the fee.

[Jan. 1186 × 18 Feb. 1187]

A = BL Harl. ch. 43 G 26. Endorsed, s. xii ex.: Confirmatio B. Cantuariensis super ecclesia de Westham; s. xii/xiii: Coll'a secunda .B. Cant'. C. ii^a . Approx. 158 × 92 + 20 mm. Sealing d. q. 2; small remains (green wax) of top of face of seal.

Omnibus Christi fidelibus ad quos presentes littere pervenerint .B. dei gratia Cantuariensis archiepiscopus . totius Anglie primas . et apostolice sedis legatus ∕ illam que est in domino salutem. Cum ad nostre sollicitudinis pertineat offitium . iustas subditorum nostrorum possessiones protegere . que in subsidium religionis pia devotione collata sunt . et episcopali auctoritate confirmata . ad maiorem securitatem protectionis et confirmationis nostre beneficio dignum duximus communire. Ea propter ad universitatis vestre noticiam volumus pervenire . nos ex auctentico scripto venerabilis fratris nostri Gileberti Londoniensis episcopi quod inspeximus intellexisse . eundem episcopum de assensu Gileberti de Muntfichet domini fundi . concessisse et dedisse dilectis filiis nostris monachis de Straford . ecclesiam de Westhamma . et eos debita cum sollempnitate in personatum eiusdem ecclesie recepisse . cuius concessionem et donationem nos ratam habentes . eandem sicut canonice et rationabiliter facta est ∕ auctoritate qua fungimur confirmamus . et sigilli nostri appositione communimus.

Probably in the lifetime of bp Gilbert Foliot; his charter does not survive (*Letters* 515 no. 10).
Probably external writing, in a good clear book-hand.

316. Tavistock abbey

Confirmation for the monastery of Tavistock of the churches of Milton Abbot and Hatherleigh, for the use of the sacristy and the infirmary respectively. The archbishop has inspected and handled the charters with which Robert (II) and Bartholomew, bishops of Exeter, granted and confirmed these churches for these uses.

[April 1185 × Jan. 1186 or Dec. 1187 × March 1190]

B = Woburn Abbey, Duke of Bedford, Muniments 3 A 3 (Tavistock cartulary) fo. 10v. s. xiii. Witness-list omitted.

Pd from B by H. P. R. Finberg in 'Some Tavistock charters' *EHR* lxii (1947) 369.

The archbp's title is 'divina miseratione Cantuariensis ecclesie minister'. It follows a general address.
The episcopal charters are also in the cartulary: *EHR* lxii 358, 366. Bp Robert's grant of Milton was confirmed by archbp Theobald.

*317. Order of the Temple: London, New Temple

Grant to all those who visit the house of the Temple at London on the Thames on the day of its dedication, and give alms to it, of an indulgence of twenty days and a share in all the prayers and spiritual benefits of the church of Canterbury. [April 1185 × Nov. 1190]

> Mentioned only, in the indulgence granted by archbp Hubert, 'ad exemplum bone memorie B. predecessoris nostri' (*EEA* iii no. 630). Since Hubert's indulgence agrees at many points with the wording of that granted by archbp Thomas (above, no. 42), Baldwin's indulgence was also probably modelled on his predecessor's.

318. Order of the Temple: Sompting

Mandate to Mr Matthew, dean, and Mr Lewis, precentor of Chichester. A dispute between the Knights Templars and the clerks of (the royal free chapel of) Steyning over the church of Sompting was delegated by the pope to bishop Seffrid of Chichester and Gervase of Petworth, and was settled by a composition. But the archbishop learns that the clerks of Steyning contravene it. He instructs the addressees to enquire carefully into the matter and if it was settled by a composition to enforce the composition. [Jan. 1186 × Dec. 1187]

B = BL ms. Cotton Nero E vi (Hospitallers' cartulary) fo. 157r. s. xv med.

B. dei gratia Cantuariensis archiepiscopus totius Anglie primas et apostolice sedis legatus dilectis filiis magistro M. decano et magistro Ludovico precentori Cicestrensis ecclesie salutem et benedictionem. Cum inter dilectos filios fratres militie Templi et clericos de Stanninges lis*a* quedam mota [fo. 157v] fuisset super corporibus mortuorum et decimis et parochianis ad ecclesiam de Suntynges, sicut a predictis fratribus dicitur, pertinentibus et venerabili fratri nostro S. Cicestrensi episcopo et dilecto filio nostro Gervasio de Pettewerd' a summo pontifice ea fuisset delegata, tandem coram eis iudicibus lis ipsa amicabili compositione inter eos facta sopita est, et forma ipsius compositionis scripto est autemptico ab ipsis iudicibus confirmata, set clerici prefati de Stanninges 'contra' iamdicte compositionis formam, sicut accepimus, venire presumunt. Quia igitur ea que auctoritate apostolica facta sunt summa debent stabilitate gaudere, discretioni vestre mandamus quatinus veritate diligentius inquisita, si rem ut prescriptum est se habere noveritis, ipsam compositionem sicut rationabiliter facta est faciatis inviolabiliter observari. Valete.

a ? lis, *om.* B

The case had been settled before the pope's delegates on 28 Oct. 1185 (on the same page of the cartulary, pd *Chichester acta* 190–1 no. 139). The dispute had previously been referred to bp Waleran and archdn Paris of Rochester by pope Lucius III (Velletri, 11 May, 1182 or 1183: *PUE* i 487 no. 212) and Waleran summoned the parties to appear at a hearing at Halling on 20 Sept. (ms. Cotton Nero E vi fo. 156v). This apparently produced no settlement, perhaps because of the death of bp Waleran in Aug. 1184.

319.   Order of the Temple: Yarmouth

Inspeximus (abridged) and confirmation of a charter of William de Vernon, granting to William Maskerel land and a dwelling at Yarmouth, which Guy the clerk held, to make a hospital in honour of God, the blessed Virgin Mary and All Saints, for the souls of king Henry, son of count Geoffrey, and of earl Baldwin, and of Richard his brother and their forebears, and for the soul of William de Vernon and the souls of William Maskerel and his forebears.

[22 Oct. 1189 × March 1190]

B = Bodl. ms. Wood empt. 10 (Sandford cartulary) fo. 72r. s. xiii ex.

Pd from B in *Mon. Ang.* vii 843b no. XLVI; and in *Sandford cartulary* ii 201 no. 283, where attributed in error to archbp Hubert. The marginal guide for an initial is 'b'.

Hiis testibus: G. episcopo Roffensi.

The archbp is not styled legate. The limiting dates are the consecration of bp Godfrey of Winchester, who authorized the founding of a hospital by the brothers William and Ralph Maskerel (*Cartulary* ii 202 no. 285) and the departure of the archbp on crusade.

We emend the cartulary text, which reads: 'cartam Willelmi Maskerelli inspeximus in hac forma. Sciant etc. et sic de verbo ad verbum ut in precedenti carta.' Since the charter later refers to the charter 'predicti W. de Vernon' (which does indeed precede as no. 282) and since the cartulary does not contain W. Maskerel's charter, this 'Maskerelli' is presumably a mistake for 'de Vernona'. Cf. *EEA* iii no. 631.

320.   Thanington: hospital of St James

Confirmation for the hospital of St James at Canterbury of the church of Bredgar, granted by king Henry II, whose charter the archbishop has inspected.   [29 Sept. 1185 × Jan. 1186]

B = BL ms. Add. 32098 (Thanington cartulary) fo. 2r. s. xv ex. C = Ibid. fo. 2v, in inspeximus by archbp Hubert.

B.*a* dei gratia Cantuariensis archiepiscopus totius Anglie primas universis sancte matris ecclesie filiis ad quos presentes littere pervenerint eternam in domino salutem. Ad universitatis vestre notitiam volumus pervenire nos ex inspectione carte domini nostri Henrici dei gratia illustris Anglorum regis intellexisse eundem dominum nostrum regem concessisse et carta sua confirmasse mulieribus leprosis in hospitali sancti Iacobi apud Cantuariam commorantibus ecclesiam de Bredegare cum universis pertinentiis suis in liberam et perpetuam elemosinam. Unde et nos quod ab ipso domino rege pia devotione actum est ratum habentes et acceptum predictam concessionem sicut rationabiliter facta est auctoritate qua fungimur confirmamus et sigilli nostri appositione communimus.[b] Hiis testibus: Gileberto Roffensi episcopo, Willelmo Glowecestriensi et magistro Petro Blesensi Bathoniensi archidiaconis,[c] magistro Silvestro, magistro Sansone, Iohanne de Exonia, Gileberto filio[d] Willelmi, Eustachio de Wilton, Galfrido Forti, et aliis multis.

[a] Bonefacius BC   [b] om. witness-list C   [c] archidiacono B   [d] folio B

After the consecration of bp Gilbert of Rochester.

Henry II's grant of the church of Bredgar to the leper women of the hospital, providing that Mr Firminus shall hold it for his lifetime, is on fo. 1v of the cartulary (pd by Somner, Canterbury part 1 app. XIIb). On fo. 2r is a letter of protection from Urban III, 23 June 1186 or 1187 (PUE i 532 no. 244). For the later persecution of the hospital and its master, Firminus (or Feraminus) see Gervas. Cant. Opp. i 427. At an uncertain date Firminus, with the consent of archbp Hubert, put the hospital under the custody of the P. & C. of Ch. Ch., Canterbury (Somner, Canterbury loc. cit. app. XIIa).

*321. Trentham priory

Mandate to the bishop of Coventry to hear the complaint of Vivian de Stoch, as proctor of Robert de Costentin, who had brought his complaint personally to the archbishop, against the prior and canons of Trentham concerning the rights of the parties in the chapels of Newcastle-under-Lyme and Whitmore.   [1188 × March 1190 ?]

Mentioned only, and possibly issued by archbp Richard: see above, no. 216.

322. Pope Urban III

Felicitations to pope Urban III, in extravagant terms, on his election to the papacy after the lamented death of Lucius III, The archbp also thanks the pope for the favours he has bestowed upon him and asks for his prayers to sustain him in his office.   [early 1186]

Petri Blesensis opera i 309–11 ep. 99; PL ccii 1533–4.

The archbp is styled 'Cantuariensis ecclesie minister (or minister humilis)'. Urban III, elected 15 Nov. 1185, was consecrated 1 Dec. 1185. By letters dated

17–18 Dec. 1185 (perhaps only despatched in mid-Jan. 1186: H. Tillmann, *Päpstl. Legaten* (Bonn 1926) 34 n. 119) he commissioned the archbp as legate and empowered him to recover alienated rights and possessions of his church (*EHR* ix (1894) 537–9; JL 15490, *Ep. Cant.* 4–5 no. 2; cf. Cheney in *Revue de droit canonique* xxviii (1978) 93). Probably the archbp refers here to these grants. The rubric in some mss. of Peter of Blois's collection describes the letter erroneously as: 'Actio gratiarum super pallio a sede apostolica misso'. Baldwin had already received the pallium from Lucius III, probably with the confirmation of his election which is dated 15 March 1185 (JL 15387, *Ep. Cant.* 4 no. 1; JL 15388, Diceto ii 36, cf. 39–40).

The final greeting is 'Vale', and there are no witnesses.

*322A. Pope Urban III

Report to the pope on one Elias, a regular canon whom he sends to the Curia after confession to the archbishop. When Elias was an acolyte he was promoted deacon, skipping the grade of subdeacon, and in course of time received the priesthood, but did not perform the office of a priest. The archbishop speaks well of him.   [April 1185 × Nov. 1187]

Mentioned only in a reply by pope Urban to Baldwin, archbp and legate, 'Sicut tue littere ... ', dated Verona, 23 June 1186 or 1187. In a group of papal letters surrounding the *Collectio Wigorniensis* in BL ms. Royal 10 A ii fo. 3r, whence pd by P. M. Baumgarten in *EHR* ix (1894) 540. The pope allows the penitent to be ordained to the grade of subdeacon if his fault was committed 'non ex industria vel contemptu set ex negligencia'. This decision did not get currency in other collections. The only ruling on the matter in *Extra* is by Innocent III in the title 'De clerico per saltum promoto' (5. 29. un.). Bernard Compostellanus antiquus had included another ruling of Innocent (*PL* ccxiv 878) which was omitted in *Compilatio III* and *Extra*.

323. Warwick: collegiate church of St Mary

Inspeximus and confirmation for the canons of St Mary's, Warwick, of a charter of bishop Roger of Worcester by which, following the example of bishop Simon, he confirmed the constitution made by bishop Simon for the canons, and confirmed the grants made by Roger earl of Warwick, corroborated by archbishop (Theobald) of Canterbury. They provided that the clergy of All Saints' in the castle should join in one chapter and fraternity with the church of St Mary, under a dean of their choice, should have the same customs and liberties as those which the churches of London, Lincoln, and Salisbury enjoy, and should control the appointments to prebends. He also confirmed their possessions, notably the churches of St Nicholas and St Lawrence, as set out in Simon's charter. The archbishop previously inspected and confirmed bishop Roger's charter when he, Baldwin, was bishop of Worcester.   [Jan. × 25 May 1186]

B = PRO E 164/22 (Warwick cartulary) fo. 24v (23v) no. 41. s. xv med. Omits bp
Roger's charter with cross-reference to fo. 23v (22v) of the cartulary, whence
the bp's charter pd by M. G. Cheney, *Roger of Worcester* 301–2 App. I no. 70.
C = Bodl. ms. Dugdale 12 (S. C. 6502) p. 81. Transcript of B. s. xvii in.

Omnibus Christi fidelibus ad quos presentes littere pervenerint B.
miseratione divina Cantuariensis ecclesie minister totius Anglie
primas et apostolice sedis legatus eternam in domino salutem. Ad
universitatis vestre notitiam volumus pervenire [nos]*ᵃ* cum administrationem episcopatus Wigorniensis domino permittente gereremus, litteras confirmationis Rogerii bone memorie Wigorniensis
episcopi super libertatibus et possessionibus ecclesie beate Marie
virginis de Warr' canonicis eiusdem ecclesie indultas inspexisse in
hac forma: Rogerius dei gratia Wigorniensis episcopus universis
sancte matris ecclesie filiis in domino salutem. Quoniam ad nostre
pondus sollicitudinis spectat ut antea [*i. e.* fo. 23v]. Et quia hanc
concessionem a memorato episcopo factam tempore quo deo disponente ecclesie Wigorniensi prefuimus confirmavimus, eandem qua
nunc fungimur auctoritate confirmamus et sigilli nostri appositione
roboramus. Hiis testibus: Willelmo archidiacono Glouecestriensi,
magistro Petro Bathoniensi archidiacono, magistro Henrico de
Norhanton', magistro Silvestro, magistro Samsone, Iohanne cancellario nostro, Galfrido filio Terrici, Rogero de Cherintun, Rogero
de Tanton', Gileberto filio Willelmi, Galfrido Forti, Henrico de
Cruce, Stephano de Campedene, Ernaldo, Eustachio clericis, et
multis aliis.

ᵃ nos?: *om.* BC

The archbp is styled legate. William of Northolt, archdn of Gloucester, was
elected bp of Worcester *c.*25 May 1186. Baldwin's inspeximus as bp of Worcester
is on fo. 24r (23r) no. 40 of the cartulary. The charter of bp Simon (1125–50)
which Roger cites is on fo. 13r (12r) no. 13 (whence pd in *Mon. Ang.* viii 1327 no.
X), abridged in the cartulary by reference to the list of possessions contained in
earl Roger's charter, ibid. fo. 12v (11v) no. 12 (whence pd in *Mon. Ang.* viii 1327
no. IX). The archbp's confirmation to which bp Roger referred is presumably
the charter attributed by the scribe of the cartulary to St Thomas; it was
probably issued by archbp Theobald, 1139 × 1145 (fo. 15r, whence pd by
Saltman, *Theobald* 500–1 no. 269).

324. Winchcombe abbey

*Confirmation for the monks of Winchcombe of the award made by the
archbishop when bishop of Worcester* ('cum Wigorniensis ecclesie
domino permittente gereremus administrationem'). *After careful
enquiry he had assigned to them two-thirds of the sheaves of Stanton
and Snowshill.*   [? April 1185 × Jan. 1186]

B = Gloucester, Glos. Record Office D 678 (Winchcombe cartulary) p. 76 (opening 25a). s. xiii med.

Pd from B in *Winchcombe cartulary* i 71–72.

The archbp is not styled legate in the title, which follows a general address; there is no witness-list or valediction. This probably antedates a confirmation by pope Urban III, dated Verona, 20 Dec. 1185 × 1186 (*Cartulary* i 72–73 and *PUE* iii 479 no. 377). The report of bp Baldwin's delegates, Peter de Withindona and Mr Peter de Lech, and his award as bp are in *Cartulary* i 70–71.

325. Wombridge priory

Confirmation for the canons of Wombridge of the charter of king Henry II granting them the church of Sutton Maddock. [Feb. × Dec. 1187]

B = BL ms. Egerton 3712 (Wombridge cartulary) fo. 70r (73r). s. xv ex.

Pd (calendar) from B by G. Morris, 'Abstracts of the ... chartulary of Wombridge priory' *Trans. Shropshire Archaeol. and Nat. Hist. Soc.* 2s. ix (1897) 106.

B. dei gratia Cantuariensis archiepiscopus totius*a* Anglie primas et apostolice sedis legatus omnibus Christi fidelibus ad quos presentes littere pervenerint eternam in domino salutem. Ad universitatis vestre notitiam volumus pervenire nos ex carta domini nostri illustris Anglorum regis Henrici secundi intellexisse ipsum concessisse et dedisse in perpetuam elemosinam ecclesiam de Suttona cum omnibus pertinentiis suis canonicis ecclesie sancti Leonardi de Wombrugg'. Et quia concessionem domini regis eisdem canonicis super dicta ecclesia factam firmam et stabilem volumus permanere, eandem sicut rationabiliter facta est et in confirmationis scripto ipsius domini regis continetur expressa auctoritate*b* qua fungimur confirmamus et sigilli nostri appositione communimus. Hiis testibus: magistro Silvestro, magistro Radulfo de Sancto Martino, Iohanne de Exonia, Galfrido filio Terrici, Willelmo*c* Prudumma, Eustachio de Wilton', Galfrido Forti, et aliis multis.

a totus B   *b* auct. expr. B   *c* add de B

This may well belong to June 1187, when the archbp was in Shropshire.

For the circumstances in which the priory acquired the church see *VCH Shropshire* ii 80b. Henry II's charter is inspected in a charter of Edward II, 15 March 1318 (*Cal. Ch. Rolls* iii 405); it is dated by Eyton (277) Feb. 1187. Pope Urban III refers to it in his privilege of 23 June 1187 (*PUE* iii 501 no. 400).

326. The church of Worcester

Notification that when the archbishop was bishop of Worcester ('dum administrationem Wigorniensis ecclesie gereremus') *he granted the church of Dodderhill and committed its care* ('curam') *to Adam son of*

Edwin, clerk, saving a yearly pension of one hundred shillings to the monks of Worcester. He has thought fit to record these facts in writing.
[April 1185 × Jan. 1186 or Dec. 1187 × Nov. 1190]

B = Worcester, D. & C. ms. A 4 (Register I) fo. 23r. s. xiii med.

Pd from B by W. Thomas, *A survey of the cathedral church of Worcester* (London 1736) appendix p. 15 no. 25; T. R. Nash *Collections for a history of Worcestershire* (London 1781–2) i 337; *Worcester cartulary* 92–93 no. 170.

The archbp is not styled legate. For other documents relating to St Augustine's, Dodderhill (in Droitwich) and its parson, Adam of Worcester, son of Edwin, see *Worcester cartulary* 88–95, 100–1, nos. 162–76, 189, and no. 228 note, above. For its later appropriation to Worcester priory see *Worcester cartulary* 260–1 no. 496 and note.

APPENDIX I

Reginald, elect of Canterbury, 27 Nov.—26 Dec. 1191

If the monks of Canterbury had had their way, archbishop Baldwin's successor would have been Reginald FitzJocelin, bishop of Bath since 1174. They elected him on 27 Nov. 1191 and wrote to the pope to ask for his confirmation and the grant of the pallium. Meanwhile, the bishops appealed against the election made by the monks.[1] On Christmas Eve the elect fell desperately ill and died on 26 December. He performed no administrative acts, to our knowledge, as unconfirmed archbishop-elect, and the only written record in his name as elect was dictated by him on his deathbed. Already printed by Stubbs, it is so brief and so poignant a note as to merit inclusion:

Reginaldus dei gratia Bathoniensis episcopus et sacrosancte Cantuariensis ecclesie electus indignus dilectis suis in Christo Gaufrido priori et conventui ecclesie Christi Cantuariensis salutem, gratiam, et benedictionem. Michi non videtur quod velit deus quod vester sim archiepiscopus. Vester autem volo et desidero esse monachus. Vos ergo cum habitu veniatis ad me quantocius apud Dokemeresfeld, domine prior et supprior, cum aliis quos volueritis. Valete, et gratia vestri incessanter, incessanter, oretis pro me.[2]

---

[1] *Fasti eccl. angl. 1066–1300* ii 5. For the circumstances of the election see *Councils & Synods* i. 1035–7.

[2] Lambeth Palace ms. 415 fo. 92r. Printed thence by Stubbs, in *Ep. Cant.* 355 no. 388. Reginald dictated this letter on Christmas Eve at Dogmersfield, a hundred miles from Canterbury (cf. his clerk's, Roger de Bonneville's, letter to the prior, ibid. 354 no. 387), so his wish that the prior should receive him 'ad succurrendum' cannot have been satisfied. The martyrology of Christ Church records his obit 'sicut pro uno archiepiscopo' (ibid. 561: VII kal. Ian.).

Richard of Devizes, monk of Winchester, gives another account of bp Reginald's last days which is, however, not incompatible with the despatch of this letter. According to Richard, Walter prior of Bath was with the bp at the last and gave him the monk's habit. Accepting the habit, Reginald said 'Deus noluit me esse archiepiscopum, et ego nolo. Deus voluit me esse monacum et ego volo.' (*Chron. reigns of Stephen* (etc.), ed. R. Howlett, (RS, vol. iii 1886) 421, *Chron. of Richard of Devizes* ed. J. T. Appleby (Nelson's Med. Texts 1963) p. 56).

APPENDIX II

ITINERARIES OF THE ARCHBISHOPS, 1162–90

Itinerary of archbishop Thomas

Note: The only dated actum is no. 34, which records the day on which the earl of Essex promised the archbishop at Windsor to make amends for his father's offences against Ramsey abbey. Apart from this, the itinerary is constructed mainly out of records of the king's court and the indications given by Becket's biographers. Since the royal charters are undated and the biographers are generally imprecise and not necessarily accurate, there is good reason for taking the dates listed below as only an approximate guide to the archbishop's movements. See the Introduction: criteria for dating, pp. lxxvi–viii.

1162	May 23	Westminster	Diceto i 306–7
	June 2–3	Canterbury	Gervas. i 170–1
	Aug. 10	Canterbury	Gervas. i 172
	Dec. 25	London	Gervas. i 172
1163	Jan. 25	Southampton	Diceto i 308
	Feb.	Oxford	Eyton 58–9
	Mar. 8	Westminster	*Lincoln reg. ant.* i 65
	Mar. 17	Canterbury	Gervas. i 173
	Mar. 19	Dover	*Foedera* (Rec. Com.) I i 23
	Mar. – Apr.	Windsor	Foliot *Letters* 185–6
	Apr. 6	Windsor	above, no. 34
	May	Romney	*MTB* iii 253
	May	Gravelines	*MTB* iii 253
	May 16–21	Tours	*MTB* iii 254
	July 1	Woodstock	Eyton 63
	Oct. 1	Westminster	*MTB* iv 201
	Oct. 13	Westminster	Barlow, *Edward the Conf.* (1970) 325
	Nov. x Dec.	Teynham	*MTB* iv 30
	Nov. x Dec.	Harrow	*MTB* iv 31
	Nov. x Dec.	Woodstock	*MTB* iv 32
	Dec. 22	Canterbury	Gervas. i 176
1164	Jan. 13–28	Clarendon	*MTB* v 71–9
	end Jan.	Winchester	Gervas. i 181
	? Feb.	Romney	Gervas. i 181

? Feb.	Aldington	*MTB* ii 325
? Feb.	Canterbury	Gervas. i 182
Mar.	Woodstock	Eyton 70
Apr. 19	Reading	above, no. 35 n.
Aug. 23	Canterbury	*Ann. mon.* i 49
Sept.	Woodstock	*MTB* iii 49
Sept.	Canterbury	*MTB* iii 49
Sept.	Romney	*MTB* iii 49
Oct. 6–13	Northampton	*MTB* iii 50–6
Oct. 14	Grantham	*MTB* iii 324
Oct. 15	Lincoln	*MTB* iii 324
Oct. 16–18	Bridgend (?)	*MTB* iii 324
Oct. 19	Boston	*MTB* iii 324
? Oct. 20	Haverholme	*MTB* iii 324
late Oct.	Chicksands	*MTB* ii 399
Oct. 25	Eastry	*MTB* iii 324
Nov. 2	Sandwich	*MTB* ii 400
Nov. 2	Oye, Gravelines	*MTB* iii 325
Nov. 3	Clairmarais	*MTB* iii 329
c. Nov. 5–10	St-Omer, St-Bertin	above, nos. 39–40
mid-Nov.	Thérouanne	*MTB* iv 58
mid-Nov.	Soissons	*MTB* iv 58
c. Nov. 29	Sens	*MTB* ii 341
Dec.	Pontigny	*MTB* ii 344
1165 Jan. – Apr.	Pontigny	*MTB* ii 344
? late Apr.	St-Benoît-sur-Loire	*MTB* iii 59
May	Bourges	*MTB* ii 347
May	Pontigny	*MTB* ii 347
1166 May 31–June 3	Soissons	*MTB* v 382
June 10	Rigny	*MTB* v 382
June 12	Vézelay	*MTB* v 383
late June–? Nov.	Pontigny	*MTB* iv 65
? Nov.	Sens, St Colombe	*MTB* ii 415, iii 404–7
1167	chiefly at Sens ?	*MTB* iv 65
Nov. 18	Trie	*MTB* iv 95, vi 262
1168–9	chiefly at Sens ?	*MTB* iv 65
1169 Jan. 6	Montmirail	*MTB* iii 430, vi 507
Jan. 7	Chartres	*MTB* iii 436–7
Jan. 9	Sens	*MTB* iii 437
Feb. 7	St-Léger-en-Yvelines	*MTB* vi 519
Apr. 13	Clairvaux	*MTB* iii 87
Nov. 14	Corbeil ?	*MTB* vii 154
Nov. 18	Paris, Montmartre	*MTB* ii 97
Nov. 19	Paris, Temple	*MTB* iii 451
late Nov.	Sens	*MTB* iii 451
1170 Jan.–Nov.	chiefly at Sens ?	*MTB* iv 65
July 22	Fréteval	*MTB* iii 466
early Oct.	Tours	*MTB* iii 114–5, 469
Oct. 12	Amboise	*MTB* iii 115
late Oct.	Chaumont, Sens	*MTB* iii 470–471
late Oct.	Rouen ?	*MTB* iii 116

? Nov. 29	Male	*MTB* iv 262
? Nov. 30	Wissant	*MTB* iii 117
Dec. 1	Sandwich	*MTB* iii 476
? Dec. 2–10	Canterbury	*MTB* iii 121, 478
? Dec. 11	Rochester	*MTB* iii 122
? Dec. 12	Southwark	*MTB* iii 122–3
? Dec. 13–17	Harrow	*Gesta abb. S. Albani* (RS) i 184
? Dec. 17–18	Southwark	Diceto i 342
? Dec. 19–24	Canterbury	*MTB* iii 124–6
Dec. 25–29	Canterbury	*MTB* iii 484–95, 132

Itinerary of archbishop Richard

1173	June 3	Westminster	*Fasti* i 4
	June 9	Canterbury	Gervas. i 244–5
	Dec. 25	Piacenza	Diceto i 388
1174	Jan. 14	Genoa	Diceto i 388
	Jan. 23	Civitavecchia	Diceto i 388
	late Jan.	Rome	Diceto i 388
	Apr. 2, 7	Anagni	Diceto i 388
	Apr. 9	Anagni	*Gesta regis Henrici* i 70
	Apr. 27–8	Anagni	*PUE* ii 326–7
	May 26	(Stura) ? Ostia	Diceto i 391
	early June	Genoa	Diceto i 391
	June 23	St-Jean-de-Maurienne	Diceto i 391
	c. Aug. 9	Barfleur	Diceto i 385, 391
	Sept. 3	London	Diceto i 391
	Oct. 5, 6	Canterbury	Diceto i 392
	Oct. 24	London, St Paul's	Diceto i 395
	Oct. × Nov.	Waltham	Diceto i 396
	Nov.	Gloucester	Diceto i 396
	Nov. 24	Bath	Diceto i 398
	? Nov.	Winchester	Diceto i 396
1175	Feb. 10	Dover	above, no. 124
	? May 11–18	Westminster	*Councils & Synods* i 965
	May 28	Canterbury	Gervas. i 256
	June 27	Lambeth	above, no. 182
	c. July 1 × 9	Woodstock	above, no. 177 n.
	Sept. 28	South Malling	*Chron. mon. de Bello* 162
	Oct. 12	Westminster	Diceto i 402
	Dec.	Peterborough	*Gesta regis Henrici* i 106
	Dec. 14	Lambeth	Diceto i 403
1176	Jan. 26	Northampton	Eyton 198
	Mar. 14–19	Westminster	Diceto i 405
	Aug. 15	Winchester	*Gesta regis Henrici* i 118–9
	Sept.	to St-Gilles	*Gesta* i 119; Gervas. i 260
	Nov. 28 × Dec. 24	to England	*Gesta* i 127
1177	c. Jan. 20	Waltham	*Gesta* i 135
	? Jan.–Feb.	to Flanders	*PR 23 Henr. II* 207–8, cf. Eyton 210
	Mar. 13	Westminster	*Gesta* i 144–54

	? Mar. 19	Westminster	*Hereford charters* 30
	Apr. 23	Wye	*Gesta* i 165
	May 22	Amesbury	*Gesta* i 165
	May 29	Winchester	*Gesta* i 166
	July 1	Winchester	*Gesta* i 177–8
	July 12	Stanstead	*Gesta* i 180–2
1178	? June	Canterbury	*Gesta* i 209
	Dec. 25	Winchester	Eyton 224
1179	? March	Paris	Gervas. i 276
	Aug. 23	Canterbury	Diceto i 433
1180	Feb.	Oxford	*Eynsham cart.* i 58
	Aug. 10	Lambeth	Gervas. i 294
	Nov. 16	Canterbury	Gervas. i 295
1181	June 26	London	Gervas. i 296
	Aug.	Nottingham, Lincoln	*Gesta* i 280
1182	Jan. 6	Marlborough	Diceto ii 10
	Oct. 10	Rochester	Diceto ii 13
	Nov. 13	Dover – Normandy	Diceto ii 14
	Dec. 18–19	Lisieux	Gervas. i 306
	Dec. 25	Caen	*Gesta* i 291
1183	Mar. 8	Poitiers	above, no. 91 n.
	May 26	Caen	above, no. 323
	c. June 24	Le Mans	Gervas. i 305
	July 3	Angers	Diceto ii 15
	Aug. 11	to England	Diceto ii 20
	Aug. 19	Canterbury	Gervas. i 307
	Sept. 25	Canterbury	Gervas. i 307
1184	Feb. 16	Halling	*Fasti* i 5

Itinerary of archbishop Baldwin

Note: Baldwin, bishop of Worcester, was elected in Dec. 1184 but Lucius III did not confirm and send the pallium until mid-March. Urban III appointed him legate by letters of 17–18 Dec. 1185 (which may not have been immediately delivered: above, p. lvii n. 81, cf. no. 322). There are some problems in this fairly fully documented itinerary. The circumstantial account by Gervase of Canterbury of the archbishop's movements 11–31 January 1188 cannot be verified from other sources and does not square with the statement in *Gesta regis Henrici* ii 30 (cf. Hoveden ii 337) that Baldwin and Hugh, bishop-elect of Coventry, were with the king at Le Mans after he met the king of France near Gisors on 21 Jan. (cf. *Gesta* ii 29, Hoveden ii 334; cf. Diceto ii 51: 22 Jan.). Rigord dates the Gisors meeting, naming Baldwin as present, 13 Jan. (*Œuvres de Rigord*, etc. (Soc. de l'histoire de France. 1882) i 83 c. 56). Gervase's recollections of Baldwin's return to England in Jan. 1188 may be confused with the archbishop's movements after his next arrival from France in July–Aug. 1189. The itinerary provided by Gerald of Wales for Spring 1188 is valuable, and for the route taken by Baldwin is probably reliable; but as Stubbs observes (*Ep. Cant.* p. lxiv n. 4), the exact dating is not so sure.

1184	Dec. 16	Westminster	Gervas. i 324–5
1185	Mar. 18	London, Clerkenwell	Diceto ii 33
	Apr. 21	Otford	above, no. 280
	May 19, 26	Canterbury	Gervas. i 326
	late Sept.	Teynham	Gervas. i 327
	Sept. 29	Canterbury	Gervas. i 330–1
	Dec. 16	Canterbury	Gervas. i 332
1186	May 1	Winchester	Diceto ii 41
	c. May 24–30	Eynsham	Diceto ii 41, *Magna vita Hugonis* (RS) 102, Gervas. i 335
	June 15	Canterbury	Gervas. i 335
	Aug. 10	Lambeth	Diceto ii 41
	Sept. 5	Woodstock	*Gesta* i 351
	Sept. 14	Marlborough	*Gesta* i 352
	Sept. 21	Westminster	*Gesta* i 352–3
	Oct. 5	Westminster ?	Diceto ii 43
	c. Oct. 20	Reading	*Gesta* i 353–4
	Nov. 25	Canterbury	Gervas. i 338
	Dec. 8–14	Gillingham, Kent	Gervas. i 343 cf. 38, 352
	Dec. 16	Canterbury	Gervas. i 344
	Dec. 17	Hackington	Gervas. i 344
	Dec. 25	Otford	Gervas. i 345
1187	Jan. 1	Westminster	Gervas. 1 346, *Gesta* ii 4
	Feb. 11, 18	Canterbury	Gervas. i 354, 356
	Mar. 8	London	Diceto ii 47–8
	Mar. 25	Otford	Gervas. i 359
	Mar. 26–29	London	Diceto ii 48
	May 17	Wingham	Gervas. i 365
	late May	London	Gervas. i 365
	June 10	Bredon	*Ep. Cant.* 61
	June 23	Shrewsbury	*Ep. Cant.* 61
	June 24–27	Chester	above, no. 258 n.
	Aug. 11	Dover	Gervas. i 379
	Aug. 28	Alençon	Gervas. i 380, cf. above, no. 262 n.
	? Nov.	Caen	Gervas. i 388
1188	? Jan. 11	Dover	Gervas. i 398
	? Jan. 13–19	Wingham	Gervas. i 398, 402
	? Jan. 19	Hackington	Gervas. i 402
	? Jan. 20	London	Gervas. i 402
	Jan. 31	Lambeth	Gervas. i 406
	Feb. 11	Geddington	Gervas. i 409–10

mid Feb.	Brigstock	*Annales cestrienses* (Rec. Soc. Lancs. & Cheshire 14. 1886) 40
? late Feb.	Charing	Gervas. i 418
? Feb. × Mar.	Cirencester	Gervas. i 419
early Mar.	Hereford	Gir. Cambr. vi 13–4
early Mar.	New Radnor	Gir. Cambr. vi 13–4
Mar.	Hay (Breconsh.)	Gir. Cambr. vi 20
Mar.	Llanddew	Gir. Cambr. vi 20
Mar.	Brecon	Gir. Cambr. vi 20
Mar.	Abergavenny	Gir. Cambr. vi 47–8
Mar.	Usk	Gir. Cambr. vi 55
Mar.	Caerleon	Gir. Cambr. vi 55
Mar.	Newport	Gir. Cambr. vi 55
Mar.	Cardiff	Gir. Cambr. vi 62
? Mar. 22	Llandaff	Gir. Cambr. vi 67, *Ep. Cant.* p. lxiv n.
Mar.	Ewenny	Gir. Cambr. vi 67
Mar.	Margam	Gir. Cambr. vi 67
Mar.	Swansea	Gir. Cambr. vi 73
Mar.	Kidwelly	Gir. Cambr. vi 78
Mar.	Carmarthen	Gir. Cambr. vi 80
Mar.	Whitland (Pembr.)	Gir. Cambr. vi 82
Mar.	Haverford West	Gir. Cambr. vi 82
Mar.	Camrose	Gir. Cambr. vi 99
Mar.	Newgale	Gir. Cambr. vi 100
Mar. × Apr.	St David's	Gir. Cambr. vi 100
Mar. × Apr.	St Dogmaels	Gir. Cambr. vi 112
Mar. × Apr.	Cardigan	Gir. Cambr. vi 112
Apr.	Lampeter	Gir. Cambr. vi 118
Apr.	Llanddewi Brefi	Gir. Cambr. vi 119
Apr.	Strata Florida	Gir. Cambr. vi 119
Apr.	Llanbadarnfawr	Gir. Cambr. vi 120
Apr.	Towyn	Gir. Cambr. vi 122
Apr.	Llanfair (Merion.)	Gir. Cambr. vi 122
Apr. 9	Nevin	Gir. Cambr. vi 124
Apr. 10	Caernarvon, Bangor	Gir. Cambr. vi 124–5
? Apr. 11	Anglesey, Bangor	Gir. Cambr. vi 126, 133
Apr. 12	Rhuddlan, St Asaph	Gir. Cambr. vi 137
Apr. 13	Basingwerk ?	Gir. Cambr. vi 137
Apr. 14–18	Chester	Gir. Cambr. vi 139, 142
Apr. 18	Whitchurch, Oswestry	Gir. Cambr. vi 142
late Apr.	Shrewsbury	Gir. Cambr. vi 144
late Apr.	Wenlock	Gir. Cambr. vi 144
late Apr.	Bromfield	Gir. Cambr. vi 146
late Apr.	Ludlow	Gir. Cambr. vi 146
late Apr.	Leominster	Gir. Cambr. vi 146
late Apr.	Hereford	Gir. Cambr. vi 146
? early June	London	Gervas. i 426
June 16	Winchelsea	Gervas. i 433
? July × Aug.	Tours	*Ep. Cant.* 227 no. 245
? Aug. × 14 Sept.	Normandy	*Ep. Cant.* 256 no. 274
1189 Feb. 1–3	Le Mans	*Ep. Cant.* 282 no. 297
Mar.	Normandy	above, no. 290

	June 4	La-Ferté-Bernard	Hoveden ii 362
	June 9	Le Mans	Gervas. i 446
	bef. July 20	Sées	Diceto ii 67
	July 31	Dover	Gervas. i 451
	Aug. 1	Wingham	*Ep. Cant.* 298 no. 314
	Aug. 5–6	Canterbury	*Ep. Cant.* 299 no. 314
	Aug. 8	Teynham	Gervas. i 453
	Sept. 3–5	Westminster	*Gesta* ii 79–84
	Sept. 15–16	Pipewell	*Gesta* ii 85
	Sept. 18	Geddington	*It. Ric.* 8
	Sept. 20	Warwick	*It. Ric.* 9
	Sept. 22	Feckenham	*It. Ric.* 9
	Oct. 4	Teynham	Gervas. i 459
	Oct. 5–6	Canterbury	Gervas. i 459–60
	Oct. 22	Westminster	*Gesta* ii 96–7, Diceto ii 71
	Nov. 8, 9, 12	Westminster	*It. Ric.* 13–4,
			Gervas. i 464–72,
			Ep. Cant. 315–7 no. 329
	Nov. 25, 28	Canterbury	*It. Ric.* 17–8
	Nov. 29, 30	Canterbury	Gervas. i 474–81
	Dec. 1–7, 28	Canterbury	*It. Ric.* 19–24
	Dec. 31	Lambeth	Gervas. i 483
1190	aft. Jan. 13	Canterbury	Gervas. i 484
	Feb. 19	London	Gervas. i 484
	Feb. 24	Canterbury	Gervas. i 484
	Mar. 6	Dover	Gervas. i 485
	Mar. 18, 20, 24	Rouen	*It. Ric.* 27–9
	Mar. 29–30	Gisors	*It. Ric.* 30
	Apr. 27	Dijon ?	*BIHR* liv (1981) 253
	Aug. 1, 3–5	Marseille	*It. Ric.* 38
	Sept. 16	Tyre	above, no. 253
	Oct. 12	Acre	above, no. 253
	Nov. 19	Acre	Gervas. i 488